THE ARDEN EDITION OF THE
WORKS OF WILLIAM SHAKESPEARE

HAMLET

Edited by
HAROLD JENKINS

THE ARDEN SHAKESPEARE

GENERAL EDITORS:
RICHARD PROUDFOOT, ANN THOMPSON
and DAVID SCOTT KASTAN

HAMLET

THE ARDEN SHAKESPEARE

* Third Series

The general editors of the Arden Shakespeare have been
W. J. Craig and R. H. Case (first series 1899-1944),
Una Ellis-Fermor, Harold F. Brooks, Harold Jenkins
and Brian Morris (second series 1946-1982)

Present general editors (third series)
Richard Proudfoot, Ann Thompson and David Scott Kastan

This edition of *Hamlet*, by Harold Jenkins,
first published in 1982 by
Methuen & Co. Ltd
Reprinted eleven times

Reprinted 1997 by Thomas Nelson & Sons Ltd

Thomas Nelson & Sons Ltd
Nelson House Mayfield Road
Walton-on-Thames Surrey
KT12 5PL UK

I(T)P® Thomas Nelson is an International
Thomson Publishing Company
I(T)P® is used under licence

Editorial matter © 1982 Methuen & Co. Ltd

Printed in Italy

British Library Cataloguing in Publication Data
A catalogue record for this book is available from
the British Library

Library of Congress Cataloguing in Publication Data
A catalogue record has been applied for

ISBN 0-416-17910-X (cased)
ISBN 0-17-443469-3 (paperback)
NPN 9 8 7 6 5 4 3

ISBN 0-17-443602-5 (playgoers edition)
NPN 9 8 7 6 5 4 3 2 1

CONTENTS

PREFACE

This new edition of *Hamlet*, although wholly independent of that with which Dowden inaugurated the original Arden Shakespeare some eighty years ago, has necessarily the same broad aims. These, as Dowden's opening statement announced them, are to give a trustworthy text, to show the relation of the text to its Quarto and Folio sources, and to add explanatory notes. The plan of an Arden volume, as it has later developed, has come to require also a full-scale introduction discussing such matters as date, text, source, and critical interpretation in a way that would not have been possible, if at that time at all, in Dowden's brief twenty pages.

The present text differs from Dowden's principally, though by no means solely, in preferring the readings of the Second Quarto over those of the Folio, which earlier tradition favoured. This follows the revolution in the textual approach to *Hamlet* effected by Dover Wilson, now half a century ago, when he established that the Second Quarto, with its signs of a close adherence to Shakespeare's manuscript, was therefore the more authoritative. The nature and status of all three original texts and the problems they confront us with are discussed in the Introduction. In writing it I have had constantly in mind a remark of Alice Walker's which still holds good, that, as a result of important work in progress, any discussion of textual matters in Shakespeare may be in need of revision before it is even in print;[1] but I have at least attempted to base my edition on a coherent textual theory.

A reader who wants to go straight to an account of my detailed procedure is referred to pp. 74–80. An account of the Textual Apparatus follows on pp. 80–1.

For all its textual complexity, I have found the bigger task with *Hamlet* to be that of annotation. Like Dover Wilson before me, I have been surprised at how many passages in Shakespeare still lack satisfactory exegesis. Some explanations handed on from editor to editor I believe to be quite wrong. (See, for minor

1. *RES*, n.s. VIII (1957), 299.

examples, II. ii. 395, V. ii. 260.) Yet such is the fascination of this play, the most discussed in the world, that hardly a line of dialogue has failed to attract comment and an article or two in the journals. Beyond linguistic dubieties, there are puzzles concerning the meaning of episodes (of which Hamlet's visit to Ophelia's closet and his bidding her to a nunnery are only the most notorious) which an annotator can hardly ignore. The sheer bulk of previous commentary creates its own practical difficulties; and although much can be silently passed over, I have not shirked the task of contesting what I see as misinterpretations. Just how full the annotation should be, and in the Arden format can be, has been a continual problem. My solution of a double set of notes has its disadvantages; but it preserves the principle and the convenience of notes on the same page as the text while allowing for expanded discussion in the LONGER NOTES at the end of the book.

The sign LN directs the reader to these LONGER NOTES, which are further described on pp. 81–2.

A consequence of the priority I have thought it right to give to fullness of annotation is that it denies space for something which most but not all new Arden volumes have, an appendix reprinting sources. This I regret the less because of the impossibility of supplying one which could be wholly satisfactory. Gollancz's *The Sources of Hamlet* (1926), which prints (in over 200 pages) Saxo and Belleforest with English translations face to face, has been of great use to me; but a desideratum of scholarship, not less important than much of the compositor analysis now in vogue, is a new edition of the relevant parts of Belleforest with a note of textual variants and an accurate modern translation. (Cf. pp. 89–90 and n.)

Every editor of Shakespeare must be heavily indebted to those who are beyond receipt of thanks. The work of the eighteenth- and nineteenth-century scholars is admirably sorted and assembled by Furness in his two-volume Variorum (1877), which, even when I have needed to look behind it, has been to me as to others an inestimable boon. Among the editors of the century since, the two whose notes I have found by far the most useful are Dover Wilson (this quite apart from his pioneer work on the text) and especially Kittredge. If their names occur more often than some others in notes which express dissent, this is because in the interests of scholarship, where names are mostly of small account, with scholars of their distinction and influence, when I hold them to be wrong I think it necessary to say so explicitly. If I have seemed sometimes to show less than respect, I am glad to right that here. I take no pleasure in disagreement with the illustrious dead, especially when this coexists, as in the case of Dover Wilson and McKerrow, with the memory of their personal kindness to me.

I have been fortunate in my friends. Whom better could I ask than Randolph Quirk what was and was not possible in Elizabethan English, than Rosamond Sprague where precisely to find what I wanted to in Plato? When I needed an expert in French or German, John Weightman nobly went over my attempts at translating Belleforest, Mary Beare my account of *Der Bestrafte Brudermord*. Kathleen Tillotson generously read the section on the date. My account of the Folio text has benefited from discussion with Richard Proudfoot. Marvin Spevack went to great trouble to assist me with the Collation, George Walton Williams to supply me with material for some notes. The stimulus which my thinking on many points derived from talking about Shakespeare with Arthur Sprague will be best understood by those who have shared this privilege. What I have gained from my fellow editor Harold Brooks is not limited to his reading of my manuscript: my particular work on one play has profited greatly from our collaborative work on many.

I give particular thanks to Reavley Gair for letting me see before publication the introduction to his edition of *Antonio's Revenge*, with its discussion of the relation between that play and *Hamlet*. It is a matter of great regret to me that since his work was ahead of mine, I could not then reciprocate, nor forewarn him of my different conclusion. I am grateful to John Tobin for suggestions I have used about the naming of the characters and some possible minor sources. To the many others who have given me information in conversation or correspondence, who have procured or lent me books, and who have sent me offprints, I hope I have made due acknowledgement; but I thank them all again now. I warmly appreciate also the expert help I have received from Magdalen Pearce, Jennifer Chandler and Linden Stafford in seeing through the press a work involving many typographical complications.

To my wife I owe a very special debt, and not only for the encouragement and endurance for which wives are often justly thanked. In daily conversation I have had available to me her intimate and wide-ranging knowledge of things Elizabethan and her wise, and sometimes sceptical, comments.

Two paragraphs in the section of the Introduction on *Der*

Bestrafte Brudermord (pp. 119–21) were first published in *Notes and Queries* (ccxxvi, 135–6) under the title of 'Hamlet's Voyage', and I record my thanks to the editors for their kindness in permitting me, with only slight verbal changes, to reproduce them here.

H. J.

ABBREVIATIONS AND REFERENCES

Titles of Shakespeare's works are abbreviated as in Onions, *A Shakespeare Glossary* (p. x). Quotations of Shakespeare's works other than *Hamlet* are from Peter Alexander's one-volume Shakespeare (Collins, 1951), which in line-numbering follows the revised Cambridge edition of 1891–3.

I. EDITIONS

The following editions are cited in the Textual Apparatus and/or Notes.

Adams	*Hamlet*, edited by Joseph Quincy Adams. 1929.
Alexander	*William Shakespeare, The Complete Works*, edited by Peter Alexander. 1951.
Boswell	*The Plays and Poems of William Shakespeare*, with . . . a life of the Poet . . . by the late Edmond Malone. [Edited by James Boswell.] 1821. [The Third Variorum, or the Malone-Boswell.] (Vol. 7.)
Caldecott	*Hamlet, and As You Like It*, a Specimen of an Edition of Shakespeare. By Thomas Caldecott. 1832. [A revision of Caldecott's edition of 1819.]
Cambridge	*The Works of William Shakespeare*, edited by William George Clark, (John Glover,) and William Aldis Wright. 1863–6. [The Cambridge Shakespeare.] (Vol. 8, 1866.)
	Revised edition by William Aldis Wright. 1891–3. (Vol. 7, 1892.)
Capell	*Mr William Shakespeare, his Comedies, Histories, and Tragedies.* [Edited by Edward Capell.] 1768. (Vol. 10.)
Chambers	The Warwick Shakespeare. *Hamlet*, edited by E. K. Chambers. 1894.
Chambers (RL)	The Red Letter Shakespeare, edited by E. K. Chambers. *Hamlet*. 1907.
Clarendon	The Clarendon Press Shakespeare. *Hamlet*, edited by W. G. Clark and W. A. Wright. 1872.
Collier	*The Works of William Shakespeare* . . . [edited] by J. Payne Collier. 1842–4. (Vol. 7, 1843.)
Collier[2]	*The Plays of Shakespeare*: The Text regulated by the old copies, and by the recently discovered folio of 1632. Edited by J. Payne Collier. 1853.
Dover Wilson	The Works of Shakespeare, edited by John Dover Wilson. *Hamlet*. 1934. [The New Cambridge Shakespeare.]
Dowden	The Arden Shakespeare. *Hamlet*, edited by Edward Dowden. 1899.
Dyce	*The Works of William Shakespeare.* The Text revised by the Rev. Alexander Dyce. 1857. (Vol. 5.)
Dyce[2]	[As above.] Second Edition. 1864–7. (Vol. 7, 1866.)

Evans	*The Riverside Shakespeare.* Textual Editor, G. Blakemore Evans. [Notes to the Tragedies by Frank Kermode.] 1974.
F	*Mr William Shakespeares Comedies, Histories, and Tragedies.* 1623. [The First Folio.]
F2	[As above.] The Second Impression. 1632. [The Second Folio.]
F3	[As above.] The Third Impression. 1663, 1664. [The Third Folio.]
F4	[As above.] The Fourth Edition. 1685. [The Fourth Folio.]
Farnham	*William Shakespeare: the Complete Works.* The Pelican Text Revised. 1969. *Hamlet,* edited by Willard Farnham.
Furness	A New Variorum Edition of Shakespeare, edited by Horace Howard Furness. *Hamlet.* 2 vols. 1877.
Globe	*The Works of William Shakespeare,* edited by William George Clark and William Aldis Wright. The Globe Edition. 1864.
Halliwell-Phillipps	*The Works of William Shakespeare,* edited by James O. Halliwell[-Phillipps]. 1853–65. (Vol. 14, 1865.)
Hanmer	*The Works of Shakespear.* [Edited by Sir Thomas Hanmer.] 1744. (Vol. 6.)
Herford	*The Works of Shakespeare,* edited by C. H. Herford. The Eversley Edition. 1899. (Vol. 8.)
Hoy	*Hamlet.* Edited by Cyrus Hoy. (Norton Critical Edition.) 1963.
Jennens	*Hamlet . . .* collated with the old and modern editions [by Charles Jennens]. 1773.
Johnson	*The Plays of William Shakespeare . . .* with the corrections and illustrations of Various Commentators; to which are added notes by Samuel Johnson. 1765. (Vol. 8.)
Keightley	*The Plays of William Shakespeare . . .* edited by Thomas Keightley. 1864. (Vol. 5.)
Kittredge	*Hamlet.* Edited and with Notes by George Lyman Kittredge. 1939.
Malone	*The Plays and Poems of William Shakespeare.* [Edited] by Edmond Malone. 1790. (Vol. 9.)
Munro	*The London Shakespeare.* A new annotated and critical edition of the complete works . . . edited by . . . John Munro. 1958. (Vol. 5.)
NCS	The New Cambridge Shakespeare. See Dover Wilson.
Parrott-Craig	*The Tragedy of Hamlet.* A Critical Edition of the Second Quarto. [By] Thomas Marc Parrott and Hardin Craig. 1938.
Pope	*The Works of Shakespear . . .* Collected and Corrected by Mr [Alexander] Pope. 1723 [1725]. (Vol. 6.)
Q1	*The Tragicall Historie of Hamlet Prince of Denmarke.* By William Shake-speare. 1603. [The First Quarto.]
Q2	*The Tragicall Historie of Hamlet, Prince of Denmarke.* By William Shakespeare. Newly imprinted and enlarged . . . according to the true and perfect Coppie. 1604 (uncorr.). 1605 (corr.). [The Second Quarto.]

Q3 [As above.] 1611. [The Third Quarto.]

Q4 [As above] according to the true and perfect Copy lastly Printed. [1622?] [The Fourth Quarto.]

Q5 [Substantially as above.] 1637. [The Fifth Quarto.]

Q 1676 *The Tragedy of Hamlet Prince of Denmark.* As it is now Acted at . . . the Duke of York's Theatre. By William Shakespeare. 1676. [The two quartos of this date, one printed from the other, are distinguishable by the imprint, which one sets in four and the other in five lines. My citations are from the former, which I take to be the earlier.]

Q 1683 [As above.] 1683.

Q 1695 *The Tragedy of Hamlet Prince of Denmark.* As it is now Acted at the Theatre Royal. By William Shakespeare. 1695.

Rann *The Dramatic Works of Shakespeare,* with notes by Joseph Rann. 1786[–94]. (Vol. 6.)

Reed *The Plays of William Shakespeare.* With . . . Notes by Samuel Johnson and George Steevens. Fifth edition. Revised and augmented by Isaac Reed. 1803. [The First Variorum, so called.] (Vol. 18.)

Ribner *Hamlet,* edited by George Lyman Kittredge. Revised by Irving Ribner. 1967.

Ridley The New Temple Shakespeare, edited by M. R. Ridley. *Hamlet.* 1934.

Riverside See Evans.

Rowe *The Works of Mr. William Shakespear.* Revised and Corrected by N[icholas] Rowe. 1709. (Vol. 5.)

Singer *The Dramatic Works of William Shakespeare.* The Text . . . revised with notes by Samuel Weller Singer. The Life of the Poet . . . by William Watkiss Lloyd. 1856. [A revision of Singer's edition of 1826.] (Vol. 9.)

Sisson *William Shakespeare, The Complete Works.* Edited by Charles Jasper Sisson. [1954.]

Spencer The New Penguin Shakespeare. *Hamlet,* edited by T. J. B. Spencer. 1980.

Staunton *The Plays of Shakespeare.* Edited by Howard Staunton. 1858–60. (Vol. 3, 1860.)

Steevens *The Plays of William Shakespeare* . . . With . . . Notes by Samuel Johnson and George Steevens. 1773. (Vol. 10.)

Steevens[2] [As above.] The Second Edition. 1778. (Vol. 10.)

Steevens[4] [As above.] The Fourth Edition. 1793. (Vol. 15.)

Theobald *The Works of Shakespeare.* Collated with the Oldest Copies . . . with Notes . . . by Mr [Lewis] Theobald. 1733. (Vol. 7.)

Theobald[2] [As above.] 1740. (Vol. 8.)

Tschischwitz *Shakspere's Hamlet, Prince of Denmark.* [Edited by] Dr Benno Tschischwitz. Halle, 1869. [English text, with commentary in German.]

Verity *Hamlet,* edited . . . by A. W. Verity. 1904.

Warburton *The Works of Shakespear.* The Genuine Text . . . with . . .

Notes by Mr Pope and Mr [William] Warburton. 1747. (Vol. 8.)

White   *The Works of William Shakespeare* . . . edited . . . by Richard Grant White. 1857–65. (Vol. 11, 1861.)

Wilson   (in Textual Apparatus) = Dover Wilson.

2. OTHER WORKS

The following abbreviations are used. Works which are sufficiently identified in the places where they are cited are not included in this list.

Abbott   E. A. Abbott, *A Shakespearian Grammar*. Second edition. 1870, etc.
Reference is to numbered paragraphs.

AN&Q   *American Notes and Queries.*

Archiv   *Archiv für das Studium der neueren Sprachen und Literaturen.*

Bailey   Samuel Bailey, *On the Received Text of Shakespeare's Dramatic Writings and its Improvement*. 2 vols. 1862–6.

BB   *Der Bestrafte Brudermord.*

Becket   Andrew Becket, *Shakespeare Himself Again* . . . A full . . . examen of the Readings and Interpretations of the several editors. Vol. 1. 1815.

Bradley   A. C. Bradley, *Shakespearean Tragedy*. 1904.

Bright   Timothy Bright, *A Treatise of Melancholy*. London, Vautrollier. 1586.
(Reprinted Facsimile Text Society, 1940.)

Bullough   Geoffrey Bullough, *Narrative and Dramatic Sources of Shakespeare*. Vol. 7. 1973.

Chambers, *WS*   E. K. Chambers, *William Shakespeare*. A Study of Facts and Problems. 2 vols. 1930.

Chambers, *El.St.*   E. K. Chambers, *The Elizabethan Stage*. 4 vols. 1923.

Chappell   William Chappell, *Popular Music of the Olden Time*. 2 vols. 1855–9.

Coghill   Nevill Coghill, *Shakespeare's Professional Skills*. 1964.

Coleridge   Samuel Taylor Coleridge, *Shakespearean Criticism*, edited by T. M. Raysor. Everyman's Library edition. 2 vols. 1960.

Corson   Hiram Corson, *Jottings on the Text of Hamlet*. 1874.

Cotgrave   Randle Cotgrave, *A Dictionary of the French and English Tongues*. 1611.
Second edition. 1632.

Dollerup   Cay Dollerup, *Denmark, 'Hamlet', and Shakespeare*. A Study of Englishmen's Knowledge of Denmark . . . with Special Reference to *Hamlet*. (Salzburg Studies in English Literature.) 1975.

Dover Wilson   See *MSH, WHH*, and Section 1 above.

Duthie   George Ian Duthie, *The 'Bad' Quarto of 'Hamlet'*. 1941.

EC   *Essays in Criticism.*

EETS   Early English Text Society.

ELH   *ELH: A Journal of English Literary History.*

ELN   *English Language Notes.*

ES	*English Studies.*
FQ	Edmund Spenser, *The Faerie Queene.*
Franz	Wilhelm Franz, *Die Sprache Shakespeares.* Halle, 1939.
Gollancz	Sir Israel Gollancz, *The Sources of 'Hamlet'.* 1926.
Greene	*The Life and Complete Works in Prose and Verse of Robert Greene,* edited by A. B. Grosart. 15 vols. 1881–6.
Greg	See *SFF.*
Hinman	Charlton Hinman, *The Printing and Proof-Reading of the First Folio of Shakespeare.* 2 vols. 1963.
HO	Harold Jenkins, *Hamlet and Ophelia,* British Academy Shakespeare Lecture, 1963. (*Proceedings of the British Academy,* XLIX, 135–51.)
Hulme	Hilda M. Hulme, *Explorations in Shakespeare's Language.* 1962.
JEGP	*Journal of English and Germanic Philology.*
Jervis	Swynfen Jervis, *Proposed Emendations of the Text of Shakespeare's Plays.* 1860.
Kökeritz	Helge Kökeritz, *Shakespeare's Pronunciation.* 1953.
Lavater	Lewes Lavater, *Of Ghosts and Spirits Walking by Night,* translated into English by R.H. 1572. [In Latin 1570.] Edited by J. Dover Wilson and May Yardley. 1929. Reference is to parts and chapters.
Le Loyer	Pierre Le Loyer, *IIII Livres des Spectres ou Apparitions et Visions d'Esprits, Anges et Demons.* Angers, 1586. Reference is to books and chapters.
Linthicum	M. C. Linthicum, *Costume in the Drama of Shakespeare and his Contemporaries.* 1936.
Lyly	*The Complete Works of John Lyly,* edited by R. Warwick Bond. 3 vols. 1902.
Marshall	Frank A. Marshall, *A Study of Hamlet.* 1875.
Misc.Obs.	*Miscellaneous Observations on the Tragedy of 'Hamlet'.* 1752.
Minsheu	John Minsheu, *Ductor in Linguas, the Guide into Tongues.* 1617.
MLN	*Modern Language Notes.*
MLR	*The Modern Language Review.*
MP	*Modern Philology.*
MSH	J. Dover Wilson, *The Manuscript of Shakespeare's 'Hamlet' and the Problems of its Transmission.* 1934.
MSR	Malone Society Reprint.
N&Q	*Notes and Queries.* For the first 12 series of 12 volumes each, reference is by series and volume; subsequent volumes are continuously numbered from CXLV on.
Nares	Robert Nares, *A Glossary . . . of Words, Phrases, Names and Allusions.* 1822. Revised J. O. Halliwell[-Phillipps] and T. Wright. 2 vols. 1859.
Nashe	*The Works of Thomas Nashe,* edited by Ronald B. McKerrow. 5 vols. 1904–10. Revised by F. P. Wilson. 1958.
NCS	See Section 1 above.
Nosworthy	J. M. Nosworthy, *Shakespeare's Occasional Plays.* 1965.

NR	See Sisson.
OED	*A New English Dictionary on Historical Principles.* 1884–1928. Reissued as *The Oxford English Dictionary.* 1933.
Onions	C. T. Onions, *A Shakespeare Glossary.* 1911, etc.
PBSA	*Papers of the Bibliographical Society of America.*
PMLA	*Publications of the Modern Language Association of America.*
PQ	*Philological Quarterly.*
Prosser	Eleanor Prosser, *Hamlet and Revenge.* 1967. Second edition, revised. 1971. Page numbers refer to the first edition, but those of the second edition, when they differ, are added in brackets.
RES	*The Review of English Studies.*
SAB	*The Shakespeare Association Bulletin.*
SB	*Studies in Bibliography.*
Schmidt	Alexander Schmidt, *Shakespeare-Lexicon.* 2 vols. 1874–5. Revised G. Sarrazin. 1902, etc.
SEL	*Studies in English Literature.*
Seng	P. J. Seng, *The Vocal Songs in the Plays of Shakespeare.* 1967.
SFF	W. W. Greg, *The Shakespeare First Folio.* 1955.
Sh.Jahr.	*Shakespeare-Jahrbuch.*
Sh.'s Eng.	*Shakespeare's England*: an Account of the Life and Manners of his Age. [By various authors.] 2 vols. 1916.
Sh.Studs.	*Shakespeare Studies.*
Sisson (*NR*)	C. J. Sisson, *New Readings in Shakespeare.* 1956.
SP	*Studies in Philology.*
SQ	*Shakespeare Quarterly.*
SS	*Shakespeare Survey.*
Taillepied	Noel Taillepied, *Traité de l'Apparition des Esprits.* 1588.
Theobald (*SR*)	Lewis Theobald, *Shakespeare Restored.* 1726.
Tilley	Morris Palmer Tilley, *A Dictionary of the Proverbs in England in the Sixteenth and Seventeenth Centuries.* 1950.
TLS	*The Times Literary Supplement.*
Walker	William Sidney Walker, *A Critical Examination of the Text of Shakespeare.* 3 vols. 1860.
WHH	J. Dover Wilson, *What Happens in 'Hamlet'.* 1935.

References to Elizabethan dramatists are as far as possible to act, scene, and line, so that they may be easily located in any edition. References to Ben Jonson accord with the standard edition by Herford and Simpson (11 vols, Oxford, 1925–52); and to Marlowe with the one-volume edition of *The Plays* by Roma Gill (Oxford, 1971).

3. MISCELLANEOUS ABBREVIATIONS

Most will be familiar, but the following may be noted.

conj.	conjecture(d)	n(n).	note(s)
corr.	corrected state	n.s.	new series
c.w.	catchword	O.E.	Old English
eds.	editors	O.N.	Old Norse
F	Folio	Q(q)	quarto(s)
Fr.	French	S.D.	stage-direction
L.	Latin	st.	stanza
lit.	literally	subst.	substantially
LN(N)	(See) Longer Note(s)	uncorr.	uncorrected state
M.E.	Middle English		

INTRODUCTION

I. THE DATE

Hamlet, Shakespeare's most famous play, was written and produced at about the midpoint of his playwriting career. A conflict of evidence has made its precise date, like most other things about *Hamlet*, a problem;[1] but certain limits are clear. It cannot have been known to Francis Meres in the autumn of 1598 when it failed to find mention in his *Palladis Tamia* among the plays there listed in witness of Shakespeare's excellence as a writer for the stage.[2] It must have been later than *Julius Caesar*, which it echoes in the account of the portents preceding Caesar's death (I.i.116–23) and which, as performed by Shakespeare's company, it makes the occasion of a joke (III.ii.102–3). *Julius Caesar*, also unmentioned by Meres, was being played in 1599: it was seen by Thomas Platter on 21 September.[3] *Hamlet* itself, as 'latelie Acted by the Lord Chamberleyne his servantes', was entered on the Stationers' Register on 26 July 1602;[4] and since a line in the bad quarto of *The Merry Wives of Windsor*, 'What is the reason that you use me thus?' (l. 1188), was lifted from it (*Ham.*, V.i.284), *Hamlet* must have been in the repertory for some time before *The Merry Wives* was registered on 18 January 1602.[5] A date between the middle of 1599 and the end of 1601 appears thus beyond dispute.

Moreover, within those limits a striking topical allusion would seem to place *Hamlet* firmly in 1601. The passage about the 'little eyases' who are 'now the fashion' and 'berattle the common stages' (II.ii.336–58) is universally recognized as an account of the boy actors who from Michaelmas 1600 were established at the Blackfriars,[6] where, according to Jonson's own dates, they acted

1. There is a helpful survey of the evidence by E. A. J. Honigmann in 'The Date of *Hamlet*', *SS* 9, 24–34, from some conclusions of which, however, I find myself having to dissent.

2. Chambers, *WS*, ii. 193–4.   3. Chambers, *El.St.*, ii. 364–5.

4. Arber, *Transcript of the Registers of the Company of Stationers*, iii. 212. See below, p. 13.

5. Ibid., iii. 199.

6. Chambers, *El.St.*, ii. 41–3; Hillebrand, *The Child Actors*, pp. 151–7; Irwin Smith, *Shakespeare's Blackfriars Playhouse*, pp. 177–8.

his *Cynthia's Revels* before the end of the year and *Poetaster* in 1601, both of them gibing at the plays and playwrights of the public playhouses. One particular taunt seems to put *Poetaster* in the spring: a professional player is made to say

> This winter has made us all poorer than so many starved snakes; nobody comes at us, not a gentleman, nor a—
> (III. iv. 328–30)

And since Jonson knew that his opponents were already preparing to retaliate (see III. iv. 322–3; IV. vii. 26–7), the play in which they did so, *Satiromastix*, must have followed within a few months if not weeks, being eventually entered for publication on 11 November.[1] All this is what lies behind Shakespeare's references to the gentlemen who forsake the 'common stages' (II. ii. 340–2) and to the poetical 'throwing about of brains' (II. ii. 353–6).[2] Since he speaks of 'much to do on both sides', it is not easy to believe that Shakespeare got in even before *Satiromastix*, as is sometimes contended on the ground that the pictures of two Horaces juxtaposed in *Satiromastix* (v. ii. 251–64) imitate the two pictures Hamlet shows his mother (III. iv. 53).[3] But whatever the precise order of events, the account of the theatre quarrel in *Hamlet* must date about or soon after the middle of 1601.[4] This would still allow time for *Twelfth Night*, which adds its mite to the quarrel by developing a joke from *Satiromastix*,[5] to come before the end of the year.

Now it is true that the passage about the child actors, present in the Folio text (F) and represented in the First Quarto (Q1), is not found in the Second Quarto (Q2), so that it is sometimes taken to be a later insertion.[6] But there is in this very same scene another substantial omission in Q2 which, by reason of what Dover Wilson has called the frayed edges it has left, is clearly recognizable as a cut (II. ii. 239–69),[7] and it is natural to assume

1. Arber, iii. 195.
2. See also notes *ad loc.*
3. *SQ*, III, 280–1; IX, 494–5.
4. Of other alleged topical allusions, one to the production of *Every Man Out of his Humour* late in 1599 cannot be demonstrated (see II. ii. 321 LN; W. J. Lawrence, *Shakespeare's Workshop*, pp. 98 ff.), and the theory that IV. iv. 18–26 alludes to the siege of Ostend has been demolished (LN).
5. See Arden *Tw.N.* III. i. 58–60 n. and Intro., pp. xxxi–xxxii.
6. Lawrence, *Shakespeare's Workshop*, pp. 106–8; Honigmann, *SS 9*, 26–7.
7. See LN; *MSH*, p. 97. Cf. Chambers, *WS*, i. 414. The only other substantial omission in Q2 (v. ii. 68–80) must surely be an error. There is no evidence in F of any material interpolations (as distinct from actors' elaborations). On the Q2 omissions, see also below, p. 44.

the two belong together. Moreover, although Lawrence thought the absence of the account of the 'little eyases' improved and Honigmann that at least it did not damage the texture of ideas,[1] the reverse can be shown to be the case. In Q2 the bare statement that the tragedians have lost their following (II. ii. 334) is succeeded immediately by Hamlet's comment, 'It is not very strange; for my uncle is King of Denmark, and those that would make mouths at him while my father lived give twenty, forty, fifty, a hundred ducats apiece for his picture in little' (II. ii. 359–62). Thus two instances of the public's fickleness are brought together, but while the first concerns the loss of popularity by those who formerly had it, the second shows an access of popularity by a man formerly disliked. The two instances are not comparable. But when we interpose the account of the boy actors we see that it is their sudden and irrational leap into favour that leads on to the equally new and irrational acclaim of another upstart. It is no more strange for them to dominate the Globe than for him to be King of Denmark, and it is the rage for the miniature actors which suggests that for the 'picture in little'. Hence I think we must accept the child actors as essential to the dialogue and 1601 as the date of its composition.

This fits with another presumed topical allusion in the text immediately preceding. 'The late innovation' (II. ii. 330–1) which has occasioned an inhibition on the players is not in itself sufficiently explicit to guide us to a date; but a date established on other grounds may attach an identity to it. The word *innovation* must of course be understood in its then common sense of insurrection. If it meant simply a novel practice it would need more explanation than Rosencrantz thinks to offer or Hamlet to solicit. Attempts to relate it to the novelty of child actors telescope, as Q1 does, what in the full text appear to be two separate things. But an insurrection, even without elaboration, is enough to account for an inhibition; and an allusion to 'the late' one in 1601 would inevitably bring to mind the Essex rebellion in February of that year (see II. ii. 330–1 LN).

Gabriel Harvey

So far so good. Perplexity begins with a reference to *Hamlet* which is not reconcilable with the date of 1601. On a blank half-page in his copy of Speght's edition of Chaucer (fol. 394ᵛ) Gabriel Harvey wrote a longish note in the course of which he said

1. See p. 2, n. 6, above.

> The younger sort takes much delight in Shakespeares Venus,
> & Adonis: but his Lucrece, & his tragedie of Hamlet, Prince of
> Denmarke, haue it in them, to please the wiser sort.
>   (*Marginalia*, ed. Moore Smith, p. 232)[1]

When exactly, after his purchase of the book in 1598, Harvey
wrote this note can only be inferred from other allusions in it; and
these are strangely conflicting. The inclusion among our 'florishing metricians' of Spenser, who died on 16 January 1599, is
apparently not indicative since the same list oddly includes
Watson, who had died in 1592; but a statement of what 'the Earle
of Essex commendes' and what 'the Lord Mountioy makes the
like account of' points to a time not only before Mountjoy was
made Earl of Devonshire in July 1603 but before Essex met his
death on 25 February 1601. The need to accommodate this to
the date of 1601 for *Hamlet* has prompted various attempts to
explain, or explain away, a present tense that is none the less
hardly credible after Essex's execution.[2] Chambers was driven to
the desperate guess 'either that "commendes" is a scribal error
for "commended", or that Harvey had access to some letter or
other writing by Essex . . . which has not come down to us'.[3] Yet
Hamlet aside, Harvey's comments on contemporary literature are
more appropriate to a time before the death of Essex, or indeed
of Spenser.[4] The possible exception is the reference to 'Owens
new Epigrams', which have taken Harvey's fancy, as they at once
did that of Latinists in general when published in 1606. As they
then appeared, however, they included, along with epigrams of
quite recent date, others of much earlier composition;[5] so it is

1. For the passage in full see Appendix (pp. 572-3). It has sometimes been
connected with one on the previous leaf (fol. 393ᵛ) which speaks of Cecil, to
whom the volume was dedicated, as 'the new patron of Chawcer'. Both
passages refer to Essex, to several of the same poets, and to publications yet to
come, and if it could ever be shown that they were written at the same time,
this would be strong evidence for 1598 or soon after as the date of the second as
well as the first. But it is at least as likely that the author some time later was
prompted to the second by coming upon the first. A new book on Harvey is
'inclined' to date both notes after 1 June 1599 (Virginia Stern, *Gabriel Harvey*,
1979, pp. 127-8); but even if one could infer that references to his own unpublished works reflected the ban on their publication, this would do little to
advance the solution of our problem.

2. Kirschbaum's contention that it accords with Harvey's practice elsewhere
(*SP*, xxxiv, 168-75) is refuted by Honigmann, *SS 9*, 25-6.

3. *Shakespearean Gleanings*, p. 68.

4. Cf. Boas, *Shakespeare and the Universities*, pp. 256-60.

5. E.g. II.21 on Burghley, dated 1596; II.29 on Sidney; II.39 on Drake
(written, according to Camden, by a pupil of Winchester school).

possible that Harvey saw some of them in manuscript,[1] though it is not clear in that case what distinguished them as 'new'. For the rest, the English works 'now freshest in request' are the *Arcadia* and *The Faerie Queene* (presumably in the enlarged editions of 1598 and 1596 respectively); and though Harvey is concerned not only with what English poetry has done but with what one may still 'looke for', the most recent in his list of poets were already prominent by the middle 1590s. Yet if Harvey were acquainted with *Hamlet* at any time before 1601, it obviously cannot have contained allusions to the theatrical events of that year. This need not imply a 1601 rehandling such as Dover Wilson characteristically envisages and Chambers rules out.[2] There has been too much irresponsible conjecture about Shakespeare's supposed revisions of supposed earlier attempts. My conception of Shakespeare is of a supremely inventive poet who had no call to rework his previous plays when he could always move on to a new one.[3] But minor changes to suit changed circumstances are another matter. I see no reason why some such, amounting perhaps to no more than the insertion of topicalities, might not have been made in *Hamlet*. Can it be then that the account of the boy actors, though clearly cut from rather than added to the Q2 text, was, after all, an addition to the original play? If so, it must have been part of a larger addition including the topical reference to the 'innovation' as well as Hamlet's remark about the King's 'picture in little'. It is not hard to envisage as an interpolation the whole passage about the players and their misfortunes, from the query 'What players are they?' to the announcement of their arrival (II.ii.324–64). Their arrival is what matters to the play and it needs no explanation. That a passage of topical interest should be inserted in a play and when no longer topical removed is not inherently unlikely; nor is it that less should be removed than was put in.

This hypothesis has admittedly objections. One might not have supposed that an addition to a play already in performance would attach itself to the author's foul papers from which we believe Q2 to have been printed. A more serious objection, although the

1. Virginia Stern (as above, p. 4, n. 1) similarly accepts this as possible, while suggesting as an alternative that the allusion to Owen may be a later addition.

2. NCS, p. xxii; *Shakespearean Gleanings*, p. 68.

3. If it comes to be accepted that the Quarto and Folio texts of *King Lear* represent two Shakespearean versions, the exception will be of a kind, I think, to prove the rule.

point is usually disregarded,[1] is that nothing Harvey says suggests
that he is concerned with *Hamlet* in performance. On the contrary
he appears to refer to a work that could be read along with *Venus
and Adonis* and *Lucrece*.[2] The possibility of its manuscript circula-
tion is one to view with scepticism: however appropriate it might
seem for the author of the narrative poems, it is not what we think
of as the way of a professional playwright and a sharer in a company jealous to protect its scripts. On the other hand, since it is
incredible that the abridged and garbled Q1 would have been
recommended for 'the wiser sort', a printed *Hamlet* would imply
for Harvey's note a date after the appearance of Q2 in 1604–5.[3]
And although a date as late as this might get support from Owen's
Epigrams if 'new' were taken to mean newly published, it has,
besides fitting less well with Harvey's other literary allusions, a
double obstacle to face: not merely the death of Essex in February
1601 but the elevation of Mountjoy in 1603.

Hence the balance of probabilities suggests that even without
a reading text Harvey was able to commend *Hamlet* before
Essex's death in February 1601.[4] And if it could once be granted
that his knowledge of the play might have come simply from the
theatre, then the likeliest solution to the puzzle would be that
Hamlet reached the stage in or shortly before 1600 (certainly after
Julius Caesar) and had the topicalities about the players grafted
on to it the next year. This solution would have the advantage of
explaining how a work of the dimensions of *Hamlet* could be
referring to the events of 1601 so soon after their occurrence, and,
incidentally, how *Satiromastix* might both have imitated *Hamlet*
and been glanced at in it. It would similarly allow more time for
the vicissitudes of the actors which planted a line of *Hamlet* in the
quarto of *The Merry Wives* as well as for the composition of *Twelfth*

1. Except by the authors of '*Hamlet, Antonio's Revenge*, and the *Ur-Hamlet*',
SQ, IX, 493–8, who in their turn ignore the counter-indications for an early date.

2. Yet Harvey's reference to Shakespeare's poems accords with opinion at
Cambridge, as shown by *The Return from Parnassus*, pt 1, ll. 1201–3, pt 2,
ll. 300–4 (cf. Nosworthy, pp. 168–70), and it may be that his mention of
Hamlet along with them reflects the impact that it made on Cambridge when,
as the Q1 title-page informs us, it was performed there. Cf. below, p. 14 and
n.1.

3. I discount Boas's suggestion of a possible lost quarto. Apart from the lack
of reference (e.g. in Meres, the Stationers' Register) the title-page of Q2
(describing the text as 'almost as much againe as it was') refers to the reported
text of Q1 and implies that there was no other.

4. A further reference by Harvey to 'the Tragedie of Hamlet' in a list of
admired works written in a book now in the Folger Library (see *SQ*, XVII,
151–5), while confirming Harvey's interest in it, gives no help with the date.

Night. It might also be expected to illuminate, and perhaps to be illuminated by, the relation between *Hamlet* and Marston's *Antonio's Revenge.*

Antonio's Revenge

The relation between these two plays has long been a matter of controversy. In each a son is visited by the Ghost of his father, who reveals that he has been poisoned, laments that his wife has yielded to the murderer, and calls on his son to revenge. The son, already separated from his beloved, whose chastity is put in question, becomes melancholy and impersonates a fool or madman. He forgoes an opportunity to stab the murderer for the sake of a fuller revenge later, and the Ghost appears to him again in his mother's chamber. Apart from the basic identity of plot there are many incidental similarities. Each play opens with a night-scene which ends with a description of dawn; the hero is shown in black and reading a book; the voice of the Ghost is heard beneath the stage; there is a dumb-show in which the widow seems first to reject but then accepts the villain's love; the beloved dies broken-hearted off stage. Often similar sentiments are expressed in different terms, as when, to take obvious examples, Hamlet says

> or ere those shoes were old
> With which she follow'd my poor father's body,
> (1. ii. 147–8)

and Antonio

> my father's trunk scarce cold,
> (11. ii. 150; G 11. iv. 14[1])

or when Hamlet says 'Now could I drink hot blood' (111. ii. 381) and Antonio 'I'll suck red vengeance' (111. i. 129; G 111. ii. 78). Critics contradict one another about whether there are verbal parallels: it depends on the significance you attach to the common use of not uncommon words. Both ghosts part from the sons they have called to vengeance upon the word 'Remember'; both on reappearing use the verb 'forget'. Both sons assert that nothing else will have place in their 'brain' (*AR* 111. i. 89; G 111. ii. 38: *Ham.* 1. v. 103); Antonio has 'a prayer or two to offer up' (111. i. 96;

---

1. Act, scene, line (1) as in the edition by G. K. Hunter (Regents Renaissance Drama Series), which approximates to Bullen's edition, except that in Act v Bullen counts one scene less; (2) preceded by G, as in the Revels edition by W. R. Gair, which reverts to the neo-classical scene-division of the quarto. Harvey Wood's Marston inconveniently gives the scene-division of the quarto with no line-numbering.

G III.ii.45) and Hamlet says he 'will go pray' (I.v.138). Shakespeare's Ghost, in pity of his wife, says 'Conceit in weakest bodies strongest works' (III.iv.114); Marston's says 'Thy sex is weak' (III.ii.70; G III.v.8). What has never been disputed is that the resemblances are 'too strong to be merely coincidental'.[1]

Older scholars, believing *Antonio's Revenge* the earlier play, accepted Shakespeare's debt to it.[2] More recently some have seen Marston as the borrower,[3] even if this has meant sidestepping the chronology. Clearly the dates are crucial.

Antonio's Revenge is the sequel to *Antonio and Mellida*, which brings on stage two pictures (v.i) bearing the inscriptions '*Anno Domini* 1599' and '*Aetatis suae* 24', and it is a very reasonable assumption that these otherwise pointless labels give the current date and the author's age. Since Marston, christened 7 October 1576, began his twenty-fourth year about Michaelmas 1599, *Antonio and Mellida* is thus fairly safely assigned to the autumn or winter of 1599–1600. The sequel, especially as it differs from that promised, may not have followed at once; and since it proclaims its own season to be winter[4] and must have preceded *Poetaster*, which ridicules it, it can be dated with something approaching certainty in the winter of 1600–1.[5] Both plays were entered on the Stationers' Register on 24 October 1601.[6]

Antonio's Revenge, then, must have preceded the description in *Hamlet* of the boy actors and their doings. The belief that there was not sufficient interval between the two plays to allow either to imitate the other has recently led some scholars to ascribe their likeness to a common source in the lost pre-Shakespearean play which is conveniently referred to as the *Ur-Hamlet*.[7] Yet obviously

1. G. K. Hunter, ed., *Antonio's Revenge*, p. xviii. See D. J. McGinn, *Shakespeare's Influence on the Drama of his Age*, pp. 19–23, and for the fullest, but not a complete, list of verbal parallels, pp. 135–8.

2. Thorndike, *PMLA*, XVII (1902), 125–220; Radebrecht, *Shakespeares Abhängigkeit von John Marston* (1918). Thorndike regards the proposition that '*Antonio's Revenge* preceded Shakspere's *Hamlet*' as 'one which can hardly be questioned' (p. 141).

3. Best, I think, D. L. Frost, *The School of Shakespeare*, pp. 173–80. See also McGinn, as above.

4. I cannot agree with Hunter (ed. *Antonio and Mellida*, p. x), that the description of winter in the Prologue is merely metaphorical. While the purpose of the lines is to evoke the tragic mood, they stress its 'congruence' with the actual 'time'.

5. A year later than was formerly supposed. See Chambers, *El.St.*, iii. 429–30.
6. Arber, iii. 193.

7. See Smith, Pizer, and Kaufman, *SQ*, IX, 493–8; Gair, ed. *Antonio's Revenge*, pp. 13, 16–19; Hunter, ed. *Antonio's Revenge*, p. xx. Reavley Gair's

if *Hamlet,* though necessarily without the account of the boy actors, was already in existence and familiar to Gabriel Harvey by 1600, it could have been familiar to Marston too. Comparison of the two plays in the light of this possibility convinces me beyond any doubt that it was.

So long as chronology does not forbid, the natural assumption would see Marston rather than Shakespeare as the borrower, if only because Shakespeare's tragedy, based on the well-known Danish story, could have no need of any supplementary source. Marston by contrast was fashioning a revenge sequel for *Antonio and Mellida,* which had little enough to offer in that genre and had to be filled out with incidents and motifs drawn from other plays.[1] Once it is accepted that his play may be the later, it becomes clear that many of these incidents and motifs had their source in *Hamlet.*

Illustration may conveniently begin with the episode of the ghost in the cellarage, already discussed at length by Nevill Coghill.[2] Its nature and purpose in *Hamlet* may be a matter of opinion (see I.v.157 LN); but it will be readily agreed that in itself it is homogeneous, that it sustains the terror of the Ghost, and that by involving Hamlet's companions it both enlarges and diversifies the action. None of these things can be said about the subterranean voice in Marston: it is heard on disconnected occasions, once in an echoing chorus 'above and beneath', once in a groan when a murder is committed (III.i.125, 194; G III.ii.75, iii.50), and although briefly acknowledged by Antonio alone, it contributes nothing to the action. It is hard to see it as more than a theatrical sensation, in which Marston simultaneously elaborates Shakespeare's device and attenuates its effect.

The clearest demonstration that the indebtedness is on Marston's side comes when features common to the two plays have a significance in *Hamlet* which in *Antonio's Revenge* they have lost. Perhaps the most striking of these is the linking of the hero's mother with the heroine's fate. In Marston the actual infidelity of the mother and the suspected infidelity of the heroine are connected simply through the murderer, whose villainy is

---

kindness in allowing me to see the relevant pages of his Introduction in advance of publication is referred to in my Preface and again acknowledged here.

1. E.g. the eating of the child's flesh from Seneca's *Thyestes* and *Titus Andronicus;* the exhibition of the hanging corpse, the plucking out of the tongue from *The Spanish Tragedy;* etc. For Marston's use of stock devices see McGinn, p. 18; Gair, pp. 18–19.

2. *Shakespeare's Professional Skills,* pp. 9–15.

responsible for both. But Hamlet's doubts of Ophelia's honesty spring from that belief in the 'frailty' of all womanhood which his mother's conduct has inspired (I.ii.146).

> Rebellious hell,
> If thou canst mutine in a matron's bones,
> To flaming youth let virtue be as wax
> And melt in her own fire.   (III.iv.82–5)

The pervasiveness of this motif in *Hamlet* gives rise to piercing ironies, as when the Queen hopes that love for Ophelia may be the 'cause of Hamlet's wildness' (III.i.38–41) or recalls how she had once hoped that Ophelia would be Hamlet's wife (v.i.237–9); and the irony has a dramatic climax when the Queen appears as the narrator of Ophelia's lovelorn death (IV.vii.163–82). There is nothing in *Antonio's Revenge* of this profound connection, but, as an interesting relic of it, it is again the hero's mother, now pointlessly, who reports the heroine's death (IV.i.283–310; G IV.iii. 160–86).

Another relic of *Hamlet* is Marston's player. In fact *Antonio's Revenge* has no player and needs none. But that does not prevent a bereaved father from saying

> Would'st have me cry . . .
> Or wring my face with mimic action,
> Stamp, curse, weep, rage, and then my bosom strike?
> Away, 'tis apish action, *player*-like.
>   (I.ii.312–16; G I.v.76–80)

No doubt this is not so unusual a simile that Marston could not have thought of it unaided. Yet, a connection between the two plays once granted, it is obvious that this 'mimic action' and this 'player-like' weeping are the same as cause Hamlet to protest

> that this *player* here,
> But in a fiction, in a dream of *passion*,
> Could *force* his soul so to his own conceit

that he had 'tears in his eyes' (II.ii.545–9). When subsequently Marston's hero says

> I will not swell like a tragedian
> In *forced passion*,   (II.ii.105–6; G II.iii.104–5)

the connection is confirmed by the verbal correspondence. But whereas Shakespeare's player is one of the troupe the plot requires, is brought to tears by speaking the thematically crucial speech about Pyrrhus and Hecuba, and hence could never have

derived from Marston's, it is easy to see how Marston's could have
derived from him.[1]

A not dissimilar link between the two plays occurs when the
murderer Piero boasts of having killed his victim by dropping
poison in the bowl in which he drank his health. This inevitably
recalls how Claudius, drinking Hamlet's health, throws a 'pearl'
or 'union' in the cup (v. ii. 268–9, 284–5); and again the connection seems established by a verbal correspondence:

> I myself *carous'd* unto his health
> And future *fortune* of our unity.   (i. i. 69–70)

> The Queen *carouses* to thy *fortune*, Hamlet.   (v. ii. 292)

But when the Queen carouses, Claudius's stratagem of course
miscarries and wife and husband, through the 'union' in the cup,
are joined in death. An incident that in Marston is briefly narrated
for the sake of a moment's villainous gloating is in *Hamlet* fully
dramatized and the indispensable means to a very significant
catastrophe. Again it is easy to see how Marston could have
derived the incident from *Hamlet* (and even the irony of Piero's
drinking to their *unity* is perhaps an echo of Claudius's *union*), but
the converse is inconceivable.

There are other incidents in the two plays in which drinking is
important. Corresponding to the King's '*revel*' in *Hamlet* (i. iv),
in *Antonio's Revenge*

> *triumphant revels* mount aloft;
> The Duke drinks deep to overflow his grief.
> The court is rack'd to pleasure; each man strains
> To feign a *jocund* eye.   (v. ii. 21–4; G v. iii. 6–9)

And again, for Marston here is revealingly repetitive,

> Proud pomp shoots mounting *triumph* up,
> Borne in loud accents to the front of Jove.
>   (v. ii. 84–5; G v. iii. 64–5)

These revels are important in Marston's catastrophe since it is in
the course of them that the masquers perform their ritual killing;
but why, one wonders, does pomp *shoot* and triumph (twice)
mount? The answer is supplied by *Hamlet*, where each '*jocund*
health that Denmark drinks' is signalled to the 'cannon', which
then resound to 'the heaven' 'the *triumph* of his pledge' (i. ii. 125–7,
i. iv. 6–12. See also v. ii. 272–5). The Shakespearean passages together give a quite precise description of the Danish custom of

1. See also ii. ii. 515–16 LN.

cannon-healths,[1] which have their place in the local colour of
Hamlet as well as in the structure of the plot. What we get in
Marston is the rhetoric of recollected noise without the specific
cause. Other verbal echoes here which individually might pass
for coincidence add cumulative weight. Marston's Duke 'drinks
deep' just as they do in Denmark (i.ii.175); but 'the front of
Jove', which in the description of Hamlet's father's portrait
(iii.iv.56) combines hyperbole with precision, has become no
more than a vague cliché for heaven.

This contrast between imaginative vagueness and imaginative
precision would seem to be characteristic; in the question of indebtedness it is clearly evidential. It may be detected even in
apparently straightforward verbal parallelisms (for it will be
beyond doubt by this time that these plentifully exist). A phrase
often cited is Marston's 'The other ghost *assum'd my father's shape*'
(i.ii.109; G i.iii.45), which appears to amalgamate Shakespeare's
'If it *assume my* noble *father's* person' (i.ii.244) and 'the devil hath
power T'*assume* a pleasing *shape*' (ii.ii.595–6). But Shakespeare's
assume brings into sharpest focus the crucial question whether the
Ghost is or only simulates Hamlet's father, and in Marston, where
a ghost is merely dreamt of, the verb lacks any comparable point.
When Hamlet asks why his father's 'bones . . . Have burst their
cerements' and why 'the sepulchre' has 'cast . . . up' the 'dead corse'
(i.iv.47–52), this concern with the physical is proper because he
has just decided to accept the Ghost as his father returned to
earth; but when in Marston it is 'the ghost' whose '*cerecloth*' (a
notably more commonplace word) is ripped up and who 'forsakes
his coffin' (iii.i.32–4), there is some confusion of body and spirit,
as in Shakespeare's exacter apprehension there is not. Again it
seems quite clear which passage is the echo of the other.

Other examples, both of conception and language, could be
added.[2] But this is not the place for a detailed study of *Antonio's
Revenge*. Enough, I think, has been said to prove its indebtedness
to *Hamlet*, which must therefore have been known to Marston
before the end of 1600. The existence of the play by that date,
which from Harvey's note seemed probable (see above, p. 6) is
now fully confirmed. I suppose there may be some who would
still contend that all Marston need have known was Shakespeare's
own source; but with links between *Hamlet* and *Antonio's Revenge*
as numerous, as detailed, and, since parallels are often in different

---

1. Dollerup, pp. 123–4, 216–17.
2. For some incidents in *Antonio's Revenge* explained as 'vestiges of *Hamlet*',
see Frost, p. 179.

contexts, as complex as they are, this would be asking too much of coincidence. It would also imply that Shakespeare followed the *Ur-Hamlet* more slavishly than we have right or reason to suppose, and even that what we think of as one of Shakespeare's supreme masterpieces was largely taken over from a predecessor. Rather, the links between the two plays, which affect every act and most scenes of *Hamlet*, suggest that what Marston knew when he wrote *Antonio's Revenge* was substantially the *Hamlet* we know now. Hence they afford no grounds for supposing that, topical allusions aside, there was ever an earlier Shakespearean version. Moreover, the nature of Marston's borrowings, abundant in incidents, in ideas, and even in little verbal echoes but without sustained identity of phrase, suggests that what Marston had to rely on was rather a retentive memory than any written text, in short that he acquired his knowledge of *Hamlet* from performances (of which he may of course have attended several). This perhaps makes it more likely that Gabriel Harvey did the same. The praise the play drew from Harvey and the imitation it received from Marston together give powerful testimony to its immediate success.

Conclusion

The conclusion I am brought to concerning the date of *Hamlet* is that as it has come down to us it belongs to 1601; but that nevertheless the essential *Hamlet*, minus the passage on the troubles of the actors, it is true, but otherwise differing little if at all from it, was being acted on the stage just possibly even before the end of 1599 and certainly in the course of 1600.

2. PUBLICATION

The history of the play's publication begins with its entry on the Stationers' Register on 26 July 1602, when James Roberts

> Entred for his Copie . . . A booke called the Revenge of Hamlett Prince [of] Denmarke as yt was latelie Acted by the Lord Chamberleyne his servantes
> (Arber, *Transcript of the Registers of the Company of Stationers*, iii. 212)

It was not, however, Roberts who brought out the First Quarto (Q1), which appeared in 1603. The title-page reads:

> THE / Tragicall Historie of / HAMLET / *Prince of Denmarke* / By William Shake-speare./ As it hath beene diuerse times acted

by his Highnesse ser- / uants in the Cittie of London: as also in the two V- / niuersities of Cambridge and Oxford, and else-where / [Device of Nicholas Ling] / At London printed for N.L. and Iohn Trundell. / 1603.

The printer has been identified as Valentine Simmes.

The unauthorized nature of this quarto is matched by the corruptness of its text. The naming of 'his Highnesse seruants' indicates publication after 19 May, when the former Lord Chamberlain's Company was taken under the patronage of the new king, James I. Nothing is known, beyond the title-page statement, of the university performances.[1]

Only two copies of this quarto are known (in the British Library and the Huntington). Before 1823, when the first of these came to light, its existence was unsuspected.

The Second Quarto (Q2) was printed, this time by Roberts, in 1604, and evidently late in the year, since of the seven extant copies[2] three are dated 1604, the others 1605. The title-page is as follows:

THE / Tragicall Historie of / HAMLET, / *Prince of Denmarke.* / By William Shakespeare. / Newly imprinted and enlarged to almost as much / againe as it was, according to the true and perfect / Coppie. / [Ling's device] / AT LONDON, / Printed by I.R. for N.L. and are to be sold at his / shoppe vnder Saint Dunstons Church in / Fleetstreet. 1604.   [*corr.* 1605.]

The claim to give 'the true and perfect Coppie' is evidently in-tended to stigmatize the defects of Q1, and with a little latitude allowed to 'almost' the assertion of almost double length is fair enough. The variance of date, though due simply to an alteration during printing, was formerly taken to indicate two editions; and this still may cause confusion, since the 1605 copies figure in older collations (Cambridge, Furness, Dowden) as Q3, with consequent misnumbering of succeeding quartos too.

What is declared about the publication of these two quartos has created a number of puzzles about what is not. Roberts's claim to *Hamlet*, his two-year delay before printing, his relations

1. It does not follow from the statement that these performances were of the Q1 text. I suppose it could have been at Cambridge that *Hamlet* was seen by Gabriel Harvey (see pp. 6–13). Nosworthy's idea that the play was specially written for a university audience (*Shakespeare's Occasional Plays*, ch. 11) is of course an engaging, but an improbable, conjecture.

2. At the British Library, the Bodleian, and Trinity College, Cambridge; the Huntington, the Folger, and the Elizabethan Club at Yale; and at the Uni-versity of Wroclaw, Poland.

with Ling, publisher of both quartos, have been the subject of ingenious speculation. But the most straightforward explanations are still also the most probable. Since nothing at all connects Roberts with Q1, we must infer that this was brought out by Ling and Trundle in spite of, not in accordance with, the entry in the Stationers' Register. Yet from Roberts's co-operation with Ling in the publication of Q2, it follows that they came to an accommodation. The participation in Q1 of Trundle, a very much junior partner, with Ling, an established bookseller, together with Trundle's disappearance when the bad quarto was succeeded by the better, has sometimes led to a guess – it can be no more – that it was he who secured the unauthorized copy. Suppositions that it came through Roberts, in league with Ling from the beginning,[1] are of course baseless.

A little light may be shed on Roberts's dealing with *Hamlet* by the partial analogy of *The Merchant of Venice*, which Roberts entered on the Stationers' Register on 22 July 1598 (Arber, iii. 122) but also failed to print till more than two years later. He printed it then for Thomas Hayes, who registered the book as his on 28 October 1600 explicitly with Roberts's consent (Arber, iii. 175). If Ling did not do the same with *Hamlet*, it must have been because he had no need to, having established the copyright as his through his prior publication of Q1. We may infer that Roberts again consented to the transfer while retaining the right to print, an arrangement the less surprising if we remember that he was essentially a printer[2] and had printed for Ling a number of times before.[3] Certainly Ling's copyright was openly accepted: *Hamlet* was one of sixteen books specified as his when they passed together to John Smethwick in 1607 (Arber, iii. 365).

In the case of *The Merchant of Venice* the reason for Roberts's delay in printing is explicit. The entry which grants it to him adds the proviso that it is not to be printed by him or anyone else without licence from the Lord Chamberlain; and this brings us to the problem – and the controversy – of Roberts's relations with the Lord Chamberlain's men. The books which he entered on the Stationers' Register include just five plays: all were entered within the period 1598–1603, all belonged to the Lord Chamberlain's

1. See below, p. 16 and n. 5.

2. Greg counts 150 imprints containing Roberts's name and only 15 original entries in the Stationers' Register over fourteen years, and concludes 'It is clear that Roberts was mainly a trade-printer, printing books for other stationers and only occasionally venturing on a serious publication of his own' (*Some Aspects and Problems of London Publishing between 1550 and 1650*, pp. 114–15).

3. Cf. Kirschbaum, *Shakespeare and the Stationers*, p. 305.

Company, and four of the five were registered with the stipulation
that they were not to be printed till further authority had been
obtained.[1] The exception in the case of *Hamlet* may be more
apparent than real; for although there was no express proviso,
Roberts did defer printing. Two of the five entries were followed
by no publication, the other three by the appearance of a quarto
after an interval of two years, each showing a change of ownership
but two of them printed by Roberts none the less. It would be
difficult not to agree with Greg[2] that there is something odd about
Roberts's entries of these Lord Chamberlain's plays. A favourite
interpretation has been that these were 'blocking' entries made
by Roberts in the interests of the players with the object not of
publishing the plays himself but of preventing others from doing
so;[3] but this has recently been challenged, I think successfully,
by Cairncross, whose view of Roberts as in conflict rather than in
concert with the players seems more apt to the nature of the
records.[4] Yet the theory he discredits does not appear more
fanciful than the one he sets up against it, in which Roberts, far
from assisting the players against the pirates, was himself the
'pirate king' trying to outmanœuvre the players with copies
surreptitiously obtained. All that we actually know is that
Roberts five times entered a Lord Chamberlain's Company play
without prospect of, four times without authority for, immediate
publication. But it will not be a wild conjecture that he hoped,
and was allowed to hope, to be able to proceed later, as with two
of the plays – *The Merchant of Venice* and *Hamlet* – to the extent of
having the printing of them, he in fact did.[5]

1. *The Merchant of Venice*, as above; *Cloth Breeches and Velvet Hose*, 27 May
1600; *A Larum for London*, 29 May 1600; *Troilus and Cressida*, 7 Feb. 1603 (Arber,
iii. 161, 226). The first required the Lord Chamberlain's licence; the next two
needed 'further' and one of them also 'better' authority and had attention
drawn to them as being Lord Chamberlain's plays (Arber, iii. 37); the last,
deferred for 'sufficient' authority, was dealt with 'in full court'.

2. *London Publishing*, pp. 117–21.

3. Pollard, *Shakespeare Folios and Quartos*, pp. 66–73, and *Shakespeare's Fight
with the Pirates*, pp. 43–4. This view was cautiously accepted by Greg (loc. cit.)
after a full review of the evidence. Chambers, however, was sceptical (*El.St.*,
iii. 188–9; *WS*, i. 146).

4. 'Shakespeare and the "Staying Entries" ', in *Shakespeare in the Southwest*, ed.
T. J. Stafford (El Paso, 1969), pp. 80–93.

5. Cairncross relies much upon what he calls 'evasive', apparently meaning
unrecorded, transfer. But of the five plays in question the transfer of *The
Merchant of Venice* was entered in the Register, that of *Hamlet* is easily explained,
while two others were not transferred at all, their registration lapsing. Moreover, Cairncross's whole hypothesis depends upon at least two quite unwarrant-
able assumptions. (1) The well-known entry of 4 August 1600 listing four other

When Roberts entered *Hamlet*, then, in July 1602, with or without the Lord Chamberlain's men's blessing, it is to be supposed that what he hoped to print was what he later did print, the genuine text. But before he could do so, he was anticipated by Q1, which led to Ling's having publication rights and subsequently partnering Roberts in Q2. It is difficult to see how Roberts can have obtained his text except from the company itself. It is often assumed, and is likely enough – as with *Romeo and Juliet* and perhaps *Love's Labour's Lost*[1] – that the players consented to replace a bad text with a good. No doubt we must be careful before speaking of Q2 as an authorized edition; but there is no ground for suspicions, too readily expressed, that Roberts acquired his copy by other than an authorized route.[2]

It was three years after the publication of Q2, on 19 November 1607, that *Hamlet* was transferred, along with other of Ling's copyrights, to John Smethwick; and Smethwick in due course published three more quartos, each printed from its predecessor:[3] Q3, 1611; Q4, undated but most probably 1622; Q5, 1637.

The undated quarto calls for a brief comment. The probable date for it is indicated by the parallel case of *Romeo and Juliet*, which too was among the copyrights which Smethwick acquired from Ling. The two plays seem to have been twinned in later publication: after publishing the third quartos in 1609 and 1611 respectively, Smethwick added the fourth quartos, both printed

---

plays 'to be staied' (Arber, iii. 37), notwithstanding Arber's warning that this is a separate entry, is assumed to apply to Roberts. This doubles at a stroke the number of plays stayed – and the number of alleged transfers – with which Roberts is held to be concerned. (2) It is assumed that when Roberts registered *Hamlet* he 'entered a bad text', which he then made over to Ling. The Register of course, not given to such distinctions, leaves unspecified what text Roberts was proposing; but from the fact that he printed Q2 and did not print Q1 we are entitled to an inference, and one contrary to that which Cairncross makes. (Cf. Pollard, *Shakespeare Folios and Quartos*, pp. 74–5.) The idea that a professional printer arranged for another printer to print a surreptitious quarto for two still other stationers while reserving for himself 'any later, and safer, printing' (Cairncross, p. 88) has impressed some reputable scholars and would be credible in spy fiction.

1. See below, pp. 36–7.

2. Cf. S. Thomas, 'The Myth of the Authorized Shakespeare Quartos', *SQ*, xxvii (1976), 186–92. See below, p. 43 and n. 3.

3. Q3 introduces some conjectural emendations, some sophistications and some errors, in all of which, except for obvious misprints, it is almost invariably followed by Q4. The emendations and sophistications, though lacking any authority, sometimes anticipate F The process of 'correction' is taken farther by Q5, which leads on to the Restoration players' quartos and through them influences Rowe.

by William Stansby without date, and the fifth, both printed by Robert Young, in 1637.[1] It has been neatly shown,[2] from the progressive damage to a tailpiece, that Q4 of *Romeo and Juliet* was printed in 1622; and although similar demonstration is not possible for *Hamlet*, in which no tailpiece appears, the facts encourage the assumption that it was put out at the same time and for the same reason. The appearance of quartos of four other plays in 1622[3] suggests that publishers sought what profit could be had from them before the projected Shakespeare Folio came out; and Smethwick's pair may have omitted the date so as not to prejudice subsequent sales.

'The Tragedie of Hamlet, Prince of Denmarke' next appears as the eighth of the tragedies in the famous First Folio itself: 'Mr William Shakespeares Comedies, Histories, & Tragedies. Published according to the True Originall Copies . . . Printed by Isaac Jaggard, and Ed. Blount. 1623.' The Folio gives a different text (F), with some additions, more omissions, and numerous verbal variants. The three later Folios (1632, 1663, 1685), of course, each copy the one before.

3. THE TEXTS

Hamlet is unique among Shakespeare's plays in having thus three substantive texts: Q1, Q2, and F. The relation between them is complicated and in some respects more than puzzling. It may be convenient to anticipate an account of them by indicating in barest essential the character of each: Q1 is, as will be explained below, a bad quarto; Q2 is a good quarto, apparently based on Shakespeare's autograph and believed to be for the most part printed from it; F derives from a playhouse transcript showing some adaptation for the stage but also depends to some extent upon Q2.

THE FIRST QUARTO (Q1)

Since Q1 was the first text to be published, it used formerly to be assumed, though not without occasional dissentients,[4] that it was

---

1. Two other plays which Smethwick had acquired from Ling, *Love's Labour's Lost* and *The Taming of the Shrew*, had similar twin publication in the quartos of 1631.

2. By George Walton Williams, *SB*, XVIII, 253–4.

3. This includes *The Troublesome Reign of King John* (Q3); the others were *Richard III* (Q6), *1 Henry IV* (Q6), and *Othello*.

4. Notably Tycho Mommsen in *Athenaeum*, 1857, p. 182; R. Grant White in his *Shakespeare*, xi (1861), 10–21, and in the *Atlantic Monthly*, XLVIII (1881), 467–79.

the first to come into being; and that its great differences from
Q2 and F were to be explained by its being an earlier version of a
play which Shakespeare afterwards revised or rewrote. During the
present century it has been conclusively demonstrated (especially
by Duthie in *The 'Bad' Quarto of 'Hamlet'*, 1941) that the opposite
is the case: Q1 is not a prior but a posterior version, not an
original of Shakespeare's play but a reconstruction of it; and its
great difference from the later-published texts is due not to their
expansion but to its abridgement, not to their revision but to its
corruption.

The idea of an earlier version, nevertheless, dies hard. The
human mind clings to beliefs long after the foundations for them
have disintegrated, and there has been a reluctance to give up
the view of Q1 as somehow intermediate between the old *Hamlet*
play of the 1580s, referred to by scholars as the *Ur-Hamlet*,[1] and
Shakespeare's finished composition. It is as well therefore to state
that all those theories which view Shakespeare's *Hamlet* as pro-
gressing to its final shape via one or more rewritings and which
have contributed to the conception of Shakespeare as an artist
much given to the revision of his own past work are quite without
evidence or plausibility.[2]

Q1 is now recognized to belong to a category of quartos which
it is one of the achievements of twentieth-century textual scholarship to have distinguished. It is, in the sense in which the word is
now used, a 'bad' quarto, one, that is to say, whose text, deriving
from performance, lacks a direct manuscript link with what the
author wrote.[3] A comparison with the two 'good' texts, Q2 and
F, reveals in the various corruptions of Q1 – omissions, mislinings,
paraphrases, verbal and morphological substitutions, misunderstandings, transpositions, anticipations and recollections – all the
recognized signs of a play reconstructed from memory. Objectors
to 'memorial reconstruction' as the explanation of the bad
quartos[4] have sometimes complained that there is no contem-

1. See below, pp. 82 ff.

2. Cf. above, p. 5.

3. Cf. Chambers, *WS*, i. 156–9; Greg, *The Editorial Problem in Shakespeare*,
pp. 9–10, 57–61; F. P. Wilson, *Shakespeare and the New Bibliography*, rev. 1970,
pp. 83–4, 87–8.

4. The most persistent opposition (culminating in *A New Look at Shakespeare's
Quartos*, 1961) has come from Hardin Craig, whose repute in other fields has
conferred prestige upon eccentric textual theories which have helped to mislead
others. Some, though not Craig himself, would explain the bad quartos as due
merely to a process of abridgement (A. B. Weiner, ed., *Hamlet, the First Quarto
1603*, 1962; R. E. Burkhart, *Shakespeare's Bad Quartos*, 1975). Abridgement of
course there was, as the following discussion will show; but it is a strange fallacy

porary 'testimony' to such a practice; but if you come upon a
mutilated corpse you don't deny a murder because nobody has
reported one. The evidence is in the texts themselves. What
'memorial reconstruction' implies, however, is often popularly
misconceived: the notion of a traitor actor selling his memory to
a printer is another of those assumptions which have outlived the
reason for them. What used to be supposed was that pirate
printers procured texts of plays by shorthand; but once it is
perceived, from the nature of their corruptions, that certain texts
have been put together from memory, and hence by actors, it
follows that the natural object of the exercise was not to sell them
(though they evidently were sold later) but to act them. What we
have to suppose is that a group of actors, wishing to perform a
play of which they had no book, would make a book from what
could be remembered by one or more of their number who had
acted in the play before. A corollary is that such a text would
need to be not so much accurate as actable; some things that
could not be remembered would have to be supplied. So it should
occasion no surprise if a tolerably coherent plot is sometimes
carried forward by dialogue which, in language or even in substance, differs from the genuine text. There are passages in
Hamlet where Q1 corresponds with the good texts in the matter
of who speaks much more than in what they say.

It is generally accepted that the principal agent in the creation
of this text was an actor who had played the part of Marcellus.[1]
His speeches, and to a less degree the speeches of others while
Marcellus is on stage, are more faithfully rendered than the bulk
of the play. And this must be the chief, if not necessarily the sole,
reason for the progressive deterioration from the relative fidelity
of the first act, with which the part of Marcellus ends, to the freely
paraphrased and often highly condensed last two.[2] But Marcellus
presumably doubled other roles: it is noticeable that the six-line
speech of Lucianus is reproduced word perfect and that the long
and difficult speech of Voltemand (II. ii. 60–80) has no more than

---

which assumes that abridgement excludes memorial reconstruction, which it
can of course combine with or result from. The notion that abridgement, even
with its concomitants of adaptation and foul copy, could account for the kind
and degree of corruption exhibited in *Hamlet* Q1, were it not that it is sometimes miraculously swallowed (as in *SEL*, XVI, 333–4), might more happily be
ignored.

1. First pointed out by H. D. Gray, *MLR*, x, 171–80.
2. The act- and scene-divisions are of course those of later editors. Neither
Q1 nor Q2 has any division at all.

a few trivial discrepancies.[1] That the actor of such minor roles should be a hired man, who afterwards left or was turned off by the company, taking his memory with him, is plausible enough. In Voltemand's speech some small correspondences of punctuation between Q1 and F, together with an unusual metrical correctness, have permitted the assumption, though I think hardly proved, that the actor's written part was available.[2]

The most obvious, though not the most significant, feature of Q1 is that referred to on the title-page of Q2. With 2154 lines against the 3723 of Q2,[3] it is not very much more than half the length. Such shortening is general in memorially reconstructed, or, as they are often called, reported texts. The 'reporter' may have been familiar only with an abridged stage version; or, perhaps with a provincial tour in prospect, he may have desired a shorter play; or abridgement may have been forced on him, consciously or not, by gaps of memory. With *Hamlet* all three of these causes would seem to have been operative. Q1 evidently derives from the already shortened version represented in F, which it often concurs with in variant readings and for the most part follows in cuts (though of two of the passages cut from F it shows some recollection[4]). But Q1 makes many more omissions of its own, notably including: the first part of the King's first speech (I. ii. 1–25); well over half of Laertes's long speech to Ophelia (I. iii. 11–13, 17–28, 39–44); over twenty lines from the Pyrrhus speech (II. ii. 470–93); a dozen lines from Hamlet's eulogy of Horatio (III. ii. 63–74); all but the first two and the last four lines of the long speech of the Player King (III. ii. 183–206); the King's dialogue with Rosencrantz and Guildenstern at the beginning of the prayer scene (III. iii. 1–26); the King's tête-à-tête with Laertes before the arrival of the messenger (IV. vii. 1–35); the account of the gentleman from Normandy (IV. vii. 75–99); and Hamlet's account of his adventures on board ship (V. ii. 1–74), although the gist of this last passage is given in a new scene which replaces IV. vi. Some, perhaps most, of these, like the clean cut in the Player King's speech, must have been deliberate excisions.[5]

---

1. As observed in 1880–1, apparently independently, by W. H. Widgery (Harness Prize Essay, p. 138) and by Grant White (*Atlantic Monthly*, XLVIII, 478), who accordingly saw the actor of Voltemand as the culprit in the enterprise.

2. Dover Wilson, *Library*, 3rd ser. IX, 156–60; Duthie, pp. 134–5.

3. i.e. lines as printed, discounting stage-directions.

4. For F's cuts see below, p. 55 and (for Q1's retention of details cut) p. 56, n. 3.

5. Cf. Nosworthy, ch. 12, esp. pp. 201–5. But while Nosworthy's textual analysis is always acute and valuable, the theories he erects upon it concerning the occasion and composition of the play seem no more than, and often to be

Stage abridgement may have been progressive. Yet there is good reason to believe that even the initial playhouse cuts exceeded those shown by F. In the Pyrrhus speech the beginning of the Q1 cut coincides with the loss of a half-line in Q2, a pretty clear indication that a deletion was marked in the Q2 copy.[1] On the other hand in the King's opening speech and in the Laertes speech the confusion in what remains in Q1 suggests that some at least of the omission is due to the reporter's inadequacy. And besides clearly definable cuts there is a great deal of haphazard shortening, due to failure of memory, of a kind later examples will bring out.[2]

It is impossible to give here anything like full demonstration of the memorial characteristics, but since Q1 is too often discussed in merely general terms, some sample illustration is demanded.[3] One of its commonest features, as revealed by a comparison with Q2 and F, is the replacement of one word by another which is more or less synonymous. Thus, the Majesty of buried Denmark did sometimes *walk* instead of *march* (I.i.52);[4] Fortinbras sharked up a *sight* instead of a *list* of resolutes (I.i.101); foreknowledge of fate may *prevent* instead of *avoid* it (I.i.137); Ophelia is asked about her *cross* instead of her *hard* words to Hamlet (II.i.107); the noisy actor splits the ears of the *ignorant* instead of the *groundlings* (III.ii.11); the Queen explains the Ghost as the *weakness* instead of the *coinage* of Hamlet's brain, and Hamlet replies that his pulse doth *beat* like hers rather than *keep time* (III.iv.139–42); and so on. In one sentence of Hamlet's five of the six significant words are varied:

The first *verse* of the *godly Ballet* / Wil *tel* you *all*
(Q2: The first *rowe* of the *pious chanson* will *showe* you *more*).
(II.ii.415–16)

---

offered as no more than, entertaining speculation. I do not share some recently expressed beliefs that Q1 may preserve amid its corruptions traces of a hypothetical theatrical abridgement (and revision) by Shakespeare himself.

1. See II.ii.470–93n. and below, p. 43.

2. See especially pp. 26–8 below.

3. For a full and instructive demonstration in another exemplar, see H. R. Hoppe, *The Bad Quarto of Romeo and Juliet*, 1948. Faced with the more complex problems of *Hamlet*, Duthie, in his concern to show the reporter at work in passages which are not paralleled in the genuine texts, omits to show his characteristics in passages which are. Some can be sorted out from A. Hart's collective examination of *Stolne and Surreptitious Copies*, 1942.

4. Whereas quotations from a specified text normally retain the spelling of that text, in the present account of Q1, in which the point of the examples lies in substantive and not accidental differences, isolated words and phrases are more profitably cited in a standard (and hence modern) spelling.

Here, however, Q1's last word is not a synonym but a stopgap: since the 'first verse' does not give all the story, it shows an imprecise grasp of the sense. In a passage conveying the broad meaning vagueness as to particular detail (the *weakness* for the *coinage* of the brain) is common. There is a shift, with an enfeeblement, of the idea when appetite is said to have grown by what it *looked on* instead of what it *fed on* (I. ii. 145) or when the time gives *scope* for the corruption of virtue and not *proof* of it (III. i. 115). A misconception, due no doubt to the dominant sense of the verb, makes the Ghost usurp *the state* instead of *this time of night* (I. i. 49). The dawn light appears more vaguely on a *mountain top* than on an *eastward hill*, and the metaphor is confused when the russet mantle clothes the *sun* instead of the *morn* (I. i. 171–2). It seems strange that a text strewn with corruptions of this sort should ever have been taken for a preliminary draft; and they must equally confound attempts to explain Q1 as merely an abridgement.

By contrast with the different word of similar sense, sometimes the sound of a word is retained while being associated with a wrong meaning. So Horatio bids Hamlet to *ceasen*, not *season*, his admiration (I. ii. 192) at what is *right done*, instead of *writ down*, in their duty to inform him (I. ii. 222).[1] The bedrid Norway is absurdly described as *impudent* instead of *impotent* (I. ii. 29); *with tongue invenom'd speech* is the best the reporter can do for *with tongue in venom steep'd* (II. ii. 506). Such misunderstandings of things heard used once to be ascribed to a shorthand writer, but they are of course equally characteristic of an actor recalling what he has heard recited but not seen written. What more clearly points to faults of memory than of hearing is the occurrence of the right words in wrong order – at its simplest in 'So *gracious* and so *hallow'd*' for 'So *hallow'd* and so *gracious*' (I. i. 169) – or of a right word recollected at the wrong point. An example shows 'the *scorns* and flattery of the world' replacing 'the whips and *scorns* of time' (III. i. 70). After the Ghost has been sent to his *grave* instead of his *account*, the displaced word appears nevertheless in the next line:

> With all my *accompts* and sinnes vpon my head
> (Q2: With all my *imperfections* on my head).   (I. v. 78–9)

Anticipations and recollections of words from neighbouring contexts, as in other memorial texts, are symptomatic. The absurdity

---

1. Such homonymic errors support the assumption that *pollax* is a miswriting of *Polacks* (see I. i. 66 LN).

of the sepulchre which has *burst*, instead of *oped*, its marble jaws
(I.iv.50) is explained by the repetition of *burst* from two lines
above. Less unfortunately, fatherly advice is for costly *apparel*
instead of *habit* (I.iii.70) because two lines later the *apparel* will
proclaim the man.

The retention of words with a confused memory of their context is a source of tell-tale misunderstandings. Q1 has it that
Hecuba, who 'in th' alarm of fear caught up' a blanket (II.ii.505),

> in the alarum and feare of death rose vp.

There is a striking example in the famous soliloquy which, after
comparing death to a sleep, reflects

> in that sleep of death what *dreams* may come . . .
>   (III.i.66)

When Q1 says

> in that *dreame* of death, when wee awake,

by making death itself the dream it muddles the whole conception; and when it surprisingly continues

> And *borne* before an euerlasting Iudge,
> From whence no passenger euer retur'nd,

it seems to have been confused by the *bourn* from which 'no
traveller returns' (III.i.79–80). On the question of the 'estimation'
in which the players are held (II.ii.332–6), Q1 contradicts itself;
for having answered that

> their reputation holds as it was wont,

it explains that their audience has deserted them. The answer is
absent from Q2, but F shows what was meant:

> their indeauour keepes in the wonted pace . . .

Q1, harking back to a word the good texts have used half a dozen
lines earlier, has substituted *reputation* for *endeavour*, thus obliterat-
ing the fact that performance and estimation do not always go
together. When Ophelia begs to be spared the *path and ready way*
to heaven instead of the *steep and thorny way* (I.iii.48), Q1 has
stopped a gap in a manner that preserves the metre but again
destroys the point.

The examples so far given of Q1's variance have shown, in
different degrees, a verbal memory of the genuine text. Often in
the first act the change affects only a single word. Yet it may
happen, and especially as the text proceeds, that the sense of a

whole phrase is rendered by another, though usually enfeebled in the process, without any verbal coincidence. Thus 'that is the question' (III.i.56), a phrase not yet preserved by fame, becomes, with a metrical expletive, 'ay there's the point'. The Queen's admonition to Polonius, 'More matter with less art' (II.ii.95), is reduced to 'Good my lord be brief'. When we come to the last act, in the dying Laertes's account of himself—

> Why, as a woodcock to mine own springe, Osric.
> I am justly kill'd with mine own treachery
>
> (v.ii.312–13)

—Q1, with no more than an echo of the *woodcock* in its *coxcomb*, drops metaphor and abstraction, and incidentally metre, to give the literal fact:

> Euen as a coxcombe should,
> Foolishly slaine with my owne weapon.

In Hamlet's death-speech

> O, I die, Horatio,
> The potent poison quite o'ercrows my spirit
>
> (v.ii.357–8)

the metaphor again gives way to something triter eked out with actual symptoms:

> O my heart sinckes *Horatio*,
> Mine eyes haue lost their sight, my tongue his vse.

An example of how the sense pattern may be followed with only the minimum of verbal correspondence is provided by the Priest's speech at Ophelia's burial (v.i.219–27):

> Her obsequies have been as far enlarg'd
> As we have warranty. Her death was doubtful;
> And but that great command o'ersways the order,
> She should in ground unsanctified been lodg'd
> Till the last trumpet: for charitable prayers
> Shards, flints, and pebbles should be thrown on her.
> Yet here she is allow'd her virgin crants,
> Her maiden strewments, and the bringing home
> Of bell and burial.

In Q1 this becomes:

> My Lord, we haue done all that lies in vs,
> And more than well the church can tolerate,
> She hath had a Dirge sung for her maiden soule:

> And but for fauour of the king, and you,
> She had beene buried in the open fieldes,
> Where now she is allowed christian buriall.

What are here preserved of the original speech, along with the general ceremony in which the particular rites are now submerged, are traces of the original framework in *And but, been, allowed, burial*. The word *maiden* also survives in a different context, while the *soul* that it now describes and the dirge that is *sung* for it anticipate the priest's next speech:

> To sing sage requiem and such rest to her
> As to peace-parted souls.   (v. i. 230–1)

Q 1, however, has reversed the effect by allowing instead of denying Ophelia what belongs only to the 'peace-parted'.

It used to be believed that passages in Q 1 which are not parallel to the Shakespearean text were survivals from the *Ur-Hamlet*, which Shakespeare had as yet only partially revised. But it was Duthie's greatest triumph in his study of the bad quarto to show that these passages of non-Shakespearean blank verse were often put together from remembered scraps of Shakespeare's play (and occasionally of other plays as well).[1] From this it follows not merely that such passages do not represent some lost original but also that they were not the work of a hack poet who has sometimes been postulated as called in to make good the reporter's gaps. An invention which is helped out by words and phrases rising in the mind from a previous contact with the play must be that of the actor-reporter himself.

It is only to be expected that for all the reporter's efforts many things elude recall. In the Priest's speech just considered the last trumpet, the flints and pebbles, have vanished with the crants and strewments. The feeble retention of Hamlet's dying speeches suggests that the absence from them of any reference to Fortinbras and the succession is more accidental than deliberate. Even though the omission of the middle of a long speech was a regular method of abridgement,[2] there are cases where vestiges of the middle reveal an attempt to give at least its gist. In Ophelia's soliloquy after the nunnery episode (III. i. 152–63) Q 1 reduces twelve lines to four:

> Great God of heauen, what a quicke change is this?
> The Courtier, Scholler, Souldier, all in him,

1. Duthie, pp. 90–131.
2. See above, p. 21.

> All dasht and splinterd thence, O woe is me,
> To a seene what I haue seene, see what I see.

The first two lines of the full speech are very inaccurately, the last line and a half quite accurately reproduced. The eight lines intervening are not, however, suppressed so much as condensed into a single phrase, 'All dash'd and splinter'd thence'. This is a freshly imported metaphor, which nevertheless betrays its source in Shakespeare's '*glass* of fashion' and so in an effort to remember.[1]

One extended example of the condensation which results from imperfect memory must suffice. In Q1 the grave-digger's song with its dependent dialogue (corresponding to v.i.61–97) goes thus:

Clowne	A picke-axe and a spade,
	A spade for and a winding sheete,
	Most fit it is, for t'will be made,
	For such a ghest most meete.
Ham.	Hath this fellow any feeling of himselfe,
	That is thus merry in making of a graue?
	See how the slaue joles their heads against the earth.
Hor.	My lord, Custome hath made it in him seeme
	nothing.
Clowne	A pick-axe and a spade, a spade,
	For and a winding sheete,
	Most fit it is for to be made,
	For such a ghest most meet.
Ham.	Looke you, there's another *Horatio*.
	Why mai't not be the scull of some Lawyer?

What one immediately notices is that the grave-digger's song is reduced from three stanzas to two – and not, apparently, for reasons of economy, since the two turn out to be the same one (the third) repeated. After the first singing of it Hamlet's question and Horatio's answer, despite some approximations, correspond with the full text, though Hamlet's further rejoinder (v.i.68–9) is missing. But then after the grave-digger has sung his stanza the second time we proceed straight to the skull of the lawyer, which in the full text follows not the second verse but the third. Yet since Q1's single repeated stanza is in fact the full text's third, the dialogue now appears to resume at the right place. What has happened is that the second and third verses have been telescoped in Q1 and the thirteen lines of dialogue which separate them in Q2 (ll. 74–91) have gone. Yet they have not entirely disappeared:

1. Possibly assisted by a recollection of the glass in *Richard II*, which 'crack'd in a hundred shivers' (IV.i.289).

for out of those thirteen lines Hamlet's 'How the knave jowls it
to th' ground' (l. 75) – though with a threefold verbal substitution – has attached itself to his earlier comment on the song, and
his reflection on Lord Such-a-one (ll. 82–5) will be inserted later.
After the talk about the lawyer and his parchments (l. 114) Q1
has:

> There's another, why may not that be such a ones
> Scull, that praised my Lord such a ones horse,
> When he meant to beg him?

It is obvious that what we have here is not purposeful abridgement but the best that the reporter's memory can do. In the
succeeding dialogue remembered fragments are similarly put together in haphazard order: the tanner (ll. 158–66) occurs before
instead of after the discussion of 'young Hamlet' (ll. 138–57), who
is said to have lost his wits upon the ground of Denmark (ll. 154–6)
before instead of after we hear of his being sent to England
(ll. 143–50). This is a fair sample of what may happen in the last
two acts.

A rearrangement of the order often betrays the vagaries of the
memory even when there is no loss of substance. A compact
illustration is afforded by Hamlet's three-line speech when the
Ghost leaves the Queen's chamber (III.iv.136–8). For convenience
it may be divided into five members:

> Why, look you there (1), look how it steals away. (2)
> My father, in his habit as he liv'd! (3)
> Look where he goes (4) even now out at the portal. (5)

What Q1 makes of it is this:

> why see (1) the king my father (x), my father, in the
> habite
> As he liued (3), looke you how pale he lookes (y),
> See how he steales away (2) out of the Portall (5),
> Looke, there he goes. (4)

The little omissions (*you there*, *even now*), the incidental substitutions (*see* for *look*, which nevertheless turns up in the next line,
he for *it*, *the* for *his*, *there* for *where*), with the ruin and mislineation
of the verse, will be recognized as characteristic. More notable,
along with the transposition of the phrases, are the additions. Of
these *x* recalls Hamlet's dramatic exclamation from I.ii.191, and
y, less apt now the Ghost has turned away, is recollected (with the
substitution of *looks* for *glares*) from a previous speech of Hamlet's
ten lines back (III.iv.125).

One of the surest indications of a text reconstructed from memory is the recollection, and still more the anticipation, of phrases at a distance from where they belong, showing that widely separated parts of the play were present in the reporter's mind at the same time. In II.i the father's first speech to the servant goes in Q1:

> these letters to my sonne,
> And this same mony with my blessing to him,
> And bid him ply his learning . . .

Here, apart from the substitution of *letters* for *notes* and their exchanging places with the money, we remark the addition of the *blessing*, recollected from I.iii.57, to which is further added, in this opening of the conversation, an anticipation of its ending,

> And let him ply his music, (II.i.72)

which nevertheless comes again in its right place. When Hamlet shows his mother the pictures of her two husbands (III.iv.53 ff.), Q1 describes the first as one

> Whose heart went hand in hand euen with that vow,
> He made to you in marriage,

and thus makes Hamlet say to his mother what in the true text the Ghost has said to him two acts before (I.v.49–50). When he reproaches her with her second husband (III.iv.91–2), the accusation in Q1

> To liue in the incestuous pleasure of his bed

makes him now apply to the Queen what he said of the King (in Q1 as in Q2) in the scene before (III.iii.90). When the King explains Hamlet's conduct at Ophelia's grave with 'he is mad' (V.i.267), Q1 adds 'as is the sea', remembering the Queen's description of Hamlet when he left her, 'Mad as the sea and wind' (IV.i.7, where Q1 itself has 'as raging as the sea').

A final example will show Q1 using with slight variation the same line four times over. When Rosencrantz and Guildenstern come to Hamlet after the play, they ask him

> what is your cause of distemper? (III.ii.328)

In Q1 this becomes

> let vs againe intreate
> To know of you the ground and cause of your distemperature.

Again is fair enough, for in their earlier scene, when they admit they have been sent for (II.ii. 292), Q1 already makes them wish to

> Know the cause and ground of your discontent

– and so to satisfy the King's request of them (II.ii. 15–17), which in Q1 is to wring from Hamlet

> The cause and ground of his distemperancie.

For good measure their report of failure (at the beginning of III.i) is also echoed in Q1 by Corambis (Polonius):

> We cannot yet finde out the very ground
> Of his distemperance.

The words of their question are thus anticipated three times before we come to it in its right place. And the first time that they ask it in Q1 they also get Hamlet's answer,

> I want preferment,

instead of having to wait till after the play for

> I lack advancement.   (III.ii. 331)

This gives a neat example of what only memory can explain: at the distance of an act there occurs an anticipation which, through the correspondence of sentiment and rhythm, is clearly recognizable as such, yet, discounting the subject pronoun, lacks any verbal link.

A reporter who thus works into his version fragments thrown up in his memory from other parts of the play may also have recourse upon occasion to bits of other plays in which he has, presumably, acted. To take one illustration, the instruction Ophelia receives from her father in their first scene together (I.iii. 120–34) includes in Q1 the warning that

> such men often proue,
> Great in their wordes, but little in their loue.

This is recognizably an echo of the recently performed *Twelfth Night*, where Viola says that 'we men'

> prove
> Much in our vows, but little in our love.
>   (II.iv. 116–17)[1]

---

1. Cf. Crompton Rhodes, *Shakespeare's First Folio*, p. 80; Duthie, p. 115. For further instances of Q1's borrowings from other plays, not all equally convincing, see Hart, *Stolne and Surreptitious Copies*, pp. 394–402; and cf. Chambers, *WS*, i. 422.

Such echoes need not of course be confined to Shakespeare. When Laertes forbids his tears at Ophelia's death (IV. vii. 185–90) he adds in Q1

> Reuenge it is must yeeld this heart releefe,

just as in *The Spanish Tragedy* Hieronimo asserts that

> in revenge my heart would find relief.   (II. v. 41)

And the same play supplies matter for the Queen when at the end of the scene in her closet (III. iv) Q1 makes her say, in agreeing to assist Hamlet in revenge,

> I will conceale, consent, and doe my best,
> What stratagem soe're thou shalt deuise.

In comparable circumstance Belimperia had said, 'I will consent, conceal' and had been told by Hieronimo to grace 'whatsoever I devise' (IV. i. 46–9).[1] *The Spanish Tragedy*, no doubt by reason of its similar theme, proved fruitful to the reporter; a number of echoes of Kyd in Q1,[2] once thought to be survivals of the *Ur-Hamlet* on the assumption that Kyd, its putative author, repeated himself, must now be ascribed to an actor's familiarity with Kyd's lines on the stage.[3]

As well as bringing in stray phrases where they do not belong, Q1 sometimes transfers whole stretches of dialogue from one part of the play to another. Thus Hamlet's exchange with Ophelia in which she says he is merry and he retorts with jests about a jig-maker and a hobby-horse that is forgot (III. ii. 120–33), instead of preceding the dumb-show, is incorporated in their later conversation at the entry of Lucianus (i.e. after III. ii. 242). Hamlet's lecture to Guildenstern on the recorder (III. ii. 336–63) leads straight on to the passage (advanced from IV. ii. 11–20) in which he lectures Rosencrantz about a sponge. In a precisely similar way the most remarkable of such transpositions brings forward the 'nunnery' scene and with it the 'To be or not to be' soliloquy (III. i. 56–163) from the third act to the second, where the entry of Hamlet immediately after the plan to 'loose' Ophelia to him (II. ii. 168) precipitates the encounter itself, while the 'fishmonger' dialogue is postponed.

---

1. Numbering as in Boas's Kyd, following the 1592 edition's division into four acts.

2. For a list see Boas's Kyd, pp. l–lii; Duthie, pp. 181–4.

3. Cf. Duthie, pp. 184–6.

The 'nunnery' scene

This change in the sequence of episodes, because of the controversy it has occasioned, demands a little attention. Those who have believed that Q1 represents an earlier version of the play have assumed its order the original; but the truth is the reverse. After all the talk at court about Hamlet's madness (II.ii. 1–167), the play must mean him, on entering at II.ii. 168, to show signs of madness, as in the 'fishmonger' dialogue he conspicuously does and in the 'To be or not to be' soliloquy does not. And the book that he enters reading, in Q1 as in the other texts, is required not for the soliloquy but for the fishmonger dialogue (see II.ii. 191–202), which, when postponed till after the nunnery scene, necessitates Hamlet's entry with the book a second time. Moreover, the nunnery scene, far from initiating the question of breeding sinners (III.i. 121–2) which the fishmonger dialogue then expands on (as suggested by Virgil Whitaker[1]), is itself prepared for by the talk of the fishmonger's daughter (II.ii. 181–9) and actually brings to a culmination a motif which the fishmonger begins.[2]

That the position of the nunnery scene in Q1 is erroneous has been perceived by the leading modern scholars,[3] but their view that it represents a deliberate alteration and not just a lapse of memory I find wholly unacceptable. This prevalent belief is simply another legacy of former misconceptions about the status of Q1. Once this is accepted as a production of the memory, the displacement of the nunnery scene requires no further explanation. Duthie makes much[4] of the skill with which Q1 effects the transition from the nunnery to the fishmonger. But this is surely what we should expect of a reporter intent on concocting a coherent play and capable elsewhere of improvising to bridge gaps. Even so he has left the tell-tale book as witness of an error which on Duthie's own showing has not been patched over. I take it he unwittingly slipped into the nunnery scene too soon and could not retrieve a mistake that he was unaware of having made. Except in scale there is no essential difference between this shift and the others (of the sponge and the jig-maker) which I have cited.[5]

1. *Shakespeare's Use of Learning*, pp. 343–4.
2. As I have shown in 'Hamlet and the Fishmonger', *Sh.Jahr.* (West), 1975, pp. 109–20. See II.ii. 174 LN.
3. Chambers, *WS*, i.417; Duthie, pp. 211–14; Greg, *SFF*, pp. 302–3.
4. pp. 214–17.
5. It is sometimes taken as evidence of design that Q1, in contrast to the Shakespearean text, brings Ophelia on with her father at II.ii. 39, so that it has

Divergences in Q1

Some other modifications in Q1 are more problematical. A new scene between Horatio and the Queen is introduced, and two of the dramatis personae are given different names; and these things, unlike the repositioning of the nunnery scene, can hardly have been entirely inadvertent. The scene between Horatio and the Queen was presumably suggested by a recollection of the tête-à-tête between these two which F's contracted stage version gives us at the beginning of iv. v, but in matter it replaces iv. vi: instead of our seeing Horatio receiving Hamlet's letter, Q1 has Horatio telling the Queen he has received it. An account of Hamlet's changing the commissions is also incorporated here instead of being left for Hamlet to give in person at the beginning of v. ii. A scene which thus amalgamates three episodes in one may seem a well-contrived abridgement, but how far abridgement was voluntary and how far compelled by imperfect recollection is impossible to say. Hamlet's adventures at sea are left in some obscurity: we hear nothing of the pirates, nor, beyond his 'being set ashore', of how he got back to Denmark. Instead there are some non-Shakespearean details. Hamlet's changing the commissions is linked with his 'being crossed by the contention of the winds'.[1] More important, there is a divergence in the attitude of the Queen, who is shown in league with Hamlet against the King; and Q1 has anticipated this development by making her promise Hamlet, at the end of the scene in her closet (iii. iv), to assist in his revenge. This seems to bring the plot a little closer to the story as we have it in Belleforest, of whom Duthie even finds verbal echoes when in Q1 Hamlet refers to his mother's 'infamy' and she vows by God's 'majesty'.[2] It is often suggested that details from Belleforest may have been transmitted through the *Ur-Hamlet*. Yet the words of the Queen's vow are manifestly

her on stage ready for the nunnery scene. But since this leaves her a silent presence throughout the reading of Hamlet's letter to her, the cost in dramatic ineptitude is high. The truth surely is that in making Ophelia enter with her father Q1 does not look forward but back: it remembers the father's proposal for his daughter to go with him to the King (II. i. 101, 117) and does not perceive the change of plan by which the letter takes her place. The reporter is better able to improvise in tight corners than to avoid them by looking ahead. See II. ii. 39 S.D. LN.

1. A correspondence here with contrary winds in *Der Bestrafte Brudermord* (for which see below, pp. 112 ff.) has suggested to some scholars that we have here a relic of a different version of the story and hence of the *Ur-Hamlet*. But for a refutation see pp. 119–21.

2. Cf. Belleforest, 'la plus infame', 'celle infamie'; 'par la haute majesté des Dieux'; and see Duthie, pp. 199–200.

echoes from *The Spanish Tragedy*[1] and her dialogue with Horatio is partly put together, after the reporter's customary fashion, from recollections of the Shakespearean text, as Duthie has excellently shown.[2] It follows that these speeches of the Queen peculiar to Q1 do not preserve passages of the *Ur-Hamlet*. They appear to derive from the reporter's own attempt to sustain a coherent plot when memory faltered. A characteristic tendency to be at the same time too vague and too explicit lands him in inconsistencies. For example, whereas Shakespeare makes it apparent that the Queen knows nothing of the murder, the reporter makes her swear, 'I never knew of this most horrid murder', thereby betraying that she does know now although Hamlet has given her no account of it. This cannot have come from the *Ur-Hamlet*. The most we can say is that if the reporter had previously acted in the old *Hamlet*, some recollections of it, as of other plays, may have mingled with his attempts at reproducing Shakespeare's.

Corambis

There remains the substitution of the names Corambis and Montano for Polonius and Reynaldo. The general assumption that Q1 preserves the original names, natural enough when it was thought to be an earlier version of the play, often persists now that it is recognized as derivative. But the thing we must be clear about is that, whatever occurred in the *Ur-Hamlet*, Polonius, not Corambis, was the original name in Shakespeare's play. And since Shakespeare very often departed from the nomenclature of his sources, the problem in any case is not why he but why Q1 made the change. No satisfactory solution has ever been suggested. It is difficult to think that a reporter who had acted in the play would forget the name of so important a character as Polonius; but we who are used to seeing it in stage-directions and speech-headings might do well to note that it occurs only five times in Shakespeare's dialogue and always in passages which are ill remembered in Q1.[3] There is no instance where Corambis is

1. Cf. above, p. 31.

2. Duthie, pp. 150–5. Cf. Q1 'his lookes That seem'd to sugar o're his villanie' and III.i.48; Q1 'Be wary of his presence' and I.iii.43, 121.

3. I.ii.57; IV.i.34; IV.iii.16, 32; IV.v.83. It should also be noted that the reporter had a bad memory for names as for numbers. (See v.i.139–57 LN on Hamlet's age.) Apart from his consistent corruptions (Leartes, Rossencraft, Gilderstone, Voltemar), he leaves Francisco, Barnardo, and Osric anonymous. The name of the ruler murdered in the play (III.ii.233) is given as Albertus instead of Gonzago, and it was done in 'Guyana' in place of Vienna.

simply slotted in in place of it: its elimination, in a memorial text, may have been less purposeful than it is usual to suppose. Yet with Reynaldo also replaced by Montano, the one thing we can feel certain of is that the double substitution is part of a single process; and a double forgetting is perhaps less probable than some now irrecoverable design (whether on the part of the reporter or, perhaps more probably, of the stage version he was recalling). The chance of a topical allusion is always alluring to commentators; but the notion that Polonius, on the strength of his similar role at court, was a caricature of Burghley is sheer conjecture;[1] and in any event, a caricature would not be concealed by a change of name. Any personal satire must have lain in the name Polonius itself, presumably because it pointed, or was thought to point, to a man of Polish – or Polonian – connection; and if it could ever be shown that one such had an associate or underling who could be recognized in the name Reynaldo (which gets stress in each of Polonius's first three speeches to the man), the case might be held to be proved. Otherwise the problem is likely to remain unsolved. Whatever the cause of the change, it is of course possible that the names in Q1, whether through design or confusion, revive those of the *Ur-Hamlet*. The one point in favour of supposing so is that Shakespeare must have come across the names somewhere, since he used them shortly after, Montano for a character in *Othello* and Corambus (perhaps the correct form) incidentally in *All's Well that Ends Well* (IV.iii.153). But we can have no assurance that these names were in the *Ur-Hamlet*,[2] or even that the *Ur-Hamlet* had a Reynaldo character at all.[3]

1. This was believed to be supported by an analogy between Burghley's *Precepts* for his son and the 'precepts' delivered by Polonius to Laertes. But now that these have been shown to derive from a long literary tradition, a reflection upon any individual can no longer be supposed. See I.iii.58–80 LN. Gollancz (*A Book of Homage*, pp. 173–7) believed that Corambis was Burghley and that by a change of name Shakespeare, writing after Burghley's death in 1598, directed the portrait at *The Counsellor* of the 'Polonian' Goslicius (English translation, 1598). But since the change, as I have insisted, was in the opposite direction, it could not introduce, though it might remove, an allusion to a Pole. See *Dramatis Personae*, Polonius, LN.

2. There are various other possibilities: e.g., if Shakespeare's company made a tactful change of names in performance, that in itself might have lodged the new names in Shakespeare's mind, available for further use when they had served their turn. Any such change (unlike the change from Oldcastle to Falstaff, or from Brooke to Broome in *Wiv.*) can only have been temporary; but it could through the reporter have been transmitted to Q1 (and incidentally *BB*, on which see below, p. 117) while leaving no trace in the later quartos or in F. 3. Cf. below, p. 100.

The usefulness of Q1 is not that it offers clues to the *Ur-Hamlet* but that it throws light on the theatrical and textual history of Shakespeare's play. It suggests something of the performances, presumably on tour, for which such a version was provided, and it tells us something of the performances which the actor-reporter had known. Hamlet's instructions to the players are expanded by a piece of actor's gag (see III.ii.44–5n.). The stage-directions indicate not what the author envisaged but what an actor remembered actually taking place. They reveal that the Ghost appeared in the Queen's chamber 'in his night gown' (III.iv.103) and that the mad Ophelia came in 'playing on a lute, and her hair down singing' (IV.v.20). It is Q1 that tells us not only, like F, that Laertes 'leaps into the grave', but that 'Hamlet leaps in after' him (V.i.251), and that in the crisis of their fencing-match 'they catch one another's rapiers' (V.ii.306). And Q1, in spite of all its corruptions, can provide some check on the two better texts, helping now to authenticate their readings, now to identify or explain their errors.[1] On rare occasions it can supply, or guide us to, a reading which both better texts have lost. Thus, where they make Hamlet exclaim (at II.ii.579)

> That I the sonne of a deere murthered, (Q2)

or

> That I, the Sonne of the Deere murthered, (F)

the reading of Q1,

> that I the sonne of my deare father,

though without *murder'd* it lacks the keyword, yet confirms a conjecture that the word *father* has dropped out. One very crucial reading that Q1 enables us to recover is the threat of Laertes against Hamlet, 'Thus *diest* thou' (IV.vii.56), instead of the *diddest* by which for over three and a half centuries the play has been impoverished.[2]

THE SECOND QUARTO (Q2)

The Second Quarto, variously dated 1604 and 1605 and claiming to be printed 'according to the true and perfect Coppie', was evidently intended to supersede the First – just as the bad quarto

---

1. As in suggesting where Q2 has strayed through following Q1 or where F preserves a theatrical variation. See below, pp. 46–52, 62–3.

2. See IV.vii.56n.

of *Romeo and Juliet* had been succeeded after a two-year interval by one claiming to be 'newly corrected, augmented, and amended'.[1] The character of the Q2 text supports the assertion that it comes from an authentic manuscript, and, for reasons which will follow, it is usually held that this manuscript was the author's own foul papers.[2]

The stage-directions, casual about characters' names and often indefinite about numbers, are those of an author rather than the playhouse. They correspond moreover to what other texts lead us to think Shakespeare's practice in composition. He will use a collective or group phrase instead of specifying individuals. Cornelius and Voltemand are not mentioned among the '*Counsaile*' at the beginning of I.ii, but are named when the dialogue requires them (l. 34). Even so the stage-directions on their entry and exit in II.ii are content to describe them as '*Embassadors*'. The entry direction at v.ii.80 makes do with the generic '*a Courtier*', which continues in speech-headings; it is only when he has to be referred to in the third person that the courtier becomes '*Ostricke*' (v.ii.193). The King and Queen of 'The Mousetrap' have no names till Hamlet chooses to announce them in a speech which calls the King the Duke (III.ii.233–4). The speeches of the '*two Clownes*' in the graveyard (v.i) are assigned simply to '*Clowne*' and '*Other*'.[3] Unspecified '*others*' are common.[4] They enter with Laertes in IV.v and with Horatio in IV.vi. In IV.ii, when Hamlet appears with Rosencrantz '*and others*', these are evidently Guildenstern and the 'further ayde' the King has directed to seek Hamlet out (IV.i.33). When next they come on stage the direction is for

1. It is plausibly supposed that the same thing happened in the case of *Love's Labour's Lost*, of which the 1598 Q is said to be 'newly corrected and augmented' although no earlier quarto has survived.

2. This is an elastic term: since 'foul papers' may obviously have still fouler ones behind them, it need not imply a mere rough draft but can cover anything from that to a manuscript containing final revisions, in fact any manuscript in a condition which presupposes that it will be succeeded by a fair copy. Greg takes as characteristic of foul papers 'that they retained recognizable evidence of free composition and that they were not in a tidy enough condition to serve the prompter'. See Bowers, *On Editing Shakespeare*, pp. 13–14, 107–8; Greg, *SQ*, VII, 102; Honigmann, *The Stability of Shakespeare's Text*, pp. 17–18.

3. Cf., to take one example among many, how the Q of *LLL* introduces the Princess's '*three attending Ladies*' and throughout their first dialogue assigns speeches by numbers only. When they come to be given names later, there is much confusion about which is which. In the Shakespearean scene in *Sir Thomas More* the author (Hand D) has prefixed speeches 'other' and even 'oth' and 'o', leaving the playhouse scribe to make precise assignment. See Addn II, 126 ff. (numbering as in MSR).

4. Cf. *Rom.* Q2, III.i.33, *and others*.

Rosencrantz '*and all the rest*' (IV.iii.12), which we are not to take
too literally, since some remain outside till told to bring Hamlet
in, whereupon '*They enter*'. The beginning of this scene is numeric-
ally imprecise: '*Enter King, and two or three*'.[1] Similar is the much-
noted opening of II.i, '*Enter old Polonius, with his man or two*', which
suggests that the author, with the scene still shaping in his mind,
is as yet undecided how many he may want. In the event no more
than one was called for,[2] but a name for him was immediately
forthcoming when he had to be addressed. All this is quite compatible with a care to define status and relationship when the
main characters are introduced: I.ii, '*Enter Claudius, King of
Denmarke, Gertrad the Queene, Counsaile: as Polonius, and his Sonne
Laertes . . .*'; I.iii, '*Enter Laertes, and Ophelia his Sister*'.[3] The King
is given a name at once, which then after his first speech-prefix is
never used again; his wife in her speech-prefixes is indiscriminately 'Gertrard' or Queen.[4]

Yet although stage-directions of this kind come evidently from
the author, theoretically it might not be impossible for them to
be transmitted through fair copy.[5] What weighs heavily against
fair copy or any scribal transcript is the abundance of errors in
the printing, many of them indicative of misreading.[6] This not
seldom results in nonsense, as in *the vmber* (F *thumbe*, III.ii.349),
a heaue, a kissing hill (III.iv.59), *pardons* for *panders* (III.iv.88), *so
loued Arm'd* for *so loud a wind* (IV.vii.22), *the King* for *checking*
(IV.vii.61), *sully and hot, or my complection* (V.ii.97–8), *trennowed* for
winnowed (V.ii.189). Among less absurd errors which F corrects
are *fearefull* for *fretfull* (I.v.20), *euer happy* for *ouer-happy* and *lap*
for *cap* (II.ii.228, 229), *let me* for *lest my* (II.ii.369), *friendly* for
French (II.ii.426), *that* for *the cue* (II.ii.555), *lowlines* (F *lonelinesse*,
III.i.46), *breakes* for *breathes* (III.ii.380), *showe* for *shoue* (III.iii.58),
base and silly (F *hyre and Sallery*, III.iii.79),[7] *greeued* for *grained*

---

1. Cf. *Rom.* Q2, IV.ii.1, *two or three*; I.i.70 and IV.iv.13, *three or foure*; etc.

2. Which appears to rule out the theoretical alternative that *or two* is an addition. The conjecture has also been made that *man or two* might arise from a misreading of Montano.

3. Cf. *Ado* (also held to be from foul papers), I.i, '*Enter Leonato gouernour of
Messina, Innogen his wife, Hero his daughter, and Beatrice his neece*'; and for other
examples, *SFF*, pp. 124–5.

4. On the inconsistency of nomenclature in foul papers see McKerrow, *RES*,
XI, 459–65; Greg, *SFF*, pp. 113–14.

5. As may have happened with *Mer.V.*, where alternative nomenclature
and indefinite directions survive in Q1, though a much less troublesome copy
has to be inferred.

6. For classified lists, see *MSH*, pp. 106–14. I give a selection only.

7. But see LN.

(III.iv.90), *kyth* (F *tythe*, III.iv.97), *criminall* for *crimefull* (IV.vii.7), *ore-reaches* for *ore-offices* (v.i.78), *waters* for *winters* (v.i.209), *sure* for *afeard* (v.ii.303), *for no* for *forc'd* (v.ii.388), and many others. Several of these look like guesses at what could not be made out.

Some readings are hardly even guesses, but apparently mere stopgaps to fill in some kind of sense when the printer accepts defeat. This at any rate is the likeliest explanation of the Q2 *heated* (F *tristfull*) *visage* (III.iv.50); *in, and* (F *to Yaughan*, v.i.60); *a* (F *sage*) *Requiem* (v.i.230); *all* (F *impon'd as*, perhaps for *impaun'd as*) *you call it* (v.ii.160); *A did sir* (corr. *A did so sir*, F *He did Complie*, v.ii.184).[1] Inability to decipher an unfamiliar word may also be surmised when, for example, *Shards* (F *Shardes*, v.i.224), is omitted altogether, leaving a metrical gap. There are many other omissions of single words and some of phrases or even of whole lines, ·whether of verse or prose (e.g. at I.iii.18; II.ii.212; II.ii. 322–3; II.ii.394–5*; III.ii.113–14*; III.ii.260; v.i.104–5*; v.ii.57).[2] Most of these F is able to supply: in passages cut from F a word in III.iv.171, a half-line at IV.i.40, and a presumed omission after I.i.119 are gone beyond recovery. The asterisked examples are cases of haplography; but when all allowance is made for the negligence of compositors, a good deal must be ascribed to the nature of their copy. Dover Wilson's pleasant hypothesis of a bungling, inexperienced, and hurried workman has had to give way before the demonstration that there were two compositors; and since these were the same as the Roberts pair who set up the first quarto of *The Merchant of Venice* and the second of *Titus Andronicus* as well as other books, they are seen elsewhere to be competent.[3] The inevitable inference that the copy for *Hamlet* gave difficulty points strongly to foul papers, and hence to autograph.

Such indications as there are of the hand in which the manuscript was written at least do not conflict with this. From errors cited (*the King* for *checking*, *sure* for *afeard*) it was obviously a secretary hand, but this is to say little. Such characteristic errors as, to cite fresh examples, *feare* for *feard* (I.i.124), *stature* for *feature* (III.i.161), *vnfold* for *vnsele* (i.e. unseal, v.ii.17) could fairly easily occur in most hands of the period, and although Shakespeare's hand may have been unusually susceptible to the confusion of *d*

1. See also p. 60 below.
2. For a few longer omissions, see below, pp. 44–5.
3. J. R. Brown, 'The Compositors of *Hamlet* Q2 and *The Merchant of Venice*', *SB*, VII, 17–40.

and *e*, especially in final positions, more individual clues are necessarily precarious. There are nevertheless a few suggestive items. The misreading of the letter *a* as *or*, to which we must ascribe *or* for the article (I.ii.96) and probably *sort* for *sate* (I.v.56),[1] and the misreading of *u* as *a* which gives us *raine* for *ruine* (III.iii.22) and *quietas* for *quietus* (III.i.75), could well arise from just such letter formations as in fact occur in the Shakespearean pages of *Sir Thomas More*.[2]

To argue much from spelling, in view of the vagaries of Elizabethan practice and the intervention of compositors, might seem to build on sand. Yet again there are indications. Since unusual spellings in a printed text[3] are likely to reflect copy, interest attaches to *hiddious* (II.ii.472), *element* (IV.vii.179), *deule* (III.ii.127) when these are also found in the Shakespearean pages of *More*.[4] Among other coincidences cited by Dover Wilson there may be significance in *tha'r* (for *th'ar*, IV.vii.11) and *ar* eight times in *More* (as against *are* once) and in the error *seale slaughter* (I.ii.132) and *More's* regular spelling of *sealf*, *sealues* (six times). The evidence of *More* (supported also by some printed texts) that Shakespeare preferred *-nck* to *-nk* and tended to dispense with final *e* after *t* finds Q2 in accord (and with no significant difference between its two compositors). *More* has *banck*, *thanck*, *thinck* and Q2 *bancke*, *ranck(e)*, *blanck(s)*, *sprinckle*, etc., to a total of twenty instances with only one exception.[5] To match *desperat* and *appropriat* in *More* Q2 has, among other instances, *desp(e)rat* (five times), *importunat*, *considerat* (for *confederate*), *prenominat*, *pyrat*, *mandat*, *associats*, *temperatly*. With combinations other than *-at* the practice is less consistent, but the occurrence once each of *infinit*,

---

1. A complication here is the juxtaposition of words (*Angle linckt*) which follow the unusual spelling of Q1; but Cairncross notwithstanding, it is difficult to deny a likely manuscript influence. See Bowers, *SB*, VIII, 58–9; Cairncross in *Text* (Uppsala), I, 75–6; and cf. below, p. 48. (Even if Q2 here were to derive from an annotated Q1, the annotation would presumably derive from an authoritative manuscript.)

2. The *a* in question, a round with a following minim joined by a horizontal stroke, is illustrated in *More*, Addn II, 245 (*a hound*); the *u*, all but closed, in l. 249 (*nature*), as noted by Dover Wilson.

3. See *MSH* again (pp. 114–17) for very useful lists, among which, however, only some permit any inference as to author.

4. Addn II, 255; 259; 176, 179. We also find *elamentes* in the Q of *LLL* (IV. iii.325) and *deule* in the good Q of *Rom.* (II.iv.1, III.i.99), both believed to be from Shakespeare's foul papers. It is conjectured that *deale* (twice in II.ii.595) is a misreading of *deule*, which would afford another instance of *a* for *u*.

5. In *linckt* (I.v.55) Q2 appears to be influenced by Q1, in which, however, the *c* is very much more sporadic.

hippocrit, opposits, statuts is worth noting.[1] Finally the most striking single spelling is the *Sc-* in *Sceneca* (II.ii.396), which looks like an idiosyncrasy of Shakespeare's: it goes with the well-known *scilens* in *More* (Addn II, 173) and the speech-prefixes *Scilens* in the quarto of *2 Henry IV* and with the Folio spelling of *Scicinius* in *Coriolanus* (over thirty times[2]) and *Scicion* for *Sicyon* in *Antony and Cleopatra* (I.ii.110–16, three times).

The hypothesis of an autograph manuscript to which all these details tend is confirmed by the survival in the print of what appear to be author's first thoughts corrected *currente calamo*. The two clearest cases occur in a passage of three lines which, as evidence of foul papers, might be thought decisive in itself:

> For women feare too much, euen as they loue,
> And womens feare and loue hold quantitie,
> Eyther none, in neither ought, or in extremitie . . .
>
> (III.ii.162–3)

That the first line here is a reject is shown by its lack of a rhyme in the midst of regular couplets and by the rephrasing of the same thought in the line which follows. Then at the beginning of the third line the extra-metrical 'Eyther none', again immediately rephrased, is another evident false start. Some other textual redundancies invite similar explanation. The impossible line

> Giues him threescore thousand crownes in anuall fee,
>
> (II.ii.73)

though Theobald defended its metre and Dover Wilson insists upon the sum,[3] is best accounted for by supposing that the printer has set up the author's rejected *score* as well as the *thousand* that was meant to supersede it. The superfluous *greatnes* in

> As by your safetie, greatnes, wisdome, all things els
>
> (IV.vii.8)

may be another instance. I suspect the first *I be* in

> If once I be a widdow, euer I be a wife. (III.ii.218)

The curious *cull-cold* at IV.vii.170 appears to preserve a first miswriting of the word (perhaps helped by an anticipation of *call*

---

1. Another correspondence is pointed to by J. R. Brown (*SB*, VII, 37–8) when he finds evidence that the Q2 copy preferred *-owe* to *-ow*. The *More* pages are consistent with *knowe, showe, growe, fellowes.*

2. See Arden *Cor.*, p. 3.

3. *MSH*, p. 274. Cairncross's theory that the Q2 line is an imperfect correction of Q1 erroneously retaining *him* (*Text*, I, 73) is even more implausible. See II.ii.73n.

later in the line) along with its correction.[1] The author evidently failed to make clear deletion-marks, but one seems to have left its trace here in the otherwise inexplicable hyphen.

Such signs of the process of composition would be expected to disappear in a fair copy, and all have in fact gone from F. In Q2 some of Hamlet's interjections in the play scene (III.ii.176, 219) are printed in the margin, presumably following copy, and may therefore be author's afterthoughts. The numerous cruxes and tangles in the text, several in passages excised from F, suggest a manuscript which had had no careful revision. Altogether, Dover Wilson seems justified in holding that 'the very roughness of the Q2 text is its best guarantee'.[2]

Playhouse marking of the manuscript

We may reasonably take it, then, that Shakespeare's autograph manuscript, with the alterations natural to the author in the course of composition, but without final tidying-up, was the manuscript used for the printing. It does not follow that this manuscript reached the printers exactly as Shakespeare left it. It is likely enough that it would have been gone over in the playhouse and received some annotation – to specify characters more precisely or to clarify the action – before being transcribed for the promptbook.[3] This at least appears to have happened with some other plays believed to have been printed from foul papers. A simple illustration is afforded by a direction in *Much Ado* (III.i), '*Enter Hero and two Gentlewomen, Margaret and Ursley*', where, as the form '*Ursley*' shows, the Gentlewomen's names have been added from the dialogue. In *Hamlet* Q2 clear signs of the playhouse book-keeper are rare; but he seems necessary to account for the duplicate direction at v.ii.285, where '*Florish, a peece goes off*' looks like the author (cf. I.iv.6 S.D.) and '*Drum, trumpets and shot*' an addition, based upon the dialogue (ll. 272–4), noting more precisely the required noises off.[4] The (perhaps mistaken) direction for '*Trumpets the while*' added opposite v.ii.275–6 also looks like the book-keeper, as do the words '*Cum Alijs*' at the end of the opening direction in I.ii, which recognize that the '*Counsaile*' requires more bodies than are actually named.[5] A question might

1. Dover Wilson improbably blames the press-corrector (*MSH*, p. 144).
2. *MSH*, p. 92.
3. On 'foul papers annotated by the book-keeper' see *SFF*, p. 109.
4. *MSH*, p. 91.
5. Cf. I.ii.S.D. LN. One suspects the same hand as prepared the fair copy behind F, in which the opening S.D. of II.ii likewise ends with *Cum alijs*. Similarly the marginal direction at v.ii.354, '*A march a farre off*', looks like an

be raised concerning some of the entries squeezed into the margin instead of being centred: that at v.i.211, for example, '*Enter K. Q. Laertes and the corse*', is obviously a later addition, whether by the author or another, prompted by the dialogue. Suspicion may attach to notes at the right of the text which mark a '*Letter*' or '*Song*'. What I think is certain is that, according to a common playhouse practice,[1] the manuscript was marked for cutting. It is well known that Q2 has a number of passages that have disappeared from F, and it cannot be mere coincidence that one of F's omissions which begins in the middle of a line corresponds with the loss of the latter part of that line in Q2 (iv.i.40). And this throws light on the similar loss of a part-line in Q2 in the course of the Player's speech (ii.ii.470); for although there is this time no cut in F, there was evidently a stage cut at this point since the rest of the speech, comprising 23 lines, is totally unrepresented in Q1. What must have happened is that the compositors of Q2, who normally ignored the theatrical cuts marked in their copy, on these two occasions (a different compositor each time) misinterpreted: a sign intended to mark the second half of a line as the beginning of a cut was mistaken for an ordinary penstroke of deletion.[2]

This evidence that the manuscript had been worked over by a playhouse book-keeper has important corollaries. It implies as the probable sequence of events that Shakespeare delivered *Hamlet* to his company in the form of his 'foul papers'; that these were then transcribed for the purpose of the promptbook; and that the original thus superseded was in due course released by the company to the press.[3]

---

addition by the same hand as in the manuscript behind F added '*a farre off*' to the entry of Hamlet and Horatio at v.i.64. If so, this strengthens the likelihood that other marginal directions were the book-keeper's as well.

1. See *SFF*, pp. 145–6. It is perhaps necessary to state that there are no grounds for supposing that the cutting was done by Shakespeare. A recent generalization by Bowers (*SB*, xxxii, 62), dismissing as 'old-fashioned' the belief that a book-keeper might cut or annotate foul papers before having them transcribed, runs counter to the evidence and relies on an *a priori* and I think a fallible judgment of what is 'inherently improbable'.

2. On iv.i.40 cf. *MSH*, p. 30, and *SFF*, p. 332. Neither makes the inference concerning ii.ii.470.

3. The effect of these corollaries is to discountenance some recent speculations. If the foul papers themselves went to the playhouse, that seems to rule out, for *Hamlet* at least, the hypothesis of Shakespeare's making his own fair copy, with *its* corollary of duplicate autographs (Honigmann, *The Stability of Shakespeare's Text*); and if the printers used a copy marked by the playhouse book-keeper, it is not easy to believe they obtained it without the company's approval (S. Thomas, *SQ*, xxvii, 186–92).

There are still a number of problems concerning its transmission into print.

Omissions

In view of the preservation in Q2 of passages left out of F, it is rather surprising to find Q2 lacking some passages which F gives. Dover Wilson lists five of more than two lines in length.[1] But of these the omission at v. i. 34–7 which robs us of one of the gravedigger's jokes is plainly a case of eyeskip, the compositor jumping from the first to the second occurrence of the word *arms*; and the loss of IV. v. 161–3, three lines at the end of a speech, may be due to the same man's oversight. The longer omission of v. ii. 68–80 is more difficult to account for, but since it deprives us of the end of a sentence and a key expression of Hamlet's new-found resolution, it can hardly have been intentional.[2] The really problematical ones are two substantial omissions, both in the same scene, which do not look accidental. The first is the passage describing Denmark as a prison, the second the account of the boy actors (II. ii. 239–69, 335–58). Both certainly are omissions from Q2 and not additions in F. The excision of the first has left unmistakable clues in the adjacent *but*s, an anomalous capital and a false presumption of continuity: 'but your newes is not true; But in the beaten way of friendship . . .'[3] As for the second, the missing account of the boy actors is being led up to and reflected on in what remains in Q2: it explains the transition from the players who have lost popularity to the new king who has gained it.[4] These undramatic conversational exchanges might seem candidates for cutting; yet their presence in the shortened F text suggests that they were in fact spoken on the stage. The second, though not the first, was partially remembered by the actor-reporter of Q1. One might be tempted to guess that they were actually marked as possible cuts, like the 23 lines of the Player's speech which appear to have been scored for deletion in the foul papers and yet were not dropped from F. But against

1. *MSH*, pp. 96–7.
2. Although the contrary has been suggested, the incomplete sense and sentence (whereby 'is't not perfect conscience?' lacks its necessary complement) seems conclusive for omission and against an addition in F. Moreover, while an addition (1) to emphasize Hamlet's new-found resolution might be conceivable, a passage which also (2) harks back to his outburst to Laertes at the grave and (3) prepares for Osric's entry is far more likely to have been accidentally dropped than deliberately inserted.
3. See LN.
4. See above, pp. 2–3.

this, quite apart from its being the practice of Q2 to ignore theatrical cuts, are the chronological indications that the account of the boy actors was inserted after the play was already in production.[1] Why these passages were dropped in printing one can only guess. By 1604 they may have had less point or more risk or both. The boy actors had become on the one hand less notorious, on the other Children of the Queen's Revels. The new queen herself was of the country that Hamlet called a prison. But in view of the Q2 passage about the drunkenness of Danes (I. iv. 8–22) censorship is not an obvious explanation. And with the possibilities of confusion in the copy, one cannot after all be quite sure that the omissions were designed.

In the printing-house

In the printing-house the text was set up by two compositors, Roberts's regular pair, of whom X set sheets B, C, D, F, I, N, O, and Y set E, G, H, K, M. Sheet L apparently belonged to Y's share, but its first and last pages were set by X.[2] In terms of the text this works out as follows:

X	I.	i.	1	– I.	v. 191
Y		I.	v. 192	– II.	ii. 161 a
X	II.	ii. 161 b	– II.	ii. 573
Y	II.	ii. 574	– III.	iii. 20
X	III.	iii. 21	– III.	iv. 212
Y	III.	iv. 213	– IV.	v. 89
X	IV.	v. 90	– IV.	v. 121
Y	IV.	v. 122	– IV. vii.	98
X	IV. vii.	99	– IV. vii.	134
Y	IV. vii.	135	– V.	i. 277
X	V.	i. 278	– end.

X seems to have been the faster workman,[3] and Alice Walker estimates that he was appreciably more prone to error;[4] but gross and careless errors as well as misreadings and omissions come from both. It is hard to believe they did the best that was possible with their admittedly difficult copy; but the inferiority of their work on *Hamlet* as compared with their other books suggests that there may have been contributory factors. Alice Walker takes the difficulty to have been not so much that the copy was illegible as that it needed more time to decipher and comprehend than the

1. See above, pp. 5–13.
2. J. R. Brown, *SB*, VII, 17 ff.
3. Bowers, *On Editing Shakespeare*, pp. 38–9.
4. *SB*, VII, 57–60.

compositors could or chose to give. How they handled straightforward copy can be seen from Q2 of *Titus Andronicus*, which was
printed from Q1. On the whole, discounting spelling variations,
they followed very faithfully; but they felt themselves free to
modernize – as in substituting *whilst* for *whiles* – and they sometimes tried to correct what they took to be mistakes. They might
regularize grammar or metre. Thus a verb is made plural to agree
with its subject; *overcome* is contracted to *orecome*. *Th'* is expanded
to *the*, or the converse if metre requires. I have observed Y
(though not X) changing *ye* to *you* and *my* or *thy* before a vowel to
mine or *thine*. That similar little things happened in *Hamlet* is
apparent from Y's mistaken expansion *the vmber* where the copy
presumably had *th umbe* (III.ii.349, F *thumbe*). Punctuation the
compositors, like most others in their age, considered within their
province, and though they often reproduced that of their copy,
their tendency, even with printed copy, was to add to it. They
were notably partial to the colon. These are things which ad-
mirers of the Q2 punctuation[1] often fail to reckon with. By
comparison with the same compositors' other texts, the *Hamlet*
punctuation, consisting mainly of commas but with a sprinkling
of colons and semicolons, is uncharacteristically light, and one
has to infer that the punctuation of the copy was considerably
lighter still – as indeed the Shakespearean pages in *Sir Thomas
More* would lead one to expect.

The use of Q1 in the printing of Q2

The most remarkable thing about the 'copy' for Q2 is yet to be
mentioned. Although the printers had what the title-page claimed
to be the 'true' copy of the play in what the accumulated evidence
leads us to believe was the dramatist's own hand, they actually
combined reliance on this manuscript with use of the bad quarto
it was meant to supersede.[2] Exactly how and to what extent Q1
was used in the printing of Q2 is a matter of dispute,[3] but that it
was used is shown by a number of little similarities, among which
a curious typographical correspondence is conclusive. In both
quartos the speech-prefixes on the first page, instead of being
indented in the usual fashion, are set flush with the margin; and

1. Notably Dover Wilson, *MSH*, pp. 196–205. In my experience many
Shakespeare editors have a regard for the punctuation of the original texts
which, in the light of what we now know of compositors (as Dover Wilson of
course did not), verges on the superstitious.

2. *MSH*, pp. 158–62; A. Walker, *RES*, n.s. II, 328–31.

3. See A. Walker, as above; Bowers, *SB*, VIII, 39–66; Cairncross, *Text*
(Uppsala), I, 67–77; below, pp. 48–52.

in both the speech-prefixes begin to be indented at the same point in the text (I.i.33). But whereas in Q1 the change connects with the beginning of the second page, in Q2's longer text there is no such connection and we are a third of the way down the second page when the point of change is reached. The inference is inescapable that Q2 sets the speech-prefixes as it does because it is copying Q1. Given this clue, we note further correspondences extending through the first act. Unusual spellings in which the two quartos agree include the phonetic *pollax* (I.i.66), *ship-writes* (I.i.78), *sallied* (I.ii.129), *pre thee . . . studient* (I.ii.177), *Capapea* in italic, *tronchions, gelly* (I.ii.200, 204, 205), *glimses* (I.iv.53), *the Nemeon Lyons nerue* (I.iv.83), *wharffe* (I.v.33), *Angle linckt*, the unmetrical *leaprous, allies* (I.v.55, 64, 67), *i'st* (I.v.119, 148), *sellerige* (I.v.159). There is a correspondence of superfluous apostrophes in *bak't, look't* (I.ii.180, 230), *can'st, dream't* (I.v.170, 175); of unexpected but perhaps significant commas in *Saw, who?* (I.ii.190), *Pale, or red?* (I.ii.232); of occasional colons, as at I.i.176, I.ii.211. The intrusive point after *gelly* (I.ii.205), though a full stop is varied to a comma, shows the same misconception of the syntax. Dover Wilson notes the correspondence of 'Speake to me(e)' printed on a separate line (I.i.135), and there is a similar instance in '*Marcellus*' (I.ii.165). More significant may be a number of common errors, most notably *cost* (F *cast*, I.i.76) and *interr'd* (F *enurn'd*, I.iv.49), possibly also *of a most select* (I.iii.74). An influence is apparent in the mixed form *horrowes* (Q1 *horrors*, F *harrowes*, I.i.47). But scholars are not always agreed about what are errors: *rootes* (I.v.33, F *rots*), which most include, is almost certainly the correct reading (see I.v.32–3 LN). On the other hand, I think we should add *Hebona* (I.v.62): for it is much more likely that Q2 accepted Q1's corruption of an unusual word than that a reporting actor independently arrived at Shakespeare's exact spelling.

It will be noticed that the correspondences between the quartos tend to occur in clusters, one striking resemblance having others in its context. In the same area of the text (I.v.157–88) as the anomalous apostrophes in *can'st* and *dream't* we find capitals for *Gentlemen, Mole, Pioner, Anticke*, the strange spelling *sellerige*, the ampersand in *Hic & vbique*, and the centred stage-direction for the Ghost to speak '*vnder the stage*'. The tangled speech on the 'Anticke disposition' is so closely similar in the two texts as to excite in itself a suspicion of dependence. '*Lethe* wharffe' is in both texts followed after five lines by a colon after *abusde* and capitals for *Youth* and *Crowne* (I.v.38–40). The notorious *pollax* comes as

the climax of four lines which, apart from the capital in *Armor*
and the variant spelling of *ice* (Q1 *yce*), are identical:

> Such was the very Armor he had on,
> When he the ambitious *Norway* combated,
> So frownd he once, when in an angry parle
> He smot the sleaded pollax on the ice.
>
> (1.i.63–6)

The error of *cost* is followed in the same line (1.i.76) by a capital
for *Cannon* and then by two lines which, even to the hyphen in
ship-writes, are the same in every respect.

On the other hand striking correspondences are often found
together with no less striking differences. The most notable
example is perhaps that afforded by the Q2 lines

> So but though to a radiant Angle linckt,
> Will sort it selfe in a celestiall bed   (1.v.55–6)

– where the spellings (*Angle linckt*) which indicate dependence on
Q1 are found adjacent to the erroneous readings *but* and *sort* for
Lust and *sate* (Q1 *fate*), for which Q1 can have given no excuse
and which betray a manuscript origin.[1] Although *of a most select*
(1.iii.74) may have been taken by Q2 from Q1, the preceding
word *Or* (Q1 *Are*) again looks like a manuscript misreading. In
the 'Anticke disposition' speech, mid-way between the common
apostrophe in *dream't* and the capital in *Anticke*, Q2 replaces *soere*
by *so mere*, which, on the analogy of *someuer* elsewhere from both
compositors (1.ii.249, 1.v.84, iii.ii.389), one would suppose the
manuscript form. Bowers detects a manuscript influence when a
compositor (X), as with *saies* and *eies* (1.i.26, 61), goes against the
spelling of Q1 and his normal preference.[2]

The curiously mixed nature of the copy thus revealed leaves
the textual experts divided as to what exactly the Q2 compositors
handled. There is, and must be, general agreement that Q1 was
used in some way, at least for the first act;[3] but whereas Alice
Walker, who has done most to enforce the recognition of its use,
maintains that an exemplar of Q1 corrected by collation with the
manuscript was the actual printer's copy for the first act, Fredson
Bowers has argued from the mixture of similars and dissimilars

---

1. Cf. Bowers, *SB*, viii, 58–9. Cairncross's attempt to explain the Q2 errors as
due to 'correction' by guesswork is an obvious rationalization.

2. *SB*, viii, 55–6.

3. Or rather the first act minus the last seven lines, with which sig. E and the
second compositor begin.

that the compositor must have worked from both print and manuscript, conflating as he went along.[1]

Alice Walker has, unquestionably, pertinent evidence for her view. The business of the speech-prefixes shows that the Q2 compositor (X) must have begun with Q1 open before him. And when we observe that his opening direction, '*Enter Barnardo, and Francisco, two Centinels*', reproduces that of Q1 save for the insertion of the names, it begins to look as though his copy of Q1 may have been one with corrections written in. This appears to be confirmed when ll. 6 and 16 each anomalously end a speech with a comma inherited from Q1. In l. 6,

> You come most carefully vpon your houre,
> (Q1: O you come most carefully vpon your watch,)

it is easier to explain the retention of the comma if we suppose that the altered wording, instead of being taken directly from the manuscript, had been entered in Q1; and in l. 16 the comma, which in Q1 does not end the speech, only comes to do so in Q2 because a new speech (l. 17) is inserted. The hypothesis of corrected copy may seem, moreover, to be strengthened by Bowers's own eminently reasonable assumption that, in a quarto divided between two compositors, the extraordinary division whereby the first man (X) composed the first three sheets (B–D) while the second (Y) concurrently began with the fourth sheet (E)[2] must have had something to do with the nature of their copy. It suggests that Compositor X had the use of something that could not be simultaneously available to Y; and the most likely thing for this to have been is a particular copy of Q1 which had been specially prepared and marked. For if Roberts was minded to use Q1, we cannot reasonably assume with Bowers[3] that he was limited to a single copy of it. Yet as an alternative to annotated copy a more plausible supposition is that there was something in the character of the compositor's task which only X was qualified to undertake.[4] And indeed the hypothesis of corrected copy, in

1. Bowers's unfinished article in *SB*, VIII, leaves unstated the conclusion to which its whole argument tends, but elsewhere he refers to 'conflation in the course of type-setting in the printer's shop, as I suspect happened with the first act of *Hamlet*' (*Shakespeare 1971*, ed. Leech and Margeson, p. 56). Cf. 'The unannotated bad quarto of *Hamlet* seems to have been consulted in the first act . . . to help the compositor of the good Second Quarto decipher the difficult manuscript' (*SB*, XXXI, 1978, 120–1).

2. Bowers, 'The Printing of *Hamlet*, Q2', *SB*, VII, 41–50.

3. *On Editing Shakespeare*, p. 43.

4. Cf. p. 50, n.4.

spite of the initial signs in favour of it, also encounters difficulties
from the start which its proponents too readily brush aside: the
opening lines of Q1 are more than trebled in Q2, and the additions on the first page, quite apart from alterations, are more than
there would be space to insert. In contending that 'correction as
far as the end of Act I would certainly have been practicable',[1]
Dr Walker overstates her case; and a subsequent restatement of it
which to 'correction' adds 'and amplification'[2] has a touch of the
disingenuous. Amplification implies that passages totally lacking
in Q1 would need to be supplied from the manuscript. One may
point to I.i. 111–28; ii. 1–26, 44–50; iv. 17–38, 75–8; and odd
lines or groups of lines elsewhere. But beyond these missing
passages, there are episodes which in Q1 are so compressed and
travestied that, however fully 'corrected', they could not possibly
have served as copy for Q2. These include the larger part of I.ii
(to l. 159) and over two-thirds of I.iii (1–51, 90–136). The
amount even of the first act which could only have been set up
directly from the manuscript is considerably more than a third.[3]

Any confident pronouncement of what happened appears impossible. One surmises that when Roberts received his 'true and
perfect coppie', he saw that it would be difficult, or at least
inconvenient, to work from and therefore had the idea of getting
what help he could from the despised Q1, specimens of which the
publisher Ling would be able to supply. The bibliographical links
at the beginning suggest that the experiment of annotating Q1
for use as copy, for all the difficulties of the opening page, was
actually tried out. After that it would presumably prove feasible
for the first scene. At the beginning of the second it would in any
case have to be abandoned, at least temporarily, though it could,
conceivably, have been resumed for parts of iv and v. But even
when Q1 did not serve as copy it was still on hand for the compositor to have recourse to, as in varying degrees he seems to have
done throughout Act I, now taking from it perhaps a single word,
now several lines together, and now, as he compared it with his
manuscript, producing a mixture of the two.[4] The uncertainties

---

1. *RES*, n.s. II, 330.

2. *Textual Problems of the First Folio*, p. 121: 'Q2 was printed, I think, from Q1
. . . throughout . . . Act I, with correction and amplification from the foul
papers.'

3. Cairncross, who seeks to establish the Walker thesis, has to make the proviso that 'the correction or annotation was intermittent in Act I' (*Text*, I, 76)
and falls back upon 'a pattern of alternation' (p. 71).

4. I am forced to agree with Nosworthy (p. 135) against Cairncross that the
kind of copy that would result from any full correction of Q1 would be 'a

of such 'consultation' of Q1 (or of any combination of annotation and consultation) inevitably shake somewhat the authority of Q2 for the first act.[1]

After the first act, with increasing divergence between the quartos, it is clear that Q1, however extensively annotated, could not have made practicable copy. The only two passages which are verbally close enough to appear possible exceptions are sufficiently accounted for by the hypothesis that the actor or actors of Voltemand and Lucianus contributed to the memorial report. Voltemand's long speech (II.ii.60–80), for all its verbal correspondence in the two texts, lacks just those little resemblances of spelling, punctuation, and typography which would betray that one was printed from the other, and, Cairncross notwithstanding, I am satisfied that it was not. The utmost use to which, after the first act, Q1 could have been put is to have been occasionally consulted when the manuscript proved obscure. Alice Walker chooses to think this did not happen, but others, including Bowers,[2] have thought it did; and Nosworthy, who alone believes Q1 was used by Y as well as X, goes so far as to identify ten passages which he supposes influenced by it, varying from 3 to 75 lines in length.[3] But for over half of these his evidence, when not illusory, is featherweight. Among the spellings which he holds beyond coincidence, *chuse* and *yce* were in frequent use, while *bloudily*, if Q2 of *Romeo and Juliet* is anything to go by (*bloud*- 23 times as against *blood* once), was probably Shakespeare's own. For the rest, *duckats* is found in *Much Ado* (IV.ii.44), another quarto thought to be printed from autograph (as well as *duckets* in *Romeo* and in *Hamlet* elsewhere); *randeuous* in *1 Henry IV* (IV.i.57), as well as in other authors; and even *penitrable* can be matched in *The Merchant of Venice* (*impenitrable*, III.iii.18): so that

compositor's nightmare'; but the task of setting up from two texts and conflating them in the process, in the manner supposed by Bowers, could hardly have been less so. It is not easy to imagine how a journeyman could be directed or could take upon himself to construct a text in this improvisatory way. But if Compositor X had special privileges or special responsibilities – if, for example, he were Roberts himself – the probabilities might be different.

1. Any postulate of 'consultation' is of course anathema to Alice Walker, because it leaves an editor not knowing at any point 'where he stands'. But one cannot resist the impression that her wish for a clear-cut editorial situation – corrected Q1 as Q2 copy for the first act, foul papers for the rest – has done much to persuade her that it exists. (See *RES*, n.s.II, pp. 329–30.) Cf. Honigmann, *The Stability of Shakespeare's Text*, pp. 151–2.

2. *On Editing Shakespeare*, pp. 43–4 (instancing Hamlet's talk with the players on sig. F3).

3. Nosworthy, pp. 135–7.

among the allegedly significant spellings, only *crocadile* appears to be unique. Nevertheless some are rare enough for the concurrence of both quartos to be remarkable; and some are associated with other correspondences, as with the capitals in

a Rat, dead for a Duckat . . .   (III. iv. 23)

For my part I might cite *Mallico* (F *Malicho*, III. ii. 135), and ask what one is to make of the following stage-directions:

Enter Gilderstone, and Rossencraft.   Q1
Enter Guyldersterne, and Rosencraus.   Q2
(II. ii. 214, Q1; 217, Q2)

Here the Q2 compositor (X) relies upon his own knowledge of the names; yet (1) he spells *Guyldersterne* with an *r* in the middle syllable instead of his normal *n* (and apparently does this deliberately, since he repeats it seven lines below); (2) he reverses the usual order of the names; and (3) he inserts a comma after the first. None of these details is unique, but all are exceptional, and the concurrence of Q1 in all three indicates that as their likely source. If so, this affords an illuminating instance of the kind of consultation there might be. There is no question of an influence of Q1 on the adjacent text; it appears to have been referred to for the stage-direction only.[1] And this, together with the alteration of the names, shows the intervention of an individual judgment.

I believe, then, that the debt of Q2 to Q1, though it necessarily diminishes, does not cease after Act I, but that Q1 continued liable to be resorted to, certainly by X and probably, on occasions of difficulty, by Y as well (*Mallico* is his).[2] The consequence for the editor is, as Alice Walker saw, disquieting. To say that 'all readings of Q2 which agree with those of Q1 incur suspicion' is unduly pessimistic; for agreement between the quartos will most often be due to their being right. Yet since we can never be sure at any point that Q2 is not in debt to Q1,[3] they can never corroborate one another; and paradoxically, the authority of Q2 (and especially against F) is less when it agrees with Q1 than when it differs.

---

1. It is not the task of an observer to offer conjectural explanations, but that would not be difficult. If the manuscript lacked or compressed the stage-direction, what more natural than that the compositor should seek confirmation of it in the print to which he has been shown to have had access?

2. I cannot see why Bowers assumes that X's having major responsibility for the use of Q1 excludes Y from any access to it at all.

3. Cf. v. i. 256 n.

Press correction

One final complication of the printing was more usual. According to a familiar practice, the sheets were subject to correction while being printed off. The extant copies reveal variants on seven formes – B (outer), C (inner), D (inner), G (outer), N (outer and inner), O (inner), the last including the title-page with its variant date. Outer N occurs in three states, the British Library copy having only seven of the nine corrections. With inner D, though it is convenient to speak of the 'corrected' state, it is in fact not clear whether in the only variant the word *Lord* at the end of a line (I.iv.69) was supplied by a correction of the type or in some copies failed to print. The other substantive variants are noted at I.iii.48, II.ii.584, III.i.163, v.i.293, v.ii.9, 109, 114 (two), 126, 157, 184, 269.[1]

The corrector is sometimes wrong. He tried to make sense of his own without referring to the copy, and an editor must not be guided by his guesses. At v.i.293 his replacement of the erroneous *thirtie* by *thereby* (F *shortly*) is an obvious piece of guesswork;[2] while at v.ii.114 he rejected the good and apt word *yaw*, presumably because he did not know it.[3] One has of course to recognize that he may also have altered readings on sheets where no evidence survives; but this is a possibility we cannot check and one which conjecture has been too ready to exploit.

THE FIRST FOLIO (F)

In the First Folio of 1623 *Hamlet* occupies signatures nn4^v–qq1^v, pp. 152–282 in the third section (*Tragedies*). But even such record of matters of fact cannot, with *Hamlet*, be simple: by a printer's error the page numbers leap a hundred after 156 to 257, and the last page (282) is misnumbered 280.

The play was set by (at least) three compositors, those customarily referred to as B and E and a third whose identity is not established. Reliable opinion divides their work as follows:[4]

1. A full list is given in *MSH*, pp. 123–4. To the information about their distribution it can now be added that the Wroclaw copy has inner C, inner D and inner O in the corrected and outer B, outer G, and outer and inner N in the uncorrected state. My inspection of this copy shows that Hinman's belief (in his Note to the Second Impression of the Clarendon Press facsimile) that it had two other variant formes is mistaken.

2. Cf. v.ii.184, 269.

3. See also notes on v.ii.9, 114 (*dozy*), 125–6 (LN).

4. Hinman, *The Printing and Proof-Reading of the First Folio*, ii.208–75, 516–17. For the unidentified compositor Hinman hesitated between A and C. His summary list prefers A for nn6–6^v and C elsewhere; but the probability that the

Comp.	Sigs	pp.	Text
B	nn4^v–5^v	152–4	I.i.1–ii.164
?	nn6–oo1	155–257 except last 36 lines[1]	I.ii.165–v.21[1]
B	oo1	257 last 36 lines[1]	I.v.22[1]–57
?	oo1^v–2	258–9	I.v.58–II.i.103
B	oo2^v–3	260–1	II.i.104–II.ii.214
?	oo3^v	262	II.ii.215–339 (the)
B	oo4–pp4	263–75 except last 20 lines[1]	II.ii.339 (fashion)– IV.vii.49[1]
?	pp4	275 last 20 lines[1]	IV.vii.49[1]–83
?	pp4^v	276	IV.vii.84–v.i.22
E	pp5–6^v	277–80	v.i.23–ii.271 (worn)
B	qq1–1^v	281–2	v.ii.271 (give) – end.

Thus, of the 31 pages some twenty were set by B, whose in-accuracy has become notorious, and four others, covering most of the fifth act, by E, 'certainly the least skilful' of all the Folio compositors[2] with a propensity for bad mistakes. If F were our only, or even our major, text for *Hamlet*, the implications would be very serious. As it is, what E is capable of perpetrating can be seen when the *Sexten* becomes *sixteene* (v.i.156), *treble woe* is turned into a *terrible woer* (v.i.239) and Hamlet hurts not his

---

doubtful pages all had the same compositor is admitted in his discussion, which provisionally assigns them all to C and suspects that A had no part in *Hamlet* (ii.217, 249). Since there are considerable objections to both, I have, while believing in a single compositor, preferred to leave him as a question-mark. Cairncross (*PBSA*, LXV, 50, 52) rejected both A and C, but his assignment of the pages in question to E (*PBSA*, LXVI, 390, 406) is unlikely to gain acceptance. His attribution of oo4^v to E as well, rejected by Howard-Hill, appears to be a slip. Perhaps it should be added that Howard-Hill finds some warrant for tentatively transferring three of E's four pages to B (*Compositors B and E . . . and Some Recent Studies*, privately circulated, 1976, pp. 16–17; *A Reassessment of Compositors B and E in the First Folio Tragedies*, privately circulated, 1977, p. 52). His later 'New Light on Compositor E' (*Library*, 6th ser., II, 1980, 156–78) sheds no further light on this. (P.S. The disqualification of A and C has now been effected by Gary Taylor in favour of a new compositor I. See *SB*, XXXIV (1981), 103–6.)

1. Approximate. The compositor's partner appears to have finished the page for him (Hinman, ii.256–7).

2. Hinman, ii.264. The case for his being an inexperienced workman is very strong and brilliantly made out. That he was therefore only an apprentice, as commonly stated, is an inference. That he was therefore John Leason, who began his apprenticeship in November 1622 (*SB*, XIII, 125) only five months before the printing of the Tragedies, is a further inference and one which even a combination of distinguished bibliographers (Hinman, ii.513; Bowers, *Bibliography and Textual Criticism*, p. 181) will not persuade us to believe. Has not Euclid taught us that a conclusion which is obviously absurd requires us to reject the premise?

brother but his *Mother* (v. ii. 240). B's high-handed way with copy is presumably to be detected when the text is expanded to fill out his page (see ii. ii. 213 n.)[1] as well as when *nor man* is emended to *or Norman* (iii. ii. 32), and the life-rendering *Pelican* is changed to a *Politician* (iv. v. 146). But with Q2 to expose such errors for what they are, the important questions about F concern less its printing than its provenance. The precise relation between the two texts – their divergences and correspondences – is one of the most puzzling of *Hamlet*'s many problems; but at least it is evident that behind F lies a manuscript other than that from which Q2 was printed.

F's divergences are not all easy to account for. But they are not beyond description and an attempt at classification.

(*i*) We begin with its *additions and omissions*. While including over seventy lines that are not found in Q2,[2] F lacks something like 230 lines that Q2 has; and although one or two of the briefer omissions may be accidental,[3] most look like deliberate cuts. 'The more important', as listed by Greg, are the long speeches that lead up to the appearances of the Ghost at i. i. 128 and i. iv. 38; twenty-seven lines of Hamlet's in the scene with his mother (iii. iv); most of the Fortinbras scene (iv. iv); 'twenty-five lines of the plot between Claudius and Laertes (in iv. vii); and fifty-four lines in the first part of the last scene, including a good deal of Osric and the whole of the Lord who so superfluously repeats his message'.[4] Shorter omissions include the description of the terror of the cliff (i. iv. 75–8); two separate couplets from the 'Mouse-trap' play (iii. ii. 166–7, 213–14); and Claudius's reflection on slander (iv. i. 41–4). It is noticeable that the cuts get rid of several passages which are tangled or defective in Q2;[5] their obscurity may have contributed to their suppression. Scholars have liked to picture Shakespeare neglecting to straighten out what he did not expect to preserve. But what is not always remembered is that the relative frequency of cruxes in the passages dispensed with must be a consequence as well as a cause of their occurrence in one text only; and although some of the cuts appear to have been marked

1. This happens at the foot of sig. oo3. At the foot of nn5ᵛ, also the ending of a B stint, three lines in Q2 become six in F (i. ii. 160–3).

2. See above, p. 44.

3. E.g. iv. iii. 26–8, and perhaps i. ii. 58–60. Both of these passages were present in the stage version reported in Q1 and the disappearance of the former breaks the connection of ideas. Cf. *MSH*, pp. 22–3.

4. *SFF*, p. 317. Cf. *MSH*, pp. 25–33.

5. E.g. i. i. 120–1; i. iv. 36–8 (the famous 'dram of eale' crux); iii. iv. 163–4.

in the foul papers,[1] it by no means follows that they were made by the author himself. Indeed the most remarkable omission, that of Hamlet's soliloquy on Fortinbras (IV.iv.32–66), while leaving Fortinbras's part intact, robs it of its most significant function. But it is no exception to the rule that excisions are of what the plot can easily spare; and their frequency over the second half of the play strengthens the impression of a theatrical abridgement.[2] Yet the loss of a mere 230 lines from a play the length of *Hamlet* can hardly represent a serious attempt at shortening. It is significant that Q2 gives evidence that additional cuts were marked in the original manuscript, and Q1 that further cuts were actually made in performance.[3] I think one has to conclude that F, while manifestly having undergone some preparation for the stage, itself contains more than can be supposed to have been regularly played at the Globe.[4]

(*ii*) The *stage-directions* of F are fuller and more systematic. But the system is somewhat mixed and not always in the interests of staging. A dozen or so missing exit-directions are supplied (though nearly as many are still wanting). An entry for the Queen when she is already on is deleted (IV.i.1). On the other hand, where Q2 reflects the author's sense of stage-grouping by naming Hamlet last when the court first enter (I.ii) and Laertes last when they come in for the fencing-match (V.ii.220), F substitutes a social for a theatrical arrangement: '*Enter Claudius King of Denmarke, Gertrude the Queene, Hamlet . . .*'; '*Enter King, Queene, Laertes and*

1. See above, p. 43.

2. Philip Edwards in an unpublished lecture has argued that Shakespeare himself took the opportunity to tighten up the action and to clarify Hamlet's motivation in the later part of the play. Not everyone will agree that the play is strengthened by the loss of the carefully prepared-for soliloquy on Fortinbras. See below, pp. 136–9.

3. See above, pp. 21–2, 43. Curiously, the converse also occurs: some of what is omitted from F has left traces in Q1. In this the fact that Fortinbras is 'nephew to old Norway' (IV.iv.14) is added to the mention of him in IV.iv.2, and the unnamed lord's announcement that the King and Queen 'are coming down' for the fencing (V.ii.200) is incorporated into Osric's part. Yet the reporter shows no further awareness of the episodes from which these phrases are taken, and they are just such bits of information as abridgement might wish to rescue. It is tempting to suppose that it was the abridger who transferred them to the surviving dialogue in the course of his cutting operation, except that one would expect them then to figure in F. (Perhaps in some promptbook they did.)

4. Cf. *SFF*, pp. 317–18. I see little to favour Nosworthy's view that Shakespeare himself devised two versions of different length to suit different occasions. See above, p. 21, n. 5. One possibility is that F restored some cut passages in the process of collation with Q2 (see below, pp. 65–73).

Lords . . .'. In the first of these directions, where Q2 introduces *'Polonius, and his Sonne Laertes'*, F as though to complete the family brings in *'his Sister Ophelia'* a scene too soon. The author's generic and collective character indications are now made precise by individual names: Cornelius and Voltemand are named when entering, not merely when addressed (I.ii.25, II.ii.58); Rosencrantz and Guildenstern are specified among those 'coming to the play' (III.ii.90); the *'Courtier'* of Q2 (v.ii.81) becomes *'young Osricke'*.[1] This last designation is taken from the dialogue (l. 193), which is fairly obviously the source also of such descriptive stage-directions as *'Enter Hamlet reading on a Booke'* (II.ii.167) and *'Exit Hamlet tugging in Polonius'* (III.iv.219), where *'tugging'* must, I think, be a misprint for *'lugging'* (cf. *lug*, l. 214). Many of F's directions are of this descriptive kind, making explicit what the dialogue implies. They are not, as Greg assumed, author's directions going back to the foul papers but the additions of a scribe or editor. I suppose they might not be beyond a playhouse transcriber of foul papers,[2] but they more suggest a text prepared for reading than performance. For example, in the play-scene F adds *'Sleepes'* (III.ii.222) and *'Powres the poyson in his eares'* (l. 254) and during the fencing-match *'Prepare to play'* (v.ii.263), *'They play'* (l. 278), *'Play'* (l. 304), *'Hurts the King'* (l. 327), and several others. But in this last scene *'In scuffling they change Rapiers'* (l. 306) seems a necessary clarification and goes beyond what can be inferred from the dialogue alone. Production rather than the reader is served by more specific directions not only for supernumeraries but for properties and noises off. The *'table prepard'* for the fencing scene in Q2 is defined in F as *'a Table and Flagons of Wine on it'*. The King enters for the play *'with his Guard carrying Torches'*, Fortinbras in the last scene *'with Drumme, Colours, and Attendants'*. To the *'march a farre off'* which heralds Fortinbras's arrival F adds *'shout [for shot] within'*; at the end *'a Peale of Ordenance are shot off'*. There are also a number of theatrically significant substitutions: the *'Danish March'* for the *'Trumpets and Kettle Drummes'* of Q2 when the King comes to the play, the *'Hoboyes'* instead of *'Trumpets'* to introduce the dumb-show, the *'Foyles, and Gauntlets'*, which

1. With this goes a care to correct the forms of characters' names (see below, p. 71) and to standardize speech-prefixes. Whereas Q2 alternates between *Gertrard* and *Queen(e)* and their abbreviations, F consistently prefers the second and in speech-prefixes (with one exception, presumably an oversight) distinguishes the Player Queen as *Bap(t)* (for *Baptista*). The single speech-prefix *Claud.* is replaced by *King*. The *Doct.* at Ophelia's burial (v.i) becomes *Priest*.

2. Especially if it were he who added *'a farre off'* to the entry of Hamlet and Horatio in the churchyard. See above, p. 42, n.5.

replace the foils and daggers of the fencing scene, even though 'Rapier and Dagger' continue in the dialogue (v.ii.142). Once or twice an extra line of dialogue is supplied, notably in the calling *'within'* at III.iv.5 and IV.ii.1 and on the entry of the messengers at IV.v.97 and IV.vii.35.[1]

Along with such indications of a text prepared for performance go alterations evidently intended to reduce the cast. The elimination of the Lord who follows Osric to inquire if Hamlet is ready to fence is no doubt prompted by the desire to dispense with an actor as much as with ten lines of dialogue. For the entry of *'three'* of the players (III.ii.1) F substitutes *'two or three'*; for the *'three or foure'* companions of the poisoner in the dumb-show *'two or three'*; for *'the Players with Recorders'* (III.ii.336) *'one with a Recorder'*; for Rosencrantz *'and others'* (IV.ii.3) Rosencrantz *'and Guildensterne'*; for *'Horatio and others'* (IV.vi.1) *'Horatio, with an Attendant'*; for *'Saylers'* (IV.vi.5) *'Saylor'*; for *'the Embassadors'* (v.ii.366) *'English Ambassador'*. Occasionally the dialogue is modified to fit: the passage about the recorders, though not that about the sailors, is translated into the singular. Or there may be a redistribution of speeches, as when the suppression of an unnamed gentleman in IV.v necessitates the transfer of his lines to Horatio and some of Horatio's inappropriately to the Queen. There are drastic economies in IV.iii which can only be achieved at some dramatic cost. The disappearance of the *'two or three'* who enter with the King leaves as a soliloquy what Shakespeare evidently intended to be a public utterance. Q2's vague but prodigal requirements, *'Enter Rosencraus and all the rest'* and, for Hamlet under guard, *'They enter'*, are ruthlessly cut down to the entry first of Rosencrantz alone and then of Guildenstern as Hamlet's solitary escort. The scene is thus deprived of throng and turmoil, Guildenstern is relegated to an inappropriate status, and the nature of these two, who never otherwise enter separately, is subtly falsified. By making Rosencrantz call to Guildenstern off stage (Q2 'How', F 'Hoa, *Guildensterne*') the adapter again shows his willingness to extend his operations to the dialogue. In IV.i, when Rosencrantz and Guildenstern enter and then promptly leave at the Queen's request, F eliminates both the entry and the relevant line of the Queen's speech (IV.i.4).

All this has usually led to the assumption that F has the promptbook behind it. But Greg found the evidence not clear.[2] No great significance need attach to the absence of some necessary

1. Cf. below, pp. 62-3, 64.
2. *SFF*, pp. 316, 323.

exits, such oversights being common in prompt texts; and the
literary character of some of the stage-directions could be due to
editorial revision. But there are other directions which lack the
definiteness normally expected of a promptbook. Where Q2 and
presumably Shakespeare are content to bring on '*the Players*'
(II.ii.416), F and presumably the book-keeper acknowledge a
need to be more specific without deciding beyond '*foure or fiue*'.
Cast reductions already cited show a similar hesitation with '*two
or three of the Players*' for Q2's '*three*' (III.ii.1) and '*some two or three
Mutes*' for Q2's '*three or foure*'. What such adjustment suggests is
perhaps not so much a promptbook as a preliminary revision of
the manuscript upon which a promptbook might be based. With
the stage-directions as with the cutting we seem to have a
text adapted for the theatre but with some options still left
open.

(*iii*) Apart from the marks of adaptation for performance, F shows
numerous *variants in the dialogue*. To see how some of these correct
Q2 it may be instructive to glance again at a few of the instances
already cited where the Q2 compositors seem to have misread
Shakespeare's manuscript or, failing to read it, guessed or resorted
to Q1.[1] Even where the result was obviously nonsense, we might
well not have seen what the true reading should be if it had not
been preserved in F. This is probably so, for example, with *that*
for *the cue* (II.ii.555) or *so loued Arm'd* for *so loud a wind* (IV.vii.22).
Other errors might almost have passed muster in Q2 without F
to expose them. One might, I suppose, have wondered about
friendly falconers (II.ii.426) or deaths put on *for no* cause (v.ii.388),
yet not have perceived that the cause was properly *forc'd* or been
certain that the falconers were *French*. In still other instances an
obviously superior F reading reveals an error in Q2 which we
should have been unlikely even to suspect: it gives us a *fretfull*
rather than a *fearefull* porpentine (I.v.20), a corpse *enurn'd* rather
than *interr'd* (I.iv.49); it makes Hamlet *affear'd* instead of *sure* what
Laertes is about (v.ii.303); its gravedigger *o're Offices*, not *ore-
reaches*, the owner of the skull (v.i.78). When this last example is
lamented as a characteristic blunder of the Folio compositor E,[2]
we may legitimately inquire how a blunderer arrived at a word
which is in Shakespeare's finest manner, both inventive and

1. See above, pp. 38–9, and, for use of Q1, p. 47.
2. Hinman, i.302–3, ii.257. Lest my confidence in the contrary be thought a
merely personal judgment, cf. H. Hulme (*EC*, xv, 220–3), 'a brilliant emendation surely if it is one'.

exact. In all these cases F surely makes it clear that Q2 mis-
rendered Shakespeare's autograph and that whoever transcribed
it for the playhouse read it right. Often the Q2 compositor, as
with *friendly* for *French* falconers, *greeued* for *grained* spots (III. iv. 90),
criminall for *crimefull* feats (IV. vii. 7), seems to have read the
beginning of a word and then assumed the rest. But it is difficult
to think that *offices* can have looked enough like *reaches* to make
that a plausible guess. It seems rather that *ore* (o'er) suggested
reaches as a stopgap when the printer was defeated by an unexpected word. And I have suggested that other puzzling variants
may be similarly explained as compositorial stopgaps, like the
visage which is *heated* in Q2 but *tristfull* in F (III. iv. 50).[1] Hence it
is unnecessary to indulge in the fancy of Shakespearean revision in
order to accept *tristful* as Shakespeare's word, or to suppose that
F's preferred variants give us his second instead of his first
thoughts. From the preservation of what we take to be authentic
readings corrupted in Q2, along with the inclusion of passages
which Q2 omits altogether, F has its inestimable value.

But while many of F's variants may confidently be taken to
correct errors of Q2, more, it is equally apparent, are themselves
corruptions. Apart from those grosser perversions already cited,
a comparison with Q2 reveals many careless errors, including
talkes for *takes* (I. i. 168), *wake* for *walke* (I. ii. 243), *euents* for *intents*
(I. iv. 42), *speed* for *heede* (II. i. 111), *two* for *tenne* (II. ii. 179), *valiant*
for *valanct* (II. ii. 419), *warm'd* for *wand* (II. ii. 548), *like* for *licke*
(III. ii. 60), *excellent* for *eloquent* (III. ii. 350), *ran* for *can* (IV. vii. 83).
There is a tendency for F to vary a word in a final unaccented
syllable, usually with a more commonplace result: it has *Easterne*
for *Eastward* (I. i. 172), *nightly* for *nighted* (I. ii. 68), *grisly* for *grissl'd*
(I. ii. 240), *knotty* for *knotted* (I. v. 18), *Imperiall* for *Imperious* (v. i. 206).
There are also numerous synonymous substitutions not to be
accounted for by any similarity in word form. We find *See* for
Looke (I. iii. 59), *ground* for *earth* (I. v. 170), *Chamber* for *closset*
(II. i. 77), *buriall* for *funerall* (IV. v. 210), *hast* for *speede* (IV. vi. 21),
past for *topt* (IV. vii. 87), *hardly* for *scarcely* (v. i. 109), *Away* for *hold
off* (v. i. 256), *teach* for *learne* (v. ii. 9), and so on. If these are due to
the compositor, theoretically it could be the compositor of Q2,
but sometimes F is clearly weaker, or less apt, as when we *waile*
instead of *mourne* for Hamlet's madness (II. ii. 151) and the skull is
Ieering instead of *grinning* (v. i. 186). Just as Q2 sometimes resorted

---

1. Cf. Q2 *a*, F *sage* (requiem), v. i. 230. Thus I choose, as throughout this
paragraph, examples from both Q2 compositors. For other probable stopgaps
in Q2 see v. i. 60 LN, v. ii. 160 LN, v. ii. 184 n. and p. 39 above.

to a stopgap for what could not be read or understood, so in its turn F may replace an unusual word by a commoner or less specific one, like *tunes* for *laudes* (IV. vii. 176) or *Rites* for *Crants* (v. i. 225). Sometimes the change extends to a whole phrase, like *my sweet Queene* for *my deere Gertrard* (II. ii. 54). Variation in forms of address, as with *my good Lord* for *mine owne Lord* (IV. i. 5), is frequent. Some substitutions are not even approximate: we have *vilde* for *Lords* (II. ii. 457), *whole* for *owne* (II. ii. 547), *poore* for *proude* (III. i. 71), *rude* for *madde* (v. i. 99), and among phrases, *how sweet Queene* for *but stay, what noyse* (IV. vii. 161), *let me see* for *shall you see* (v. ii. 1), *in good faith* for *good my lord* (v. ii. 105). In all of these the F variant is noticeably inferior, sometimes the merest stopgap and sometimes only groping for the sense.

Apparently casual substitutions are common in little unstressed words, especially prepositions: characteristic are (*Ioyntresse*) *of* for Q2 *to* (I. ii. 9), (*flushing*) *of* for *in* (I. ii. 155), (*Tribute*) *of* for *on* (II. ii. 319), (*Fetters put*) *vpon* for *about* (III. iii. 25); *in* for *of* (*the afternoone*) (I. v. 60), *To* for *In* (*censure*) (III. ii. 87), *at* for *in* (*grauemaking*) (v. i. 65). Among numerous other minor variants are the interchange of *and* and *but* or of *you* and *ye*, the replacement of the demonstrative by a possessive pronoun or the article, variations in personal pronouns and auxiliary verbs, changes in tense or in grammatical number (through the loss or addition of a final *s*), inversions of the *will I* for *I will* type. These are the common accidents of copying, though much multiplied. But there are also deliberate alterations. As commonly happens in Folio texts, some, but not all, oaths are removed or weakened.[1] There is some sophistication. F, a more literary text, smooths out colloquialisms: it regularly gives us *he* for the pronoun *a* which is common in Q2.[2] It tends, though less systematically, to expand *th'* to *the*. It changes *my* and *thy* before a vowel into *mine* and *thine*; it often contracts pronoun-verb combinations (*Ile, I'm, I'ue, he's, 'tis,* etc.), and in verse this is often in accordance with the metre, though practice is not consistent and opposite changes sometimes occur. There is also modernization: *whiles* is replaced by *while, sithence* by *since, someuer* by *soeuer, hath* by *has*. The past participles *tooke* (v. i. 135) and *bore* (v. i. 179) give way to *taken* and *borne*. Grammar

1. It is usually supposed that this was consequent upon the Act of 1606 forbidding profanity on the stage and accordingly that texts in which it occurs derive from promptbooks. But Greg (*SFF*, pp. 149–52) shows that there was also a tradition of literary expurgation, so that oaths may have been removed or toned down specifically for printing. Cf. A. Walker, *Textual Problems*, pp. 30–1.

2. One instance of *a* survives at v. i. 173.

is tidied up, so that we no longer say, as in Q2, '*this* three yeeres' (v.i.135) or 'two men there *is* not liuing' (II.ii.20). Adverb forms in -*ly* are preferred – *likely* for *like* (II.ii.152), *conueniently* (I.i.180), *royally* (v.ii.403). There are little attempts at improvement, as when the indefinite article is strengthened to *one* ('With one Auspicious, and one Dropping eye', I.ii.11) or *nothing but* to *no other thing than* (II.ii.302). When Claudius is said to be distempered not with drink but 'with choller', F points this by '*rather* with choller' and then increases 'more choller' to '*farre* more choller' (III.ii.295–9). Hamlet now specifies '*two* Prouinciall Roses' on his shoes (III.ii.270–1) and is to do not just 'a turne' but 'a *good* turne' for the pirates (IV.vi.20). An odd adjective or adverb could of course have been accidentally omitted in Q2, but collectively these are more like accretions for the sake of extra point or emphasis – or the embellishments of an actor making the most of his part.

(*iv*) That the habits of *the actors* have indeed left their mark upon F appears from a further category of variant. There are little scraps of dialogue incorporated in F for which Q2 gives no warrant. These are often repetitions of a word or phrase which occurs singly in Q2: 'yes, yes' (I.v.104), 'My Tables, my Tables' (I.v.107), 'farre gone, farre gone' (II.ii.189), 'well, well, well' (III.i.92), 'Wormwood, Wormwood' (III.ii.176), and so on. Occasionally repetition is accompanied by expansion, as when Polonius's 'That's good' becomes 'That's good: Inobled [for *mobled*] Queene is good' (II.ii.500). Reynaldo repeats more cue (II.i.53), the grave-digger more song (v.i.118) in F than in Q2. We find interpolated exclamations – 'Looke you' (I.v.138), 'Why' (II.ii.278), 'I sure' (II.ii.578), 'pox' (III.ii.247), 'la' (IV.v.57), 'O' several times – and occasionally interjections of a more striking character, as when Hamlet takes up his mother's word 'Extasie' at III.iv.142. His cry 'Oh Vengeance!' in the middle of a soliloquy (after II.ii.577) is probably an actor's interpolation, and his dying groans, 'O, o, o, o' (v.ii.363) have long been recognized as such.[1] That all these and others like them are additions in F rather than omissions in Q2 follows from the fact that their absence does not impair the sense while their presence sometimes vulgarizes the dramatic effect or damages the metre. There is sometimes extra dialogue to emphasize the action: 'Alacke, what noyse is this?' (IV.v.96); 'How now? What

1. Except by those who regard them as additional directions *to* the actor. Either way they represent theatrical accretions to Shakespeare's dialogue.

Newes?', with the messenger's reply, 'Letters my Lord from
Hamlet' (before IV. vii. 36); Hamlet's 'Let me see' on taking the
skull from the grave-digger (v.i. 178). The confessional 'A touch,
a touch' of Laertes in the fencing-match (v. ii. 289) has more art
than these other examples, but in view of them must be suspect.[1]

How much of the verbal corruption which I have shown to be
characteristic of F may also have originated with actors rather
than with scribes and compositors is a question not possible to
answer. Such typical approximations as 'Heere's a Napkin' for
'Heere *Hamlet* take my napkin' (v. ii. 291) are more easily attributable to a slipshod memory than to copyists' errors. Confusion of
memory is also the likely explanation when F wrongly introduces
in one place a word which occurs correctly in another. Thus,
among variants already cited, *in good faith* for *good my lord*
(v. ii. 105) is immediately repeated in what follows; 'his *whole*
conceit' for 'his *owne* conceit' (II. ii. 547) is evidently prompted by
what comes three lines later, 'his *whole* function suting With
formes to his *conceit*' (I cite from Q2); the *excellent* instead of *eloquent* music that Hamlet associates with the recorder (III. ii. 350)
anticipates the '*excellent* voyce' he credits it with in his next speech.
Similarly, the cock becomes in F 'the Trumpet to the *day*' instead
of *morne* (I. i. 155) through confusion with 'the God of *day*' it is to
awake two lines below.[2] Such anticipations might not be beyond a
scribe, or even a compositor, given to glancing forward in his copy
and trying to carry too much in his head. But sometimes what is
anticipated is not the immediate context but a passage remote in
the play. Thus, when in F Hamlet speaks of a 'Satyricall *slaue*'
instead of *rogue* (II. ii. 196), this may be explained by his having to
say 'a *rogue* and pesant *slaue*' over three hundred lines farther on
(II. ii. 544); and when Fortinbras *claimes* instead of *craues* a passage
over the Danish 'Kingdome' (IV. iv. 3), that may be because he
will have to *clame* rights 'in this kingdome' later (v. ii. 394–5).
Dover Wilson, who first demonstrated this element of memorial
corruption, attributed it to a playhouse transcriber with a too
active memory of a familiar text;[3] but it seems more likely that
the confusion arose in the memory of the actors and that F here
reproduces what was actually spoken on the stage. The notion
that the actors' deviations and elaborations might be deliberately
recorded in the promptbook has, not surprisingly, been ridiculed;

1. For a fuller discussion of 'Playhouse Interpolations in the Folio Text of
Hamlet', see *SB*, XIII, 31–47.
2. Cf. *MSH*, pp. 57–8.
3. *MSH*, pp. 59–64.

but with a simple theory of promptbook origin inadequate to account for F, other hypotheses are possible, and the difficulty of explaining, with this as with some other Folio texts, how the actors' modifications came to be incorporated must not prevent our accepting that they did.

F is then a very mixed text. It differs from Q 2 partly by preserving what Q 2 omits or misrenders, but more through theatrical modifications both deliberate and accidental, through literary sophistication and modernization, and through the inevitable corruptions incident to the processes of transcription and printing. To attribute particular variants to a specific stage in the transmission is often impossible; nor is there perhaps great point in the attempt. Much of the verbal corruption – Alice Walker would apparently think most – was no doubt due to the Folio compositors. Misreadings and approximations on the one hand, modernizations and grammatical corrections on the other, were certainly within their scope. Yet some of the grammatical corrections belong to compositor E, the seemingly unconfident workman, who tends to be influenced by his copy; and apart from the variation between *ye* and *you*, which reflects an individual preference (of compositor B), no type of variant is confined to one compositor alone. Along with this even distribution the actual amount of deviation seems to imply the co-operation of a scribe; and indeed that initial fair copy of Shakespeare's autograph to which we owe the preservation of authentic readings lost by Q 2 must be presumed itself to have begun the process of corruption. The elimination of colloquialisms may have begun early: at least it is noticeable that *a* for *he* does not appear in Q 1. Theatrical adaptations made in anticipation of production one can be more certain of; but again, not every theatrical modification can be assigned to a particular phase of transmission. The 'within' speeches, for example, which F adds at III. iv. 5 and IV. ii. 1, might have been written into the first playhouse transcript so that they would be spoken in performance, or they might have arisen in the course of performance and then found their way into the written text. The evidence suggests that more than one transcript intervened between Shakespeare's manuscript and the Folio: I envisage a fair copy which was preparatory for but did not become the promptbook, and a subsequent transcript of this. Actors' alterations and embellishments, designedly or not, may have been incorporated in such a transcript; alternatively they might have been written in when copy for the Folio was prepared. The pruning of oaths was presumably carried out before copy reached the printers; and some editing for print (including some verbal sophistication and some additional stage-directions) is probable. That there was at least some half-hearted preparation for a reading text appears from the beginning of a division into acts and scenes: but marking only three scenes in the first act, this is perfunctory at best,[1] and after '*Scena Secunda*' in the second act it ceases altogether.[2]

F's use of Q2

To these various complexities of the F text there is still one crucial element to add; and that is Q2 itself. Much as F deviates from Q2, it also copied from it. For just as tell-tale features of Q1 reappear in Q2, so incidental details of Q2 reappear in F; and the problem of a text which is contaminated by one it purposes to supersede is thus repeated.

Irregular details which are identical in Q2 and F may of course have a common source in Shakespeare's original manuscript: an ill-written word may have been twice independently misread, some oddity in a stage-direction more than once reproduced. But there are numerous little correspondences which one would not expect to survive repeated transcription.[3] Common errors which suggest that F copied from Q2 include (the reading required being given in modern spelling in parenthesis): i.i.97 Q2 *desseigne*, F *designe* (design'd); i.ii.209 *Whereas* (Where as); i.v.43 *wits* (wit); ii.ii.484 Q2 *A rowsed* F *A ro wsed* (Aroused); ii.ii.579 Q2 *deere*, F *Deere* (dear father); iii.iii.18 *somnet* (summit); iv.vii.56 Q2 *didst* F *diddest* (diest); iv.vii.98 *t'would* ('twould); iv.vii.123 *indeed(e)* (in deed); v.ii.29 *villaines* (villanies). Among these the capital at ii.ii.579 shows that F was misled by the absence of the noun (which Q3, however, had supplied), and the obvious explanation at iv.vii.56 is that someone expanded for the metre when confronted by the erroneous *didst*. Similarly the F errors *Sonnet* (i.iv.70) and *maruels* (ii.i.3) were probably induced by Q2 *somnet* (summit) and *meruiles* (marvellous). An occasional

---

1. Thus resembling the act- and scene-division of *Richard III*, also, in Greg's view (*SFF*, p. 197), 'most likely introduced at the time of printing'. It can hardly come from the promptbook (as supposed by Alice Walker in *RES*, n.s. ii, 337–8).

2. The rest of the present act-division in a quarto of 1676, of the scene-division with the eighteenth-century editors.

3. For instances, see Dover Wilson, *MSH*, p. 297; A. Walker, *RES*, n.s. ii, 331–8; A. Walker, *Textual Problems of the First Folio*, pp. 123–35; Jenkins, *SB*, vii, 71–5; Nosworthy, pp. 144–51. The examples I give now, not always the same ones, are illustrative rather than exhaustive.

grammatical confusion – like the plural verbs with the subject *haire* (III.iv.121–2), already emended in Q3 – remains in F unaltered.

A number of unusual spellings are also common to both texts, such as *farwell* (F *farwel*, I.i.18), *of* for *off* (which some copies of F have, I.i.43), *brazon* (F *Brazon*, I.i.76), *Hiperion* (I.ii.140), *reakes* (F *reaks*, I.iii.51), *ranck* (I.iii.73), *ore-teamed* (II.ii.504), *dosen* (II.ii.535), *fixion* (F *Fixion*, II.ii.546), *paiock* (F *Paiocke*, III.ii.278), *boudge* (III.iv.17), *ardure* (F. *Ardure*, III.iv.86), *impitious* (F *impittious*, IV.v.100), *soopstake* (F *Soop-stake*, IV.v.142), *vnsinnow'd* (F *vnsinnowed*, IV.vii.10), *&* (v.i.18), *Renish* (v.i.174), *spleenatiue* (F *Spleenatiue*, v.i.254), *Woo't* (v.i.270–1), *cuplets* (F *Cuplet*, v.i.282), *how* (F *How?* through a misunderstanding, v.ii.317). An uncorrected page of F follows Q2 in *a sunder* (v.i.257) and *Crocadile* (v.i.271).[1] But it is not merely a question of unusual spellings or actual errors: agreement even in usual spellings where there were equally usual alternatives may be cumulatively suggestive.[2] To take but one brief example, in 'Nimph (F Nimph,) in thy orizons (F Orizons) Be all my sinnes remembred' (III.i.89–90), though none of the spellings is unique, the identity of all is remarkable. F sometimes conforms with Q2 against a compositor's usual preference, as when *leasure*, the regular spelling of Q2, turns up once in F in spite of *leysure* twice on the same page. The significance of capitalization is diminished by F's manifest addiction to it; but it is very rare for a capital in Q2 not to reappear in F. In the ten-line speech which opens IV.iii, for example, Q2's single capitalized word *Law* is one of only two words to have a capital in F; and there are a few instances of capitals – like *Chaplesse* (v.i.87) as against *chopfalne* (v.i.186) – which even in F might not have been expected[3] and which are anticipated in Q2.

In punctuation the two texts differ very greatly, largely but not solely through F's much heavier stopping. In view of this general independence it becomes the more significant when F concurs, for instance, in some inessential comma or in the adoption of a colon. There are a score of cases spread over three compositors in which a Q2 colon or (less often) semicolon is repeated in F and nearly as many in which a semicolon is raised to a colon. Sometimes F appears to have been misled by wrong

1. Hinman, i.303.
2. See Nosworthy, pp. 145–7.
3. Though this is scarcely true of most of those cited by Nosworthy, p. 148. Nevertheless his argument on the many coincidences of upper and lower case is weighty.

pointing in Q2. A notable example is at II.ii.396–8, where Q2 reads:

> *Sceneca* cannot be too heauy, nor *Plautus* too light for the lawe of writ, and the liberty: these are the only men.

F inserts a comma after *light* and raises the colon to a full stop, but shows the same misunderstanding. The Q2 line

> May fit us to our shape if this should fayle,
>
> (IV.vii.149)

typically acquires in F a comma in the middle and a semicolon at the end, but thus attaches the condition even more clearly to what precedes instead of to what follows. Errors of line-division are the same in both texts at I.i.132–3 and I.iii.113–14, and largely the same, in spite of F's unsuccessful effort to put things right, at V.ii.224–6.

Stage-directions are sometimes identically abbreviated even where F was under no pressure of space: *Exit Fran.* (I.i.19); *Exeunt Gent.* (III.iii.26); *Enter Ros. & Guild.* (IV.i.32). All these are placed in the right margin, the entry irregularly so. With *A Noise within* (IV.v.96) also at the right and level with the last line of the King's speech F again duplicates the Q2 layout. A clearer typographical link occurs when Hamlet's verses to Ophelia (II.ii.115–18) are in each text set flush with the margin instead of being indented. Especially interesting are features in F which, without reproducing Q2, appear to be influenced by it. An entry-direction which Q2 squeezes into the margin, '*Enter K.Q. | Laertes and | the corse*' (V.i.211), is expanded and centred in F yet positioned where Q2 begins it even though in the middle of a sentence:

> But soft, but soft, aside; heere comes the King.
> *Enter King, Queen, Laertes, and a Coffin,*
> *with Lords attendant.*
> The Queene, the Courtiers.

At IV.v.152 F's mistaken transfer of 'Let her come in' from the dialogue to the stage-direction is an attempt to correct the error of a misaligned speech-prefix which in Q2 gives these words to Laertes.[1]

Particular significance attaches to the retention in F of small anomalous details when Q2 appears already to have taken them from Q1.[2] The extraordinary spelling *pollax* (F *Pollax*, I.i.66), along with such other unusual ones as *allies* (F *Allies*, I.v.67) and

---

1. See *MLR*, LIV, 391–3.   2. See above, p. 47.

the *ea* in *leaprous* (F *leaperous*, I.v.64), continues, as do the apostrophes in *can'st* and *dream't* (I.v.170, 175), the ampersand in *Hic &
vbique* (I.v.164), the capital for the adjective *Anticke* (I.v.180), and
the separate line for *Marcellus* (I.ii.165). With these may go one
or two phrases in stage-directions, like the '*two Centinels*' of the
opening and the Ghost crying '*vnder the Stage*' (Q1 *stage*, I.v.157),
which also occur in all three texts. Of marks of punctuation
already found notable through Q2's agreement with Q1, F
follows the comma in 'Pale, or red?' (I.ii.232) and the colons at
I.i.176, I.v.38, I.v.190. Indicative also are the comma after *vs* at
I.i.28 and the full stop after *loue* at I.v.23. These are all small
things, but since they originate in a reported text and therefore
cannot derive from Shakespeare's manuscript, their combined
evidence seems to be decisive.[1]

Hence although F relies upon an independent manuscript, it
cannot have been printed directly and simply from it. What is
often supposed, and what I now accept as probable, is that it
depends, though not necessarily directly, upon a copy of Q2[2]
which had been collated with the manuscript and emended to
conform with it.[3]

Such use of a printed text can in itself occasion no surprise.
That Jaggard the printer himself preferred printed copy is customarily asserted but has never, I think, been shown; and one

1. It is perhaps worth noting that of the items listed in which Q2 is followed
by F several are not copied in the close reprints Q3 and Q4. Besides supplying
the missing word *father* and giving *haire* its singular verbs, Q3 changes *meruiles*
to *maruelous*, *of* to *off*, *brazon* to *brazen*, *Hiperion* to *Hyperion*, *impitious* to *impetuous*,
how to *hoe*; it drops the comma in 'Pale, or red?' and the apostrophe in *can'st*.
Additional changes in Q4 are *ranck* to *ranke*, *Centinels* to *Sentinels*, and *&* to *and*
(both at v.i.18 and in IV.i.32 S.D.) and *leasure* consistently to *leisure*.

2. A conjecture by Cairncross that F may in part have used Q4 is not
supported by the evidence. There are a few rare coincidences between F and
Qq 3 and 4, but collation shows F often agreeing with Q2 when these later
quartos depart from it. (The previous note incidentally gives a sample.) If Q4
often anticipates F in things like capitals, that surely means that it conforms to
the practice of its later time. Cf. Walker, *Textual Problems*, pp. 124–5.

3. The shift in my own position since I first wrote on the subject over twenty
years ago, from the acceptance of an occasional to a conviction of a general
dependence, has been determined by my increased familiarity with the minutiae of the texts and my consequent awareness of much more correspondence
than had then been pointed out. The difficulty of demonstration, of which I
have been very conscious in writing the foregoing paragraphs, is that while indebtedness in exceptional details can readily be shown, it is the cumulative
effect of numerous similarities not individually significant which finally convinces one that F's use of Q2 was a matter of much more than sporadic consultation.

may reasonably suspect that the embranglements of a heavily corrected quarto would outweigh any advantage it had in casting off. That printers who were, in that age, necessarily accustomed to setting up from handwriting and who had in any case to do it for half of the Folio plays should prefer a much-altered quarto to a clean manuscript, and even go to the trouble of replacing the second by the first, is something that defies belief. But that Shakespeare's fellow actors, with printed playbooks in their locker (as, for the plays already published, they must have had), should make use of them to furnish the printers with copy is the most natural thing in the world. And it is becoming increasingly evident that that is what they did. The pattern that is emerging shows Heminge and Condell, or whoever assisted them in assembling material for the Folio, making use of a good quarto wherever one was available, sometimes adding touches from the promptbook, sometimes – as with *Titus Andronicus* and *Richard II* – inserting an extra scene or passages, sometimes by a detailed process of correction from another source substituting what is in effect a different text. When research has shown that quartos provided the Folio copy even for plays where the texts are widely divergent, like *Richard III*, *Troilus and Cressida*, and *King Lear*, there is no *a priori* reason why the same should not have happened with *Hamlet*. It has been confidently asserted, especially by Alice Walker, that it did, with a corrected Q2 serving as the copy from which F was set up.[1]

Yet the evidence does not all point one way. Agreements between the texts are mingled with divergences, often in the same passage, of a kind difficult to reconcile with a belief that F was printed from Q2.[2] To set against errors which F appears to have

1. *RES*, n.s. ii, 328–38; *Textual Problems of the First Folio*, pp. 121–37. The credit for recognizing F's dependence on Q2 and confuting the previous belief that they were independent texts belongs to Alice Walker, though her demonstration that the dependence was general rather than occasional was sparse. It has since been supplemented by Nosworthy but with only part acceptance of her case for Q2 copy. The whole case for F's dependence on Q2 has been attacked by J. K. Walton (*The Quarto Copy for the First Folio of Shakespeare*, 1971), who, however, minimizes or ignores indubitable correspondences between them. It would be a strong argument in favour of Q2 copy if one could accept Hinman's conclusion, from his study of the Folio printing, that Compositor E was not employed on plays set from manuscript; but the conclusion has recently been challenged, not only by Cairncross (*PBSA*, lxvi, 369–406) but also by Howard-Hill (in *A Reassessment of Compositors B and E*, 1977), and may have to meet further challenge from the study of other Folio texts.

2. The difficulties are still, I think, most fully presented in *SB*, vii, 69–83, though there with a conclusion I am not now able to maintain. Dr Walker herself was happy to ignore them; but Greg, who found the case for F's having been printed from Q2 'not far short of proof', added a cautionary note (*SFF*,

taken from Q2, there are others of its own making which suggest
the misreading of handwritten copy, and they occur in places
where a satisfactory Q2 reading should have required no handwritten emendation. Instances are: Q2 *fear'd*, F *feare* (II.i.112);
Q2 roman *pious chanson*, F italic *Pons Chanson* (II.ii.415); Q2
totall, F *to take* (II.ii.453); Q2 *mobled* twice, F *inobled* three times
(II.ii.498–9); Q2 *wand* (=wann'd), F *warm'd* (II.ii.548); Q2
sugar, F *surge* (III.i.48); Q2 *their perfume lost*, F *then perfume left*
(III.i.99); Q2 *sole*, F *foule* (III.iii.77); Q2 *brother*, F *breath* (III.iv.
65); Q2 *th'incorporall*, F *their corporall* (III.iv.118); Q2 *neuer*, F
neerer (IV.iii.7); Q2 *cunnings*, F *commings* (IV.vii.154); Q2 *lay*, F
buy (IV.vii.181); Q2 *For*, F *Sir* (V.i.254). For individual variants
in this list it would not perhaps be hard to think up other possible
explanations. Some, like the supplanting of the unfamiliar
mobled or the metaphor in '*sugar* ore the deuill', could inspire conjectures of conjectural emendation. Some might be ascribed to
the inaccuracy of Compositor B, in whose work most of them
occur. But collectively they make it difficult to deny in F an element of graphic error. Moreover, besides some correspondences
in punctuation, there are many striking divergences: if Q2 sometimes misled F, at other times, as F's copy, it ought to have prevented F from such misinterpretations as the following:

Q2   Goes slowe and stately by them; thrice he walkt
F   Goes slow and stately: By them thrice he walkt,
                                                         (I.ii.202)

Q2   variable seruice, two dishes but to one table, that's the end.
F   variable seruice to dishes, but to one Table that's the end.
                                                         (IV.iii.24–5)

Q2   to morrow shall I begge leaue to see your kingly eyes,
     when I shal first asking you pardon, there-vnto recount
F   To morrow shall I begge leaue to see your Kingly Eyes.
     When I shall (first asking your Pardon thereunto) recount
                                                         (IV.vii.43–4)

Further instances may be found at I.iii.8–10, I.iii.57, II.i.42,
II.ii.133, II.ii.156, II.ii.294–5, III.i.126–7, III.i.186, III.iv.197,

pp. 329, 333) and Hinman, after categorically asserting it, found the evidence
'inconclusive'. (Cf. *The Printing and Proof-Reading of the First Folio, passim,* and the
Norton Facsimile, p. xv. See also his Introduction to the Clarendon Press
facsimile of Q2: 'Dr Walker's view is not likely to find unqualified acceptance
until there is a better understanding of how, in any text set from printed copy,
there can be so little correspondence in accidentals, such as the spelling of
speakers' names, and in typographical detail generally.')

IV. v. 112, IV. vii. 56–7. Not all of these are from Compositor B. Variation of spelling is of course normal practice; but while some aberrant spellings identical in both texts therefore attract attention, F often deserts Q2 just where it might be expected to follow copy – in the spelling of foreign, or foreign-seeming, words and in unusual proper names. Q2 *Mallico* becomes F *Malicho* (III. ii. 135), Q2 roman *Esill* F italic *Esile* (v. i. 271). F has no sooner conformed to Q2 in *Hiperion* (I. ii. 140) than it replaces Q2's regular *Elsonoure* with *Elsenour* (I. ii. 174),[1] and then *Nemeon* with *Nemian* (I. iv. 83). Q2 has *Pollack* or *Pollacke*, F *Poleak* or *Polake*; Q2 *Valtemand* F *Voltemand* in the first act, Q2 *Voltemand* F *Voltumand* in the second. With the names of other characters, by contrast, F shows unusual consistency in its own different practice. It changes *a* to *o* in *Reynoldo*, always omits the *t* which in the first eight of ten occurrences Q2 puts in *Ostr*(*ick*(*e*). Q2 *Gertrard* is regularly F *Gertrude*, Q2 *Fortinbrasse* or (as in Q1) *Fortenbrasse* F *Fortinbras*, Q2 *Rosencraus* and *Guyldensterne* F *Rosincrance* and *Guildenstern*(*e*). And since, except for *Reynoldo* in his single scene, these new name-forms are all shared by more than one compositor, they must reflect the copy, and some copy other than Q2. Moreover, they are extended even to abbreviated speech-headings. *Ros.* (with a single exception, where space was short) is always (35 times) expanded to *Rosin.*, *Rey.* (13 times) to *Reynol.*, as though to insist on the changed middle vowel; *Guyl*(*d*) always (24 times) becomes *Guil*(*d*). It may be that the manuscript which F aims at reproducing, whether directly or indirectly, was one that took particular care over the form of characters' names. In view of the other signs of its theatrical provenance,[2] this is no more than we might expect; and that anyone who corrected the quarto by the manuscript in preparing it for printers' copy should likewise give attention to the names is credible enough.[3] What I have found harder to credit, given the latitude of the times both in spelling and in speech-prefixes, is that the putative corrector should go to the trouble of persistently expanding speech-prefixes already perfectly clear and making such seemingly pointless alterations as deleting the *t* in *Ostrick*(*e*) and the final *-se* of *Fortinbrasse* and even substituting *i* for *y* in *Guyl*(*densterne*) no fewer than 39 times. Yet

---

1. In II. ii two compositors of F both spell this *Elsonower*.

2. See above, pp. 56–9.

3. Even minor changes in the spelling of characters' names can be paralleled in other F texts known to have been printed from corrected quartos. Where *Hamlet* appears to be unique is in the consistency of F's alteration of the speech-prefixes.

if Q2 was the copy, how else are we to explain the absolute consistency in this sustained by three compositors?

An assumption that F was printed directly from Q2 requires us to accept a largely mechanical collator, negligent enough to overlook some textual errors yet in the detail of character-names and speech-headings unexpectedly and unnecessarily meticulous, and along with him compositors who, while exercising their customary freedom in rendering their printed copy, yet followed manuscript corrections of it with fidelity to the letter. The mechanical collator seems also requisite to explain the importation into F of those apparently scribal errors which displace Q2's true readings. He might help one to understand how the use of Q2 copy could combine with the persistent petty corruption, not all to be blamed on compositors, which has been shown to be a feature of F. Yet the hypothesis of a collation, supposedly undertaken to ensure reliable copy, which could nevertheless supplant the printed sense of Q2 with nonsense from a manuscript is bound to be disconcerting, and to provoke a little scepticism. It cannot in any case account for F's erroneous punctuation. F's style of pointing is in general that of Jaggard's printing-house, where the compositors, for all their individual habits, shared a common system based on heavier and more frequent stops, in favour of which, except seemingly by accident, Q2 was disregarded. All the same, if they actually had Q2 in front of them, it is strange that it so often failed to guide them, even inadvertently, to better sense.

There have been some recent attempts to resolve these difficulties by refining on the theory of Q2 copy. Cairncross, one of its strongest advocates, came to maintain that the copy alternated print and manuscript. Some manuscript leaves it must certainly have had to provide the three F additions which are too long to have been written upon the quarto margins;[1] and if some, then conceivably others. The first part of II.ii is sometimes made a candidate for manuscript setting and Nosworthy confidently contends for Voltemand's speech on the evidence of its spelling divergences (which include *Voltumand*, *Poleak*, and *Norwèy*).[2] Yet the problem is not local but pervasive, and recognizing that likenesses and differences between the two texts often occur in close proximity, Nosworthy argues that for the most part printed and manuscript copy were used simultaneously, the compositor being

1. II.ii.239–69; II.ii.335–58; v.ii.68–80.
2. p. 155. The case here is fairly strong, but the point that Compositor B would not have substituted the archaic form *Norwey* if setting from Q2 would be refuted if I.i.64 were also set from Q2.

directed by a mark in his printed copy when to take something from the manuscript.[1] But even if the analysis which is supposed to reveal the constant switching back and forth were more convincing than it is, I could not see this as a workable procedure. One thing that is surely axiomatic is that the copy Jaggard handed out to his compositors, whatever form it took, must have been reasonably coherent and of a kind that could be manageably distributed between them, as such twofold copy could not. I am sometimes forced to wonder if the idea of putting together a copy with scissors and paste or of having it put together by compositors as they worked would have had the same appeal for the practical men of the Jacobean theatre and printing-shop as it has for some modern scholars.[2]

A somewhat more plausible hypothesis, I think, is that between the annotation of Q2 and the printing of F a transcript intervened. It is a hypothesis that has of course serious difficulties of its own: not all the correspondences between Q2 and F – especially oddities of spelling and layout – are of a kind that would be expected to persist through transcription, and the very notion of a transcript postulates what one would have supposed the whole process of collation and correction undertaken to avoid. But at least it affords an explanation for those F errors which betray a misreading of handwriting and for the strangely consistent changes in the forms of characters' names. Some of the scribal corruption could also have occurred at this stage. One thing we cannot know is how much annotation of a copy of Q2 may have been specifically undertaken in preparation for F and how much may already have been done for some purpose of the playhouse (where a copy could, after all, have been in use for nearly twenty years). With any or all of the group of plays having widely divergent texts there may well have been some factor in the transmission of which we know and can guess nothing. What, however, is certain, on the evidence contained in the *Hamlet* texts themselves, is that F combines the authority of an independent manuscript with derivation in some way from Q2.

---

1. p. 160.
2. The analogy between F's use of Q2 and Q2's use of Q1, for all the similarity of the resultant textual problems, is liable to mislead. The printing situations were really very different. The printers of Q2 were faced with some difficult foul papers as their primary copy and resorted to the print for help; but for F a good quarto was available to serve as basic copy and should have given no great trouble if, after suitable correction, it was chosen to be used.

Press correction

Extant copies of the Folio show press correction on eight pages of *Hamlet*; but whatever the bibliographical interest of this, it is of scant textual significance. The corrector was evidently less concerned with accuracy than tidiness. He attended to obvious misprints and little typographical faults like turned letters and inked quads; but it is apparent that he neither checked proof with copy nor made any serious attempt to discover or emend errors. Three times wrong or defective punctuation is put right; occasionally spelling is altered, most notably when the maimed burial *rights* more properly become *rites* (v.i.212). The only genuinely substantive variant is the correction of *take* to *thanke* at II.ii.83. The existence in the uncorrected state of a page set by Compositor E and containing one wrong word-division and one rejected spelling (*a sunder*, *Crocadile*) which also occur in Q2 is important as corroborating the use of Q2.[1] Full details of the variants are given in Hinman, i.301–4.

4. THE EDITORIAL PROBLEM AND THE PRESENT TEXT

The textual situation discussed above confronts an editor with the following complications. Of three texts, each of the last two, though largely substantive, owes something to its predecessor, while the first, the only wholly independent text, has all the unreliability of a memorial reconstruction. Q2, the one which stands closest to the author, leaves obscure a number of passages which are not represented in the other two at all. These include some, though not all, of the famous cruxes (cf. above, p. 55). On the other hand, F contains passages not in Q2 which are certainly authentic as well as incidental additions almost as certainly spurious. In the matter of variant readings, since F as well as Q1 reflects playhouse deviation from the Shakespearean original, agreement between these two does not authenticate a reading against Q2; and in view of Q2's partial dependence on Q1, agreement between those two, especially in the first act, does not authenticate a reading against F. Moreover, with F also dependent on Q2, agreement even between the two good texts affords no guarantee, and it is obviously possible for all three texts to be wrong together. The most famous instance of this is the word *pollax* (F *Pollax*) at I.i.66; but the crux at I.iii.74, 'of a most select', may be another.

This edition, like most others since Dover Wilson established

1. Cf. above, p. 66.

Q2 as the most authoritative text, is based primarily upon it. Earlier editors, who tended to follow F, still of course incorporated from Q2 or its descendants passages which F lacks; and since some at least of these were apparently cut before the foul papers were transcribed (see above, p. 43), it is as well to recognize that the editorial tradition from Rowe on has always included things which, though indubitably of Shakespeare's composition, were probably never spoken on the stage. In seeking to present the play as Shakespeare wrote it rather than as it was shortened and adapted for performance I do no more than follow tradition. Even those who insist that a play is created only in the theatre would hardly, I think, prefer the contrary procedure; and those who like to imagine that some passages were cut by Shakespeare himself[1] will not quarrel with their retention. While following Q2's fuller version, I naturally include also anything preserved in F which I take to have been lost from Q2; but all words and phrases in F which I judge to be playhouse additions to the dialogue (see above, pp. 62–3) I omit. Some readers may regret the disappearance of some words – like the exclamations 'O Vengeance' at II.ii.577 and 'Ecstasy' at III.iv.142 – which have become part of the familiar text; but an editor who sees no reason for attributing them to Shakespeare while recognizing that they often disturb metre or dramatic sense or both has no alternative but to reject them.[2] Yet decision is sometimes difficult (as with IV.ii.29, 'hide Fox, and all after' and V.ii.289, 'A touch, a touch'); and where words occurring in F only are more easily attributable to Shakespeare than to the actors (as with III.i.32, 'lawful espials') I accept the probability of omission by the Q2 compositors.

On the assumption that F inherits from a corrected quarto, it might in theory be expected to give the better text. Sometimes,

1. But see above, p. 43, n.1, pp. 55–6.

2. For fuller justification see *SB*, XIII, 31–47, esp. 42–3. The demonstration there of theatrical accretions has, I think, been generally accepted. Some recent editors (notably Hoy, but also in part Evans) have already been persuaded to drop them. The sole articulate objector to their omission – on the ground that what arises in performance becomes an integral part of the play – should in logic welcome with them F's cuts and cast-reductions (to say nothing of its memorial corruptions). No doubt he will approve the Penguin editor's inclusion of an added piece of dialogue known only to the reported text Q1, perhaps even share the pleasure of one reviewer in being thus given 'more *Hamlet*' for his money than ever before. The metaphysical question of what *Hamlet* is is not one to be gone into here. But there may be something to be said for identifying Shakespeare's *Hamlet* with what there is evidence to believe that Shakespeare wrote.

as has been shown (pp. 59–60), it does; but its reliability is of course no higher than that of the manuscript it draws upon; and since this was evidently at a greater remove from the autograph, its 'corrections' were in fact often corruptions, while the actual process of correcting (and perhaps transcribing), however carried out, gave opportunity for more. Where variants appear to be indifferent the belief that Q2 rests on the foul papers naturally gives it preference. But the editor must be eclectic; every variant imposes upon him the inescapable responsibility of choice. My judgment will often confirm that of my predecessors but will occasionally go against it, as when I unhesitatingly follow Q2 at II.ii.553 (*her*) and F at v.i.78 (*o're Offices*). Such decisions will usually be defended in the notes. Upon occasion both variants have to be rejected; for it seems clear that some F readings are attempts at correcting deficiencies in Q2 by not very inspired guesswork. When the editor believes this to have happened, he need accord to F no higher authority than belongs to later Folios and editors: Dover Wilson established the principle that in such cases the editor should proceed not by accepting F but by himself attempting to emend Q2. One instance in which I have done this occurs at v.ii.219. Where both texts are wanting, as at III.iv.171 and IV.i.40, I have been assisted but not felt bound by previous attempts to fill the gap.

Q1 has had its greatest value in suggesting the source of corruption where the two better texts are at variance – in exhibiting, for example, the probable contamination of Q2 through its use of its predecessor or of F through the influence of stage performance. But, though instances are necessarily rare, I have been glad to accept the guidance of Q1 when it confirms that both the other texts are wrong. (See above, p. 36.)

The newly perceived relation of the three texts, with Q2 conceivably taking errors from Q1 and F likewise from Q2, greatly enlarges of course the invitation to emend. I have little hesitation in accepting Theobald's *bawds* for *bonds* at I.iii.130. The emendation *diest* at IV.vii.56, though hitherto adopted only by Dover Wilson in a late reprint, is beyond any question. Readings common to Q2 and F which have incurred suspicion include IV.iii.7, *smooth and euen* ('hypermetrical and tautologous'[1]), IV.v.119 *browe* (F *brow*), v.ii.274 *heauen* (F *Heauen*); but these seem all sufficiently within the range of Shakespeare's carelessness for emendation to be resisted. Conjectures like *stings* for *slings* (III.i.58) and *sconce* for *silence* (III.iv.4) may receive more con-

1. Nosworthy, p. 156.

sideration in future than they have always had; but the questioned readings here are certainly defensible and error no more than possible. Some textual scholars busy themselves with calculations of the probable number of errors; but sobering as statistics may be, since they cannot locate the errors they presume, they hardly authorize much loosening of editorial restraint.[1] It remains true that, even though F cannot corroborate Q2 in what it may have derived from it, agreement between them will more often be due to their both being right than to the handing on of a mistake. In some cases, however, as at I.iii.74 (where all three texts challenge if they do not positively defy both sense and metre) what most prevents editorial intervention is the lack of any proposal for a plausible alternative.

In stage-directions I have normally followed Q2 in preference to F; but I have incorporated the additional directions of F and Q1 where they specify action the dialogue implies or provide for its ordinary stage accompaniments (such as properties, noises, or lights). Directions, however, which change what is called for by Q2 I have rejected. These would have their place in a record of the play's stage history rather than in its accepted text; but they are of course given in the collation. Stage-directions added by later editors, i.e. all originating later than F, are placed within square brackets; but brackets are not used for mere verbal variations such as conventionalize the form of directions while leaving the substance unaffected. These are noted in the apparatus when the original wording may be of interest in itself, but otherwise not: e.g. *Cum alijs* for 'with Others', but not *Exeunt Embassadors* (F *Exit Ambass.*) for 'Exeunt Voltemand and Cornelius'. The names of characters in stage-directions and speech-prefixes are standardized without notice.

In the modernization of spelling the criterion must be that accidents are relinquished while substance is preserved; but it is difficult, as all modernizing editors find, to know where to draw the line. Some early volumes in this series – unwisely as we now think – permitted occasional archaisms, such as *murther* and *vilde*; but with the present general editors the practice has now changed. If *murder* and *murther* are, as one editor insists, 'more than variant spellings', they are no more than accidental variants of the same word. To follow Q2 in *murther*, its preponderant and so conceivably

1. This is the fallacy that haunts all the current research on compositors. Useful as it is to have knowledge of their stints and the errors each was prone to, this can still not identify errors. What it may do is to give confirmation of errors suspected on other grounds.

Shakespearean form, would logically involve printing also *hundreth* (I.ii.237) and *fadoms* (I.iv.77), and even *tider* (I.iii.125), with a result that could neither be consistent nor a modern text at all.[1] On the other hand, modernization is not extended to grammar and vocabulary. I have not replaced such words as *whiles* and *somever* with their modern equivalents, even though this was already done in F. My principle is to preserve archaic forms in the following cases only:

(*i*) Where they are a matter not of spelling but of grammar, as in Q2, 'hee hath bore me' (F *borne*, v.i.179). Q2 *strooken* (III.ii.265) may become *strucken* (as in F) but not *stricken*.

(*ii*) Where, as in *whiles* and *somever*, or in *sith* for *since*, the archaic form may reasonably be regarded as a separate word. In this category the *OED* has been, though not an arbiter, a useful guide.

(*iii*) Where the archaism is one to which modern readers are habituated, so that in its context it is likely to seem less strange than the modern equivalent would. Thus in the context of II.ii.437 *sallets* will, I judge, be more acceptable than *salads*. But I see no reason why *margin* in its ordinary mundane sense (v.ii.152) should disguise itself as *margent*.[2]

(*iv*) Where the archaic spelling indicates a pronunciation that is required for the verse. Thus I print *crownet* (Q2 *cronet*) rather than *coronet* (F) at IV.vii.171 and at I.iv.82 follow F *artire* (for which Q2 *arture* may be a misprint) rather than the *artery* of Q5 or the contracted *art'ry* of many editors.

(*v*) Where the form suggests a dialect or colloquial usage. Some forms of course may belong to more than one category: *crowner* (v.i.4, 22), I take it, would be admissible in the third if not already in the fifth. But, unlike some recent editors, I find no place for *heraldy* (I.i.90, II.ii.452) or *caviary* (II.ii.433), which, like *romage* (I.i.110), obtrude an antiquarian pedantry. Words which have gone out of use should adapt to modern spelling. F *tarre* (cf. *farre*) is naturally acclimatized as *tar* (II.ii.351), and *mobled* (II.ii.498–9) – though here the tradition which has rhymed it with *ennobled* presents us with a dilemma – is better matched with *cobbled* (spelt *cobled* in F *Cor.* I.i.194). By contrast the common *and* in the sense of 'if' is left unchanged: it is the editors' *an*, neither original nor modern, which here is artificial.

1. F occasionally modernizes to *murder* but at least once does the reverse. It permits both forms in the same speech. *Vile*, the invariable form in Q2, becomes *vilde* in F when the compositor is B. A moral seems clear.

2. Cf. note on *ribbon*, IV.vii.76.

I have retained the colloquial forms of Q2, and on the assumption that the Q2 compositors were capable of occasional sophistication, I have introduced a few from F (III.ii.235, v.i.75, 91, etc.).

On the evidence of Q2 I have regarded *my* and *thy* before a vowel as the usual Shakespearean forms instead of the more literary *mine* and *thine*, which are frequent in F; and holding again that the Q2 compositors may sometimes have sophisticated, I have adopted *my* and *thy* whenever they occur in either text. But as I do not suppose that Shakespeare himself would necessarily be consistent, where *mine* and *thine* are found in both texts I have made no emendation.

Elision is a very difficult matter and not one to be determined by the Q2 spelling. This will often afford a clue, but we can never be sure in an individual case that it reproduced the copy; and even if we could, we should not be entitled to assume that Shakespeare's own spelling was systematic on the point. His pages in *Sir Thomas More*, indeed, suggest the contrary. I have never deferred to a contracted spelling in Q2 against the obvious requirements of the metre (e.g. II.ii.97, III.iii.6). In the past forms of verbs the criterion must unquestionably be the metrical requirement and not the Q2 spelling. The Arden convention is to print *'d* where the metre requires elision, *-ed* where it does not (except that words ending in *-ied* are not in any case contracted). The ending *-led* takes no elision since it is necessarily syllabic, and with *-red*, *-ned* elision is always in the final syllable. I decline to believe that a distinction can or should be made between *offer'd* and *off'red*, *poison'd* and *pois'ned* on the basis of the Q2 spelling. Where *the* occurs before a vowel, Q2 usually marks the elision (*th'*) while F is liable to expand. But since Q2 could also expand upon occasion (as shown by *the vmber* for *thumbe* and the practice of the same compositors in reprinting *Titus Andronicus*) and the evidence suggests that the contracted form is more Shakespearean, I have chosen it wherever it occurs with metrical propriety in either text. Thus I follow F at I.i.64 (where Q2 may be contaminated by Q1), I.iii.45, II.ii.505. Occasionally Q2 contracts unmetrically and I expand – sometimes, as at II.ii.450, with the support of F, and sometimes, as at v.ii.356, without it. In all other cases where elision is in question I have been guided by Q2 to the extent that I have used contracted spellings only where it gives precedent. When, as often happens, F alone contracts, it has no clear authority and may possibly be mistaken. For example, where Q2 has 'I am too much in the sonne' and F contracts to 'I am too much i'th' Sun' (I.ii.67), it would be possible to prefer

'I'm too much in the sun'. Where Q2 reads 'you are in the right' (I.v.132), it might be better to contract 'you are' rather than read, as F does, 'you are i'th' right'. The retention of the un-contracted Q2 phrase at least gives the reader the opportunity of choice. The frequent failure of both Q2 compositors to provide for elision in pronoun–verb combinations (I will, he will, he would, etc.) suggests that Shakespeare himself may not have done so, and since the rhythm may often be kept by running syllables together without actual elision, the editor should, I think, be sparing of contractions. Similarly with the unaccented vowels in polysyllabic words. It must be admitted that Q2 here is a very dubious authority: it prints *sulphrus* at I.v.3 but has just had *soueraigntie* and *desperate* (I.iv.73, 87) and will go on to *adulterate* and *trayterous* (I.v.42, 43). In these and other cases I have not wished to mark an elision where the original does not.

The problem of elision of course concerns verse only. The contractions that modern spelling permits in prose are limited to those of colloquial speech.

The punctuation of Q2 deserves to be treated with respect both for the signs of intelligent handling and the presumed closeness of the text to Shakespeare. But the idea that it relies almost entirely upon the punctuation of its copy is impossible to endorse.[1] The *Titus Andronicus* reprint shows the compositors, though attentive to their copy, ready to depart from it on occasion, and they may well have been the more so when the copy was foul papers (see above, p. 46). I have normally retained their punctuation where it seems compatible with sense and modern practice, but I have not hesitated to vary it as a modernized text requires. The Elizabethans used commas or colons in many cases where modern writers would use full stops, which I have often therefore sub-stituted. I do not subscribe to the view that to follow an Eliza-bethan quarto in punctuating long speeches almost entirely with commas somehow makes them more dramatic. The dramatic aims of Elizabethan pointing will often be better fulfilled by translating than preserving it.

In the textual apparatus no notice is usually taken of spelling and punctuation (including presumed misprints), except where they affect, or may affect, the sense; of variations in spacing (as in *a while, to day, me thinks, a sunder*); or, in stage-directions and speech-

1. *MSH*, pp. 196–7. The rival hyperboles of Dover Wilson ('a thing of sheer beauty') and the recent Penguin ('The punctuation is chaotic') may be allowed to cancel one another out.

prefixes, of variant nomenclature for the same characters. Insignificant verbal differences in equivalent stage-directions are likewise ignored. Variations in line-division are recorded when they are, or may be, metrically or bibliographically significant, but not when, as in F's frequent division of the first line of a speech, their interest is no more than typographical. With these exceptions all F variants are naturally given. Owing to the extent of divergence it would not be profitable, or indeed possible, to list the variants of Q1; but the agreement of Q1 with either Q2 or F where these differ is usually noted, and its independent readings are occasionally cited, especially where they may conceivably assist in establishing the text. In the interests of both clarity and economy and to avoid the frequent repetition of such locutions as *Q1 subst.*, it will I hope be sufficient for me to remark here that while variants are cited in the spelling of the text in which they occur, where two or more texts are listed as having the same variant the spelling may be that of the first only. Since Quartos later than the second and Folios later than the first were each printed from their respective predecessors, their variants, when they are not merely errors, have only the status of editorial emendations and are accordingly noted only when they have intrinsic intèrest or historical importance.

A word should perhaps be added on one innovation in the Commentary. Not all that has made *Hamlet* the most discussed play in the world is matter for an editor; but there are numerous detailed controversies on points of interpretation which no annotator can ignore. It has become increasingly obvious to me that annotation of this play, if it is not to be hopelessly inadequate, cannot be accommodated, according to the much-valued Arden practice, at the foot of the page; and this practical difficulty I have sought to cope with by a compromise. While retaining the usual format of a footnote-commentary, I have supplemented this by a series of 'Longer Notes'. The existence of a 'Longer Note' on any passage is always signalled by the letters LN. Nevertheless I have tried in the footnote always to give a sufficient gloss for the reader to get at the bare sense without having to look beyond the page; when he seeks supporting argument he may perhaps be willing to. Since the determinant of the Longer Notes, however, is primarily the call on space, they are necessarily miscellaneous. Some defend the readings of the text, or debate interpretations. Some supply source material or contemporary illustration of manners or linguistic usage; some, in however inadequate a summary, indicate a context of ideas. It is, moreover, only by means of Longer Notes that one can do justice to the many questions which criticism has by now made inescapable – like the question of Hamlet's age (see v.i. 139–57) or of the King's behaviour at the dumb-show (III.ii. 133 S.D.). Some famous matters of debate find a focus in Notes on single words, like *fishmonger* (II.ii. 174) or *nunnery* (III.i. 121). Other Notes range beyond word or phrase to engage with a whole speech. To take contrasting examples, Hamlet's soliloquy beginning 'To be or not to be' (III.i. 56–88) and Ophelia's running commentary on her distribution of flowers (IV.v. 173–83), the one already too much discussed, the other – for this play strangely – too little, call in my judgment for fresh interpretation. Such speeches as the recital about Troy and Pyrrhus (II.ii. 448–514), the Queen's description of Ophelia's death (IV.vii. 165–82), Hamlet's apology to Laertes (v.ii. 222–40) cannot be properly understood if they are merely viewed, as they have too often been, in relation to the motives and reactions of the characters. In the editorial task of explanation, the Longer Notes have not their least important function when what has to be explained is not just the verbal meaning, which may even be plain enough, but the place and purpose of a speech or episode in the play's large design.

In one other respect I am aware of departing from custom. It seems to me a rational procedure when commenting on a modernized text of Shakespeare to give quotations from other authors, save those whose language is that of an older period, in modern spelling too; and except when the original spelling is or may be relevant to the point at issue, this is what I have normally done. The reader will not be surprised therefore if references to a standard edition in old spelling are accompanied by a modern-spelling quotation. Occasionally, for the sake of intelligibility, I have not shrunk from modernizing punctuation also.

5. SOURCES

The Ur-Hamlet

It is reasonably and inevitably supposed that the immediate source of *Hamlet* was an earlier play on the same subject, which scholars have come to call the *Ur-Hamlet*. This play is not extant and was apparently never printed, but that it did exist is well known from a number of contemporary references. Its performance in or before 1596 is witnessed to by Thomas Lodge's allusion to what seems to have been a notorious feature, the pale-vizarded 'ghost which cried so miserably at the Theatre, like an oyster-wife, *Hamlet, revenge*'.[1] It is usually assumed that the play thus acted at the Theatre was the same as the *Hamlet* of which Henslowe's Diary records a single performance at Newington Butts in June 1594, and that this in turn was a revival of the *Hamlet* play already being satirized by Nashe in a famous passage in his Preface to Greene's *Menaphon* in 1589:

> It is a common practice nowadays amongst a sort of shifting companions, that run through every art and thrive by none, to leave the trade of *Noverint*, whereto they were born, and busy themselves with the endeavours of art, that could scarcely Latinize their neck-verse if they should have need; yet English Seneca read by candle-light yields many good sentences, as *Blood is a beggar*, and so forth; and if you entreat him fair in a frosty morning, he will afford you whole Hamlets, I should say handfuls of tragical speeches. But . . . Seneca, let blood line by line and page by page, at length must needs die to our stage; which makes his famished followers to imitate the kid in Aesop, who, enamoured with the fox's newfangles, forsook all hopes of life to leap into a new occupation; and these men, renouncing all possibilities of credit or estimation, to intermeddle with Italian translations . . .   (Nashe, iii. 315–16).

This passage not only vouches for the existence of the old *Hamlet* play as early as 1589 but may be thought to give a clue to the author of it. The fable of the kid, in any case more Spenser's than Aesop's,[2] appears to be brought in less for its aptness than for the pun on a writer's name. Although speaking of 'a common practice', Nashe is focusing on one practitioner. For it cannot be a coincidence that Thomas Kyd had been born the son of a scrivener; not keeping to this 'trade of *Noverint*', took to literary composition; not having been to a university, could be said to have had a limited classical education; was nevertheless an imitator of Seneca, from whom he culled many sententious sayings in his *Spanish Tragedy* and elsewhere; but forsook that occupation for a new one when in 1588 he published *The House-holder's Philosophy* 'first written in Italian by . . . Tasso'. To remark with McKerrow that others as well as Kyd meddled with Italian

1. *Wit's Misery*, 1596, p. 56. 'Hamlet, revenge' became a byword. See Dekker, *Satiromastix*, IV.i.121; Rowlands, *The Night-Raven*, 1620, sig. D2.
2. *The Shepherd's Calendar*, May, 174–305. Spenser's story is a variation on Aesop's fable of the wolf and the kid, substituting a fox for the wolf and an ending in which the kid, instead of staying unharmed, is 'so enamored with the newell' that he succumbs.

translation is beside the point. Not all who did can also, for example, have had scriveners for their fathers; it is not singly but all together that the items listed are conclusive of identity.[1] Of course Nashe never actually says that it is Kyd who is the object of his ridicule; but when the whole satiric technique is one of allusion and innuendo, it would surely be naïve to assume that what is not literally spelled out is therefore not implied. McKerrow's judgment that 'there is no reason for supposing' that Kyd is here referred to must be regarded as a rare but astonishing aberration.[2]

Yet while there can be no reasonable doubt that Kyd is the prime butt of Nashe's ridicule, the ridicule is, ostensibly at least, not of one man but of a class of writers; so that it does not inevitably follow that the *Hamlet* play for which the class of writers is mocked must have been by Kyd himself. Yet when every other gibe about 'these men' has its application to Kyd and none has been shown to point to anyone else,[3] it is a natural assumption that in his mockery of *Hamlet* Nashe was glancing at Kyd too. His little joke would have a sharper point if he could count on his readers' knowing that Kyd and the author of *Hamlet* were the same. When we add that this *Hamlet* play, its plot necessarily one of murder, madness, and revenge and its style evidently remarkable for its Senecan sententiousness, must therefore have had a strong likeness to Kyd's own *Spanish Tragedy*, we cannot justly regard Kyd's authorship of it as less than highly probable.[4] The

1. With the dismay one feels when Homer nods, one may venture to observe that McKerrow's other arguments are no more logical. He draws an analogy between Nashe's reference to 'the kid in Aesop' and his reference to 'the glowworm mentioned in Aesop's Fables' while admitting what makes it invalid, that there was no writer called Glow-worm; he acknowledges no distinction between Nashe's general scorn of *noverint*-writers and a particular gibe about being born to the trade and leaving it (Nashe, iv. 449–51). In favour of Kyd see Østerberg, *RES*, xviii, 385–94. I have found McKerrow pronounced admirable and Østerberg unconvincing (see *Spanish Trag.*, Revels edn, pp. xxiii, 139–40), but my assessment of their arguments is exactly the opposite.

2. It is regretfully necessary to insist on this because the authority of Nashe's distinguished editor has done more than anything else to dissuade scholars from accepting Nashe's meaning. Even the most judicious recent appraisal, that of Arthur Freeman (*Thomas Kyd*, pp. 39–48), still stops short of the obvious conclusion.

3. We may discount Baldwin's attempt to identify the man born to 'the trade of *Noverint*' with the draper's son Anthony Munday (*Literary Genetics of Shakespeare's Plays*, p. 20).

4. In view of some recent speculations, it may be as well to emphasize that there are no grounds whatever for supposing it a youthful work by Shakespeare which he afterwards rewrote.

point will be of some importance as a further clue to what it may have been like.[1]

Since the play does not exist, not much can be known for certain about its nature and contents. There have been numerous attempts to reconstruct it in detail; but since they depend on working back from one or both of the First Quarto and the German play *Der Bestrafte Brudermord* on the now untenable assumption that these somehow derive from it rather than from Shakespeare's play,[2] such attempts need not concern us.[3] The supposition which they usually involve that Shakespeare simply took over the structure of the *Ur-Hamlet* more or less scene for scene while rewriting most of the dialogue is the height of improbability.[4] On the other hand it is not quite true to say, with Chambers and Kittredge, that we know no more of the lost play than that it was of a Senecan type and had a ghost which called 'Hamlet, revenge'. We also know from his name that the revenger was a legendary Danish hero. For the essentials of his story and hence of the plot that was handed on to Shakespeare we may turn to earlier accounts.

Saxo

The first connected account of the hero whom later ages know as Hamlet is that of Saxo, called Grammaticus, in his *Historiae Danicae*, written at the end of the twelfth century and first published in 1514.[5] But that some of the legends upon which Saxo

1. See below, p. 97.

2. For Q1 see above, pp. 18 ff.; for *BB* below, pp. 112 ff. Argument based on the hypothesis that *Antonio's Revenge* derives from the *Ur-Hamlet* and not *Hamlet* (as in *SQ*, IX, 493–8) is similarly invalid. See above, pp. 7–13.

3. Among representative examples are C. M. Lewis, *The Genesis of Hamlet* (1907), pp. 64–76; H. D. Gray, 'Reconstruction of a Lost Play', *PQ*, VII, 254–74; Parrott and Craig (ed.), *Hamlet*, pp. 7–15; Bowers, *Elizabethan Revenge Tragedy*, pp. 89–93; V. K. Whitaker, *Shakespeare's Use of Learning*, pp. 329–46. The last, though still cited with respect, suffers from the same misconceptions as the rest. F. Carrère, *Le Théâtre de Thomas Kyd*, pp. 187–226, is the exception in accepting the priority of *Hamlet* to *BB* but proceeds on the equally untenable assumption that one can distinguish the legacy of Kyd in *Hamlet* on the basis of Kyd's known work elsewhere. I do not believe, to take but one example, that a Latin tag and the swearing on a sword can justify a conclusion that the cellarage scene (I.v.157–90) existed in the *Ur-Hamlet*.

4. See below, pp. 99–100.

5. *Danorum Regum heroumque Historiae*, Paris, 1514; variously referred to as *Historiae Danicae* from the running title and less correctly *Historia Danica* from the prologue and preface. Saxo's Latin was translated by Oliver Elton (*The First Nine Books of the Danish History of Saxo Grammaticus*, 1894). The relevant portion of it, from Books 3 and 4, is most conveniently given with the English

drew were current ages before his time is evident from some lines of the ninth-century poet Snæbjörn, preserved by Snorri Sturlason in his so-called *Prose Edda*. Here in a reference to the sea-maidens who ground Amloði's meal[1] we recognize a connection with the incident in Saxo in which the sand on the seashore is spoken of as meal and Amleth observes that it has been ground fine by stormy seas. The enigmatic sayings of the seeming madman, whose very name seems to have signified a fool or simpleton, are from the first at the centre of his story. After his father has been murdered by his uncle he simulates stupidity but ultimately contrives and executes revenge. Reduced to its bare outline this is the same story as the Romans told of Lucius Junius Brutus (a name which likewise indicates a simpleton), who avenged the murder of his father when he drove the Tarquins out of Rome; and it is often supposed, but cannot be proved, that Saxo transferred some details from one hero to the other.[2]

Saxo tells how Amleth's father and uncle, Horwendil and Fengo,[3] ruled Jutland under Roric King of Denmark. The valiant deeds of Horwendil inspired the rivalry of the King of Norway,[4] whom he slew in single combat. He won the favour of Roric, whose daughter Gerutha became his wife and gave birth to their son Amleth. Fengo, jealous of his brother's success, killed him and, adding incest to murder, married Gerutha. The young Amleth, fearful for his own safety, took refuge in a pretence of imbecility, going about morose and covered in dirt. He took to shaping hooked sticks, their tips hardened in the fire, and said, when asked, that these were javelins to avenge his father. Such behaviour aroused as much as quieted suspicion and led to attempts to trap him. In the belief that dissembling is defeated by concupiscence, a beautiful woman was appointed to waylay him; but he avoided this trap through the warnings of a foster-brother and the compliance of the woman, who had been a companion of his

---

face to face in Gollancz, *The Sources of Hamlet*, 1926. Both are also printed in the margins of Dover Wilson's Cranach *Hamlet* (1930). The English only is most easily accessible in Bullough's *Narrative and Dramatic Sources of Shakespeare*, vol. vii. See also below, p. 90 n. A new translation of Saxo by Peter Fisher, but not noticeably better for our purposes, has recently appeared (1979), and a companion volume of commentary is promised.

1. Gollancz, pp. 1–8.

2. See Gollancz, pp. 27–33. Incidents in which the hero conceals gold in hollow sticks are too close for mere coincidence; but important differences in the circumstances and purport do not suggest direct borrowing.

3. So in Saxo; Englished by Elton as Feng; Fengon in Belleforest.

4 Coller(us) in Saxo, Collere in Belleforest, becomes in Elton Koll.

childhood. She agreed to deny that he had had her, so that when he told the truth it was taken as a sign of madness. But a sceptical friend of Fengo devised a second test whereby Amleth would be overheard in conversation with his mother, to whom he would speak without guile. The friend hid beneath the bedding in her chamber,[1] but Amleth in his mad antics (crowing, flapping his arms, and jumping up and down on the bedding) discovered him and killed him, cutting up his body and throwing it into a sewer, where it was devoured by pigs. He harangued his mother on her incestuous marriage with his father's murderer and, bringing her to repentance, confided to her the truth about his madness and his intention of revenge. His account of the eavesdropper's disappearance, again the truth disbelieved, seemed once more to confirm his madness while strengthening the suspicions of Fengo, who planned to do away with him. He despatched him to England with an escort of two retainers carrying a letter directing the King to put him to death; but Amleth changed the letter while his companions slept, substituting their deaths for his and requesting the King instead to give him his daughter in marriage; and all happened as he devised. Before leaving home Amleth had instructed his mother to put up woven hangings in the hall and in twelve months' time to celebrate his obsequies; and on the appointed day he returned in the middle of his funeral rites to the astonishment of the lords, whom he feasted till they were drunk. Then he brought down upon them the hangings which his mother had put up and secured them with the hooked sticks he had long before prepared. Next he set fire to the hall and proceeded to the chamber where Fengo was asleep. His own sword, because he kept wounding himself with it, had been nailed to his scabbard, and he now changed it for Fengo's, so that when his uncle awoke, to be told that vengeance was now come, it was he who was left with the sword that would not draw and was killed with his own weapon. Next day Amleth justified himself in an oration to the people, who acclaimed him as their king.

Amleth's further adventures do not concern Shakespeare. It is plausibly supposed that they may not always have concerned Amleth, and that two originally different heroes have here coalesced. Yet it contributes to our impression of Amleth that the continuation of his story repeats several of its motifs. He makes a

1. In the straw, according to the translators and the ordinary meaning of *stramentum*; but the word can mean a coverlet, so that Belleforest is probably right to render it by *loudier* (quilt), and the primitiveness of Amleth's world is a degree less than has been made out.

second visit to England, where the King, to avenge Fengo's death, repeats Fengo's plan to have him killed by another ruler's hand. He is sent on an embassage to a fearsome Scottish queen, but by another substitution of letters while the bearer is asleep, death is once more changed to marriage and Amleth wins a second bride. By a characteristic trick, propping up yesterday's dead to look like today's army, he defeats the English king in battle and returns with his two wives to his own land. Roric is now dead and his successor regards Amleth as a usurper. In the ensuing war between them Amleth knows that his doom has come and dies a heroic death. His Scottish wife, notwithstanding a vow to be united with him in death, repeats the frailty of his mother and marries her husband's killer.

In this primitive and sometimes brutal story the essentials of Shakespeare's plot – fratricide, an incestuous marriage, feigned madness, and the ultimate achievement of a long-delayed revenge – are already present. And it is already the kind of potentially dramatic story in which 'carnal, bloody, and unnatural acts' show 'purposes mistook Fall'n on th'inventors' heads' (v. ii. 386–90). The woman who waylays the hero, the man who spies on him in his mother's chamber, and the retainers who escort him to England to be killed already adumbrate the roles of Ophelia, Polonius, and Rosencrantz and Guildenstern. Less obviously the foster-brother, the one friend among foes, holds the germ of Horatio. Incidents in Shakespeare which have their origin in Saxo include the combat with King Fortinbras; and even in Shakespeare's very different catastrophe the hero gets back to Denmark in the middle of a funeral and achieves the crowning act of vengeance by way of an exchange of swords.

Likenesses do not stop at incidents. In Shakespeare's big set scene between Hamlet and his mother the very drift of the dialogue is anticipated in Saxo. With this passage from Elton's translation compare iii. iv. 64–94:

> Most infamous of women! dost thou seek with such lying lamentations to hide thy most heavy guilt? Wantoning like a harlot, thou hast entered a wicked and abominable state of wedlock, embracing with incestuous bosom thy husband's slayer, and wheedling with filthy lures of blandishment him who had slain the father of thy son. This, forsooth, is the way that the mares couple with the vanquishers of their mates; for brute beasts are naturally incited to pair indiscriminately; and it would seem that thou, like them, hast clean forgot thy first husband.

Something of Saxo also remains in Hamlet's savage contempt for Polonius's corpse, as when he decides to 'lug the guts' from the room (III.iv.214) or expatiates on its being eaten (IV.iii.16–20). And other parts of the play reveal similar survivals: the filth that Amleth is smeared with in his pretended madness has left its traces on Hamlet's garb in the 'foul'd' stockings (II.i.79) which figure with the lover's more conventional dishabille; and Fengo's fear of his wife's displeasure becomes one of Claudius's reasons for not proceeding against Hamlet (IV.vii.9–16).

Belleforest

All this is not to imply that Shakespeare ever read Saxo. Direct indebtedness is improbable, and arguments in favour of it[1] appear to be without substance. What made the story available to the Elizabethans[2] was its retelling in their own day by the Frenchman Belleforest as the third story of the fifth series of his popular *Histoires Tragiques*. Of the very complicated bibliography of the *Histoires Tragiques* it will be enough here to say that the seven volumes were published individually over the period 1559 to 1582, that each volume continued to be separately reprinted, and that the fifth, first appearing in 1570, had as many as eight editions before the end of the century. In English *The Hystorie of Hamblet*, published in 1608, turns out to be an unacknowledged translation of Belleforest; but it is of course too late for Shakespeare, and indeed appears at one point to be drawing on Shakespeare's play. It makes the spying counsellor hide not under the quilt (*loudier*), as in Belleforest, but 'behind the hangings', once even 'behind the arras' (cf. III.iii.28; IV.i.9). So Hamblet, instead of jumping on the bed, beats with his arms 'upon the hangings', and it is 'into the hangings' that he thrusts his sword. Moreover, this English version, without any equivalent in Belleforest, makes Hamblet

1. As by Dover Wilson (NCS, p. xvi), citing certain 'germinal phrases'. But these show similarities of the kind I have been illustrating, without any verbal parallel. Once given the spy in the closet, Shakespeare did not need to know Saxo's phrase *praesumptione quam solertia abundantior* in order to call Polonius a 'rash, intruding fool' (III.iv.31). And it is not that Saxo's *laceratam matrem* influences Shakespeare to write 'Thou hast cleft my heart in twain' (III.iv.158), but that Elton is influenced by Shakespeare to translate 'He rent the heart of his mother'. See also A. P. Stabler, 'The Sources of Hamlet: Some Corrections of the Record', Washington State U. *Research Studies*, XXXII, 207–16.

2. Shakespeare's acquaintance with other early accounts of Hamlet is from time to time suggested, but is unlikely and unshown. See Olsson (*Sh.Studs.*, IV, 183–220) for Albert Krantz's *Chronica Regnorum Aquilonarium*, and T. S. Ormsby-Lennon (*Library Chronicle*, U. of Pa., XLI, 119–48) for R. Nannini's *Orationi in materia civile*.

cry 'A rat, a rat!' (cf. III.iv.23; IV.i.10), and when he pulls his victim out, adds 'by the heels'. The translator's deviations are slight; but since he held himself free to make them, it is necessary, in any discussion of Belleforest's version, to consult the original French.[1]

Belleforest sticks fairly faithfully to the events of Saxo's story, the principal difference being that he tells it at twice the length. He drops some inconsequential incidents, notably those clever sayings of Amleth which belong to the oldest part of his legend and perhaps have lost their point, but more characteristically expands. He has little narrative invention but likes to make the most of the episodes he finds, sometimes with unfortunate results. For example, Saxo is able to say that Fengo slaughtered his brother and then gave out that he had done it to protect his brother's wife; but Belleforest makes the villain first fall upon his brother at a banquet and then pretend that he has killed him in the act of assaulting his wife. Elaborating the circumstance each time, he ends with a contradiction. Most of his elaboration, however, comes from his ubiquitous moralizing comment. Unlike Saxo, who, with an occasional terse observation on the ways of men, takes all in his stride, Belleforest is not always at ease with the story he is telling: he apologizes for what will seem barbarity to more polished and enlightened times; and although he can respond to the folk hero who comes out of degradation to triumph, Amleth's more fabulous achievements cause him some misgiving. Feats of clairvoyance at the English court elicit, instead of admiring wonder, an excursus on the dangers of divination and its association with the devil. The revenge itself gives less disquiet, though Belleforest is over-anxious to defend it as giving the wicked their true deserts. So Saxo's elemental story is now introduced by an 'argument', decked out with classical and biblical parallels, as an instance of how murder is followed by God's vengeance; and

1. From which I shall therefore translate direct. Belleforest's French version is reprinted in Gollancz and the Cranach *Hamlet* (as above, p. 85, n. 5) from the 1582 edition face to face with the 1608 translation. But the 1582 text has a number of corruptions and I have used the more reliable 1576. I have not had access to 1572, which Stabler finds the 'most authentic'. The English version only is given in Collier's *Shakespeare's Library*, in Furness, and in Bullough. Complaints that this is not always an accurate translation fail to recognize that it makes no claim to be. It has its particular interest as a work of Shakespeare's time, but in so far as it has stood in the way of a more serviceable translation of Belleforest its existence has proved a disadvantage. Saxo, Belleforest, and *The Hystorie of Hamblet* may be found together, as well as in Gollancz and the Cranach *Hamlet*, in R. Gericke and M. Moltke, *Shakespeare's Hamlet-Quellen*, Leipzig, 1881.

Fengon's crimes are magnified by stressing not only fratricide and incest but tyranny and the oppression of his people. Amleth's address to the people after he has put his uncle to death places all its emphasis on the justice of his deed, which rights their wrongs as well as his. The primitive hero, whom Saxo praised for his combination of courage and cunning, now acquires an aura of chivalry in his pursuit of honour and glory. At his death Belleforest repeats Saxo's laments for one whose fortune was not equal to his gifts; but even so, remembering Amleth's two wives, he sees also the tragedy of a noble hero undone by his one weakness of susceptibility to women. Yet although the urge to improve every occasion leads the author into inconsistencies, what runs through Belleforest's narrative is the effort to view the tale of violence in a universal and edifying perspective; and one can hardly doubt that this was part of his appeal in the age of *A Mirror for Magistrates*. In fact Belleforest's prose comment did something to prepare for those high-flown philosophizing speeches which Nashe was to sneer at in the first dramatic *Hamlet*.

Belleforest himself did not neglect his opportunities for big set speeches. Those already existing in Saxo – Amleth's denunciation of his mother and his oration to the people – are done at much greater length; and the mother who only wails in Saxo has a long speech of her own to give still greater importance to the interview in her chamber. A passage from Belleforest, set against the one already cited from Saxo, will illustrate not only the characteristic difference between the two authors but how far this episode is developed in the narrative before it reaches the stage.

What perfidy is this, O most infamous of all who have ever prostituted themselves to the will of an abominable whoremonger, that under the guise of a dissembling tear[1] you should conceal the most wicked and detestable crime that man could ever imagine or commit? What trust can I have in you, who, like a lascivious wanton breaking out into every immodesty, run with outstretched arms after that villainous, treacherous tyrant who is the murderer of my father, and incestuously caress the robber of the lawful bed of your faithful spouse . . .? Is it the part of a queen and daughter of a king to give way to the appetites of the brutes, and, like mares who couple with the vanquishers of their first mates, to submit to the will of the abominable king who has murdered a more valiant and virtuous man than himself and who, in massacring Horwendile, has extinguished the honour and glory of the Danes, who are

1. *un pleur dissimulé*; 1582 erroneously *un plus dissimulé*, whence 1608 a dissembling creature.

of no account for strength, courage, or valour[1] now that the
lustre of knighthood has been brought to an end by the cruellest
and most dastardly villain living upon earth? I will never
acknowledge him my kinsman, and I cannot regard him as my
uncle nor you as my beloved mother – the man who has shown
no respect for the blood which ought to have united us more
closely than any union with you, and the woman who could
never, without dishonour and the suspicion of having consented
to her husband's death, have agreed to a marriage with his
cruel foe. Ah, Queen Geruth, it is the way of bitches to consort
with several partners and to desire marriage and coupling with
various mates: it is nothing but licentiousness that has effaced
from your mind the memory of the virtues and valiant achievements of the good king, your husband and my father . . .

(Cf. Gollancz, pp. 210–12.)

The comparison to beasts, taken directly from Saxo, is emphasized
by repetition and the addition of bitches (*chiennes*) to mares. And
Belleforest takes it still further, even at the cost of diminishing his
hero, by making Amleth accuse his mother of leaving him to the
mercy of a murderer when even the beasts – lions, tigers, ounces,
leopards are enumerated – fight in defence of their young. It is
Belleforest also who extends and heightens the antithesis between
the brother-husbands which will be structural to Shakespeare's
play. The charge, already in Saxo, that Amleth's mother has
replaced the virtuous man by the bad man who has killed him is
repeated no less than four times in the passage I have quoted.
Moreover, this contrast between the two husbands is already
made in Belleforest, as it is not in Saxo, from the moment the
marriage takes place:

That wretched woman, who had had the honour to be the wife
of one of the wisest and most valorous princes of the north,
allowed herself to sink to such vileness as to break her faith to
him; and what is worse, even to marry him who was the cruel
murderer of her lawful husband.

(Cf. Gollancz, p. 188.)

Shakespeare of course likewise introduces the contrast from the
start (even before the murder itself is known) with Hamlet's first
soliloquy (I.ii.139–57; see also I.v.47–52).

Belleforest's persistent endeavour to heighten things contributes, along with a verbal copiousness, some new details to the
story. The most sensational of these is the adultery of Amleth's
mother. With nothing in Saxo to suggest this, Belleforest specific-

1. *force, cœur ny vaillance*; 1582 *force ny cœur de vaillance*.

ally says that before Fengon had murdered his brother he had incestuously seduced his brother's wife (*incestueusement soüillé la couche fraternelle, abusant de la femme . . .*), and again that he had already dishonoured her (*entretenoit execrablement*) during her husband's life. This is consistent with the aim of magnifying the villain's crimes, but the blackening of the wife undermines the excuses that Belleforest will presently give her in the interview with Amleth. Shakespeare omits the excuses, but takes over the extra dimension of her guilt[1] and accordingly of Hamlet's anguish.

Occasionally some circumstantial detail added by Belleforest gives the story a new direction, which may have far-reaching results. An instance occurs in his account of the combat with the Norwegian king. In Saxo there was simply a pact for the burial of the vanquished; but Belleforest adds that the loser should forfeit his ships' treasure. And once the idea of forfeiture takes root and – again with the help of Belleforest, who has the victor overrun the coast of Norway – is joined with the loss of lands, the way is open for Young Fortinbras and his enterprise to recover them. The episode of the woman employed to waylay Amleth supplies a more striking example. Saxo explains her co-operation with Amleth by the intimacy (*familiaritatem*) due to their common upbringing, but Belleforest, perhaps unwittingly going farther, says that she had loved him (*l'aymoit*) from childhood and adds that she would have been sorry not to enjoy the man whom she loved more than herself (*jouyr de celuy qu'elle aimoit plus que soymesme*). The lady's equivocal role as both temptress and lover is thus strengthened, and the first hint is given for that selfless devotion which is at the heart of Ophelia's tragedy. It is even possible that Belleforest helped to suggest the Ghost; for, as pointed out by Stabler,[2] he twice refers to the shade (*ombre*) of the murdered man. When Amleth finally dispatches his uncle, he bids him report to his brother in the underworld that his son has avenged him, so that his shade may rest in peace (*son ombre s'appaise*). From a metaphorical shade to a visible speaking ghost is an immense imaginative leap and one for which Belleforest alone could provide no adequate springboard. But the errand to the underworld is of a kind to gratify the vengeful spirits of

1. The adultery of the Queen in *Hamlet* is sometimes disputed, but when Hamlet accuses his mother of being false to her marriage-vows (III. iv. 44–5) and his uncle of having whored her (v. ii. 64), the matter is more than implicit. See I. v. 42 LN, III. iv. 42–8 n.

2. *PMLA*, LXXVII, 18–20 (partly anticipated by Charlotte Stopes in *Trans. of the Roy. Soc. of Lit.*, 2nd ser. XXXIII (1915), 158).

Seneca, whose vogue could facilitate the leap; and a tradition
once established,[1] a dramatist wishing to bring a ghost on to the
stage might well find in Belleforest suggestions for its use. The
Ghost in Shakespeare's *Hamlet*, unlike Belleforest's shade, is not
mentioned at the end,[2] but they have in common the need for
vengeance from a son, who seeks to give the spirit rest (I. v. 190);
and it is especially interesting that the other reference in Belleforest occurs just where in Shakespeare the Ghost makes a reappearance, during the son's interview with his mother. Amleth
accuses her of failing to respect the manes of his father (*les ombres
de Horwendille*), undeserving (*indigne*[3]) of being treacherously
murdered by his brother and shamefully betrayed by the wife he
so well treated; and this of course is the burden of the Ghost's tale
to Hamlet in an earlier scene in Shakespeare (I. v. 42 ff.). Thus the
functions of Shakespeare's Ghost – to tell of his murder and
betrayal, to demand vengeance of his son, and to appear again
in the Queen's chamber – whether or not they owe anything to
Belleforest, may be said to be anticipated by him.

Verbal echoes of Belleforest in *Hamlet* are few; they could
hardly be expected to carry across the linguistic gap. Yet occasionally a word in Shakespeare, more often a turn of thought, may
be traced back to a possible or probable origin in Belleforest. The
interview between Amleth and his mother is again fruitful. He
tells her not to be offended if he speaks to her severely; Shakespeare's Hamlet 'will speak daggers to her' (III. ii. 387) and 'must
be cruel only to be kind' (III. iv. 180). Geruthe laments how
women's infidelities have bandaged their eyes (*bandé les yeux*);
Hamlet accuses Gertrude of playing 'hoodman-blind' (III. iv. 77).
Dissembling lamentations and incestuous embraces are already
in Saxo, but Belleforest, with a dissembling tear (*un pleur dissimulé*)
and the image of running with outstretched arms to incestuous
caresses (*allez courant les bras tenduz . . . et caressez incestueusement le
vouleur du lict legitime de vostre loyal espoux*), moves closer to the
'unrighteous tears' and the speedy posting 'to incestuous sheets'
in Hamlet's first soliloquy (I. ii. 154–7). Elsewhere Belleforest
thinks of Amleth's supposed madness as a hindrance to his
advancement (*un si grand defaut à son avancement*), Shakespeare's

1. See Moorman, 'The Pre-Shakespearean Ghost', *MLR*, I, 85–95.
2. It is perhaps curious that he is not, but see below, p. 159. One naturally
wonders if in the pre-Shakespearean *Hamlet*, as in *The Spanish Tragedy* and *The
Misfortunes of Arthur*, he was. Cf. below, p. 159.
3. Stabler, following 1572, reads *indigné*, incensed. The accent, also present in
1583 and 1601, is missing in 1576 and 1582. The 1608 translation has *unworthy*.

Hamlet complains 'I lack advancement' (III.ii.331). Amleth presents himself to the people as the minister and executioner (*le ministre et executeur*) of just vengeance, Hamlet is made Heaven's 'scourge and minister' (III.iv.177). Faced with the problem of miraculous knowledge, Belleforest speculates whether Amleth, instructed by the 'malign spirit' which 'abuses men', has become susceptible through his 'melancholy' to diabolic revelations;[1] and Hamlet, when he comes to question the honesty of the spirit he has seen, reminds himself that

> the *devil* hath power
> T'assume a pleasing shape, yea, and perhaps,
> Out of my weakness and my *melancholy*, . . .
> *Abuses* me to damn me. (II.ii.595–9)

Even the famous 'To be or not to be' soliloquy appears to derive something from Belleforest. Vowing to his mother that he will avenge his father, Amleth asks, 'What is the good of living when shame torments our conscience and cowardice holds us back from gallant enterprises?'[2] But the comparison with Shakespeare –

> Thus *conscience* does make cowards of us all . . .
> And *enterprises* of great pitch and moment
> . . . their currents turn awry (III.i.83–7)

– reveals a profound difference. Belleforest does not regard such failures as the common lot of men. The choice he offers Amleth is between two kinds of glory, either a glorious death or by the use of arms (*les armes au poing*) a glorious triumph over foes: the alternatives Hamlet debates, 'to suffer' life's misfortunes or 'to take arms' in a hopeless cause,[3] afford no such simple heroics. Belleforest, following Saxo, likens Amleth to Hercules: the comparison persists in Shakespeare, but those who were like are now unlike (I.ii.152–3). The mind of Hamlet, confronting the enigma of man's life, is not in Belleforest at all.[4]

1. 'Amleth . . . avoit esté endoctriné en celle science, avec laquelle *le malin esprit abuse* les hommes, et advertissoit ce Prince (comme il peut) des choses ja passees . . . et si ce Prince, pour la vehemence de la *melancholie*, avoit receu ces impressions, devinant ce qu'autre ne luy avoit jamais declairé . . .' A word of caution is necessary here, since the Belleforest occurs in a different context and both the idea and the keywords were widespread. See II.ii.597 LN.

2. 'Dequoy sert vivre, où la honte, et l'infamie . . . tourmentent nostre *conscience*, et la poltronnerie . . . retarde le cœur des gaillardes *entreprises* . . .?'

3. See III.i.57–60 LN.

4. For Shakespearean debts to Belleforest, not all equally convincing, see Stabler, *PMLA*, LXXXI, 207–13, and *Sh.Studs.*, V, 97–105; also Bullough's notes on the English version.

Belleforest nevertheless is clearly revealed as, directly or indirectly, a main source. A question that arises but is hardly possible to answer is whether all that Shakespeare inherited from Belleforest came to him through the *Ur-Hamlet*; or whether the resemblances (including even odd verbal parallels) are such as to suggest that while working from the stage play he also looked beyond it and read Belleforest for himself. The second alternative presents us with the possibility that some things common to Belleforest and Shakespeare were not in the *Ur-Hamlet*. Yet it is as inconceivable that the *Ur-Hamlet* did not use Belleforest as it is that Shakespeare did not use the *Ur-Hamlet*. He cannot have been unfamiliar with a play which was acted at the Theatre and which probably therefore belonged to his own company; and in it he would find the story of Hamlet's revenge upon his uncle already thrown into dramatic form. We must suppose that it already contained at least the leading episodes in the traditional Hamlet story – the feigned madness; the encounter with a fair lady; the killing of the spy; the Queen denounced in a big scene in her chamber; Hamlet's voyage for England and the death of his two escorts; his return, and, whether or not these resembled what happens in Shakespeare's ending, a funeral, an exchange of swords and the killing of the King. It seems likely that the earlier play developed, from hints already in Belleforest, the love interest and the contrast between the dead and living brothers. We know that it had a ghost which called for revenge, and we may presume that this was the ghost of the murdered father and that it appeared at or near the beginning. Since it addressed the hero directly, unlike the ghosts in Seneca and that of Andrea in *The Spanish Tragedy*, it would seem to have progressed from the position of a prologue or chorus to take part in the action of the play.[1] Whether, like the ghost of Andrea, it reappeared at the end to celebrate vengeance achieved;[2] whether the hero survived his revenge, as in Belleforest, or, as in Shakespeare and *The Spanish Tragedy*, perished while achieving it – these are things that can only be surmised. Most important of all in the matter of the transformation of Belleforest, we cannot tell how far the pre-Shakespearean play had gone in developing the sub-plot which makes the man that Hamlet kills the father of a son who will avenge him as well as of the woman who loves Hamlet.

1. Hence the murder need not have taken place before the play began. Yet the dramatist can hardly have had it both ways, as in *The Spanish Tragedy*, which opens with Andrea's ghost and murders Horatio in Act II.

2. Cf. above, p. 94, n. 2.

The Ur-Hamlet and The Spanish Tragedy

Speculation is better kept in check; but this does not mean that probabilities need go unacknowledged. The probability that the *Ur-Hamlet* was by Kyd, though not an essential premise, makes it easier to regard Kyd's *Spanish Tragedy* as in some sort a companion-piece. The *Ur-Hamlet*, with its apparently less conventional and more integrated ghost, is sometimes argued,[1] and more often assumed, to be the later; but the order must, I think, be the reverse.[2] Indeed without the *Ur-Hamlet*, *The Spanish Tragedy* might not have been possible. Belleforest provides the source for a play on Hamlet, which is then available as a model for a further revenge tragedy for which no independent source is known. First we have the archetypal revenge situation, the son's revenge for his father; and then, with the father's revenge for his son, *The Spanish Tragedy* gives us the converse. If Kyd's *Spanish Tragedy* and Shakespeare's *Hamlet* thus in different ways derive from the *Ur-Hamlet*, some of the things they have in common, over and above the paradigm of murder, ghost, madness, revenge, may be due to this common source. Something has to be allowed for coincidence and a possible influence of *The Spanish Tragedy* on Shakespeare; but these cannot adequately explain why so many features of *The Spanish Tragedy* have an analogy in *Hamlet*.[3] It has a background of wars and politics, with ambassadors going back and forth. Hieronimo distrusts the letter which reveals the murderer just as Hamlet distrusts the Ghost.[4] He reproaches himself for delay, even accuses himself of preferring words to blood.[5] He has thoughts of suicide. His situation is reflected in that of other fathers as Hamlet's is in that of other sons. He takes one father for a spirit come to rebuke his tardiness. He arranges the performance of a play which is less innocent than it seems. Instead of mirroring the crime, as in *Hamlet*, this play presents the vengeance; yet the image of the crime is still there in the exhibition of Horatio's corpse, and the play, by effecting vengeance in the guise of an entertainment before an unsuspecting

1. See, e.g., Bullough, pp. 17–18.

2. Cf. Stoll, *MP*, xxxv, 33–4; Bowers, *Elizabethan Revenge Tragedy*, pp. 95–9.

3. I am not of course the first to remark them. See e.g. Stoll, *MP*, xxxv, 32–3; Carrère, *Le Théâtre de Thomas Kyd*, pp. 146–7. Bullough (pp. 16–17) lists 'over a score', but some of these seem insignificant and others give a separate listing of different aspects of the same thing.

4. *Spanish Trag.* III.ii. 37–8; *Ham.* II.ii. 598–9. If Shakespeare took the idea of this from the *Ur-Hamlet*, then the verbal reminiscence of Belleforest (see above, p. 95) may be due to the *Ur-Hamlet* too.

5. *Spanish Trag.* III.vii. 67–8; cf. *Ham.* II.ii. 581, IV.iv. 66.

court, extends the analogy with *Hamlet* to include the fencing-match as well. In an ironic prelude to it the avenger and his destined victim, like Hamlet and Laertes, have a public reconciliation. For the rest, *The Spanish Tragedy* has a heroine whose love is opposed by her father and brother, and another woman, Hieronimo's wife, who goes mad and kills herself.

The cumulative effect of such parallels suggests that of the incidents which make up Shakespeare's plot some at least of those not in Belleforest were added in the *Ur-Hamlet*. Saxo and Belleforest tell a basically simple tale of a revenge that is ultimately achieved after being long and steadily purposed; but before Shakespeare came to the story doubts and delays and reproaches, of which there was earlier no sign, would seem to have begun. The madness of heroine as well as hero, a play within the play as part of the strategy of vengeance are among the probable embellishments. Yet *The Spanish Tragedy* may be equally suggestive of what the *Ur-Hamlet* lacked. I do not mean that there is nothing to correspond with, for example, the grave-digger or the pirates, the mad visit to Ophelia's closet or the villain spared at prayer: one can deduce little from omissions.[1] More significant is it that sensational episodes in *The Spanish Tragedy* are often merely episodic. Two instances spring to mind. The old man petitioning for his murdered son provokes Hieronimo to comparisons and a hallucinatory outburst; but he appears suddenly without history and vanishes without consequence. One cannot quite say this of Hieronimo's wife Isabella. Her three scenes, in which she respectively laments, 'runs lunatic', and kills herself, show at least progression; but her role really duplicates Hieronimo's and, except for the spectacle and clamour, could be omitted without loss. Shakespeare's minor figures are imagined with more circumstance; even Reynaldo belongs rather to life than the stage; and Rosencrantz and Guildenstern are a part of Hamlet's environment long before the plot requires them. But more than this greater naturalism is a new moral and psychological depth. Kyd's much-praised inventiveness is largely of the surface;[2] but an incidental stage excitement may correspond to something which

1. Nevertheless the emblematic function of these last two episodes, the one dramatizing Hamlet's farewell to love, the other his inactivity in revenge, has, I believe, the stamp of Shakespeare's creative imagination. See below, pp. 135, 140.

2. An exception occurs in the treatment of justice. That Hieronimo, who has to give justice to others, cannot get it for himself is dramatically neat; but the justice he administers to Pedringano has an irony that goes deeper. No such subtleties appear in the treatment of Hieronimo's revenge.

in the marvellous integration of Shakespeare's play connects with an inner core of meaning. In *Hamlet* the series of avenging sons sets up a pattern of contrasts which illumine the dilemmas and frustrations of the hero in a world of mingled good and evil. Lorenzo in *The Spanish Tragedy*, opposing his sister's love or embracing the man by whose hand he will presently die, has suggestions of Laertes; but if, as seems therefore probable, the *Ur-Hamlet* invented a son for the man that Hamlet killed, the profound implications of this seem to have been left for Shakespeare to explore. At least *The Spanish Tragedy* gives no hint that the agent of revenge may also be its object. Hieronimo's soliloquies, rhetorical and histrionic, apart from an occasional 'sentence' have few of those reflections on life and death which Hamlet's predicament evokes; and his madness, though it may sometimes combine the theatrical and the plausible, lacks the 'method' whereby Hamlet glances at truths that sanity cannot discover. Ophelia's madness is also used to reveal what reason would not: but by contrast with that of Isabella, it is in no sense a variation on the hero's; and her 'doubtful' death, with all the ripples that it stirs in the world of Elsinore,[1] is the direct antithesis of Isabella's stagy suicide.[2] Rightly understood, the wreckage of her mind through a devoted and rejected love is supremely moving.[3] Her sufferings, both a counterpoint to and a consequence of Hamlet's, add an important dimension to his tragedy.

The Spanish Tragedy, then, by the evidence it gives of what it could take from the *Ur-Hamlet*, shows what Shakespeare could, and even sometimes must, have taken too; but by its limitations it also points to the limitations of the *Ur-Hamlet*. The more controlled yet complex unity of *Hamlet*, which has been seen as a sign that the *Ur-Hamlet* came later than *The Spanish Tragedy*,[4] is rather, I think, to be ascribed to Shakespeare's profoundly imagined transformation of what the *Ur-Hamlet* had to offer.

One has accordingly to admit the chance that the given plot underwent considerable reshaping. Discussions of the source-play

1. It is one of the ironies of criticism that the confusion of gossip and report which so superbly brings a whole community to life should have been attributed to Shakespeare's inconsistency or revision. See v.i.2 n.

2. If the Queen's report of the drowning was echoed in *Locrine* (as suggested in *N&Q*, ccxxiv, 121–2), so much presumably would have been in the *Ur-Hamlet*. I find this somewhat improbable. But though it would lessen Shakespeare's originality in one way, in another, since Sabren in *Locrine* explicitly 'sought her death', it would emphasize it.

3. See below, pp. 151–2 and IV.v.23 LN, 23–40 LN, 48–66 LN.

4. Bullough, pp. 17–18.

have unreasonably assumed that *Hamlet* followed it closely in the order and the matter of its scenes. Shakespeare's practice elsewhere in rehandling source materials, including the particular example of *King Lear*, gives us no reason to pre-suppose that he would rigidly adhere to the scheme of an earlier play; and apart from the general improbability, there are signs in *Hamlet* itself that he did not. To take perhaps the most striking, the role and character of Fortinbras can be seen evolving as the play proceeds. The war with which he threatens Denmark (I.i) is suddenly called off for an expedition against Poland, and the hot-headed youth with his band of desperadoes becomes the leader of a disciplined army (IV.iv) and ultimately a fit ruler of Hamlet's realm (V.ii.355ff.). His 'lawless resolutes', however, are not dispensed with; they have attached themselves to Laertes (IV.v.101–11). Whether or not these avenging sons figured in the *Ur-Hamlet*, they were being fashioned, or refashioned, by Shakespeare in the course of composition.[1] It is apparent from the opening scenes that the function of Laertes, as well as of Ophelia, was clearly conceived by Shakespeare from the start; but there were details still to be worked out. The little inconsistency whereby Polonius first proposes that Ophelia shall go with him in person to the King and then substitutes the letter betrays a change of plan,[2] which may encourage a guess that Hamlet's visit to Ophelia's closet and Polonius's consequent theory of love-madness were Shakespeare's own elaborations. Horatio, like Ophelia, must have been in the *Ur-Hamlet* by virtue of his descent from Saxo; but Shakespeare's uncertainty about him, now well-informed now ignorant about affairs in Denmark,[3] shows that his role and status had not been predetermined. A vagueness as to minor characters, evident from the stage-directions,[4] suggests that these are being created by Shakespeare as he writes: hence the episodes of Reynaldo, who crystallizes the stage-direction's 'man or two' (II.i), and of the 'Courtier' who develops into Osric,[5] look like Shakespearean inventions.

1. Cf. below, p. 142. For a full discussion see 'Fortinbras and Laertes and the Composition of *Hamlet*', *Rice U.Studs.*, LX, 95–108. I do not agree with Gray and Carrère (see above, p. 85, n. 3) that the change of plan they duly note after the first scene involves a shift of interest from an external action of revenge through war, inherited from the *Ur-Hamlet*, to the internal workings of the hero's mind. The war can never have been more than a background and as such it continues to be important; and Fortinbras, through his various avatars, never ceases to be a military leader.

2. See II.ii.39S.D. n.   3. See I.iv.12–13 LN.
4. See above, pp. 37–8.   5. Cf. V.ii.88 LN (end).

Beyond recognizing these small but unmistakable signs of an author working freely on an action still being shaped, unrestricted to lines laid down, I will permit myself one conjecture. The circumstantiality with which Shakespeare endows his characters is nowhere more apparent than with the Ghost. We know that the Ghost in the *Ur-Hamlet*, with its white vizard and its cry of 'Revenge', left a deep impression on the memory of a spectator. But I think we too readily suppose that it must therefore have been like the Ghost in Shakespeare. *The Spanish Tragedy* suggests that it was not. For I find it impossible to believe that the author of *The Spanish Tragedy* knew (much less had written) anything at all closely resembling the early scenes of *Hamlet*.[1] It is not merely that his ghost is a conventional literary figure still trailing on to the stage all the trappings of classic myth while Shakespeare gives visible form to the fears of the popular mind. In *Hamlet*, from the first apprehensions of the soldiers on the watch to the moment when the apparition at length breaks silence with its dreadful tale, the circumstance with which it is imagined is in accord with the progression of events. Unless we are to suppose, in spite of appearances, that the earlier play gave Shakespeare not merely a ghost but his conception of the Ghost, it can hardly have had his disposition of the scenes of the first act.[2]

The Murder of Gonzago

It is often assumed that the introduction of the Ghost into the story involved the change in the method of the murder. In Saxo Hamlet's father was butchered (*trucidatus*), with bloodshed (*manu cruenta*), and Belleforest adds explicitly that he was set on at a banquet. The murder done in secret was an innovation. But although a secret murder might require a ghost to reveal it, the converse does not follow. We may accept the usual complaint that the secret murder deprives Hamlet of his traditional motive for pretending madness; but this weakness, if it is one, can easily be

1. Cf. Bullough, p. 28. He finds 'a degree of sophistication in Shakespeare's treatment entirely lacking in *The Spanish Tragedy* and probably only dimly foreshadowed in the *Ur-Hamlet*.'

2. So much so that when we find another play actually beginning with the sentry's challenge 'Who's there?' and following, as concerns the ghost, the same course of events, I would think this in itself a strong argument for inferring it a copy and not a source. *BB* has, in this order, the challenge, the cold, talk of the Ghost, the apparition itself, Horatio's report of it to Hamlet, the Ghost beckoning Hamlet, the Ghost's account of the murder, Hamlet rejoining his companions, the swearing on the sword, the decision to feign madness. I cannot feel the slightest doubt that this derives from Shakespeare's *Hamlet* and not from Shakespeare's source.

exaggerated – indeed Shakespeare seems to capitalize it by linking
the pretended madness with a genuine emotional disturbance –
and the corresponding advantages are great. There are consequences for the murderer's character as well as for the revenger's
task, and a revenge that cannot be openly declared invites a
subtler intrigue. The King's moves to penetrate Hamlet's madness are matched with Hamlet's to establish the King's guilt. The
device of imaging the crime in a play requires, if it is to be unmistakable both by the perpetrator and by us, a murder of a
singular kind; and a model for this was found, whether by
Shakespeare or his predecessor, in an actual occurrence in Italy.

Francesco Maria I della Rovere, Duke of Urbino, died in
October 1538. There were rumours of poison, and the barber-
surgeon who had attended him confessed under torture that, at
the instigation of Luigi Gonzaga, a kinsman of the Duchess, he
had poisoned him by a lotion in his ears.[1] The affair remains
mysterious, for although the barber was put to death, Gonzaga's
guilt was never proved; but the combination of his name with
the unusual method of killing leaves no doubt that we have here
the prototype of the murder in *Hamlet*. The statement that 'the
story is extant, and written in very choice Italian' (III. ii. 256–7)
may have been true to fact, but no printed source has been traced.
The name of the alleged murderer has been switched to his victim,
but Luigi may have suggested Lucianus; and though the Duchess
was called not Baptista but Leonora, an earlier Duke of Urbino
had married Battista Sforza. For dramatic reasons the murderer
is made the 'nephew',[2] and the better to mirror Claudius and
Gertrude the Duke and Duchess become a King and Queen.
When Hamlet nevertheless says 'Gonzago is the Duke's name'
(III. ii. 233–4), this is presumably a relic of the source. As a relic
unlikely to survive rehandling it points rather to Shakespeare than
his predecessor as the innovator in the matter of the poisoning;[3]
and the freedom with adopted names is quite in Shakespeare's
manner. The dead Duke was a famous soldier, a portrait of him
in armour by Titian is in the Uffizi Gallery in Florence, and
Bullough conjectures that the dramatist may have been familiar
with an engraving of it, perhaps in the hypothetical source. The
idea that this bearded figure 'in complete steel' with hand on
truncheon and a helmet behind him with its 'beaver up' may have

1. See Bullough, pp. 28–34, and *MLR*, xxx, 433–44.

2. See III. ii. 239 and LN.

3. Of course the *Ur-Hamlet* might have had the play about a duke and Shakespeare then improved on it; but what I see as the greater probability remains.

suggested some details for the description of King Hamlet[1] is not intrinsically implausible.

Possible sources of other episodes

The idea of a murderer betraying his guilt on seeing his crime represented in a play was not novel; and popularly reported instances were presumably known to Shakespeare. Yet a play which, on the evidence of its title-page, his company had 'lately' acted may have been particularly in his mind when he made Hamlet say that

> guilty creatures *sitting at a play* . . .
> . . . have proclaim'd their malefactions.
> For murder, though it have no tongue, will speak
> With most *miraculous* organ. (II. ii. 585–90)[2]

In *A Warning for Fair Women*, published 1599, an episode in which a murdered man revives to accuse his murderer prompts the reflection that in a case of blood God's justice is 'miraculous', and this in turn leads on to an account of a woman at Lynn in Norfolk who, 'sitting to behold a tragedy' in which a wife was haunted by the ghost of the husband she had murdered, confessed to a similar crime. A tale that is common knowledge is not incompatible with a particular reminiscence, as is also perhaps suggested by 'Aeneas' tale to Dido' as retold in the Player's speech. The incident in the 'tale' of Priam's slaughter by Pyrrhus belonged to literary tradition: it descends from the account of the fall of Troy in the *Aeneid*; and that Shakespeare knew the Virgil for himself might have been a fairly safe assumption even without the evidence of *Lucrece*.[3] Yet the recital in *Hamlet* corresponds in one or two details with the version by Marlowe and Nashe. In their *Tragedy of Dido* (published 1594) Aeneas tells how Pyrrhus came with 'his harness dropping blood' and how he 'whisk'd his sword about' with the result that Priam 'fell down' (II. i. 214, 253–4); in Shakespeare the 'sable arms' of Pyrrhus are transformed to 'total gules, horridly trick'd With blood', and 'with the whiff and wind of his fell sword', Priam 'falls' (II. ii. 453–4, 469–70). But the rest of Shakespeare's account differs both from *Dido* and from Virgil; and it shows him, far from relying on a single source, selecting and adapting and inventing to fit the purposes of his own play.[4]

1. See the engraving reproduced in Bullough, facing p. 31, and cf. I. ii. 199–242.
2. See LN on this passage.
3. For which see *Poems* (Arden), ll. 1501–68n.
4. See II. ii. 448–514 LN.

For the episode of the pirates, which neatly tightens the plot by returning Hamlet to Denmark without the digression of English adventures, it is still less necessary to seek a specific source. In tales either of fact or fancy pirates were familiar enough. Bullough cites Sidney's *Arcadia*, in which Pyrocles is captured by pirates and afterwards fights alongside them (I. viii); but a likelier connection would be with an incident that Shakespeare must recently have come upon in the course of writing *Julius Caesar*. In the beginning of his *Life* of Caesar Plutarch tells how Caesar in his youth was captured by pirates and spent thirty-eight days on their ship while his ransom was being procured. They waited on him with much courtesy and he was merry with them. But, in contrast with Hamlet, the 'turn' that Caesar did them was to have them captured and crucified. Whether or not Shakespeare remembered this incident, the 'mercy' of his variation (IV. vi. 18–20) is significant.

Pierce Penniless His Supplication to the Devil

The characterization of the Danish court and especially of its drinking owes something to Nashe's pamphlet, *Pierce Penniless His Supplication to the Devil* (1592).[1] The story in Saxo requires the courtiers to get drunk, and Shakespeare evidently knew of the Danish practice of accompanying the drinking of healths with cannon;[2] but for Hamlet's famous speech about the custom 'more honour'd in the breach than the observance' he appears to have drawn on a passage in Nashe's pamphlet. When the King 'takes his rouse', Hamlet deplores the effect of the custom upon the national reputation:

> This *heavy-headed* revel east and west
> Makes us traduc'd and tax'd of other nations –
> They clepe us drunkards, and with *swinish* phrase
> Soil our addition . . .   (I. iv. 17–20)

This, as other accounts attest, was accurate enough; but Nashe in particular, as soon as he starts to describe the Danes, thinks of them as 'bursten-bellied sots' and decries 'this surly *swinish* generation' (Nashe, i. 180); and later, when his account of the deadly sins has brought him via gluttony to an attack on drunkenness, he refers to 'the *heavy-headed* gluttonous house-dove' (i. 210). In the passage on drunkenness itself Nashe has lamented the

---

1. *N&Q*, cxcviii (1953), 371–4, 377–8; Muir, *The Sources of Shakespeare's Plays*, pp. 167–8.
2. See I. ii. 125–6, I. iv. 7–12; Dollerup, pp. 123–4.

custom whereby 'superfluity in drink', instead of causing a man, as formerly, to be called 'foul drunken swine', is nowadays 'counted honourable'; and he has been led to reflect how 'this unnecessary vice' so disfigures a man that, whatever his 'virtues', 'that one beastly imperfection will utterly obscure' them (i. 204–5). In a similar way Shakespeare, while extending what Nashe says of drunkenness to apply to any vice, goes on to observe that when a man carries 'the stamp of one defect',

> His virtues else, be they as pure as grace,
> As infinite as man may undergo,
> Shall in the general censure take corruption
> From that particular fault.   (i. iv. 33–6)

The result in Nashe is that the drunkard's 'good qualities sink . . . to the bottom of his carousing cups . . . like lees and dregs, dead and unregarded'; and Shakespeare, if my interpretation of this famous crux is right, concludes that a 'dram' of evil will submerge, or 'dout', the 'noble substance'.[1]

Nashe's discussion of 'the heavy-headed gluttonous house-*dove*' leads into an account of Sloth which has its echoes in that soliloquy of Hamlet's in which he calls himself a 'dull and muddy-mettled rascal'. Nashe says that if a man, in neglect of arms and honour, 'sit dallying at home, nor will be awaked by any indignities out of his love-*dream*, but suffer every upstart groom to defy him, set him at naught, and shake him by the *beard* unrevenged . . ., he shall be suspected of *cowardice*' (i. 210–11). Hamlet compares himself with 'John-a-*dreams*', asks 'Am I a *coward*?', pictures himself accepting such indignities – 'Who calls me villain, . . . plucks off my *beard*?' – and concludes that he is '*pigeon*-liver'd' (ii. ii. 561–73). For Nashe 'Sloth in *nobility, courtiers, scholars* . . . is the chiefest cause that brings them in contempt', in contrast with the warrior who shares the hardships of 'his *soldiers*'; and the antidote for sloth is to emulate one who is 'the only *mirror* of our age' (i. 210–11). It is just such a one that Ophelia recalls when she laments the '*noble* mind',

> The *courtier's, soldier's, scholar's* eye, tongue, sword . . .
> The *glass* of fashion and the mould of form.
>   (iii. i. 152–5)

Hamlet's attack on women's painting exploits a traditional topic of satire; yet the recurrent correspondences with *Pierce Penniless* suggest that more than coincidence is involved when Nashe, going

---

1. See i. iv. 36–8 LN, and for Nashe i. iv. 17–20 LN, 23–38 LN.

on from the drunken Danes to a diatribe against cosmetics, sneers at women with wrinkled '*cheeks*' who 'have their deformities new *plastered* over' (i. 181) and Shakespeare makes Claudius refer to 'the harlot's *cheek*, beautied with *plast'ring* art' (III. i. 51).[1]

A Treatise of Melancholy

In all these parallels the essential words and phrases and, in one signal instance, the sequence of ideas are anything but commonplace. In *Pierce Penniless*, moreover, they occur in the passages about drunken Danes and drunkenness in general, or in passages in the immediate vicinity of these, so that they fall within a limited stretch of about thirty pages. It is as though Shakespeare actually turned up these pages, possibly in search of local colour, while *Hamlet* was gestating; and this may have been connected, whether as cause or consequence, with his making Danish intemperance part of the moral framework of his play. However that may be, the nature of the correspondences puts Shakespeare's indebtedness to *Pierce Penniless* beyond question. The status of Timothy Bright's *Treatise of Melancholy* (1586) is less certain.

In Bright's account of melancholy and its victims we have little difficulty in detecting affinities with Hamlet. The melancholy man, we are told, is 'doubtful before, and long in deliberation: suspicious, painful in study, and circumspect' (p. 124); he is more given to 'contemplations' and 'not so apt for action' as other men are (p. 200). A passage like the following might be taken as a summary of much that Bright elaborates elsewhere: 'The perturbations of melancholy are for the most part sad and fearful, and such as rise of them: as distrust, doubt, diffidence, or despair, sometimes furious, and sometimes merry in appearance, through a kind of Sardonian and false laughter' (p. 102).

Yet the Elizabethan malady, as it has been called, was a subject of wide interest, and one on which Shakespeare must have been in any case well informed. The suggestion that he 'turned to' Bright for help in creating his hero seems unlikely. Still less can we suppose that he envisaged and worked out a character who would conform to type as a melancholy man: the belief that he formed his tragic heroes to exemplify 'slaves of passion' is happily outmoded.[2] The lines of Hamlet's character were laid down, to

1. For possible reminiscences of *Pierce Penniless* see also II. i. 25 LN, v. ii. 82–3 LN; of some other works by Nashe, *Hamlet Studies*, II (1980), 37–46.

2. For the melancholy type, see e.g. Schücking, *Character Problems in Shakespeare*, trans. 1922, pp. 153–71. 'Slaves of passion' is the subtitle of Lily Campbell's *Shakespeare's Tragic Heroes*, 1930, where Hamlet exemplifies 'grief'.

begin with, by the story he belonged to. Saxo's hero had to be one who, to be sure, could act with fury, yet passed his time in meditating an action long deferred; who simulated foolish lethargy, yet mocked anyone who questioned him with cryptic and Sardonian replies. With Belleforest even supplying the word,[1] there is enough here to suggest the man with

> something in his soul
> O'er which his melancholy sits on brood.
>
> (iii. i. 166–7)

What Shakespeare does is to take us into Hamlet's mind, to intellectualize the character, and, by doing so, transform it. But many of the ideas he gives Hamlet to express belong to the common intellectual currency of his age, so that it cannot be surprising if some are also found in Bright. Certainly Shakespeare did not need Bright to tell him that the mind of man can look before and after, that his faculties owe allegiance to the 'sovereignty' of reason, and that his body is a mechanism animated by the soul.[2] Among phrases which have been noted as common to them both, 'discourse of reason' was a term in regular use, 'custom of exercise' is hardly out of the ordinary, and 'posset and curd', for all the shudder these words cause when Shakespeare describes the poisoning of the blood, are too natural a conjunction to be explained by Bright's equally unremarkable reference to a 'posset curd'.

In view of the traditional nature of the melancholic traits in Hamlet, the author of *The Elizabethan Malady* thinks it 'not necessary to assume that Shakespeare had read a book about melancholy'.[3] Yet it would be strange if the most available and authoritative treatment of the subject had not come under his eye. A few details of a more particular kind may suggest that it had. The sufferer from melancholy, as Bright describes him, is 'given to fearful and terrible *dreams*' (p. 124); his house 'seemeth unto the melancholic a *prison* or *dungeon*, rather than a place of assured repose and rest' (p. 263), 'the air meet for melancholic folk ought to be . . . open and patent to all winds . . . especially to the *south* and *south-east*' (p. 257). Hamlet, we remember, confesses to 'bad *dreams*' (ii. ii. 256 ff.), insists that 'Denmark's a *prison*' in a world of many '*dungeons*' (ii. ii. 243–51), and explains, 'I am but *mad north-north-west*. When the wind is *southerly*, I know a hawk

---

1. See above, p. 95 and n. 1.
2. See iv. iv. 37; i. iv. 73; ii. ii. 122–3; with notes.
3. Lawrence Babb, p. 107n.

from a handsaw' (II.ii.374–5). Here we are among the conundrums with which Hamlet's wit, amid the seemingly spontaneous
flow of mad-talk, bewilders such as Rosencrantz and Guildenstern; but the conundrums may have had their origin in what
Bright states soberly as fact. His phrases are less picturesque and
memorable than Nashe's, so that echoes are less easily evoked: it
also follows that any that there may be are less easily detectable.
Nevertheless there is an occasional image which anticipates
Hamlet. Bright refers to 'the lists of reason' being 'broken through'
(p. 250), Shakespeare to an excessive humour 'breaking down the
pales and forts of reason' (I.iv.28). And for all that descriptions
of man's gorgeous heavenly canopy are something of a Renaissance set-piece, the melancholy which in Bright 'obscureth the
sun and moon and all the comfortable planets of our natures' so
that 'they appear . . . more than half eclipsed of this *mist* of blackness' (p. 106) is perhaps recognizable when Hamlet says, 'This
brave o'erhanging firmament, this majestical roof fretted with
golden fire . . . appeareth nothing to me but a foul and pestilent
congregation of *vapours*' (II.ii.300–3).[1]

Altogether, while I think the influence of Bright on Shakespeare's conception of Hamlet has been much exaggerated and
that many of the examples which are alleged to show it are without weight, there seems sufficient evidence to justify us in including *A Treatise of Melancholy* among the subsidiary sources of the
play.[2]

Montaigne's Essays

The case of Montaigne is still more difficult. Again it is not a
matter of concentrated borrowings such as we have seen from
Nashe, but of widely scattered correspondences of thought. That
Montaigne and *Hamlet* have many of these is undeniable: it is
equally undeniable that many of them voice traditional Renaissance wisdom ultimately deriving from the classical moral writers.
Montaigne is more likely to cite, and perhaps to know, his source;
but he and Shakespeare shared an inexhaustible interest in the
vagaries of the human mind as it confronts the great issues of life

1. For citations from Bright, not necessarily pointing to indebtedness, see
notes on I.iv.28, 73; II.ii.243, 298–303, 374–5; III.i.160; III.ii.54; IV.iv.37.

2. The case for Shakespeare's use of Bright, long ago accepted by Dowden
(see his II.ii.310n.), is most fully advocated by M. I. O'Sullivan (*PMLA*, XLI,
667–79) and Dover Wilson (*WHH*, pp. 309–20) and endorsed by Muir (*The
Sources of Shakespeare's Plays*, pp. 166–7). Hardin Craig was more cautious, but
concluded (in his Introduction to the Facsimile Text Society reprint) that the
case was 'nevertheless . . . good'.

and death, and were liable to make their own 'what oft was thought' about them. If therefore they frequently give expression to the same sentiments, this in itself is not evidence of any direct relationship. Shakespeare did not have to read Montaigne in order to remark that 'there is nothing either good or bad but thinking makes it so' (II.ii.249–50); and although Montaigne preceded him in saying that death was like a sleep (III.i.64) and that, since death must come, it need not matter when (V.ii.216–20), he was not the first to do so.

What is well known and demonstrable is that Montaigne was Shakespeare's source for certain passages in *The Tempest*.[1] The question of his wider influence on Shakespeare has been endlessly debated.[2] There have also been many attempts to show it on *Hamlet* in particular, among which those which once contrived to see the whole *raison d'être* of the play in the pillorying of Montaigne and his philosophy are least in need of resurrection.[3] After a reaction against earlier excesses, Montaigne is now reasonably regarded as a source for some ideas in *King Lear*, and a growing consensus sees Shakespeare coming under his influence following the publication of Florio's translation in 1603.[4] This of course post-dates *Hamlet*.

Nevertheless, apart from the obvious possibility that Shakespeare knew Montaigne in the French, translations were being undertaken from at least 1595, when one was entered in the Stationers' Register; and Sir William Cornwallis specifically says in 1600 that he has read Montaigne in English.[5] Whether or not these references are to Florio's version, as is sometimes doubted but more often assumed, this was itself registered on 4 June 1600 and there is some evidence that it was well under way at least by

1. In addition to the long-recognized borrowing, in *Tp.* II.i.141 ff., from Montaigne's essay 'Of the Cannibals', see Eleanor Prosser in *Sh.Studs.*, 1, 261–4.

2. A bibliography is impossible here. Large claims for Shakespeare's use of Montaigne were made by J. M. Robertson, *Montaigne and Shakespeare*, 1897, revised 1909, and G. C. Taylor, *Shakespeare's Debt to Montaigne*, 1925. The parallels which are alleged to show it are assembled in Susanne Türck, *Shakespeare und Montaigne*, 1930. Necessary cautions are put by Churton Collins, *Studies in Shakespeare*, 1904, and especially Alice Harmon, *PMLA*, LVII, 988–1008. The article by R. Ellrodt, *SS 28*, 37–50, arguing for Montaigne's influence on *Hamlet* and succeeding plays, covers the more recent debate in its excellent notes.

3. G. F. Stedefeld, *Hamlet, ein Tendenzdrama Shakespeare's*, 1871; J. Feis, *Shakspere and Montaigne*, 1884.

4. See Muir, *Lr* (Arden), pp. 249–53, and *The Sources of Shakespeare's Plays*, pp. 8, 206.

5. *Essays*, ed. D. C. Allen, p. 42.

1598.[1] There is thus no insuperable objection to supposing that
Shakespeare was acquainted with Montaigne in Florio's translation at the time of writing *Hamlet*, if apparent instances of verbal
reminiscence should point in that direction.[2] In both Florio and
Shakespeare death is not only like a sleep but comes as a 'consummation'. Men 'rough(ly) hew' what heaven perfects. In
Florio 'a *wisdom* . . . so *precisely* circumspect' is the enemy of doing,
in Shakespeare the 'thinking too *precisely*' which leaves a thing
undone 'hath but one part *wisdom*'. Florio has it that they are 'the
weakest . . . whose *conceit* . . . is so seized upon that they imagine
. . . what they see not', Shakespeare that '*conceit* in *weakest* bodies
strongest works'.[3] In none of these examples is the thought
exactly the same, and in some it takes in Shakespeare a strikingly
different turn. The sleep of death is not, as in Montaigne, 'without
dreams'; the 'wisdom' of thinking too precisely is for Hamlet
three parts cowardice; his mother does not 'imagine' what she
sees not, but fails to see the Ghost at all. Nevertheless such signs
of an ever-active mind putting what it borrows to new use do not
in any way diminish the likelihood of a debt. Perhaps no single
word or group of words is sufficiently remarkable for its use to be
conclusive in itself; but they have a cumulative weight. Moreover,
a temptation to dismiss them as insignificant is met with the
curious fact that the words which specifically link Florio with
Shakespeare are often absent from the French.[4] I incline therefore
to think that of the ideas which Shakespeare so lavishly bestowed
on Hamlet a few at least were prompted by his recent reading in
Florio's Montaigne.

Attempts to identify further sources have been numerous: *Hamlet*
notoriously excites the ambition of critical discoveries. We know
that Shakespeare read Adlington's translation of *The Golden Ass*
of Apuleius, but coincidences of motif and vocabulary[5] are not

1. When the imagery of Montaigne's I. 24 ('Of Pedantism') is made use of in
Florio's preface to his *World of Words*. See Frances Yates, *John Florio*, p. 213.

2. It seems proper to point out that some of the closest parallels are with
Book 1; but no sharp distinctions can be drawn. It would be very hard to contend for an acquaintance while limiting it to the earlier portions of the work.

3. For these and other parallels, not necessarily suggesting indebtedness, see
notes on II.ii.249–50, II.ii.515–16, III.i.56–88 (end), III.iv.114, IV.iii.21, IV.iv.
18–26, IV.iv.41–2, v.ii.10–11, v.ii.218–20 (end).

4. Cf. *consummation*, aneantissement; *roughly hew*, esbauche; a *wisdom* so
tenderly *precise*, and so *precisely* circumspect, la prudence si tendre et circon-
specte; the minds of . . . the *weakest*, les ames . . . plus molles; whose *conceit* and
belief is so seized upon, on leur a si fort saisy la creance.

5. See *SS 31*, 34–6.

enough to show that it had an effect on *Hamlet*. Anything that
Shakespeare read could have contributed to the play which
perhaps more than any other reflects the intellectual interests of
his time. But claims that this or that work had a pervasive influence are very difficult to substantiate. Hardin Craig's discovery
in Cardan's *De Consolatione* of sentiments similar to Hamlet's does
not warrant the conclusion that that was where Hamlet found
them.[1] An attempt to show that Shakespeare went to Erasmus's
Praise of Folly for help in giving Hamlet a humanist cast of mind
is unsuccessful.[2] The whole question of the sources of ideas, in an
age much given to repeating proverbial wisdom, discourages
confident assertions. It has often happened that investigators
concerned with one source have attributed to it what could have
come equally well from another. Thus the passage on the 'particular fault' which brings a man's virtues into disrepute (I.iv.23–
38), now recognized as having its original in Nashe, was formerly
derived by Robertson from Montaigne and by Miss O'Sullivan
from Bright. Miss O'Sullivan and Dover Wilson both connected
Bright with Hamlet's observation on the wisdom of 'thinking too
precisely' which is actually closer to Montaigne as Florio renders
him. Taylor ascribed to the influence of Montaigne those 'precepts' to a son in which Polonius echoes a whole host of Elizabethan fathers.[3] The editor of the translation of Guazzo's *Civil
Conversation* connects his author with Hamlet's feeling of being in
prison, for which we have found a fuller analogy in Bright.
Identifications proposed for the book Hamlet is reading at
II.ii.168ff., even if one could suppose a particular book intended,
would cancel one another out. The incident of Osric's hat,
paralleled both in Guazzo's *Civil Conversation* and in Florio's
Second Fruits,[4] appears to be based on a stock joke. It is not surprising that Shakespeare's dialogue shares a number of topics with
the *Civil Conversation*.[5] Yet when Hamlet taunts Ophelia on the
subject of women's beauty there is a close enough resemblance to

1. *Huntington Library Bulletin*, VI, 17–37.
2. *SS 27*, 59–69.
3. I.iii.58–80 LN.
4. V.ii.94 n.
5. See *The Civile Conversation of M. Steeven Guazzo*, ed. Sullivan (Tudor Translations), i.l–lvi. On the general question of Shakespeare's knowledge of this
book, see J. M. Ellis d'Alessandro, 'Guazzo and Shakespeare', *Rivista di
letterature moderne e comparate*, XXXI, 85–108. J. L. Lievsay's *Stefano Guazzo and the
English Renaissance* (1961), while showing that Guazzo was well known in
England, unaccountably refrains from considering his influence on Shakespeare
and the drama.

suggest a possible direct link.[1] The more plausible hypotheses of such localized indebtedness to this or other works I hope to have mentioned in the notes.[2]

6. DER BESTRAFTE BRUDERMORD (BB)

What has proved to be one of the most puzzling of all the *Hamlet* problems is presented by the existence of a German play called *Tragoedia der Bestrafte Brudermord oder Prinz Hamlet aus Dännemark* (often referred to in English as *Fratricide Punished*). Mercifully the difficulty of the problem is in excess of its importance. Since *BB* is neither a text nor a source of Shakespeare's play, it cannot legitimately claim extended treatment here. But since it has often been held (wrongly in my belief) to descend from the *Ur-Hamlet* and so to afford illumination on Shakespeare's source, the question of its precise relation to Shakespeare's *Hamlet* cannot quite be ignored. Fortunately, the thorough investigation by Duthie (in *The 'Bad' Quarto of 'Hamlet'*), although in one respect mistaken,[3] makes it unnecessary to repeat either his references to earlier controversy[4] or his detailed demonstration from the texts.

BB turns out to be a version of *Hamlet* in a very degenerate form. It is assumed to descend from one taken to Germany, perhaps already much corrupted, by one of the bands of English actors who are known to have toured there from Elizabethan times. A *Tragoedia von Hamlet einen Printzen in Dennemarck* was performed by an English troupe at Dresden in 1626;[5] but it is likely that *Hamlet* first reached Germany years earlier, quite possibly, as happened with some other English plays, even before it had

---

1. See III.i. 107–8, 144 and LNN; Tudor Trans., ii. 10–13.

2. While most claims referred to in the last paragraph invite a degree of scepticism, there are others which should perhaps be explicitly rejected. Those of the anti-Jesuit pamphlet, *A Sparing Discovery of our English Jesuits* (1601), even if the verbal parallels could be seen as significant, would be ruled out by the date (David Kaula, *SS 24*, 71–7, and *Shakespeare and the Archpriest Controversy*, pp. 30–41). Resemblances alleged between the 'Second History' in Henry Wotton's *Cupid's Cautels* and the story of Ophelia seem to me illusory (*Emporia State Research Studies*, 1966, pp. 18–26). Dover Wilson's fantasy about the Earl of Essex as a model for Hamlet ought not now to be repeated in a responsible work of reference.

3. See below, pp. 119–21.

4. The important early studies are those of Creizenach, expressing a minority view which has proved substantially correct: '*Der bestrafte Brudermord* und ihre Bedeutung für die Kritik des Shakespeare'schen Hamlet' (*Berichte der philol.-histor. Classe der Königl. Sächs. Gesellschaft der Wissenschaften*, 1887, pp. 1–43); *Die Schauspiele der englischen Komödianten* (*Deutsche National-Litteratur*, ed. J. Kürschner, XXIII, 1889), pp. 127–45; *MP*, II (1904–5), 249–60.

5. Cohn, *Shakespeare in Germany* (1865), p. cxv.

appeared in print. Opportunities for alteration and textual deterioration during the century that elapsed before the date of the surviving German text are obvious.

BB is known to us only through a manuscript said to have borne the date 'den 27. Oktober 1710' and to have been in the possession of the actor Conrad Ekhof, who died in 1778. It came into the hands of H. A. O. Reichard, who, after giving an abstract in the Gotha 'Theater-Kalender' for 1779 (pp. 47–60), published it in full in the periodical *Olla Potrida* in 1781 (Part II, pp. 18–68). This, with the disappearance of the manuscript, is now our sole authority for the text.[1]

What we have in *BB* is a short play, slightly less than half as long as Q1. But it contains most of the Shakespearean action, often corresponding scene by scene, if in the barest form. Avoiding all long speeches, it lacks the famous soliloquies save the one debating whether to kill the King at prayer. Absent also are Hamlet's conversations with Rosencrantz and Guildenstern, the Player's speech on the sack of Troy, the dialogue of the play within the play, which is thus confined to dumb-show, Ophelia's songs, and the whole of the scene in the churchyard. On the other hand, the play has acquired from somewhere an allegorical prologue and much new farcical matter, the tone of which is set at the beginning when the Ghost boxes the sentry's ear. Ophelia, in the delusions of her madness, sees her lover in an absurd courtier called Phantasmo, who has developed out of Osric. There is a peasant in trouble for unpaid taxes and a notorious 'banditti' episode in which two ruffians (*Banditen*) are under orders to go with Hamlet to England and kill him. They land with him on an island, where they propose to shoot him, but he by a trick falls forward so that they shoot one another instead. From the local allusions and the traditional motifs employed, it appears that much of the farcical matter must have accrued in Germany.

The style, with only a few exceptions, notably in the Prologue, is spare and abrupt. Typically, Ophelia accosts Hamlet un-addressed: 'I pray your highness to take back the jewel which you presented to me.' In the scene with his mother Hamlet starts straight off with 'Lady mother, did you really know your first

---

1. It was reprinted by Albert Cohn in *Shakespeare in Germany* (1865), 237–304, and again by Creizenach in *Die Schauspiele der englischen Komödianten*, pp. 125–86. Cohn provided side by side a translation by Georgina Archer, and subsequent ones include those in Furness, Bullough (adapted from Furness), and Brennecke, *Shakespeare in Germany* (1964). Except when it is necessary to quote the German, I use the translation by Furness.

husband?' On the other hand, what we have already seen in action may be described again in speech. What happens is often made crudely explicit. The King tells us, 'I hope that when they both drink of the wine they will then die', and Leonhardus (Laertes) explains, 'It is a poisoned sword . . . I was to have wounded you with it'. Yet stripped of all refinement, the bald sense of the dialogue often corresponds to Shakespeare closely. The first court scene, albeit repositioned, begins 'Although our brother's death is still fresh in the memory of us all . . .' (cf. I.ii. 1–2). Hamlet's reply to his mother's request to stay is 'Your command I will obey with all my heart' (cf. I.ii. 120). The Ghost, once alone with Hamlet, begins, 'Hear me, Hamlet, for the time draws near when I must betake myself again to the place whence I have come; hear, and give heed to what I shall relate to thee' (cf. I.v. 2–6). Hamlet says 'Speak', addresses the shade of his 'father' (cf. ll. 6–9), exclaims at hearing of 'unnatural death' (cf. ll. 25–6), and the Ghost tells of the juice of hebenon (*Saft von Ebeno*) poured into the ear (cf. ll. 62–3). The effect of the poison is that 'as soon as a few drops of it mix with the blood of man, they at once clog the veins' (cf. ll. 65–70). When Hamlet requires his companions to swear, Horatio says 'Only just propose the oath to us' and Hamlet replies 'Then lay your finger on my sword' (cf. I.v. 160, 166). On the appearance of the Ghost in the Queen's chamber Hamlet asks 'What wouldst thou?' and the Queen interrupts with 'What are you about? and to whom are you talking?' Notably more explicit than in Shakespeare ('Do you see nothing there?'), Hamlet rejoins, 'See you not the ghost of your departed husband?', and the Queen answers, 'I see nothing at all'. (Cf. III.iv. 105, 116–18, 131–3.) Sometimes even the vocabulary is the same, when a word unusual in German carries over from the English. The 'consent' Polonius gives for his son's return to France (I.ii. 60) becomes the subject of a joke with the word (*Consens*) repeated five times.[1] The pictures of the Queen's two husbands, their 'counterfeit presentment' (III.iv. 54), are referred to once each as '*das Conterfait*'.[2]

Sometimes a correspondence of topic goes with a variation in

1. Creizenach argued that this borrowed word must come from the Q2 text.
2. I have to content myself, and hope to content my readers, with sample illustration of *BB*'s numerous resemblances to the Shakespearean text as we have it in Q2 and F. It should perhaps be pointed out that both Creizenach and Duthie are concerned to show where *BB* agrees with either Q1 or Q2 against the other, and accordingly omit its agreements with them both. But Duthie (p. 253) stresses that a complete list of correspondences between *BB* and Q2 would make 'an extremely lengthy catalogue'.

the thought. Whereas in Shakespeare Hamlet confesses to the Ghost his neglect of its command (III. iv. 107–9), in *BB* he simply vows to fulfil it. The weather in the opening scene, instead of being 'bitter cold', is, more feebly, 'not so cold' as it was. It is fairly obvious that *BB* has been much corrupted by memorial transmission. Its dialogue sometimes lacks the context which in Shakespeare makes the point clear. The King asks if there is nothing offensive in the play before anything has occurred to arouse suspicion. Osric's counterpart lets Hamlet persuade him that it is now cold, now hot, but the joke is not led up to by his standing uncovered. Among what look like memory confusions is the transfer of the name Francisco from the first sentinel to the character Shakespeare calls Marcellus. Pyrrhus, eliminated along with the excerpt from the Troy play, gives his name to the king in the other inset play who in Shakespeare is Gonzago. Shakespearean material often appears in the wrong order. In the opening the sentry refers to his relief before not after the remark about the cold. The King's drunken revelry is already heard off stage in this first scene. Hamlet's encounter with the Ghost (I. v) precedes the scene at court (I. ii), where Hamlet's return to Wittenberg is discussed before, instead of after, that of 'Leonhardo' to France. The Ghost, instead of repeating Hamlet's injunction to swear, echoes the swearing itself; and Horatio does not wait for the ghostly voice before saying it is strange (I. v. 172; *BB* I. vi. 6). Ophelia's father reports Hamlet's madness to the King before, not after, Ophelia is frighted by it. His remark that he too suffered for love in his youth occurs in his discussion with the King instead of during his subsequent tête-à-tête with Hamlet. When Leonhardus appears demanding revenge the King at once proposes the wager and the fencing-match, and this all happens before the King and Queen see Ophelia mad. When they do, she already has flowers to distribute. Phantasmo (Osric) comes to announce the wager before the Queen reports Ophelia's death, and he manages to deliver his message before, not after, Hamlet teases him about being hot and cold. And so on. It is obvious that such transpositions are for the most part inadvertent. A typical mix-up involves Hamlet's injunction to Polonius to entertain the players well, with Polonius's reply that he will treat them 'according to their desert' (II. ii. 518–23). *BB* loses Hamlet's witty retort to this ('Use every man after his desert, and who shall scape whipping?') and transfers the rest from its appropriate place on the occasion of the players' arrival to follow upon the play scene, where it is provoked by the chamberlain's comment that the players may get scant reward because of the King's displeasure, which replaces Guildenstern's announcement that the King is 'marvellous distempered' (III.ii.291–3).

From these and other examples of memory's mingled recollections and distortions it is evident that *BB*, except where it introduces matter extraneous to the traditional Hamlet story, is not merely a dependent text but one which derives either from Shakespeare's *Hamlet* or from something so like it as not really to be a different play at all. In theory of course this could be the *Ur-Hamlet*. But all those who hold to such a theory commit themselves to the belief that Shakespeare, while no doubt heightening effects with powerful diction and writing in some brilliant soliloquies, was for large parts of *Hamlet* content to follow a source-play step by step, not only incident by incident but often speech by speech.[1] To object to such a view is not bardolatry; it is merely to resist the absurd.[2] For although I am not sure, not having written one, how a masterpiece is created, I cannot believe that one has ever come into being in that way. All we know of Shakespeare suggests a capaciousness of imaginative grasp which transcends such piecemeal working. A play like *Coriolanus*, to take one which keeps in places verbally very close to its source, shows at the same time great boldness in the selection, rehandling, and recombination of parts. Nowhere are we more aware than in *Hamlet*, with its vitality of dramatization and its profound reflections on human life, of an imagination reaching out beyond the surface of a plot.

What primarily convinces me that *BB* is substantially derived from the Shakespearean *Hamlet* is, then, a comparison of the texts; and I find it hard to believe that anyone who makes the same comparison without any predilection is likely to come to a different conclusion.[3] But there are of course historical reasons

1. For the contrary view, see above, pp. 99–101.

2. Cf. Duthie, who, emphasizing *BB*'s 'frequent closeness to the full Shakespearean version of Q2', decides that if *BB* represents the *Ur-Hamlet*, 'then the latter resembled Shakespeare's full play very much more than I should be prepared to suppose' (p. 253); and Creizenach, who says that the assumption that the *Ur-Hamlet* is the source of those parts of *BB* that agree with Shakespeare makes Shakespeare 'a plagiarist' and the author of the *Ur-Hamlet* 'one of the greatest poets of all time' (*MP*, II, 250).

3. Cf. Chambers, *WS*, i.422. Significantly the study by R. Freudenstein (*Der Bestrafte Brudermord: Shakespeares 'Hamlet' auf der Wanderbühne des 17 Jahrhunderts*, Hamburg, 1958), though vitiated by a failure to allow for oral transmission and a consequent assumption that *BB* was an actual adaptation of the printed texts, came down in favour of Q1 and Q2 and against the *Ur-Hamlet* as the origin of *BB*.

why there have been predilections and why alternative hypotheses have often been preferred. So long as it was widely believed that Q1 was an earlier version of *Hamlet* than the one represented in Q2 and F,[1] it was natural to suppose that *BB* preserved an earlier version too. For one of the remarkable things about *BB* is that in certain conspicuous features it accords with Q1 instead of with the genuine text. Notoriously, it calls Ophelia's father *Corambus* (Q1 *Corambis*); and from his plan to set Hamlet and Ophelia together *BB*, like Q1, proceeds directly to their encounter, so that the nunnery scene comes before the arrival of the players.[2] Among other likenesses, Hamlet expects the King at the enactment of his crime not simply to betray his guilt but specifically to 'turn pale'; and it is the King, not his accomplice, who proposes not only the unbated sword but the poisoned point as well. When these things were thought, from their presence in Q1, to be marks of an earlier version which Shakespeare subsequently modified, it was reasonable to believe that *BB* stemmed from the *Ur-Hamlet*. But now that it has to be accepted that Q1 is not a preliminary draft of Shakespeare's play but a corrupt derivative of it,[3] it follows, and ought to have been more generally perceived, that *BB* must be a derivative version also. To take what is perhaps the most striking of the correspondences between *BB* and Q1, I have already shown that in the position of the nunnery scene Q1 is in error:[4] the book with which Hamlet enters in both Q1 and Q2 (II.ii.168) is required for the fishmonger dialogue which follows immediately in Q2 and not for the nunnery scene which follows in Q1, where the fishmonger dialogue is postponed. *BB* has neither book nor fishmonger, but the order which it shares with Q1 cannot be the original.

The most curious thing about *BB* is not just that it sometimes corresponds with Q1 but that it combines features belonging to Q1 with others belonging to Q2. Echoes of the memorial reconstruction merge with others of the genuine text. Duthie lists 21 instances of agreement between *BB* and Q1 where Q2 differs; but against these he has 36 instances of *BB* in agreement with Q2 where Q1 differs.[5] From this textually hybrid character of *BB*

1. Since in what is material to this discussion F agrees with Q2, it may henceforth be ignored.
2. Cf. above, pp. 31–2.
3. See above, pp. 19ff.
4. Cf. above, p. 32.
5. Very clearly set out on pp. 240–52. Bullough thinks that the parallels with Q1 are 'more significant with regard to action and characters' (pp. 21–2). But this really only means that in a few conspicuous deviations one memorial

Creizenach long ago inferred that it descended from a stage-version of *Hamlet* which itself contained ingredients of both Q2 and Q1. In some sense this must be true, but whereas Creizenach postulated a version already deviant from Q2 from which Q1 would then move away farther, Duthie (pp. 255–7) pointed to some specific instances in which Q1 was manifestly intermediate between Q2 and *BB*. In the passage where Hamlet expects the King to betray himself on witnessing his crime (III.ii.80–1) he says in Shakespeare 'If his occulted guilt Do not itself unkennel' without defining what the signs of guilt will be. But *BB* has '*wo er sich entfärbt oder alterirt*', 'if he turn pale or change colour', which, save that it puts the condition affirmatively, exactly corresponds to Q1 'If he doe not bleach, and change'. Q1 appears to derive its word *bleach* from a recollection, and perhaps a misunderstanding, of an earlier passage, in which Hamlet says 'if a do *blench*' (II.ii.593); and if this is so, then it must have been *bleach* that gave rise to *entfärbt* and the converse is not possible. In another example (I.ii.115–16) we find the King saying to Hamlet in Q2 'We beseech you . . . to remaine Heere in the cheare and comfort of our eye', in Q1 'let mee intreat you stay in Court', and in *BB* '*bleibt bey uns am Hofe*', 'stay with us at court'. Here Duthie shows that Q1 has not simply paraphrased Q2; it has substituted words remembered from another passage, where the King makes a similar request to Rosencrantz and Guildenstern: Q2 'I *entreate* you both . . . That you voutsafe your rest heere *in our Court*' (II.ii.10–13). Since Q1 incorporates both the entreating and the court while *BB* has only the court, *BB* must derive from Q1 and not the other way about. The effect of such examples is of course to confirm that *BB* has developed out of Shakespeare's play and to refute again the notion that it is based on the *Ur-Hamlet*.

Yet if *BB*'s inheritance from Shakespeare had come solely via Q1, it could not correspond with Q2 as it does in details which Q1 lacks. To account for its combination of elements from both there are a number of possible explanations. An acting version of Shakespeare's play might have had adjustments made to it when a quarto became available; but the memorial characteristics of *BB* suggest that any influence from the printed text was small. A likelier explanation, as Duthie saw, is that an acting text was evolved by a group of actors whose collective memory embraced

---

version influenced another. It is the number of parallels in unobtrusive details that is 'more significant' for textual relationships, and both Creizenach and Duthie are emphatic that the closer affinities are with Q2. So too Greg, *SFF*, p. 308.

more than one version of the play. In the conditions of Shakespeare's time, with bands of strolling players readily forming and re-forming, it is not difficult to envisage the coming together of some who could draw on recollections of having acted the authentic text with others who knew only the Q1 version.

In such a mingling of versions it is also possible of course that a contribution might be made by an actor or actors whose memory was of the *Ur-Hamlet*, of which a relic might thus survive. Those scholars who have liked to suppose that *BB* derives from the *Ur-Hamlet* rather than from Shakespeare's *Hamlet* have often fastened upon the episode of the banditti commissioned to kill Hamlet and tricked into killing one another (*BB* iv.i, v.ii); and Duthie himself maintained, erroneously, that this non-Shakespearean episode in *BB* was a relic of the *Ur-Hamlet*. It will be remembered that in Belleforest on the voyage to England Hamlet reads and alters the letters of his escorts so that it is not he but they who are put to death. Except for the suppression of Hamlet's adventures in England and the introduction of the pirates to effect his prompt return to Denmark, what happens in Belleforest is substantially what happens in Shakespeare; and the natural assumption is that Shakespeare found Belleforest's version of events, with or without the pirates, in the *Ur-Hamlet*. The idea that the *Ur-Hamlet* substituted the quite different banditti episode in which Hamlet disposed of his two companions on an island and that Shakespeare then reverted to Belleforest is implausible on the face of it; and moreover, the whole business of these banditti is of a piece with the other farcical accretions in *BB*.[1] What persuades Duthie that it was in the *Ur-Hamlet* is his belief that it contributed certain details to Q1. It is here, in its account of Hamlet's voyage, that Q1 deviates farthest from the genuine text. Instead of having the events of the voyage told by Hamlet to Horatio (iv.vi, v.ii. 1–56), Q1 in a scene not paralleled in Q2 has them told by Horatio to the Queen; and although the events, minus the pirates, are substantially the same, the account of them is muddled and incomplete. When Q1 says of Hamlet on board ship,

> Being crossed by the contention of the windes,
> He found the Packet sent to the king of *England*,

the connection of the two things is not obvious; and although Q1 goes on to tell how Hamlet changed the instructions in the packet so that the doom appointed for him was diverted to his companions, all it says about how he got back to Denmark is

1. Cf. Bullough, pp. 46–7; Greg, *SFF*, p. 306.

He being set ashore, they went for *England.*

The curious touch about 'the contention of the windes', which is not heard of in Q2, appears to connect with the 'contrary winds' (*contrairen Wind*)[1] in *BB* (v. ii), which led the ship to anchor off an island where Hamlet went ashore with the banditti and they shot one another while he escaped. What Duthie infers is that Q1 has supplied some gaps in its ill-remembered story from a recollection of a different episode which has survived in *BB* and which, for it to be thus recollected, must have figured in the *Ur-Hamlet.*

This, I am afraid, is where Duthie is mistaken. To begin with, a 'contention of the winds' and 'contrary winds' are not the same, although. in a confused memory one might suggest the other. *Contrary* winds blow against voyagers whose progress they impede; but a *contention* of the winds occurs when they blow against one another in a turmoil of the elements. There is no hint of a storm in *BB*, and Q1 gets the hint for it, I believe, not from some presumed original of *BB* but from the turbulence in Q2. There Hamlet says

> Sir in my hart there was a kind of fighting
> That would not let me sleepe,   (v. ii. 4–5)

and it was because he could not sleep that he got up and, as Q1 puts it, 'found the Packet'. Hamlet's sleeplessness is not mentioned in Q1, but it is surely that which tacitly connects his being 'crossed by the contention of the windes' with his finding of 'the Packet'. A confused recollection of the Shakespearean text has transferred the disturbance within Hamlet to the elements around him, so that the 'fighting' in his heart becomes the 'contention' of the winds. And when the contention of winds in Q1 gives rise in due course to the contrary winds of *BB*, this affords yet another example of the genesis of *BB* in places where it develops from the authentic Shakespearean text by way of the perversions of Q1. As for Q1's reference to Hamlet's 'being set ashore', that too has nothing to do with anchoring off an island nor the machinations of banditti, and never could have seemed to have except to the minds of scholars under the intoxicating influence of *BB*. What it has to do with is the Queen's question,

> But what became of *Gilderstone* and *Rossencraft*?

– to which Horatio replies,

> He being set ashore, they went for *England,*

the point of this being that they went forward to their doom

1. The more so since translators always render this as plural.

leaving Hamlet behind. Where he was 'set ashore' is not specified, it is true, but it does not need to be because in the first line of this Q1 scene Horatio has already told the Queen and us that Hamlet is 'safe arriv'de in *Denmarke*'. With no word of the pirates, Q1 also leaves untold how he came to be '*set* ashore' in Denmark; but it evidently remembers a passage in Q2 where Hamlet announces in a letter to the King, 'I am *set* naked on your kingdom' (iv.vii. 42). Thus Q1's account of Hamlet's voyage, for all its short-comings, is one version and not two: it contains nothing that is not derived from the Q2 text, needs and receives no enlightenment from *BB*, and gives no support whatever to the theory that *BB* preserves an episode from the *Ur-Hamlet*.[1]

This disposes of Duthie's 'strongest point' (p. 263) for supposing that *BB*, while primarily based on Shakespeare's play, yet shows traces of the *Ur-Hamlet*. Nevertheless, there remains one series of possible clues less easy to dismiss. *BB* oddly corresponds with Belleforest in some details which Shakespeare omits. Hamlet vows that his vengeance will be such that 'posterity shall talk of it for ever'.[2] The Queen blames herself for Hamlet's madness, which she thinks due to her marriage, though in *BB* not, as in Belleforest, as a punishment from God.[3] Hamlet accuses her of hypocritical tears.[4] All of these are sentiments quite natural in the circumstances; but together they suggest more than coincidence, and since it is difficult to postulate an actor with a first-hand knowledge of Belleforest, the most probable explanation is that they came into *BB* from the *Ur-Hamlet*, and if so through an actor who had taken part in it.[5] We must therefore accept that some

1. The issue is not affected by the anonymous play *Alphonsus Emperor of Germany*, which has been linked by Bowers with *BB* and *Hamlet* (*MLN*, xlviii, 101–8) but appears to be a red herring. In this two German peasants have orders from the Emperor to kill a prince, who tricks them by shamming dead, after which one kills the other for the spoils and is himself killed by the prince, who then, like Hamlet in *BB*, finds the incriminating letters. But such resemblances as there are between this play, *BB*, and *Hamlet* show the use of the same stock motifs rather than a common source in the *Ur-Hamlet*, about which nothing could in any case be inferred from a play of very uncertain date. Cf. Bullough, pp. 46–7.

2. *BB*, i.vi; cf. Gollancz, pp. 194, 216.   3. *BB*, iii.vi; Gollancz, p. 208.

4. *BB Crocodillsthränen* (iii.v); Belleforest *un pleur dissimulé* (see above, p. 91 and n.).

5. Cf. above, pp. 33–4, and Duthie, pp. 200–4, 260. Further instances of survivals from Belleforest in *BB* have been suggested, especially by Stabler, most of them unconvincing because commonplace or not parallel (*Sh.Studs.*, v, 97–105). The attempt to argue, on the strength of them, that *BB* simply derives from the *Ur-Hamlet* and not from Shakespeare is made possible only by ignoring the whole of the contrary evidence.

vestiges of Shakespeare's source-play may have been preserved in *BB*; and these may even suggest that the source-play followed Belleforest fairly closely: but since they can only be ascribed to the *Ur-Hamlet* when there is nothing to correspond to them in Shakespeare, *BB* cannot show us, except negatively, the use that Shakespeare made of it.

BB emerges as a very mixed text. It is essentially an acting version, initially put together, it appears, by a varied group of actors with experience of different *Hamlets* and a readiness to put their memories to use, and subsequently much debased, as it passed through generations of actors, by progressive adaptations and corruptions. It seems to preserve a few pre-Shakespearean strands, but for the most part it originates in Shakespeare. It has therefore a unique interest in revealing the transformation his play could undergo in the course of a century or so of popular performance. What it cannot reveal, unless in some fragmentary relics of Belleforest, is what has been most looked for in it, the content of the *Ur-Hamlet*.

This necessary conclusion is likely, I am aware, to be unwelcome. Scholars and sentimentalists alike will continue to hanker after a sight of the lost *Hamlet* which served as Shakespeare's source. But the belief that this is somehow to be seen through *BB*, with or without the help of Q1, has for far too long bedevilled the study of *Hamlet*, which will do better without the mirage.

7. CRITICAL INTRODUCTION[1]

(i) Problems

Few, I imagine, would challenge the assertion that '*Hamlet* is the most problematic play ever written by Shakespeare or any other playwright'.[2] Of its numerous problems some are adventitious, arising from the texts in which it has survived or from its indefin-

---

1. For an outline of *Hamlet* criticism, see '*Hamlet* Then and Now', *SS 18* (1965), 34–45. In the present critical essay I have occasionally incorporated a phrase or sentence from this and other previously published essays: 'The Tragedy of Revenge in Shakespeare and Webster', *SS 14* (1961), 45–9; 'Hamlet and Ophelia', Brit. Acad. Shakespeare Lecture, 1963; 'Fortinbras and Laertes and the Composition of *Hamlet*', *Rice U.Studs.*, LX (1974), 95–108; 'Hamlet and the Fishmonger', *Sh.Jahr.* (West), 1975, 109–20. A number of points are further elaborated in the LONGER NOTES, but only the more important can be given cross-reference.

2. Harry Levin, *SQ*, VII, 105.

able relation to the source-play which has not. Some, we may as well admit, are due to ambiguities left unresolved by the dramatist; more have been created by the critics: but some permanent and deep-seated problems of the meaning of the play remain.

For his part, Shakespeare seems undecided whether Horatio is in Elsinore as a visitor or a denizen;[1] he describes Fortinbras as a hot-headed rebellious youth and then presents him as a dignified commander fit to inherit the realm;[2] he allows 'young Hamlet' at one point to be thirty.[3] These, however, are less 'problems' to be solved than local discrepancies which have to be accepted – sometimes even gratefully for the clues they give to Shakespeare's mind. But audiences, and still more readers, have looked for a kind of consistency Shakespeare does not always bother to supply. Perhaps no play has suffered more than *Hamlet* from what Waldock christened the 'documentary fallacy',[4] the habit of treating a work of fiction as though it were a record of historical fact, from which inferences about other supposed facts could be drawn. Hence the critical arguments as to which were the 'dozen or sixteen lines' which Hamlet contributed to *The Murder of Gonzago* and when he wrote the letter to Ophelia which Polonius produces, not to mention such awkward questions as who could have witnessed Ophelia's drowning without attempt to save her. Most such 'problems', I suppose, have now gone from the critical repertory: we no longer much ask with Bradley, 'Where was Hamlet at the time of his father's death?'; but there is still an active controversy on why Claudius failed to react to the dumb-show, about which the text is equally silent.[5]

The proliferation of such unanswerable questions is not, I think, caused by the play's having more loose ends than most, but rather by its unrivalled imaginative power. *Hamlet* is so much a part of our lives that it encourages us to expect its people to behave as they would in the real world. We impute our attitudes to them. An amusing instance is afforded by a recent comment that foolish counsellors should take warning from the 'fidgety impatience' of

1. I.iv.12–13 LN.

2. Cf. above, p. 100, and see *Rice U.Studs.*, LX, 95–108.

3. V.i.139–57 LN.

4. A. J. A. Waldock, *Hamlet: A Study in Critical Method*, p. 78 and *passim*, but especially *Sophocles the Dramatist*, pp. 11 ff.

5. III.ii.133 S.D. LN. And even while this book is in the press an article appears maintaining that Hamlet's 'tenders' of 'affection' to Ophelia (I.iii.99–100) must have been made after his return from Wittenberg for his father's funeral and that they therefore 'prove' that he is trying to replace a dead love-object with a living one (*EC*, XXXI, 116).

Laertes during Polonius's advice.[1] Ignoring the dramatic function
of the episode, this tells us less about the play than about the
critic, and perhaps the stage production. Such additions to the
text may lead to serious misinterpretation. It is generally assumed
that Hamlet was offended with Ophelia because she refused his
letters and took part in a little plot to test him; but nothing that
he says suggests this, and preconceptions of what must be in his
mind have distracted attention from the evidence of what is.[2]
Sometimes criticism has even denied what is in the text: for well
over a century it was almost universally accepted that when
Hamlet proposed to defer his revenge till he could send the King's
soul to damnation, he could not have meant what he said. In our
day a race of critics has arisen who maintain that Hamlet should
have disapproved of his father's ghost as much as they do themselves.[3]

The desire to explain what the play does not by supplying the
characters with motives and reactions on the model of our own
is part of that demand for psychological realism which has dominated dramatic criticism since the eighteenth century, encouraged
by the rise of the novel, which can trace the inner workings of its
characters' minds to a degree that a play, presenting its persons
through speech and action, cannot.[4] The greatest of all solilo-
quizers, who does so much to lay bare his heart and mind to us,
yet leaves some of his actions with their motives undisclosed; so
that attempts to understand them created the problem of Hamlet's character. By the end of the nineteenth century, the great
age of character criticism as of the novel, it was possible to read,
in a work significantly published in the year of Bradley's *Shakespearean Tragedy*, that *Hamlet* 'is, in relation to its motive and main
interest, a purely psychological study, and to that study the whole
action of the drama is subordinated'.[5] It is no less possible, however, to see the matter in reverse, with the 'action of the drama'
pre-eminent in shaping a significant design while the 'psychological' interest of the characters' motivation has a subsidiary
importance in giving the action plausibility. The play is organ-
ized, for example, about the crime which is already past when it

1. *TLS*, 1980, p. 392.
2. See below, pp. 149–51.
3. 'If this ghost turns out to be one who clamours for revenge, then we have
every reason to suppose that Shakespeare entertained some grave doubts about
him' (L. C. Knights, *An Approach to 'Hamlet'*, p. 46). See below, p. 154.
4. See *SS 18*, 36–40.
5. Churton Collins, *Studies in Shakespeare*, 1904, p. 289. Cf. Bradley, p. 89,
'The whole story turns upon the peculiar character of the hero.'

begins but which is re-enacted in its central scene, and this re-enactment is plausibly motivated by Hamlet's thought that the Ghost may be a deceiving spirit. But those who interpret this thought either as an excuse for hesitation or as a valid reason for delay extend its 'psychological' significance with small warrant from the text. Hamlet's madness is useful to account for such strange episodes as the visit to Ophelia's closet and the fight with Laertes at her grave; but – in this unlike Ophelia's – it does not illumine what the episodes it occasions contribute to the play; and this no doubt is why they have left most critics at a loss. When we make inferences about the characters from Hamlet's declaration that his madness and not he has hurt Laertes and from Ophelia's lie that her father is at home, we find ourselves ascribing to them casuistries and subterfuges which the play may not intend. 'Hamlet sees himself as Pyrrhus', says Clifford Leech, percipiently noting resemblances; and he goes on to infer that Hamlet 'sensed a relationship between himself and Claudius'.[1] But the perception of affinities between them takes place in the dramatist's mind rather than in Hamlet's. In having Hamlet recite the lines describing Pyrrhus, as in having the Queen speak the account of Ophelia's death, there is a fine dramatic point – what is said reflects back upon the speaker – but it is not one that has to do with characterization or psychology.

All this is not to say that psychological verisimilitude is unimportant. The characters in what they do must at least not offend credibility. Shakespeare is justly famed for holding the mirror up to human nature; but a Shakespearean play may have purposes which reach beyond those of its characters. One of the problems for us now, in an age which has lost familiarity with those Elizabethan techniques which allow actions to speak for themselves, is to detect when such purposes are present and to assess the significance of actions which contribute to them.

Even the perennial questions, Why does Hamlet delay his revenge? ('the problem of problems', as it has been called), Why is Hamlet so cruel to Ophelia?, seem to invite something more than a psychological explanation. Hamlet himself seems always to be asking questions much bigger and more searching than those we ask of him. When we expect him to be discussing whether and why and how he should revenge, he is liable to be ruminating on the mysteries of our being:

1. 'The Hesitation of Pyrrhus', in D. W. Jefferson (ed.), *The Morality of Art*, pp. 47–9.

> What is a man
> If his chief good and market of his time
> Be but to sleep and feed? A beast, no more.

This sounds very like a retort to his earlier eulogy,

> What piece of work is a man, how noble in reason, how infinite in faculties, . . . in apprehension how like a god.

The consciousness of neglecting his revenge draws forth the protests that 'godlike reason' was not given 'to fust in us unus'd'. Ideas of man's dual nature – mind and body, reason and appetite, blood and judgment, god and beast – are recurrent. Ophelia provokes Hamlet not to resentment at her having 'denied his access' but to the bewildered exclamation, 'What should such fellows as I do crawling between earth and heaven?' And the central act of the play, the act in which he is both to 'affront Ophelia' and to 'catch the conscience of the King', launches itself forth in a soliloquy on the choice of 'To be or not to be'. Many critics, feeling this a little remote from the business Hamlet has in hand, have persuaded themselves that it somehow conceals a debate on whether to act or not to act, to kill or not to kill the King.[1] But Hamlet voices a larger dilemma than this. Practical as he can be on occasion, the big moral and metaphysical issues are rarely far from his mind. So much is this so that some criticism in our century has maintained that, for all the endless controversy over the character of Hamlet, the hero himself is less important than the views he expresses on the subject of human life. Thus C. S. Lewis in a lecture aptly titled 'Hamlet: the Prince or the Poem?' suggested that the poem was more important than the prince, and that Hamlet's speeches derive their interest less from the man who speaks them than from the things he speaks of.[2] But this, I think, is a somewhat dangerous line. For *Hamlet* is essentially dramatic, and in all the hero's utterances about the human lot we must retain an awareness of who it is who utters them and how they relate to his own particular predicament – the predicament, quite simply, of a man in mourning for his father, whose murder he is called on to avenge. Perhaps we may say that it is only this prince who could evoke this poem. For it is from the character that the command to revenge assumes in

1. III.i.56–88 LN.

2. 'I believe that we read Hamlet's speeches with interest chiefly because they describe so well a certain spiritual region through which most of us have passed . . . rather than because of our concern to understand how and why this particular man entered it.' (Brit. Acad. Shakespeare Lecture, 1942, p. 15.)

the dramatist's imagination that the profoundest meanings of the play arise.

Bradley himself derived from the action of the play a sense of 'some vaster power' working through the deeds of men; and he recognized that 'concentration on the character of the hero is apt to withdraw our attention from this aspect of the drama'.[1] Tillyard, in seeking, like Lewis, to reverse the critical emphasis, insists that 'criticism has erred in treating the profundities and paradoxes and the turnings of Hamlet's mind as the substance of the play rather than as the means of expressing another substance';[2] but this stops short of explaining how one conveys the other. 'The difficulty, in ultimate terms,' says Waldock, 'is to know what the play is really about'.[3] He is not alone in finding 'suggestions of meanings not fully worked out in the action'.[4] This surely has something to do with Eliot's feeling that Hamlet 'is dominated by an emotion which is . . . in *excess* of the facts as they appear'. Unfortunately Eliot was led to exaggerate the 'excess' by his limited and indeed perfunctory view of the play – apparent in his accepting from Robertson 'that the essential emotion of the play is the feeling of a son towards a guilty mother' – and so to pronounce the play, notoriously and absurdly, 'an artistic failure'.[5] But many others have felt that *Hamlet* is concerned with more than its revenge plot can easily support. A recent essay by Philip Brockbank has duly observed that 'Shakespeare takes only a limited interest in Hamlet as an avenger. His deeper interest is in Hamlet the tragic-hero, required to take upon himself the moral distress of the whole community.'[6] But this again, in discussing the 'deeper interest', does little to pursue the connection between the two.

What, then, is the relation between Hamlet's task of revenge and the universal mysteries of man's being which occupy his mind? How is it that the first is able to suggest the second? This, as I see it, is the fundamental problem in *Hamlet* if the play is to be revealed as a coherent dramatic design and its significance

1. pp. 171–4.
2. *Shakespeare's Problem Plays*, p. 28.
3. *Hamlet*, p. 7.
4. *Sophocles the Dramatist*, p. 169.
5. *Selected Essays*, 1932, pp. 143–6. Cf. below, p. 134, n. 2. Unfortunately, though inevitably, so startling a pronouncement attracted more attention than the more perceptive judgment that '*Hamlet* the play is the primary problem, and Hamlet the character only secondary' (p. 141). For a reply to Eliot, see F. Fergusson, *The Idea of a Theater*, pp. 99–102.
6. 'Hamlet the Bonesetter', *SS 30*, 110.

understood. No one will be so foolish as to suppose that a definitive answer is either attainable or, since the greatness of a work of art is in its infinite suggestiveness, desirable. But I am bold enough to believe that an answer is nevertheless not impossible.

(ii) *The prince and the brother kings*

It seems proper to begin where Shakespeare must have begun himself. A man who is murdered by his brother is to be avenged by his son: that is the essential *donnée* of the story of Hamlet as it came to Shakespeare from Saxo through Belleforest and, with the addition of the father's ghost, the old lost play of *Hamlet* which was on the stage in the 1590s. In this plot of a son's revenge he found the basis of a structure linking beginning, middle, and end. An exposition opening with the ghost of the father already dead and then presenting his successor has its tremendous climax in the revelation of the murder to the son, who accepts the charge of revenge. In the big central scene the murder is not once but twice re-enacted on the stage and the murderer confronted with his crime. But as this also alerts him to the threat of vengeance, it precipitates counter-plots which lead to a catastrophe in which the hero at length achieves revenge at the moment of his own death. In the three ceremonial court scenes in which at the beginning, middle, and end son and uncle face one another in mutual but undeclared hostility, there is a kind of theatrical symmetry.

The first of them, placed between the Ghost scenes, contributes to an exposition shaped by the triangle of father, uncle, son. The much-praised opening scene has already presented to us in the most startling way the figure 'like the King that's dead', and the expectancy created by this silent apparition has come to focus on 'young Hamlet', who must be told about the ghost, they say, because

> This spirit, dumb to us, will speak to him.

Before we even see the hero of the play, he is already known to us as the son of a dead king and the intended recipient of a message from his ghost. Now that we do see him he appears at court isolated and in black, mourning for his father. His resentment of the new king manifests itself as soon as he is addressed:

> But now, my cousin Hamlet, and my son . . .
> How is it that the clouds still hang on you?
> —Not so, my lord, I am too much in the sun.

In this first quibbling retort Hamlet repudiates the new king's attempt to claim him for his son and declares his allegiance to his father. His resistance to the efforts of King and Queen to console him for his father's death makes the burden of the dialogue which follows. What Shakespeare stresses from the first is the bond between son and father. And when the son at length faces his father's ghost it is this that will be stressed again as the compulsion to revenge:

> If thou didst ever thy dear father love . . .

Or, what is practically synonymous,

> If thou hast nature in thee . . .

An antithesis between the brother kings is part of the moral and dramatic structure. Before we behold the reigning king, the dead king has already been presented, through the Ghost, as a man of heroic valour; and as soon as the new king has left the stage, the first of Hamlet's soliloquies explicitly contrasts them. And then, the soliloquy dividing and yet linking the two halves of the scene, our attention swings back to the former king as the watchers duly come to 'young Hamlet' to report the apparition. Thus, while the action is moving forward towards the moment when Hamlet will encounter the Ghost, his attitude to his dead father is being impressed upon us. This 'goodly king' appears in his mind's eye as a model of human perfection:

> A was a man, take him for all in all:
> I shall not look upon his like again.

After his distrust of the new king who seeks to usurp his father's place in his affection comes this veneration for his father, whom, in between these two episodes, the soliloquy praises as

> So excellent a king, that was to this
> Hyperion to a satyr.

Hyperion of course is the god of the sun in human form and a satyr is a creature half man half beast; so that this early image vividly suggests to us that dual nature of man upon which Hamlet will repeatedly reflect. We must never forget that the two are brothers. When one destroys the other, their kinship adds to murder something 'most foul, strange and unnatural'. Yet what is unnatural is also natural: the god and the beast in human nature belong to the same life-tree. Aristotle found it best for tragedy when brother killed brother or child parent; and one begins to see what it was in the old Danish legend that laid hold of Shakespeare's imagination. The brother kings are never reduced to allegory, but in them we are aware of the good and evil in man, the magnanimous soul and the sensual appetite, represented in the persons and actions of the play. The situation in which Hamlet finds himself before he as yet knows anything of the murder is one in which the godlike man is dead and supplanted by the beastlike. And what is worse, his own mother has ceased to mourn Hyperion and taken the satyr-brother in his place, becoming worse than a beast herself:

> A beast that wants discourse of reason
> Would have mourn'd longer.

The surprise is not that her son should long to be free of his 'sullied flesh', but that Eliot, a poet so responsive to imagery and myth, should think Hamlet's grief excessive for what is here suggested. With the bad man in possession of queen and kingdom, Hamlet's plight extends to the whole 'state of Denmark', where what is 'rotten', we may say, is that the god in man has succumbed to the beast. This we may find reflected in that drunken revelry which gives Denmark, in the word from Nashe which Hamlet makes his own, its 'swinish' reputation and which echoes through the night even as we wait for the Ghost to appear. The dreadful tale it ultimately tells further develops the likeness to the brutes:

> Ay, that incestuous, that adulterate beast
> . . . won to his shameful lust
> The will of my most seeming-virtuous queen.

For

> lust, though to a radiant angel link'd,
> Will sate itself in a celestial bed
> And prey on garbage.

The vocabulary here, alternating words like *angel* and *celestial* with those verbs of animal connotation, *sate* and *prey*, suggests a descent from heavenly embraces to bestial feeding. This is the condition of things that Hamlet is called on to redeem. In the words of the Ghost's command,

> Let not the royal bed of Denmark be
> A couch for luxury and damned incest.[1]

Hamlet's task, when placed in the widest moral context, is not

---

1. This passage receives little comment from those who think the command is one that Hamlet should resist (see below, p. 154). Miss Prosser, however, while claiming to read 'without preconceptions', sees in such exhortations a morbid obsession with the sensual (pp. 134–5).

simply to kill his father's killer but by doing so to rid the world of the satyr and restore it to Hyperion. It is the son of a murdered father, but also perhaps the scion of the human stock, who can be heard in that lament which ends the first act:[1]

> The time is out of joint. O cursed spite,
> That ever I was born to set it right.

It is characteristic of the play to avoid artificially imposed patterns: the moral contrast between the brothers does not become schematic. But the pattern, once suggested, continues in the mind. It is momentarily revived when Hamlet remarks of the fickle public that those who 'would make mouths' at his uncle while his father lived now give good money for the new king's picture. And in the interview between Hamlet and his mother, so prominent in the sources, with its denunciation of her second marriage, the dramatist takes the opportunity to bring portraits of her two husbands into the centre of the play and through them to develop the antithesis which the comparison of 'Hyperion to a satyr' had begun. Hamlet depicts his father to her and to us:

> See what a grace was seated on this brow,
> Hyperion's curls, the front of Jove himself,
> An eye like Mars to threaten and command

– we remember the martial hero of the opening scene –

> A station like the herald Mercury
> New-lighted on a heaven-kissing hill . . .

Each separate feature in this portrait shows the majestic beauty of a god, while they combine together in a form

> Where every god did seem to set his seal
> To give the world assurance of a man.

This is a portrait of a man in his highest capability, the man whom Hamlet said was 'all in all'. And the rule of this complete man has been stolen (it is Hamlet's word) by 'a king of shreds and patches'. After the description of the godlike king one might perhaps have expected a companion portrait in terms of the beast. Shakespeare's dynamic scene, again, avoids such formal symmetries; yet the bestial character of the second king comes out in

1. The act-divisions are of course not Shakespeare's (see above, p. 65 and n.), but may nevertheless be used as a convenient register of the way the action is disposed. Except for the premature ending of Act III they correspond to the natural divisions of the subject. The end of Act I corresponds with the end of the exposition.

the ensuing dialogue in images of appetite and lust. Hamlet marvels how his mother could cease 'to feed' on her 'fair mountain' and – in another brutish verb – 'batten on this moor'. The coupling of her second marriage shows her

> In the rank sweat of an enseamed bed,
> Stew'd in corruption, honeying and making love
> Over the nasty sty.

It is just as Hamlet is beginning a tirade against his father's 'murderer' that he is suddenly interrupted by the reappearance of the Ghost, as though the dramatist means to reinforce the contrast between the brother kings by bringing the dead one back on to the stage at the centre of the play and showing Hamlet's father yet again 'in his habit as he liv'd'.

Yet Shakespeare's purposes are rarely single. This is not the only reason for the Ghost's return. When the Ghost parted from Hamlet on the battlements its last words were 'Remember me', and Hamlet swore in a twenty-line soliloquy to do precisely that; but now on its reappearance the Ghost's first words are 'Do not forget', the same command repeated with a significant shift of phrase. When the Ghost first called on him to revenge the murder Hamlet had exclaimed

> Haste me to know't, that I with wings as swift
> As meditation or the thoughts of love
> May sweep to my revenge.

Yet the first thought that occurs to him when he sees the Ghost again is that he has not swept, has not been swift, but the opposite:

> Do you not come your *tardy* son to chide,
> That, laps'd in time and passion, *lets go by*
> Th'important acting of your dread command?

And that this is the reason for its coming the Ghost explicitly confirms:

> This visitation
> Is but to whet thy almost blunted purpose.

The structure of the action emphasizes that the 'command' that made the climax of the exposition has failed to be performed.

(iii) *The sons*

This we shall find to be further emphasized by the behaviour of others in comparable situations. It is a principle of Shakespeare's

dramatic art to combine his plot with sub-plots which will repeat
or contrast with it, and his exposition accordingly has been ready
with other sons besides Hamlet. This is the more remarkable in
that the story in Saxo and Belleforest had no other sons; but it
had other men who were killed, in a challenge to single combat or
through hiding in the Queen's chamber, and these men could
become fathers with sons who would have to avenge them.
Whether Shakespeare himself invented these other sons or found
them in the *Ur-Hamlet* may ultimately not matter: what does is
the prominence he accords them from the start. In the first court
scene Hamlet is the last of three young men with whom the new
king has to deal; and while this, as the critics say,[1] by holding us
in suspense enhances the impact of the King's first words to
Hamlet, the important thing is that Fortinbras and Laertes here
lead up to Hamlet because their situations are designed to reflect
his. The first, as the son of a dead king and nephew of a reigning
king, invites obvious comparisons, and is actively campaigning to
right his father's alleged wrongs. Even in the opening scene,
before we had heard anything of 'young Hamlet', we had the
story of 'young Fortinbras', putting himself at the head of a band
of desperadoes and endangering the peace of Denmark in the
process. The harmful aspects of a son's zeal for restitution are
recognized from the first. Laertes has as yet no story, his father
not yet dead; but the permission granted him to return to France
neatly sets him against Hamlet, dissuaded from going back to
Wittenberg; and since he is to have a story later, we must know
who he is. This is the obvious reason why the King addresses him
by name four times in nine lines. If this also shows him to be in the
King's favour, it will prepare for their later alliance; but what
matters at the moment, as our attention is held on him, is that he
no less than Hamlet is being connected with his father. The King
will grant Laertes his request because of the service his father has
done to Denmark; he asks if he has his father's leave; and
Polonius's first speech in the play is to say that he has given it
him. Shakespeare's art of preparation here is as masterly as it is
unobtrusive; and before Laertes finally gets away there will be a
scene of leave-taking which not only introduces his sister and
with her the sub-plot of Hamlet's love but shows Laertes twice
receiving his father's blessing. With it comes a famous speech of
fatherly advice, which, though often regarded as a set-piece of
dubious relevance, and with a bored and fidgety Laertes even

1. Dover Wilson, *WHH*, p. 31; Granville-Barker, *Prefaces to Shakespeare*,
iii. 39.

turned into a joke, is not too long for its dramatic purpose of holding father and son together on the stage in their father-and-son relationship. The traditional nature of the maxims bestowed on a son being launched into the world[1] shows Polonius in his generic paternal role. This need not exclude an individual trait, and the turn for pompous platitude ('And it must follow as the night the day') we shall see more of later. The little scene with Reynaldo develops the fussy meddlesomeness and the love of subterfuge which will thrust Polonius into the King's affairs and take him along some secret corridors of power to his death behind the arras; but in this scene he is still basically the anxious father directing his attention, and ours, to the son away in France. No sooner have we seen Hamlet staggering under the weight of the Ghost's command than we are asked to imagine Laertes busy sowing some wild oats; so that when the play now goes on to concern itself with Polonius's daughter, already appearing 'affrighted' on the stage before Reynaldo has quite left it, we shall surely not forget that Polonius has also a son, who may, when his father is killed, even without a ghost to summon him, be expected to return. Nothing could be clearer than that this second revenge action is all along being envisaged within the dramatist's design.[2]

It is hardly less clear that Fortinbras, a son all 'hot' for action, was envisaged at the beginning as yet another revenger, who would contrast with Hamlet. But the strange thing about Fortinbras is that the sonship which brought him into the play is very soon being discarded.[3] When the ambassadors dispatched early in the first act have returned early in the second, his efforts for his father's lands are over, and his soldiers, diverted 'against the Polack', are no longer a threat to Denmark. We have still, I suppose, some expectation of seeing them in some other guise; but for the present Fortinbras waits, like Laertes, both ready to appear on the scene when, in the fourth act, occasion will demand them.

(iv) Embroilment

Before then the play has much to do. It is often spoken of as though it were loosely, even carelessly constructed, and it is true

1. I.iii. 58–80 LN.

2. Eliot's comment that 'there are unexplained scenes – the Polonius-Laertes and the Polonius–Reynaldo scenes – for which there is little excuse' (*Selected Essays*, p. 143) is staggering. A critic who fails to perceive that *Hamlet* is a play about sons and fathers seems unlikely to have anything useful to say about it. But see above, p. 127, n.5.

3. On the change in Fortinbras's role see *Rice U.Studs.*, LX, 95–108.

that it seems to proceed in a leisurely, meditative fashion, surrounding its exciting incidents with an amplitude of soliloquies and conversational exchanges and little digressive episodes with all the time in the world to enlarge upon the nature of the world. But through it all, and nowhere more than in these crowded middle acts, Shakespeare holds in assured grasp the many threads of his complicated plot. The 'antic disposition', which, however we interpret it, is Hamlet's immediate response to the charge the Ghost has laid upon him, receives prompt demonstration in Ophelia's account of the visit to her closet. By the time the threat of Fortinbras is disposed of Polonius is bursting with his theory of Hamlet's madness and Rosencrantz and Guildenstern, whose mission it will be to escort Hamlet to England (their sole function in Belleforest), have already come to court. Hamlet's encounters with these, as well as revealing something of his mind to us, baffle the King's attempts to ferret out his secret: at the same time they serve to announce the players, through whom Hamlet's assault upon the King's conscience will be able to take shape. And while the way is thus preparing for the focal scene which will give an image of the murder, opportunities are afforded for perspectives on Hamlet's role. The representation on the stage of what the Ghost has narrated is the outstanding example in the play of the device whereby a key incident or motif is repeated or anticipated in a different mode; but by a not dissimilar technique Hamlet's visit to Ophelia's closet is a proleptic emblem of the farewell we shall actually hear spoken in the 'nunnery' scene, and the speech which gives a taste of the Player's quality is used to bring in Pyrrhus, who, whatever you choose to make of him, in some sort images Hamlet. The account of how his sword 'seem'd i'th' air to stick' while he 'stood, and . . . did nothing' describes what a later scene will show. Finally, the performance of the Player in his part elicits from Hamlet a contrast with his own performance in his:

O what a rogue and peasant slave am I!

In this soliloquy at the end of the second act Hamlet reproaches himself for his inaction. A player reciting an imaginary tale about the slaughter of a king and father so identifies himself with his part that he actually sheds tears, while Hamlet, with a real cause of grief in the murder of the King his father, is making no response.

There will presently be another soliloquy which will likewise 'inform against' him; and since the soliloquy on the Player anticipates the soliloquy on Fortinbras, they ask to be considered together. Fortinbras, when at length we see him in the fourth act, is a rather different person from the headstrong youth we were prepared for at the opening of the play: it is not as a son seeking to recover what his father lost that he is ultimately juxtaposed with Hamlet. Yet he can still contrast with Hamlet as a man of action in a daring enterprise, and the sight of his army risking death for a worthless patch of ground comes to Hamlet as a rebuke. A second time confronted by a man who is greatly stirred when he seemingly need not be, Hamlet is again reminded of what he himself needs must but does not do. Superficially the Player reciting a speech and the prince leading troops to war have little in common; but the very difference between them serves to emphasize the one thing in which they are like one another and both unlike the hero of the play. Each gives himself whole-heartedly to his vocation and Hamlet neglects his.

Thus Fortinbras pairs with the Player in that each prompts Hamlet to a soliloquy of self-reproach. The Ghost's return to his 'tardy son' who 'lets go by' the 'acting' of the 'dread command' is doubly reinforced.

(v) Delay

Why, then, does Hamlet delay? After more than two centuries of debate on this celebrated question one detects in some quarters a critical weariness with it as intrinsically less important than it has been made to seem.[1] But a problem does not diminish because it becomes familiar; and Hamlet himself was of course the first to raise it, and to be defeated by it:

> I do not know
> Why yet I live to say this thing's to do.

It is true that there are some who deny that Hamlet procras-tinates. They point out that to kill a king surrounded by guards is not a simple matter, or that once Hamlet has dispelled a

---

1. 'It is not fashionable to consider Hamlet as a man who delays' (*EC*, XXIII, 1973, p. 232). 'The issue of Hamlet's delay . . . is, on the whole, a pretty boring one by now' (*Hudson Rev.*, XXVI, 1973, p. 518). Philip Brockbank calls it 'the question that academic courtesy should perhaps never again allow' (*SS 30*, 1977, p. 109); Ruth Nevo dismisses it as 'misconceived' (*Tragic Form in Shakespeare*, 1972, pp. 129–30). Both of these, however, see Shakespeare ex-ploiting delay and would probably agree with the writer in the *Hudson Review* (p. 520) that 'we should not be looking for an objective correlative that will explain Hamlet's motives but for an aesthetic one that might explain Shake-speare's'.

reasonable doubt of the Ghost's story he is given no opportunity.[1]
But that is not Hamlet's view. What he says is:

> I have cause, and will, and strength, and means
> To do't.

And I think we must conclude that it is not Shakespeare's view
either. Prominent in the centre of the play, the fact of delay,
whatever may be said about the reason for it, is not so easily
escaped.[2]

There have, however, been attempts to minimize the effect of
the soliloquies in which Hamlet reproaches himself for what he
has not done. Stoll is the chief of those who insist that delay is
simply inherent in the story.[3] The axiom 'No delay, no play' is
ultimately incontestable, but it need mean little more than that
the course of revenge, like that of true love, must not run smooth
too soon. In Saxo and Belleforest an interval of many years before
revenge is finally achieved suggests not procrastination but sustained determination and calls for no accusing comment. So long
as a hero is thought to be planning something it is unlikely to
strike us that he ought by now to have done it. It is often remarked
that through all the excitements of Shakespeare's unfolding drama
it would never occur to us that Hamlet was neglecting his revenge
if he refrained from saying so himself. Stoll finds that the charges
Hamlet brings against himself are not substantiated in the action
of the play. He maintains that Shakespeare, necessarily deferring
the achievement of revenge until the end, 'slurred over' the delay,
and that the soliloquies which draw attention to it serve to

1. E.g. Kittredge, pp. xi–xvi, making, notably, no reference to Hamlet's self-
reproaches or his confession to the Ghost; Hazelton Spencer, *The Art and Life
of William Shakespeare*, pp. 313–17.

2. Cf. D. G. James, *The Dream of Learning*, p. 47: 'Few of us will deny that
Hamlet's procrastination is the major fact in the play and that it was intended
by Shakespeare to be so.' The word *delay*, never used by or of Hamlet in the
play but traditional in criticism, is in some respects an unfortunate one: unlike
procrastination it may apply to either the agent or the event, and the ambiguity
has occasioned some critical confusion. Neither word is entirely satisfactory, for
although they correspond to Hamlet's *tardy*, by putting the emphasis on postponement they diminish the impression of neglect.

3. The point was trenchantly put by an 18th-century critic (said by Rawlin-
son to be George Stubbes) in *Some Remarks on the Tragedy of Hamlet*, 1736, p. 34:
'The poet was obliged to delay his hero's revenge; but then he should have contrived some good reason for it.' The romantic critics, of course, and their
successors thought he gave ample reason for it in the character of his hero. An
obvious fact often overlooked is that as determinants plot and character are not
mutually exclusive. It is hard to see why Stoll (see next note) should be so
anxious to relieve the hero of all responsibility.

reassure the audience that what the hero has not done yet he ultimately will.[1] I doubt if this explanation would occur to anyone who had not read *The Spanish Tragedy*, to which it is more appropriate; it is hardly necessary to remark that the soliloquies stress much more what is not done than what will be.

A different explanation is given by Waldock, who, in his brilliant little book on the critical reactions to *Hamlet*, holds that the self-reproach of these soliloquies, although indicative of delay, is only a minor motif of the play. The Player weeping for Hecuba, Fortinbras leading an army to capture a mere eggshell – these, he says, are little curiosities of life which happen to strike Hamlet's imagination and prompt him to consider his own conduct as he might not spontaneously have done, so that the notion of delay which they give rise to, although admittedly in the play, is not 'a prominent feature of the design'.[2] But the answer to this, I think, is that the doings of Fortinbras and the Player are more than interesting curiosities, because Hamlet's encounters with them are not chance encounters such as might occur in life. They occur in a dramatic composition; and why should they occur at all except to elicit from Hamlet the reflections which we have seen they do? And if the play without them would not give the impression of delay, may that not be the reason why the dramatist, so pointedly as it seems, has brought them in?

A closer look at these two soliloquies of self-reproach seems desirable. For all their matching reflections, they have an air of naturalness rather than contrivance. Characteristically there is no formal or stylistic correspondence: indeed the ruminations on the 'delicate and tender prince' are very different from the passionate outburst on 'this player here'. But there are detailed analogies of thought which reach below the surface and suggest an underlying dramatic purpose. The Player is moved to tears by a 'fiction', Fortinbras finds quarrel in a 'straw', in each case something of no substance. The one has his 'dream' of passion, the other his 'fantasy' of fame. Hamlet by contrast has a powerful and genuine incitement – 'a dear father murder'd' as the one soliloquy puts it, 'a father kill'd, a mother stain'd' as the other – yet according to the first soliloquy 'can say nothing', according to the second lets 'all sleep'. Each soliloquy asks whether he is therefore a 'coward';

---

1. *Hamlet: an Historical and Comparative Study*, 1919, pp. 16–25, 70. See also *Art and Artifice in Shakespeare*, 1933, pp. 94–101.

2. *Hamlet*, pp. 30, 85–6, 91–5. It is strange that Waldock should here slip into that confusion between life and art which, under the term 'documentary fallacy', he discusses with such beautiful lucidity elsewhere. See above, p. 123.

and each works to a climax of self-accusation, which leads to a resolve in terms appropriate to it. The speech on the Player ends:

> The play's the thing,
> Wherein I'll catch the conscience of the King,

that on the soldier:

> From this time forth
> My thoughts be bloody or be nothing worth.

In addition to such parallels there is also an unobtrusive but significant verbal link which joins the two soliloquies in a larger composition which embraces both. That a contrast between Fortinbras and Hamlet was in mind from the outset I hope I have shown; and how the contrast was to go can be seen with a little hindsight from the description of 'young Fortinbras' in the first scene as being of '*mettle* hot and full'. But Hamlet does not wait to meet Fortinbras in order to call himself 'a *dull* and muddy-*mettled* rascal'. In this phrase from the soliloquy on the Player one epithet contrasts with what we remember Fortinbras was and the other with what he still will be when the actual encounter with him spurs Hamlet's '*dull* revenge'. This repeated word *dull* shows Hamlet aware of having become what the Ghost had specially warned him not to be:

> I find thee apt.
> And *duller* shouldst thou be than the fat weed
> That roots itself in ease on Lethe wharf,
> Wouldst thou not stir in this.

It is when he becomes 'dull' that the Ghost returns. The play has manifestly been preparing from the first for the moment when Hamlet beside Fortinbras would be shown as 'dull', and it is as though the Player has slipped in to take Fortinbras's turn. Yet Fortinbras, although no longer the revenger we expected, still enters in his own turn, so that a design duplicates itself to produce two soliloquies, which achieve a natural symmetry. One preceding and one succeeding the reappearance of the Ghost, they unite in confirming by their 'dull' motif the 'almost *blunted* purpose' which occasions it. The 'dull' revenge reveals itself as a creative element in a developing pattern.

Hence a consideration of the two soliloquies makes it impossible to agree with Stoll that Hamlet's delay is in any way 'slurred over' or with Waldock that it is not prominent in the play's design. *Hamlet* is not simply a tragedy of revenge in which the crucial deed has to be deferred until the end: it is a play about a man with a deed to do who for most of the time conspicuously fails to do it.

Nor can we accept that delay is more talked about than exhibited. Why else do we have the prayer scene directly upon the play scene? Partly of course to show the King's conscience duly caught; but as he kneels, we see the revenger, like Pyrrhus, with drawn sword arrested and his enemy at his mercy; and when, unlike Pyrrhus, he puts his sword up, whatever we choose to think of his reasons, the tableau of an opportunity let slip is unforgettable.[1]

Moreover, the theme of purpose unfulfilled, of which Hamlet here presents a vivid and particular example, has its reflection in general terms elsewhere. Later in the play the King reminds another revenger how the human will is subject to 'abatements and delays'. Hamlet, in between the two soliloquies which lament his own inaction, has another soliloquy in which, looking beyond his own case to the case of humanity at large, he muses upon 'resolution' which is weakened by 'thought' until 'enterprises of great pitch and moment . . . lose the name of action'. The Player King, in those gnomic couplets which reduce large truths to truisms, plants the same thought like a motto in the centre of the play:

> What to ourselves in passion we propose,
> The passion ending, doth the purpose lose.

(vi) The central act

This speech of the Player King is but one of many things which, in the shaping of *Hamlet*, demand and receive a central place. The soliloquies of self-reproach for a deed undone, one at the end of the second act and the other near the beginning of the fourth,[2] have made themselves into a kind of frame for a sequence of crucial scenes which Shakespeare's easy mastery of the constructive art accommodates within the middle act. At the centre of all,

1. Cf. P. Alexander, *Shakespeare's Life and Art*, p. 157: 'Here Shakespeare has reduced almost to visual terms the whole of Hamlet's problem.' See III.iii. 89–95 LN (end).

2. In what we call IV.iv. But apart from the fact that the first three scenes are short (140 lines altogether), it is frequently observed that the traditional beginning of Act IV, first marked in the 1676 quarto, is unsatisfactory. (See IV.i n.) The phase of the action which culminates in the slaying of Polonius is not concluded when Hamlet lugs off the body but continues for three more scenes of aftermath. The link scene of Fortinbras would more suitably be the first of Act IV or, as some would have it, even the last of Act III.

with the nutshell truths inside it, is the play-within-the-play which re-enacts the murder. This also contains an image of the Queen as an inconstant wife. It is followed by the tableau of the inactive revenger, the 'pictures' of the Queen's two husbands, and the startling reappearance of the Ghost. The King is shown confessing, if not repenting, his sin, the Queen taxed with hers. Hamlet's verbal onslaught on his mother after the play balances his denunciation of Ophelia before it: revulsion from marriage is exhibited both in effect and cause. In and around these highly dramatic scenes a seemingly unhurried amplitude persists in many brief encounters which are always liable to give some fresh perspective while sustaining the impression of natural court activity. Even as we prepare for the murder play, room is found for Hamlet to lecture the actors on their art, after it to mock Guildenstern with the recorder: we are reminded that art holds a mirror up to nature, but that the heart of a man's mystery is not easily plucked out. Polonius continues as a butt for Hamlet's wit, and the jest about the 'brute part' of killing him in a play is another of the little previews of what will later happen in earnest. Between the play scene which strengthens Hamlet's resolve to kill the King and the prayer scene which gives him his opportunity, Rosencrantz and Guildenstern, in reflections on 'the cess of majesty', remind us of what killing a king may mean. The necessary participation of Horatio in Hamlet's plot to catch the King permits a vignette of the man who, rising above fortune, is not 'passion's slave', and who thus contrasts with the revenger as well as with others with whom the revenger is himself contrasted. (The weeping Player, the time-serving Rosencrantz and Guildenstern immediately come to mind.) More than Horatio is of course involved here: indeed the character is not obviously correspondent, though equally not incompatible, with what we see of him elsewhere; but it brings a sketch of one kind of ideal man into the centre of the play. Most significantly perhaps, preluding the whole sequence is the soliloquy on 'To be or not to be', in which Hamlet's personal plight is transcended in the plight of being man suffering all the 'natural shocks that flesh is heir to', and he debates what will reveal itself as the basic issue of the play, whether this is better escaped from or endured.

In Shakespeare's art of construction here thematic expansion does not weaken, but combines with, concentration in the plot. In this central sequence the movement of events intertwines the two actions of revenge and marriage and brings them to their crises together. The meeting between Hamlet and Ophelia, now that we come to it, not only disappoints Polonius's plan but simultaneously tells Ophelia that Hamlet will not marry, the King that he *will* revenge:

> I say we will have no mo marriage. Those that are married already – all but one – shall live; the rest shall keep as they are.

This is still the gist of what Hamlet says to each of them in his excited comments as they watch the acting of the play. What one crisis means for Ophelia a later act will show. In the other, just when revenge brings its threat to a climax as the King is confronted with his guilt, it begins to recoil upon itself. Hamlet has his moment of triumph, which strengthens his grim resolve ('Now could I drink hot blood'), but his eagerness to kill the King is first paralysed in the prayer scene and then in the Queen's chamber frustrated by his killing Polonius instead. When the Ghost now suddenly returns and Hamlet stands convicted of neglect, the corpse of Polonius lies before them and the second revenge action is ready to begin.

(vii) *The second revenge*

This, along with the fate of Ophelia, occupies most of the fourth act. But before Polonius's son has time to arrive from France, Hamlet is shipped away from Denmark, meeting Fortinbras en route for Poland as he goes. Fortinbras, as we have seen, is no longer of interest as his father's son, and as an improving example makes a parallel with the Player; yet he is still sufficiently a revenging son to be, as before, a precursor for Laertes. The Fortinbras episode looks both ways: it closes that part of the play which emphasizes the inactive hero; but it simultaneously serves to introduce the counter-action which will present his opposite. 'Young Laertes', however, has apparently absorbed the fiery role originally envisaged for 'young Fortinbras'; for while Fortinbras's troops 'go softly on' obedient to command, the 'lawless resolutes' he 'shark'd up' at the beginning seem to have attached themselves to Laertes, who advances 'in a riotous head', while 'the rabble call him lord'. The threat to the peace of the kingdom is significantly not dropped: Shakespeare does not forget the dangers of vengeance let loose.

As the son of a murdered father Laertes is all the situation asks for. He appears indeed to have been conceived to exhibit, even to the verge of caricature, all that Hamlet as revenger might have been; and no soliloquy is needed to point the difference out. Laertes rushes into the presence, overbearing the King's officers:

critics who choose to suppose that the King's guards were an obstacle to Hamlet should note that it is just fifteen lines from 'Where is my Switzers? Let them guard the door' to 'The doors are broke.' When Laertes confronts the King with 'Where is my father? . . . How came he dead? . . . I'll be reveng'd Most throughly for my father', it can hardly fail to strike us that this is what Hamlet might have but has not said. It may also strike us, however, that whereas Hamlet took pains to establish the King's guilt by confronting him with his crime, Laertes challenges the King about a crime he has not done. In his second scene with the King, when initial fury has cooled down, Laertes is still unquestioningly confident: the thought of 'a noble father lost' is followed by 'But my revenge will come', and he welcomes the killer's return so that he may 'tell him to his teeth, "Thus diest thou"'. His every word and gesture invites comparison with Hamlet. When he says he would 'cut his throat i'th' church' we recall the sight of Hamlet sparing the King at prayer. Here is a man whose resolution does not pale with thought. Hamlet knew 'the dread of something after death' and the 'conscience' that makes men 'cowards'; but Laertes consigns 'conscience' to 'the profoundest pit' of hell and says 'I dare damnation'.

This effectively appalling speech (IV. v. 130–6) can only confirm our view that the contrast with Laertes is not one by which Hamlet is disparaged. And indeed those earlier 'occasions' which made Hamlet call himself 'dull' were not wholly to his discredit. For although there is fineness in the actor's tears and greatness in the soldier's quest of 'honour', yet tears that are shed for fictitious woes and honour that risks the lives of twenty thousand men for a plot of land not big enough to hold them are, it would seem, excessive. What we see of Laertes as revenger, unhesitant and violent, with neither awe nor scruple, careless both of the safety of the realm and of his own salvation, makes Hamlet's deficiencies in this part such as we can hardly wish away. In the end both meet their deaths because Hamlet is too magnanimous to 'peruse the foils', Laertes mean enough to take advantage of it.

(viii) The dual role

The contrast between these two revengers has often been remarked on. What is rarely emphasized, is mostly ignored altogether,[1] yet is vastly more important, is that the revenge of Laertes

1. Exceptions include N. Alexander, *Poison, Play, and Duel* (1971), and W. Hutchings in *Critical Quarterly*, xx (1978), 23–32, who observe that 'Hamlet is to

for his father involves Hamlet as its object. If Fortinbras is to re-cover his father's lands, he must make war on Denmark: and if Laertes is to take vengeance upon his father's killer, he must seek Hamlet's life. Fortinbras's war on Denmark Shakespeare, no doubt for good artistic reasons, decided not to pursue; but the campaign of Laertes brings into the play a second revenge action in which the first revenger appears at the other end. The hero charged with a deed of vengeance now also incurs vengeance. The situation of revenge is revealed as one in which the same man may act both parts; and the paradox of man's dual nature, compound of nobility and baseness, god and beast, repeatedly placed before us in the words of the play and represented in its action in the contrasting brother kings, is also exemplified in the hero's dual role. Both parts are poignantly recognized by Hamlet himself when, looking down at Polonius's dead body, he says,

> Heaven hath pleas'd it so,
> To punish me with this and this with me.

When he says, comparing himself with Laertes,

> By the image of my cause I see
> The portraiture of his,

he does not add that the image may be inverted. But if he sees himself mirrored in Laertes, it follows and must not escape us that the same mirror shows an image of Claudius in him. What was being prepared for from the beginning, with the careful build-up of Polonius's son alongside the Ghost of Hamlet's father, is subsequently acted out. The hero who is both punisher and punished finally kills the King only on receiving from Laertes his own death-wound.

It may seem strange that, for one who is eloquent on so many things, Hamlet does not expatiate more upon his dual role. Perhaps this is the reason why it has had so little critical notice.[1] But drama has other means than verbal statement of expressing

---

Laertes what Claudius is to Hamlet' (Hutchings), but do not enlarge on the moral and structural significance of this. Critical introductions by scholars of the highest distinction, from Kittredge to Kermode, do not so much as mention it. Nor is there any hint of it in either Bradley or Dover Wilson; nor, I think, in any of the other critics to whom this introduction refers.

1. The general silence has naturally made me ask myself whether I make too much of something which most of my predecessors have been content to make little or nothing of. But repeated reconsideration only confirms my view that the duality of the revenger, agent and victim, is the essential foundation on which the play is built, that it was seen to be so by Shakespeare, and that accounts of the play which ignore it are necessarily inadequate and usually misleading.

its designs, and what is apparent in the action (unlike the significance of Fortinbras and the Player, which action alone cannot bring out) need not also be expounded. Here at any rate we have, in the centre of the play, no less conspicuous than the re-enacting of the villain's crime, the revenger committing his own crime on the stage and brutally dragging the body off before our eyes. And unless we perceive the significance of Hamlet's guilty deed – the revenger of his father killing another man's father – it is difficult to see how the ending of the play can be understood, as too often it is not.[1] Moreover, the importance which the play attaches to Hamlet's dual role is confirmed and clearly signalled by its reflection in other figures. It is one of the functions of a play-within-a-play to give opportunity for such reflections, and it will by now be somewhat clearer in what sort Pyrrhus images Hamlet. The dramatic pause with arrested sword before

> Aroused vengeance sets him new awork

represents only a small part of Pyrrhus. Slayer of Priam the archetypal father, emblem of black designs and bloody execution, this savage and brutal killer,[2] when viewed through the outlandish diction as in some distorting mirror, presents a monstrous and horrific figure in which the alarming potentialities of both murderer and revenger are contained.[3] In the other inset play Lucianus, entering to poison the sleeping king, is abruptly introduced not as the brother we expect but as 'nephew to the King'.[4] Attempts to explain this as a Freudian slip on Hamlet's part gain nothing, I think, but anachronism. The double status of Lucianus, like the fearsome destructiveness of Pyrrhus, arises not so much in Hamlet's mind as in the design of his creator. Superimposed upon the image of Claudius is this sudden glimpse of Hamlet, so that Lucianus becomes identified with both.

It will hardly be necessary to observe that while murderer and revenger thus merge into one another, likeness does not imply equation. Pyrrhus, mercifully, is not Hamlet; and the guilt of Hamlet and Claudius is not the same. We require no treatise in ethics to differentiate between thrusting a sword into an intruder

1. Laertes's reference to 'my father's death' when Hamlet dies avenging *his* father's death reminds us of the wrong Hamlet has done. Each, while killing his father's killer, forgives and is forgiven by his own. See v. ii. 332–7 and nn.; *Rice U.Studs.*, LX, 106–7.

2. Cf. II. ii. 446 nn.

3. II. ii. 448–514 LN.

4. III. ii. 239 LN.

behind the arras and secretly poisoning a brother for his crown; and it is a critical aberration which attributes the rottenness in the kingdom to the prince who broods over its ills[1] rather than to the King who through fratricide 'stole' it. About such matters, notwithstanding some critical confusion, the play is, I take it, more than clear. (The poisoning, with a 'leperous distilment' of 'cursed hebenon' and the hideous disfigurement it brings, is made a deed of fabulous horror, but the 'wretched, rash, intruding fool' is killed contemptuously like 'a rat'.) Yet a pattern of analogies is able to suggest to us that the hero, although unlike Claudius he can deny 'a purpos'd evil', has yet 'hurt' his 'brother',[2] and that the prince who reveres Hyperion and aspires to redeem his kingdom has also the satyr in him.

It is, I think, in this dual role of Hamlet's that we may see the genesis of his character. For it is of course, in the dramatization of the Hamlet story, the role that determines the character, not the psychological make-up of the man that determines what he will do; and as soon as the spying counsellor, instead of being finished with, as in Saxo and Belleforest, when the pigs have finished with him, is allowed to leave a son behind him, the killer of this counsellor appears in a different light. So Hamlet has to become a different kind of revenger. Instead of the hero of concealed but unswerving purpose, celebrated for his courage and virtue, we have a hero who in seeking to right a wrong commits one, whose aspirations and achievements are matched by failures and offences, and in whom potentialities for good and evil hauntingly coexist. And this is what transforms the single-minded revenger into the complex representative of us all.

May we perhaps also find here the reason for Hamlet's delay? A hero whose tragic role it is to punish and be punished, to do evil along with good, might well be reluctant to perform it. That is not of course to say that Hamlet at the beginning of the play, as he mourns his father's death and his mother's marriage, can be prophetically aware that before the play is done it will be his destiny to kill Polonius and be killed by Laertes. But the play itself is aware of the destiny it is preparing for him and of that larger destiny of which the dual revenge becomes the symbol; and as the play shapes itself in the dramatist's imagination it is able to communicate to its hero a reluctance – not indeed to kill Polonius, which Hamlet does not show, but to live the life required of him in a world which seems dominated by evil, which he does show

1. As in Wilson Knight, *The Wheel of Fire*, 1949 edn, pp. 32–42.
2. v. ii. 237–40.

from the beginning. It is in this sense, I think, that it is possible to say that delay is inherent in the story: it is not merely that the story requires revenge to be deferred till the end (which, as I have suggested, need not imply procrastination), but that it leads the hero towards a destiny which a man who aspires to virtue does not willingly accept. Such a destiny in a tragic play is best suited by a reluctant hero, and not the less so because it leaves him saying 'I do not know Why . . .'

(ix) Hamlet in his world

All this is not to suggest that one can explain just how the character of Hamlet, the most discussed of all the characters of literature, grew in Shakespeare's mind. Initially conceived, as it must have been, in relation to the plot's demands, it grew no doubt beyond them until what Hamlet shrinks from is not the act of vengeance but the whole burden of living. The questions we find him asking, as Shakespeare takes us into Hamlet's mind and imparts to him his own intellectual curiosity, concern not so much the nature of revenge as the nature of man;[1] but they are questions which he is able, and indeed impelled, to ask by reason of what in his revenger's dual role he has become.

Any attempt at exemplification by selecting supposedly significant traits from the hero Shakespeare puts upon the stage risks making the character seem artificially contrived, whereas no character, surely, is less composed to a formula than Hamlet. Yet as, with seeming naturalness, he passes from melancholy brooding to sudden acts of passion, from lofty contemplation to rage or scorn or enigmatic thrusts of wit, we are fairly consistently aware of a man at odds with his environment and with its reflection in himself. He laments the state of things in Denmark, where his father has been succeeded by his uncle, to whom the fickle public have transferred allegiance and the Queen her wifely embraces. He wants to get away to Wittenberg, where I suppose he would pursue things of the mind, but stays at home by the persuasion of his mother. For all his objection to the customs of the Danish court he has to admit that he is 'native' there and 'to the manner born'. He knows himself inescapably a part of what he loathes. His nature has its symbol in his parentage; for if he is the son of his father, the godlike model of perfection, whom he venerates and would obey, he is also the son of her who replaced Hyperion with the satyr. In the big scene between them in the middle of

1. See above, pp. 125–6.

the play, when she asks if he has forgot her, he spells out the fact
of her incest:

> You are the Queen, your husband's brother's wife,

and significantly adds:

> And, would it were not so, you are my mother.

But it is not only what she is that contaminates him. He has a
sense of belonging to a diseased stock. And his disgust with what
he is extends beyond his personal inheritance to 'all the uses' of a
world in which only 'rank and gross' things flourish. He is haunted
by all the ills and wrongs of this life from which only death can
bring release.

The burden of the indissoluble 'flesh' is with him from the
beginning, and we may remember it ironically, if he temporarily
does not, when he vows that the Ghost's commandment shall live
in his brain 'Unmix'd with baser matter'. Even before the
commandment is given he feels in advance his weakness and
inadequacy. When in his first soliloquy he contrasts his uncle
with his father, he adds

> No more like my father
> Than I to Hercules,

thus opposing himself to the doer of great deeds and implicitly to
the father he would emulate. After the elation of his meeting with
the Ghost and his eagerness to 'sweep' to his revenge, he is soon
apologizing to his companions for 'so poor a man as Hamlet is'.

In the leisurely dialogues of the second act his maladjustment
can be more explicit. He has lost all his mirth; Denmark is a
prison; the world is one; and the whole created universe, even
while he celebrates the glory of it after the best Renaissance
fashion, appears to him also in a very different aspect:

> This goodly frame the earth seems to me a sterile promontory,
> this most excellent canopy the air . . ., this brave o'erhanging
> firmament, this majestical roof fretted with golden fire . . .
> appeareth nothing to me but a foul and pestilent congregation
> of vapours.

The wonderful 'piece of work' that is a man is to him a 'quintessence of dust'. The 'antic disposition', which justifies itself
psychologically as a cover for feelings genuinely distraught and
dramatically as a source of the arresting question or retort, is able
to glance at more than 'reason and sanity' can easily expound.
There are quips on the lack of honesty in the world, on what every

man deserves, on the iniquities of fortune, the decrepitude of age; and in reply to Polonius's innocent inquiry, 'Will you walk out of the air, my lord?' the death-wish suddenly resurfaces: 'Into my grave?' Many scattered thoughts are ultimately distilled into that soliloquy in which the death-wish finds an answer in the dread of what comes after. Although it is a soliloquy which transcends, as I have said, Hamlet's personal plight, it can now perhaps be seen to be generated by it. For it projects into a quasi-formal debate near the mid-point of the play the question which hovers over Hamlet's dramatic role: the 'mortal coil' being what it is, would one choose 'to be', or not? The choice – which is, however, no choice – between accepting and rejecting the human lot is central. The scene with Ophelia which immediately follows gives an abrupt change of mood and focus but, in its renunciation of love, a variation upon the same theme.

(x) Ophelia

The 'nunnery' scene, as it is called, and indeed Ophelia's whole part in the play, has generally been misunderstood: it is not too much to say that the failure to get Ophelia right has frustrated the interpretation of the tragedy. Bradley doubted 'whether from the mere text of the play a sure interpretation' could 'be drawn',[1] and I suspect that it is still the usual view that 'we are left with an unsolved puzzle'.[2] Those who think that Shakespeare 'deliberately' kept Ophelia's story 'vague' and that the 'uncertainty' contributes to the 'attractiveness' of the play even try to make a virtue of defeat.[3] Yet if we grasp the implications of what Hamlet says to Ophelia and to her father about her, the reason for Hamlet's treatment of her is, I believe, clearly and powerfully given.[4]

The essential of her story is that she is the woman Hamlet might have married and did not. What we learn from the opening act is that he had wooed her with 'holy vows of heaven' but that she in obedience to her father afterwards repelled his suit. The critics, confusing an Elizabethan play with life, or at least a romantic novel, assume that Hamlet must react to this and so

1. p. 153.
2. Bullough, p. 52.
3. J. M. Patrick, 'The Problem of Ophelia', in A. D. Matthews and C. M. Emery (eds.), *Studies in Shakespeare*, 1953, pp. 139–44; L. Kirschbaum, 'Hamlet and Ophelia', *PQ*, xxxv, 376–93.
4. For fuller exposition, see *HO*; *Sh.Jahr.* (West), 1975, 109–20.

project on to him the resentment they would feel themselves. They accuse Ophelia of rejecting him, suppose him to feel jilted or betrayed, and, all prepared for a lovers' tiff, make a problem of what happens. To assume that Hamlet's behaviour to Ophelia is due to her refusal of his love letters is to make the mistake of Polonius, whose view the play specifically repudiates. His view has its importance because the testing of it is what leads to the nunnery scene itself; but when we reach the nunnery scene, if we read what it says instead of what we expected it to say, we find that it is Hamlet who rejects Ophelia's love and not she his. He says nothing of her repelling him; he astonishes her by asking if she is honest and, holding that honesty is incompatible with beauty, implies that she will not be. The frailties he will later denounce in his mother he foresees in her. He directs at her a diatribe against face-paintings and cuckoldings and all the sins traditional to women. Yet, though this is not always noted, the sins he first refers to are his own:

> Nymph, in thy orisons
> Be all my sins remember'd.

And he presently goes on:

> I could accuse me of such things that it were better my mother had not borne me.

What things they are we are not told; for his sins, like hers, are less actual then potential, what he calls 'offences at my beck', the sins inherent in the nature of a man 'crawling between earth and heaven'. He confesses that he loved her once and then immediately denies it; and the paradox of love that is not love is, I take it, in the nature of the lover. His heavenly vows have the satyr lurking in them. With the example of his mother, who has made 'marriage vows as false as dicers' oaths', it is not difficult to see why he should say to Ophelia 'We will have no mo marriage'. But more than this, while he fears that Ophelia will prove false, the greater fear is that she has valued his love, and even has returned it. It is her confession that she believed in it that provokes the horrified exclamation, 'Wouldst thou be a breeder of sinners?' For that is what love and marriage lead to, the propagation of one's kind, and it explains the nature of Hamlet's recoil.

It is a recoil for which the play has prepared: for the present dialogue with Ophelia only brings to the surface what has been in Hamlet's mind before, as the 'method' of his madness has been used to show. He has associated Polonius's daughter with ideas of mating and breeding and the sort of life they may bring forth. In his mad talk he called Polonius 'a fishmonger' and then suddenly interjected 'Have you a daughter?' It was believed that the daughters of fishmongers were unusually prone to breed;[1] and the thought of the daughter here comes straight upon a nauseous example:

> If the sun breed maggots in a dead dog, being a good kissing carrion . . .

With the word in a double sense, 'a good kissing carrion' may be one way of describing the fair Ophelia herself, and the point of requiring her to be protected from the sun, though much obscured by critical ingenuities, should be clear. 'Conception is a blessing', Hamlet goes on, 'but as your daughter may conceive –' With the sun and the maggots in mind it may be better that she should not. The warning has been given. But on Polonius's next appearance Hamlet addresses him as Jephthah; and Jephthah too had a 'fair daughter', as Hamlet reminds us by quoting a popular ballad while leaving us to complete her story. And what we shall, or should, recall, if Polonius does not, is that Jephthah's daughter notoriously did not breed but could only bewail her virginity before being sacrificed by her father. As between the fishmonger's daughter and Jephthah's Hamlet makes the choice for Ophelia when he consigns her to a nunnery. He cannot resist her attraction, as is shown by his behaviour at the play; but his obscene jests there make her whom he has so ambiguously loved the focus of his disgust with the whole sexual process. His last word to her is a jest about how women 'mis-take' their husbands.

On her side, the pathos of Ophelia's rejection is eloquent in her memory of Hamlet's 'music vows'. When he has killed her father and himself been shipped away from Denmark there is little left for Ophelia but, like Jephthah's daughter, to bewail her virginity, as she does in the songs and the fantasies of her madness, which betray a frustrated love.[2] Her forsaking has its emblems in her death from the breaking of a willow[3] and the 'maimed rites' this leads to, which Hamlet has to watch. But neither the 'churlish priest', nor indeed the uncomprehending critics,[4] can refuse 'her

1. II. ii. 174 LN.   2. See IV. V. 23 LN, 23–40 LN, 48–66 LN, 184 LN.
3. IV. vii. 165–82 LN.

4. One would have thought the point of the virginal allusions here could not be missed. Those who assert that Ophelia 'was not a chaste young woman' (Rebecca West, *The Court and the Castle*, p. 15) and even that she had been seduced by Hamlet would appear not merely to have misunderstood earlier parts of the play but to have left the end unread.

virgin crants, her maiden strewments' as 'her fair and unpolluted flesh' is committed to the earth. It is only the most obvious of the ironies in these last words that they are spoken by the brother who began her story with a warning not to yield Hamlet her 'chaste treasure'. Her tragedy of course is that Hamlet has left her treasure with her; and it is also a large part of his. In the final conjunction of epithets – 'fair and unpolluted' – the play allows her in her death to confute those fears of Hamlet's about honesty and beauty which were partly responsible for it; but she is buried in her maiden purity with her true love unfulfilled. The beautifully imagined and beautifully wrought sub-plot of Ophelia's constant and forsaken love is one of the most poignant things in Shakespeare; and the final irony of her fate is that it has been so often misconceived.

Bradley thought Shakespeare restricted his scope with Ophelia so that 'too great an interest should not be aroused in the love-story';[1] and Schücking likewise saw it as a thing apart, with 'the figure of Ophelia . . . a beautiful dramatic luxury . . . superfluous' to Shakespeare's main design.[2] Yet Shakespeare's more usual way was to let a sub-plot illumine, not distract from, his central theme. And that is what the story of Ophelia, once we have understood it, may be seen to do in *Hamlet*. Hamlet's revulsion from love and marriage and from whatever would perpetuate a loathed life is the obverse of that wish for release from life's ills which opens his first soliloquy and has its fullest expression in the soliloquy which the meeting with Ophelia interrupts. His own nature of man, including bestial lusts and lethargies as well as godlike reason, mingles good and evil; and he is placed in a situation – his ideally virtuous father destroyed by a wicked brother who is now in possession of his kingdom and his queen – which shows evil prevailing over good. So although he sees the nobility of man, the beauty of women, the majesty of the universe, what his imagination dwells on is the quintessence of dust, the reason unused, the mutiny in the matron's bones, the nasty sty, the prison. His vision of the world may be said to exemplify the process which a famous speech of his describes whereby 'some vicious mole of nature' in a man extends itself in the general view till 'all the noble substance' is obscured. Hamlet sees evil flourish and spread. His first soliloquy links the death-wish with his image of a world where corrupt growth is unchecked.

1. p. 160.
2. *Character Problems in Shakespeare's Plays*, p. 172.

> 'Tis an unweeded garden
> That grows to seed; things rank and gross in nature
> Possess it merely.

Later he will exhort his mother not to

> spread the compost on the weeds
> To make them ranker.

The 'mildew'd ear', the ulcer, the impostume grow and infect. Fertility manifests itself in vile forms of life; and in this teeming life of weeds, and maggots, and sinners, to which his being commits him, Hamlet wishes to have no part. He wishes he had never been born; he cannot bear to bring his love to fruition; he shuns marriage and procreation.

Thus Hamlet denies his own nature, declining to act out the part that life purposes for him. And is this not also what happens when he eagerly responds to the Ghost's 'If thou hast nature in thee . . .' and then fails to fulfil what nature is demanding? It is not necessary that a turning away from love and a reluctance in revenge should be connected in the plot: below the level of explicitness a correspondence is not difficult to detect. Hamlet 'importun'd' Ophelia with 'holy vows' of love, and his vows to remember the Ghost palpitate all through his speech at the Ghost's departure; and then, for reasons which the drama, in respect of love, makes clear, nature is resisted and vows are unfulfilled. May we not say that the love plot gives expression to what the revenge plot too, if it stops short of articulating it, nevertheless suggests?

(xi) Revenge

It has often been observed that Hamlet has very little to say about the nature of his task, as distinct from his failure to perform it. In the presentation of Hamlet – and here a contrast with Hieronimo is instructive – the revenger recedes behind the human creature he has come to symbolize. But this does not and cannot mean that Shakespeare had no views about revenge, nor that they are less than fundamental to the shaping of his play. They are, however, such as a hero can more appropriately enact than expound.

It is the premise of Shakespeare's *Hamlet*, as of the traditional Hamlet legend, that a son should avenge a father's murder. In Bradley's words, 'Hamlet, it is impossible to deny, habitually assumes, without any questioning, that he *ought* to avenge his father'.[1] Waldock, endorsing this as being 'perfectly clear', adds

1. p. 97.

a pertinent warning against 'unguarded importations of modern feeling into our responses'.[1] Yet critics have emerged in recent years who blame Hamlet for submission to the Ghost. To Hamlet's 'The spirit that I have seen May be a devil' Wilson Knight retorts 'It was', pointing to its effect on Hamlet's mind.[2] Others, though not Knight himself, regard all revenge as necessarily evil. L. C. Knights refers to 'that Ghost whose command had been for a sterile concentration on death and evil',[3] and Eleanor Prosser has devoted a book[4] and much erudition to an attempt to demonstrate that the Ghost was an evil spirit whose command should not have been obeyed. Such critical discoveries only succeed in standing the play on its head. Shakespeare's conception of revenge is less simple. What the Ghost appeals to in Hamlet is the 'nature' that is in him; and if the play imposes on its hero the duty of revenge, it does not follow that revenge, any more than the 'nature' that prompts it, has unqualified approval. Is it not indeed the ambivalence which Shakespeare perceives in revenge that invites into the play all those ideas about the dual nature of man, mingling good and evil, which ultimately give it shape?

Instead of a debate upon the ethics of revenge we have something much more exciting. We have revenge commanded by a ghost; and whether the Ghost is good or bad is a matter of much concern in the early part of the play. The danger it may bring is recognized in advance – in the apprehensions of the opening scene, in Hamlet's

I'll speak to it though hell itself should gape,

and in that fearful speech of Horatio's,

What if it tempt you toward the flood, my lord . . . ?

Hamlet's bravery in entering into converse with it contributes to our impression of his heroic stature. The uncertainty about its character, where it comes from and what it means, reaches a

1. *Hamlet*, p. 26.

2. *The Wheel of Fire*, 1949 edn, p. 39. Knight, however, could conceive of a prompt killing as an act of creative assassination. He makes a distinction between the Ghost's command to revenge and the command to remember (pp. 44–5). But the two are of course the same.

3. *An Approach to 'Hamlet'*, p. 89. See also above, p. 124, n.3.

4. *Hamlet and Revenge*, 1967; 2nd edn 1971. For others recorded to have taken a similar line, see there, pp. xiin., 138n. For a reply, see K. Muir, *Shakespeare's Tragic Sequence*, pp. 57–60. Even Miss Prosser finds in the theatrical and critical history of the play 'almost unanimous agreement . . . that Hamlet is morally obligated to obey the Ghost': p. 238 (242).

climax in the words in which he addresses it, with all the dramatic
emphasis which this culminating moment gives:

> Be thou a spirit of health or goblin damn'd,
> Bring with thee airs from heaven or blasts from hell,
> Be thy intents wicked or charitable . . .

Three times the alternatives are put. But whichever it is, whether
of heaven or hell, Hamlet accepts the Ghost as the spirit of his
father which it claims to be and which later events confirm it to
be. As the spirit of his father it speaks to the deepest springs of
feeling in him, to the primitive allegiance of the blood, to filial
duty and love; and the voice of nature with which it speaks is
reinforced by some power beyond the confines of our human
world. In his first words after the Ghost has left him, 'O all you
host of heaven! O earth!', Hamlet acknowledges both the force of
nature and the power that governs nature. But he ominously goes
on, 'What else? And shall I couple hell?' Later he does precisely
that when, in the soliloquy on the Player at the end of the second
act, he says he is

> Prompted to my revenge by heaven and hell.

Those who maintain that the prompting is wholly diabolical and
so to be resisted are confuted by the text. But if they ignore the
heavenly component in revenge, we must not ignore the hellish.
The dread command which 'earth' and 'nature' call on Hamlet
to obey belongs to some universal order in which good and evil
both have part. The father in whom he saw the highest perfection
of manhood in the image of the gods was yet a man possessing a
human nature, from the guilt of which he is not yet released. His
Ghost still suffers for 'the foul crimes done in my days of nature';
it adds to the horror of the murder that he was

> Cut off even in the blossoms of my sin,

or, as Hamlet puts it,

> With all his crimes broad blown, as flush as May.

These are the sins of natural growth, such as Hamlet laments in
'our old stock'. As he explains to Ophelia,

> Virtue cannot so inoculate our old stock but we shall relish of it.

Even the noblest of heroic fathers could not be free of the evil
which blossoms in all life. And the command to revenge, coming
from father to son and not one for nature to resist, is enforced by
a power beyond nature in which it would seem that heaven and

hell conjoin. There are times indeed when the hellish influence is dominant and Hamlet gives himself over to cruel and vengeful passions. There has been a prefiguring of this in the savage and bloody Pyrrhus, significantly called 'hellish'; and the play-murderer, with his 'damnable faces', is identified, we remember, as 'nephew to the King'. His single speech has its echoes in the dreadful words of Hamlet at the end of the play scene when elation at the proof of the King's guilt gives him a thirst for blood:

> 'Tis now the very witching time of night,
> When churchyards yawn and hell itself breathes out
> Contagion to this world. Now could I drink hot blood,
> And do such bitter business as the day
> Would quake to look on.

This is the mood, I take it, in which he might 'do it pat' when he finds the King at prayer and then forbears for 'a more horrid hent' which would ensure the King's damnation. As Wilson Knight observes, 'Hamlet's thoughts here, by pushing revenge to its logical and hateful conclusion, make an ironical comment on the nature of revenge as such'.[1] But we must not suppose that the shudders which many readers have experienced at such sentiments were not felt first by Shakespeare; and it undermines the purposes of his play to suppose a revenger who could not mean them.[2] It is with his bloody passion still unassuaged that Hamlet at the first stir behind the arras, to quote the Queen on this,

> Whips out his rapier, cries 'A rat, a rat',
> And . . . kills . . .

and thus becomes the villain in a cause which images his. The evil implicit in the task which nature imposes on him now finds expression in a way which, as we have seen, is integral to the plot.

In Hamlet Shakespeare presents a revenger who is both ruthless and reluctant. As a revenger he must act, on behalf of outraged virtue, to restore a violated order, set right what is 'out of joint'. But the act he is impelled to involves him in evil of the kind which he would punish. As the ruthless revenger he exemplifies in his own person the evil which is inseparable from the good in human nature; as the reluctant revenger he can symbolize the good's abhorrence of it.[3]

---

1. *The Wheel of Fire*, 1949, p. 318n.
2. See III.iii. 89–95 LN.
3. Cf. 'What is intolerable in Hamlet's situation is that it cannot be reduced to the familiar antitheses of right and wrong: conscience both demands and opposes action' (Catherine Belsey, 'The Case of Hamlet's Conscience', *SP*,

The essential subject of *Hamlet*, suggested by and focused in the old story of a son's revenge, is, then, as I see it, the intermingling of good and evil in all life. The world to which the hero's human destiny commits him is one in which Hyperion and the satyr are brothers, sprung from the same stock, which also lives in him. Seeing the satyr apparently triumphant, he is possessed by a sense of the all too fertile viciousness of the life in which his own life shares. It is a life in which he must yet is reluctant to participate. He longs for death, refuses marriage and procreation, his nature resistant to what nature wills. This, I think, is the fundamental conflict the play exhibits in Hamlet; and it is a conflict which accords with his neglect to perform his destined task.

(*xii*) *The final act*

In the last act, however, there comes a change. We find Hamlet in the churchyard meditating on death. But death is not now something to be longed for as a release from the ills of the flesh, nor something to be shunned from the dread of what comes after. Born on the day that the grave-digger began his occupation, Hamlet has lived all his life under death's shadow; and in the skulls the grave-digger throws up he sees quite simply the common destiny of men. It is a destiny he appears now to accept. In the final scene, just before the fatal fencing-match, he says

> If it be now, 'tis not to come; . . . if it be not now, yet it will come,

and adds 'The readiness is all'. Thus ready for the death which completes life's universal pattern, he is also reconciled to the pattern of life which death completes. For he now perceives in the universe, embracing all its apparent good and evil, a supreme if mysterious design. Instead of inveighing against 'all the uses of this world', instead of regarding the 'goodly frame' of the earth as 'a sterile promontory', instead of lamenting that he was born to set right what was 'out of joint', he now asserts his faith in

> a divinity that shapes our ends,
> Rough-hew them how we will.

LXXVI, 147–8). This article, though it appeared too late for me to make use of, seems to me one of the very few to perceive the significance of revenge in *Hamlet*. Yet whereas the writer stresses that Hamlet is corrupted by the evil in his mission, the profounder implication, I think, is that, the evil being ineradicable, the mission requires Hamlet to submit to its corruption. A man who embraces his human lot must consent to be a sinner.

In what has happened to him on his voyage he sees this shaping influence at work. Describing the sealing of the commission which he substituted for the one Rosencrantz and Guildenstern were bearing, he says

> Why, even in that was heaven ordinant.

The divine power which seems to be ordering things has brought him back to Denmark, where, instead of

> I do not know
> Why yet I live to say this thing's to do,

he can now exclaim

> Is't not perfect conscience
> To quit him with this arm?

Revenge still has its ruthlessness, as witness what it does to Rosencrantz and Guildenstern; but reluctance, now that he recognizes and submits to a universal order, is at an end. The question of 'to be' or 'not to be' is finally answered. He can now accept his place in this mortal world, and instead of recoiling from what life involves, he is willing to play his part. There has been more than one indication of this. Breaking in upon Ophelia's funeral to make his presence known, he proclaims himself 'Hamlet the Dane'. Thus he not only accepts that he is 'native here' but takes to himself the monarch's title, hitherto applied to Claudius. Denmark, which he once called a prison, he now claims as his kingdom. Moreover, the love which he repudiated in the middle of the play he now asserts:

> I lov'd Ophelia. Forty thousand brothers
> Could not with all their quantity of love
> Make up my sum.

For the fulfilment of love and marriage it is now tragically too late. And belated protestations quickly become ridiculous, as he recognizes in his ranting to Laertes. But there remains his long-neglected deed. The fight with Laertes at the grave, and the subsequent reconciliation, in this like the visit to Ophelia's closet or the arrested sword of Pyrrhus, are examples of the prefiguring in another mode of what will shortly follow. Laertes is the villain's tool and ally, and a poisoner in his own right; but he is the 'brother' Hamlet has injured, in whose cause Hamlet sees his own. In the final contest between them two sons avenging their fathers, yet each tainted with the evil he would destroy, punish one another, yet die forgiving one another. With evil itself in the person of the King there is of course no reconciliation. The avenger who kills him when he has himself received his own death-wound at last fulfils his dual role.

It is difficult to imagine a comment from a ghost that could be fitting for this outcome. No doubt Shakespeare could have managed something less jarring than the satisfied gloatings of the ghost in *The Spanish Tragedy*; but a finer dramatic tact forgoes the formal pattern which a reappearance might have given and lets the Ghost pass unnoticed from the play. We may respond to promptings from the powers beyond but not presume to pronounce their judgments. What we more appropriately have instead are the expression of a faith in providence and the prayer of a fellow creature, in the lovely words of Horatio, for a heavenly benediction:

Flights of angels sing thee to thy rest.

Johnson is well known to have said that Shakespeare 'seems to write without any moral purpose'; but this is perhaps a play in which a moral is implicit, both simple and profound. For it commends a man who, after questioning the meaning of creation, comes to accept a design in it beyond our comprehending, and who therefore, after seeking to withdraw from life through an abhorrence of all that is ugly and vicious in it, is finally – though tragically not until death approaches – content to live life as it is, able to acknowledge, in word and deed, 'The readiness is all'.

HAMLET

[DRAMATIS PERSONAE

HAMLET, *Prince of Denmark.*
CLAUDIUS, *King of Denmark, Hamlet's uncle.*
The GHOST *of the late king, Hamlet's father.*
GERTRUDE, *the Queen, Hamlet's mother, now wife of Claudius.*
POLONIUS, *councillor of State.* 5
LAERTES, *Polonius's son.*
OPHELIA, *Polonius's daughter.*
HORATIO, *friend and confidant of Hamlet.*
ROSENCRANTZ, ⎱ *courtiers, former schoolfellows of Hamlet.*
GUILDENSTERN, ⎰ 10
FORTINBRAS, *Prince of Norway.*
VOLTEMAND, ⎱ *Danish councillors, ambassadors to Norway.*
CORNELIUS, ⎰
MARCELLUS,
BARNARDO, ⎱ *members of the King's Guard.* 15
FRANCISCO,
OSRIC, *a foppish courtier.*
REYNALDO, *a servant of Polonius.*
Players.
A Gentleman *of the court.* 20
A Priest.
A Grave-digger.
The grave-digger's Companion.
A Captain *in Fortinbras's army.*
English Ambassadors. 25
Lords, Ladies, Soldiers, Sailors, Messengers, and Attendants.

SCENE. *Elsinore: the Court and its environs.*]

DRAMATIS PERSONAE. 1–27.] *This edn; a list of 'The Persons Represented' appeared in Q 1676 and subsequent editions.*

162

1. *Hamlet*] The name (from O.N. Amloði) apparently denoted one who was, or pretended to be, dim-witted (see *Lond. Mercury*, XI, 510–11). Amleth(us) in Saxo and Belleforest, it had already become Hamlet in the play presumed to be Shakespeare's source (See Intro., pp. 82–3).

2. *Claudius*] The King's name is known from his first entry-direction and first speech-heading, after which, however, it is never used again. (See I.ii S.D. LN.) It was evidently suggested by that of the Roman emperor who married Agrippina, his niece and the mother of Nero, referred to at III.ii.384–5. Claudius was cited by Erasmus (*Institutio Principis Christiani*) along with Caligula as the type of the bad ruler, and in the incestuous marriage and the uncle-stepfather the analogies with *Hamlet* are obvious. Equally obviously, since the emperor was murdered by his wife, who was murdered by her son, one must resist the temptation to extend them.

4. *Gertrude*] The standard form in F for the Q2 Gertrard (which is possibly a misreading) and Q1 Gertred; an anglicization of Saxo's Gerutha and Belleforest's Geruthe.

5. *Polonius*] LN.

6. *Laertes*] A name which recalls, and may have been suggested by, a famous father–son relationship; but it is odd to find Shakespeare, who knew that Laertes was the father of Odysseus (*Tit.* I.i.380), giving it to a son. It became Leartes in Q1.

7. *Ophelia*] The name, from the Greek, meaning succour, is usually thought inappropriate, although Rus-

kin (*Munera Pulveris*) connects it with Ophelia as 'a ministering angel' (v.i.234). But the choice perhaps confused Opheleia with Apheleia, simplicity, innocence. Cf. Jonson, *Cynthia's Revels*, v.vii.51 ff.: 'The fourth, in white, is Apheleia, a nymph as pure and simple as the soul, or as an abrase table, and is therefore called Simplicity', etc. (See *AN&Q*, XVI, 134–5.) This, without suggesting an actual source, seems more relevant than the use of Ofelia (along with Montano) as a man's name in Sannazaro's *Arcadia*.

8. *Horatio*] The name echoes *The Spanish Tragedy*, where Horatio, the murdered son, is also the loyal friend.

9–10. *Rosencrantz, Guildenstern*] LN.

11. *Fortinbras*] This French name ('strong-in-arm') brings the aura of a warrior of romance. Like Hamlet, it is given to father as well as son, thus replacing Saxo's Coller(us). The similarly named Starcatherus of Saxo's books 6–8, who has been cited as a prototype (*ES*, LV, 235–7), offers an analogy rather than a source.

12. *Voltemand*] This spelling alternates with Valtemand in Q2 and with Voltumand in F. F2, and accordingly the early editorial tradition, has Voltimand, Q1 Voltemar. The name is a corruption of Valdemar, owned by several Danish kings.

13. *Cornelius*] May have been taken for a Danish name, from bearers of it settled in Denmark, though actually Dutch (Dollerup, pp. 187–8).

14–16. *Marcellus, Barnardo, Francisco*] LN.

17. *Osric*] Though sometimes classed

as Danish, this is a notable Anglo-Saxon name, and as such occurs in earlier Elizabethan drama, as in the pseudo-historical *A Knack to Know a Knave* and the titles of two other plays in Henslowe. It is not apparent why Shakespeare gives it, like Oswald, to one who inspires contempt. Merely 'a Courtier' on entering in Q2, he becomes 'young Ostricke' when a name is required. Q2 later, and F regularly, omits the *t*. Q1 remembers him only as 'a Bragart Gentleman'.

18. *Reynaldo*] So Q2; Reynoldo in F. A variant of Reynard, the name is no doubt apt for the wiles required of the man. Cf. *Mother Hubberd's Tale*, 917–18, 'a Reynold . . . That by his shifts his Master furnish can'. The change to Montano in Q1, along with that of Polonius (q.v.) to Corambis, is unexplained.

21. *A Priest*] At Ophelia's funeral. So F, Q1; but Q2 has only the speech-heading *Doct.* (twice), which Dover Wilson takes for a costume note and a sign for a Protestant clergyman. See v.i.219 n.

22. *A Grave-digger*] Called Delver, v.i.14.

23. *Companion*] The second 'clown', the straight man of the pair, is not, as commonly supposed, a grave-digger. See v.i S.D. n.

THE TRAGEDY OF
HAMLET, PRINCE OF DENMARK

ACT I

SCENE I

Enter BARNARDO *and* FRANCISCO, *two Sentinels.*

Bar. Who's there?

Fran. Nay, answer me. Stand and unfold yourself.

Bar. Long live the King!

Fran. Barnardo?

Bar. He.   5

Fran. You come most carefully upon your hour.

Bar. 'Tis now struck twelve. Get thee to bed, Francisco.

Fran. For this relief much thanks. 'Tis bitter cold,
　　　And I am sick at heart.

Bar. Have you had quiet guard?   10

Fran. Not a mouse stirring.

Bar. Well, good night.

Title. TRAGEDY] *Q2,F;* Tragicall Historie *Q1.*

ACT I

Scene 1

ACT I SCENE I.] *F (Actus Primus. Scæna Prima.); not in Q2.*   S.D.] *Q2,F;*
Enter two Centinels. Q1; Francisco upon his Post; Enter, to him, Bernardo. Capell.
12–14.] *As Q2; prose F.*

S.D. *Sentinels*] The scene is the platform of the battlemented castle.
Cf. I.ii.213.

1–25.] LN.

2. *me*] Emphatic. It is the sentry
on guard who has the right to
challenge.

3. *Long live the King!*] Whether or
not this is the formal password, as
often supposed, Barnardo identifies
himself as one on lawful business.
Cf. Marcellus at l. 16. But the speech

'is dramatically ironical in view of all
that follows' (Dover Wilson).

6. *upon your hour*] on the stroke of
your appointed time.

8. *much thanks*] 'Thanks' was often
used as singular. Cf. II.ii.25; *Ant.*
II.vi.47 ('a liberal thanks').

9. *sick at heart*] Francisco's melancholy, for which no reason is given,
contributes to the impression that all
is not well. It 'foreshadows Hamlet'
(Dover Wilson).

If you do meet Horatio and Marcellus,
The rivals of my watch, bid them make haste.
Fran. I think I hear them.

          Enter HORATIO *and* MARCELLUS.

                      Stand, ho! Who is there?   15
Hor. Friends to this ground.
Mar.   And liegemen to the Dane.
Fran. Give you good night.
Mar. O, farewell honest soldier, who hath reliev'd you?
Fran. Barnardo hath my place. Give you good night.   *Exit.*
Mar. Holla, Barnardo!   20
Bar. Say, what, is Horatio there?
Hor. A piece of him.
Bar. Welcome, Horatio. Welcome, good Marcellus.
Hor. What, has this thing appear'd again tonight?
Bar. I have seen nothing.   25
Mar. Horatio says 'tis but our fantasy,
    And will not let belief take hold of him,

15 S.D.] *As Sisson; after 14 Q2,F; after 15 Dyce.*   15. ho] *Q2; not in F.*
Who is] *Q2;* who's *F.*   18. soldier] *F,Q1;* souldiers *Q2.*   19. hath]
Q2,Q1; ha's *F.*   24. *Hor.*] *Q2; Mar. F,Q1.*

14. *rivals*] partners, which Q1 reads. Cf. rivality, *Ant.* III.v.8, and Chettle, *Hoffman,* 'I'll seat thee by my throne of state, And make thee rival in those governments' (MSR, l. 735).

16. *the Dane*] the Danish king. Cf. I.ii.44, v.i.251.

17. *Give*] i.e. (may) God give. Cf. *LLL* IV.ii.78, 'God give you good morrow'.

21. *what*] It is difficult to attach a precise value to these little interjections, which give the effect of both naturalness and urgency. This seems to combine the *what* of a call (in reply to Marcellus's *Holla*) with the *what* which preludes a question (cf. l. 24, II.i.107, and see *OED* What A 21).

22. *A piece of him*] The hand he offers is solid enough, but the dark which conceals the rest of him enables him to reserve full participation. The sceptic is already characterized by his

tone of humorous deflation. Cf. his rejoinders to Hamlet at I.ii.169, I.v.131–2, III.ii.273, 279, v.i.199.

23. *Welcome . . . Marcellus.*] Coleridge (i.39) distinguishes the 'gladness' of 'Welcome, Horatio!' from the mere 'courtesy' of 'Welcome, good Marcellus!'

24. *this thing*] The dramatic requirement supports the authority of Q2 in the attribution of this line to Horatio rather than Marcellus. It is the unbeliever who describes as 'this thing' what Marcellus will presently refer to as 'this dreaded sight', 'this apparition'. By these unspecific allusions Shakespeare wonderfully keeps us in suspense. Only when the Ghost has actually appeared does he particularize it as a figure 'like the King that's dead'.

26. *fantasy*] delusive imagination. LN.

Touching this dreaded sight twice seen of us.
Therefore I have entreated him along
With us to watch the minutes of this night,   30
That if again this apparition come,
He may approve our eyes and speak to it.
Hor. Tush, tush, 'twill not appear.
Bar.   Sit down awhile,
And let us once again assail your ears,
That are so fortified against our story,   35
What we have two nights seen.
Hor.   Well, sit we down.
And let us hear Barnardo speak of this.
Bar. Last night of all,
When yond same star that's westward from the pole,
Had made his course t'illume that part of heaven   40
Where now it burns, Marcellus and myself,

29–30. along With us] along, With vs *Q2;* along With vs, *F.*   36. have two
nights] *Q2,Q1;* two Nights haue *F.*

29.] An explanation for the benefit
of the audience rather than Barnardo, who was expecting Horatio to
come (l. 21).

along] With the common omission
of the verb of motion. Abbott 30.

30. *With us*] The Q2 punctuation
as well as the metre connects this
primarily with 'to watch' rather
than with 'along'; but the word
order permits us to take it with both.

32. *approve*] confirm the trust-
worthiness of.

speak to it] LN.

33. *Sit down*] This may seem incongruous for a sentry. W. J. Lawrence
(as in I.i.42 S.D. LN) argues that 'The
seated attitude was adopted to concentrate attention on the spectre',
which would emerge 'in front of
them through a trap'. But cf. I.i.42
S.D. LN.

36. *What*] Object of the verb of
saying implied in *assail your ears*

(= attempt to get you to listen to).

38. *of all*] Emphatic; cf. last of all.

39. *yond same star*] Though there
need be no reference to an identifiable star, Shakespeare had presumably seen the brilliant star
Capella, which would appear in the
winter sky 'westward from the pole'
(= pole-star), as the stars of the
Great Bear, which have also been
suggested, would not (*N&Q*, ccviii,
412–13).

40. *his*] its. *His* was the ordinary
form of the neuter, as well as masculine, possessive. The Elizabethan
alternative was *it*, as at I.ii.216,
v.i.214. *Its* occurs in some late
Shakespearean quartos (including
Ham. Q4) and rarely in the Folio,
where it is presumably an editor's or
printer's modernization. Cf. Abbott
228.

illume] Apparently a Shakespearean
coinage.

The bell then beating one—

Enter GHOST.

Mar. Peace, break thee off. Look where it comes again.
Bar. In the same figure like the King that's dead.
Mar. Thou art a scholar, speak to it, Horatio.   45
Bar. Looks a not like the King? Mark it, Horatio.
Hor. Most like. It harrows me with fear and wonder.
Bar. It would be spoke to.
Mar.   Question it, Horatio.
Hor. What art thou that usurp'st this time of night,
    Together with that fair and warlike form   50
    In which the majesty of buried Denmark
    Did sometimes march? By heaven, I charge thee speak.
Mar. It is offended.
Bar.   See, it stalks away.

---

42 S.D.] *Q2,Q1; after* off *F.*   44. figure] *Q2,Q1;* figure, *F.*   46. a] *Q2;*
it *F,Q1.*   47. harrows] *F;* horrowes *Q2;* horrors *Q1.*   48. Question]
F,Q1; Speake to *Q2.*   52. thee] *Q2,F,Q1;* thee, *Rowe.*

42. *beating*] striking, though the
suggestion is rather of rhythmic
repetition than of a single stroke.
Cf. to beat a drum, and Q1 *towling.*
    42 S.D. *Enter Ghost.*] LN.
    44. *the same*] i.e. the same as on
previous occasions.
    like the King] Note the refraining
from accepting that it is in fact the
King. Cf. below, ll. 46–7, 50–2, 84,
112–13; I.ii.199, 244. Doubt as to
the Ghost's identity is present from
the first.
    45. *scholar*] Cf. l. 32 LN. Though
Latin, as editors remark, was necessary for the exorcism of spirits, that
is not the point here. The purpose of
questioning a ghost is to discover
'who it is, and what is its business'
(Grose, *Provincial Glossary*).
    46. *a*] Colloquial for *ha* = he;
common in the Elizabethan drama,
but often (improperly) represented
by *a'* in modern texts. It is frequent
in Q2 (Dover Wilson counted 37
instances), but is retained in F only

at v.i.173. Though Q1 and F
regularize here to *it*, both retain the
masculine pronoun in l. 69. In later
scenes, *he* and *it* alternate, partly
according as the Ghost is thought
of in its character of apparition or as
the spirit of Hamlet's father (see e.g.
III.iv.136–8); but it would be wrong
to look for any consistent distinction.
    47. *harrows*] lacerates (*OED* 4).
Cf. I.v.16. Q1 shows an interesting
confusion, but the Q2 *horrowes* finds
a precedent in *A Remedy for Sedition*
(1536), 'They . . . horrowe with
spades' (E4).
    48. *It would be spoke to.*] Cf. l. 32 LN.
    49. *usurp'st*] Horatio challenges
both the Ghost's right to invade the
night and its right to assume the
form of the dead King.
    51. *Denmark*] the King of Denmark.
Cf. Norway, l. 64.
    52. *sometimes*] formerly.
    53. *It is offended.*] Not (as Prosser,
pp. 98–9) because it is invoked 'by
heaven' but because this inter-

Hor. Stay, speak, speak, I charge thee speak.   *Exit Ghost.*
Mar. 'Tis gone and will not answer.   55
Bar. How now, Horatio? You tremble and look pale.
     Is not this something more than fantasy?
     What think you on't?
Hor. Before my God, I might not this believe
     Without the sensible and true avouch   60
     Of mine own eyes.
Mar.   Is it not like the King?
Hor. As thou art to thyself.
     Such was the very armour he had on
     When he th'ambitious Norway combated.
     So frown'd he once, when in an angry parle   65
     He smote the sledded Polacks on the ice.
     'Tis strange.
Mar. Thus twice before, and jump at this dead hour,

54. thee] *Q2,Q1;* thee, *F.*   64. he] *Q2,Q1; not in F.*   th'] *F;* the *Q2,Q1.*
66. Polacks] *Malone;* pollax *Q2,F* (Pollax), *Q1;* Poleaxe *F4,* Pole-axe *Rowe;*
Polack *Pope.*   68. jump] *Q2,Q1;* iust *F.*

locutor is not the one it seeks. See
next note.
   55. *will not answer*] Ghosts, even
when questioned, will speak only to
those for whom they have a message.
Cf. 1.i.176.
   58. *on't*] For *on* where we use *of,*
see Abbott 181. Cf. l. 92(F).
   59. *might*] was still commonly used
in its original sense of 'could'. Cf.
1.ii.141.
   60. *the sensible . . . avouch*] the
assurance given by the evidence of
the senses. *avouch,* testimony. Cf.
'vouch', *Meas.* 11.iv.156. The conver-
sion of the sceptic (cf. ll. 26–7) will
persuade the audience to accept
the objective reality of the Ghost.
But it will only enhance uncertainty
as to its nature and purpose. Cf.
ll. 70–2, 131–42; 1.iv.40–57; 11.ii.594–
9.
   63. *the very armour*] There is perhaps
an inconsistency in allowing Horatio
to know this detail of what the play
will later say happened thirty years

before. Dowden remarks that the
armour would be remembered and
long pointed out; but the truth, I
think, is that although it later suits
Shakespeare to date the victory over
Fortinbras on the day of Prince
Hamlet's birth, he does not at this
stage attach any precise date to it.
Cf. v.i.139–57 and LN.
   64. *Norway*] the King of Norway,
the elder Fortinbras. The combat is
described ll. 85 ff.
   65. *frown'd*] As befitted a martial
hero. Cf. 1.ii.230 and n.
   parle] parley, encounter (and perhaps one not limited to words). See
l. 66 LN.
   66. *sledded Polacks*] Poles borne in
sleds. LN.
   68. *jump*] exactly. Cf. v.ii.380, and
Oth. 11.iii.374, 'bring him jump where
he may Cassio find.'
   dead] has ominous connotations of
'the dead of night' (cf. *Tit.* 11.iii.99),
the time of stillness and darkness,
when the normal activities of life

With martial stalk hath he gone by our watch.
Hor. In what particular thought to work I know not,   70
But in the gross and scope of my opinion,
This bodes some strange eruption to our state.
Mar. Good now, sit down, and tell me, he that knows,
Why this same strict and most observant watch
So nightly toils the subject of the land,   75
And why such daily cast of brazen cannon
And foreign mart for implements of war,
Why such impress of shipwrights, whose sore task
Does not divide the Sunday from the week.
What might be toward that this sweaty haste   80
Doth make the night joint-labourer with the day,
Who is't that can inform me?
Hor.   That can I.
At least the whisper goes so: our last King,

---

71. my] *F,Q1;* mine *Q2.*   76. why] *F,Q1;* with *Q2.*   cast] *F;* cost
Q2,Q1.

---

are suspended. Cf. i.ii.198. Applied
to midnight, as often (*Meas.* iv.ii.59,
R3 v.iii.180), it concentrates these
suggestions upon an exact point of
time, and so here, though the hour
is one not twelve (l. 42), it has the
additional effect of reinforcing *jump.*

70. *to work (in)*] to let my mind be
occupied (with).

71. *the gross and scope*] the general
drift, as contrasted with the 'particular thought' (l. 70).

72. *This bodes . . . state.*] Compelled
by his 'own eyes' (l. 61) to abandon
the theory of 'fantasy' (l. 26), Horatio
adopts an orthodox alternative. Cf.
Lavater, ii.xvi: 'If they be not vain
persuasions, or natural things, then
are they forewarnings of God.'

eruption] violent outbreak. Cf. *Caes.*
i.iii. 78, 'strange eruptions'.

73. *Good now*] An expression of
entreaty, 'good' being a vocative
with the omission of the noun. Also
at *Err.* iv.iv.21. Abbott 13.

75. *toils*] (transitive) imposes toil
on. Cf. Abbott 290.

subject] subjects (collective), as in
i.ii.33. Cf. *Meas.* ii.iv.27, 'The
general subject to a well-wish'd
king Quit their own part'.

76. *why*] With ellipsis (there is).

cast] casting.

76–8. *brazen cannon . . . shipwrights*]
A reflection of Denmark's contemporary war preparations under Christian IV. A decade earlier Sir Jerome
Horsey (*Travels*, Hakluyt Soc., pp.
243–4) had complained to Christian's
predecessor of 'the enticing away' of
English 'shipwrights to fashion your
navy' and 'the carrying away' from
England (cf. *foreign mart*) of 'much
ordinance, both brass and iron,
pieces and other munition'.

77. *mart*] (= market) trading.

78. *impress*] impressment (for forced
service), conscription, as in *Troil.*
ii.i.95.

80. *toward*] imminent. Cf. v.ii.370.

82. *That can I.*] Horatio's position
as informant here contrasts with his
unfamiliarity with affairs in Denmark in i.iv. See i.iv.12–13 LN.

Whose image even but now appear'd to us,
Was as you know by Fortinbras of Norway,　　　85
Thereto prick'd on by a most emulate pride,
Dar'd to the combat; in which our valiant Hamlet
(For so this side of our known world esteem'd him)
Did slay this Fortinbras, who by a seal'd compact
Well ratified by law and heraldry　　　　　90
Did forfeit, with his life, all those his lands
Which he stood seiz'd of to the conqueror;
Against the which a moiety competent
Was gaged by our King, which had return'd
To the inheritance of Fortinbras,　　　　　95
Had he been vanquisher; as, by the same cov'nant
And carriage of the article design'd,
His fell to Hamlet. Now, sir, young Fortinbras,
Of unimproved mettle, hot and full,

90. heraldry] heraldy *Q2*, Heraldrie *F,Q1*.　　　91. those] *F,Q1*; these *Q2*.
92. of] *Q2,Q1*; on *F*.　　　94. return'd] *F*; returne *Q2*.　　　96. cov'nant] *F*;
comart *Q2*; compact *Q 1676*.　　　97. article design'd] *F2*; article desseigne
Q2; Article designe *F*; articles deseigne *Q3*.

86. *emulate*] emulous, eager to
excel.

88. *this side of our known world*]
'= the whole western world (as we
should say)' (Dover Wilson).

89. *compact*] The stress on the
second syllable is usual in Shakespeare.

90. *heraldry*] the recognized usages
of chivalry, of which the heralds were
arbiters. Elsewhere Shakespeare em-
ploys the word in its more usual sense
of the lore of armorial bearings or, by
synecdoche, for the coat-of-arms
itself. (Cf. ii. ii. 452; *All's W*. ii. iii. 256.)
Law and heraldry, though sometimes
taken as a hendiadys for heraldic
law, more probably implies that the
agreement was executed by a legal
instrument (cf. *seal'd*) as well as
having heraldic approval.

91. *Did forfeit . . . all*] LN.

92. *seiz'd of*] possessed of. Still of
course the regular legal term.

93. *moiety*] portion (not necessarily
limited to a half).

competent] sufficient. Hamlet stakes
lands enough to match all those of
Fortinbras.

94. *return'd*] A loose use, not to be
taken as implying that Fortinbras
would have got *back* possessions
originally his.

96. *the same cov'nant*] i.e. the 'compact' of l. 89. LN.

97. *carriage . . . design'd*] purport
of the article referred to. LN.

99. *unimproved*] unrestrained. 'To
improve' is (1) to turn to good
account, as in the only Shakespearean
use, 'his means, if he improve them,
may well stretch' (*Caes*. ii. i. 159);
whence *unimproved*, either (*a*) 'not
yet used for advantage' (Skeat,
Glossary), untried, 'waiting to be
given shape or purpose' (Alexander), or (*b*) with *un-* denoting
reversal rather than mere negation,
undisciplined, ill-regulated, 'allowed
to run riot' (Verity): (2) to reprove,
condemn (L. *improbare*), whence
unimproved = 'unreproved' (Nares),

Hath in the skirts of Norway here and there   100
Shark'd up a list of lawless resolutes
For food and diet to some enterprise
That hath a stomach in't, which is no other,
As it doth well appear unto our state,
But to recover of us by strong hand   105
And terms compulsatory those foresaid lands
So by his father lost. And this, I take it,
Is the main motive of our preparations,
The source of this our watch, and the chief head
Of this post-haste and rummage in the land.   110
Bar. I think it be no other but e'en so.
Well may it sort that this portentous figure

101. lawless] *Q2,Q1;* Landlesse *F.*   104. As] *Q2;* And *F.*
106. compulsatory] *Q2;* Compulsatiue *F.*   110. rummage] *Q2* (Romadge),
F (Romage).   111–28.] *Q2; not in F,Q1.*

unrebuked, uncensured.

100. *skirts*] outlying parts.

101. *Shark'd up*] got together by snatching up indiscriminately, as a shark does its food. *OED* presents 'shark' as a variant of 'shirk', to trick and hence to prey on others, in which this sense is strengthened by the predatory connotations of the noun. The suggestion of the shark's savage rapacity anticipates *lawless*. Cf. *Sir Thomas More* (MSR, Addn II.207–9), 'ruffians as their fancies wrought . . . would shark on you', and Dover Wilson, NCS, pp. xxxvi–xxxvii.

list] lit. a catalogue of soldiers' names, and so a troop.

lawless resolutes] desperadoes. When we see Fortinbras's men in IV.iv they are a well-disciplined army. Shakespeare probably changed his design in course of composition, while fulfilling an original idea of introducing a revenging son with an unruly mob of followers by transferring these to Laertes (IV.v). See Intro., pp. 100, 142, and *Rice U. Studs.*, LX, 100–3.

102. *For*] denoting purpose. The sense is not, as sometimes supposed, that the resolutes are hired for (no

pay but their) food. Rather they are to serve as 'food . . . to some enterprise'. Cf. next note.

103. *a stomach*] The enterprise is personified by its possession of a stomach, or a spirit of daring, the stomach being traditionally the seat of courage. Cf. *Caes.* v.i.66, 'If you dare fight today, come to the field; If not, when you have stomachs'. There is a play on the literal sense, the stomach of the enterprise being supplied with 'food' in the shape of the 'lawless resolutes'.

109. *head*] fountain-head, origin, as at II.ii.55.

110. *post-haste*] furious activity. Cf. l. 80.

rummage] (of which the QF readings are merely old spellings), bustling activity, turmoil. Primarily a nautical term for the removal and rearrangement of a ship's cargo.

111–28.] With the omission of this passage in F (and Q1), cf. the cut at I.iv.17–38, and see note there.

112. *sort*] accord. Cf. *H5* IV.i.63; *MND* v.i.55. The appearance of the Ghost accords with the fact that King Hamlet is the *question* or

Comes armed through our watch so like the King
That was and is the question of these wars.
Hor. A mote it is to trouble the mind's eye.   115
In the most high and palmy state of Rome,
A little ere the mightiest Julius fell,
The graves stood tenantless and the sheeted dead
Did squeak and gibber in the Roman streets;
As stars with trains of fire and dews of blood,   120
Disasters in the sun; and the moist star,
Upon whose influence Neptune's empire stands,

---

115. mote] moth *Q2*, mote *Q4*.   119.] *Omission marked after this line/ Jennens.*
120–3.] *As Q2; after 128 Tschischwitz.*

---

occasion of the war. Its being 'armed' accords with the danger of war.

portentous] in the strict sense. Cf. Lavater, I.i, '*Portentum* is that which forsheweth some thing to come, as when strange bodies appear in the air, or blazing stars . . .'

115. *A mote it is*] Not, *pace* Dover Wilson, because Horatio sees the incident as insignificant but because it sets up irritation in the (mind's) eye. Tilley M 1189. The Q2 *moth* is an alternative, and probably a Shakespearean, spelling. Cf. QF of *LLL* IV.iii.157 and F of *John* IV.i.92, *H5* IV.i.177.

to trouble] Hugh of St Cher, commenting on Psalm iv.4 (see Vulgate, Basle, 1504), distinguishes between the sinful anger which blinds, and the zealous anger which merely troubles (*turbat*) the eye for a time, like a collyrium, so that it may later see more clearly. So the mind, now troubled by the Ghost, may later see what it betokens, as happened with the Roman portents Horatio now cites. The emphasis, however, is on present perplexity rather than on future clarification.

the mind's eye] Cf. I.ii.185 and n.

116. *palmy*] flourishing, with reference to the palm as the symbol of victory. Apparently a Shakespearean coinage.

state] in the territorial and political sense, as at l. 72. Christopher North (*Blackwood's*, LXVI, 252–4) insists that it implies 'at once Place and indwelling Power'. 'The high and palmy state of Rome' thus corresponds to Virgil's 'rerum . . . pulcherrima Roma' (*Georgics*, II.534).

117–23.] For the prodigies preceding Caesar's death, LN.

119. *squeak*] Ghosts traditionally spoke in a thin shrill voice. In the *Odyssey* the souls of Penelope's suitors squeak like bats (XXIV. 5). Cf. *Aeneid*, VI.492–3, 'vocem exiguam'; *Locrine*, III.vi.19, 'shrieking notes'; I.v.2 n. below.

120. *As*] The awkward connection suggests possible omission. LN.

121. *Disasters*] signs of ill omen. A 'disaster' (cf. L. *astrum*) is etymologically 'an unfavourable aspect of a star or planet' (*OED*).

the moist star] the moon (cf. *Wint.* I.ii.1), often called 'watery' with reference not simply to its pallid light but to the belief that it drew up moisture from the sea. It has power over 'Neptune's empire' through its control of the tides.

122. *influence*] An astrological 'influence' was an emanation by means of which a heavenly body exerted power over mundane things.

stands] depends.

Was sick almost to doomsday with eclipse.
And even the like precurse of fear'd events,
As harbingers preceding still the fates   125
And prologue to the omen coming on,
Have heaven and earth together demonstrated
Unto our climatures and countrymen.

Enter GHOST.

But soft, behold. Lo, where it comes again.
I'll cross it though it blast me.   *Ghost spreads its arms.*
                    Stay, illusion: 130
If thou hast any sound or use of voice,
Speak to me.

---

124. fear'd] *Parrott-Craig, conj. Collier;* feare *Q2;* fearce *Q3.*   128. climatures]
Q2; climature *White, conj. Dyce.*   130 S.D.] *It spreads his armes.* Q2 *(opp.*
130–1); He spreads his arms. *Q 1676; not in* F,Q1.   132–3.] *As Pope; one line*
Q2,F.

123. *almost to doomsday*] 'almost to
the point of complete darkness,
alluding to the biblical prophecy
that at the second coming of Christ
"the moon shall not give her light"
(Matthew xxiv. 29)' (Herford).

124. *precurse*] that which precedes
(and foretokens).

fear'd] In view of (1) the sense and
(2) the confusion of *d* and *e* in the
Elizabethan hand, there can be little
doubt that this is the correct emendation instead of the *fierce* which most
editors have taken over from Q3.
Cf. F's error at II. i. 112.

125. *still*] always. A normal Elizabethan use. Cf. I. ii. 104, II. ii. 42,
IV. vii. 115, etc.

fates] Though 'fate' often means
no more than pre-ordained end, it
often retains also, esp. in the plural, a
quasi-personal significance. (Cf. *3H6*
IV. iii. 58, 'What fates impose, that
men must needs abide'.) The suggestion here is not only of calamities
to come but of powers ordaining and
working them.

126. *omen*] strictly, that which
foreshadows an event, but here the

event foretold. Cf. Heywood, *Life
of Merlin* (1641, frontispiece), 'Merlin
. . . His country's omen did long
since foretell'.

127–8. *demonstrated . . . climatures*]
Cf. *Caes.* I. iii. 31–2, 'portentous things
Unto the climate that they point
upon'. *climatures*, climes.

128. *our*] Clearly identifying Horatio as a Dane. But cf. I. iv. 12–13 LN.

129. *soft*] peace, break off. So at
I. v. 58, III. i. 88, III. ii. 383, IV. ii. 2,
v. i. 210. See *OED* soft *adv.* 8.

130. *cross it*] i.e. cross its path,
confront. This, according to popular
belief, would be to expose oneself
to its baleful influence. The death in
1594 of Ferdinando, 5th Earl of
Derby (famous in dramatic annals
as Lord Strange), was said to have
occurred after a mysterious tall man
had appeared in his chamber and
'twice crossed him swiftly' (Lodge,
Illustrations of Brit. History, 1791,
iii. 48). The context rules out the
interpretation 'make the sign of the
cross', which would be to guard
against rather than to invite blasting.

130 S.D. *spreads its arms*] LN.

If there be any good thing to be done
That may to thee do ease, and grace to me,
Speak to me;   135
If thou art privy to thy country's fate,
Which, happily, foreknowing may avoid,
O speak;
Or if thou hast uphoarded in thy life
Extorted treasure in the womb of earth,   140
For which they say your spirits oft walk in death,
Speak of it, stay and speak.   *The cock crows.*
               Stop it, Marcellus.
Mar. Shall I strike at it with my partisan?
Hor. Do if it will not stand.
Bar. 'Tis here.
Hor. 'Tis here.   145
                        Exit Ghost.
Mar. 'Tis gone.
    We do it wrong, being so majestical,
To offer it the show of violence,

134–5.] *As Q2,Q1; one line F.*   137–8.] *As Q2; one line F,Q1 (subst.).*
141. your] *Q2;* you *F,Q1.*   142 S.D.] *Q2 (opp. 141–2); not in F,Q1.*
143. at] *F; not in Q2.*   146 S.D] *As Sisson; after 147 F; not in Q2.*

133–42. *If . . . If . . . Or if . . . stay and speak.*] LN.

137. *happily*] haply, perchance.

141. *your*] Commonly used indefinitely, without reference to a particular person addressed, but imputing to hearers in general knowledge of the object condescendingly referred to. *OED* 5 b. Cf. I.v.175, III.ii.3, IV.iii.21–3, v.i.56–7, 165–6. The touch of familiarity, if a little surprising amid this solemn speech, accords with the sceptically tinged 'they say' and is more in keeping than the quite different familiarity of the F *you spirits*, which is additionally awkward when only one is being addressed.

142. *speak. Stop it*] For the Ghost's behaviour here see I.ii.216ff. Warton noted as 'a most inimitable circumstance in Shakespeare' the aggravation of suspense when the Ghost,

hitherto silent, at length prepares to speak, only to be interrupted.

143. *partisan*] 'a long-handled spear, the blade having one or more lateral cutting projections' (*OED*). It was borne by officers of the guard. See *Sh.'s Eng.*, i.137–8, and cf. Cotgrave, *pertuisane*, 'leading-staff'.

146 S.D. *Exit*] McManaway supposes the Ghost disappears through one trap and rises again through another (*PBSA*, XLIII, 315); W. J. Lawrence (*Pre-Restoration Stage Studies*, pp. 107–8), following Calvert (*An Actor's Hamlet*), that the illusion of the Ghost's being in two places was effected by having two ghosts (a practice still sometimes followed). But I suspect that the actors could manage the business, then as now, without such expedients.

148–50.] Cf. Lavater, III.xi, 'Some others, when spirits appear unto

For it is as the air, invulnerable,   150
And our vain blows malicious mockery.
Bar. It was about to speak when the cock crew.
Hor. And then it started like a guilty thing
Upon a fearful summons. I have heard
The cock, that is the trumpet to the morn,   155
Doth with his lofty and shrill-sounding throat
Awake the god of day, and at his warning,
Whether in sea or fire, in earth or air,
Th'extravagant and erring spirit hies
To his confine; and of the truth herein   160
This present object made probation.
Mar. It faded on the crowing of the cock.

155. morn] *Q2*; day *F;* morning *Q1*.

them, will by and by set on them, and drive them away with naked swords . . . not considering . . . that spirits are nothing hurt with weapons'.

150. *as the air*] The orthodox view. Cf. Le Loyer, III, 8, 'Si elles [les Ames] apparaissent à nous . . . ce n'est qu'un fantôme d'air qu'elles ont vêtu seulement'; Taillepied, ch. 16, 'Les corps des esprits, quand ils se veulent apparaître, sont de l'air'.

151. *malicious mockery*] 'a mere semblance of malice' (Schmidt), 'malice' here being not ill-will but 'power to harm' (*OED* 2). The Ghost being 'invulnerable', the power of the blows to harm is illusory. Cf. *John* II.i.251–2, 'Our cannons' malice vainly shall be spent Against th'invulnerable clouds'. See H. Hulme, *ES*, XLVII, 190–2.

155. *The cock*] LN.

trumpet] trumpeter, as often (e.g. *3H6* V.i.16; *Troil.* IV.v.6). The image was not new: cf. Drayton, *Endimion and Phoebe* (1595), l. 387, 'the cock, the morning's trumpeter'.

156. *lofty*] Suggesting both the cock's upstretched throat and the trumpeter's proud, majestic sound.

158. *Whether in sea . . . air*] quali-

fying *confine* (l. 160). It was held that there were four different orders of spirits according to which of the four elements they inhabited. Cf. *Il Penseroso*, 93–6.

159. *extravagant*] straying beyond its proper bounds. Both this and *erring* (wandering) have the strict Latin sense. Cf. *Oth.* I.i.137, 'an extravagant and wheeling stranger Of here and everywhere'; Chapman's *Odyssey*, IX, '*Erring* Grecians we, From Troy returning homewards'. There is no suggestion (as Prosser, p. 122) that an 'erring spirit' is an evil one.

160. *confine*] place of confinement. Cf. II.ii.245; *Tp.* IV.i.121. For *his*, see above, l. 40 n.

161. *object*] A word often applied to a spectacle which excites a strong emotional reaction (of horror, dread, admiration, etc.). See *OED* 3 b. Cf. *Oth.* V.ii.367, 'The object poisons sight'; *Tit.* III.i.64, 'This object kills me'; *Cym.* I.vi.101, 'This object, which Takes prisoner the wild motion of mine eye'; *Per.* I.i.43; *Mer. V.* I.i.20; *Lr* V.iii.238.

probation] proof.

Some say that ever 'gainst that season comes
Wherein our Saviour's birth is celebrated,
This bird of dawning singeth all night long;   165
And then, they say, no spirit dare stir abroad,
The nights are wholesome, then no planets strike,
No fairy takes, nor witch hath power to charm,
So hallow'd and so gracious is that time.
Hor. So have I heard and do in part believe it.   170
But look, the morn in russet mantle clad
Walks o'er the dew of yon high eastward hill.
Break we our watch up, and by my advice
Let us impart what we have seen tonight
Unto young Hamlet; for upon my life   175
This spirit, dumb to us, will speak to him.
Do you consent we shall acquaint him with it
As needful in our loves, fitting our duty?

163. say] *Q2,Q1*; sayes *F*.   165. This] *Q2*; The *F,Q1*.   166. dare stir]
Q2; can walke *F*; dare walke *Q1*.   168. takes] *Q2,Q1*; talkes *F*.
169. that] *Q2,Q1*; the *F*.   172. eastward] *Q2*; Easterne *F*.

163–9. *Some say . . . that time.*] See
l. 155 LN.
163. *'gainst*] in expectation of the
time when. Cf. II.ii.479, III.iv.50.
Abbott 142.
165. *bird of dawning*] i.e. the cock,
of course; not, as Wilson Knight
once supposed, the lark.
167. *strike*] destroy by evil influence, blast. Cf. *Cor.* II.ii.111,
'struck Corioli like a planet'; *Tit.*
II.iv.14; *Wint.* I.ii.201. Cf. *moon-
struck*.
168. *takes*] bewitches (especially
by infecting with disease). Cf. *Gam-
mer Gurton's Needle*, I.ii.25–6, 'They
sit as still as stones in the street As
though they had been taken with
fairies'; *Wiv.* IV.iv.27–32, 'Herne
the Hunter . . . takes the cattle, And
makes milch-kine yield blood'; *Lr*
II.iv.161–2, 'Strike her young bones,
you taking airs, with lameness.'
169. *gracious*] associated with divine
grace, blessed.
170. *in part believe*] Note the art
with which Horatio is made to re-

linquish some but not all of his original scepticism (cf. ll. 26–7, 33–5,
59–61, 160–1) and with which Shakespeare uses the suggestiveness of
supernatural beliefs without committing himself to them ('Some say',
'I have heard'), thus leaving the
episode mysterious.
171–2. *the morn . . . eastward hill*] A
very literary description. LN.
175. *young Hamlet*] Coleridge (i. 19)
notes 'the unobtrusive and yet fully
adequate mode of introducing the
main character, *young* Hamlet, upon
whom transfers itself all the interest
excited for the acts and concerns of
the king, his father'.
176. *will speak to him*] Cf. above,
l. 55 n., I.v.2.
178. *loves*] Elizabethan idiom permits the plural of an abstract noun
which refers to a quality as possessed
by more than one person. Cf.
I.ii.251, 254; III.ii.196; wisdoms,
I.ii.15; modesties, II.ii.280; companies, II.ii.14.

Mar. Let's do't, I pray, and I this morning know
    Where we shall find him most convenient. *Exeunt.* 180

SCENE II

Flourish. Enter Claudius KING *of Denmark, Gertrude the* QUEEN,
Council, *including* VOLTEMAND, CORNELIUS, POLONIUS *and
his son* LAERTES, HAMLET [*dressed in black*], *with* Others.

King. Though yet of Hamlet our dear brother's death
    The memory be green, and that it us befitted
    To bear our hearts in grief, and our whole kingdom
    To be contracted in one brow of woe,
    Yet so far hath discretion fought with nature   5
    That we with wisest sorrow think on him

179. Let's] *Q2,Q1;* Let *F.*   180. convenient] *Q2;* conueniently *F,Q1.*

Scene II

SCENE II] *F* (*Scena Secunda*); *not in Q2.*   S.D.] *Florish. Enter Claudius, King of
Denmarke, Gertrad the Queene, Counsaile: as Polonius, and his Sonne Laertes, Hamlet,
Cum Alijs. Q2; Enter Claudius King of Denmarke, Gertrude the Queene, Hamlet,
Polonius, Laertes, and his Sister Ophelia, Lords Attendant. F; Enter King, Queene,
Hamlet, Leartes, Corambis, and the two Ambassadors, with Attendants. Q1.*

180. *convenient*] For adjectival forms
in adverbial use, see Abbott 1.

Scene II

S.D.] LN.
1–39.] On the style of this speech,
LN.
   1. *Hamlet our dear brother*] On the
succession, LN.
   2. *that*] 'Used (like Fr. *que*) as a
substitute instead of repeating a
previous conjunction' (*OED* that
conj. 8).
   us] Referring to all present, as is
indicated by 'our hearts' (l. 3). By
the artful mingling of the plural with
the royal use (our 'brother', our

'kingdom', etc.) Claudius effects an
identification of his audience with
himself.
   4. *contracted in one brow*] Combines
the suggestions of being knit together
in one united feeling and of the
expression of this feeling by the
knitting of the brow. For the idiom,
see Palsgrave's *Acolastus* (EETS, pp.
84–5), '*Contrahere frontem*, to drawe
the forheed to gyther, signifieth to
lowre or bende the browes: which
countenance we make, whan we be
miscontented or angry'. Cf. Wm.
Burton's trans. of *Clitophon and Leu-
cippe*, 1597 (ed. Gaselee and Brett-
Smith, p. 109), 'grief and sorrow
contracteth her brows'.

Together with remembrance of ourselves.
Therefore our sometime sister, now our queen,
Th'imperial jointress to this warlike state,
Have we, as 'twere with a defeated joy,   10
With an auspicious and a dropping eye,
With mirth in funeral and with dirge in marriage,
In equal scale weighing delight and dole,
Taken to wife. Nor have we herein barr'd
Your better wisdoms, which have freely gone   15
With this affair along. For all, our thanks.
Now follows that you know young Fortinbras,
Holding a weak supposal of our worth,
Or thinking by our late dear brother's death

8. sometime] *Q2;* sometimes *F.*   9. to] *Q2;* of *F.*   11. an . . . a] *Q2;* one
. . . one *F.*   17. follows that you know] *Q2;* followes, that you know *F;*
follows that you know: *Dowden, conj. Walker.*

7. *ourselves*] Though Claudius is no
doubt making it appear that the
marriage concerns not merely himself but the whole state (Kittredge),
it is not true that 'ourselves' could
not refer to the monarch alone. Cf.
R2 I.i.16, III.iii.127.

8. *sometime*] former.

sister, now our queen] The incestuous
nature of the marriage is made clear
to the audience from the first. Cf.
l. 157.

9. *jointress*] Not earlier recorded.
Literally, a woman who is in joint
possession, and hence sometimes
explained as 'joint-ruler'. But nothing
else in the play gives Gertrude that
status and even here 'our queen'
seems to regard her as Claudius's
consort. The word may already have
had its later sense of the holder of a
jointure, i.e. an estate which is settled
on a wife and passes to her on her
husband's death.

11.] LN.

13. *dole*] grief.

14. *barr'd*] 'excluded, acted without
the concurrence of' (Caldecott).

15. *better wisdoms*] Not better than
mine, but better than ordinary, of a

superior kind. For the plural, cf.
I.i.178n.

16. *this affair*] strictly, the marriage.
Thanks for his accession may be included in 'for all'. A report of the
coronation of Christian IV in 1596
describes his crowning by the councillors with the words 'Accept from
us the Crown of this State' (*SQ*,
xvi, 156).

17. *follows that you know*] Walker's
attempted improvement (*know:*) is
adopted by many editors, who thus
make the Council already acquainted
with the matter that 'now follows'.
But I agree with Sisson (*NR*) that
the sense is not 'follows what you
already know, namely' but 'the next
point is, you must be told that'. It
may be objected that Fortinbras's
warlike preparations are in fact
known (I.i.98–107); but it is his
formal demands (*message*, l. 22) that
the Council are now to be told.

young Fortinbras] Cf. 'young Hamlet',
I.i.175. Shakespeare evidently intends a parallel between the two
princes.

18. *weak supposal*] low opinion.

Our state to be disjoint and out of frame,   20
Colleagued with this dream of his advantage,
He hath not fail'd to pester us with message
Importing the surrender of those lands
Lost by his father, with all bonds of law,
To our most valiant brother. So much for him.   25
Now for ourself, and for this time of meeting,
Thus much the business is: we have here writ
To Norway, uncle of young Fortinbras—
Who, impotent and bedrid, scarcely hears
Of this his nephew's purpose—to suppress   30
His further gait herein, in that the levies,
The lists, and full proportions are all made
Out of his subject; and we here dispatch

21. Colleagued] *F;* Coleagued *Q2;* Co-leagued *Capell.*   this] *Q2;* the *F.*
advantage,] aduantage *Q2;* Aduantage; *F.*   24. bonds] *F;* bands *Q2.*
25. him.] *Q2;* him. / *Enter Voltemand and Cornelius. F.*   31. herein,] *Q2;*
heerein. *F.*   33. subject] *Q2,F;* subjects *Q5.*

20. *disjoint and out of frame*] Cf.
ironically I.v.196, I.i.72, I.iv.90, etc.
frame, systematic order, often referring to the created universe. Cf.
II.ii.298; *1H4* III.i.16; *Mac.* III.ii.16
('Let the frame of things disjoint').

21. *Colleagued*] allied. The assumption that it must qualify the subject,
Fortinbras (l. 17), led Warburton
and others to explain that Fortinbras
had only his own dream for an ally.
Dowden and Dover Wilson, with
better sense if not syntax, take it with
'supposal'. But I think it is to be
taken as applying to the general
idea of ll. 18–20. In Fortinbras's
motives his notion of Denmark's
weakness is linked with his dream
concerning himself.

dream of his advantage] either the
illusion of his (present) superior position, or the vision of his (prospective)
gain. The first goes better with *this,*
the second with *colleagued.*

22. *message*] Possibly plural, as
'pester' would suggest. On the suppression of the inflexion after *-ge*
see Abbott 471.

23. *Importing*] having for its substance. Dowden rightly rejects
Abbott's 'importuning'.

24. *with all bonds of law*] Cf.
I.i.89–98.

25. *So much for him.*] Not of course
that Fortinbras is now disposed of.
But 'so much' for what he has done
and 'now' for my reaction to it.

26. *for*[2]] the reason for.

28. *Norway, uncle of young Fortinbras*]
Fortinbras's uncle has succeeded to
his father's throne. This adds to the
parallel between the situations of
Hamlet and Fortinbras, which
Shakespeare may have initially designed to be more important than it
subsequently becomes. It should also
refute suggestions that Claudius is in
some way a usurper.

31. *gait*] going, proceeding. *OED*
gate *sb*[2] 6.

32. *lists*] Cf. I.i.101.

proportions] numbers, especially in
military contexts; forces. Cf. *H5*
I.ii.304, 'Let our proportions for
these wars Be soon collected'.

33. *subject*] Collective, as in I.i.75.

You, good Cornelius, and you, Voltemand,
For bearers of this greeting to old Norway,   35
Giving to you no further personal power
To business with the King more than the scope
Of these dilated articles allow.
Farewell, and let your haste commend your duty.

Cor. ⎫
        ⎬ In that, and all things, will we show our duty.   40
Volt. ⎭

King. We doubt it nothing. Heartily farewell.

                     Exeunt Voltemand and Cornelius.

And now, Laertes, what's the news with you?
You told us of some suit: what is't, Laertes?
You cannot speak of reason to the Dane
And lose your voice. What wouldst thou beg, Laertes, 45
That shall not be my offer, not thy asking?
The head is not more native to the heart,

---

35. bearers] *Q2,Q1; bearing F.*   38. dilated] *F; delated Q2; related Q1.*
40. *Cor. Volt.*] *Q2; Volt. F; Gent. Q1.*   41 S.D.] *F subst.; not in Q2,Q1.*
45–6. Laertes, . . . asking?] *F; Laertes,? . . . asking, Q2.*

37. *To*] for (Abbott 186). But Kittredge takes 'to business' as an infinitive.

38. *dilated*] set out at length. The Q2 *delated*, which editors have made heavy weather of, is simply a variant spelling, recorded in Minsheu ('to *Delate*, or speak at large of anything') and amply demonstrated in *OED*. Neither the common interpretation 'conveyed' nor Dover Wilson's 'accusing' commends itself.

allow] Possibly subjunctive ('may allow'), more probably 'attracted into the plural by the plural noun *articles*' (Kittredge). Cf. III.ii.192 and Abbott 412.

39. *your haste commend your duty*] i.e. your haste rather than your words. Claudius anticipates the usual parting formula, exemplified in l. 253 and v.ii.179. Cf. *LLL* IV.ii.135, 'Stay not thy compliment; I forgive your duty'. See *PQ*, I, 71–3.

41. *nothing*] This adverbial use is common. Cf. *Cor.* I.iii.99, 'they nothing doubt prevailing'; Abbott 55.

42. *Laertes*] 'Caressing him with his name four times in nine lines' (Dover Wilson), the King shows his graciousness to Polonius's son. But much more important, Shakespeare takes this opportunity of spotlighting the youth who is to be Hamlet's 'image' (cf. v.ii.77), foil, foe, and ultimately killer. Cf. Intro., p. 133.

44. *the Dane*] the Danish king. Cf. I.i.16, v.i.251.

45. *thou*] The change from *you* to *thou* expresses friendly intimacy.

46. *my offer . . . asking*] given by me spontaneously without your having to ask.

47. *The head . . . the heart*] Claudius's assertion gains strength from the traditional correspondence between the human organism, with the interdependence of its various members, and the body politic. The king is naturally the *head*, and in mediaeval allegory the councillors are often referred to as the *heart*. See Kellett,

The hand more instrumental to the mouth,
Than is the throne of Denmark to thy father.
What wouldst thou have, Laertes?

Laer.   My dread lord,   50
Your leave and favour to return to France,
From whence though willingly I came to Denmark
To show my duty in your coronation,
Yet now I must confess, that duty done,
My thoughts and wishes bend again toward France   55
And bow them to your gracious leave and pardon.

King. Have you your father's leave? What says Polonius?

Pol. He hath, my lord, wrung from me my slow leave
By laboursome petition, and at last
Upon his will I seal'd my hard consent.   60
I do beseech you give him leave to go.

King. Take thy fair hour, Laertes, time be thine,
And thy best graces spend it at thy will.
But now, my cousin Hamlet, and my son—

50. My dread] *Q2;* Dread my *F;* My gratious *Q1.*   55. toward] *Q2;*
towards *F.*   58. He] *F,Q1; not in Q2;* A *Parrott-Craig.*   58–60. wrung . . .
consent] *Q2; not in F;* wrung from me a forced graunt *Q1.*   64. Hamlet,]
Q2,F; Hamlet, Exit [*Laertes*]. *Q1.*

Suggestions, p. 31, and cf. *Cor.* i.i.113–
14, 'The kingly crowned head . . . The
counsellor heart'. *native,* closely
joined in nature. Cf. *All's W.* i.i.209,
'kiss like native things'. In the next
line the king as the *hand* is the provider
for his subjects.

49. *the throne . . . father*] From this
acknowledgement of Polonius's service there is no justification for
inferring that he has helped Claudius
to the throne. It is the throne itself,
not its present occupant, that is indebted to him. Note that the first
reference to Polonius is to him as the
father of Laertes, stressing what is to
be a determining factor of the plot.

56. *leave and pardon*] Kittredge compares More, *Richard III* (ed. Lumby,
p. 76), 'When the duke had this
leave and pardon to speak'. *pardon,*
indulgence, as at iv.vii.44.

58. *He hath*] Dover Wilson explains

the omission of the pronoun in Q2 by
suggesting that '*Polo.* Hath' represents
a misreading of 'Pol a [= he] hath'
(*MSH,* pp. 110–11). Yet although Q2
invariably uses '*Pol.*' for the speech-
heading elsewhere, it would not be
unlike Shakespeare to write 'Polo'
on the first occasion and 'Pol' subsequently.

60. *seal'd*] The metaphor is that of
affixing a seal to a document (with
a play on *will*) to give it authority.
hard] reluctant.

62. *Take thy fair hour*] Enjoy the
favourable season of your life; roughly
equivalent to *carpe diem.*

63. *graces*] attractive qualities; en-
dowments and accomplishments. Cf.
Mer. V. ii.vii.33, 'I do in birth deserve
her, and in fortunes, In graces, and
in qualities of breeding'; *Ant.* ii.ii.134;
H8 i.ii.122.

64. *cousin*] any kinsman more dis-

Ham. A little more than kin, and less than kind.   65
King. How is it that the clouds still hang on you?
Ham. Not so, my lord, I am too much in the sun.
Queen. Good Hamlet, cast thy nighted colour off,
    And let thine eye look like a friend on Denmark.
    Do not for ever with thy vailed lids   70
    Seek for thy noble father in the dust.
    Thou know'st 'tis common: all that lives must die,
    Passing through nature to eternity.
Ham. Ay, madam, it is common.
Queen.   If it be,
    Why seems it so particular with thee?   75
Ham. Seems, madam? Nay, it is. I know not 'seems'.
    'Tis not alone my inky cloak, good mother,
    Nor customary suits of solemn black,
    Nor windy suspiration of forc'd breath,

65.] *Aside | Theobald* ². 67. so] *F;* so much *Q₂.* in the sun] *Q₂* (sonne); i'th' Sun *F.* 68. nighted] *Q₂;* nightly *F.* 72. common:] common; *Theobald;* common *Q₂;* common, *F.* lives] *Q₂,F;* live *F₂.* 77. good] *F;* coold *Q₂.*

tant than a brother; often used of a nephew.

65. *more than kin . . . kind*] more than kinsmen in our actual relationship and less than kinsmen in our likeness to one another and in our mutual feelings and behaviour. *kind*, members of a family as naturally united in community of feeling. LN.

67. *in the sun*] With pun on *son.* LN.

68. *nighted*] night-like. Cf. Abbott 294.

69. *Denmark*] Whether this means the King (as at I.i.51, I.ii.125) or the kingdom is hardly possible to say.

70. *Do not for ever*] Ironical in view of ll. 145–51.

vailed] lowered. *OED v².*

72. *'tis common*] This sentiment, to be amplified in the King's next speech, is a traditional commonplace of consolation. Cf. Ovid, *Met.*, tr. Golding, xv. 550, (to Egeria weeping for her husband's death) 'Thy mourning moderate . . . Not only thou hast

cause . . . '; Seneca, *Ad Polybium, Works,* tr. Lodge, 1614, p. 692, 'It is therefore a great comfort for a man to bethink himself that the same hath happened unto him, which all others have suffered before him, and all that follow him must endure, and therefore . . . nature hath made that most common which is most grievous'. For other classical and Renaissance instances see B. Boyce, *PMLA,* LXIV, 771–80.

all that lives] For the not uncommon use of the inflexional *s* with a plural subject, see Abbott 333.

75. *particular with thee*] to affect you as a thing peculiar to yourself.

77. *'Tis not alone*] Implying a contrast with the character of his mother's own mourning.

79. *suspiration*] sighing. *OED* cites this passage to illustrate the sense 'breathing'; but the literal meaning is more apt.

forc'd] forcibly expelled.

No, nor the fruitful river in the eye,   80
Nor the dejected haviour of the visage,
Together with all forms, moods, shapes of grief,
That can denote me truly. These indeed seem,
For they are actions that a man might play;
But I have that within which passes show,   85
These but the trappings and the suits of woe.
King. 'Tis sweet and commendable in your nature, Hamlet,
To give these mourning duties to your father,
But you must know your father lost a father,
That father lost, lost his—and the survivor bound   90
In filial obligation for some term

---

82. moods] *Q2,F;* modes *Q 1695.*   shapes] *Q3;* chapes *Q2;* shewes *F.*
83. denote] *F;* deuote *Q2.*   85. passes] *Q2;* passeth *F.*

---

81. *haviour*] demeanour, expression.
Cf. *Cym.* III. iv. 9.

82. *moods*] A 'mood' is 'a frame of
mind or state of feelings' (*OED* mood
sb.[1] 3) but may come to mean the
outward expression of this. Schmidt
glosses 'external appearance, countenance expressive of disposition',
citing *Sonn.* XCIII, 'In many's looks
the false heart's history Is writ in
moods and frowns and wrinkles
strange'. Cf. *Compl.* 201, 'the en-
crimson'd mood' (of rubies as emblems of passion). The frequent
interpretation 'mode' is unauthenti-
cated. For though there was some
merging of *mood* (O.E. *mōd*) and *mode*
(L. *modus*), the use of the latter in
its modern non-technical sense was a
17th-century development, which
was no doubt responsible for the
reading *modes* in Q1695 as well as
for *mode* in F3 of *2H4* IV. v. 200.

shapes] This 'correction' of the Q2
chapes is supported by Shakespeare's
frequent use of *shape* in the sense of
appearance, sometimes in conjunction with 'form', often denoting
illusory appearance, and sometimes
in reference to grief. See *Ado* v. i. 14,
'such a grief . . . In every lineament,
branch, shape, and form'; *LLL*
v. ii. 751; *R2* II. ii. 22. F *shewes* is more

likely to have had its source in the
show of l. 85 than, as Furness and
Dowden held, to have been deliberately repeated in it; *show* does not
repeat one item but sums up the
whole of ll. 77–82.

85.] It was a commonplace that
the greatest griefs were inexpressible.
Cf. Seneca, *Hippolytus*, 607, 'Curae
leves loquuntur, ingentes stupent.'

87. *commendable*] The stress on the
first syllable was normal usage.

89–90. *your father . . . lost his*] Here
and in ll. 103–6 cf. Seneca on death:
'Hoc patri tuo accidit . . . hoc
omnibus ante te, hoc omnibus post
te' (*Epistles*, 77). See above, l. 72 n.

90. *the survivor bound*] Grammar and
Kittredge suggest '(that father) bound
the survivor', sense 'the survivor
(was) bound'.

91. *some term*] Cf. l. 70, 'Do not for
ever'. Such advice is again traditional. See esp. Ecclesiasticus xxxviii.
17, 'Weep bitterly, and make great
moan . . . and that a day or two . . .
and then comfort thyself'; Seneca
(Lodge, p. 706), 'Let our sighs be
drawn from the bottom of our hearts;
yet let them have an end'. Plutarch
similarly deprecates 'making no end
of sorrow' (tr. Holland, 1603, p.510).
Cf. *All's W.* I. i. 48–9.

To do obsequious sorrow. But to persever
In obstinate condolement is a course
Of impious stubbornness, 'tis unmanly grief,
It shows a will most incorrect to heaven,   95
A heart unfortified, a mind impatient,
An understanding simple and unschool'd;
For what we know must be, and is as common
As any the most vulgar thing to sense—
Why should we in our peevish opposition   100
Take it to heart? Fie, 'tis a fault to heaven,
A fault against the dead, a fault to nature,
To reason most absurd, whose common theme
Is death of fathers, and who still hath cried
From the first corse till he that died today,   105
'This must be so'. We pray you throw to earth
This unprevailing woe, and think of us
As of a father; for let the world take note
You are the most immediate to our throne,

96. a] *F;* or *Q2.*

92. *obsequious*] appropriate to obse-quies (funeral rites). Cf. *Tit.* v.iii.152; *3H6* ii.v.118.

persever] With stress on the second syllable, the regular form down to the mid-17th century.

93. *condolement*] grieving.

95. *incorrect*] uncorrected, undisciplined; hence not submissive, recalcitrant.

97. *simple*] untutored, ignorant.

99. *any . . . to sense*] that which is most familiar to common observation of anything there is. Cf. Abbott 419a and, for 'any' with superlative, *Cym.* i.iv.57, 'any the rarest of our ladies'. *vulgar*, widely current (cf. *Lr* iv.vi. 212, 'Most sure and vulgar; everyone hears that'); *sense*, perception through the senses.

100. *peevish*] foolishly perverse.

102. *fault to nature*] offence against the natural order of things.

103–4. *whose . . . who*] 'The antecedent seems to be *nature* rather than *reason*' (Kittredge). For the use of *who* to refer to personified abstractions, see Abbott 264.

104. *still*] always. Cf. i.i.125, ii.ii.42, iv.vii.115.

105. *the first corse*] Abel's. An unhappy instance on Claudius's part, with the irony of an analogy which goes beyond what the speaker intends. Cf. iii.iii.37–8.

he] for *him.* See Abbott 205–6.

106. *throw to earth*] The phrasing suggests that he should *bury* it (along with his father).

107. *unprevailing*] unavailing. Cf. *OED* prevail *v.* 4; *Rom.* iii.iii.60.

109. *immediate*] next in succession. Cf. *2H4* v.ii.71, 'th'immediate heir of England' (Prince Hal). The King's statement need not be inconsistent with an elective monarchy (see i.ii.1 LN). Indeed in a hereditary monarchy there would be no occasion for it.

And with no less nobility of love   110
Than that which dearest father bears his son
Do I impart toward you. For your intent
In going back to school in Wittenberg,
It is most retrograde to our desire,
And we beseech you bend you to remain   115
Here in the cheer and comfort of our eye,
Our chiefest courtier, cousin, and our son.

Queen. Let not thy mother lose her prayers, Hamlet.
I pray thee stay with us, go not to Wittenberg.

Ham. I shall in all my best obey you, madam.   120

King. Why, 'tis a loving and a fair reply.
Be as ourself in Denmark. Madam, come.
This gentle and unforc'd accord of Hamlet
Sits smiling to my heart; in grace whereof
No jocund health that Denmark drinks today   125

112. toward] *Q2;* towards *F.*   you.] *F;* you *Q2.*   119. pray thee] *Q2;*
prythee *F.*

110. *nobility*] Though variously
glossed, this word should give no
difficulty. Shakespeare often describes as 'noble' feelings or attributes
of mind that are held up for admiration, and *no less* refers to quality not
quantity. Paternal love is regarded
as a noble passion, and Claudius says
that his love for Hamlet is not inferior in kind to that of an actual
father for his son.

112. *impart*] deal liberally. Such
intransitive use does not occur elsewhere. It may be that by the time
he had reached the verb Shakespeare
regarded *nobility* as its object, forgetting that he had begun with *with.*
But Kittredge compares Porter, *Two
Angry Women of Abington* (MSR,
l. 258), 'With all the parts of neighbour love, I impart myself to Master
Goursey'; and it is possible that
Shakespeare used *impart* for 'impart
myself'. So Johnson interpreted it.

113. *Wittenberg*] LN.

114. *retrograde*] lit., going back-
wards; hence contrary. Chapman,
May Day, III.iii.196, 'Come, be not

retrograde to our desires', is probably
an echo.

115. *bend you*] Not '(we) bend you'
as a reinforcement of 'we beseech
you', but 'bend yourself,' i.e. submit
yourself.

116. *eye*] A frequent metonymy for
the royal presence, as in *Mac.*
IV.iii.186, 'Your [Malcolm's] eye
in Scotland would create soldiers'.
Cf. IV.iv.6, IV.vii.44.

117. *cousin . . . son*] As observed by
Kittredge, the King repeats the
words which gave offence before
(l. 64), and the Queen for the second
time intervenes.

120. *in all my best*] to the best of
my ability.

obey you] Pointedly ignoring the
King's persuasions.

124. *to*] 'Sits *at* my heart' would be
normal, but the preposition is influenced by 'smiling'.

grace] thanksgiving. The French
sense (L. *gratiae*) was formerly
common.

125. *Denmark*] the King of Denmark. Cf. I.i.51.

But the great cannon to the clouds shall tell,
And the King's rouse the heaven shall bruit again,
Re-speaking earthly thunder. Come away.
                              Flourish. Exeunt all but Hamlet.
Ham. O that this too too sullied flesh would melt,
     Thaw and resolve itself into a dew,   130
     Or that the Everlasting had not fix'd
     His canon 'gainst self-slaughter. O God! God!

127. heaven] *Q2;* Heauens *F.*   128 S.D. *Flourish.*] *Q2;* not in *F,Q1.*
129. sullied] *Wilson;* sallied *Q2,Q1;* solid *F.*   132. self-slaughter] *F;* seale
slaughter *Q2.*   God! God] *Q2;* God, O God *F.*

drinks] 'The King's intemperance
is very strongly impressed; everything that happens to him gives him
occasion to drink' (Johnson). Cf.
I.ii.175, I.iv.8–22, II.ii.84, III.ii.294,
III.iii.89, v.ii.264ff., and, for an
appropriate nemesis, 330–1.
    126. *the great cannon . . . shall tell*]
They do so at I.iv.6. Cf. the King's
similar directions at v.ii.267–75.
Such celebrations were a Danish
custom and, like the references to
Wittenberg, they show Shakespeare
taking some care with local colour.
See I.iv.12–13 and LN.
    127. *rouse*] 'Prob. an aphetic form
of *carouse*, due to the phrase *to drink
carouse* having been apprehended as
to drink a rouse' (*OED*). Either a
bumper drunk as a toast, as here, or a
drinking session. Cf. I.iv.8, II.i.58.
The Danish word was *rus* and Dekker
(*Gull's Hornbook*) refers to 'the Danish
rowsa'; but the suggestion that
Shakespeare uses *rouse* to give a
Danish colouring is countered by its
occurrence in *Faustus*, IV.i.19, *Oth.*
II.iii.60, and indeed *Ham.* II.i.58.
    bruit] noise abroad. *Bruit again* is
often glossed as 'echo'. But the noise
in the heavens will echo not the rouse
but the cannon. The King's drinking
will be signalized by the cannon (the
'earthly thunder'), the echoing of
which will then 'bruit' or proclaim
it again.
    129. *too too*] A very common dupli-

cation in the 16th century, especially
to intensify the expression of regret.
OED too 4.
    sullied] LN.
    129–30. *melt . . . dew*] Warhaft (see
l. 129 *sullied* LN) stresses as the contrast to 'self-slaughter' (l. 132) the
resolving of the baser element into
the higher, whereby Hamlet might
return from melancholy to normal
health, or, if to become dew is to die,
then from 'misery' to 'felicity'. But
there is surely no thought here of being
restored to health or happiness, only
of being free of the 'flesh' whether
through its own deliquescence or
through suicide. Cf. Paul on the
desire to be *dissolved* and the necessity
of living in the *flesh* (Philippians
i.23–4, as regularly cited in the
Homily on the Fear of Death and elsewhere. Cf. also 2 Corinthians v.1). To
resolve (change into another form or
element) into a *dew* (moisture) is another synonym for *melt* and *thaw*, and
does not imply (as Warhaft would
suggest) a further transformation into
vapour.
    132. *canon 'gainst self-slaughter*]
Again referred to in *Cym.* III.iv.74–5.
Commentators have puzzled unnecessarily over this; for while a
'divine' prohibition may be easier to
accept than to demonstrate, what is
easily demonstrated is that the Church
regularly regarded 'self-slaughter' as
forbidden by the sixth commandment.

How weary, stale, flat, and unprofitable
Seem to me all the uses of this world!
Fie on't, ah fie, 'tis an unweeded garden   135
That grows to seed; things rank and gross in nature
Possess it merely. That it should come to this!
But two months dead—nay, not so much, not two—
So excellent a king, that was to this
Hyperion to a satyr, so loving to my mother   140
That he might not beteem the winds of heaven
Visit her face too roughly. Heaven and earth,
Must I remember? Why, she would hang on him
As if increase of appetite had grown
By what it fed on; and yet within a month—   145
Let me not think on't—Frailty, thy name is woman—
A little month, or ere those shoes were old
With which she follow'd my poor father's body,

133. weary] *F;* wary *Q2.*   134. Seem] *Q2;* Seemes *F.*   135. ah fie] *Q2;*
Oh fie, fie *F.*   136–7. nature . . . merely. That] *F;* nature, . . . meerely
that *Q2.*   137. to this] *F;* thus *Q2.*   141. beteem] *Q2;* beteene *F.*
143. would] *F,Q1;* should *Q2.*   147. ere] *Q2,F;* e'er *Rowe.*

See, e.g., Augustine, *De Civitate Dei,*
1.20; Bishops' Bible, margin on 1
Maccabees vi.46 and 2 Maccabees
xiv.41; Henry Smith, on Philippians
i.23 (*Sermons,* 1592, p. 543). Donne,
Biathanatos (III.ii.8), while contesting
the interpretation, acknowledges that
'the Commandment . . . is cited by all
to this purpose'.

133. *How weary, stale, flat, and unprofitable*] Cf. La Primaudaye, *The
French Academy,* pt 2, 1594, p. 254:
'When grief is in great measure, it
bringeth withal a kind of loathing
and tediousness, which causeth a
man to hate and to be weary of all
things. . . . Some grow so far as to hate
themselves, and so fall to despair,
yea many kill and destroy themselves.'

135. *an unweeded garden*] Kittredge
notes the echo in Rowlands, *Hell's
Broke Loose* (1605), 'this unweeded
garden of the world'.

136. *in nature*] i.e. inherent in
nature. Shakespeare recognizes that

the weeds are a part of natural
growth.

137. *merely*] entirely (L. *merus,*
unmixed).

140. *Hyperion to a satyr*] LN.

141–2. *he might not beteem . . .
roughly*] Cf. Wager, *Mary Magdalene*
(B2), 'My parents . . . would not
suffer the wind on me to blow'.
Shakespeare transforms a common
expression so as to suggest something
uncommon and grand. By contrast
Gertrude's love is made to seem
(ll. 144–5) sensual. *beteem,* permit.

147. *or ere*] before. *Or,* from O.E.
ǣr, itself means 'before', as at l. 183
(Q1 *Ere*), v.ii.30. But once it had
weakened in emphasis and perhaps
intelligibility, it was very often reinforced by *ere,* itself from O.E. *ǣr*
and so another form of the same word.
(*Lr* II.iv.285; *Mac.* IV.iii.173; etc.)
But *or ever* is also common (see l. 183
below; A.V. as in Proverbs viii.23,
Daniel vi.24), and it may be that

Like Niobe, all tears—why, she—
O God, a beast that wants discourse of reason   150
Would have mourn'd longer—married with my uncle,
My father's brother—but no more like my father
Than I to Hercules. Within a month,
Ere yet the salt of most unrighteous tears
Had left the flushing in her galled eyes,   155
She married—O most wicked speed! To post
With such dexterity to incestuous sheets!
It is not, nor it cannot come to good.

---

149. she—] *This edn;* she *Q2;* she, euen she. *F.*   150. God] *Q2,Q1;*
Heauen *F.*   151. my] *Q2;* mine *F,Q1.*   155. in] *Q2,Q1;* of *F.*

---

ere here is really the contraction of *ever*. So *OED* regards it (Or B 1 b, C 1 d, e; Ere C 1 d). Cf. Abbott 131.

149. *Niobe*] The type of sorrowing womanhood. In the Greek myth she wept inconsolably for the deaths of her children, slain by Apollo and Diana, until grief turned her into a stone, from which tears continued to fall. See Ovid, *Met.,* VI. 146–312.

she—] The F *even she,* which fills out the metre, may be Shakespearean but is comparable to the F repetitions at ll. 135, 224, 235, etc. See Intro., p. 62. As suggesting that better had been expected of her than of other women, it adds no doubt a note of poignancy but goes somewhat against the rest of the speech. And it weakens the sudden breaking off for the passionate exclamation which follows.

150. *a beast*] Anticipating Hamlet's reproaches to his mother in III.iv, where the corresponding passage in Belleforest has, 'Est-ce à une Royne . . . de suivre les appetits des bestes . . . ?', with much elaboration of beast analogies. See Intro., pp. 91–2. Cf. also I.v.56–7; and LN on l. 140 above.

wants discourse of reason] LN.

153. *Hercules*] who performed superhuman tasks. Already, before *his* task has come to him, Hamlet gives an indication of his feeling of inadequacy. This is the more significant in that he is made to negative in advance a comparison found in earlier versions of the story. Saxo concluded that if fortune had been as kind to him as nature, he would have outdone the labours of Hercules; and Belleforest likened him to Samson, the 'Hercules of the Hebrews'.

154. *unrighteous*] Because the grief they express is belied by her conduct (l. 157). Cf. Belleforest, *un pleur dissimulé,* and see Intro., p. 94.

155. *flushing*] Referring to the redness caused by weeping. Cf. *tears, galled.* Before the salt had gone from her reddened eyes = before her tears had ceased.

157. *dexterity*] nimbleness. Cf. *1H4* II.iv.251, 'You carried your guts away as nimbly, with as quick dexterity . . .'

incestuous] Incest formerly included the union of a woman with her husband's brother. (See Leviticus xviii.16; xx.21.)

But break, my heart, for I must hold my tongue.

Enter HORATIO, MARCELLUS, *and* BARNARDO.

Hor. Hail to your lordship.
Ham.   I am glad to see you well.   160
  Horatio, or I do forget myself.
Hor. The same, my lord, and your poor servant ever.
Ham. Sir, my good friend, I'll change that name with you.
  And what make you from Wittenberg, Horatio?—
  Marcellus.   165
Mar. My good lord.
Ham. I am very glad to see you.—[*To Barnardo*] Good even,
    sir.—
  But what in faith make you from Wittenberg?
Hor. A truant disposition, good my lord.
Ham. I would not hear your enemy say so,   170
  Nor shall you do my ear that violence
  To make it truster of your own report
  Against yourself. I know you are no truant.
  But what is your affair in Elsinore?

159. break,] *F4;* breake *Q2,F,Q1.*   160–1. I am . . . myself.] *As F; one*
line Q2.   162–3.] *As Q2;* 4 lines ending Lord, / euer. / friend, / you: *F.*
165. Marcellus.] *Q2,F; Marcellus? Capell.*   167. *To Barnardo*] *White.*
170. hear] *Q2;* haue *F.*   171. my] *Q2;* mine *F.*

159. *break, my heart*] Silent griefs
were said to make the heart break.
Cf. *Mac.* IV.iii.209–10; Ford, *Broken
Heart*, v.iii.75. Corson has the approval of Furness, Dowden, and others
in taking 'break' as subjunctive with
'my heart' as its subject. But the
absence of a comma from the early
texts accords with Elizabethan practice before a vocative. Cf. *Lr* v.iii.312
(F), 'Breake heart, I prythee breake'.
163. *change that name*] exchange the
name of 'servant', i.e., I am *your*
servant. Alternatively the *name* is
that of 'friend', i.e., Friend (not
servant) is what we will call one
another. Cf. below, ll. 253–4 (*duty
. . . loves*).
164. *what make you*] The common
phrase for 'What are you doing?'

OED make *v.*[1] 58. Cf. II.ii.270.
165. *Marcellus.*] Though most eds.
add a question-mark, this is surely a
simple greeting, to which Marcellus
replies.
167. *Good even*] A normal greeting
at any time after noon. Cf. *Rom.*
II.iv.105 ff.
174. *Elsinore*] the Danish Hel-
singör. Not mentioned in Saxo or
Belleforest, who locate the story in
Jutland. But Elsinore was well known
to the Elizabethans by reason of its
fortress at the entrance to the Sound,
where the Danes exacted tribute of
passing ships; and some of Shakespeare's fellow actors had played
there. Q2 always spells *Elsonoure*,
Q1 *Elsenoure* or *Elsanoure*, F *Elsenour*
or *Elsonower*.

We'll teach you to drink deep ere you depart.   175
Hor. My lord, I came to see your father's funeral.
Ham. I prithee do not mock me, fellow-student.
    I think it was to see my mother's wedding.
Hor. Indeed, my lord, it follow'd hard upon.
Ham. Thrift, thrift, Horatio. The funeral bak'd meats   180
    Did coldly furnish forth the marriage tables.
    Would I had met my dearest foe in heaven
    Or ever I had seen that day, Horatio.
    My father—methinks I see my father—
Hor. Where, my lord?
Ham.   In my mind's eye, Horatio.   185
Hor. I saw him once; a was a goodly king.

175. to drink deep] *F,Q1;* for to drinke *Q2.*   177. prithee] *Q2* (prethee),
Q1 (pre thee); pray thee *F.*   178. see] *F,Q1; not in Q2.*   183. Or ever I
had] *Q2;* Ere I had euer *F;* Ere euer I had *Q1.*   185. Where] *Q2,Q1;* Oh
where *F.*   186. a was] *Q2;* he was *F,Q1.*

175. *to drink deep*] A reflection on
the Danish drinking habits, already
instanced at l. 125 and enlarged on in
i.iv.8–22.
    176. *I came to see . . . funeral.*] Verity
contrasts Laertes's reference to the
'coronation', l. 53. Quite apart from
whether or not Horatio belonged to
the court circle, about which the
play seems curiously undecided (cf.
nn. on l. 186 below and i.iv.12–13),
Shakespeare here ignores the fact
that if he has been a month and more
(ll. 138, 147) in Denmark, Hamlet
would have been likely to know of his
presence.
    180. *bak'd meats*] meat pies. Cf.
White Devil, iv.ii.20, 'as if a man
Should know what fowl is coffin'd in
a bak'd meat Afore you cut it up'.
Often *bakemeats* (as Genesis xl.17),
where *bake* is past participle (orig.
baken).
    181. *coldly*] in the literal sense. The
funeral left-overs were served up cold
for the wedding.
    182. *dearest foe*] Cf. *1H4* iii.ii.123,
'my nearest and dearest enemy'. The
phrase is influenced by the analogy
of 'dearest friend'. But for *dear* =

grievous, cf. *R2* i.iii.151, 'dear exile';
Tim. v.i.226, 'dear peril'. This seems
to be etymologically a different
word (O.E. *dēor*) from *dear* = loved
(O.E. *dēore*), though the two inevitably became indistinguishable, so
that *dear* was naturally applied to
whatever affects us closely, whether
in a good or bad sense. (Cf. iii.iv.193;
iv.iii.41.) See *OED* dear *a.*[1] and *a.*[2].
    183. *Or ever*] before. Cf. i.ii.147 n.
    185. *Where*] Horatio starts at what
seems a reference to the Ghost.
    my mind's eye] A traditional meta-
phor, going back to Plato (ψυχῆς
ὄμμα, *Republic,* vii, 533 D; cf. *Sophist,*
254 B). Cf. e.g. Aristotle, *Nichomachean Ethics,* vi.12 (1144a 30);
Cicero, *De Oratore,* iii.163 ('mentis
oculi') and elsewhere; Chaucer, *Man
of Law's Tale,* 552; Sidney, *Apology,*
6th para.; Ephesians i.18 (Bishops'
Bible, 'the eyes of your minds'). See
SQ, vii, 351–4. For the phrase, cf.
above, i.i.115, *Lucr.* 1426; and for
the expansion of the idea, *Sonn.*
xxvii and cxiii.
    186. *once*] Conflicting with the
impression given by i.i.62ff., as
well as by ll. 211, 241–2 below, that

Ham. A was a man, take him for all in all:
    I shall not look upon his like again.
Hor. My lord, I think I saw him yesternight.
Ham. Saw? Who?
Hor.   My lord, the king your father.   190
Ham. The king my father?
Hor. Season your admiration for a while
    With an attent ear till I may deliver
    Upon the witness of these gentlemen
    This marvel to you.
Ham.   For God's love let me hear!   195
Hor. Two nights together had these gentlemen,
    Marcellus and Barnardo, on their watch
    In the dead waste and middle of the night
    Been thus encounter'd: a figure like your father

---

187. A] *Q2;* He *F,Q1.*   in all:] *F;* in all *Q2;* in all, *Q1.*   190. Saw?
Who?] *F;* saw, who? *Q2,Q1;* Saw who? *Q 1676.*   195. God's] *Q2,Q1;*
Heauens *F.*   198. waste] wast *Q2,F,* waste *F2;* vast *Q1,Q4;* waist *Malone.*

Horatio had seen him often. P.
Simpson (*MLR,* XIII, 321–2) tries to
resolve the inconsistency by supposing
that Horatio is about to refer to some
particular occasion when Hamlet
interrupts. But cf. I.iv.12–13 LN.

    187. *a man*] 'Edwin Booth . . .
paused after "man", giving it as if
something higher than "king" ' (Dowden). Rightly so. He was the embodiment of the ideal of manhood. Cf.
III.iv.62; *Caes.* v.v.75, 'Nature might
stand up And say to all the world
"This was a man!" '

    all in all] perfect in all things (with
take subjunctive rather than imperative). LN.

    190. *Saw? Who?*] Dyce, arguing
for the punctuation *Saw who?,* adds,
'No pause . . . was made . . . by the
two Kembles, Kean, and Young –
none is made by Macready and the
younger Kean'. *Who* for *whom* was
common; cf. Abbott 274.

    192. *Season*] temper, moderate.
Cf. II.i.28; *Mer. V.* IV.i.192, 'When
mercy seasons justice'.

admiration] astonishment, as at
III.ii.318.

    196–206.] Horatio's speech, 'a
perfect model of dramatic narration
and dramatic style, the purest poetry
and yet the most natural language'
(Coleridge, i.35).

    198. *waste*] Furness, Clark and
Wright (Camb.), Dowden, Kittredge are among editors who have
adopted Q1's *vast,* with the support
of *Tp.* I.ii.327, 'that vast of night'
(when spirits 'work'). But Greg
(*Principles of Emendation,* p. 66) and
Sisson (*NR*) find it unreasonable to
depart from the more authoritative
Q2 and F. Though *wast* would be an
easy misreading of *vast,* it was a
normal spelling of *waste,* the sense of
which is reinforced by *dead* (cf.
I.i.68 n.); and the association with
its homonym *wast* = waist may have
suggested *middle* (cf. II.ii.232). The
hint of a pun is 'improved' on by
Marston, *Malcontent,* II.v.91, "Tis
now about the immodest waste of
night'.

Armed at point exactly, cap-à-pie,   200
Appears before them, and with solemn march
Goes slow and stately by them; thrice he walk'd
By their oppress'd and fear-surprised eyes
Within his truncheon's length, whilst they, distill'd
Almost to jelly with the act of fear,   205
Stand dumb and speak not to him. This to me
In dreadful secrecy impart they did,
And I with them the third night kept the watch,
Where, as they had deliver'd, both in time,
Form of the thing, each word made true and good,   210
The apparition comes. I knew your father;
These hands are not more like.

Ham.   But where was this?
Mar. My lord, upon the platform where we watch.

---

200. at point exactly,] at poynt, exactly *Q2;* to poynt, exactly *Q1;* at all
points exactly, *F.*   cap-à-pie] *Capapea Q2,Q1, Cap a Pe F.*   202. stately by
them;] *Q2;* stately: By them *F.*   204. distill'd] *Q2,Q1;* bestil'd *F.*
205. jelly with . . . fear,] *F;* gelly, with . . . feare *Q2;* gelly. With . . . feare
Q1.   209. Where, as] *Q 1683;* Whereas *Q2,F;* Where as *Q1,Q5.*
210. thing,] *Q2;* thing; *F;* thing. *Q1.*   213. watch] *Q2;* watcht *F,Q1*
(watched), *Q3.*

---

200. *at point*] correctly in every
detail. Cf. Sir G. Haye, *Law of Arms*,
1456, Scot. Text Soc., p. 113, 'Ane
gude knycht . . . suld seth all his
study till arm him at poynt'; *Lr*
i.iv.325, 'keep At point a hundred
knights'.

cap-à-pie] head to foot. Cf. l. 227.
This French phrase was familiar in
description of arms. The Q2 spelling
presumably derives from Q1.

203. *fear-surprised*] *surprised* = over-
powered, made helpless. Cf. *Wint.*
iii.i.10, 'the ear-deaf'ning voice o'th'
oracle . . . so surpris'd my sense That
I was nothing'; *Tit.* ii.iii.211; Isaiah
xxxiii.14.

204. *truncheon*] a staff carried as a
symbol of military command.

distill'd] dissolved. See *OED* distil
v. 7. Some earlier eds. made a difficulty of this, and the F *bestil'd*, though
without parallel, has been defended

as going aptly with *stand dumb*. But
it is not by being struck motionless
that bodily substance turns to *jelly*,
which makes the sense quite clear.

205. *act*] action, effect, as in *Oth.*
iii.iii.332, 'poisons, . . . with a little
act upon the blood, Burn . . .'

209-10. *both in time, Form*] For
omission of *and*, cf. *Lr* i.i.48-9, 'we
will divest us both of rule, Interest of
territory, cares of state'.

211. *knew*] I see no good reason for
taking this, with Dover Wilson, to
mean 'recognized' rather than 'was
well acquainted with'. As Wilson
himself notes, Horatio is careful not
to say that the Ghost *was* Hamlet's
father, only that it was like him.

213. *platform*] the terrace of a fort
where guns were mounted.

watch] Some copies of Q2 show the
type disturbed and the end of the
line not printing properly. But that

Ham. Did you not speak to it?

Hor.   My lord, I did,
　　But answer made it none. Yet once methought   215
　　It lifted up it head and did address
　　Itself to motion like as it would speak.
　　But even then the morning cock crew loud,
　　And at the sound it shrunk in haste away
　　And vanish'd from our sight.

Ham.   'Tis very strange.   220

Hor. As I do live, my honour'd lord, 'tis true;
　　And we did think it writ down in our duty
　　To let you know of it.

Ham. Indeed, sirs; but this troubles me.
　　Hold you the watch tonight?

All.   We do, my lord.   225

Ham. Arm'd, say you?

All.   Arm'd, my lord.

Ham. From top to toe?

All.   My lord, from head to foot.

---

216. it] *Q2,F;* its *Q4.*   224. Indeed] *Q2;* Indeed, indeed *F,Q1.*
225, 226, 227. *All.*] *Q2,Q1; Both. F; Mar. Ber. Capell.*

watch is in fact the reading is established by the visibility of a final point
in other copies.

214. *speak to it*] Cf. I.i.32, 45, 48
and nn.

216. *it*] A regular form for the
neuter possessive, alternative to the
original *his* before both were replaced
by *its.* Cf. v.i.214; *Lr* I.iv.215. See
I.i.40 n.

218. *even then*] at that very moment.

224-43.] Here we pass, without
abrupt or even definable transition,
into one of those passages of rapid
colloquial dialogue which are neither
prose nor regular metre. It is with
hesitation that I set out ll. 225-7,
233-5, as verse; for Shakespeare
clearly makes no sustained attempt
to fit short speeches into pentameter
lines. Yet the verse rhythm is never
quite suspended; speeches of a five-

foot length form single lines of blank
verse (229, 231, 237); and as longer
speeches supervene (241 ff.) the regular metre is resumed with perfect
naturalness. Cf. I.i.1-25 and LN.

224. *Indeed*] assuredly. Not emphasizing what follows but approving
what has just been said. For the F
reduplication, cf. ll. 135, 235, and
Intro., p. 62.

225. *All*] F's *Both* perhaps recognizes that Horatio is not one of the
appointed watch, or, as Parrott and
Craig suppose, that Barnardo does
not watch in I.iv. But no such justification holds for ll. 226, 227, and the
reverse substitution occurs (mistakenly) at l. 238; so that F's variation of the speech-headings shows no
systematic purpose. Shakespeare presumably intended a full chorus.

Ham. Then saw you not his face?

Hor. O yes, my lord, he wore his beaver up.

Ham. What look'd he, frowningly?   230

Hor. A countenance more in sorrow than in anger.

Ham. Pale, or red?

Hor. Nay, very pale.

Ham.   And fix'd his eyes upon you?

Hor. Most constantly.

Ham.   I would I had been there.

Hor. It would have much amaz'd you.

Ham.   Very like.   235

    Stay'd it long?

Hor. While one with moderate haste might tell a hundred.

Mar. ⎫

Bar. ⎬ Longer, longer.

Hor. Not when I saw't.

Ham. His beard was grizzled, no?   240

Hor. It was as I have seen it in his life,

    A sable silver'd.

---

228. face?] *F,Q1; face. Q2.*   230. What look'd he,] *This edn;* What look't he *Q2;* What, lookt he *F;* How look't he, *Q1.*   235–6. like. / Stay'd] *This edn;* like, stayd *Q2;* like, very like: staid *F,Q1 (subst.).*   238. *Mar. Bar.*] *Q2 (Both.); All.F; Mar. Q1.*   240. grizzled] *Q2,Q1;* grisly *F.*   241. was ... life,] *Q1;* was ... life *Q2;* was, ... life, *F.*

228. *face?*] The question-mark in F is supported by Q1, and its absence in Q2 is paralleled by l. 240. But Dover Wilson and Sisson regard this speech as a deduction rather than an inquiry.

229. *beaver*] Originally the beaver was drawn up from the chin and the vizor let down from the forehead. But in 16th-century helmets beaver and vizor had ceased to be distinct, and either word was applied to the whole face-guard, which 'could be pushed up entirely over the top of the helmet' (Planché, *Cyclopaedia of Costume,* i. 39), thus leaving the face free.

230. *What*] Not an exclamation, as the F punctuation, which eds. invariably follow, might suggest. Hamlet is not taking up anything that has been said but introducing a new question. Either then a mere interrogative particle, as at I.i.21, 24, II.i.107 (*OED* What A 21), or, better, *What* = How, as Q1 shows it to have been understood. See *OED* What A 20. Cf. *Ant.* I.v.50 (F), 'What was he sad, or merry?'

frowningly] i.e. with the mien appropriate to an armed warrior. See I.i.65, and cf. *Mer. V.* III.ii.85, 'Hercules and frowning Mars'; *Cym.* II.iv.23, 'Julius Caesar . . . found their courage Worthy his frowning at'.

235. *amaz'd*] lit. 'put into a maze'; hence not merely 'astonished' but 'bewildered', as by something defying explanation. Cf. II.ii.559, III.iv.112; *Meas.* IV.ii.192, 'Put not yourself into amazement how these things should be'; *John* IV.iii.140.

Very like] For the F reduplication,

Ham.   I will watch tonight.
  Perchance 'twill walk again.
Hor.   I war'nt it will.
Ham. If it assume my noble father's person,
  I'll speak to it though hell itself should gape   245
  And bid me hold my peace. I pray you all,
  If you have hitherto conceal'd this sight,
  Let it be tenable in your silence still;
  And whatsomever else shall hap tonight,
  Give it an understanding but no tongue.   250
  I will requite your loves. So fare you well.
  Upon the platform 'twixt eleven and twelve
  I'll visit you.
All.   Our duty to your honour.
Ham. Your loves, as mine to you. Farewell.
                    Exeunt [Horatio, Marcellus, and Barnardo].

242-3. I . . . again] As *Q2; one line F,Q1.*   242. I will] *Q2,Q1;* Ile *F.*
243. walk] *Q2,Q1;* wake *F.*   war'nt] *Q2* (warn't)*;* warrant *Q1;* warrant
you *F.*   248. tenable] *Q2,Q1;* treble *F.*   249. whatsomever] *Q2;*
whatsoeuer *F,Q1,Q3.*   251. you] *Q2,Q1;* ye *F.*   254. loves] *Q2,Q1;*
loue *F.*   254 S.D.] *Exeunt. Manet Hamlet. (opp. 253-4) Q 1676; Exeunt (after
253) Q2,F,Q1.*

cf. l. 224 and Intro., p. 62. It is
highly improbable that Q2 omitted a
repetition in its copy twice in 15
lines.

  243. *war'nt*] The colloquial contraction of 'warrant' was common.

  244. *If it assume . . . person*] Contrast
l. 255. Hamlet alternates between
regarding the Ghost as an unknown
spirit in his father's shape and as his
'father's spirit' itself. There being no
question of mere hallucination (cf.
I. i. 26-7), it must be one or the other.

  245. *I'll speak to it*] Cf. I. i. 32 LN.

  though hell . . . gape] as ready to receive one who converses with a
devil. A spirit which assumed another's shape might well be, and in
the belief of such Protestants as
James I would certainly be, a devil. Cf.
II. ii. 595-6 and LN. A gaping hell
would be easily visualized by an
audience used to seeing hell-mouth
represented not only in pictures
but as an actual stage-property.

  246. *bid me hold my peace*] What 'bids'
him is not hell's command but the
threat of hell if he does otherwise.
Cf. preceding note.

  249. *whatsomever*] The older, and
evidently Shakespearean, form is
modernized in F, as also at I.v.84,
178. But F keeps *How . . . somever* at
III. ii. 389, and comparable instances
occur in other F texts. Q2 itself has
whensoever at v. ii. 199.

  251. *loves*] For the plural, as at
l. 254, cf. I. i. 178 and n.

  253. *Our duty*] The plain man's
abbreviation of the more elaborate
formula used by Osric, v. ii. 179.

  254. *loves*] Hamlet emends 'duty'
to 'love' as earlier he had done
'servant' to 'friend' (ll. 162-3).

My father's spirit—in arms! All is not well.   255
I doubt some foul play. Would the night were come.
Till then sit still, my soul. Foul deeds will rise,
Though all the earth o'erwhelm them, to men's eyes.

Exit.

SCENE III

Enter LAERTES *and* OPHELIA, *his sister.*

Laer. My necessaries are embark'd. Farewell.
          And sister, as the winds give benefit
          And convoy is assistant, do not sleep,
          But let me hear from you.
Oph.   Do you doubt that?
Laer. For Hamlet, and the trifling of his favour,   5
          Hold it a fashion and a toy in blood,

---

255. spirit—in arms!] spirit (in armes) *Q2; Spirit in Armes? F.*   257. Foul]
F,Q1; fonde *Q2.*

Scene III

SCENE III] *F (Scena Tertia); not in Q2.*   S.D. *his sister] Q2; not in F.*
3. convoy is assistant,] *Theobald;* Conuoy is assistant; *F;* conuay, in assistant
Q2.   5. favour] *Q2;* fauours *F.*

255. *My father's spirit*] Contrast
l. 244. That ghosts were the spirits
of the departed was the traditional
view from classical times and reinforced by the Catholic doctrine of
purgatory. That Protestants disputed
it and denounced it as 'a foolish
opinion' (Burton, 1.ii.1(2)) is not
dramatically relevant. Shakespeare
is aware of various beliefs and allows
Hamlet to be the same. Cf. West,
'King Hamlet's Ambiguous Ghost',
PMLA, LXX, 1107ff., and notes on
1.i.26, 1.iv.40, 1.v.10–13, 25.

256. *doubt*] fear, suspect (as often).
Cf. 11.ii.56, 111.i.168.

foul play] The disclosure of a crime
was held to be one of the common
reasons for a ghost's appearance.
Cf. 1.v.25 LN. It was not, however,
among those speculated on by Horatio

and his companions (1.i.72, 112–41).
It is left for Hamlet to divine the
nature of the Ghost's errand (though
not as yet, of course, its import).
With this first clear hint not of what
but of what kind the Ghost's communication will be Shakespeare still
further heightens suspense.

Scene III

2. *as*] at such times as.

3. *convoy is assistant*] means of conveyance are available. Fr. *assister* =
to be in attendance. Shakespeare
thinks of communication between
Denmark and France as being necessarily by sea (cf. *embark'd, winds*).

6. *a toy in blood*] an amorous sport
of impulsive youth. LN.

A violet in the youth of primy nature,
Forward, not permanent, sweet, not lasting,
The perfume and suppliance of a minute,
No more.

Oph.　　　　No more but so?

Laer.　　　　　　　Think it no more.　　　　10

For nature crescent does not grow alone
In thews and bulk, but as this temple waxes,
The inward service of the mind and soul
Grows wide withal. Perhaps he loves you now,
And now no soil nor cautel doth besmirch　　　15
The virtue of his will; but you must fear,

8. Forward] *Q2*; Froward *F.*　　8–10. lasting, / The perfume and suppliance
of a minute, / No more.] *Q2 (subst.)*; lasting / The suppliance of a minute? No
more. *F.*　　10. so?] *Rowe*; so. *Q2,F.*　　11. crescent] cressant *Q2,F.*
12. bulk] *F*; bulkes *Q2.*　　this] *Q2*; his *F.*　　16. will] *Q2*; feare *F.*
fear,] *Q2*; feare *F.*

7. *primy*] A Shakespearean coinage.
In its prime or springtime, the period
when youth is at its flower. Cf. *Sonn.*
XII, 'When I behold the violet past
prime'. This whole passage suggests
a youthful Hamlet (cf. l. 124,
I.v.16), in contrast to the thirty
years attributed to him at v.i.139–
57 (on which LN).

8. *Forward*] prompt to act, hence
quickly coming into flower.

8–9. *not lasting . . . of a minute*] As it
will seem ironically to prove – cf.
III.i.99, and see v.i.233 n.

9. *suppliance*] something which
supplies or fills up (a vacancy);
pastime.

10. *No more but so?*] Parrott and
Craig follow Corson in rejecting the
editorial question-mark, taking Ophelia to accept her brother's view. But
this removes the justification of
Laertes's long hortatory speech and
is hardly consistent with ll. 110–14.
It is because she does not find it easy
to agree with her brother (and her
father) that she does 'not know' what
she 'should think' (l. 104).

11. *crescent*] as it grows. L. *crescere.*
The *ss* spelling (from Fr.) in Q2 and

F was normal until the 17th century
re-formed the word according to the
Latin.

12. *thews and bulk*] *thews*, physical
parts, strength. *Bulk* here combines
the senses of (1) physical size and
(2) the trunk of the body, for which
see II.i.95 n. Cf. *2H4* III.ii.251–2, 'the
thews, the stature, bulk, and big
assemblance of a man' (in contrast
to 'the spirit').

this temple] The familiar scriptural
image for the body as the house of
the spirit. See 1 Corinthians iii.16–17,
vi.19 ('Your body is the temple of the
Holy Ghost which is in you'), etc.

13. *service*] Continuing the religious
metaphor of the temple, while referring directly to the social and
political duties enlarged on in ll. 17–24.

15. *cautel*] '*Cautelle*: A wile, cautel,
sleight; a . . . guileful device or
endeavour; also craft, . . . deceit'
(Cotgrave). Cf. *Cor.* IV.i.33, 'caught
With cautelous baits and practice'.

16. *The virtue of his will*] the purity
of his intention (with sexual overtones in both nouns). *virtue*, moral
integrity. Cf. *Caes.* II.i.133, 'do not
stain The even virtue of our enter-

His greatness weigh'd, his will is not his own.
For he himself is subject to his birth:
He may not, as unvalu'd persons do,
Carve for himself, for on his choice depends   20
The sanity and health of this whole state;
And therefore must his choice be circumscrib'd
Unto the voice and yielding of that body
Whereof he is the head. Then if he says he loves you,
It fits your wisdom so far to believe it   25
As he in his particular act and place
May give his saying deed; which is no further
Than the main voice of Denmark goes withal.
Then weigh what loss your honour may sustain
If with too credent ear you list his songs,   30
Or lose your heart, or your chaste treasure open
To his unmaster'd importunity.
Fear it, Ophelia, fear it, my dear sister,

18] *F; not in Q2.*   21. sanity and] *Hanmer, conj. Theobald (SR)* ; safty and *Q2*;
safety and *Q3*; sanctity and *F*; safety and the *Warburton.*   this whole] *Q2*;
the weole *F.*   26. particular act and place] *Q2*; peculiar Sect and force *F.*

prise' (in the manner of 'cautelous'
men).

17. *His greatness weigh'd*] his exalted
position being considered.

20. *Carve for himself*] A proverbial
phrase, Tilley C 110. Cf. *R2* II.iii.144,
'Be his own carver and cut out his
way'; Swinburn, *Testaments and Last
Wills*, 1590, p. 50, 'It is not lawful
for legataries to carve for themselves,
taking their legacies at their own
pleasures'. On the last as a possible
source, see Muir, *Sources of Sh.'s
Plays*, pp. 169–70.

21. *sanity*] well-being. LN.

23. *yielding*] consent. The word
need not imply submission; it can
mean a giving forth (in words), hence,
like *voice*, a proclaimed opinion. Cf.
Sir T. Smith, *Commonwealth of England*, 'The order of proceeding to
judgment is by assent of voices, and
open yielding their mind in court'
(1589 edn, p. 121). For *yield* =

declare, utter, cf. also IV.V.11, *All's
W.* III.i.10; *OED* yield 12.

24. *he is the head*] Granted the or-
thodoxy of these sentiments on the
marriage of a prince, this anticipation
of Hamlet's succession to the throne
seems more in accord with a hereditary than an elective monarchy. See
I.ii.1 LN. There is no thought here of
Hamlet's having or needing the King's
'voice' (cf. III.ii.331–3, I.ii.109).

26. *in his particular act and place*] in
the action and position which belong
to him as one differentiated from
other men; 'acting as he must in his
special circumstances and under the
restrictions of his rank' (Kittredge).

28. *main*] general. Cf. *H8* IV.i.31,
'the main assent Of all these learned
men'. *OED* main *a.* 7 b.

30. *list*] listen to (as often).

31. *chaste treasure*] i.e. virginity. Cf.
Meas. II.iv.96, 'the treasures of your
body'; *Cym.* II.ii.42, 'I have pick'd

And keep you in the rear of your affection
Out of the shot and danger of desire.   35
The chariest maid is prodigal enough
If she unmask her beauty to the moon.
Virtue itself scapes not calumnious strokes.
The canker galls the infants of the spring
Too oft before their buttons be disclos'd,   40
And in the morn and liquid dew of youth
Contagious blastments are most imminent.
Be wary then: best safety lies in fear.
Youth to itself rebels, though none else near.

---

34. you in] *Q2;* within *F.*   40. their] *Q2;* the *F.*

---

the lock and ta'en The treasure of her honour'. The question of Ophelia's chastity will not be less important than that of Isabella and Imogen, and is given early prominence.

34.] In this military metaphor Ophelia's affection is figured as the forward troops, exposed to danger, while she herself is to stay behind out of reach of the enemy shot.

36.] This and ll. 38, 39 are preceded in Q2 by the inverted commas which are often used in Elizabethan texts to signalize sententious sayings. So too IV. v. 17–20.

chariest] most modest. The general sense of *chary* as the opposite of *prodigal* combines with its particular sexual use. Cf. Rich, *Apolonius and Silla* (1921 repr., p. 79), '[I] that have so charely preserved mine honour'; *Tw.N.* III. iv. 192, 'laid mine honour too unchary out'; *Wiv.* II. i. 87, 'sully the chariness of our honesty'.

38. *Virtue . . . strokes.*] Cf. III. i. 137–8 and n.

scapes] The aphetic variant of *escape* was in common use not only in verse. The apostrophe which editors like to insert is strictly proper only in 18th-century and later texts.

39–40.] The sentiment is commonplace and the language, conventional-poetic, appropriate. That 'the most forward bud Is eaten by the canker

ere it blow' is cited as a common saying in *Gent.* I. i. 45–6. See also Day, *Law Tricks*, 1608, MSR, ll. 704–6, 'Do not let despair Like the rank canker . . . Eat the young rose of beauty in the bud'. *Infants of the spring* echoes *LLL* I. i. 101. *Button* (Fr. *bouton*) is, since the *Roman de la Rose*, poetic for 'bud' (cf. *2 Noble Kinsmen*, III. i. 6). To *disclose*, lit. to open, was a normal verb to describe the process of buds unfolding (cf. *Sonn.* LIV. 8) – as also of eggs hatching (see III. i. 168, v. i. 282).

41. *liquid*] has, as in Latin, the connotation 'bright'.

42. *Contagious blastments*] disease-bringing blights. Cf. *blasting*, III. iv. 65. This meaning of *blast* comes from the attribution of disease in plants to blasts of foul air. As these are associated with morning dampness, so the 'morn' of 'youth' is the time both of bright promise and of greatest susceptibility to corruption. Cf. *Meas.* II. iii. 11, 'falling in the flaws [= blasts] of her own youth'.

43. *safety lies in fear*] Cf. *Mac.* III. v. 32–3, 'Security [= freedom from fear] Is mortals' chiefest enemy'.

44. *rebels*] The stirring of passion, or sexual desire, is often spoken of as *rebellion* (against one's higher nature). Cf. III. iv. 82 ff.; *All's W.* IV. iii. 18, v. iii. 6; *Mer. V.* III. i. 31.

Oph. I shall th'effect of this good lesson keep   45
        As watchman to my heart. But good my brother,
        Do not as some ungracious pastors do,
        Show me the steep and thorny way to heaven,
        Whiles like a puff'd and reckless libertine
        Himself the primrose path of dalliance treads,   50
        And recks not his own rede.
Laer.   O fear me not.
        I stay too long.

Enter POLONIUS.

        But here my father comes.
        A double blessing is a double grace:
        Occasion smiles upon a second leave.
Pol. Yet here, Laertes? Aboard, aboard for shame.   55
        The wind sits in the shoulder of your sail,

---

45. th'] *F;* the *Q2.*   46. watchman] *Q2;* watchmen *F,Q3.*   48. steep]
Q2 corr., F; step *Q2 uncorr.*   49. Whiles] *Q2;* Whilst *F.*   like] *F; not in*
Q2.   52 S.D.] *As Sisson; after* rede (*51*) *Q2; after 51 F; after 52 Capell.*

45–6. *I shall . . . my heart.*] The critics read Ophelia's speech according to their different conceptions of her character. Some who regard her as fickle detect indications of lightness already. Yet her spirited rejoinder notably begins with the earnest reception of her brother's counsel. I see no mockery in *lesson.* Cf. ll. 85–6, and Greene's Dorothea (*James IV*, I.i.167), 'I will engrave these precepts in my heart'. *effect,* i.e. substance.

47. *ungracious*] lacking (spiritual) grace, ungodly. Cf. *R2* II.iii.89; *1H4* II.iv.430.

49. *Whiles*] F modernizes, as also at I.v.96, III.iv.150. But contrast v.ii.399.

puff'd] lit. swollen. Falstaff is 'puff'd' (*Wiv.* v.v.146). Here usually glossed 'bloated'. But heedless man on the way to hell may be 'puff'd' with pride. Cf. 'puff'd' with ambition, IV.iv.49.

50. *Himself*] With the switch to the singular cf. I.iv.33. Here it focuses the comparison more sharply on Laertes. The opposite change from singular to plural occurs at III.ii.183–6.

primrose path] Shakespeare's own variation on the traditional metaphor of the broad way to destruction. See Matthew vii.13–14. Cf. *Mac.* II.iii. 18–19, 'the primrose way to th'everlasting bonfire'; *All's W.* IV.v.48–9, 'the flow'ry way that leads to the broad gate and the great fire'.

dalliance] The general sense of careless pleasure includes the particular one of amorous flirtation. Cf. *1H6* v.i.23, 'wanton dalliance with a paramour'.

51. *recks not his own rede*] heeds not his own counsel. *Rede* (O.E. *rǣd*), though it occurs only once in Shakespeare, was still in common use.

54. *Occasion smiles upon*] It is a happy circumstance which gives opportunity for. *Occasion,* cf. II.ii.16.

And you are stay'd for. There, my blessing with thee.
And these few precepts in thy memory
Look thou character. Give thy thoughts no tongue,
Nor any unproportion'd thought his act.   60
Be thou familiar, but by no means vulgar;
Those friends thou hast, and their adoption tried,
Grapple them unto thy soul with hoops of steel,
But do not dull thy palm with entertainment
Of each new-hatch'd, unfledg'd courage. Beware   65
Of entrance to a quarrel, but being in,
Bear't that th'opposed may beware of thee.
Give every man thy ear, but few thy voice;
Take each man's censure, but reserve thy judgment.
Costly thy habit as thy purse can buy,   70
But not express'd in fancy; rich, not gaudy;
For the apparel oft proclaims the man,
And they in France of the best rank and station

---

57. for. There,] *Theobald (subst.); for, there* Q2,Q1; *for there: F.*   thee]
Q2,Q1; you *F.*   59. Look] Q2; See *F.*   62. Those] Q2,Q1; The *F.*
63. unto] Q2; to *F.*   65. new-hatch'd] Q2; vnhatch't *F;* new Q1.   courage]
Q2,Q1; Comrade *F.*   68. thy ear] Q2; thine eare *F.*

---

57. *There*] Goes with the 'blessing', as suggested by Q2 (and Q1). Theobald's S.D., 'Laying his hand on Laertes' head', is adopted by many editors. Corson, implausibly defending the F punctuation, held *there* to refer to the port where the 'sail' was.

58–80.] For such advice to a son, LN.

59. *character*] engrave. The accent could fall on either the first or (as here) the second syllable. Cf. *Sonn.* CXXII. 2, 'Full character'd with lasting memory'.

60. *unproportion'd*] unruly, intemperate. Cf. *R2* III.iv.41, 'Keep law and form and due proportion'.

his] its. See I.i.40 n.

62. *and their adoption tried*] and their acceptance as your friends having been justified by experience. It is the friendship rather than the 'adoption' that has been 'tried', or proved. See *OED* try *v.* 13. The nominative absolute introduced by *and* is quite a regular construction. The effect of *and* is that of adding a further circumstance to what has already been said (almost 'moreover'). So too III.iii.62. See Abbott 95.

63. *hoops*] Pope's notion that grappling implied *hooks* rather than *hoops* is a piece of 18th-century literalism.

65. *courage*] gallant, swashbuckler. LN.

69. *censure*] opinion, judgment (not necessarily, or even usually, condemnatory). Cf. I.iv.35; III.ii.27, 87.

70. *habit*] clothing. Cf. III.iv.137.

71. *fancy*] fantasticalness, ornamentation.

Are of a most select and generous chief in that.
Neither a borrower nor a lender be,   75
For loan oft loses both itself and friend,
And borrowing dulls the edge of husbandry.
This above all: to thine own self be true,
And it must follow as the night the day
Thou canst not then be false to any man.   80
Farewell, my blessing season this in thee.
Laer. Most humbly do I take my leave, my lord.
Pol. The time invests you; go, your servants tend.
Laer. Farewell, Ophelia, and remember well
    What I have said to you.
Oph.   'Tis in my memory lock'd,   85
    And you yourself shall keep the key of it.

74. Are of a most select and generous chief] *F* (cheff); *Or* of a most select
and generous, chiefe *Q2;* Are of a most select and generall chiefe *Q1;* Ar
of a most select and generous, cheefe *Q3;* Are most select and generous,
chief *Rowe;* Are of a most select and generous *White;* Are of a most select and
generous choice *Collier*[2] (choice *conj. Steevens*).   75. be] *F;* boy *Q2.*
76. loan] *F* (lone); loue *Q2.*   77. dulls the] *F;* dulleth *Q2;* dulleth the
Q3; dulleth th' *conj. Parrott-Craig.*   83. invests] *Q2;* inuites *F.*

74. *Are of a most select . . . that.*]
Select, lit. picked out, hence distinguished from the ordinary by superior
quality of rank (cf. Drayton, *Barons'
Wars,* VI.xvi, 'Men most select, Of
special worth and sort'); *generous*
(L. *generosus*), of, or having the
characteristics associated with, noble
birth (cf. IV.vii.134, V.ii.238); *chief,*
head, top, and so the height of anything (as in 'the chief of summer'),
its point of maximum intensity or
excellence. One may therefore paraphrase, '[Frenchmen of the highest
rank] are of a most distinguished and
noble pre-eminence in that respect'
(i.e. in unostentatious richness of
dress). LN.
    77. *dulls the edge*] Parrott and Craig
suggest that *Q2 dulleth edge* is an error
for *dulleth th'edge* and F a modernization.
    husbandry] saving. Cf. *Mac.* II.i.4,
'There's husbandry in heaven; Their
candles are all out'.

78. *to thine own self be true*] be constant, be consistent in your opinions.
See ll. 58–80 LN.
    81. *season*] 'mature, ripen'
(Schmidt). Cf. III.ii.204. The effect
of adding the blessing is not to make
the advice more palatable *to* Laertes
but to enrich and mature it *in* him.
    83. *invests*] besieges, hence presses
upon. (So Theobald.) F *invites* has
usually been preferred and accords
with Shakespearean usage: cf. *Cym.*
III.iv.104, 'the time inviting thee';
Mac. II.i.62, 'The bell invites me'.
Time *calls upon us* at *Mac.* III.i.36 and
Ant. II.ii.162. But *invests,* if without
parallel, has the character of a
Shakespearean metaphor and is not
easily attributable to the Q2 compositor.
    tend] attend (Fr. *attendre*), i.e. wait.
So too at IV.iii.45.
    86. *yourself shall keep the key*] She will
remember it till he permits her to
forget it. The echo of this phrase in

Laer. Farewell.   *Exit.*

Pol. What is't, Ophelia, he hath said to you?

Oph. So please you, something touching the Lord Hamlet.

Pol. Marry, well bethought.   90
   'Tis told me he hath very oft of late
   Given private time to you, and you yourself
   Have of your audience been most free and bounteous.
   If it be so—as so 'tis put on me,
   And that in way of caution—I must tell you   95
   You do not understand yourself so clearly
   As it behoves my daughter and your honour.
   What is between you? Give me up the truth.

Oph. He hath, my lord, of late made many tenders
   Of his affection to me.   100

Pol. Affection? Pooh, you speak like a green girl,
   Unsifted in such perilous circumstance.
   Do you believe his tenders, as you call them?

Oph. I do not know, my lord, what I should think.

Pol. Marry, I will teach you. Think yourself a baby   105
   That you have ta'en these tenders for true pay
   Which are not sterling. Tender yourself more dearly

---

105. I will] *Q2;* Ile *F.* 106. these] *Q2;* his *F.*

Northward Ho, 1.i.71, however, promises not remembrance but secrecy. So too *A Fair Quarrel,* ii.ii.66.

 93. *free*] liberal.

 94. *put on*] pressed upon, as in *AYL* 1.ii.85 ('his mouth full of news.—Which he will put on us as pigeons feed their young'). Cf. *Tw.N.* v.i.61.

 101. *green*] Cf. Chapman, *All Fools,* iv.i.18, 127, 'You're green, you're credulous, easy to be blinded', 'young and green'.

 102. *Unsifted*] untried; inexperienced in resisting temptation. Cf. Luke xxii.31, 'Satan hath desired to have you, that he may sift you as wheat'.

 106. *tenders*] *Tender,* offer, is especially used in connection with (1) expressions of feeling (cf. tender thanks, sympathy), and particularly

(in Elizabethan use) love; (2) the formal presentation of money in payment (cf. legal tender). Used by Ophelia in the first context (l. 99), the word is taken up by Polonius (l. 103) and now switched into the second, with the effect that what is for her an affair of the heart now appears as a commercial transaction. The contrast here is not, as has been thought, between 'tenders' and 'true pay', but between tenders which are and are not 'true pay' or 'sterling' (see next note).

 107. *sterling*] genuine money. Cf. *Mamillia,* 'It is ... hard to descry the true sterling from the counterfeit coin' (Greene, ii.256).

 Tender yourself more dearly] (1) Offer yourself at a higher rate. The commercial sense continues, with Ophelia

Or—not to crack the wind of the poor phrase,
Running it thus—you'll tender me a fool.
Oph. My lord, he hath importun'd me with love   110
In honourable fashion.
Pol. Ay, fashion you may call it. Go to, go to.
Oph. And hath given countenance to his speech, my lord,
With almost all the holy vows of heaven.
Pol. Ay, springes to catch woodcocks. I do know,   115
When the blood burns, how prodigal the soul
Lends the tongue vows. These blazes, daughter,
Giving more light than heat, extinct in both

---

109. Running] *Collier*[2]*;* Wrong *Q2;* Roaming *F;* tendring *Q1;* Wronging
Pope; Wringing *Theobold, conj. Warburton.*   113. speech, my lord] *Rowe;*
speech / My Lord *Q2,F (subst.).*   114. With almost all the holy] *Q2;* with
all the *F.*   115. springes] *F,Q1;* springs *Q2.*   117. Lends] *Q2,Q1;*
Giues *F.*

---

herself becoming now the object of
exchange. With it combines a further
sense of *tender,* to feel tender towards,
be solicitous for (cf. IV.iii.41),
whence also (2) Show greater care for
yourself.

109. *Running*] In this generally
accepted emendation *running* completes the metaphor of the broken-
winded horse in the previous line.
LN.

tender me a fool] Polonius sustains
the notion of the offer of a bad bargain, but is now himself the victim.
The *fool* Ophelia will offer to him is
of course herself. Though it might
not be beyond him, there is no justification for supposing that Polonius
has a bastard in mind. *Fool* unqualified does not mean 'baby' – when the
child in *Rom.* I.iii.32, 49, is called
pretty fool, this is a normal term of
endearment. The further suggestion
that Polonius may mean that Ophelia
will make a fool of him – 'present me
(to the public) as a fool' (Dowden) –
also strains the text.

112. *fashion*] Polonius again takes
up Ophelia's word in a different
sense. Cf. l. 6.

113. *countenance*] approval, sanction,
confirmation.

114. *With almost . . . heaven.*] A suspicion that Q2 *almost* and *holy* are
metrical fill-ups is hard to reconcile
with the belief that Q2 was printed
from autograph. Omissions in F may
connect with an attempt to adjust the
metre following the mislining of 'my
lord'.

115. *springes to catch woodcocks*]
springes, snares. A proverbial phrase,
Tilley S 788. The woodcock was
supposed easily caught. See Gosson,
Apology for the School of Abuse (Arber,
p. 72), 'Cupid sets up a springe for
woodcocks, which are entangled ere
they descry the line, and caught
before they mistrust the snare'. Cf.
v.ii.312.

116. *the blood*] Cf. I.iii.6 LN.

117.] The metrical deficiency of this
line has given rise to many suggestions
for supplying a supposed omission.

blazes] *Blaze* often has the suggestion of a short spurt of flame. Cf.
Greene's *Never Too Late,* 'Lightning,
that beautifies the heaven for a blaze'
(Greene, viii. 142).

Even in their promise as it is a-making,
You must not take for fire. From this time   120
Be something scanter of your maiden presence,
Set your entreatments at a higher rate
Than a command to parley. For Lord Hamlet,
Believe so much in him that he is young,
And with a larger tether may he walk   125
Than may be given you. In few, Ophelia,
Do not believe his vows; for they are brokers
Not of that dye which their investments show,
But mere implorators of unholy suits,
Breathing like sanctified and pious bawds   130

120. From] *Q2;* For *F.*   time] *Q2;* time Daughter *F.*   121. something]
Q2; somewhat *F.*   123. parley] *F;* parle *Q2.*   125. tether] tider *Q2,*
tether *F.*   128. that dye] *Q2;* the eye *F.*   130. bawds] *Pope², Theobald,*
conj. SR; bonds *Q2,F.*

119. *it*] the promise. The blazes
give promise of light and heat but die
down even at the moment that the
promise is being made.

122. *entreatments*] negotiations. A
military metaphor, as is clear from
parley. It was of course traditional
to represent courtship in terms of war.
Ophelia, as defender of a citadel, is
not to accept the besieger's call for a
parley as a sufficient reason for her to
treat, or enter into negotiations, with
him.

125. *tether*] *Ted(d)er* (cf. *Q2 tider*)
is the commoner Elizabethan form.

126. *In few*] i.e. in a few words, in
short. A common idiom.

127. *brokers*] A *broker,* properly an
agent or middleman, often meant a
go-between in love affairs and hence
a bawd. The word is applied to
Pandarus (*Troil.* III.ii.199–200, v.x.
33), and in *John* II.i.582 *broker* and
bawd are equivalents. (Cf. *brokes,*
said of one who negotiates for a maid's
honour, *All's W.* III.v.68.) This sense
of *brokers,* latent here, becomes active
with l. 129. There is probably also a
quibble as in *John* II.i.568, 'That
broker that still breaks the pate of
faith, That daily break-vow'. A

broker popularly suggested dishonest
dealing.

128. *investments*] (1) clothes; (2)
sieges (*OED* invest *v.* 7). The metaphor asserts that the language in
which the vows are couched does not
indicate their real nature. The only
other instance of this word in Shakespeare (*2H4* IV.i.45) also refers to
vestments of a colour which belies the
wearer's inward character. Its conjunction here with *brokers* suggests to
Dover Wilson and others a further
pun on monetary investments, but it
is not clear that the activities of
Elizabethan brokers (in laying out
money on goods for resale) were
commonly so called.

129. *implorators*] A word not otherwise recorded, but corresponding to
Fr. *implorateur* (obs.), for which
Cotgrave gives 'An implorer, be-
seecher, . . . humble and earnest
entreater'.

unholy suits] Contrast 'holy vows',
l. 114. Polonius has said (l. 128) that
the vows are only *clothed* in holiness.
The disparity between their *invest-*
ments and their *suits* is sharpened by
the pun.

130. *bawds*] LN.

The better to beguile. This is for all.
I would not, in plain terms, from this time forth
Have you so slander any moment leisure
As to give words or talk with the Lord Hamlet.
Look to't, I charge you. Come your ways.   135
Oph. I shall obey, my lord.   *Exeunt.*

[SCENE IV]

Enter HAMLET, HORATIO, *and* MARCELLUS.

Ham. The air bites shrewdly, it is very cold.
Hor. It is a nipping and an eager air.
Ham. What hour now?
Hor.   I think it lacks of twelve.

---

131. beguile] *F;* beguide *Q2.*   133. moment] *Q2,F;* moments *Q3,*
moment's *Pope.*

Scene IV

SCENE IV] *Capell.*   1. shrewdly] *F;* shroudly *Q2;* shrewd *Q1.*   it is] *Q2;*
is it *F.*   2. a] *F;* not in *Q2;* An *Q1.*

---

131. *for all*] once for all, as in *Cym.*
II.iii.106.

133. *slander*] disgrace, abuse.

moment] For the noun used adjec-
tivally, cf. *1H6* I.iv.54, 'every minute
while' (F). Later idiom prefers the
genitive, as in Q3 and *Gent.* I.i.30,
'one fading moment's mirth'. But cf.
'the region kites' (II.ii.575), and see
Abbott 22, 430.

135. *Come your ways.*] A common
idiom, in which *ways* shows an old
adverbial use of the genitive. See
OED way *sb.*[1] 23. Cf. III.i.130.

Scene IV

I.iv] This scene, like I.i, takes place

on the platform of the battlements.
See I.ii.213, 252.

S.D.] The absence of Barnardo
receives no explanation, and needs
none beyond dramatic convenience.
Hamlet, like Horatio before him, is
provided with two companions; the
third is redundant.

1. *shrewdly*] keenly.

2. *eager*] sharp, bitter. The original
sense; cf. Fr. *aigre,* and I.v.69.

3. *lacks of*] Formerly a common
idiom in telling the time and still
surviving regionally in such phrases
as 'It wants ten minutes of (to) six'.
See *OED* want *v.* 1c, 2d.

Mar. No, it is struck.

Hor.   Indeed? I heard it not.

It then draws near the season   5
Wherein the spirit held his wont to walk.

A flourish of trumpets, and two pieces [of ordnance] go off.

What does this mean, my lord?

Ham. The King doth wake tonight and takes his rouse,
Keeps wassail, and the swagg'ring upspring reels;
And as he drains his draughts of Rhenish down,   10
The kettle-drum and trumpet thus bray out
The triumph of his pledge.

Hor.   Is it a custom?

Ham. Ay marry is't,
But to my mind, though I am native here
And to the manner born, it is a custom   15
More honour'd in the breach than the observance.

4–5. Indeed . . . season] *This edn; one line Q2,F.*   5. It then] *Q2;* then it *F.*
6 S.D.] *Q2 (subst.); not in F;* Sound Trumpets *(after 3) Q1.*   9. wassail]
Q2,Q1; wassels *F.*   14. But] *Q2;* And *F.*

4. *it is struck*] The time exactly
corresponds with that of the opening
scene. Cf. I. i. 7.

6 S.D. *pieces*] The cannon of
I. ii. 126. It is with an effective irony –
which perhaps the audience does not
always note – that the cannon by
which Claudius celebrates Hamlet's
staying on in Denmark are heard by
Hamlet at the very moment when he
waits for his father's ghost. And the
echoes of the new King's revelry
(ll. 8 ff.) will still be in our ears when
the ghost of the King he has murdered
tells how he got the crown.

8. *wake*] stay up and awake, often
implying nocturnal revelry.

takes his rouse] carouses. Cf. I. ii. 127
and n., II. i. 58.

9. *the . . . upspring reels*] riotously
dances the upspring (a wild dance).
LN.

10. *Rhenish*] The common name
given to Rhine wine, also at v. i. 174.
It was the characteristic drink of the
Danish upper classes (Dollerup, pp.
124–6).

11. *kettle-drum and trumpet*] Characteristically Danish. Though not referred to in I. ii. 125–8, their function
as a signal to the cannon (l. 6 S.D.) is
made clear by v. ii. 272–5.   LN.

12. *triumph*] festive celebration,
often accompanied by trumpets or
other sounds of rejoicing. Cf. *OED*
4–6; *MND* I. i. 19, 'With pomp, with
triumph, and with revelling'.

pledge] The 'jocund health' of
I. ii. 125. Cf. l. 6 S.D. n.

12–13. *Is it a custom?—Ay*] LN.

15. *to the manner born*] Not merely
familiar with the custom from birth,
but committed to it by birth. It is
part of his heritage (possibly with a
play on 'manor'). Lewkenor, in a
passage (immediately preceding an
account of Wittenberg) which Shakespeare may well have read, speaks of
the drunkenness of the people of
Leipzig as an 'innated and incor-
rigible vice, which custom hath
drawn to a nature among them'
(*Discourse of Foreign Cities*, E3). Cf.
note on *habit* (l. 29) below.

This heavy-headed revel east and west
Makes us traduc'd and tax'd of other nations—
They clepe us drunkards, and with swinish phrase
Soil our addition; and indeed it takes   20
From our achievements, though perform'd at height,
The pith and marrow of our attribute.
So, oft it chances in particular men
That for some vicious mole of nature in them,
As in their birth, wherein they are not guilty   25
(Since nature cannot choose his origin),

17–38. This . . . scandal.] *Q2; not in F,Q1.*   19. clepe] clip *Q2,* clepe *Q5.*

17–38.] The omission in F (and Q1) of this discursive passage before the appearance of the Ghost corresponds to the similar cut at I.i.111–28. It cannot therefore be attributed, as is often suggested, to the fear of offending James I's Danish Queen. Though evidently cut as being 'undramatic', the passage both prolongs expectancy and at the same time gives to the Ghost's appearance the dramatic effect of a sudden interruption. Cf. I.i.42, 128. See Dover Wilson, *MSH*, p. 25.

17–20. *This heavy-headed revel . . . addition*] LN.

17. *heavy-headed*] Transferred epithet. The revellers are lumpish, their wits dulled with drink. This echoes Nashe (LN).

east and west] Not, of course, describing *revel* but modifying *traduc'd.*

18. *tax'd of*] censured by. *Of* was commonly used before a word denoting the agent. Cf. IV.ii.11.

19. *clepe*] call.

20. *addition*] Something added to a man's name which distinguishes or describes him. Cf. II.i.48; *Mac.* I.iii.105; *Lr* I.i.135, II.ii.22; etc. The name of Dane is regularly accompanied by an allusion to swine.

20–2. *it takes . . . attribute*] This 'revel', this drunkenness, causes our achievements, even when these attain the acme of possible performance, to lose the best and most vital part of the esteem we should enjoy. With *pith and marrow* cf. Tindale, *Answer to More,* Pref., 'He never leaveth searching till he come at the bottom, the pith, the quick, the life, the spirit, the marrow'. Our *attribute* is the character attributed to us, our reputation. Cf. *Troil.* II.iii.112, 'Much attribute he hath, and much the reason Why we ascribe it to him'. By contrast, Hamlet's point is that the Danes have not 'much attribute' even though their actual achievements would give reason for it.

23–38. *So, oft it chances . . . scandal.*] LN.

23. *particular men*] individuals (the previous sentence having been concerned with the case of a whole people).

24. *for*] on account of.

some vicious mole] Corresponding to 'the stamp of one defect' (l. 31). The figure has its literal counterpart in *Cym.* V.v.364–6, 'Upon his neck a mole . . . that natural stamp'.

25–30. *As in their birth . . . manners*] An expansion of l. 24. The syntax is clear if one understands that *as* is equivalent to 'namely' (cf. I.i.120) and introduces a specification of various categories. The 'mole' or 'defect' may occur in men (1) 'in their birth', (2) 'by their o'ergrowth of some complexion', or (3) 'by some habit'.

26. *his*] its. Cf. I.i.40.

By their o'ergrowth of some complexion,
Oft breaking down the pales and forts of reason,
Or by some habit, that too much o'erleavens
The form of plausive manners—that these men,   30
Carrying, I say, the stamp of one defect,
Being Nature's livery or Fortune's star,
His virtues else, be they as pure as grace,
As infinite as man may undergo,
Shall in the general censure take corruption   35

27. their] *Q2;* the *Pope.*   33. His] *Q2;* Their *Pope², Theobald, conj. SR.*

27. *complexion*] properly the *combination* of the four humours (blood, choler, melancholy, phlegm) in a man's bodily constitution; hence the temperament or disposition, considered as determined by which of the four humours was dominant; hence (as here) a single dominant humour or the temperamental characteristic derived from it.

28. *breaking down . . . reason*] This description of the growth of a humour until it gets out of control echoes Bright, who calls for the strictest restraint 'where the lists of reason are most like to be broken through' (p. 250).

29. *habit*] Onions cites this as one of only three instances in Shakespeare in which *habit* has its ordinary modern sense of 'settled practice'. (But see III.iv.164.) Note, however, that a 'habit' is not regarded as an acquired characteristic merely (cf. nn. on ll. 25–30, 32). It may have been the idea of habit as a manifestation of nature, a form that nature assumes, that here suggested the word *habit* itself. The common Elizabethan meaning, 'dress' (as in I.iii.70, III.iv.137), seems to be latent, giving rise to 'Nature's livery' in l. 32. Cf. III.iv.163–7.

29–30. *o'erleavens The form of plausive manners*] corrupts the pattern of approved behaviour. LN.

30. *that*] Resuming the *That* of l. 24.

32. *Fortune's star*] As distinct from the *mole of nature*, l. 24. *Star* refers both to the supposed source of Fortune's influence and to its effect. (Cf. II.ii.141.) Associated with *stamp* and *livery*, the word suggests a visible mark – like an unfavourable counterpart of Guiderius's mole ('a sanguine star', *Cym.* V.v.364) or the 'star', a white patch, on a horse's forehead. LN.

33. *His*] Referring to *these men* (l. 30). For the change in number, cf. I.iii.50. It provides no ground for supposing that Hamlet has his own case in mind, but may well be due to the influence of the singular *defect*.

34. *undergo*] sustain. Dowden ('support') and Onions ('bear the weight of') both compare *Meas.* I.i.24, 'To undergo such ample grace and honour'. *OED* (6d), citing both these instances but no others, less plausibly explains as 'partake of, enjoy'.

35. *the general censure*] either (1) public opinion, or (2) the appraisal of the man as a whole, the overall estimate, in contrast with the '*particular* fault'. For *censure*, see I.iii.69n. What the single fault corrupts is not, as so widely assumed, the man's character, but the opinion that is formed of it, his reputation, or 'image'.

From that particular fault. The dram of evil
Doth all the noble substance often dout
To his own scandal.

Enter GHOST.

Hor.　　　　　　Look, my lord, it comes.
Ham. Angels and ministers of grace defend us!
　　Be thou a spirit of health or goblin damn'd, 40
　　Bring with thee airs from heaven or blasts from hell,
　　Be thy intents wicked or charitable,
　　Thou com'st in such a questionable shape
　　That I will speak to thee. I'll call thee Hamlet,

36. evil] *Keightley, conj. Jervis;* eale *Q2;* ease *Q3;* base *Theobald;* ill *Jennens;* e'il *Kittredge;* ev'l *Evans.*　　37. often dout] *Steevens⁴;* of a doubt *Q2;* of worth out *Theobald;* of worth dout *Malone;* to a doubt *Sisson.*　　38. To] *Q2;* Of *Sisson.* 42. intents] *Q2,Q1;* euents *F.*

36–8. *The dram of evil . . . scandal.*] The little drop of evil often blots out all the noble substance and so (the evil but not the nobility being visible) brings it into disrepute. LN.

37. *substance*] the essential nature of a thing in contrast with that which is accidental.

38. *To*] with the consequence of.

his] Probably neuter (cf. I.i.40n.), referring either to the *dram of evil* or (preferably) the *noble substance.* Kittredge, however, makes it correspond to *his* in l. 33 and refer to 'the man in question'. Ambiguity may be partly due to the preceding crux.

39. *Angels . . . defend us!*] A prayer for protection against a possible evil spirit. *ministers,* messengers of God. Cf. III.iv.177; *Meas.* V.i.115, 'you blessed ministers above'.

40. *a spirit of health or goblin damn'd*] *health,* salvation. 'A spirit of health', however, is not, as often interpreted, a saved soul but a good angel. Hamlet addresses the Ghost not as his father's spirit but as a spirit in his father's shape. Cf. I.ii.244 and n. The question is not whether his father is saved or

damned but whether this is a good spirit or an evil one. Cf. *Caes.* IV.iii. 277, 'Art thou some god, some angel, or some devil . . . ?' *goblin,* demon.

41. *airs*] breezes.

blasts from hell] Taillepied (ch. 15) records that those who have seen spirits often find their lips crack and faces swell as if they have been struck with an ill wind.

43. *questionable*] which invites questioning. Cf. I.i.48. Not 'dubious', which the spirit may be but the *shape* is not. Cf. *Mac.* I.iii.43, 'Are you aught That man may question?'

shape] the bodily form which a spirit assumes. Cf. I.ii.244.

44. *I'll call thee Hamlet*] Notwithstanding the uncertainty about the Ghost's nature (ll. 40–2, I.ii.244), Hamlet now chooses to suppose it his father's spirit. Confirmation will come when the Ghost asserts its identity (I.v.9), which Hamlet unquestionably accepts (cf. I.v.144); and though he will later wonder if it may not after all be a deceiving devil (II.ii.594ff.), his play will finally convince him (III.ii.280–1).

King, father, royal Dane, O answer me. 45
Let me not burst in ignorance, but tell
Why thy canoniz'd bones, hearsed in death,
Have burst their cerements, why the sepulchre
Wherein we saw thee quietly inurn'd
Hath op'd his ponderous and marble jaws 50
To cast thee up again. What may this mean,
That thou, dead corse, again in complete steel
Revisits thus the glimpses of the moon,
Making night hideous, and we fools of nature

45. O] Q2,Q1; Oh, oh F.　　49. inurn'd] F; interr'd Q2,Q1.　　53. Revisits]
Q2 (Reuisites), F; Revisitst F2.

45. *royal Dane*] i.e. King of Denmark. Cf. i.i.16, i.ii.44, v.i.251. Some eds. call for a pause after *father*, seeing this rather than *royal Dane* as the natural climax. But the point of the various titles is that Hamlet hopes to hit on the one that will induce the Ghost to speak.

46. *burst*] This anticipates *burst* in l. 48; but though in theory it could be a reporter's error taken from Q1 into Q2 and thence into F, it seems more reasonable to conclude that Shakespeare could use the same expressive word twice within three lines.

47–9. *thy canoniz'd bones . . . inurn'd*] LN.

47. *canoniz'd*] having received the most sacred rites of the Church. The accent on the second syllable was normal. See Abbott 491.

hearsed] coffined. *Hearse*, originally denoting a structure carrying lighted tapers under which the bier with the coffin was placed in church, came to be used for the bier or for the coffin itself. This seems to be the usual sense in Shakespeare (e.g. *R3* i.ii.2; *Mer. V.* iii.i.77).

48. *cerements*] A Shakespearean coinage for 'burial clothes', the unusual word adding to the solemnity. Though Q1 corrupts to *ceremonies*, the word connects not with this but with *cerecloth*, lit. waxed cloth (to

cere = to wax, Fr. *cirer*), which will indicate pronunciation. Cf. F *cerments*, F2–4 *cearments*.

49. *inurn'd*] entombed. LN.

50. *marble jaws*] Battenhouse (*PMLA*, XLVIII, 173) finds a reminiscence of Christ's emergence from the tomb and its prefiguring in Jonah's from the whale (Matthew xii.39–40), and concludes that Shakespeare has 'fused the imagery of sepulchre and whale'. But a sepulchre can have 'jaws', and they open in *Rom.* v.iii.47.

52. *in complete steel*] Cf. i.ii.200, 226–7. *Complete*, like many other disyllabic adjectives, takes the stress on either syllable. See Walker, *Sh.'s Versification*, pp. 291–5. Hence *cómplete* will be normal before a noun accented on the first syllable, *compléte* predicatively. Cf. *secure*, i.v.61; *absurd*, iii.ii.60; *profound*, iv.i.1.

53. *Revisits*] In the 2nd pers. sing. the final *t* is often dropped for the sake of euphony, especially when the verb-stem itself ends in *t*. See Abbott 340.

glimpses of the moon] fitful moonlight.

54. *hideous*] Not, as usually now, physically repulsive, but terrifying. Cf. *Rom.* iv.iii.50, 'these hideous fears'; etc. So at ii.ii.472.

we] For this use of the nominative before an infinitive, see Abbott 216.

fools of] playthings of, subject to the

to tickle his spine

So horridly to shake our disposition   55
With thoughts beyond the reaches of our souls? *to give him a*
Say why is this? Wherefore? What should we do? *teddy bear*
to lie against him   to break   to flirt w/Ghost beckons.
his neck   him

Hor. It beckons you to go away with it,
As if it some impartment did desire
To you alone.

Mar.   Look with what courteous action   60
It waves you to a more removed ground.
But do not go with it.

Hor.   No, by no means.

Ham. It will not speak. Then I will follow it.

Hor. Do not, my lord.

Ham.   Why, what should be the fear?
I do not set my life at a pin's fee,   65
And for my soul, what can it do to that,
Being a thing immortal as itself?
It waves me forth again. I'll follow it.

Hor. What if it tempt you toward the flood, my lord,
Or to the dreadful summit of the cliff   70

---

56. the] *Q2,Q1*; thee; *F.*   61. waves] *Q2,Q1*; wafts *F.*   63. I will] *Q2*;
will I *F,Q1.*   69. lord] *Q2 (some copies)*, *F,Q1*; *lacking in some copies of Q2.*
70. summit] *Rowe*; somnet *Q2*; Sonnet *F.*

caprices of. Cf. 'Time's fool' (*Sonn.* cxvi.9), 'fortune's fool' (*Rom.* III. i.133), 'Death's fool' (*Meas.* III.i.11). We are 'fools of nature' in being at the mercy of nature's limitations (and hence confounded by what is beyond nature, l. 56).

55. *disposition*] mental constitution. Cf. *Wiv.* IV.v.101, 'more than . . . man's disposition is able to bear'.

57. *What should we do?*] Hamlet (like Horatio in I.i.133ff.) supposes that the Ghost requires *some* action from them.

62. *do not go*] Notwithstanding its 'courteous' invitation, they still fear the Ghost may be evil. Cf. ll. 69ff.

65–6. *my life . . . my soul*] It is one of these that the Ghost, if it were a

devil, would be aiming at. Cf. James I, *Demonology*, III.2, where the devil is said to trouble men 'to obtain one of two things . . . The one is the tinsel of their life . . . The other . . . is the tinsel of their soul'.

69–70. *toward the flood . . . the cliff*] Horatio still fears that the Ghost may be a manifestation of the devil, who aims at the lives of his victims 'by inducing them to such perilous places at such time as he either follows or possesses them, which may procure the same' (James I, loc. cit.). Dover Wilson compares *Lr* IV.vi.67–72, where Edgar pretends that it was 'some fiend' that brought Gloucester to the cliff-top.

That beetles o'er his base into the sea,
And there assume some other horrible form
Which might deprive your sovereignty of reason
And draw you into madness? Think of it.
The very place puts toys of desperation,   75
Without more motive, into every brain
That looks so many fathoms to the sea
And hears it roar beneath.

Ham.   It waves me still.
Go on, I'll follow thee.

Mar. You shall not go, my lord.

Ham.   Hold off your hands.   80

Hor. Be rul'd; you shall not go.

Ham.   My fate cries out
And makes each petty artire in this body
As hardy as the Nemean lion's nerve.
Still am I call'd. Unhand me, gentlemen.
By heaven, I'll make a ghost of him that lets me.   85
I say away.—Go on, I'll follow thee.

Exeunt Ghost and Hamlet.

71. beetles] *Q2* (bettles), *F;* beckles *Q1.*   72. assume] *Q2,Q1;* assumes *F.*
75–8. The . . . beneath.] *Q2; not in F,Q1.*   78–9. It . . . thee.] As *Q2; one*
line F.   78. waves] *Q2;* wafts *F.*   80. hands] *Q2;* hand *F.*   82. artire]
F,Q3 (artyre)*;* arture *Q2;* Artiue *Q1;* artery *Q5.*   84. call'd.] *Q2* (cald,)*;*
cal'd? *F.*

71. *beetles*] overhangs. The verb is
a Shakespearean nonce-word but
obviously derives from *beetle brows,*
which Shakespeare was not the first
to ascribe figuratively to a hill (see
OED beetle *a.* 2 b). But though the
word has gained currency from F,
I take it that *bettles* was Shakespeare's
form. For it is far better to explain
Q1 *beckles* as the actor's corruption
of this (how else?) than, like Bowers,
'to suppose with Dover Wilson and
Alice Walker that Q2 *bettles* owes its
odd form to contamination from Q1'
(*Textual and Literary Criticism,* p. 154).

73. *deprive your sovereignty of reason*]
Not, of course, take reason away from
your sovereignty, but take your
sovereignty of reason away. LN.

75–8. *The very place . . . beneath.*]

Cf. 'the place' described by Edgar,
Lr IV.vi. 11–24.

75. *toys*] freaks, irrational impulses.
Cf. I.iii.6 LN and *Rom.* IV.i. 119, 'If
no inconstant toy nor womanish fear
Abate thy valour'.

82. *artire*] = artery. Both the disyllabic form (indicated by the Q and F
spellings and corresponding to Fr.
artère) and the meaning 'sinew'
(Kittredge) are paralleled in other
writers. The commoner trisyllable
(arteries) occurs in *LLL* IV.iii. 302.

83. *Nemean lion*] the slaying of which
was the first of the labours of Hercules.
Also referred to in *LLL* IV.i.81, where
the accent is again on the first syllable,
as also in Golding's Ovid, IX.242.

85. *lets*] hinders.

Hor. He waxes desperate with imagination.
Mar. Let's follow. 'Tis not fit thus to obey him.
Hor. Have after. To what issue will this come?
Mar. Something is rotten in the state of Denmark.   90
Hor. Heaven will direct it.
Mar.   Nay, let's follow him.   *Exeunt.*

[SCENE V]

Enter GHOST *and* HAMLET.

Ham. Whither wilt thou lead me? Speak, I'll go no further.
Ghost. Mark me.
Ham.   I will.
Ghost.   My hour is almost come
    When I to sulph'rous and tormenting flames
    Must render up myself.
Ham.   Alas, poor ghost.
Ghost. Pity me not, but lend thy serious hearing   5

---

87. imagination] *F,Q1;* imagion *Q2.*

Scene v

SCENE v] *Capell.*   1. Whither] *Q2* (Whether), *Q1;* Where *F.*

87. *imagination*] 'Imagination bodies forth the forms of things unknown', *MND* v.i.14. These include the fantasies of the madman, which might be the work of spirits. Cf. III.ii.83. See *Wiv.* III.iii.191, 'What spirit, what devil suggests this imagination?'; *2H4* I.iii.31–2, 'Imagination Proper to madmen'. Horatio, still fearing for Hamlet's 'sovereignty of reason' (ll. 73–4), sees him succumbing to the influence of the spirit.

89. *Have after.*] Let's pursue.

91. *it*] the issue (l. 89).

Nay] i.e. 'let us not leave it to Heaven, but do something ourselves' (Clarendon).

Scene v

2. *Ghost*] Only now, alone with Hamlet and in response to his questioning, does the Ghost speak for the first time. Cf. i.i.48, 55, 176 and nn. For the voice associated with ghosts, see i.i.119 and n. The ghost in the pre-Shakespearean *Hamlet* was said by Lodge to have 'cried . . . miserably . . . like an oyster-wife'. The 'whining ghost' of the popular stage, 'screaming like a pig half-stick'd', was mocked in *A Warning for Fair Women* (1599), Ind.

My hour] daybreak. Cf. ll. 58, 89 and i.i.152–62.

3. *sulph'rous and tormenting flames*] LN.

To what I shall unfold.

Ham.   Speak, I am bound to hear.

Ghost. So art thou to revenge when thou shalt hear.

Ham. What?

Ghost. I am thy father's spirit,
    Doom'd for a certain term to walk the night,   10
    And for the day confin'd to fast in fires,
    Till the foul crimes done in my days of nature
    Are burnt and purg'd away. But that I am forbid
    To tell the secrets of my prison-house,
    I could a tale unfold whose lightest word   15
    Would harrow up thy soul, freeze thy young blood,
    Make thy two eyes like stars start from their spheres,
    Thy knotted and combined locks to part,
    And each particular hair to stand an end
    Like quills upon the fretful porpentine.   20

---

11. confin'd to fast] *Q2,F;* confined fast *Tschischwitz, conj. Misc.Obs.*
18. knotted] *Q2,Q1;* knotty *F.*   19. an] *Q2,F;* on *Q1.*   20. fretful] *F,Q1;*
fearefull *Q2.*

---

6. *bound*] Commentators say that
Hamlet means *bound,* 'prepared'
(< O.N. *búinn,* pp. of *búa,* as in 'bound
for England'), which the Ghost con-
verts into *bound,* 'under obligation'
(pp. of *bind*). But I take it that Hamlet
is 'bound' in duty and also by inescapable fate (cf. I.iv.81). Cf. III.
iii.41.

10-13. *Doom'd . . . purg'd away.*]
LN.

11. *to fast*] The idea that fasting is
inappropriate to spirits has led to such
conjectural emendations as *waste* and
confinèd fast. The latter has support
from More's *Supplication of Souls* (see
ll. 10-13 LN), which tells how in
purgatory souls are kept *fast* in fire
till their sins are purged. But hell,
after all, was physical, and its torments often included hunger. Cf.
Chaucer, *Parson's Tale,* 194, 'moore-
over the myseyse of helle shal been in
defaute of mete and drinke'; *Pierce
Penniless,* 'whether it be a place . . .

where men see meat, but can get
none' (Nashe, i. 218).

12. *crimes*] The 'imperfections' of
l. 79. Cf. III.iii.81. We need not
suppose that 'crimes' implies offences
of great gravity. Cf. II.i.44.

15. *I could a tale unfold*] How much
more effective than the explicit narrative of the Ghost of Andrea (*Spanish
Trag.*)!

16. *harrow*] Cf. I.i.47.

18. *combined*] wound together – as
opposed to the separation into single
(*particular*) hairs.

19. *an end*] *An* is not just a variant
spelling of *on* but the preposition *a,*
the weakened form of O.E. *on* (cf.
afire, afoot, II.ii.484 *awork*) with *n*
retained before a vowel. So at III.
iv.122, *R3* I.iii.304 (F), *2H6* III.ii.318
(F). See *OED* A *prep.*[1], An *prep.,*
An-end *phr.* Most eds. accordingly
retain *an end* but (inconsistently)
modernize *an edge* (*1H4* III.i.133,
Wint. IV.iii.7).

SC. V]   HAMLET   217

But this eternal blazon must not be
To ears of flesh and blood. List, list, O list!
If thou didst ever thy dear father love—
Ham. O God!
Ghost. Revenge his foul and most unnatural murder.   25
Ham. Murder!
Ghost. Murder most foul, as in the best it is,
But this most foul, strange and unnatural.
Ham. Haste me to know't, that I with wings as swift
As meditation or the thoughts of love   30
May sweep to my revenge.
Ghost.   I find thee apt.
And duller shouldst thou be than the fat weed
That roots itself in ease on Lethe wharf,
Wouldst thou not stir in this. Now, Hamlet, hear.
'Tis given out that, sleeping in my orchard,   35
A serpent stung me—so the whole ear of Denmark
Is by a forged process of my death

22. List, list] *Q2;* list *Hamlet / F;* Hamlet *Q1.*   24. God] *Q2,Q1;* Heauen *F.*
29. Haste] *Q2,Q1;* Hast, hast *F.*   know't] *Q2;* know it *F,Q1.*   I] *Q2; not
in F,Q1.*   33. roots] *Q2,Q1;* rots *F.*   35. 'Tis] *Q2,Q1;* It's *F.*
my] *Q2,Q1;* mine *F.*

21. *eternal blazon*] depiction of the
world beyond. A richly suggestive
phrase. *Eternal,* referring to what is
beyond mortal experience (contrast
flesh and blood), enhances the notion
of dread (cf. *Caes.* I.ii.160, 'Th'eternal
devil'). *Blazon* has the usual figurative
sense (influenced by *blaze*) of publication loudly and at large, while
retaining, from the literal meaning of
a coat-of-arms on a heraldic shield,
the idea of a vivid representation (cf.
Sonn. CVI.5, 'the blazon of sweet
beauty's best').

22. *List, list*] F's substitution of the
vocative for the repetition may follow
the stage practice (cf. Q1). Again at
l. 91.

25. *Revenge his . . . murder.*] LN.

28. *unnatural*] The reiteration of this
word (from l. 25) emphasizes the
violation of the natural tie between kin.
Its sense is also reinforced by *strange.*

29–30. *as swift . . . thoughts*] An
elaboration of the proverbial 'swift as
thought' (Tilley T 240), a favourite
comparison of Shakespeare's (see e.g.
LLL IV.iii.326, v.ii.261; and for
'thoughts of love' *Rom.* II.v.4–8). In
Wily Beguiled, printed 1606, 'I'll make
him fly swifter than meditation'
(Prol. 37) may be an echo of this
passage.

32–3. *duller . . . Lethe wharf*] *Lethe,*
the underworld river of forgetfulness;
dull, lethargic, inert. LN.

35. *orchard*] garden.

36. *A serpent*] In Belleforest the
murder took place at a banquet. The
secret poisoning recalls the allegory
of the sleeping king and the serpent's
sting in *2H6* III.ii.254ff.

37. *forged process*] fabricated account.
Cf. *forgeries,* II.i.20. *Process* was often
used for a relation of events.

Rankly abus'd—but know, thou noble youth,
The serpent that did sting thy father's life
Now wears his crown.   40
Ham. O my prophetic soul! My uncle!
Ghost. Ay, that incestuous, that adulterate beast,
With witchcraft of his wit, with traitorous gifts—
O wicked wit, and gifts that have the power
So to seduce!—won to his shameful lust   45
The will of my most seeming-virtuous queen.
O Hamlet, what a falling off was there,
From me, whose love was of that dignity
That it went hand in hand even with the vow
I made to her in marriage, and to decline   50
Upon a wretch whose natural gifts were poor
To those of mine.
But virtue, as it never will be mov'd,
Though lewdness court it in a shape of heaven,
So lust, though to a radiant angel link'd,   55

41. My] *Q2,Q1;* mine *F.*   43. wit] *Pope;* wits *Q2,F.*   with traitorous
gifts —] *Q2* (gifts,)*;* hath Traitorous guifts. *F;* with gifts, *Q1.*   45. to his]
Q2; to to this *F.*   47. a] *F; not in Q2.*   52-3.] *As Pope;* one line *Q2,F.*
55. lust] *F,Q1;* but *Q2.*

41. *prophetic*] Referring to Hamlet's
divination not of the murder (the
revelation of which has taken him by
surprise, l. 26) but of his uncle's true
nature.

42. *adulterate*] LN.

43. *witchcraft*] Cf. *Antonio's Revenge*
(III.v.8–9), where the Ghost of
Andrugio ascribes his wife's defection
to the 'black incarnate fiend' who
trips her faith.

traitorous gifts] Kittredge understands 'gifts of mind and manner';
but possibly 'presents', which did
what 'natural gifts' (l. 51) could not.
Cf. in *H5* the '*treacherous* crowns'
(II.Prol.22), which a traitor claims
'did not *seduce*' (II.ii.155).

47. *a*] Metre favours the article,
which F supplies. But cf. Q2 *What*,
F *What a* at II.ii.303.

48. *dignity*] worthiness. Cf. *Troil.*
I.iii.204, 'not a finger's dignity'; etc.

53. *virtue*] 'Sometimes a noun occurs
in a prominent position at the
beginning of a sentence, to express
the subject of the thought, without
the usual grammatical connection
with a verb or preposition' (Abbott
417).

54. *a shape of heaven*] 'The devil hath
power T'assume a pleasing shape'
(II.ii.595–6. See LN). Lavater (II.xv)
specifies 'the shape of a prophet, an
apostle, evangelist, bishop, and
martyr'. The Bible says that 'Satan
himself is transformed into an angel
of light' (2 Corinthians xi.14), and in
Christian legend he often tempted
saints and ascetics by appearing to
them in dreams in the likeness of
another saint or a beautiful woman.
See *Meas.* II.ii.179–81. The word
shape, denoting an assumed appearance or an acted role, often in itself
implied deception.

Will sate itself in a celestial bed
And prey on garbage.
But soft, methinks I scent the morning air:
Brief let me be. Sleeping within my orchard,
My custom always of the afternoon,   60
Upon my secure hour thy uncle stole
With juice of cursed hebenon in a vial,
And in the porches of my ears did pour
The leperous distilment, whose effect
Holds such an enmity with blood of man   65
That swift as quicksilver it courses through
The natural gates and alleys of the body,
And with a sudden vigour it doth posset
And curd, like eager droppings into milk,
The thin and wholesome blood. So did it mine,   70
And a most instant tetter bark'd about,

---

56. sate] *F;* sort *Q2;* fate *Q1.*   56–7.] *As Q2; one line F.*   58. morning]
Q2; Mornings *F,Q1.*   59. my] *Q2,Q1;* mine *F.*   60. of] *Q2;* in *F,Q1.*
62. hebenon] *F;* Hebona *Q2,Q1.*   63. my] *Q2,Q1;* mine *F.*   68. posset]
F; possesse *Q2.*   69. eager] *Q2,Q1;* Aygre *F.*   71. bark'd] *Q2,Q1;* bak'd *F.*

---

56. *sate itself*] gratify its appetite
to the point of being wearied or
disgusted.

61. *secure*] free from care or anxiety
(like L. *securus*). The two senses of
the word gave rise to many paradoxes
and quibbles. Cf. the proverb, 'The
way to be safe is never to be secure'
(Tilley W 152). With the stress on
the first syllable cf. *Oth.* IV.i.71, 'To
lip a wanton in a secure couch';
I.iv.52 n.

62. *hebenon*] LN.

63. *in . . . my ears did pour*] Pliny
speaks of this being done with henbane (see l. 62 LN). But Shakespeare
probably took the idea from reports
of the actual murder of the Duke of
Urbino in 1538, allegedly by poison
dropped in his ears. See Intro.,
p. 102.

64. *leperous*] creating scales on the
body like leprosy. Cf. ll. 71–2.

68. *vigour*] Staunton thought *rigour*
'more suitable to the context'. But
cf. *Comus,* 627, 'shew me simples . . .

Telling their strange and vigorous
faculties'.

posset] thicken and curdle like a
posset, i.e. hot milk in which ale
or wine is mixed.

69. *eager*] (continuing the posset
comparison) acid, sour. This sense
from the French is emphasized by the
F spelling *Aygre.* Cf. I.iv.2 and *Sonn.*
CXVIII.2, 'With eager compounds we
our palate urge'.

70. *thin*] The natural condition of
the blood in health. Cf. Bright, p. 270,
'Melancholy blood is thick and gross,
and therefore easily floweth not
though the vein be opened'.

71. *tetter*] eruption of the skin. Cf.
Duchess of Malfi, II.i.81, 'a foul tetter,
that runs all over a man's body'.
Hence *bark'd.* Dover Wilson compares
Deloney's ballad on the poisoning of
Edward II (*Works,* ed. Mann, p. 405):
'An ugly scab o'erspreads his lily skin',
'foul blotches' break out on his face,
and he becomes like 'a lazar'.

Most lazar-like, with vile and loathsome crust
All my smooth body.
Thus was I, sleeping, by a brother's hand
Of life, of crown, of queen at once dispatch'd,   75
Cut off even in the blossoms of my sin,
Unhousel'd, disappointed, unanel'd,
No reck'ning made, but sent to my account
With all my imperfections on my head.
O horrible! O horrible! most horrible!   80
If thou has nature in thee, bear it not,
Let not the royal bed of Denmark be
A couch for luxury and damned incest.
But howsomever thou pursuest this act,
Taint not thy mind nor let thy soul contrive   85
Against thy mother aught. Leave her to heaven,
And to those thorns that in her bosom lodge
To prick and sting her. Fare thee well at once:

75. of queen] *Q2,Q1;* and Queene *F.*   76. blossoms] *Q2,F;* blossom *White.*
80–1. O . . . If] *Q2,F,Q1 subst.;* Ham. O . . . Ghost. If Rann, *conj. Johnson.*
84. howsomever] *Q2;* howsoeuer *F,Q1.*   pursuest] *F;* pursues *Q2.*
85. mind] minde, *Q2;* mind; *F.*

75. *dispatch'd*] deprived (by death).
76. *in the blossoms of my sin*] Cf.
ll. 12–13, III.iii.81. For the plural
blossoms, cf. *Wint.* v.vii.121, 'in the
blossoms of their fortune'.
77. *Unhousel'd, disappointed, unanel'd*]
collectively, deprived of the last rites.
Unhousel'd, not having received the
'housel' or eucharist; *unanel'd,* not
having been anointed with holy oil
(i.e. without extreme unction); *disappointed,* not having made proper
'appointment' (cf. *Meas.* III.i.61) or
preparation, and hence referring in-
clusively to such rites (e.g. confession
and absolution) as are not specified
by the other two words.
80.] Johnson remarks that it was
'ingeniously hinted' to him 'by a very
learned lady' that this line should
belong to Hamlet. Many eds., including Kittredge, have given it him,
and many actors of Hamlet, including
Garrick,   Irving,   and   Forbes
Robertson, have spoken it. But it is

not out of character for the Ghost,
who would appear from Q1 to have
spoken it on the Elizabethan stage,
and who is not to be deprived of it
against the united authority of all
three texts.
81. *nature*] natural feeling. Cf.
III.ii.384, III.iii.32, v.ii.227, 240;
2H4 IV.v.37–40, 'Thy due from me
Is tears and heavy sorrows of the
blood Which nature, love, and filial
tenderness, Shall, O dear father, pay
thee'.
83. *luxury*] lust (the usual Elizabethan sense).
84. *howsomever*] Cf. *whatsomever,*
I.ii.249.
pursuest] Q2 *pursues,* which F
corrects, may conceivably be Shakespearean. Cf. *Revisits,* I.iv.53. But the
loss of *t* in the 2nd pers. sing. is
commoner when the verb-stem itself
ends in *t.*
85. *Taint not thy mind*] i.e. with evil
thoughts. LN.

The glow-worm shows the matin to be near
And gins to pale his uneffectual fire.　　　　　　　　90
Adieu, adieu, adieu. Remember me.　　　　　　　*Exit.*

Ham. O all you host of heaven! O earth! What else?
And shall I couple hell? O fie! Hold, hold, my heart,
And you, my sinews, grow not instant old,
But bear me stiffly up. Remember thee?　　　　　　95
Ay, thou poor ghost, whiles memory holds a seat
In this distracted globe. Remember thee?
Yea, from the table of my memory

91. Adieu, adieu, adieu] *Q2;* Adue, adue, *Hamlet | F;* Hamlet adue, adue, adue *Q1.*　91 S.D.] *F,Q1; not in Q2.*　93. O fie! Hold, hold] *Q2;* Oh fie: hold *F,Q3 (subst.);* oh hold *Pope;* Hold, hold *Capell.*　95. stiffly] *F;* swiftly *Q2.*　96. whiles] *Q2;* while *F.*

89–90. *The glow-worm . . . fire.*] The poetic diction (*matin*) gives heightened significance to the familiar ritual of dawn. Cf. 1.i.171–2. But whereas the mortals spoke of daylight beginning, the spirit speaks of darkness ending. *uneffectual,* not, as Warburton supposed, because the glow-worm gives light without heat, but because its light is now disappearing. Cf. *Per.* 11.iii.43–4, 'a glowworm . . . which hath fire in darkness, none in light'. 'As uneffectual as the glow-worm's fire' in the anonymous *Charlemagne* (Bullen, *Old Eng. Plays,* iii.170) is probably an echo rather than a source.

91. *adieu³*] With F's substitution of '*Hamlet*' for one of the repetitions cf. l. 22.

91 S.D. *Exit*] Probably vanishing through a trap-door, which will give greater verisimilitude to the voice 'under the stage' in the episode which follows.

93. *hell*] Uncertainty about the Ghost's provenance (cf. 1.iv.40–1), quieted during its presence, returns when it is gone. Hamlet does not ignore that that to which he now pledges himself may embrace both good and evil. (Cf. 11.ii.580.) Cf.

Spanish Trag., 111.xiii.109, where Hieronimo, failing to find justice on earth, will 'down to hell'.

O fie] Omitted by Capell and others, in defiance of textual authority, as extra-metrical and inappropriate. But cf. 1.ii.135, 11.ii.583.

96. *whiles*] Q2's older form is modernized in F. Cf. 1.iii.49 and n.

97. *globe*] head; perhaps with a suggestion of its being a microcosm. Modern commentators like to point out that for an audience in the Globe theatre there would be a triple pun.

98. *table*] tablet; a flat surface bearing, or designed to bear, an inscription, effigy, etc. Cf. l. 100n. Theobald shows that the metaphor was as old as Aeschylus. Cf. Sidney, *Apology,* 'Let Aeneas be worn in the tablet of your memory', and the injunction of Proverbs (iii.3; vii.3) for a 'son' to write 'commandments' 'upon the table of thine heart'. The allusion is not, as often supposed, specifically to the 'tables' carried by gentlemen for noting down memoranda. Yet it evidently brought such writing-tablets into Shakespeare's mind (cf. *saws, copied*) and suggested the business of l. 107. Cf. the conceit of *Sonn.* cxxii.

I'll wipe away all trivial fond records,
All saws of books, all forms, all pressures past   100
That youth and observation copied there,
And thy commandment all alone shall live
Within the book and volume of my brain,
Unmix'd with baser matter. Yes, by heaven!
O most pernicious woman!   105
O villain, villain, smiling damned villain!
My tables. Meet it is I set it down
That one may smile, and smile, and be a villain—
At least I am sure it may be so in Denmark.   [*Writes.*]
So, uncle, there you are. Now to my word.   110
It is 'Adieu, adieu, remember me.'
I have sworn't.

Enter HORATIO *and* MARCELLUS [*calling*].

104. Yes] *Q2;* yes, yes *F,Q1.*   107. tables] *Q2,Q1;* Tables, my Tables *F.*
109. I am] *Q2,Q1;* I'm *F.*   109 S.D.] *Rowe (subst.); not in Q2,F,Q1;*
after 107 Wilson.   111–12.] *As Q2;* one line *F.*   112 S.D.] *Q2; after 113*
F,Q1; after 118 Capell.   calling] This edn.

99. *fond*] foolish (the commonest sense at this date).

100. *forms*] shapes drawn or imprinted upon the 'table'. Cf. *pressures,* impressions, and III.ii.24, 'his form and pressure'. Shakespeare often uses *form* to refer to an exact image such as is given by a wax impression; e.g. *MND* I.i.49, *Tw.N.* II.ii.28.

104. *Unmix'd with baser matter*] Yet it is the essence of Hamlet's plight that he can neither eliminate the 'baser' elements from his human nature nor obliterate them from his consciousness.

107. *tables*] writing-tablets (often made of ivory). Cf. l. 98n. Blakemore Evans (*MLN,* XLII, 235–6) cites an emblem by Whitney (1586, p. 100), on hypocrites ('saints in show, with Judas hearts'), which recommends testing the correspondence of a man's words and deeds by noting them on 'a table'.

108. *one may smile . . . be a villain*]

Cf. Richard of Gloucester, 'I can smile, and murder whiles I smile' (*3H6,* III.ii.182).

110. *there you are*] Referring to what he has just 'set down'.

to my word] He adopts the Ghost's parting phrase as his 'word' or motto. For *word* in this sense, see *Lr* III. iv.179; *Per.* II.ii.21; Nashe, iii.30, 'resolving to take up for the word or motto of my patience, *Pedere posse sat est*'. Presumably Hamlet inscribes the word as a mnemonic on his 'tables' (l. 107) as well as on the metaphorical 'table' and 'book' of his brain (ll. 98, 103).

112 S.D. *Enter*] They enter searching for Hamlet and F reasonably makes the calling begin off stage. But the postponement of their actual entry, by Capell and many subsequent eds., goes against all three texts. The illusion of darkness permits them to be on stage with Hamlet without perceiving him. Cf. *Rom.* II.i.

Hor. My lord, my lord.
Mar. Lord Hamlet.
Hor. Heavens secure him.　　　　　　　　　　　　　　115
Ham. [*aside*] So be it.
Mar. Hillo, ho, ho, my lord.
Ham. Hillo, ho, ho, boy. Come, bird, come.
Mar. How is't, my noble lord?
Hor. What news, my lord?　　　　　　　　　　　　120
Ham. O, wonderful!
Hor. Good my lord, tell it.
Ham. No, you will reveal it.
Hor. Not I, my lord, by heaven.
Mar. Nor I, my lord.　　　　　　　　　　　　　　125
Ham. How say you then, would heart of man once think it—
　　　But you'll be secret?
Hor. ⎫
　　　⎬ Ay, by heaven.
Mar. ⎭
Ham. There's never a villain dwelling in all Denmark
　　　But he's an arrant knave.　　　　　　　　　　130
Hor. There needs no ghost, my lord, come from the grave
　　　To tell us this.
Ham.　　　　　　Why, right, you are in the right.

---

113. *Hor.*] *Q2,Q1; Hor. & Mar. within. F.*　　115. Heavens] *Q2,Q1;* Heauen *F.*
116. *Ham.*] *Q2; Mar. F.*　　aside] *Wilson.*　　117. *Mar.*] *Q2; Hor. F,Q1.*
118. *Ham.*] *Q2,F; Mar. Q1.*　　bird]*F;* and *Q2;* boy *Q1.*　　119. is't] *Q2,Q1;*
ist't *F.*　　123. you will] *Q2;* you'l *F,Q1.*　　128. heaven.] *Q2;* Heau'n, my
Lord. *F,Q1.*　　129.] *As F,Q1; 2 lines divided* villaine, / Dwelling *Q2.*
never] *Q2,Q1;* nere *F.*　　131-2. There . . . this.] *As Q2; prose F.*
132. in the] *Q2,Q1;* i'th' *F.*

---

115. *secure*] keep safe, protect.

116. *So be it.*] Capell noted the solemn effect of this amen. F's taking these words away from Hamlet would itself impugn its redistribution of the speeches.

118. *Hillo . . . come.*] Hamlet answers Marcellus's halloo in familiar fashion (cf. *Birth of Merlin*, II.i.61–3, 'So ho, boy, so ho . . . – So ho, boy, so ho, illo ho, illo ho'). *Come, bird, come* was properly the cry of a falconer recalling his hawk but easily extended to any call or enticement. Steevens cites Tyro's *Roaring Megge*, 1598, 'I'll go see the kite: come, come bird, come'. Cf. also Cutwode, *Caltha Poetarum*, st. 136; Marston, *Dutch Courtesan*, I.ii.131.

126. *once*] ever.

130. *But he's an arrant knave*] The disclosure which Hamlet was apparently about to make he suddenly turns into a jest.

131. *come*] Infinitive (rather than past pple.).

And so without more circumstance at all
I hold it fit that we shake hands and part,
You as your business and desire shall point you—   135
For every man hath business and desire,
Such as it is—and for my own poor part,
I will go pray.

Hor. These are but wild and whirling words, my lord.

Ham. I am sorry they offend you, heartily—   140
Yes faith, heartily.

Hor.   There's no offence, my lord.

Ham. Yes by Saint Patrick but there is, Horatio,
And much offence too. Touching this vision here,
It is an honest ghost, that let me tell you.
For your desire to know what is between us,   145
O'ermaster't as you may. And now, good friends,
As you are friends, scholars, and soldiers,
Give me one poor request.

Hor.   What is't, my lord? We will.

Ham. Never make known what you have seen tonight.

---

135. desire] *Q2;* desires *F,Q1.*   136. hath] *Q2,Q1;* ha's *F.*   137. my]
Q2,Q1; mine *F.*   138. I will] *Q2;* Looke you, Ile *F;* ile *Q1.*
139. whirling] *Q2,Q1;* hurling *F.*   140. I am] *Q2,Q1;* I'm *F.*
142. Horatio] *Q2,Q1;* my Lord *F.*   143. too. Touching . . . here,] *Rowe*
(here—)*;* to, touching . . . heere, *Q2;* too, touching . . . heere: *F.*
146. O'ermaster't] *F,Q3;* Or'emaister it *Q1;* Oremastret *Q2.*

---

133. *circumstance*] elaboration of
detail. Cf. *John* II.i.77, 'The interruption . . . Cuts off more circumstance'; *2H6* I.i.100; *Ado* III.ii.91.

138. *I will go pray*] Perhaps for
strength to carry out his task. But
perhaps because 'it behoveth them
which are vexed with spirits, to pray
especially' (Lavater, III.vi).

139. *whirling*] violently excited.

142. *by Saint Patrick*] An apt oath.
For 'St. Patrick, you know, keeps
purgatory' (Dekker, *2 Honest Whore*,
I.i.42). To seek a particular source
for this belief is to ignore the very
great fame of St Patrick's Purgatory,
in an Irish cave, much visited by
pilgrims. The story was that all who
spent a day and night there would

both be purged of their sins and have
visions of the damned and the blest.
See Holinshed, *Chronicles*, 1587, ii.28;
D. P. Barton, *Ireland and Shakespeare*,
1919, pp. 30 ff.

143. *Touching this vision*] Dover
Wilson suggests (*WHH*, p. 79) that
'Hamlet is on the point of revealing
the secret'. Cf. ll. 123–7. But the
assumption that while he wishes to
tell Horatio he is checked by the
presence of Marcellus is an embroidery upon the text. That he does
subsequently inform Horatio becomes
clear from III.ii.77.

144. *honest*] genuine.

145. *what is between us*] what the
Ghost and I have to do with one
another.

Hor. ⎱
Mar. ⎰ My lord, we will not.   150

Ham. Nay, but swear't.

Hor. In faith, my lord, not I.

Mar. Nor I, my lord, in faith.

Ham. Upon my sword.

Mar. We have sworn, my lord, already.   155

Ham. Indeed, upon my sword, indeed.

Ghost. (*Cries under the stage*) Swear.

Ham. Ah ha, boy, say'st thou so? Art thou there, truepenny?
Come on, you hear this fellow in the cellarage.
Consent to swear.

Hor.   Propose the oath, my lord.   160

Ham. Never to speak of this that you have seen.
Swear by my sword.

Ghost. Swear.   [*They swear.*]

Ham. *Hic et ubique?* Then we'll shift our ground.
Come hither, gentlemen,   165
And lay your hands again upon my sword.
Swear by my sword
Never to speak of this that you have heard.

Ghost. Swear by his sword.   [*They swear.*]

Ham. Well said, old mole. Canst work i'th' earth so fast? 170

---

158. Ah ha] *F; Ha, ha Q2,Q1.*   158–9.] *As Q2; prose F.*   161. seen.] *F;*
seene Q2.   163 S.D.] *This edn; they lay their hands upon the hilt | Wilson.*
164. our] *Q2,Q1; for F.*   167–8.] *As Q2; lines transposed F,Q1 (subst.).*
169. by his sword] *Q2; not in F,Q1.*   169 S.D.] *Wilson (subst.).*
170. earth] *Q2,Q1; ground F.*

152. *not I*] i.e. 'I will not make it
known', not 'I will not swear', which
he does ('in faith'). Cf. l. 155.

154. *Upon my sword*] The cross of
the sword was often used for this
purpose. Cf. *H5* II.i.98, 'Sword is
an oath'.

157. *Ghost . . . under the stage*] LN.

158. *truepenny*] honest fellow. Truepenny is the name of a trusty servant
in *Ralph Roister Doister* and other
plays. A supercilious scholar calls a
countryman 'old truepenny' in
2 Return from Parnassus (l. 654). The
mocking familiarity with which

Hamlet now addresses the Ghost continues the levity in front of his companions which began at l. 118.

159. *you hear*] There is no ground
for the suggestion of Verity and Kitto
(*Form and Meaning in Drama*, p. 263)
that they do not hear. Lines 168, 172
point to the contrary.

163 S.D. *They swear.*] LN.

164. *Hic et ubique*] See l. 157 LN.

166. *again*] Not as beginning the
process afresh but as repeating it.
Cf. l. 163 S.D. LN.

170. *mole*] See l. 157 LN.

A worthy pioner! Once more remove, good friends.
Hor. O day and night, but this is wondrous strange.
Ham. And therefore as a stranger give it welcome.
There are more things in heaven and earth, Horatio,
Than are dreamt of in your philosophy.   175
But come,
Here, as before, never, so help you mercy,
How strange or odd some'er I bear myself—
As I perchance hereafter shall think meet
To put an antic disposition on—   180
That you, at such time seeing me, never shall,
With arms encumber'd thus, or this head-shake,
Or by pronouncing of some doubtful phrase,

175. your] *Q2,Q1*; our *F.*   175–6.] *As Hanmer; one line Q2,F.*
178–86. How strange . . . never shall, . . . giving out, to note] *Steevens⁴*; (How
strange . . . neuer shall . . . giuing out, to note) *Q2*; How strange . . . neuer
shall . . . giuing out to note, *F.*   178. some'er] *so mere Q2; so ere F,Q1.*
181. time] *F*; times *Q2,Q1.*   182. this head-shake] *Theobald*; this head shake
Q2,Q1; thus, head shake *F.*

171. *pioner*] This QF spelling was
usual and indicates the stress. A *pioneer*
was originally a foot-soldier who preceded the main army with spade or
pickaxe, hence a digger, and so, as
here, a miner. Cf. *H5* III.ii.81. See
l. 157 LN.

173. *as a stranger . . . welcome*] The
Christian ethic of Matthew xxv.35
('I was a stranger, and ye took me in')
and many scriptural exhortations.
Cf. Middleton, *Women beware Women,*
II.ii.225, 'She's a stranger, madam. –
The more should be her welcome'.

175. *your philosophy*] Not some particular philosophy of Horatio's but
philosophy in general, *your* being used
in the indefinite sense then common.
Cf.   I.i.141,   III.ii.3,   IV.iii.21–3,
v.i.56–7, 165–6.

176. *But come*] A phrase like this,
calling attention to what follows, is
often extra-metrical. Cf. II.i.42, 62;
II.ii.105. Only the last of these is
printed as a separate line in Q2 and
none of them in F.

177–87. *Here, as before, . . . swear*]

The oath, 'as before', begins with
never (cf. ll. 161, 168), but then goes
off into conditions and explanations,
only to emerge (181) in an anacoluthon,   the   syntax   reflecting
Hamlet's excited state. The main
construction is: 'swear (187) here,
as before (177) . . . that you . . . never
shall (181) . . . (to) note (186) that
you know aught of me'. See nn. on
ll. 182, 186.

178. *How . . . some'er*] Cf. i.v.84,
I.ii.249n.

180. *To put . . . on*] The famous
announcement of his intention to
affect madness. *antic*, grotesque =
'strange or odd' (l. 178). Cawdrey,
A   Table   Alphabetical,   1604,   defines
'*anticke*, disguised'. The word is particularly used of an actor with a
false head or grotesque mask. For
put on see III.i.2n.

182. *encumber'd*] folded. No parallel
use has been found, but the general
sense is entangled, impeded in movement, and an 'encumbered labyrinth'
(translating Fr. *touffe trop épais*) occurs

As 'Well, we know', or 'We could and if we would',
Or 'If we list to speak', or 'There be and if they
    might',   185
Or such ambiguous giving out, to note
That you know aught of me—this do swear,
So grace and mercy at your most need help you.
Ghost. Swear.   [*They swear.*]
Ham. Rest, rest, perturbed spirit. So, gentlemen,   190
With all my love I do commend me to you;
And what so poor a man as Hamlet is
May do t'express his love and friending to you,
God willing, shall not lack. Let us go in together.
And still your fingers on your lips, I pray.   195

---

184. Well] *F;* well, well *Q2,Q1.*   185. they] *Q2,Q1;* there *F.*
187–8. do swear, / . . . you.] *Q2;* not to doe: / . . . you: / Sweare. *F,Q1 (subst.).*
189 S.D.] *Kittredge; after* spirit (*190*) *Globe.*

in Fenton's *Monophylo,* 1572 (sig.
T4ᵛ). 'Arms across', 'folded',
'wreathed', in a 'knot', etc., are
regularly associated by Shakespeare
and others with sighs, melancholy
brooding, and a mind occupied with
more than it can utter.

this head-shake] The hyphenation of
head-shake seems the best way of
making sense of Q2, which most eds.
follow. But it creates a dubious noun
and puts some strain on *this* (= such
as this), and I wish I could feel
certain that Q2 is not merely copying
Q1 here. F may be right in repeating
thus to balance with the previous
phrase but hardly in regarding *shall
. . . shake* as the main verb.

184. *Well*] The duplication of *well*
(Q1,Q2) has all the air of an actor's
repetition, which Q2 may have taken
from Q1. The close correspondence
of the two quartos throughout this
awkward speech casts doubt on
several of the Q2 readings (cf.
l. 182n.).

184, 185. *and if*] = if.

185. *There be . . . might*] i.e. There
are (those who could tell) if they were
permitted to.

186.   *giving   out*]   intimation
(Dowden), publication. Cf. *Meas.*
I.iv.54.

to note] to indicate (*OED* note *v.*² 5).
To is often inserted before an infinitive, even one which would not
normally require it, when the infinitive stands at a distance from its
preceding verb (here *shall,* l. 181).
Cf. ll. 17–18, 'Make . . . to part'. See
Abbott 350, and, for instances of
shall . . . to, ES, xxvi, 142–4.

192. *so poor a man*] Dover Wilson
notes that Hamlet 'drops many hints
of his lack of means and of power.' See
II.ii.268–72, III.ii.93–4, 331. But
these are all in a half-mocking tone.
He may here be thinking rather of
himself as poor in spirit. This is his
third use of the word *poor* since the
Ghost left him.

195. *still*] always. Cf. I.i.125 and n.

The time is out of joint. O cursed spite,
That ever I was born to set it right.
Nay, come, let's go together.   *Exeunt.*

198. Nay, come,] Nay, come *F;* Nay come, *Q2.*

196. *out of joint*] in utter disorder. For this idiom see Horsey, *Travels* (Hakluyt Soc., p. 262), 'This turbulent time . . . all out of joint, not likely to be reduced a long time to any good form of peaceable government'; Tilley J 75. Cf. 1.ii.20, 'our state . . . disjoint and out of frame'.

198. *Nay . . . together.*] Evidently they stand aside to give him precedence, which he, characteristically (cf. 1.ii.163, 253–4), declines.

ACT II

[SCENE I]

Enter old POLONIUS, *with his man* REYNALDO.

Pol. Give him this money and these notes, Reynaldo.
Rey. I will, my lord.
Pol. You shall do marvellous wisely, good Reynaldo,
　　Before you visit him, to make inquire
　　Of his behaviour.
Rey.　　　　　　My lord, I did intend it.　　　　　5
Pol. Marry, well said, very well said. Look you, sir,
　　Inquire me first what Danskers are in Paris,
　　And how, and who, what means, and where they keep,
　　What company, at what expense; and finding

ACT II

Scene 1

ACT II] F (*Actus Secundus*); *not in* Q2.　　SCENE I] Q *1676*.　　S.D.] *Parrott-Craig; Enter old Polonius, with his man or two.* Q2; *Enter Polonius, and Reynoldo.* F; *Enter Corambis, and Montano.* Q1.　　1. this] Q2,Q1; his F.　　3. marvellous] Q3; meruiles Q2; maruels F.　　wisely,] wisely Q2; wisely: F. 4. to make inquire] Q2; you make inquiry F.

S.D.] The Q2 *old* gives a clue to Shakespeare's conception of the character, and occurring now instead of at Polonius's first appearance, perhaps suggests that the conception has developed. Q2's (and presumably Shakespeare's) *or two* is redundant; the scene as it came to be written envisages one man only.

3. *shall*] expressing not mere futurity but inevitability (= cannot but, are certain to). Cf. *Mac.* III. iv. 57, *Oth.* I. i. 44.

marvellous] This adverbial use is very common, and the Q2,F spellings (cf. *Troil.* I. ii. 130, Q,F *maruel's*) indicate pronunciation. Cf. III. ii. 293.

4. *inquire*] Shakespeare often uses a verb as a noun. Cf. I. i. 60, *avouch*; III. i. 168, 'hatch . . . disclose'; v. ii. 23, *supervise*, etc. See Abbott 451.

6. *Look you, sir*] This manner of insisting on attention to what he is about to say is characteristic of Polonius. Cf. ll. 15, 42, 62; II. ii. 105, 107. In several instances the arresting phrase is made more emphatic by being extra-metrical.

7. *Danskers*] Danes. LN.

8. *keep*] lodge.

By this encompassment and drift of question   10
That they do know my son, come you more nearer
Than your particular demands will touch it.
Take you as 'twere some distant knowledge of him,
As thus, 'I know his father, and his friends,
And in part him'—do you mark this, Reynaldo?   15

Rey. Ay, very well, my lord.

Pol. 'And in part him. But', you may say, 'not well;
But if't be he I mean, he's very wild,
Addicted so and so'—and there put on him
What forgeries you please—marry, none so rank   20
As may dishonour him—take heed of that—
But, sir, such wanton, wild, and usual slips
As are companions noted and most known
To youth and liberty.

Rey.   As gaming, my lord?

Pol.   Ay, or drinking, fencing, swearing,
Quarrelling, drabbing—you may go so far.   26

Rey. My lord, that would dishonour him.

Pol. 'Faith no, as you may season it in the charge.
You must not put another scandal on him,

---

14. As] *Q2,Q1; And F.*   25-6. swearing, / Quarrelling,] *Q2,F;* swearing,
quarrelling, / *Capell.*   28. no] *F; not in Q2.*

---

10. *encompassment*] roundabout
course.

11. *come . . . nearer*] i.e. to the real
object of your inquiry. Dowden insists
that the comparison is not between
particular and general questions
(*demands*) but between putting questions and affecting knowledge.
Though Kittredge regards *come you* as
indicative, it may be taken as imperative, parallel with *Inquire* (l. 7)
and *Take* (l. 13). When Reynaldo has
first found out that Laertes is known,
he is then to come nearer to the
crucial matter than is possible by
specific questions (*particular demands*);
and Polonius proceeds to instruct him
how to do this (by talking about
Laertes in such a way as to draw the

others on).

13. *Take*] assume.

20. *forgeries*] fabrications. Cf. I.
v. 37; *MND* II.i.81.

24. *To*] Follows on *companions*, the
sense being 'such slips (= lapses) as
are well known to be associated with
youth'.

25. *fencing*] LN.

26. *drabbing*] whoring.

28. *season*] temper. Cf. I.ii.192.

29. *another*] Not implying that the
things already mentioned are scan-
dals, which Polonius has denied. In
Elizabethan usage *other* may refer to
an instance of a different kind instead
of to a different instance of the same
kind. See *OED* other *adj.* 7.

That he is open to incontinency—   30
That's not my meaning; but breathe his faults so
    quaintly
That they may seem the taints of liberty,
The flash and outbreak of a fiery mind,
A savageness in unreclaimed blood,
Of general assault.   35
Rey. But my good lord—
Pol.   Wherefore should you do this?
Rey. Ay, my lord, I would know that.
Pol. Marry, sir, here's my drift,
    And I believe it is a fetch of warrant.
    You laying these slight sullies on my son,   40
    As 'twere a thing a little soil'd i'th' working,
    Mark you,
    Your party in converse, him you would sound,

34-5. A ... assault.] *As Q2; one line F.*   37. Ay, my lord, ... that.] *As*
Q2,F; Ay, my good lord, | ... that. Capell; Ay, my lord | ... that. Steevens².
39. warrant] *F; wit Q2.*   40. sullies] *F,Q3; sallies Q2.*   41. i'th'] *F; with*
Q2; wi'th' Alexander.   42-3.] *As Malone; one line Q2,F.*   you, ... converse,]
Q2; you ... conuerse; F.

30. *incontinency*] The distinction between this and 'drabbing' is a question
of how it is regarded – whether as
confirmed libertinism or merely as the
natural hot-bloodedness of youth
(ll. 22-4, 32-5).

31. *quaintly*] artfully (the usual
Elizabethan sense).

34. *savageness*] The characteristic
of wild creatures, whose animal
instincts, supposedly situated in the
blood (see I.iii.6 n., and cf. *Tp.* IV.
i. 53, 'th' fire i'th' blood'), are *unreclaimed*, i.e. untamed.

35. *Of general assault*] which assails
men in general, i.e. to which most
men are liable.

38. *drift*] underlying purpose,
scheme. Cf. IV.vii. 150.

39. *fetch of warrant*] legitimate trick.
Cf. *fetches*, subterfuges, *Lr* II.iv.87.
Verity takes *of warrant* to mean
'warranted to succeed', but Polonius's
point is that the end justifies the
means. Cf. *Oth.* I.ii. 79, 'arts inhibited

and out of warrant'. Q2's *wit*, like its
wait at III.iv.5, appears to be a misreading of an abbreviation of *warrant*.
Errors with this word in other texts
(see *MSH*, p. 108) suggest that
Shakespeare was in the habit of contracting it. Cf. *warn't*, I.ii.243.

40. *sullies*] Q2 *sallies* is apparently
an alternative form. See I.ii. 129 LN.

41. *soil'd i'th' working*] Like something (e.g. in needlework) which is
soiled by being handled in the course
of being made, the young man will
seem to have become sullied by that
worldly contact through which he
acquires his accomplishments.

42. *Mark you,*] Though F by its
punctuation tries to make *your party*
the object of *Mark*, this is an inter-
jectional phrase, as made clear by
the Q2 comma and the metre, and
as such in Polonius's characteristic
manner. See II.i.6 n., I.v. 176 n.

43. *converse*] conversation. Stress on
the second syllable was normal.

Having ever seen in the prenominate crimes
The youth you breathe of guilty, be assur'd   45
He closes with you in this consequence:
'Good sir', or so, or 'friend', or 'gentleman',
According to the phrase or the addition
Of man and country.

Rey.   Very good, my lord.

Pol. And then, sir, does a this—a does—what was I about   50
        to say? By the mass, I was about to say something.
        Where did I leave?

Rey. At 'closes in the consequence'.

Pol. At 'closes in the consequence', ay, marry.
        He closes thus: 'I know the gentleman,   55
        I saw him yesterday', or 'th'other day',
        Or then, or then, with such or such, 'and as you say,
        There was a gaming', 'there o'ertook in's rouse',
        'There falling out at tennis', or perchance
        'I saw him enter such a house of sale'—   60
        Videlicet a brothel, or so forth.
        See you now,

---

44. seen] *Q2; seene. F.*   48. or] *Q2; and F.*   50. a this—a does—] a this,
a doos, *Q2;* he this? He does: *F.*   50-2.] *Prose Malone; 3 lines ending* say?
| something, | leaue? *Q2; ending* this? | say? | leaue? *F.*   51. By the mass]
Q2; not in F.   53. consequence'.] *Q2;* consequence: / At friend, or so, and
Gentleman. *F.*   54. closes] *Q2;* closes with you *F;* closeth with him *Q1.*
56. th'other] *Q2;* tother *F,Q1.*   57. such or] *Q2;* such and *F.*   58. a] *Q2;*
he *F.*   gaming', 'there o'ertook] *F (subst.);* gaming there, or tooke *Q2.*
61-2.] *As Capell; one line Q2,F.*   62-3. now, . . . takes] *F (subst.);* now, . . .
take *Q2;* now . . . take *Alexander.*

---

44. *prenominate*] aforenamed.

crimes] The word was often used in
a less restricted sense than now.
Cf. I.v.12.

46. *closes with*] agrees with, falls in
with (lit. comes close to).

in this consequence] Not merely 'in
the following way' but pointing to
what follows as a natural result.

48. *addition*] form of address (i.e.
whatever is *added* to one's name).
Cf. I.iv.20.

53.] The extra words in F, though
they have usually been regarded as
an omission in Q2, have the air of

an actor's elaboration. It is noticeable
that Polonius ignores them in taking
up the cue. Cf. Intro., p. 62, and see
SB, XIII, 40-1. F's *closes with you* in
l. 54 (repeated from l. 46) shows a
similar expansion.

58. *a*] pronoun (he).

o'ertook] i.e. by the effects of drink.
A recognized euphemism for 'drunk'.
See *OED* overtake 9.

in's rouse] in his cups. Cf. I.ii.127,
I.iv.8.

59. *tennis*] LN.

62. *See you now*] Cf. I.v.176 and n.,
II.i.42 and n., II.ii.105 and n.

Your bait of falsehood takes this carp of truth;
And thus do we of wisdom and of reach,
With windlasses and with assays of bias,   65
By indirections find directions out.
So by my former lecture and advice
Shall you my son. You have me, have you not?

Rey. My lord, I have.

Pol.   God buy ye, fare ye well.

Rey. Good my lord.   70

Pol. Observe his inclination in yourself.

Rey. I shall, my lord.

Pol.   And let him ply his music.

Rey. Well, my lord.   *Exit.*

Enter OPHELIA.

63. carp] *Q2;* Cape *F.*   69. ye . . . ye] *Q2;* you . . . you *F.*   73 S.D.] As
Q2,F; after Farewell. (*74*) *Singer.*

63. *carp*] Dover Wilson notes a
quibble on carp = talk.

64. *we of wisdom and of reach*]
Abbott (168) construed *of* as 'by
means of'. But the construction is
shown by *LLL* iv.ii.27, 'we of taste
and feeling'. Cf. *Sir Thomas More*
(MSR, Addn ii, 157), 'Are you men
of wisdom'; *Wily Beguiled* (Sc. ii,
MSR l. 137), 'Thus men of reach
must look to live'. *reach*, mental
capacity, range of comprehension.
Cf. i.iv.56.

65. *windlasses*] roundabout courses.
So in Golding's Ovid, ii.891 ('The
winged god . . . Continued not
directly forth, but gan . . . to . . . fetch
a windlass round about'), vii.1015,
and not infrequently elsewhere.

assays of bias] devious tests. In
bowls the player does not aim directly
at the jack but relies on the bias (the
curving line on which it runs) to
bring the bowl round to its object.

67. *lecture*] lesson.

69. *God buy ye*] It seems best, with
Alexander and Sisson, to retain the
original form of a contraction which
cannot be satisfactorily rendered into
modern English. The frequent edi-

torial expansion to *God b(e) wi' ye*
gives to a natural colloquialism an air
of artificiality, as also does Dover
Wilson's bold *God bye ye.* If this is on
the analogy of *Good-bye,* then *ye*
(except for metre) is redundant.
Cf. ii.ii.543, iv.iv.30, iv.v.197.

70. *Good my lord.*] Deferentially
accepting his dismissal. Cf. ii.ii.542.

71. *Observe . . . yourself.*] i.e. accommodate yourself to his bent. LN.

72. *ply his music*] Some would interpret metaphorically: let him carry on
with his tune. But music was one of
the essential accomplishments of the
gentleman, and Polonius's natural
wish for his son to acquire these goes
with his tolerance of gentlemanly
wild oats.

73 S.D. *Exit.*] Most eds. assume
that *Farewell* must precede Reynaldo's
exit. But the order of the original
texts makes good dramatic sense.
Polonius's first farewell is at l. 69.
But he follows Reynaldo with his
afterthoughts and is still talking as the
latter leaves the stage, by which time
Ophelia has entered from the other
side, to confront her father as he turns.

Pol. Farewell. How now, Ophelia, what's the matter?
Oph. O my lord, my lord, I have been so affrighted.   75
Pol. With what, i'th' name of God?
Oph. My lord, as I was sewing in my closet,
    Lord Hamlet, with his doublet all unbrac'd,
    No hat upon his head, his stockings foul'd,
    Ungarter'd and down-gyved to his ankle,   80
    Pale as his shirt, his knees knocking each other,
    And with a look so piteous in purport
    As if he had been loosed out of hell
    To speak of horrors, he comes before me.
Pol. Mad for thy love?
Oph.   My lord, I do not know,   85
    But truly I do fear it.
Pol.   What said he?
Oph. He took me by the wrist and held me hard.
    Then goes he to the length of all his arm,
    And with his other hand thus o'er his brow
    He falls to such perusal of my face   90

---

75. O my lord] *Q2;* Alas *F.*   76. i'th'] *Q2;* in the *F.*   God] *Q2;*
Heauen *F.*   77. closet] *Q2;* Chamber *F.*   80. down-gyved] *F2;* downe
gyued *Q2,F;* downe gyred *Q3.*   85–6. My . . . it.] *As Q2; one line F.*

77–100.] On the 'closet' episode, LN.

78. *unbrac'd*] unfastened. Cf. *Caes.* I.iii.48, II.i.262. The doublet was fastened with buttons all down the front. To appear with it undone was very unseemly. Cf. Rowley, *A Match at Midnight,* IV (Hazlitt's Dodsley, xiii.79), 'Widow. You will not be so uncivil to unbrace you here?'

79. *No hat*] Hats were normally worn in public, even indoors. See *Sh.'s Eng.,* ii.109. Cf. v.ii.93 ff.

stockings foul'd] A detail that perhaps derives from Saxo via Belleforest, who describes Hamlet, when simulating madness, as wallowing in the filth and sweepings of the house ('se veautrant és balieüres et immondices de la maison').

80. *down-gyved*] fallen down so as to resemble gyves (fetters). A Shake-spearean coinage.

83. *As if . . . hell*] Perhaps a traditional simile for the madman's gaze. Cf. *Marriage of Wit and Science* (MSR, l. 1239), 'Thy look is like to one, that came out of hell'.

84. *horrors*] The melancholic was thought liable to suffer from terrifying delusions of 'goblins' and other 'shapes'. See Bright, pp. 103–4. What 'horrors' are in Hamlet's mind are necessarily unknown to Ophelia but can be surmised by the audience, who have seen him with the Ghost.

88. *goes . . . arm*] He backs till he holds her at arm's length.

90. *perusal*] scrutiny. Cf. IV.vii.135. The exact meaning of *peruse,* examine detail by detail, is brought out by *Troil.* IV.v.232–3, 'I have with exact view perus'd thee, Hector, And quoted joint by joint'.

As a would draw it. Long stay'd he so.
At last, a little shaking of mine arm,
And thrice his head thus waving up and down,
He rais'd a sigh so piteous and profound
As it did seem to shatter all his bulk   95
And end his being. That done, he lets me go,
And with his head over his shoulder turn'd
He seem'd to find his way without his eyes,
For out o' doors he went without their helps,
And to the last bended their light on me.   100

Pol. Come, go with me, I will go seek the King.
This is the very ecstasy of love,
Whose violent property fordoes itself
And leads the will to desperate undertakings
As oft as any passion under heaven   105
That does afflict our natures. I am sorry—
What, have you given him any hard words of late?

Oph. No, my good lord, but as you did command,

---

91. a] *Q2; he F.*   95. As] *Q2; That F.*   97. shoulder] *Q2,Q1; shoulders
F,Q3.*   99. helps] *Q2; helpe F,Q1.*   101. Come] *Q2; not in F.*
105. passion] *F; passions Q2.*   106. sorry—] *Capell; sorry, Q2,F; sorrie; Q5;
sorry. Globe.*

---

95. *bulk*] Often equated with
'breast', as in Baret, *Alveary*, 'the bulk
or breast of a man'. But more properly
the whole trunk. See Elyot, *Castle of
Health*, IV, 'The boulke, called in
latyn *thorax*, whiche conteyneth the
brest, the sides, the stomake, and
entrayles' (1541 edn, fol. 89v). In
R3 I.iv.40, Clarence describes how
his soul could not escape from his
'panting bulk'. Cf. *Lucrece*, 467, 'her
heart . . . Beating her bulk'.

99. *helps*] The Q2 plural is
thoroughly idiomatic, as in *3H6*
IV.i.45, 'with their helps'; *Ado* II.
i.345, 'with your two helps'. Cf.
I.i.178n.

100. *bended their light*] As with
Orpheus's last look at Eurydice. (See
ll. 77–100 LN.)

101. *Come, go with me*] So at l. 117.
But at II.ii.39 Polonius arrives alone.

102. *ecstasy*] a state of mind in
which, from whatever cause, reason
is in suspense. Often synonymous
with 'madness'. Cf. III.i.162, III.
iv.74, 140.

103. *Whose . . . itself*] the violent nature of which leads to
self-destruction. Sufferers from love-
madness were held liable to suicide.
property, that which is proper or
natural to anything (cf. *proper*, l. 114),
characteristic. *fordoes*, destroys (the
Old English sense). Cf. v.i.214.
Itself refers not to *property* but to
ecstasy.

106. *I am sorry—*] Polonius breaks
off what he was going to say and
resumes it at l. 111.

107. *What*] Cf. I.i.21, 24.

108. *as you did command*] See
I.iii.121, 132–4.

I did repel his letters and denied
His access to me.

Pol.   That hath made him mad.   110
I am sorry that with better heed and judgment
I had not quoted him. I fear'd he did but trifle
And meant to wrack thee. But beshrew my jealousy!
By heaven, it is as proper to our age
To cast beyond ourselves in our opinions   115
As it is common for the younger sort
To lack discretion. Come, go we to the King.
This must be known, which, being kept close, might
    move
More grief to hide than hate to utter love.
Come.   *Exeunt.*   120

SCENE II

Flourish. Enter KING *and* QUEEN, ROSENCRANTZ *and*
GUILDENSTERN, *with* Attendants.

King. Welcome, dear Rosencrantz and Guildenstern.
    Moreover that we much did long to see you,

111. heed] *Q2;* speed *F.*   112. quoted] *F;* coted *Q2.*   fear'd] *Q2;*
feare *F.*   114. By heaven] *Q2,Q1;* It seemes *F.*   120. Come] *Q2; not
in F.*

Scene 11

SCENE II] *F (Scena Secunda); not in Q2.*   S.D. Flourish] *Q2; not in F.*
with Attendants] *Cum alijs F; not in Q2; Lords and other Attendants | Rowe.*

112. *quoted*] observed. Cf. *Rom.*
I.iv.31 ('What curious eye doth
quote deformities?'); *Troil.* IV.v.233.
Q2 *coted* is a variant form (Fr. *coter*).
    113. *wrack*] ruin, 'wreck'. Cf.
All's W. III.v.20, F 'the wracke of
maiden-hood'.
    jealousy] 'suspicion; apprehension
of evil; mistrust' (*OED* 5). So at
IV.v.19. Cf. *Tw.N.* III.iii.8, 'jealousy
what might befall your travel'.
    115. *To cast beyond ourselves*] To *cast*
in hunting is to search for the scent.
See *TLS*, 1931, p. 1053; 1932, p. 12.

Hence 'to overrun the trail' (Dover
Wilson). It is natural for old men to
suspect more than they actually
know.
    117. *go we*] Cf. above, l. 101 and n.
    118–19. *might move . . . love*] Con-
cealment might cause more grief
(presumably because of what the mad
lover might do – see ll. 103–4) than
the publication of Hamlet's love
would give offence.

Scene 11

2. *Moreover*] besides. *OED* 4b.

The need we have to use you did provoke
Our hasty sending. Something have you heard
Of Hamlet's transformation—so I call it,   5
Sith nor th'exterior nor the inward man
Resembles that it was. What it should be,
More than his father's death, that thus hath put him
So much from th'understanding of himself
I cannot dream of. I entreat you both   10
That, being of so young days brought up with him,
And sith so neighbour'd to his youth and haviour,
That you vouchsafe your rest here in our court
Some little time, so by your companies
To draw him on to pleasures and to gather,   15
So much as from occasion you may glean,
Whether aught to us unknown afflicts him thus
That, open'd, lies within our remedy.
Queen. Good gentlemen, he hath much talk'd of you,
And sure I am, two men there is not living   20
To whom he more adheres. If it will please you
To show us so much gentry and good will
As to expend your time with us awhile
For the supply and profit of our hope,
Your visitation shall receive such thanks   25

---

5. I] *F; not in Q2.*   6. Sith nor] *Q2;* Since not *F.*   10. dream] *Q2;*
deeme *F.*   12. sith] *Q2;* since *F.*   haviour] *Q2;* humour *F.*
16. occasion] *Q2;* Occasions *F.*   17.] *Q2; not in F.*   20. is] *Q2;* are *F,Q3.*

---

6. *Sith*] F modernizes, as also at
l. 12.

11. *of*] Cf. Mark ix. 21, 'Of a child';
Gent. IV.iv.3, 'one that I brought up
of a puppy'.

brought up with him] Cf. III.iv.204,
'my two schoolfellows'.

12. *sith*] O.E. *siððan,* afterwards. In
Elizabethan English rarely used, as
here, to express time-connection
merely, though common in the sense
of 'because'. Cf. l. 6, IV.iv.45, IV.vii.3.

neighbour'd to] intimately acquainted
with.

haviour] demeanour, manner(s).
Cf. I.ii.81.

13. *vouchsafe your rest*] consent to
stay. (Cf. Fr. *rester.*)

14. *companies*] For the plural, cf.
I.i.178n.

16. *occasion*] opportunity, favourable
circumstance. Cf. I.iii.54.

18. *open'd*] revealed. Ironic in view
of what the revelation would be.

20. *is*] The singular is common
after 'there' even with a plural
subject. Abbott 335.

22. *gentry*] gentlemanliness (cf.
V.ii.110), courtesy.

24. *supply and profit*] 'fulfilment and
furtherance' (Kittredge).

As fits a king's remembrance.

Ros.   Both your Majesties
Might, by the sovereign power you have of us,
Put your dread pleasures more into command
Than to entreaty.

Guild.   But we both obey,
And here give up ourselves in the full bent   30
To lay our service freely at your feet
To be commanded.

King. Thanks, Rosencrantz and gentle Guildenstern.
Queen. Thanks, Guildenstern and gentle Rosencrantz.
And I beseech you instantly to visit   35
My too much changed son. Go, some of you,
And bring these gentlemen where Hamlet is.

Guild. Heavens make our presence and our practices
Pleasant and helpful to him.

Queen.   Ay, amen.
Exeunt Rosencrantz and Guildenstern [and an Attendant].

Enter POLONIUS.

Pol. Th'ambassadors from Norway, my good lord,   40
Are joyfully return'd.

King. Thou still hast been the father of good news.

---

29. But] *Q2; not in F.*   31. service] *Q2;* Seruices *F.*   36.] *As Q2;*
2 lines divided Sonne. | Go *F.*   you] *Q2;* ye *F.*   37. these] *Q2;* the *F.*
39. Ay] *Q2; not in F.*   39 S.D. Exeunt . . . Guildenstern] *Q2;* Exit *(after*
him) *F.*   an Attendant] *This edn; Attendants Capell.   Polonius] Q2,F;*
Corambis and Ofelia Q1.

26. *fits*] For 'thanks' as singular,
cf. I.i.8 and n.

28. *dread*] held in awe, deeply
respected. Cf. I.ii.50, III.iv.109.

30. *the full bent*] the utmost to which
a bow may be drawn; hence (to) the
limit of our capacity. Cf. III.ii.375,
'to the top of my bent'; *Ado,* II.
iii.204, 'her affections have their full
bent'.

36. *some*] i.e. some one (indefinite
singular). The '*attendants*' of most
eds. at l. 39 S.D. suggests that *some* is
usually taken for a plural. But cf.

Per. v.i.9, 'there is some of worth
would come aboard; I pray greet
him fairly'; *R2* IV.i.268.

38. *practices*] doings, devices. But
the other connotations of the word
(wiles, deceits) give a touch of irony.

39. *Pleasant*] pleasing.

39 S.D. *Enter Polonius.*] Without
Ophelia, notwithstanding II.i.101,
117. Presumably Shakespeare
changed his mind in the course of
composition. LN.

42. *still*] always. Cf. I.i.125, etc.

Pol. Have I, my lord? I assure my good liege
    I hold my duty as I hold my soul,
    Both to my God and to my gracious King;   45
    And I do think—or else this brain of mine
    Hunts not the trail of policy so sure
    As it hath us'd to do—that I have found
    The very cause of Hamlet's lunacy.
King. O speak of that: that do I long to hear.   50
Pol. Give first admittance to th'ambassadors.
    My news shall be the fruit to that great feast.
King. Thyself do grace to them and bring them in.
                                    [*Exit Polonius.*]
    He tells me, my dear Gertrude, he hath found
    The head and source of all your son's distemper.   55
Queen. I doubt it is no other but the main,
    His father's death and our o'er-hasty marriage.
King. Well, we shall sift him.

        Enter POLONIUS, VOLTEMAND, *and* CORNELIUS.

                        Welcome, my good friends.
    Say, Voltemand, what from our brother Norway?
Volt. Most fair return of greetings and desires.   60
    Upon our first, he sent out to suppress
    His nephew's levies, which to him appear'd
    To be a preparation 'gainst the Polack;
    But better look'd into, he truly found
    It was against your Highness; whereat griev'd   65

43. I assure my good liege] *Q2;* Assure you, my good Liege *F;* I assure your
grace *Q1.*   45. and] *Q2,Q1;* one *F.*   48. it hath] *Q2;* I haue *F;* it had
Q1.   50. do I] *Q2;* I do *F.*   52. fruit] *Q2;* Newes *F.*   53 S.D.] *Rowe.*
54. dear Gertrude] *Q2;* sweet Queene, that *F.*   57. o'er-hasty] *F;* hastie *Q2.*
58 S.D.] *As Dyce subst.; after 57 F; Enter Embassadors (after 57) Q2.*   58. my]
Q2; not in *F.*

45. *Both . . . King*] Duty to God and
duty to king are regarded as involving
one another.

47. *Hunts not . . . policy*] does not
pursue the path of statecraft.

52. *fruit*] i.e. dessert.

53. *grace*] honour. With a play on
grace before meat the King takes up
Polonius's metaphor.

56. *doubt*] suspect.

58. *sift him*] subject him (i.e.
Polonius) to searching inquiry.

61. *our first*] i.e. our first broaching
of the matter.

61–8. *sent out to suppress . . . Fortinbras*]
Cf. 1.ii.27–31.

63. *the Polack*] the King of Poland.
Cf. 1.i.16, 'the Dane', etc.

That so his sickness, age, and impotence
Was falsely borne in hand, sends out arrests
On Fortinbras; which he, in brief, obeys,
Receives rebuke from Norway, and, in fine,
Makes vow before his uncle never more   70
To give th'assay of arms against your Majesty:
Whereon old Norway, overcome with joy,
Gives him three thousand crowns in annual fee
And his commission to employ those soldiers
So levied, as before, against the Polack,   75
With an entreaty, herein further shown,   [*Gives a paper.*]
That it might please you to give quiet pass
Through your dominions for this enterprise
On such regards of safety and allowance
As therein are set down.

King.   It likes us well;   80
And at our more consider'd time we'll read,
Answer, and think upon this business.
Meantime, we thank you for your well-took labour.
Go to your rest, at night we'll feast together.

---

73. three] *F,Q1;* threescore *Q2.*   76 S.D.] *Malone.*   78. this] *Q2;* his *F;*
that *Q1.*   83. thank] *Q2, F corr., Q1;* take *F uncorr.*

67. *borne in hand*] deluded, kept under a false belief (lit. maintained – cf. Fr. *maintenir*). Cf. *Ado* IV.i.301, 'bear her in hand until they come to take hands'; *Mac.* III.i.80; *Cym.* v.v.43. *OED* bear *v.*[1] 3e.

arrests] orders of prohibition.

71. *assay*] trial of strength, challenge.

73. *three thousand*] *Q2*'s metrically redundant *score* was presumably Shakespeare's first thought, which *thousand* was meant to supersede. It is defended by Dover Wilson (*MSH,* p. 274) on the ground that 'three thousand crowns' is inadequate for a campaign later estimated to cost 'twenty thousand ducats' (IV.iv.25). But what the text refers to here is not the financing of the Polish expedition but the gift of an 'annual' revenue, as which 60,000 crowns would be

colossal. Cf. Shakespeare's hesitation in *Tim.* about deciding on sums of money (see *SS 6,* 75–7), and see Intro., p. 41.

77–8. *pass Through your dominions*] In the geography of the play Denmark seems to be thought of as lying between Norway and Poland. Cf. LNN on I.i.66, II.i.7, IV.iv.3–4.

79. *of safety and allowance*] The document proposes the terms on which 'allowance' is sought and by which the 'safety' of the country is to be assured.

81. *at our more consider'd time*] when we have more time for consideration.

82. *Answer*] That Claudius gave consent appears from IV.iv.2–3.

84. *we'll feast*] 'The King's intemperance is never suffered to be forgotten' (Johnson). Cf. I.ii.125n.

Most welcome home.

Exeunt Voltemand and Cornelius.

Pol.   This business is well ended.   85
My liege and madam, to expostulate
What majesty should be, what duty is,
Why day is day, night night, and time is time,
Were nothing but to waste night, day, and time.
Therefore, since brevity is the soul of wit,   90
And tediousness the limbs and outward flourishes,
I will be brief. Your noble son is mad.
Mad call I it, for to define true madness,
What is't but to be nothing else but mad?
But let that go.

Queen.   More matter with less art.   95
Pol. Madam, I swear I use no art at all.
That he is mad 'tis true; 'tis true 'tis pity;
And pity 'tis 'tis true. A foolish figure—
But farewell it, for I will use no art.
Mad let us grant him then. And now remains   100
That we find out the cause of this effect,
Or rather say the cause of this defect,
For this effect defective comes by cause.
Thus it remains; and the remainder thus:

85. well] *Q2;* very well *F,Q1.*   90. since] *F; not in Q2.*   97. he is] *F;*
hee's *Q2.*   98. 'tis 'tis] *Q2;* it is *F.*   104. thus:] thus. *F;* thus *Q2.*
104–5.] *As Q2; one line F.*

86–92.] Polonius's 'mode of oratory
is truly represented as designed to
ridicule the practice of those times,
of prefaces that made no introduction, and of method that embarrassed
rather than explained' (Johnson).

86. *expostulate*] inquire into. *OED*
1 b.

87–9. *What majesty . . . and time*] Put
simply, it is as unnecessary to go into
a subject's duty as to explain day and
night.

90. *brevity is the soul of wit*] LN.

93. *Mad call I it*] i.e. without
'expostulating' the nature of madness.

to define true madness] Perhaps an
echo of Horace, *Sat.,* II.iii.41, 'quid

sit furere', translated by T. Drant
(1566) 'But what is madness to
define?' The theme of the satire is
that the accepted madman is no
madder than anyone else. Hence the
true madness is that of the world in
general (see *N & Q,* ccii, 194–6). No
doubt it is as well for Polonius to 'let
that go'.

95. *More matter with less art.*] See
l. 90 LN.

103. *comes by cause*] i.e. there must
be a cause for it.

104. *Thus . . . thus*] He loses the
thread of his argument and non-
sensically repeats himself.

Perpend,   105
I have a daughter—have while she is mine—
Who in her duty and obedience, mark,
Hath given me this. Now gather and surmise.
(*Reads*)   *To the celestial and my soul's idol, the most*
beautified Ophelia—That's an ill phrase, a vile phrase,   110
'beautified' is a vile phrase. But you shall hear—
these; in her excellent white bosom, these, &c.
Queen. Came this from Hamlet to her?
Pol. Good madam, stay awhile, I will be faithful.

        Doubt thou the stars are fire,   115
        Doubt that the sun doth move,
        Doubt truth to be a liar,
        But never doubt I love.
O dear Ophelia, I am ill at these numbers. I have not art to

---

106. while] *Q2,Q1;* whil'st *F.*   109. *Reads.*] *Q 1676; The Letter. F; Letter.*
(*opp. 115*) *Q2.*   110. *beautified*] *Q2,F;* beatified *Theobald.*   110–12.] *roman F;*
italic Q2.   111–12. hear—*these; in*] *This edn; heare: thus in | Q2;* heare these
in | *F;* hear—*These to* | *Rowe;* hear;—*These in* | *Capell;* hear. Thus: *In* | *Malone.*
112. *&c*] *italic Q2;* roman *Q 1676;* not in *F.*   119–23.] *italic F;* roman *Q2.*

---

105. *Perpend*] consider (lit. weigh),
take careful note. A word otherwise
used in Shakespeare only by Pistol
and clowns. Its absurd inflation is in
'King Cambyses' vein', as noted by
Tilley, *MLN*, xxiv, 244–7. Cf.
Cambyses, ll. 2–5, 1018. Its being extra-
metrical makes for an emphatic
pause, and it has a line to itself in
Q2. Cf. ii.i.6 n.

107. *mark*] Cf. *Perpend*, l. 105. Perhaps this also should be regarded as
extra-metrical, with *obedience* as four
syllables.

108. *gather and surmise*] draw your
conclusions.

109–23.] On the letter, LN.

110.   *beautified*] 'endowed with
beauty' (Dover Wilson). LN.

112. *these*¹] for 'these letters'. The
plural (from L. *litterae*) with singular
sense was very common. (Cf. iv.
vi.2 n.) LN.

in her . . . bosom] Where a love-letter
would be kept. Cf. *Gent.* iii.i.248–50,
'Thy letters . . . shall be deliver'd

Even in the milk-white bosom of thy
love.'

&c.] As a substitute for some
formal phrase, this again is common
in letter-headings.

116. *Doubt . . . move*] Referring to
the orthodox belief of the Ptolemaic
astronomy that the sun moved round
the earth. Since each of the poem's
first two lines assumes the certainty
of what had now begun to be doubted,
there is an irony of which Shakespeare
(though not, I take it, Hamlet) must
have been aware.

117. *Doubt*] i.e. suspect (as at l. 56).
Note the shift in meaning in this line,
which the formulaic repetition would
disguise. The possibility of alternative
meanings of the verb leaves the
status of truth and hence of Hamlet's
love in some ambiguity, which
perhaps prepares for iii.i.115–19.

119. *ill at these numbers*] bad at this
verse-making. This sense of *numbers*
continues in *art* while the other sense
suggests *reckon*; so that *have no art to*

reckon my groans. But that I love thee best, O most best, 120
believe it. Adieu.

> *Thine evermore, most dear lady, whilst this*
> *machine is to him,*　　　　　*Hamlet.*

This in obedience hath my daughter shown me,
And, more above, hath his solicitings, 125
As they fell out by time, by means, and place,
All given to mine ear.

King. But how hath she receiv'd his love?

Pol. What do you think of me?

King. As of a man faithful and honourable. 130

Pol. I would fain prove so. But what might you think,
When I had seen this hot love on the wing—
As I perceiv'd it, I must tell you that,
Before my daughter told me—what might you
Or my dear Majesty your queen here think, 135
If I had play'd the desk or table-book,
Or given my heart a winking mute and dumb,
Or look'd upon this love with idle sight—

124. shown] *Q2;* shew'd *F.*　　　125. above] *F;* about *Q2.*　　　solicitings]
Q2; soliciting *F.*　　　127–9.] *As Q2,F; 2 lines divided* she | Receiv'd *Capell.*
133. it, I . . . . that,] it (I . . . that) *Q2;* it, I . . . that *F.*　　　137. winking]
F; working *Q2.*

reckon = (1) cannot count, (2) cannot express in verse.

122–3. *whilst this machine is to him*] while this bodily frame belongs to him. The Elizabethans thought of nature in general and the human body in particular as a mechanism. The word *machine,* without the prosaic associations it has acquired in a later age, refers admiringly to a complicated structure composed of many parts. Bright, e.g., thinks of the body as an 'engine' stirred into action by the soul. Hamlet's phrase is nevertheless tinged with his contempt for corporeal life. For *to,* cf. our idiom, There is a great deal *to* him.

133. *I perceiv'd it*] We know differently; see I. iii. 91 ff.

136. *play'd . . . table-book*] been a means of communication, a go-between. A table-book was a book of writing-tablets, like the 'tables' of I. v. 107. The influence of that passage has led Kittredge and others to stress the use of tables for private note-taking and hence to suppose that Polonius alludes only to storing the information away. But the essential function of both desk and table-book concerns not privacy but writing. To play *their* part is to give active assistance as distinct from the silent connivance referred to in the next line.

137. *winking*] closing of the eyes, a very common Elizabethan sense both literal and metaphorical. Cf. *Cym.* v. iv. 184–6, 'None want eyes to direct them . . . but such as wink and will not use them'; *H5* II. ii. 55; etc. LN.

138. *look'd . . . with idle sight*] saw without noticing, without attaching importance to (as distinct from the

What might you think? No, I went round to work,
And my young mistress thus I did bespeak: 140
'Lord Hamlet is a prince out of thy star.
This must not be.' And then I prescripts gave her,
That she should lock herself from his resort,
Admit no messengers, receive no tokens;
Which done, she took the fruits of my advice,   145
And he, repelled—a short tale to make—
Fell into a sadness, then into a fast,
Thence to a watch, thence into a weakness,
Thence to a lightness, and, by this declension,
Into the madness wherein now he raves   150
And all we mourn for.
King.   Do you think 'tis this?
Queen. It may be; very like.
Pol. Hath there been such a time—I would fain know that—
That I have positively said ''Tis so',
When it prov'd otherwise?
King.   Not that I know.   155

---

140. And . . . mistress] *Q2;* And (. . . Mistris) *F.*   141. star] *Q2,F,Q1;*
sphere *F2.*   142. prescripts] *Q2;* Precepts *F.*   143. his] *F;* her *Q2.*
146. repelled—] repell'd, *Q2;* repulsed. *F.*   148. watch] *F,Q3;* wath *Q2.*
149. a] *F; not in Q2.*   150. wherein] *Q2;* whereon *F.*   151. mourn] *Q2;*
waile *F.*   'tis] *F; not in Q2.*   152. like] *Q2;* likely *F.*   153. I would]
Q2; I'de *F.*

---

deliberate connivance of the previous
line).

139. *round*] thoroughly, uncom-
promisingly. Cf. III.i.185.

140. *my young mistress*] Characteristically condescending.

141. *star*] The determinant of
fortune, and hence by metonymy the
place or condition given to one by
fortune. Cf. 'Fortune's star', I.iv.32;
and 'In my stars I am above thee',
Tw.N. II.v.128.

145. *took the fruits of*] Not merely
accepted but followed, so that the
advice bore fruit in her conduct.

146. *repelled*] The Q2 reading is
supported by II.i.109.

147–50.] Polonius tells off the successive medical stages of what he
regards as a classical case: depression, loss of appetite, insomnia, de-
bility, delirium, raving madness. The
'sadness' of the lovelorn hero is described at length in *Rom.* I.i.122ff.
Fasting and watching are among the
effects of love in *Gent.* II.i.21–2.
Weakness suggests not only an enfeebled physical condition but also a
mind losing its grip (cf. l. 597 below).
In *lightness* (cf. 'lightheaded') the
mind is actually wandering; cf. *Err.*
v.i.72, 'his head is light', said of a
supposed madman.

Pol. Take this from this if this be otherwise.

                    [Points to his head and shoulder.]

    If circumstances lead me, I will find

    Where truth is hid, though it were hid indeed

    Within the centre.

King.   How may we try it further?

Pol. You know sometimes he walks four hours together   160

    Here in the lobby.

Queen.   So he does indeed.

Pol. At such a time I'll loose my daughter to him.

    Be you and I behind an arras then,

    Mark the encounter. If he love her not,

    And be not from his reason fall'n thereon,   165

    Let me be no assistant for a state,

    But keep a farm and carters.

King.   We will try it.

        Enter HAMLET, *reading on a book.*

156. this if . . . otherwise.] this, if . . . otherwise; *Q2;* this; if . . . otherwise, *F.*
156 S.D.] *Theobald (subst.).*   160–1. You . . . lobby.] *As Q2; 3 lines ending* ●
sometimes / heere / Lobby. *F.*   161. does] *Q2;* ha's *F.*   167. But] *Q2;*
And *F.*   167 S.D. *Enter Hamlet*] *Q2,F; after 170 S.D. Dyce; at 159 Wilson.*
reading on a book] *F; not in Q2.*

156. *Take this from this*] Dowden, comparing ll. 166–7, suggests that Polonius refers to his staff of office and the hand which bears it. Yet the traditional injunction is to separate head from shoulders. Cf. *Iliad*, II. 259 (Chapman, 'If ever . . . , let not Ulysses bear This head').

159. *the centre*] the centre of the earth, traditionally thought of as its most inaccessible point and the most remote from the light of day. Cf. *Volpone*, I.i.9–10, 'the day Struck out of chaos, when all darkness fled Unto the centre'; Tourneur, *Atheist's Trag.*, IV.iii.282, 'I will search the centre'.

160. *four*] Commonly used for 'several' and hence not to be taken precisely. Cf. *Duchess of Malfi*, IV.i.9, 'She will muse four hours together'. Elze collected many examples in *Sh.Jahr.*, XI, 288–94.

162. *loose*] In reversal of l. 143.

But the mating sense of *loose . . . to him* can hardly be missed. Cf. *Wiv.* II.i.163, 'If he should intend . . . toward my wife, I would turn her loose to him'. Dover Wilson makes much of the farmyard associations (*WHH*, 103 ff.), which certainly add no dignity to Polonius's scheme. But it is not clear why they should be thought to reflect upon Ophelia, who is not present and for whose attitude to the assignation see III.i.40–2.

163. *arras*] This kind of tapestry, named after the town of Arras and commonly hung in front of the walls in wealthy houses, has become so well known through *Ham.* as scarcely to need comment.

165. *thereon*] on that account.

167 S.D. *Enter Hamlet*] LN.

reading on a book] Attempts to identify the book are pointless. Cf. l. 196 LN.

Queen. But look where sadly the poor wretch comes reading.
Pol. Away, I do beseech you both, away.

      I'll board him presently. O give me leave.   170
               Exeunt King and Queen [and Attendants].

      How does my good Lord Hamlet?
Ham. Well, God-a-mercy.
Pol. Do you know me, my lord?
Ham. Excellent well. You are a fishmonger.
Pol. Not I, my lord.   175
Ham. Then I would you were so honest a man.
Pol. Honest, my lord?
Ham. Ay sir. To be honest, as this world goes, is to be one
      man picked out of ten thousand.
Pol. That's very true, my lord.   180
Ham. For if the sun breed maggots in a dead dog, being a
      good kissing carrion—Have you a daughter?

170 S.D.] *Exeunt King and Queen | Capell; after 169 Q2 (subst.); after* presently *F (subst.).*   *and Attendants] Malone; and Train | Capell.*   174. Excellent] *Q2;* Excellent, excellent *F.*   You are] *Q2;* y'are *F,Q1.*   178–9.] *Prose F; 2 lines divided* goes, | Is *Q2.*   179. ten] *Q2,Q1;* two *F.*   182. good] *Q2,F;* God *Hanmer, Warburton.*

170. *board*] accost.
presently] at once.

give me leave] A formula not of accosting, as often supposed, but of farewell. From being a request for permission (to depart), it came to be a courteous form of dismissal. Probably addressed to attendants who do not vanish with sufficient alacrity.

172. *God-a-mercy*] i.e. God have mercy (on you). A polite response to a greeting, esp. a greeting from a social inferior. Cf. *John* I.i.185, 'Good den, Sir Richard'. – 'God-a-mercy, fellow!'

174. *a fishmonger*] In its ordinary sense ridiculously inappropriate for Polonius. But in another aspect a *fishmonger* is seen as one whose daughter had a more than ordinary propensity to breed, which leads on to ll. 181–4. LN.

176. *honest*] With a play on words; for although in the ordinary sense a fishmonger is a respectable honest tradesman, honest in another (sexual) sense is precisely what a fishmonger in another sense (cf. l. 174 LN.) is not. This again leads on to ll. 182–5, and ultimately to III.i. 103 ff.

178–9. *one man . . . ten thousand*] The more usual formula, as cited by Tilley (M 217), is 'a man among a thousand'.

181. *if the sun breed maggots in a dead dog*] That the sun creates new life from dead matter is an ancient idea, and appropriately so since Hamlet now reads, or affects to read, from his book. LN.

181–2. *a good kissing carrion*] i.e. a carrion good for kissing, or good in the kissing. LN. *Carrion* has its primary sense of a dead carcase, but also its secondary sense of live flesh, and especially flesh contemptuously regarded as available for sexual pleasure. This leads us directly enough to Polonius's daughter and what, by analogy, may happen to her.

Pol. I have, my lord.

Ham. Let her not walk i'th' sun. Conception is a blessing,
but as your daughter may conceive—friend, look 185
to't.

Pol. [*aside*] How say you by that? Still harping on my
daughter. Yet he knew me not at first; a said I was a
fishmonger. A is far gone. And truly in my youth I
suffered much extremity for love, very near this. I'll 190
speak to him again.—What do you read, my lord?

Ham. Words, words, words.

Pol. What is the matter, my lord?

Ham. Between who?

Pol. I mean the matter that you read, my lord. 195

Ham. Slanders, sir. For the satirical rogue says here that
old men have gray beards, that their faces are
wrinkled, their eyes purging thick amber and plum-
tree gum, and that they have a plentiful lack of wit,

---

185. but] *Q2;* but not *F.*   conceive—] *Malone;* conceaue, *Q2;* conceiue.
F.   187. *aside*] As *Capell; beginning* Still *Jennens; beginning* Yet *Pope.*
188-9. a said . . . A] *Q2;* he said . . . he *F.*   189. gone] *Q2;* gone, farre
gone *F.*   195. that] *Q2; not in F,Q1.*   read] *Q2,Q1;* meane *F.*
196. rogue] *Q2;* slaue *F.*   198. amber and] *Q2;* Amber, or *F.*   199. lack]
Q2; locke *F.*

---

184. *Let her . . . sun.*] literally, for
obvious reasons in view of what the
sun does to the other carrion;
figuratively, keep her away from
public places, and perhaps, with the
sun as a royal emblem, specifically
from the prince. After Polonius's plan
to 'loose' her (l. 162) the audience
may appreciate the irony of this.
Dover Wilson, though without
apparent justification, hears an echo
of the proverb, 'Out of Heaven's
blessing into the warm sun'.

Conception] (1) the power of forming
ideas in the mind, and (2) becoming
pregnant. The pun, not an uncommon one, is also used in *Lr*
I.i. 11-12.

185. *but as . . . conceive*] F *but not as*
specifically denies (that *conception* in
the second sense is a blessing) where
Q2, more artfully, leaves us with a

hint which imagination may
complete.

187. *How . . . by that?*] 'A triumphant exclamation' (Kittredge):
What do you say about that! For
by, cf. *Mer.V.* I.ii.48, 'How say you
by the French lord?'

Still] always. Cf. I.i. 125 and n.

193. *the matter*] the substance.
Hamlet deliberately misunderstands.

196. *the satirical rogue*] LN.

198. *purging*] discharging, exuding.

198-9. *plum-tree gum*] Gerard's
Herbal speaks of 'the gum which
cometh out of the plum-tree'.
Shakespeare presumably knew of it
from observation. But it may have
been proverbial: cf. Cooke, *Greene's
Tu Quoque* (Hazlitt's Dodsley, xi. 282),
'Surely I was begotten in a plum-
tree, I ha' such a deal of gum about
mine eyes'.

together with most weak hams—all which, sir, 200
though I most powerfully and potently believe, yet I
hold it not honesty to have it thus set down. For
yourself, sir, shall grow old as I am—if like a crab you
could go backward.

Pol. [*aside*] Though this be madness, yet there is method 205
in't.—Will you walk out of the air, my lord?

Ham. Into my grave?

Pol. Indeed, that's out of the air.—[*Aside*] How pregnant
sometimes his replies are—a happiness that often
madness hits on, which reason and sanity could not 210
so prosperously be delivered of. I will leave him and
suddenly contrive the means of meeting between him
and my daughter.—My lord, I will take my leave
of you.

---

200. most] *Q2; not in F.*   203. yourself] *Q2,Q1;* you your selfe *F.*
shall grow] *Q2;* should be *F;* shalbe *Q1.*   205–14.] *Prose Q2; as verse with
lines ending* madnesse, / walke / Lord? / Graue? / Ayre: / are? / happinesse, /
on, / not / of. / him, / meeting / daughter. / humbly / you. *F.*   205. *Aside*]
Johnson.   208. that's] *Q2,Q1;* that is *F.*   of the] *Q2,Q1;* o'th' *F.*
Aside] *As Capell.*   210. sanity] *F;* sanctity *Q2.*   212–13. suddenly . . . and]
F; not in Q2.   213. My] *Q2,Q1;* My Honourable *F.*   will] *Q2,Q1;*
will most humbly *F.*

---

202. *honesty*] proper behaviour,
decorum. Cf. *Oth.* IV.i.274, 'It is not
honesty in me to speak What I have
seen.'

203. *old as*] i.e. as old as.

204. *go backward*] Dover Wilson
(after Capell) imagines Hamlet bearing down upon the old man as he
emphasizes point by point until
Polonius is forced to retreat and give
a demonstration of crab-like motion.

205–6. *madness, yet . . . method in't*]
Cf. Horace, *Sat.,* II.iii.271, 'Insanire
paret certa ratione modoque', and
l. 93n. above.

206. *Will you walk . . . air*] Fresh air
was thought to be bad for invalids:
Polonius betrays what he thinks. LN.

207. *Into my grave?*] This continues
the literal-mindedness of Hamlet's
retorts. If I am to go 'out of the air'
in a strict sense, where can I go but

to my death? The absence of a
question-mark in Q2, though taken
by some as a clue to interpretation,
is clearly not significant: it is in line
with ll. 177, 191, 193, 194.

208. *pregnant*] pointed, quick-witted.
See *OED a.*² 3b and cf. *2H4* I.
ii.160–1, 'pregnancy is made a
tapster, and his quick wit wasted'.
The latent wordplay comes to the
surface in *delivered.*

209–11. *a happiness . . . delivered of*]
A hint not always taken by the
commentators.

212. *suddenly*] immediately.

213. *My lord, I will take*] The words
Honourable and *most humbly*, additional
in F, are evidently fill-ups by the
compositor (B). They are not really
in character for Polonius, and the
whole speech, the last on a page and
of the compositor's stint, is set out in

Ham. You cannot, sir, take from me anything that I will 215
    not more willingly part withal—except my life, ex-
    cept my life, except my life.
Pol. Fare you well, my lord.
Ham. These tedious old fools.

Enter ROSENCRANTZ *and* GUILDENSTERN.

Pol. You go to seek the Lord Hamlet. There he is.   220
Ros. God save you, sir.   *Exit* [*Polonius*].
Guild. My honoured lord.
Ros. My most dear lord.
Ham. My excellent good friends. How dost thou,
    Guildenstern? Ah, Rosencrantz. Good lads, how do 225
    you both?
Ros. As the indifferent children of the earth.
Guild. Happy in that we are not over-happy: on For-
    tune's cap we are not the very button.
Ham. Nor the soles of her shoe?   230
Ros. Neither, my lord.
Ham. Then you live about her waist, or in the middle of
    her favours?
Guild. Faith, her privates we.

215. sir] *F; not in Q2.*   216. not] *Q2; not in F.*   216–17. life, except
my life, except my life] *Q2;* life, my life *F.*   219 S.D.] *As Capell; after 217
Q2; after 220 F.*   220. the] *Q2;* my *F.*   221 S.D.] *Capell; exit. Q1; after
220 Pope; not in Q2,F.*   222. My] *Q2;* Mine *F.*   224. excellent] *F,Q3;*
extent *Q2.*   224–6.] *Prose F; 2 lines divided* Guyldersterne? | A *Q2.*
225. Ah] *Q2 (A);* Oh *F.*   226. you] *Q2;* ye *F.*   228–9.] *Prose F; 2 lines
divided* lap, | We *Q2.*   over-happy: . . . cap] *F;* euer happy . . . lap *Q2.*
230. shoe?] *F;* shooe. *Q2.*   233. favours] *Q2;* fauour *F.*

short irregular lines, like a sort of
free verse, with the obvious purpose
of eking out the text.
  215–16. *cannot . . . will not*] The
double negative (Abbott 406) was
not uncommon and this instance,
occurring in Q2 though 'corrected'
in F, is probably Shakespearean.
  216–17. *except my life . . . my life*]
Coleridge (i. 24) praises the repetition as 'most admirable'.
  227. *indifferent*] like the ordinary
run of mortals, neither fortunate nor

unfortunate. Cf. *Gent.* III. ii. 44.
  229. *the very button*] The button, at
the crown of the cap, is of course the
highest point.
  234. *privates*] (1) private parts of
the body; (2) ordinary subjects
without rank or public office. (Cf.
H5 IV. i. 234, 'What have kings that
privates have not too?') Explained by
OED and some editors as intimates or
favourites, which is precisely what
the context says they are not.

Ham. In the secret parts of Fortune? O most true, she is a 235
         strumpet. What news?

Ros. None, my lord, but the world's grown honest.

Ham. Then is doomsday near. But your news is not true.
         Let me question more in particular. What have you,
         my good friends, deserved at the hands of Fortune 240
         that she sends you to prison hither?

Guild. Prison, my lord?

Ham. Denmark's a prison.

Ros. Then is the world one.

Ham. A goodly one, in which there are many confines, 245
         wards, and dungeons, Denmark being one o'th'
         worst.

Ros. We think not so, my lord.

Ham. Why, then 'tis none to you; for there is nothing
         either good or bad but thinking makes it so. To me 250
         it is a prison.

Ros. Why, then your ambition makes it one: 'tis too nar-
         row for your mind.

Ham. O God, I could be bounded in a nutshell and count
         myself a king of infinite space—were it not that I 255
         have bad dreams.

236. What] *Q2;* What's the *F.*   237. but] *Q2;* but that *F.*   239–69. Let me
. . . attended.] *F; not in Q2,Q1.*

235–6. *is a strumpet*] The dialogue
confirms by a process of seemingly
rational deduction what had long
been recognized. Fortune was a
strumpet on account of her proverbial fickleness. Cf. below, l. 489.

238. *Then is doomsday near.*] Because
honesty is incompatible with the
world's nature (cf. ll. 178–9) and
hence must be destructive of it.

239–69. *Let me question . . . attended.*]
For Q2's omission, LN.

239. *question*] The intransitive use
was common. Cf. III.iv.11; *Meas.*
v.i.270, 'Give me leave to question'.

243. *a prison*] The feeling of being
in prison was a recognized symptom
of melancholy. Cf. Bright, p. 263,
'The house, except it be cheerful and
lightsome, trim and neat, seemeth

unto the melancholic a prison or
dungeon'.

245. *confines*] places of confinement.
Cf. i.i.160.

249–50. *there is nothing . . . makes it
so*] A common reflection. LN.

252. *your ambition*] They try to
'bring him on to some confession'
(III.i.9). It would be convenient to
be able to say (with Dover Wilson)
that they are employed to test a
theory of the King's that Hamlet's
'distemper' is due to frustrated ambition (for the throne), just as
Ophelia is employed to test Polonius's
theory that it is due to frustrated
love (*WHH*, pp. 116–25). But that
goes beyond the text.

256. *bad dreams*] Another symptom
of the melancholic (Bright, p. 124).

Guild. Which dreams indeed are ambition; for the very
　　substance of the ambitious is merely the shadow of a
　　dream.

Ham. A dream itself is but a shadow.　　　　　　　　260

Ros. Truly, and I hold ambition of so airy and light a
　　quality that it is but a shadow's shadow.

Ham. Then are our beggars bodies, and our monarchs
　　and outstretched heroes the beggars' shadows. Shall
　　we to th' court? For by my fay, I cannot reason.　　265

Ros. ⎱
Guild. ⎰ We'll wait upon you.

Ham. No such matter. I will not sort you with the rest of
　　my servants; for, to speak to you like an honest man,
　　I am most dreadfully attended. But in the beaten
　　way of friendship, what make you at Elsinore?　　270

Ros. To visit you, my lord, no other occasion.

Ham. Beggar that I am, I am even poor in thanks, but I
　　thank you. And sure, dear friends, my thanks are too
　　dear a halfpenny. Were you not sent for? Is it your

272. even] *F*; euer *Q2*.

257–9. *the very substance . . . a dream*]
The ambitious man first dreams of
what he then strives to attain, so that
in his achievement he imitates his
dream. Hence paradoxically his
'substance' is the 'shadow' of the
dream that creates it (and so a
shadow of a shadow).

263–4. *Then are our beggars . . .
shadows.*] Hamlet, whose two previous
speeches have countered the argument of the others, now ridicules it
by pursuing it to absurd lengths.
Since ambition is 'a shadow's shadow',
the only substantial beings must be
those with no ambition, i.e. beggars,
and the ambitious (kings and heroes),
who are by definition shadows, must
be shadows of them. The straining
heroes are *outstretched* like elongated
shadows, looking bigger than they are

265. *th' court*] Presumably the
appropriate place for their sort of
chop-logic (which Hamlet says he is
unable to supply).

266. *wait upon*] escort, attend. (Cf.
Meas. i.i.84, 'I'll wait upon your
honour.') Hamlet quibbles in replying
that he does not class (*sort*) them as
serving-men. Cf. i.ii. 162–3.

269. *dreadfully attended*] wretchedly
waited on. But is there also a further
allusion to the 'dreams', the 'horrors'
which haunt his mind?

269–70. *the beaten way*] Cf. the
beaten (well-trodden) track. Hamlet
abandons tortuous expressions for
plain, frank speech.

274. *a halfpenny*] Usually taken to
be equivalent to 'at a halfpenny',
but possibly *by* a halfpenny. Kittredge
explains that Hamlet's thanks are
not worth a halfpenny because he
lacks 'power in the state'; but may
it not be that even his poor thanks are
(a halfpennyworth) more than the
visitors deserve (if they have not
come of their own free will)? So,
substantially, Dover Wilson.

own inclining? Is it a free visitation? Come, come, 275
   deal justly with me. Come, come. Nay, speak.

Guild. What should we say, my lord?

Ham. Anything but to th' purpose. You were sent for, and
   there is a kind of confession in your looks, which your
   modesties have not craft enough to colour. I know 280
   the good King and Queen have sent for you.

Ros. To what end, my lord?

Ham. That, you must teach me. But let me conjure you,
   by the rights of our fellowship, by the consonancy of
   our youth, by the obligation of our ever-preserved 285
   love, and by what more dear a better proposer
   can charge you withal, be even and direct with me
   whether you were sent for or no.

Ros. [*aside to Guildenstern*] What say you?

Ham. Nay, then I have an eye of you. If you love me, 290
   hold not off.

Guild. My lord, we were sent for.

Ham. I will tell you why; so shall my anticipation prevent
   your discovery, and your secrecy to the King and

275–6. come, deal] *Q2;* deale *F.*   278. Anything but] *Q2;* Why any thing.
But *F.*   'to th'] *Q2;* to the *F.*   279. of] *Q2,Q1; not in F.*   287. can] *Q2;*
could *F.*   289. *aside to Guildenstern*] *Globe; To Guilden. Theobald.*
294. discovery, and] *Q2;* discouery of *F.*

278. *Anything . . . purpose.*] Although
a few eds., including Alexander,
follow F, *but to th' purpose* must surely
modify *anything. But* = except, and
anything but is good modern idiom.
Hamlet sarcastically says they may
say anything they like *other than* what
is to the purpose. The opposite
interpretation – 'Anything, only let
it be to the purpose' – much favoured
by eds., gives quite inferior sense.
Hamlet is not exhorting them to give
a straight answer; he is assuming
they won't.

280. *modesties*] For the plural, cf.
I.i.178n.

colour] give a different appearance
to, disguise. Cf. III.i.45.

284–6. *by the rights . . . love*] See
ll. 11–12 above. *rights of*, what is

due to; *consonancy*, harmonious com-
panionship.

286. *proposer*] The sense, though
often strangely mistaken, is clearly
illustrated by I.v.160, 'Propose the
oath', i.e. state the form of it. Having
specified three precious things in
turn, Hamlet envisages that 'a better
proposer', one more adept than he
at framing exhortations, might think
of something still 'more dear' to
exhort them by.

287. *even*] straightforward.

290. *have an eye of*] have an eye *on*,
am watching.

291. *hold not off*] do not hang back,
do not refrain from speaking freely.

293–4. *prevent your discovery*] forestall your revelation.

Queen moult no feather. I have of late, but where- 295
fore I know not, lost all my mirth, forgone all custom
of exercises; and indeed it goes so heavily with my
disposition that this goodly frame the earth seems to
me a sterile promontory, this most excellent canopy
the air, look you, this brave o'erhanging firmament, 300
this majestical roof fretted with golden fire, why, it
appeareth nothing to me but a foul and pestilent congregation of vapours. What piece of work is a man,
how noble in reason, how infinite in faculties, in form
and moving how express and admirable, in action 305
how like an angel, in apprehension how like a god:
the beauty of the world, the paragon of animals—

295. Queen] *Q2*; Queene: *F.*   297. exercises] *Q2*; exercise *F.*   heavily] *Q2*;
heauenly *F.*   300. firmament] *Q2; not in F.*   302. appeareth] *Q2*;
appeares *F.*   nothing . . . but] *Q2*; no other thing . . . then *F.*
303. What] *Q2*; What a *F.*   304. faculties] *Q2*; faculty *F.*   305–6. moving
. . . admirable, . . . action . . . angel, . . . apprehension . . . god:] *F subst.*
(mouing . . . admirable? . . . Action, . . . Angel? . . . apprehension . . . God?),
Q5 subst.; moouing, . . . admirable . . . action, . . . Angel . . . apprehension,
. . . God: *Q2.*

295. *moult no feather*] (in non-
figurative language) remain intact.
296–7. *forgone . . . exercises*] Contrast, however, v.ii.206–7, 'I have
been in continual practice'.
297–8. *it goes so heavily . . . that*]
There is no ambiguity if we recognize
that this is the impersonal construction, as in 'How goes it with . . .
Antony?' (*Ant.* i.v.38), etc., and that
the clause introduced by *that* is not
the complement of *it goes* but follows
on from *so.*
298–303. *this goodly frame . . .
vapours.*] LN.
298. *frame*] structure. A favourite
word to describe the earth, or the
cosmos, considered as a systematic
physical construction. Cf. *Mac.* iii.
ii.16, 'Let the frame of things disjoint'.
299. *promontory*] The metaphor
suggests that man's earthly existence
is surrounded by some different
element vastly greater than itself.
300. *brave*] splendid.

301. *fretted*] adorned. An archi-
tectural term esp. applied to ceilings
with gilded decoration.
303. *What piece*] The omission of
the article after an exclamatory *what*
(as in *Q2*) was idiomatic. Cf. *Caes.*
i.iii.43, 'What night is this'; *Tw.N.*
ii.v.104, 'What dish o'poison . . . !';
Gent. i.ii.53, 'What fool is she'. In the
last instance an apostrophe in F
'neatly illustrates the obsolescence of
the construction' (Maxwell, *RES*, n.s.
iv, 358). Hence F's *What a piece* may
be regarded as a modernization (the
acceptance of which into the editorial
tradition has prevented recognition
of the construction in *Q2*). See
Abbott 86; Franz 273; Dyce, v.368.
piece of work] a work of artistic
creation, esp. one remarkable for
fine craftsmanship. Shakespeare uses
the same term to refer to the Gonzago
play (iii.ii.46–7) and the rich tapestry
in Imogen's chamber (*Cym.* ii.iv.72).
304–6. *in form and moving . . . like a
god*] On the punctuation, LN.

and yet, to me, what is this quintessence of dust?
Man delights not me—nor woman neither, though
by your smiling you seem to say so.   310

Ros. My lord, there was no such stuff in my thoughts.

Ham. Why did ye laugh then, when I said man delights
not me?

Ros. To think, my lord, if you delight not in man, what
Lenten entertainment the players shall receive from 315
you. We coted them on the way, and hither are they
coming to offer you service.

Ham. He that plays the king shall be welcome—his Majesty shall have tribute on me, the adventurous knight
shall use his foil and target, the lover shall not sigh 320
gratis, the humorous man shall end his part in peace,
the clown shall make those laugh whose lungs are

---

309. nor] *Q2*; no, nor *F,Q1*.   woman] *F,Q1,Q3*; women *Q2*.
312. ye] *Q2*; you *F,Q1*.   then] *Q2,Q1*; *not in F.*   319. on] *Q2*; of *F,Q1*.
322-3. the clown . . . sear] *F,Q1 subst.*; *not in Q2.*

---

308. *quintessence*] lit. the fifth
essence, distinguished from the four
elements composing matter but held
to be extractable from them. Hence
the *quintessence of dust* is dust (1) in
its utmost refinement, (2) in its
most essential character. Any recognition of man's superiority as (1)
goes with the bathos of his being (2).

315. *Lenten entertainment*] frugal
reception, with a glance perhaps at
the total prohibition of plays during
Lent (reconfirmed by the Privy
Council on 22 June 1600).

316. *coted*] outstripped. (A metaphor from coursing, in which one
dog is said to cote, or run ahead of,
another.) Cf. III.i.17.

319. *tribute on*] In support of the
Q2 *on*, cf. *Lr.* v.iii.165, 'thou that
hast this fortune on me', and see
OED on, 23.

320. *target*] a small targe or shield.

321. *the humorous man*] Not of course
the jester (who is mentioned next),
but the man who is 'govern'd by
humours' (*1H4* III.i.237), moods or

caprices; as a stock stage character,
esp. one addicted to violent rages,
like the 'humorous' Duke of *AYL*
(I.ii.245, II.iii.8).

in peace] The point is in the incongruity, the part being the reverse
of peaceful. The humorous man, like
the knight with his weapon and the
lady with her tongue, is to have
full rein to enact his stock role. Hence
he will play out his peace (unmolested)
his unpeaceful part, and play it to
its peaceful end when his rages are
all spent. LN.

322-3. *whose lungs . . . sear*] 'who
are of such sensible and nimble lungs
that they always use to laugh at
nothing' (*Tp.* II.i.166-7). Cf. the
'barren spectators' of III.ii.41. The
type is well known. *Sear* is a gun-
smith's term for that part of a gun-
lock which holds the hammer in
position and is released by pressure on
the trigger. Hence *tickle of* (or *a*, for
on) *the sear*, 'easily made to go off'
(*OED*). LN.

tickle a th' sear, and the lady shall say her mind
freely—or the blank verse shall halt for't. What
players are they?   325
Ros. Even those you were wont to take such delight in,
the tragedians of the city.
Ham. How chances it they travel? Their residence, both
in reputation and profit, was better both ways.
Ros. I think their inhibition comes by the means of the 330
late innovation.
Ham. Do they hold the same estimation they did when I
was in the city? Are they so followed?
Ros. No, indeed are they not.
Ham. How comes it? Do they grow rusty?   335
Ros. Nay, their endeavour keeps in the wonted pace; but
there is, sir, an eyrie of children, little eyases, that
cry out on the top of question, and are most tyrannically clapped for't. These are now the fashion, and

---

323. tickle] *Clarendon, conj. Staunton;* tickled *F,Q1.*   a th'] *Sisson;* a'th' *F.*
324. blank] *F,Q1;* black *Q2.*   326. such] *Q2; not in F.*   334. are they] *Q2;*
they are *F.*   335–58.] *F; not in Q2.*

323–4. *say her mind freely*] Evidently
the lady of the stock role had an
unbridled tongue (cf. l. 321 n.). I do
not think it implied that her part
contained obscenities. Verity interprets *freely* as suggesting that the boy
actor forgot his words and improvised,
but since that *would* make the blank
verse go lame, it does not fit the
context.

327. *the tragedians of the city*] The
temptation to see this as an allusion
to Shakespeare's own company should
surely be resisted. Still more so the
idea that he might bestow this title
on a rival company.

328. *Their residence*] their settled
stay (in the city) as opposed to going
on tour.

329. *both ways*] i.e. in both reputation and profit.

330–1. *their inhibition . . . innovation*]
the ban on their playing (in town)
is due to the recent insurrection.
Though this is much disputed, the

allusion is probably to the Essex
rebellion rather than to troubles
occasioned by the success of the boy
actors. LN.

335–58.] For the Q2 omission, LN.

337. *eyrie of children*] A clear topical
reference to the Children of the
Chapel, who began to act at the
Blackfriars theatre towards the end
of 1600. Cf. Intro., pp. 1–2. An *eyrie*
(or *aerie*) is a nest, and hence the
young, of a bird of prey.

eyases] young hawks, notable for
their clamour. In *The Gentleman's
Recreation*, 1674 (p. 93), 'an Eyess' is
said to be so called 'as long as she is
in the Eyrie. These are very troublesome in their feeding, do cry very
much'. Cf. Fletcher, *Woman's Prize*,
I. ii. 148–50 ('Eyasses, that . . . cry
like Kites'), and see *SQ*, XXVIII, 86–8.

338. *on the top of question*] with the
maximum of contention. LN.

338–9. *tyrannically*] vehemently.

so berattle the common stages—so they call them— 340
that many wearing rapiers are afraid of goose-quills
and dare scarce come thither.

Ham. What, are they children? Who maintains 'em?
How are they escotted? Will they pursue the quality
no longer than they can sing? Will they not say 345
afterwards, if they should grow themselves to common players—as it is most like, if their means are no
better—their writers do them wrong to make them
exclaim against their own succession?

Ros. Faith, there has been much to do on both sides; and 350
the nation holds it no sin to tar them to controversy.

---

340. berattle] *F2* (be ratle)*;* be-ratled *F.*   347. most like] *Pope;* like most
F; like most will *Wilson.*   no] *F;* not *F2.*

---

340. *berattle the common stages*]
noisily assail the public playhouses.
The boy actors performed *Cynthia's
Revels* in the winter of 1600 and
Poetaster in the spring of 1601, and
it was in these plays that Jonson
satirized the plays and players of
the regular theatres and especially
the dramatists Marston and Dekker.
R. A. Small, *The Stage-Quarrel*, 1899,
is probably the best account. Among
briefer ones see Tucker Brooke, *The
Tudor Drama*, pp. 375–86.

so they call them] The term 'common
stages' was contemptuously used in
Cynthia's Revels (Ind. 182; IV.iii.118).
Cf. the Privy Council's use of 'com-
mon playhouses' (Chambers, *El.
St.*, iv.322).

341–2. *many wearing rapiers . . .
thither*] An instance of the pen's
proving mightier than the sword.
Rapier-wearing gallants are deterred
from attending the public theatres by
fear of ridicule. Cf. *Poetaster*, III.iv.
328ff., where Histrio says, 'Nobody
comes at us; not a gentleman, not
a – '.

344. *escotted*] provided for. Cf. to
pay one's *scot*, O.Fr. *escot*. Eds. usually
keep the F spelling *escoted*, but if the

infinitive is rightly *escot* (*OED*), the
preterite should retain the short
vowel. Cf. Cotgrave, *escotter*.

quality] profession (of acting).

345. *no longer . . . sing*] only until
their voices break. Essentially they
are choirboys, but the question is
whether they will necessarily cease
acting when they cease to be such.

347. *like*] likely (that they will).

347–8. *if . . . no better*] if they have
no better means of livelihood. F
has an ink-mark after *no*, but Dover
Wilson (*MSH*, pp. 291–2), along
with F2, is mistaken in seeing this
as the trace of a *t*.

349. *exclaim against . . . succession*]
decry the condition they themselves
must come to.

350. *on both sides*] While still writing
Poetaster (see above, l. 340n.) Jonson
knew that Dekker had been 'hired . . .
to abuse . . . and bring him in, in a
play' (III.iv.322), and *Satiromastix*,
acted by the Lord Chamberlain's
company, retaliated upon Jonson
shortly after. See Intro., p. 2.

351. *tar*] incite. The other two
instances in Shakespeare (*John* IV.
i.117; *Troil.* I.iii.392) both have to
do with inciting dogs to fight.

There was for a while no money bid for argument
unless the poet and the player went to cuffs in the
question.

Ham. Is't possible?   355

Guild. O, there has been much throwing about of brains.

Ham. Do the boys carry it away?

Ros. Ay, that they do, my lord, Hercules and his load too.

Ham. It is not very strange; for my uncle is King of Denmark, and those that would make mouths at him   360
while my father lived give twenty, forty, fifty, a
hundred ducats apiece for his picture in little.
'Sblood, there is something in this more than
natural, if philosophy could find it out.

A flourish of trumpets.

Guild. There are the players.   365

Ham. Gentlemen, you are welcome to Elsinore. Your

---

359. very] *Q2; not in F.*   my] *Q2;* mine *F.*   360. mouths] *Q2;* mowes
F; mops and moes *Q1.*   361. fifty] *Q2; not in F.*   361–2. a hundred]
Q2; an hundred *F.*   363. 'Sblood] *Q2; not in F.*   364 S.D.] *A Florish.*
Q2; Flourish for the Players. *F; The Trumpets sound, Q1.*

352–3. *no money . . . to cuffs*] The
only plays which paid were those in
which the children's writers and the
players of the public theatres attacked
one another. In the Apology
appended to *Poetaster* Jonson admitted
that he 'taxed' the players and said
they got food and clothes by what
they did against him (ll. 141–9). The
sense of *argument* may be the general
one of discussion, or the specialized
one of the plot or summary of a play
(cf. III.ii.227).

353–4. *in the question*] concerning
the matter at issue (rather than, as
some say, in the dialogue).

357. *carry it away*] have the better of
it, triumph. Cf. *Rom.* III.i.72, where,
since Romeo declines to fight,
Tybalt 'carries it away'.

358. *Hercules and his load*] His *load*
is the world, which Hercules was
sometimes represented bearing on
his shoulders. LN.

359–62. *It is not . . . picture in little.*]

Hamlet compares the unreasoning
adulation given to the boy actors and
to the (formerly derided) new king.

360. *make mouths*] pull faces (cf.
IV.iv.50). The variants *mouth* and
mow (Fr. *moue*) have the same sense.

362. *ducats*] Though the ducat
(*ducato*), a ducal coin, originated in
Italy, the name was given to the gold
coins of many European countries,
including Denmark.

364 S.D. *trumpets*] It was customary
for players so to announce their
arrival (as they also do in *Shr.* Ind.
i.71 ff.).

366–9. *Your hands . . . garb*] Having
brought himself to pronounce a
welcome, Hamlet recognizes that he
should go through the forms and
ceremonies that belong to welcome.
But his insistence on the forms seems
designed to leave the spirit of the
welcome in doubt. Dover Wilson
makes 'Your hands?' a question,
assuming that 'it is not Hamlet but

hands, come then. Th'appurtenance of welcome is
fashion and ceremony. Let me comply with you in
this garb—lest my extent to the players, which I tell
you must show fairly outwards, should more appear 370
like entertainment than yours. You are welcome.
But my uncle-father and aunt-mother are deceived.

Guild. In what, my dear lord?

Ham. I am but mad north-north-west. When the wind is
southerly, I know a hawk from a handsaw.   375

Enter POLONIUS.

Pol. Well be with you, gentlemen.

Ham. Hark you, Guildenstern, and you too—at each ear
a hearer. That great baby you see there is not yet out
of his swaddling-clouts.

Ros. Happily he is the second time come to them, for they 380
say an old man is twice a child.

367. then] *Q2; not in F.*   Th'appurtenance] *Q2;* The appurtenance *F.*
369. this] *Q2;* the *F.*   lest my] *F;* let me *Q2.*   370. outwards] *Q2;*
outward *F.*   379. swaddling-clouts] *Q2,Q1;* swathing clouts *F.*   380. he is]
Q2; he's *F.*

the others who offer to shake hands'.
Sisson, *NR*, with a period after *hands,*
explains, 'Hamlet offers the intimate
gesture of hand-shaking. The young
men respectfully hesitate, and Hamlet
reassures them'. *comply,* observe the
formalities of courtesy (*OED* comply
v.[1] 2). Cf. v.ii.184.

369. *my extent*] my showing, my
behaviour, that which I extend (as
we still 'extend' a welcome).

370–1. *should more appear . . . than
yours*] should make it seem that they
are being received more favourably
than you are.

374–5. *mad north-north-west . . .
southerly*] Commentators explain that,
with birds flying before the wind, if
'the wind is southerly', the watcher's
eye is turned away from the sun and
so can see more clearly. But this is
surely to be too literal-minded (and
in that case why 'north-north-west'?).
Common beliefs about madness con-

cerned its fluctuating nature and its
supposed dependence on the weather.
Hamlet's wit is in the fanciful par-
ticularization with which he applies
these to his own case. Cf. Bright,
p. 257, 'The air meet for melancholic folk ought to be thin, pure and
subtle, open, and patent to all winds:
in respect of their temper, especially
to the south, and southeast'. Hence
we may paraphrase *when the wind is
southerly* as 'in my more lucid
moments'.

375. *I know a hawk from a handsaw.*]
Hamlet issues a warning that he is
able to distinguish one thing from
another and so to see through false
pretences; perhaps also that he can
recognize a bird of prey when he
sees one. LN.

380. *Happily*] haply, perhaps, as at
I.i.137.

380–1. *they say . . . twice a child*]
Instances are given in Tilley, M 570.

Ham. I will prophesy he comes to tell me of the players.
Mark it.—You say right, sir, a Monday morning,
'twas then indeed.

Pol. My lord, I have news to tell you.   385

Ham. My lord, I have news to tell you. When Roscius was
an actor in Rome—

Pol. The actors are come hither, my lord.

Ham. Buzz, buzz.

Pol. Upon my honour—   390

Ham. Then came each actor on his ass—

Pol. The best actors in the world, either for tragedy,
comedy, history, pastoral, pastoral-comical, historical-pastoral, tragical-historical, tragical-comical-
historical-pastoral, scene individable, or poem un- 395
limited. Seneca cannot be too heavy, nor Plautus too

---

382. prophesy] prophecy, *Q2;* Prophesie. *F.*   383. a] *Q2,Q1;* for a *F.*
384. then] *Q2;* so *F,Q1.*   386. was] *Q2,Q1; not in F.*   390. my] *Q2;*
mine *F.*   391. came] *Q2;* can *F.*   393–4. pastoral-comical, historical-
pastoral] *Q2 (without hyphens);* Pastoricall-Comicall-Historicall-Pastorall *F.*
394–5. tragical-historical, tragical-comical-historical-pastoral] *F; not in Q2.*

383–4. *You say right . . . indeed.*] If
this were a nonsense remark addressed to Polonius, it would be
unique in being ignored. Rather
Hamlet ignores Polonius by pretending to be in earnest conversation.
For *a* see i.v.19n., and cf. iv.v.180;
Rom. iii.iv.20 ('a Thursday').

386. *Roscius*] The most famous
actor of antiquity. Hamlet confounds
Polonius by mentioning an actor
before he does.

389. *buzz*] A contemptuous exclamation dismissing something as idle
gossip or (as here) stale news.

391. *Then came . . . ass*] Plausibly
supposed to be a quotation from a
ballad (like ll. 403–4). It supplies a
rejoinder to '*upon* my honour'.

392–5. *tragedy . . . tragical-comical-
historical-pastoral*] The licence to act
which James I granted to Shakespeare's company specified 'comedies,
tragedies, histories, interludes, morals,
pastorals . . . ' (Chambers, *El. St.,*

ii.208). But what Polonius begins as
a sober, if inappropriate, catalogue
ends in self-parody – through which
Shakespeare no doubt smiles at contemporary dramatic olios.

394. *tragical-historical*] The first
play to be so designated on its title-
page was 'The Tragicall Historie of
Hamlet' (Q1, Q2).

395. *scene individable*] Usually explained as a play which observes the
unity of place, as distinct from *poem
unlimited,* which observes no unities.
But these meanings are not obvious,
and both terms may be more appropriately interpreted as bringing the
already ridiculous categories to a
climax in an all-inclusive (*unlimited*)
and unclassifiable (*individable*) drama.

396–7. *Seneca . . . light.*] '*Plautus* and
Seneca are accounted the best for
Comedy and Tragedy among the
Latins' (Meres, *Palladis Tamia,* 1598).
Heavy, grave, serious, characterizes
tragedy in contrast to comedy, which

light. For the law of writ, and the liberty, these are
   the only men.
Ham. O Jephthah, judge of Israel, what a treasure hadst
   thou!   400
Pol. What a treasure had he, my lord?
Ham. Why,
         One fair daughter and no more,
         The which he loved passing well.
Pol. [*aside*] Still on my daughter.   405
Ham. Am I not i 'th' right, old Jephthah?
Pol. If you call me Jephthah, my lord, I have a daughter
   that I love passing well.
Ham. Nay, that follows not.
Pol. What follows then, my lord?   410
Ham. Why,
         As by lot God wot,
      and then, you know,
         It came to pass, as most like it was.

---

397. light. For . . . liberty,] *Johnson;* light for . . . liberty: *Q2;* light, for . . .
Liberty. *F.*   writ] *Q2,F;* wit *Q 1676.*   402–4.] *As Capell; 2 lines* (Why
. . . more *as one line*) *F,Q1; prose Q2.*   405. aside] *As Capell.*   412.] *As
quotation Malone; quotation beginning by Pope; prose Q2,F.*   414.] *As quotation
Pope; prose Q2,F.*

---

is *light* or gay. It corresponds to the
gravis of the Latin rhetoricians, alluding to Seneca's weighty *sententiae* and
exalted diction. (On 'Polonius, Seneca
and the Elizabethans' see *Proc. Camb.
Philological Soc.*, CCI, 33–41.)

   397. *For the law of writ, and the
liberty*] This difficult phrase, never
very satisfactorily explained, is perhaps best paraphrased: for plays
composed according to the rules and
plays written in complete freedom
from them. LN.

   these] The actors, not (*pace* Sisson,
NR) Seneca and Plautus.

   399. *Jephthah, judge of Israel*] Judges
xi. 30–40. Jephthah sacrificed his
daughter, who bewailed her virginity.
As a type he is thus the opposite of a

fishmonger (cf. l. 174 and LN) and
recalls the warning of ll. 181–6.
Jephthah, Judge of Israel is actually the
title of a well-known ballad, from
which Hamlet proceeds to quote
(ll. 403–4, 412–14). LN.

   404. *passing*] surpassingly, exceedingly.

   405. *Still*] always, as at l. 187,
I. i. 125, etc.

   409. *that follows not*] Because
Polonius is like Jephthah in having a
daughter, it does not follow that he
is like him in loving her.

   411–14.] Hamlet affects to misunderstand and tells not what
follows logically but what follows in
the ballad. See l. 399 LN.

The first row of the pious chanson will show you 415
more, for look where my abridgement comes.

Enter the Players.

You are welcome, masters. Welcome, all.—I am
glad to see thee well.—Welcome, good friends.—O,
old friend, why, thy face is valanced since I saw thee
last. Com'st thou to beard me in Denmark?—What, 420
my young lady and mistress! By'r lady, your ladyship is nearer to heaven than when I saw you last by
the altitude of a chopine. Pray God your voice, like a

415. row] *Q2,F;* verse *Q1.*   pious chanson] *Q2; Pons Chanson F;* godly
Ballet *Q1.*   416. abridgement comes] *Q2,Q1;* Abridgements come *F.*
416 S.D. *the*] *Q2; foure or fiue | F.*   417. You are] *Q2;* Y'are *F.*   419. old]
Q2; my olde *F,Q1.*   why] *Q2; not in F,Q1.*   valanced] *Q2,Q1;* valiant *F.*
421. By'r lady] Byrlady *F;* by lady *Q2;* burlady *Q1.*   422. to] *Q2; not
in F.*

415–16. *The first row . . . more*] row,
stanza, as understood by Q1. Those
who object that the first stanza of
the ballad does not by itself show
'more' of the daughter's story fail to
take Hamlet's meaning. The first
stanza shows more of 'what follows'
than Hamlet actually recites.

415. *pious chanson*] So called because
it is a song based on holy writ. This
sounds more like a term from a song-
book title than a Shakespearean
coinage. Attempts to defend the F
Pons Chanson by linking it with the
French *chanson du pont-neuf*, a street
ballad, could afford a cautionary
tale. The synonymous substitutions
of Q1 show, again, what the actors
understood.

416. *abridgement*] The players, who
(1) cut him short and (2) entertain
him, thus shortening the time. Cf.
MND v.i.39, 'What abridgment
have you for this evening?' The contention (in *SQ,* III. 381–2) that an
abridgement is not a shortening and
the proposed alternative interpretation – epitome, image in little – are
untenable.

416 S.D. *Enter the Players.*]
Shakespeare is not specific as to how
many and it seems best to follow him.
F estimates the practical requirement.
The play of III.ii will have four
speaking parts, of which two may be
doubled, plus at least '*two or three
Mutes*' (see III.ii.133 S.D.2–11 n.), so
that at least five will be needed then.
It does not follow that all must appear
now.

419. *old friend*] F and Q1 prefix *my.*
But cf. l. 531.

valanced] draped (i.e. with a beard).

421. *my young lady*] the boy actor
who played the women's parts.

By'r lady] *By* (or *be*) *lady* seems to
have been an acceptable, and may
here be the Shakespearean, form.
(See *Tit.* IV.iv.48, and New Arden
note.) But cf. Q2 *ber Lady* at III.ii.131.

423. *chopine*] a woman's overshoe
with a high sole of cork covered with
leather and often highly decorated.
LN. It is not of course implied that
the boy wears chopines (still less that
boy actors sometimes wore them on
the stage), only that he has grown.

piece of uncurrent gold, be not cracked within the
ring.—Masters, you are all welcome. We'll e'en to't 425
like French falconers, fly at anything we see. We'll
have a speech straight. Come, give us a taste of your
quality. Come, a passionate speech.

1st Play. What speech, my good lord?

Ham. I heard thee speak me a speech once, but it was 430
never acted, or if it was, not above once—for the
play, I remember, pleased not the million, 'twas
caviare to the general. But it was, as I received it—
and others, whose judgments in such matters cried in
the top of mine—an excellent play, well digested in 435
the scenes, set down with as much modesty as cun-

---

426. French] *F,Q1;* friendly *Q2.*   429. good] *Q2,Q1; not in F.*
434. judgments] *Q2;* iudgement *F.*

424–5. *cracked within the ring*] Before
milled coins became general in 1662
coins were liable to be clipped
(*cracked*) for the metal thus obtained;
and if the clipping invaded the ring
round the sovereign's head, the coin
was no longer legal tender (hence
uncurrent). 'A cracked crown' was 'a
common saying' (Lyly, *Midas,* II.
ii. 21); and there were jests comparing a cracked coin to a woman's
cracked virtue (e.g. Lyly, *Woman in
the Moon,* III. ii. 262–6), the *ring,* or
O, with reference to the sexual
anatomy, being the seat of her
virginity. Shakespeare's pun is wittier:
if the boy actor's voice is broken, and
so *cracked* in its *ring,* it will likewise be
uncurrent (without value for women's
parts). This jest is echoed in
Beaumont's poem *The Remedy of Love*
('If her voice be bad, crack'd in the
ring'), but without the point.

425. *e'en to't*] just have a go.

426. *like French falconers . . . we see*]
A falcon was normally trained for a
particular kind of quarry. Hence
Hamlet ascribes to the French (and
so to himself) more enthusiasm than
art. Evidence cited by commentators

that the French were in fact expert
falconers – according to Sir T.
Browne 'the first and noblest' in
western Europe (*Works,* ed. Keynes,
v. 74) – cannot turn this into a compliment. Cf. Madden, *Diary of Master
Wm. Silence,* 1907 edn, p. 140.

428. *quality*] professional skill. Cf.
l. 344.

431–2. *the play*] LN.

433. *caviare*] Then a novel delicacy,
and being 'generally unpalatable to
those who have not acquired a taste
for it' (*OED*), regarded as a thing for
the connoisseur. The spellings *cauiary*
(Q2, Q1), *cauiarie* (F) indicate an
Elizabethan pronunciation in four
syllables. LN.

434–5. *cried in the top of*] confirmed
with higher authority than.

435. *digested*] ordered, shaped.
Cf. *R3* III. i. 200, 'digest our complots
in some form'.

436. *modesty*] propriety of style;
restraint, as further indicated by the
lack of affectation (ll. 438–9) and fine
writing (l. 441). Cf. III. ii. 19, and
Caes. III. i. 214, 'The enemies of Caesar
shall say this; Then, in a friend, it is
cold modesty'.

ning. I remember one said there were no sallets in the
lines to make the matter savoury, nor no matter in
the phrase that might indict the author of affection,
but called it an honest method, as wholesome as   440
sweet, and by very much more handsome than fine.
One speech in't I chiefly loved—'twas Aeneas' tale
to Dido—and thereabout of it especially when he
speaks of Priam's slaughter. If it live in your memory,
begin at this line—let me see, let me see—   445
The rugged Pyrrhus, like th'Hyrcanian beast—
'Tis not so. It begins with Pyrrhus—
The rugged Pyrrhus, he whose sable arms,
Black as his purpose, did the night resemble
When he lay couched in the ominous horse,   450

---

437. were] *Q2*; was *F,Q1*.   439. affection] *Q2*; affectation *F*.
440–1. as wholesome . . . fine] *Q2*; *not in F*; as wholesome as sweete *Q1*.
442. One] *Q2*; One cheefe *F*; a *Q1*.   in't] *Q2*; in it *F,Q1*.   tale] *F,Q1*;
talke *Q2*.   443. when] *Q2*; where *F,Q1*.   446–7.] *As Capell; prose Q2,F*.
447. 'Tis] *Q2,Q1*; It is *F*.   448.] *As F,Q1; prose Q2*.   450. the ominous]
F,Q1; th'omynous *Q2*.

---

437. *sallets*] tasty morsels, sharp
flavours, hence ribaldries. *Sallet* is
merely a variant of *salad*, which is the
form used by F in *Ant.* I.v.73 ('My
Sallad dayes') and by many eds. in
All's W. IV.v.13, 15.
439. *affection*] affectation.
441. *more handsome than fine*] with
more natural grace than artful
workmanship.
442–3. *Aeneas' tale to Dido*] See
Aeneid, II, and for 'Priam's slaughter'
esp. ll. 506–58. But though this is the
ultimate source, detailed correspondences are few.
446. *rugged*] An apt epithet for both
the landscape and the beasts of
Hyrcania (see next note), corresponding to Virgil's *horrens*. Hence
terrifyingly wild in appearance. Cf.
Mac. III.iv.100–1, 'like the rugged
Russian bear . . . or th'Hyrcan tiger'.
Hyrcanian beast] Hyrcania, a region
on the southern shores of the Caspian,
in literature famous for tigers.

Virgil's Aeneas in his tale makes no
reference to them but Virgil's Dido
(and Marlowe's) denounces Aeneas,
when he deserts her, as having been
suckled by them (*Aeneid*, IV.367).
Shakespeare refers to them not only
in *Mac.* but also in *3H6* ('more
inhuman . . . than tigers of Hyrcania',
I.iv.155). Hamlet's slip of memory
thus stresses the savagery of Pyrrhus
from the start.
448–514.] On the Player's speech,
LN.
448. *sable arms*] black armour,
appropriate to his hellish 'purpose'.
In Virgil his armour was gleaming
(*coruscus*).
450. *the ominous*] If we assumed, as
some eds. apparently do, that Q2
th'omynous followed copy, this would
suggest for Shakespeare a pronunciation *ominous*, which his practice elsewhere contradicts.
horse] The wooden horse in which
the Greeks entered Troy.

> *Hath now this dread and black complexion smear'd*
> *With heraldry more dismal. Head to foot*
> *Now is he total gules, horridly trick'd*
> *With blood of fathers, mothers, daughters, sons,*
> *Bak'd and impasted with the parching streets,*   455
> *That lend a tyrannous and a damned light*
> *To their lord's murder. Roasted in wrath and fire,*
> *And thus o'ersized with coagulate gore,*
> *With eyes like carbuncles, the hellish Pyrrhus*
> *Old grandsire Priam seeks.*   460
>   So proceed you.

Pol. 'Fore God, my lord, well spoken, with good accent
      and good discretion.

1st Play.   *Anon he finds him,*
Striking too short at Greeks. His antique sword,   465

---

452. *heraldry*] heraldy *Q2*, Heraldry *F,Q1*.   *dismal. Head to foot*] *F subst.*;
dismall head to foote, *Q2*.   453. *total*] *Q2,Q1*; to take *F*.   456. *a damned*]
Q2; damned *F*.   457. *lord's murder*] *Q2*; vilde Murthers *F*.   460–1.] *As*
Capell (subst.); *one line Q2*.   461. So proceed you.] *Q2*; *not in F*; So goe
on. *Q1*.   465. *antique*] anticke *Q2,F*, antique *Pope*.

---

451. *complexion*] colour, appearance, not necessarily of the face only, and here applied to the whole armed figure.

452. *heraldry*] *Heraldry* is concerned with armorial bearings, and so, by synecdoche, the word may refer to the coat-of-arms itself, and here specifically to its colour. At the same time, by metonymy, the heraldic colour terms appropriate to armorial bearings are applied to the whole armour, the *heraldry* of which thus changes from black (*sable*) to red (*gules*) all over.

dismal] Much stronger in meaning then than now. Literally, characteristic of the *dies mali*, days of ill omen; hence calamitous. Cf. v.ii. 372.

453. *trick'd*] delineated. A technical term in heraldry: a coat-of-arms is *tricked* when it is portrayed with the colours, instead of being painted in, indicated by conventional signs and marks.

454. *With blood*] Cf. Marlowe and Nashe, *Dido*, ii.i.214, and see Intro., p. 103.

455. *parching*] It is the heat of the burning streets that dries the blood and bakes it into a crust.

456. *tyrannous*] pitilessly harsh.

458. *o'ersized*] smeared over as with size.

459. *like carbuncles*] Carbuncles, fiery red in colour, were thought to have a light of their own by means of which they shone in the dark. Cf. l. 457, 'in wrath and fire', where the heat comes from within as well as without. For Shakespeare an eye glowing red carries particular menace. Cf. *Cor.* v.i.63, 'His eye Red as 'twould burn Rome'; *John* iv.ii.163; *2H6* iii.i.154.

465–7. *His antique sword . . . command.*] Cf. *Aeneid*, ii. 509–11: 'Arma diu senior desueta trementibus aevo Circumdat nequiquam umeris, et inutile ferrum Cingitur.' Hence *an-*

Rebellious to his arm, lies where it falls,
Repugnant to command. Unequal match'd,
Pyrrhus at Priam drives, in rage strikes wide;
But with the whiff and wind of his fell sword
Th'unnerved father falls. Then senseless Ilium,   470
Seeming to feel this blow, with flaming top
Stoops to his base, and with a hideous crash
Takes prisoner Pyrrhus' ear. For lo, his sword,
Which was declining on the milky head
Of reverend Priam, seem'd i'th' air to stick;   475
So, as a painted tyrant, Pyrrhus stood,
And like a neutral to his will and matter,
Did nothing.
But as we often see against some storm
A silence in the heavens, the rack stand still,   480
The bold winds speechless, and the orb below

---

467. *match'd*] Q2; match F.   470. *Then senseless Ilium*] F; not in Q2.
471. *this*] Q2; his F.   475. *reverend*] F; reuerent Q2.   477. *And*] F; not in
Q2.   477–8.] *As* Q2; *one line* F.

---

tique, 'which he had wielded long ago in his youth' (Kittredge). This word is always in Shakespeare accented on the first syllable. *repugnant*, recalcitrant.

469–70. *But with the whiff . . . falls.*] LN.

470. *unnerved*] enfeebled in sinew, strengthless. The first recorded use of the word. Cf. *Dido*, II.i.252, 'his want of strength'.

470–93. *Then senseless Ilium . . . fiends.*] The complete absence from Q1 of these 23 lines points to a cut in performance; and the omission in Q2 of the first three words, presumably due to a printer's misunderstanding, suggests that a cut was marked in the foul papers.

470. *senseless*] having no feeling, inanimate. It brings out the paradox of 'seeming to feel *this*'.

Ilium] The citadel rather than the city. Cf. *Aeneid*, II.555–6, 'prolapsa . . . Pergama'.

472. *his*] its. See I.i.40n.

hideous] This describes not the sound but the terror that it causes. Cf. I. iv.54.

473. *Takes prisoner . . . ear*] He is arrested in mid-action by the noise.

474. *declining*] descending. A rare use, though again said of a sword in *Troil.* IV.v.189.

476. *painted*] fixed motionless, as in a painting.

Pyrrhus stood] LN.

477. *a neutral to his will and matter*] His *matter* is that which his *will* seeks to effect. The poet envisages a conflict between them suddenly suspended, with the will neither fulfilled nor even defeated and the possessor of the will in complete passivity neither furthering nor opposing it.

479. *see*] Loosely used to include perceiving by other senses.

against] in preparation for.

480. *rack*] the clouds in the upper air driven by the wind.

As hush as death, anon the dreadful thunder
Doth rend the region; so after Pyrrhus' pause
Aroused vengeance sets him new awork,
And never did the Cyclops' hammers fall   485
On Mars's armour, forg'd for proof eterne,
With less remorse than Pyrrhus' bleeding sword
Now falls on Priam.
    Out, out, thou strumpet Fortune! All you gods
In general synod take away her power,   490
Break all the spokes and fellies from her wheel,
And bowl the round nave down the hill of heaven
As low as to the fiends.

Pol. This is too long.

Ham. It shall to the barber's with your beard.—Prithee 495
say on. He's for a jig or a tale of bawdry, or he sleeps.

482-3. *death, . . . region; so*] *Q2* (region, so); death: . . . Region. So *F*.
484. *Aroused*] *Collier;* A rowsed *Q2,F*.   486. *Mars's*] *Q2* (*Marses*); Mars
his *F*.   *armour*] *Q2;* Armours *F*.   491. *fellies*] *F4;* Fallies *F;* follies *Q2;*
felloes *Q5*.   495. *to the*] *Q2,Q1;* to'th *F*.

---

482. *hush*] A not uncommon usage,
regarded by Abbott (22) as an adjectival use of the noun, but explained
by *OED* as a modification of the
adjective *husht*, which derived from
the interjection and was then mistaken for a past pple.

483. *region*] air, heavens. Milton
speaks of birds which 'wing the
region' (*Par. Lost*, VII. 425). This
(normal) usage comes by a specializ-
ation of *region* in the sense of a
division of the universe.

484. *Aroused vengeance*] LN.

awork] for *on work*. See Abbott 24.
Especially common in this phrase;
e.g. Bacon, *Henry VII*, 'that our people
be set awork in arts and handicrafts'
(*Works*, ed. Spedding, etc., vi. 80);
Lucr. 1496; etc.

485. *Cyclops'*] The Cyclopes were
giants in the employ of Vulcan, god
of metalworkers (cf. III. ii. 84).

486. *proof*] certified strength; the
quality of armour which has been
specially 'proved' or tested for its
power of resistance. Cf. *Ant.* IV. viii.

15, 'Leap thou . . . through proof
of harness to my heart'; *R2* I. iii. 73,
'Add proof unto mine armour with
thy prayers.'

487. *remorse*] (as very often) com-
passion.

489. *strumpet Fortune*] Cf. ll. 235-6
above.

491. *her wheel*] Fortune is traditionally represented with a wheel
because, as Fluellen explains, 'she is
turning and inconstant'. It is a fine
stroke to make this emblem of her
power into an emblem of her
destruction.

492. *nave*] hub; all of the wheel
that is left when the spokes and
fellies are gone.

495. *beard*] The conspicuous feature
of an inveterate chin-wagger.

496. *jig*] a farcical afterpiece involving dancing and, usually, singing,
'wherein some pretty knavery is
acted' (Cotgrave, under *Farce*). See
Chambers, *El. St.*, ii. 551-2; C. R.
Baskervill, *The Elizabethan Jig*, 1929.

Say on, come to Hecuba.

1st Play. *But who—ah, woe!—had seen the mobbled queen—*

Ham. 'The mobbled queen'.

Pol. That's good.   500

1st Play. *Run barefoot up and down, threat'ning the flames*
   With bisson rheum, a clout upon that head
   Where late the diadem stood, and, for a robe,
   About her lank and all o'erteemed loins
   A blanket, in th' alarm of fear caught up—   505
   Who this had seen, with tongue in venom steep'd,
   'Gainst Fortune's state would treason have pronounc'd.
   But if the gods themselves did see her then,
   When she saw Pyrrhus make malicious sport
   In mincing with his sword her husband's limbs,   510
   The instant burst of clamour that she made,
   Unless things mortal move them not at all,

---

498. *ah, woe*] a woe *Q2*, ah woe *Q5*; O who *F,Q1*. 498–9. *mobbled . . . mobbled*] mobled . . . mobled *Q2,Q1*; inobled . . . inobled *F*. 499. queen.] *Q2*; Queene? *F*. 500. good.] *Q2*; good: Inobled Queene is good. *F,Q1* subst. (Mobled). 501. *flames*] *Q2*; flame *F*. 502. *upon*] *Q2*; about *F*; on *Q1*. 504–5. *loins | A blanket,*] loynes, | A blancket *Q2,F* subst. 505. *th'alarm*] th'Alarum *F*; the alarme *Q2*. 510. *husband's*] *F,Q1,Q3*; husband *Q2*.

---

497. *Hecuba*] LN.

498. *mobbled*] with face muffled. The word is readily acceptable as the past participle of the verb *to mob(b)le*, though the comments it attracts in the play suggest that it was rare. For the spelling (and pronunciation) I follow Dryden and other 17th-century authors. Note that at *Cor.* I. i. 194 F spells *cobled*. Ethel Seaton would take *mobled* as an adjective from the noun *moble(s)*, an older cognate of *movable(s)*, L. *mobilia*, and hence describing the queen as having rich possessions (*TLS*, 1947, p. 439). This would bring out the paradox of *barefoot* but lacks authentication.

499. *'The mobbled queen'*.] Eds. adopt F's question-mark, which may however signify an exclamation. It is not clear that Hamlet is questioning and not savouring the phrase.

500. *That's good*] F's addition is a characteristic piece of ad-libbing (see Intro., p. 62), still further expanded in Q1 ('good, faith very good').

502. *bisson rheum*] blinding tears. Although this generally accepted interpretation has been challenged (*Sh.Jahr.*, XCVI, 177–91), *bis(e)ne*, blind, is very well attested from Anglo-Saxon to Tudor times (see note on *Cor.* II. i. 59, bisson, F *beesome*, in Clarendon edn, 1879) and the transferred epithet offers no difficulty. *Rheum*, any watery discharge, is often used for tears in particular. Cf. Hecuba's threat in *Lucr.* 1468, 'with my tears quench Troy that burns'.

504. *o'erteemed*] exhausted with childbearing (referring to her numerous offspring and also explaining *lank*).

512.] This was the doctrine of Epicurus.

> *Would have made milch the burning eyes of heaven*
> *And passion in the gods.*

Pol. Look whe'er he has not turned his colour and has 515
　　tears in's eyes. Prithee no more.

Ham. 'Tis well. I'll have thee speak out the rest of this
　　soon.—Good my lord, will you see the players well
　　bestowed? Do you hear, let them be well used, for
　　they are the abstract and brief chronicles of the time. 520
　　After your death you were better have a bad epitaph
　　than their ill report while you live.

Pol. My lord, I will use them according to their desert.

Ham. God's bodkin, man, much better. Use every man
　　after his desert, and who shall scape whipping? Use 525
　　them after your own honour and dignity: the less
　　they deserve, the more merit is in your bounty. Take
　　them in.

Pol. Come, sirs.

Ham. Follow him, friends. We'll hear a play tomorrow. 530
　　[*To First Player*] Dost thou hear me, old friend? Can
　　you play *The Murder of Gonzago*?

515. whe'er] *Capell* (whe'r); where *Q2,F.*　　516. Prithee] *Q2*; Pray you *F.*
517. of this] *Q2*; *not in F.*　　519. you] *Q2*; ye *F.*　　520. abstract] *Q2*;
Abstracts *F,Q1.*　　522. live] *Q2,Q1*; liued *F.*　　524. bodkin] *Q2*; bodykins
F. much] *Q2*; *not in F*; farre *Q1.*　　525. shall] *Q2*; should *F,Q1.*
531. *To First Player*] *As they follow Polonius, Hamlet detains and steps aside with 1
Player. White.*

513. *burning eyes*] presumably the
stars, which, having become *milch*
(adj. = milk-giving), give a milk of
tears.

514. *passion*] overpowering emotion
– object of *made* (= created) understood. Hecuba's afflictions similarly
stir the gods in Ovid (*Met.*, XIII. 573):
'illius fortuna deos quoque moverat
omnes'.

515. *whe'er*] i.e. whether.

515–16. *has tears in's eyes*] LN.

519. *bestowed*] lodged.

520. *abstract*] A noun, as always in
Shakespeare, and apparently synony-
mous with *brief chronicles*. Cf. *R3*
IV.iv.28, 'Brief abstract and record'.
There is nothing odd about the
combination of singular and plural

nouns: the players can collectively
produce a single effect, but it is no
doubt the sense of their severality,
assisted by the influence of *chronicles*,
that leads F into the plural. Cf.
abridgement, l. 416.

525. *whipping*] The statutory punishment for unlicensed players, who
were held to be vagabonds.

531. *Dost thou hear me*] With this
phrase (= A word with you) Hamlet
keeps the leading Player back as the
rest are beginning to depart. The
Q1 version ('Come hither maisters')
infelicitously replaces this confidential
aside with a general conversation.

532. *The Murder of Gonzago*] See
III.ii.233–4 LN.

1st Play. Ay, my lord.

Ham. We'll ha't tomorrow night. You could for a need
    study a speech of some dozen or sixteen lines, which   535
    I would set down and insert in't, could you not?

1st Play. Ay, my lord.

Ham. Very well. [*To all the Players*] Follow that lord, and
    look you mock him not.   *Exeunt Polonius and Players.*
    [*To Rosencrantz and Guildenstern*] My good friends,   540
    I'll leave you till night. You are welcome to Elsinore.

Ros. Good my lord.   *Exeunt [Rosencrantz and Guildenstern].*

Ham. Ay, so, God buy to you. Now I am alone.
    O what a rogue and peasant slave am I!
    Is it not monstrous that this player here,   545
    But in a fiction, in a dream of passion,

534. for a] *F,Q1*; for *Q2*.   535. dozen] *F,Q1*; dosen lines *Q2*.   536. you]
Q2; ye *F*.   538. *To all the Players*] *This edn.*   539 S.D. *Exeunt . . . Players*]
*As Capell; after 541 Q2; after 529 Exit Polon. F,Q1 subst.; after 529 Exit
Polonius with some of the Players | and after 539 Exit Player | Reed; after 530
Exit Polonius with all the Players except the First | and after 539 Exit First Player |
Dyce.*   540. *To Rosencrantz and Guildenstern*] *Johnson.*   542 S.D.] *Exeunt.
Q2; Exeunt. Manet Hamlet. F; after* you. (*543*) *Staunton.*   543. buy to you] *Q2*;
buy'ye *F*.

534. *for a need*] if necessary. (A
common idiom.)

535–6. *a speech . . . insert*] LN.

538. *Follow*] Repeating the instruction of l. 530, Polonius and the rest
of the players having paused to wait
for the First.

539. *mock him*] As Hamlet has done
but no one else must.

542 S.D.] The placing of the
Exeunt in Q2 and F before Hamlet's
farewell words, though reversed by
most eds., is taken by Dover Wilson
to indicate that Hamlet speaks 'in a
tone of sarcastic relief after the two
have gone'. This, however, the
corresponding instance at II.i.73
does not confirm.

543. *God buy*] i.e. good-bye. The
additional *you* is common but the
intrusive *to* is not. It shows how com-
pletely the original sense of 'God be
wi' ye' had been lost. See II.i.69n.

544. *rogue and peasant slave*] A

curious parallel in the *bad* Q of *Rom.*
(1597) – where the dying Mercutio
says 'some peasantly rogue, some
Sexton, some base slave shall write
my Epitaph' – suggests that Shakespeare is here drawing on familiar
stage-material or perhaps echoing a
lost play.

peasant] low, base fellow. Frequent
as a term of abuse. In *Shr.* IV.i.113,
Petruchio calls his 'foolish knave'
'You peasant swain! you whoreson
malt-horse drudge!'

545–6. *this player . . . passion*]
Elizabethans saw it as a characteristic
of the player's art, which was thus
distinguished from the orator's, that
he feigned a passion he did not really
feel (e.g. Thos. Wright, *The Passions
of the Mind*, rev. 1604, p. 179). Cf. the
'actions that a man might play',
I.ii.84. Hence *monstrous*. But see
ll. 515–16 LN. *But*, only.

Could force his soul so to his own conceit
That from her working all his visage wann'd,
Tears in his eyes, distraction in his aspect,
A broken voice, and his whole function suiting   550
With forms to his conceit? And all for nothing!
For Hecuba!
What's Hecuba to him, or he to her,
That he should weep for her? What would he do
Had he the motive and the cue for passion   555
That I have? He would drown the stage with tears,
And cleave the general ear with horrid speech,
Make mad the guilty and appal the free,
Confound the ignorant, and amaze indeed
The very faculties of eyes and ears.   560
Yet I,
A dull and muddy-mettled rascal, peak

---

547. own] *Q2; whole F.*   548. his] *F; the Q2.*   wann'd] *Q2* (wand);
warm'd *F.*   549. in his aspect] *Q2; in's Aspect F.*   553. her] *Q2; Hecuba
F,Q1.*   555. the cue] *F; that Q2.*   560. faculties] *Q2; faculty F.*
560–1.] *As Johnson; one line Q2,F.*

547. *to*] into accord with.
conceit] that which is conceived in the mind (and may have no external reality). So at l. 551.
548. *her*] i.e. the soul's.
548–51. *his visage . . . his conceit*] See ll. 515–16 and LN.
549. *aspect*] Nearly always with the accent on the second syllable, to effect which F contracts *in his.*
550. *function*] activity (L. *fungor*, perform); the motive force or principle which supplies the outward *forms* or gestures. Cf. *Mac.* I.iii.140, 'function is smother'd in surmise'.
553. *her*] If we believe that Q2 was printed from autograph copy, we must accept its crisp and forceful reading here. Dover Wilson's fancy that *her* derives from a Shakespeare abbreviation *hec* (*MSH*, p. 107) is obviously unacceptable and the unmetrical F *Hecuba*, which eds. prefer only through the force of custom, is as obviously an actor's (over-)

emphasis. See *SB*, XIII, 44–5.
558. *Make mad the guilty*] Note that what the Player 'would' do is what Hamlet presently does (ll. 584ff.): it is the example of the Player that leads to his device of the play.
free] guiltless. Cf. III.ii.236; *AYL* II.vii.85.
559. *amaze*] throw into confusion. Cf. I.ii.235 and n., III.iv.112; *Wiv.* III.iii.102, 'Be not amaz'd; call all your senses to you'.
562. *dull*] Cf. I.v.32; Intro., p. 139.
muddy-mettled] dull-spirited. There is also the suggestion of *metal* which has lost its brightness (*mettle* being originally the same word).
rascal] Perhaps also with a play on a second meaning – a young unantlered deer, lean and unfit for hunting, and so sluggish. It is a joke when Falstaff is called a 'muddy rascal', *2H4* II.iv.41.
peak] mope, languish. Cf. *Mac.* I.iii.23, 'dwindle, peak, and pine'.

Like John-a-dreams, unpregnant of my cause,
And can say nothing—no, not for a king,
Upon whose property and most dear life   565
A damn'd defeat was made. Am I a coward?
Who calls me villain, breaks my pate across,
Plucks off my beard and blows it in my face,
Tweaks me by the nose, gives me the lie i'th' throat
As deep as to the lungs—who does me this?   570
Ha!
'Swounds, I should take it: for it cannot be
But I am pigeon-liver'd and lack gall
To make oppression bitter, or ere this
I should ha' fatted all the region kites   575

569. by the] *Q2;* by'th' *F.*   571–2.] *As Steevens*[4]*; one line Q2,F.*
572. 'Swounds] *Q2;* Why *F;* Sure *Q1.*   575. ha'] a *Q2,Q1,* ha' *Wilson;*
haue *F,Q3.*

563. *John-a-dreams*] A nickname (like *John-a-nods*) for a listless, dreamy fellow (*a* = of). Probably current in familiar speech, though otherwise recorded only in Armin, *A Nest of Ninnies,* 1608.

unpregnant] As in *Meas.* IV.iv.18, 'unpregnant And dull to all proceedings'.

565. *property*] I take this to refer to his proper person (including all that belonged to the essential quality of the man) rather than to his possessions. Cf. *Ant.* I.i.58, 'that great property Which still should go with Antony'. The frequent assumption that it refers to his crown and queen, etc. rests on a false analogy with I.v.75.

566. *defeat*] destruction (the primary sense, from Fr. *défait,* from *défaire,* to undo). Cf. I.ii.10, v.ii.58.

566–73. *Am I a coward? . . . pigeon-liver'd*] These lines owe something to the description of the slothful man in Nashe's *Pierce Penniless.* See Intro., p. 105. But Shakespeare makes the general 'indignities' particular and concrete. Emrys Jones (*Origins of Shakespeare,* pp. 22–4) compares the self-reproaches of Atreus in Seneca's

Thyestes, ll. 176–80.

569–70. *gives me the lie . . . lungs*] give the lie, accuse of lying. A lie in the throat (a common accusation, see Tilley T 268) could be no mere slip of the tongue, and the deeper its origin the worse. Kittredge quotes Webster, *Devil's Law-Case,* IV.ii.643–4, 'I'll give the lie in the stomach – That's somewhat deeper than the throat'.

570. *me*] See Abbott 220.

573–4. *pigeon-liver'd . . . bitter*] The pigeon was a symbol of meekness, being popularly believed to have no gall, which was notoriously the source within the liver of bitter and rancorous feelings. See Browne, *Vulgar Errors,* III.3. In Dekker's *1 Honest Whore* (I.v.109) it is said of the patient man, 'Sure he's a pigeon, for he has no gall'. Cf. also *Oth.* IV.iii.90, 'We have galls; and though we have some grace, Yet have we some revenge'; Tilley D574.

575. *the region kites*] the kites of the air. For *region* = air, see l. 483 and n.; for the adjectival use of the noun cf. *Sonn.* XXXIII, 'The region cloud', and see Abbott 22, 430.

With this slave's offal. Bloody, bawdy villain!
Remorseless, treacherous, lecherous, kindless villain!
Why, what an ass am I! This is most brave,
That I, the son of a dear father murder'd,
Prompted to my revenge by heaven and hell,   580
Must like a whore unpack my heart with words
And fall a-cursing like a very drab,
A scullion! Fie upon't! Foh!
About, my brains. Hum—I have heard
That guilty creatures sitting at a play   585
Have, by the very cunning of the scene,
Been struck so to the soul that presently
They have proclaim'd their malefactions.
For murder, though it have no tongue, will speak
With most miraculous organ. I'll have these players 590
Play something like the murder of my father

---

576. offal. Bloody,] offal: bloudy, *Q5;* offal, bloody, *Q2;* Offall, bloudy:
a *F.*   577. villain!] *Q2,Q1 (subst.);* villaine! / Oh Vengeance! / *F.*
578. Why] *Q2,Q1;* Who? *F.*   This] *Q2,Q1;* I sure, this *F.*   579. a dear
father murder'd] *Q3;* a deere murthered *Q2;* the Deere murthered *F;* my
deare father *Q1.*   582–5.] *As Johnson; lines ending* foh. / heard, / play, *Q2;*
ending Drab, / Braine. / Play, *F; ending* drab, / scullion! / heard, / play, *Capell.*
583. scullion] *F;* stallyon *Q2;* scalion *Q1;* cullion *Theobald.*   584. brains]
Q2 corr.; braues *Q2 uncorr.;* Braine *F,Q1.*   Hum] *Q2; not in F,Q1.*

---

577. *Remorseless*] pitiless. Cf. l. 487
and n.
    kindless] unnatural, lacking all
feeling for one's own kind. Cf.
I.ii.65 and n.
    villain!] F's *Oh Vengeance!* has all the
marks of an actor's addition. Hamlet
accuses himself of cursing (l. 582) but
not of threats, and his change from
self-reproach to the pursuit of retri-
bution occurs only at l. 584. See
SB, XIII, 37.
    578. *brave*] becoming, admirable.
    579. *father*] Without this word
(omitted in Q2 and F) Q3 (but not
Ff 2–4 nor some later eds.) evidently
regarded the sense as incomplete.
What authenticates the addition,
however, is the presence of *father* in
the reported text Q1.
    580. *heaven and hell*] both of which

are reflected in that 'nature' to which
the Ghost has appealed (I.v.81).
Cf. I.v.93. The prompting of hell is
more fully suggested at III.ii.379–83.
    582. *drab*] whore.
    583. *scullion*] a kitchen menial of
either sex, 'proverbially foul-mouthed'
(Sisson, *NR*). The word was in
common use as a term of contempt.
LN.
    584. *About*] get going, set about it.
Cf. *Caes.* III.ii.204, 'Revenge! About!
Seek!'; *Wiv.* v.v.53.
    585–8. *guilty . . . malefactions*] LN.
    586. *cunning*] art, as at ll. 436–7.
    scene] theatrical representation.
    587. *presently*] instantly, as at l. 170.
    590–1. *I'll have these players Play*]
The plan that Hamlet seems only now
to be arriving at he has of course
already set in motion (ll. 531–8) and

Before mine uncle. I'll observe his looks;
I'll tent him to the quick. If a do blench,
I know my course. The spirit that I have seen
May be a devil, and the devil hath power   595
T'assume a pleasing shape, yea, and perhaps,
Out of my weakness and my melancholy,
As he is very potent with such spirits,
Abuses me to damn me. I'll have grounds
More relative than this. The play's the thing   600
Wherein I'll catch the conscience of the King.   *Exit.*

---

593. a do] *Q2;* he but *F.*   595. a] *Q2;* the *F.*   devil . . . devil]
deale . . . deale *Q2,* Diuell . . . Diuel *F.*

---

in a more precise form (a named
play with a proposed additional
speech) than at this point he envisages. This 'inconsistency' cannot
quite be explained away by Dover
Wilson's theory that Hamlet's soliloquy renders what has already taken
place in his mind while the Player's
recitation was proceeding (*WHH,*
p. 142 n.)

593. *tent*] probe. A *tent* was an
instrument for examining or cleansing
a wound. Sidney sees it as a virtue of
tragedy that it 'openeth the greatest
wounds, and showeth forth the ulcers
that are covered with tissue'.

blench] flinch. The word is related
to *blink* but not to *blanch,* with which
it is sometimes confused. (Hence Q1
bleach at III. ii. 80–1; see Intro., p. 118.)

595–6. *the devil . . . shape*] LN.

597. *Out of my . . . melancholy*] LN.

598. *potent*] The devil not only
exploits but is able to intensify the
melancholy which predisposes Hamlet

to be deluded. Cf. III. iv. 76–7 n.

spirits] the vapours out of which
melancholy is engendered. But Verity
takes 'such spirits' to mean such as
that referred to in l. 594 – on the
ground that Shakespeare would not
use the same word in two different
senses in the same context.

599. *Abuses*] beguiles, deludes. Cf.
Le Loyer, III. 7, 'un Diable qui se
fait Ame pour te decevoir et abuser'.
Cf. I. v. 38, IV. vii. 48. In *Per.* I. ii. 38–45
those are said to 'abuse' the King
who flatter him, encourage him to
sin and hence endanger his life. For
the word in Belleforest, see Intro.,
p. 95 n.

600. *relative*] cogent, material.
Having only the word of a ghost,
Hamlet seeks evidence more directly
relating to (connected with) the
circumstances; perhaps also (as
Hulme, pp. 30–3) relatable (able to
be told) to the public.

[ACT III]

[SCENE I]

Enter KING, QUEEN, POLONIUS, OPHELIA, ROSENCRANTZ,
GUILDENSTERN.

King. And can you by no drift of conference
  Get from him why he puts on this confusion,
  Grating so harshly all his days of quiet
  With turbulent and dangerous lunacy?
Ros. He does confess he feels himself distracted,   5
  But from what cause a will by no means speak.
Guild. Nor do we find him forward to be sounded,
  But with a crafty madness keeps aloof
  When we would bring him on to some confession
  Of his true state.
Queen.   Did he receive you well?   10
Ros. Most like a gentleman.
Guild. But with much forcing of his disposition.

ACT III

Scene 1

ACT III SCENE 1] *Q 1676.*   S.D. *Guildenstern.] Capell; Guyldensterne, Lords.*
Q2, F subst.   1. conference] *Q2;* circumstance *F.*   6. a] *Q2;* he *F.*

S.D.] The *Lords* of Q2 and F
presumably originated with Shakespeare, who then omitted to make use
of them. There is no appropriate
(and l. 42 is the only possible) point
at which they could retire.

  1. *drift of conference*] course of talk.
For this (usual) sense of *conference,*
cf. l. 187.

  2. *puts on*] Hamlet's word at
I.v.180. In itself it need not mean
'feigns'. Cf. *AYL* v.iv.175 and see

OED put 46 d. Yet it shows the King's
suspicion that Hamlet's *confusion*
(mental disturbance) is not altogether
involuntary.

  5. *distracted*] confused in his wits,
as at I.v.97. Cf. 'distraction', v.ii.225.

  8. *crafty*] full of guile. Cf. l. 2 n. and
III.iv.190, 'mad in craft'.

  12. *disposition*] 'inclination at the
time' (Kittredge) rather than general
bent. Cf. II.ii.298.

Ros. Niggard of question, but of our demands
 Most free in his reply.
Queen.   Did you assay him
 To any pastime?   15
Ros. Madam, it so fell out that certain players
 We o'erraught on the way. Of these we told him,
 And there did seem in him a kind of joy
 To hear of it. They are here about the court,
 And, as I think, they have already order   20
 This night to play before him.
Pol.   'Tis most true,
 And he beseech'd me to entreat your Majesties
 To hear and see the matter.
King. With all my heart; and it doth much content me
 To hear him so inclin'd.   25
 Good gentlemen, give him a further edge,
 And drive his purpose into these delights.
Ros. We shall, my lord.   *Exeunt Rosencrantz and Guildenstern.*
King.   Sweet Gertrude, leave us too,
 For we have closely sent for Hamlet hither
 That he, as 'twere by accident, may here   30
 Affront Ophelia.

14-15. Did . . . pastime?] *As Capell; one line Q2,F.*   19. here] *Q2; not in F.*
23-7.] *As Pope; lines ending* hart, / me / inclin'd. / edge, / delights. *Q2; ending*
me / Gentlemen, / purpose *on F.*   27. into] *Q2;* on / To *F.*   28. too] *F;*
two *Q2.*   30. here] *Q2;* there *F.*   31-2.] *As Johnson; one line F, (ending*
my selfe) *Q2.*

13-14. *Niggard . . . reply.*] Eds. note
the discrepancy with the actual
encounter in II.ii and with ll. 7-10
above. But strict accuracy is not to
be looked for from those who 'try to
piece out an account which will not
discredit them' (Dowden). *Question*
may refer to conversational interchange rather than mere interrogation, so that Rosencrantz confirms,
before going on to qualify, what
Guildenstern has said. *of* (our demands), in respect of, as regards (see
Abbott 173).
 14. *assay*] test the inclination of.
OED explains as 'challenge to a trial

of . . . skill' (with which cf. II.ii.71),
but this is not how Rosencrantz
understands it.
 15. *pastime*] Though not restricted
to, readily suggests a dramatic entertainment (Hulme, pp. 337-8).
 17. *o'erraught*] overtook.
 21. *This night*] A day has intervened since II.ii.530-4.
 26. *edge*] incitement, spur (cognate
with the verb *egg on*).
 28-37.] The scheme outlined by
Polonius at II.ii.160-4 is now to be
put into action.
 29. *closely*] privately.
 31. *Affront*] come face to face with.

Her father and myself, lawful espials,
We'll so bestow ourselves that, seeing unseen,
We may of their encounter frankly judge,
And gather by him, as he is behav'd,   35
If't be th'affliction of his love or no
That thus he suffers for.

Queen.   I shall obey you.
And for your part, Ophelia, I do wish
That your good beauties be the happy cause
Of Hamlet's wildness; so shall I hope your virtues   40
Will bring him to his wonted way again,
To both your honours.

Oph.   Madam, I wish it may.

                                      [*Exit Queen.*]

Pol. Ophelia, walk you here.—Gracious, so please you,
We will bestow ourselves.—Read on this book,
That show of such an exercise may colour   45
Your loneliness.—We are oft to blame in this,

---

32. lawful espials] *F; not in* Q2.   33. We'll] Q2; Will F.   38. your] Q2,F;
my Q3.   42 S.D.] *Theobald; not in* Q2,F.   43. please you] Q2; please
ye F.   46. loneliness] F; lowlines Q2.

---

32. *lawful espials*] The absence of
these words from Q2, together with
the metrical redundancy, has brought
them under suspicion. But it may
well have been the metrical irregu-
larity that led to their omission. They
are most unlike an actor's elaboration and they fit the line as 'Affront
Ophelia' does not. *espials*, spies.

38–40. *I do wish . . . wildness*] Having
feared that Hamlet's madness has to
do with her own conduct (II. ii. 56–7),
the Queen would no doubt be glad
to be proved wrong; but she is consistently shown as favouring Hamlet's
suit to Ophelia (cf. v.i. 236–8).

39. *beauties*] For the plural, cf.
Mer.V. III. ii. 157, 'I might in virtues,
beauties . . . Exceed account';
MND I.i. 48.

42. *it*] must be taken to refer in a
general way to the whole wish which

Ophelia echoes, not (as in Furness)
to warrant emending *beauties* and
virtues to the singular.

43. *Gracious*] Apparently a vocative.
The word is frequent in royal
address, though its use without a
noun is unparalleled.

44. *Read on this book*] In icono-
graphic convention a solitary woman
with a book represented devoutness.
Hence ll. 45–7, *exercise, devotion,* etc.
Cf. *White Devil,* v.vi, 'Enter Vittoria
with a book. . . . What, are you at your
prayers?' The book is of course
traditional in pictures of the
Annunciation.

45. *exercise*] religious observance (of
prayer or meditation).

45–6. *colour Your loneliness*] give
plausibility to your being alone.
For *colour,* cf. II.ii. 280.

'Tis too much prov'd, that with devotion's visage
And pious action we do sugar o'er
The devil himself.

King. [*aside*]   O 'tis too true.
How smart a lash that speech doth give my
    conscience.   50
The harlot's cheek, beautied with plast'ring art,
Is not more ugly to the thing that helps it
Than is my deed to my most painted word.
O heavy burden!

Pol. I hear him coming. Let's withdraw, my lord.   55
                    Exeunt [*King and Polonius*].

                    Enter HAMLET.

Ham. To be, or not to be, that is the question:
    Whether 'tis nobler in the mind to suffer

───────────────────────────────

48. sugar] *Q2;* surge *F.*   49. *aside*] As Capell; *beginning 50 Pope.*   too] *Q2;*
not in F.   55. Let's] *F; not in Q2.*   55 S.D. *Exeunt*] *F; not in Q2.*
King and Polonius] *Capell;* all but Ophelia | *Rowe.*   Enter Hamlet.] *F; before*
55 *Q2.*

───────────────────────────────

47. *prov'd*] testified to by experience.

47–8. *visage . . . sugar*] The mixed metaphor has been objected to, but the sense of providing a deceptively attractive exterior is clear.

50–4.] This is the first clear indication the King gives of his guilt. Dramatically it dispels, if that were necessary, any doubts the audience might have; but more specifically it forewarns them, by revealing the *conscience* that is to be caught, what the effect of Hamlet's play-acting device (II. ii. 584–601) will be. Thus, even while the King is enacting the plot to spy on Hamlet, expectation of Hamlet's plot to spy on the King gains force. At the same time this glimpse of the guilty conscience looks forward not only to III. ii but beyond it to III. iii.

51. *The harlot's . . . art*] A standard object of Elizabethan satire (see l. 144 LN), but in view of borrowings elsewhere (see Intro., pp. 104–6)

there may be a specific echo of *Pierce Penniless*, 'These aged mothers of iniquity will have their deformities new plastered over' (Nashe, i. 181). This begins a motif which reappears at ll. 144–6 and v. i. 187–8.

52. *to the thing that helps it*] in comparison with that (artificial beauty) which makes good its shortcomings.

53. *painted*] A word appropriate to one half of the comparison is transferred to the other: fair but false in appearance, like the beauty of the painted cheek.

56–88.] LN.

56. *To be*] to have being, to exist. See ll. 56–88 LN.

57–60. *Whether 'tis nobler . . . end them*] The 'question' is restated in amplified form. LN.

57. *in the mind*] 'This is to be connected with "suffer", not with "nobler"' (Dowden); 'This modifies *nobler*, not *suffer*' (Kittredge).

The slings and arrows of outrageous fortune,
Or to take arms against a sea of troubles
And by opposing end them. To die—to sleep,   60
No more; and by a sleep to say we end
The heart-ache and the thousand natural shocks
That flesh is heir to: 'tis a consummation
Devoutly to be wish'd. To die, to sleep;
To sleep, perchance to dream—ay, there's the rub: 65
For in that sleep of death what dreams may come,
When we have shuffled off this mortal coil,

58. slings] *Q2,F; stings conj. Misc.Obs.*
Pope; die to sleepe Q2; dye, to sleepe F.

60. die—to sleep,] die,—to sleep—
64. wish'd. To] *F; wisht to Q2.*

58. *slings*] One cannot quite dismiss the possibility of a misprint. The '*stings* of fortune' are referred to in Googe's translation of Palingenius (1576, p. 156) and Middleton, *The Old Law*, iv.ii.202. Cf. also *The Puritan*, iii.iii.70, 'let Fortune drive all her stings into me'. But Shakespeare could have read in Golding's translation of Caesar's *Gallic War* how the Romans attacked the Britons from the sea 'wyth slyngs, shot of arrowes, and other artillery' (1565, fol. 99ᵛ). 'Slings and arrows' in Fletcher's *Valentinian* (i.iii.227) is presumably an echo of *Ham.*

outrageous] Because capricious, obeying no principle.

59. *take arms . . . troubles*] Though a 'sea of troubles' is itself ancient, the 'mixed' metaphor has been much objected to. But the incongruity of taking arms against a sea is expressive of the idea – the futility of fighting against an uncontainable and overwhelming force. See ll. 57–60 LN.

60. *end them*] Not by overcoming them but (paradoxically) by being overcome by them. See ll. 57–60 LN.

61. *No more*] i.e. to die is no more than to sleep.

62. *shocks*] The primary sense of 'clashes of arms' is usual in Shakespeare (cf. *R2* i.iii.136, *R3* v.iii.93, etc.) and here resumes the battle metaphor of ll. 58–9.

63. *consummation*] final ending, as in *Cym.* iv.ii.281, 'Quiet consummation have, And renowned be thy grave'. But as variant spellings in Q2 and F indicate, the word is not distinguished from *consumation* (from *consume*). See *OED* consumation. Florio's *consummation* (see ll. 56–88 LN) translates Montaigne's *anéantissement*. Hence the primary idea seems to be of (1) being consumed or vanishing into nothingness. Cf. *Lr* iv.vi.129, 'Burning, scalding, stench, consumption' (Q 'consumation'); *Edw. III*, iv.ix.43, 'darkness, consummation, dust and worms'. But the ordinary modern sense of (2) satisfying climax may also be present, as *OED* (consummation 4) supposes.

65. *rub*] obstacle. Cf. *H5* v.ii.33, 'What rub or what impediment'. A metaphor from bowls, the rub being anything which impedes or deflects the bowl from its course.

67. *coil*] A richly suggestive word: (1) turmoil of activity, the invariable sense in Shakespeare; but here also, in a bold nautical metaphor, (2) something wound round us like a rope. This second sense seems clear from *shuffled off* (= got rid of, cast aside), but *OED* can cite no instance before Cotgrave (1611): '*Vrillonner une cable*, to coil a cable, to wind . . . it up round, or in a ring'. Unlike many commentators, I do not see

Must give us pause—there's the respect
That makes calamity of so long life.
For who would bear the whips and scorns of time,   70
Th'oppressor's wrong, the proud man's contumely,
The pangs of dispriz'd love, the law's delay,
The insolence of office, and the spurns
That patient merit of th'unworthy takes,
When he himself might his quietus make   75
With a bare bodkin? Who would fardels bear,
To grunt and sweat under a weary life,
But that the dread of something after death,
The undiscover'd country, from whose bourn
No traveller returns, puzzles the will,   80
And makes us rather bear those ills we have

71. Th'oppressor's] *Q2*; The Oppressors *F*.   proud] *Q2*; poore *F*.
72. dispriz'd] *F*; despiz'd *Q2*.   74. th'unworthy] *Q2*; the vnworthy *F*.
76. would] *Q2*; would these *F*.

this *coil* as anything so simple as the body, from which the soul frees itself at death. It includes all the appurtenances, occupations, and experiences of mortal life.

68. *respect*] as in 'with respect to'; regard (as in l. 87).

69. *of so long life*] (an adjectival phrase =) so long-lived. But although this is the strict grammatical sense, it is not easy to exclude the feeling that 'long life' is itself being regarded as a 'calamity'.

70. *time*] 'the world we live in' (Kittredge), temporal life. Not, as often explained, 'the time(s)', as though one age might be different from another.

72. *dispriz'd*] unvalued. On the principle of the more difficult reading F *dispriz'd* is less likely than Q2 *despiz'd* to be a corruption. The *z* spelling (which *OED* does not record for *despise*) lends strong support.

75. *quietus*] quittance for a debt, with a play on 'quiet' as the state 'devoutly to be wish'd'. *Quietus est*, he is quit, were the words written against an account to indicate that

payment had been made.

76. *bare bodkin*] Ernst Honigmann has drawn my attention to the anticipation of this in Seneca, *Epist.*, 70, 'scalpello aperitur ad illam magnam libertatem via et puncto securitas constat.' See *N&Q*, CCXXVI, 129–30. A bodkin was a short dagger (the original sense) or lancet. Steevens quotes Beaumont and Fletcher, *Custom of the Country* (II.iii.88), 'Out with your bodkin, Your pocket-dagger, your stiletto'. *bare*, mere (rather than unsheathed).

fardels] burdens, packs. (The word – in its variant *farthel(l)* – used of the Shepherd's bundle in *Wint.* IV. iv.707, etc.) F's *these*, though sometimes defended, unwarrantably limits the burdens to the ones just specified.

80. *No traveller returns*] LN.

puzzles] (much stronger in meaning than now) bewilders so as to make incapable of proceeding. Cf. *Tw.N.* IV.ii.42, 'more puzzled than the Egyptians in their fog'; *Ant.* III.vii.10, where Cleopatra is warned that her presence in the battle 'needs must puzzle Antony'.

Than fly to others that we know not of?
Thus conscience does make cowards of us all,
And thus the native hue of resolution
Is sicklied o'er with the pale cast of thought,   85
And enterprises of great pitch and moment
With this regard their currents turn awry
And lose the name of action. Soft you now,
The fair Ophelia! Nymph, in thy orisons
Be all my sins remember'd.

Oph.   Good my lord,   90
How does your honour for this many a day?

Ham. I humbly thank you, well.

Oph. My lord, I have remembrances of yours
That I have longed long to redeliver.
I pray you now receive them.

Ham.   No, not I.   95

---

83. of us all] *F,Q1; not in Q2.*   85. sicklied] *F;* sickled *Q2.*   86. pitch] *Q2;*
pith *F.*   87. awry] *Q2;* away *F.*   92. well.] *Q2;* well, well, well. *F.*
95. you now] *Q2;* you now, *F;* you, now *Theobald.*   not I] *Q2;* no *F.*
95–6. No . . . aught.] *As Capell; one line Q2,F.*

83. *conscience*] (1) as in ordinary
modern usage, the inner voice of
moral judgment; (2) consciousness,
the fact or faculty of knowing and
understanding. LN.

make cowards of us] The natural
sense is 'cause us to be cowards' (as
unambiguously in *R3* I.iv.133); but
the interpretation 'adjudge us (make
us out to be) cowards' is occasionally
found (e.g. H. Craig in *Hunt.Lib.Bull.*,
VI, 23).

84. *native hue*] Resolution is sanguine
and its complexion therefore red.

85. *sicklied*] A nonce-use.

thought] Often used to denote meditation of a melancholy cast. Cf.
'thought-sick', III.iv.51. See IV.
v.185 n.

86. *pitch*] height, esp. 'the height to
which a falcon soared, before she
stooped upon her prey' (Nares). Cf.
R2 I.i.109, 'How high a pitch his
resolution soars!' The association of
pitch with *resolution* confirms the more

authoritative reading of Q2.

87. *currents*] This recalls *Caes.*
IV.iii.221 ('we must take the current
when it serves'), where the imagery
of sea and tide is explicit.

88. *Soft you now*] be silent, cease.
Cf. I.i.129, etc. *OED* soft *adv.* 8.

89. *Nymph . . . orisons*] Cf. ll. 44–6.
Ophelia is seen as at her devotions.
The tone is 'grave and solemn'
(Johnson) rather than ironical (Dover
Wilson). (Cf. Coghill, pp. 29–30;
HO, p. 142.)

92. *I humbly thank you*] 'He answers
as to a stranger' (Dowden) – in fact
in the same form of words as he uses
to the Captain (IV.iv.29) and Osric
(v.ii.82).

well] The F repetition – variously
interpreted as showing impatience,
boredom, depression, or irony –
appears to be no more than an actor's
elaboration. See Intro., p. 62, and
SB, XIII, 38.

　　　I never gave you aught.

Oph.　My honour'd lord, you know right well you did,
　　　And with them words of so sweet breath compos'd
　　　As made the things more rich. Their perfume lost,
　　　Take these again; for to the noble mind　　　　　　100
　　　Rich gifts wax poor when givers prove unkind.
　　　There, my lord.

Ham.　Ha, ha! Are you honest?

Oph.　My lord?

Ham.　Are you fair?　　　　　　　　　　　　　　105

Oph.　What means your lordship?

Ham.　That if you be honest and fair, your honesty should
　　　admit no discourse to your beauty.

Oph.　Could beauty, my lord, have better commerce than
　　　with honesty?　　　　　　　　　　　　　　110

---

97. you know] *Q2*; I know *F*.　　　99. the] *F*; these *Q2*.　　　Their perfume lost,]
Q2; then perfume left: *F*.　　　107–8. your honesty . . . beauty] *F*; you . . .
beautie *Q2*; Your beauty . . . honesty *Q1*.　　　109–10.] *Prose F; 2 lines divided
comerse / Then Q2*.　　　110. with] *Q2,Q1*; your *F*.

96. *I never gave you aught.*] Dover
Wilson, stressing *you*, implies that
Hamlet sees Ophelia as a changed
person from the woman he loved
(*WHH*, p. 129). But the dialogue
might be taken to put the greater
stress (through repetition) on *I*. The
long line of critics who assume that
Hamlet's conduct to Ophelia is the
consequence of hers to him share this
assumption with Polonius, whom the
play discredits. Nothing Hamlet says
supports it, and whatever construction we place on his equivocations, it
is clearly he, not she, who repudiates
their former love. Cf. ll. 115–19
below. See *HO*, p. 140.

99. *Their perfume lost*] Ironically
recalling I.iii.7–9.

101. *Rich . . . unkind.*] The rhyming
sententia, a common feature of
Elizabethan drama, should not be
taken to imply coldness or insincerity.

103. *honest*] (1) truthful, sincere (in
what you have just said), but quickly
passing into (2) chaste. Cf. II.ii.176

and n.

107–8. *your honesty . . . beauty*]
(1) Your chastity should permit no
one to have converse with your
beauty. But what Ophelia answers is
(2) Your chastity should permit itself
no converse with your beauty. It does
not follow, though it is often supposed, that she misunderstands
Hamlet's meaning. And she may
understand, though she does not
accept, the implication that in the
association of chastity and beauty
chastity will suffer. Where the
speakers agree is in assuming that a
woman is vulnerable through her
beauty, which it is the office of her
honesty to protect; and Hamlet already
anticipates the *nunnery* of l. 121.
Emendation (as in *N&Q*, ccxxv,
1980, 166–9) is certainly not called
for. LN.

109. *commerce*] Primarily used of
business dealings, the word may also
have sexual implications, which
Hamlet's reply picks up.

Ham. Ay, truly, for the power of beauty will sooner trans-
    form honesty from what it is to a bawd than the
    force of honesty can translate beauty into his like-
    ness. This was sometime a paradox, but now the
    time gives it proof. I did love you once.   115

Oph. Indeed, my lord, you made me believe so.

Ham. You should not have believed me; for virtue cannot
    so inoculate our old stock but we shall relish of it. I
    loved you not.

Oph. I was the more deceived.   120

Ham. Get thee to a nunnery. Why, wouldst thou be a
    breeder of sinners? I am myself indifferent honest,
    but yet I could accuse me of such things that it were
    better my mother had not borne me. I am very
    proud, revengeful, ambitious, with more offences at 125
    my beck than I have thoughts to put them in, im-
    agination to give them shape, or time to act them in.
    What should such fellows as I do crawling between
    earth and heaven? We are arrant knaves all, believe

118. inoculate] *F;* euocutat *Q2;* euacuat *Q3.*   121. to] *F; not in Q2.*
Why,] *This edn;* why *Q2,F,Q1.*   126–7. in, imagination] *Q2;* in imagination, *F.*   129. earth and heaven] *Q2;* Heauen and Earth *F,Q1.*   all] *F,Q1;
not in Q2.*

113. *his*] its (honesty's).

114. *sometime*] once.

paradox] a thing contrary to
received opinion or rational explanation (the usual Elizabethan sense).

115. *gives it proof*] As in the instance
of his mother.

117–18. *virtue . . . relish of it*] A
metaphor from horticulture using
inoculate in its etymological sense (L.
oculus, bud): a graft of virtue cannot
so change our original sinful nature
that we shall not still have the flavour
of it. *But* = that . . . not; *of it,* of the
old stock. Hence the equivocation of
I loved you not, i.e. the love I had for
you was not love.

121. *a nunnery*] where she will preserve her chastity and be safe from
love, marriage, and the breeding of
sinners. *Nunnery* was sometimes used
sarcastically for a house of *un*chaste

women, and awareness of this may
add a bitter undercurrent as the
dialogue proceeds; but to insist on it
(as in *WHH,* pp. 128–34) at the
expense of the literal meaning, itself
so poignant in the context, is perverse.
LN.

Why,] Not, as almost universally
assumed, an interrogative, but an
interjection. The question is *wouldst
thou?* with Hamlet exclaiming at such
a wish, not asking the reason for it.
See *OED* Why IV. 7.

122. *indifferent honest*] (with a play
on the previous sense of *honest*)
tolerably good-living.

125–6. *at my beck*] waiting to be
committed.

129. *We*] The shift from *I* via *such
as I* to *we* shows Hamlet thinking less
of sins peculiar to him than of those
he shares with all mankind.

none of us. Go thy ways to a nunnery. Where's your 130
father?

Oph. At home, my lord.

Ham. Let the doors be shut upon him, that he may play
the fool nowhere but in's own house. Farewell.

Oph. O help him, you sweet heavens.   135

Ham. If thou dost marry, I'll give thee this plague for thy
dowry: be thou as chaste as ice, as pure as snow,
thou shalt not escape calumny. Get thee to a nunnery, farewell. Or if thou wilt needs marry, marry a
fool; for wise men know well enough what monsters 140
you make of them. To a nunnery, go—and quickly
too. Farewell.

Oph. Heavenly powers, restore him.

Ham. I have heard of your paintings well enough. God
hath given you one face and you make yourselves 145
another. You jig and amble, and you lisp, you nick-

133-4.] *Prose F; lines divided* him, / That . . . house, / Farewell. *Q2.*
134. nowhere] *Q2* (no where), *Q1*; no way *F.*   138-9. nunnery,] *Q2*;
Nunnery. Go, *F.*   143. Heavenly] *Q2*; O heauenly *F.*   144. paintings]
Q2; pratlings too *F*; paintings too *Q1.*   145. hath] *Q2,Q1*; has *F.*
face] *Q2,Q1*; pace *F.*   yourselves] *Q2,Q1*; your selfe *F.*   146. jig and]
Q2 (gig &); gidge, you *F*; fig, and you *Q1.*   lisp] *F*; list *Q2.*
146-7. you nickname] *Q2*; and nickname *F.*

130. *Go thy ways*] See I.iii.135n.

130-1. *Where's your father?*] There
is no textual basis for the common
assumption that Hamlet's question is
prompted by his having just discovered the answer to it. LN.

132. *At home*] We know differently,
but it is hard to see what in Hamlet's
succeeding speeches should persuade
the commentators that he does.

135, 143. *help . . . restore*] She
believes him to be mad.

136. *If thou dost marry*] Cf. l. 121.
Is it not clear that it is the thought of
Ophelia's marrying that enrages
him?

137-8. *be thou as chaste . . . calumny*]
A recurrent thought in Shakespeare.
See I.iii.38, now ironically echoed;
Meas. III.ii.174, 'back-wounding
calumny The whitest virtue strikes';

Wint. II.i.73, 'Calumny will sear
Virtue itself'. Cf. Tilley E 175.

140. *monsters*] Cuckolds were popularly supposed to grow horns, and
'a horned man's a monster' (*Oth.*
IV.i.62).

141. *you*] you women. He has
ceased to think of Ophelia as an
individual.

144. *paintings*] LN.

146. *jig and amble*] Both verbs are
of dancing: *jig*, move with the rapid,
jerky rhythm of the jig; for *amble* cf.
Romeo, reluctant at the ball, 'I am
not for this ambling' (I.iv.11). Hence
both suggest an unnatural gait betokening fantastical frivolity. Cf.
1H4 III.ii.60, 'The skipping King,
he ambled up and down'. To *amble*
can also imply 'to act the coquette'.
Cf. *R3* I.i.17, 'To strut before a

name God's creatures, and make your wantonness
your ignorance. Go to, I'll no more on't, it hath made
me mad. I say we will have no mo marriage. Those
that are married already—all but one—shall live;   150
the rest shall keep as they are. To a nunnery, go.   *Exit.*
Oph. O, what a noble mind is here o'erthrown!
The courtier's, soldier's, scholar's, eye, tongue, sword,
Th'expectancy and rose of the fair state,
The glass of fashion and the mould of form,   155
Th'observ'd of all observers, quite, quite down!

147–8. wantonness your] *F,Q1;* wantonnes *Q2.*   149. mo marriage] *Q2;*
more Marriages *F,Q1.*   154. expectancy] *F;* expectation *Q2.*

---

wanton ambling nymph'; 1 *Return
from Parnassus,* l. 1310, 'each mincing
dame, Each ambling minion'; Shirley,
Lady of Pleasure, v.i.395, where colts
and virgins are alike taught 'the
amble'.

lisp] Like Chaucer's Friar, who
'lipsed for his wantownesse', i.e. out
of affectation.

146–7. *nickname*] find new names
for. Kittredge thought these were
euphemisms, Dowden indecencies
(like what 'maids call medlars when
they laugh alone', *Rom.* II.i.36). But
the point of offence, I take it, is as in
making a new face (ll. 144–6).

147–8. *make your wantonness your
ignorance*] what you really do from
wilful affectation you pretend is due
to your knowing no better. *Wantonness,* with its basic sense of 'disregard
of rule', need mean no more than
affectation or caprice: Elyot's
Governour, 1.5, had referred to the
linguistic habits of foolish women,
who often omitted letters and syllables
'of a wantonnesse'; *John* IV.i.16
recalls young men who would be sad
'only for wantonness'. Yet the context
here evokes the word's sexual connotations to suggest the arts of
seduction.

149. *mo*] = *more,* but not a corruption of it. O.E. *mā.*

150. *all but one*] As with Polonius

at ll. 130–4, the effect depends on our
knowing, but not on Hamlet's
knowing, of the King's presence.

153. *courtier's, soldier's, scholar's*]
For the rhetorical scheme, see Arden
MND III.i.105–6 n. We need not
assume a textual error because the
order of *soldier's, scholar's* is reversed
in *tongue, sword.* Cf. *Lucr.* 615–16.
With the princely ideal here cf. the
Duke in *Meas.,* 'a scholar, a statesman, and a soldier' (III.ii.135–6).
There may be a recollection of a
passage on Sloth in *Pierce Penniless,*
for which see Intro., p. 105.

154. *expectancy*] Apparently regarding Hamlet as heir to the throne.

rose] As a symbol of the perfection
of young manhood, cf. 'Richard,
that sweet lovely rose', *1H4* I.iii.175.
Ophelia will be described as the
'rose of May' (IV.v.157) when she
too is 'blasted'.

155. *The glass . . . form*] 'He was the
. . . glass . . . That fashion'd others'
(*2H4* II.iii.31–2). For a possible
Nashe echo see Intro., p. 105; but
cf. also North's Plutarch, 'as if I looked
into a glass, to frame and fashion
my life, to the mould and pattern of
these virtuous noble men' (Life of
Paulus Aemilius, Tudor Trans., ii.
196).

156. *observ'd*] honoured, respected.
OED observe 4b.

And I, of ladies most deject and wretched,
That suck'd the honey of his music vows,
Now see that noble and most sovereign reason
Like sweet bells jangled out of tune and harsh,   160
That unmatch'd form and feature of blown youth
Blasted with ecstasy. O woe is me
T'have seen what I have seen, see what I see.

Enter KING *and* POLONIUS.

King. Love? His affections do not that way tend,
Nor what he spake, though it lack'd form a little,   165
Was not like madness. There's something in his soul
O'er which his melancholy sits on brood,
And I do doubt the hatch and the disclose
Will be some danger; which for to prevent,
I have in quick determination   170
Thus set it down: he shall with speed to England

157. And] *Q2;* Haue *F.*   158. music] *F;* musickt *Q2.*   159. that] *F;*
what *Q2.*   160. jangled out of tune] *F;* iangled out of time *Q2;* jangl'd,
out of tune *Capell.*   161. feature] *F;* stature *Q2.*   163. see.] *F,Q2 uncorr.;*
see. *Exit. Q2 corr., Q1.*   166. soul] *Q2;* soule? *F.*   169. for] *Q2; not*
in *F.*

157. *deject*] For this past pple., see Abbott 342.

158. *music*] Choice between the variants is difficult, but Q2 *musickt* may be an error induced by *suckt* or by a final *e* being read as *d;* and it is not so much that he spoke the vows musically as that they were like music to her. Abbott (22, 430) treats *music vows* as a noun compound.

159. *sovereign*] having the right of rule (over other faculties). See I.iv.73 LN.

160. *out of tune*] 'an adverbial element to *jangled*, and not an adjective element to *sweet bells*' (Corson). But many eds. differ. The variants present another difficult choice, with the balance favouring *tune.* LN.

161. *feature*] form, fashioning (of the whole body, not specially of the face). (Fr. *faiture.*) Cf. *R3* I.i.19,

'Cheated of feature . . . Deform'd, unfinish'd'.

blown] in full flower. Cf. III.iii.81; *LLL* v.ii.293–7; etc.

162. *ecstasy*] madness, as at II.i.102, III.iv.140.

164. *affections*] (in a more general sense than now) feelings, inclinations.

168. *doubt*] fear. Cf. I.ii.256.

disclose] synonymous with *hatch*, the revealing of the young by the breaking open of the shell. Cf. v.i.282. With the noun forms here cf. II.i.4 and n.

171. *set it down*] resolved.

he shall . . . to England] The dramatist, if not the King, is already preparing the plot against Hamlet's life. As an instance of Shakespeare's construction see this developing at III.iii.3–7 and III.iv.202–7 before becoming explicit at IV.iii.57–71.

For the demand of our neglected tribute.
Haply the seas and countries different,
With variable objects, shall expel
This something settled matter in his heart,   175
Whereon his brains still beating puts him thus
From fashion of himself. What think you on't?

Pol. It shall do well. But yet do I believe
The origin and commencement of his grief
Sprung from neglected love. How now, Ophelia?   180
You need not tell us what Lord Hamlet said,
We heard it all. My lord, do as you please,
But if you hold it fit, after the play
Let his queen-mother all alone entreat him
To show his grief, let her be round with him,   185
And I'll be plac'd, so please you, in the ear
Of all their conference. If she find him not,
To England send him; or confine him where
Your wisdom best shall think.

King.   It shall be so.
Madness in great ones must not unwatch'd go.   190
                                                    Exeunt.

176–9.] *As F; lines ending* beating / himselfe. / well. *Q2.*   179. his] *Q2;*
this *F.*   185. grief] *Q2;* Greefes *F.*   186. plac'd, . . . you,] *Q2 subst., F3;*
plac'd so, please you *F.*   190. unwatch'd] *F;* vnmatcht *Q2.*

---

172. *tribute*] This historical allusion to the Danegeld had also topical overtones, since the Danish kings had recently sought to reimpose an annual payment. See Horsey, *Travels* (Hakluyt Soc.), pp. 240–4; Cal. S.P. Dom., 1598–1600, p. 59.

173. *the seas*] A recognized cure. Cf. *Wint.* IV.iv.752, 'he is gone aboard a new ship to purge melancholy'.

174. *objects*] notable sights. Cf. I.i.161.

175. *This something settled matter*] Referring back to l. 166. *Something*, an unidentified thing, is best taken as an adjective describing *matter*. Most eds. take it as an adverb (= some-

what) with *settled*. But the King accepts without qualification that the matter is *settled*, firmly lodged, in Hamlet's heart. It is what it is that is indefinite. Schmidt compares *R2* II.ii.36, 'my something grief' ('i.e. existing, but of uncertain nature').

176. *still*] constantly.

puts] The subject is of course the whole preceding phrase. Cf. Abbott 413.

177. *fashion of himself*] his normal behaviour.

185. *round*] plain-spoken, as at II.ii.139, III.iv.5.

187. *find him*] find the truth about him.

[SCENE II]

Enter HAMLET *and three of the* Players.

Ham. Speak the speech, I pray you, as I pronounced it to
you, trippingly on the tongue; but if you mouth it as
many of your players do, I had as lief the town-crier
spoke my lines. Nor do not saw the air too much with
your hand, thus, but use all gently; for in the very   5
torrent, tempest, and, as I may say, whirlwind of
your passion, you must acquire and beget a temper-
ance that may give it smoothness. O, it offends me
to the soul to hear a robustious periwig-pated fellow
tear a passion to tatters, to very rags, to split the ears   10
of the groundlings, who for the most part are capable
of nothing but inexplicable dumb-shows and noise.

Scene 11

SCENE II] *Capell.*   S.D. *three*] *Q2; two or three | F.*   3. your] *F,Q1;* our *Q2.*
town-crier] *Q2;* Town-Cryer had *F.*   4. with] *Q2,Q1; not in F.*
6–7. whirlwind of your] *Q2;* the Whirle-winde of *F.*   9. hear] *Q2,Q1;*
see *F.*   10. tatters] totters *Q2,Q1,* tatters *F.*

S.D. *three*] F revises for economy.
Three, in Q2 and presumably Shakespeare's, is unexpectedly precise but
corresponds (if we discount the
Prologue) to the number of speaking
parts in their play. Cf. II.ii.416
S.D. n.

1–35.] On acting, LN.

1. *the speech*] See II.ii.534–6, and
cf. *my*, l. 4. But Hamlet quickly
passes from an instruction about the
speech of his own composition to
discuss acting in general.

3. *your players*] Not a reference to
the particular troupe, but the indefinite *your*, as at I.i.141, I.v.175,
IV.iii.21–3, V.i.56–7, 165–6. The Q2
error *our* is repeated at l. 159.

4. *saw the air*] Cf. Quintilian's
objection to this kind of hand movement in oratory: 'solet esse . . .
secanti similis' (*Inst. Orat.*, XI.iii.119).
Bulwer, *Chironomia*, 1644, echoing

Quintilian, refers to 'the action of
one that saws or cuts' (pp. 102–3).

5. *use all gently*] do everything (1)
with moderation (2) in the well-bred
manner of a gentleman.

7. *acquire and beget*] 'acquire,
through training and practice; beget,
through a native artistic impulse'
(Dowden).

9. *robustious*] turbulent; with more
fury than wit. Cf. *H5* III.vii.144.

periwig-pated] Wigs at this date
belonged to the stage rather than to
normal wear: the epithet stresses
what is histrionic and artificial.

11. *groundlings*] the humblest spectators, who frequented the 'ground'
or yard of the theatre.

11–12. *capable of*] appreciative of,
responsive to. Cf. III.iv.127.

12. *inexplicable . . . noise*] The
groundlings, it appears, prefer sound
and spectacle to sense. The charge is

I would have such a fellow whipped for o'erdoing
Termagant. It out-Herods Herod. Pray you avoid it.
1st Play. I warrant your honour.   .   15
Ham. Be not too tame neither, but let your own dis-
cretion be your tutor. Suit the action to the word,
the word to the action, with this special observance,
that you o'erstep not the modesty of nature. For anything so o'erdone is from the purpose of playing,   20
whose end, both at the first and now, was and is to
hold as 'twere the mirror up to nature; to show virtue
her feature, scorn her own image, and the very age
and body of the time his form and pressure. Now
this overdone or come tardy off, though it makes the   25

13. would] *Q2,Q1;* could *F.*   19. o'erstep] *Q2;* ore-stop *F.*   20. o'erdone]
Q2; ouer-done *F.*   23. her feature] *Q2;* her owne Feature *F.*
25. makes] *Q2;* make *F.*

echoed in Heywood, *Love's Mistress*
(IV.i), 'The vulgar are best pleas'd
with noise and shows'. In *dumb-shows*
Shakespeare not uncharacteristically
mocks what he is going to supply.

14. *Termagant*] a noisy violent
personage in the Mystery Plays,
traditionally   the   companion   of
Mahound,   the   false   deity   of   the
Mahommedans.

Herod] The biblical tyrant was
represented in the Mystery Plays as
a figure of violent rages, typified in
the Coventry *Pageant of the Shearmen
and Taylors* (ll. 779–83, 'I stampe!
I stare! . . . I rent! I rawe! and now
run I wode! . . . ', after which
'*Erode ragis in the pagond and in the
strete also*').

20. *from*] i.e. remote from. See
Abbott 158.

21–2. *to hold . . . nature*] Cf.
Webster's praise, in the postscript, of
the acting of *The White Devil* for 'the
true imitation of life, without striving
to make nature a monster'. The widespread Renaissance theory of drama
as an image of actual life derives from
Donatus on comedy, where it is
attributed   to   Cicero   (*Commentum
Terenti,*   ed.   Wessner,   i. 22:

'comoediam esse Cicero ait imi-
tationem vitae, speculum consue-
tudinis, imaginem veritatis'.

23. *feature*] shape, appearance, as
at III.i.161.

scorn] that which excites scorn.
Cf. *LLL* I.i.288, 'These oaths and
laws will prove an idle scorn'.

23–4. *the very age . . . time*] The
difficulty felt by Johnson and others
over the 'age . . . of the time' led to
conjectural emendations, including
visage for *very age* (Bailey, ii. 7–8) on
the analogy of *2H4* II.iii.3, 'the visage
of the times'. But the difficulty
disappears if we perceive that *age*
does not correspond with *body* as an
attribute of 'the time' but with the
whole phrase *body of the time. body,*
'the   essential   and   vital   part'
(Schmidt), but also with a suggestion
of the 'substance' of which the players
give the image (*OED* body 24).

24. *his form and pressure*] its likeness
as seen in an impression (e.g. in wax,).
Cf. I.v.100 and n. *his*, its, as at
I.i.40, etc.

25. *come tardy off*] executed inadequately (so that the attempted
realization falls short of the original).
OED tardy 3.

unskilful laugh, cannot but make the judicious
grieve, the censure of the which one must in your
allowance o'erweigh a whole theatre of others. O,
there be players that I have seen play—and heard
others praise, and that highly—not to speak it pro-   30
fanely, that neither having th'accent of Christians,
nor the gait of Christian, pagan, nor man, have so
strutted and bellowed that I have thought some of
Nature's journeymen had made men, and not made
them well, they imitated humanity so abominably.   35

1st Play. I hope we have reformed that indifferently with
us.

Ham. O reform it altogether. And let those that play your
clowns speak no more than is set down for them—
for there be of them that will themselves laugh, to   40
set on some quantity of barren spectators to laugh
too, though in the meantime some necessary question of the play be then to be considered. That's
villainous, and shows a most pitiful ambition in the

---

27. of the] *F;* of *Q2.*   30. praise] *F;* praysd *Q2.*   31. th'accent] *Q2;*
the accent *F.*   32. nor man] *Q2;* or Norman *F;* Nor Turke *Q1.*
37. us] *Q2;* vs, Sir *F.*

26. *unskilful*] undiscriminating.
27. *censure*] judgment, opinion, as
at I.iii.69, etc.
28. *allowance*] acceptance as just.
30–1. *not to speak it profanely*]
Referring to the implication that
there can be men not of God's making.
31. *Christians*] ordinary decent
beings.
32. *nor man*] i.e. nor any man whatever. Cf. Jonson, *Silent Woman,*
IV.i.1–2, 'Was there ever poor
bridegroom so tormented? or man,
indeed?' F shows misunderstanding.
34. *Nature's journeymen*] i.e. not
Nature herself but her common
workmen.
men] Theobald's conjecture *them*
(though accepted by Furness) is
unnecessary; for it is not the players
themselves but humanity at large,
when seen in the inaccurate repre-

sentation of it by the players, that
seems an inferior piece of work.
35.   *abominably*]   The   regular
Elizabethan spelling *abhominable* reflects the accepted, though false,
etymology *ab homine,* which is played
on here.
36. *indifferently*] moderately well.
Cf. III.i.122.
39. *clowns . . . set down for them*] A
traditional practice: Tarlton in particular was famed for his extempore
wit. In Brome, *The Antipodes* (II.
ii.40–9) an actor called Byplay is
rebuked for adding to what the
author has composed, as used to be
done 'to move mirth and laughter . . .
in the days of Tarlton and Kempe'.
44–5. *the fool that uses it.*] In Q1 an
addition of 10 lines at this point
provides, ironically enough, an instance of the thing complained of. LN.

fool that uses it. Go make you ready.   *Exeunt Players.* 45

Enter POLONIUS, ROSENCRANTZ, *and* GUILDENSTERN.

How now, my lord? Will the King hear this piece
of work?
Pol. And the Queen too, and that presently.
Ham. Bid the players make haste.   *Exit Polonius.*
Will you two help to hasten them?   50
Ros. Ay, my lord.   *Exeunt Rosencrantz and Guildenstern.*
Ham. What ho, Horatio!

Enter HORATIO.

Hor. Here, sweet lord, at your service.
Ham. Horatio, thou art e'en as just a man
As e'er my conversation cop'd withal.   55
Hor. O my dear lord.
Ham.   Nay, do not think I flatter,
For what advancement may I hope from thee
That no revenue hast but thy good spirits
To feed and clothe thee? Why should the poor be
flatter'd?

---

45 S.D. *Exeunt Players.*] *F subst.*, *Q1*; *not in Q2*.   *Enter . . . Guildenstern.*] *F;*
after 47 Q2.   46–7.] *Prose Q2*; *2 lines divided* Lord, / Will *F*.   49 S.D.] *F;*
not in Q2.   51. *Ros.* Ay] *Q2*; *Both.* We will *F*.   52 S.D.] *Q2*; *before 52 F*.
56. *Ham.*] *F*; *not in Q2* (*except c.w.*).

46–7. *piece of work*] artistic composition. Cf. II.ii.303 and n.
   48. *presently*] immediately.
   51 S.D. *Exeunt . . . Guildenstern.*]
The dismissal of the King's agents
(who seem to have been brought on
for no other purpose) just when
Hamlet summons his own confidant
effects a contrast between them
which the ensuing discourse on
flattery reinforces.
   53. *sweet*] A frequent epithet in
complimentary or affectionate address. Cf. v.ii.90.

   54. *just*] well-balanced, as explained
in ll. 66–72. Bright (p. 97) tells how
a 'just proportion' in the 'mixture of
the elements' or the 'humours' of the
body 'breedeth an indifferency to all
passions'. It is regularly observed that
Hamlet values in Horatio what he
knows to be lacking in himself.
   55. *conversation*] dealings (not only
talk) with people.
   cop'd] encountered.
   58. *revenue*] Often accented on the
second syllable.

No, let the candied tongue lick absurd pomp,   60
And crook the pregnant hinges of the knee
Where thrift may follow fawning. Dost thou hear?
Since my dear soul was mistress of her choice,
And could of men distinguish her election,
Sh'ath seal'd thee for herself; for thou hast been   65
As one, in suff'ring all, that suffers nothing,
A man that Fortune's buffets and rewards
Hast ta'en with equal thanks; and blest are those
Whose blood and judgment are so well commeddled

60. tongue lick] *Q2*; tongue, like *F*.   62. fawning] *Q2*; faining *F*.
63. her] *Q2*; my *F*.   64. distinguish her election,] *Q2*; distinguish, her
election *F*.   65. Sh'ath] *Q5*; S'hath *Q2*; Hath *F*.   68. Hast] *Q2*; Hath *F*.
69. commeddled] *Q2*; co-mingled *F*.

60–2. *let the candied tongue . . .
fawning*] The basic idea is that
flattery (here figured as fawning and
genuflecting) should direct its atten-
tions where it may expect profit
(*thrift*) to ensue. The *candied tongue*
suggests an obsequious dog whose
physical licking affords an image of
the flatterer's sugary words. The
association of dog and candy belongs
to a famous Shakespearean 'image
cluster' (see Spurgeon, *Sh.'s Imagery*,
pp. 194–7; Armstrong, *Sh.'s Imagination*, pp. 154–6). The candy is of
course what the tongue bestows, not
(as Spurgeon) sweetmeats the dog
has eaten. Cf. *1H4* I.iii.251–2, 'What
a candy deal of courtesy This fawning
greyhound then did proffer me!'

60. *absurd*] insipid, without savour.
This Latin sense is well demonstrated
by Hulme (pp. 160–2), citing
Cotgrave, who offers *unsavoury, insulse,
absurd* as equivalent renderings of
Fr. *sans sel ni saulge*. But the antithesis she sees between *candied* and
absurd (even though the one may by
contrast have suggested the other) is
more apparent than real. *Absurd*
corresponds to such other Shakespearean epithets for pomp as *painted*
(*AYL* II.i.3; *Tim.* IV.ii.36) and *vain*.
The sweets of flattery are lavished on

that which, in spite of its rewards
(*thrift*), affords no genuine gratification. For the accentuation of *absurd*,
see I.iv.52 n.

61. *pregnant*] ready, easily stirred.
Cf. *Lr* IV.vi.225, 'am pregnant to
good pity'.

63–4. *was mistress . . . election*] had
the power to discriminate in her
choice among men. Cf. *Meas.*
I.i.18–19, 'we have with special soul
Elected him'.

65. *Sh'ath*] *Q2 S'hath* is, apart from
the common displacement of the
apostrophe, a quite satisfactory reading difficult to account for except as
deriving from the manuscript. *F* gives
a streamlined version.

66. *in suff'ring . . . nothing*] With a
play on the different meanings of
suffer: while undergoing all things
(as the next two lines explain), is
harmed by none.

69. *blood*] As the seat of passion, and
hence the opposite of *judgment*.
Cf. I.iii.6 and n., IV.iv.58.

commeddled] commingled, which *F*
substitutes. *OED*'s only other instance
of the word is in *The White Devil*
(III.iii.36), where 'religion . . . is
commeddled with policy'. But *meddle*
in its original sense of 'mingle',
'blend' was common.

That they are not a pipe for Fortune's finger   70
To sound what stop she please. Give me that man
That is not passion's slave, and I will wear him
In my heart's core, ay, in my heart of heart,
As I do thee. Something too much of this.
There is a play tonight before the King: 75
One scene of it comes near the circumstance
Which I have told thee of my father's death.
I prithee, when thou seest that act afoot,
Even with the very comment of thy soul
Observe my uncle. If his occulted guilt   80
Do not itself unkennel in one speech,
It is a damned ghost that we have seen,
And my imaginations are as foul
As Vulcan's stithy. Give him heedful note;
For I mine eyes will rivet to his face,   85
And after we will both our judgments join
In censure of his seeming.

Hor.   Well, my lord.
If a steal aught the whilst this play is playing
And scape detecting, I will pay the theft.

Enter Trumpets *and* Kettle-drums *and sound a flourish.*

73. of heart] Q2,F; of hearts Q 1676.   79. thy] Q2; my F.   80. my] Q2;
mine F.   84. stithy] Q2; Stythe F.   heedful] Q2; needfull F.
87. In] Q2; To F.   88. a] Q2; he F.   89. detecting] F; detected Q2.
89 S.D.] *Enter . . . Kettle-drums* Q2; *Danish March. Sound a Flourish* F; *trumpets
and kettledrums heard* | Wilson.

70–1. *pipe . . . stop*] The metaphor
will recur in ll. 355–63.
     72. *not passion's slave*] See l. 54 n.
     73. *my heart's core . . . heart of heart*]
Both phrases mean the same, on the
supposed etymology of *core*, from L.
cor: in the very centre of my heart.
     78. *that act*] The 'scene' of l. 76.
The words can be equivalent because
both refer to an action performed in
the course of the play rather than to
one of its technical divisions.
     79. *the very comment*] the most
searching consideration.
     thy] The 'just' Horatio will be the
perfect witness.
     81. *one speech*] The speech of

Hamlet's composition. Cf. II.ii.535,
III.ii. 1–4.
     82. *a damned ghost*] Cf. II.ii.594–9
and I.iv.40.
     84. *Vulcan's stithy*] The smithy of
the god of blacksmiths, and hence (1)
symbolic of blackness, (2) having
affinities with hell, whence the
'damned ghost' responsible for
Hamlet's 'imaginations' (cf. I.iv.87)
will have come.
     87. *In censure of his seeming*] in
judging (forming an opinion) of his
appearance (looks, demeanour). Cf.
censure, I.iii.69, III.ii.27.
     89 S.D. *Trumpets and Kettle-drums*]
Characteristic of Denmark; the F

Ham. They are coming to the play. I must be idle.   90
   Get you a place.

Enter KING, QUEEN, POLONIUS, OPHELIA, ROSENCRANTZ,
GUILDENSTERN, *and other* Lords *attendant, with the King's*
Guard *carrying torches.*

King. How fares our cousin Hamlet?
Ham. Excellent, i'faith, of the chameleon's dish. I eat the
   air, promise-crammed. You cannot feed capons so.
King. I have nothing with this answer, Hamlet. These   95
   words are not mine.
Ham. No, nor mine now.—[*To Polonius*] My lord, you
   played once i'th' university, you say?
Pol. That did I, my lord, and was accounted a good
   actor.   100
Ham. What did you enact?
Pol. I did enact Julius Caesar. I was killed i'th' Capitol.

91 S.D.] *before 89 S.D., F subst.; after 89 S.D., King, Queene, Polonius, Ophelia.
Q2; Enter King, Queene, Corambis, and other Lords. Q1.*   92–105.] *Prose F; lines
ending* yfaith, / ayre, / so. / Hamlet, / Lord. / say, / Actor, / enact? / Capitall, /
mee. / there, / readie? *Q2.*   97. mine now.—My lord, you] *Johnson;* mine
now my Lord. / You *Q2;* mine. Now my lord, you *F;* My lord, you *Q1.*
To Polonius] *As Johnson; after* my Lord / *Rowe.*   99. did I] *Q2;* I did *F,Q1.*
101. What] *Q2,Q1;* And what *F.*

Danish March is not so much an
elaboration as an alternative wording.
See I.iv.11 LN.

90. *be idle*] (1) be unoccupied.
They must not be seen conspiring.
(So Greg, *MLR*, XIV, 362–3.) Or,
as usually taken, (2) be foolish, act
the madman (as in his next speech
Hamlet does).

92. *cousin*] Cf. I.ii.64.

93. *of the chameleon's dish*] *Fares* =
(1) does, (2) eats, and Hamlet
characteristically answers the wrong
sense. (Cf. II.ii.191–5, 206–8, 409–14,
etc.) That the chameleon feeds on
air was an ancient belief. See Ovid,
Met. XV.411 ('ventis animal nutritur
et aura'); Browne, *Vulgar Errors*,
III.21. Cf. *Gent.* II.i.160–2, 'Though
the chameleon Love can feed on the
air, I am one that am nourish'd by

my victuals'; Tilley M 226.

94. *promise-crammed*] fed with (no
more than) promises. If specific
allusion is intended, it must be to
the King's 'voice' for the succession.
See I.ii.108–9, III.ii.331–3. Dover
Wilson sees Hamlet playing up to
the King's suspicion that his trouble
is disappointed ambition. Cf. II.
ii.252. There is perhaps a play on
air, heir.

capons] which *are* crammed (though
not with air) to prepare them for the
table. A veiled hint that Hamlet suspects the King of designs against him.

96. *mine*] for me, to do with me.

97. *nor mine now*] 'A man's words,
says the proverb, are his own no
longer than he keep them unspoken'
(Johnson). Tilley W 776.

My lord] Q2 directs these words to

Brutus killed me.

Ham. It was a brute part of him to kill so capital a calf
there. Be the players ready?   105

Ros. Ay, my lord, they stay upon your patience.

Queen. Come hither, my dear Hamlet, sit by me.

Ham. No, good mother, here's metal more attractive.

[*Turns to Ophelia.*]

Pol. [*aside to the King*] O ho! do you mark that?

Ham. [*lying down at Ophelia's feet*] Lady, shall I lie in your   110
lap?

Oph. No, my lord.

Ham. I mean, my head upon your lap.

Oph. Ay, my lord.

---

107. dear] *Q2;* good *F.*   108. metal] mettle *Q2,F,* metall *Q5;* a mettle
Q1.   108 S.D.] *Wilson subst.*   109. *aside to the King*] *Capell.*
110. *lying . . . feet*] *Rowe.*   113–14.] *F; not in Q2.*

---

the King. But they are more appropriate to the person newly addressed
and Q1 suggests that they were said to
Polonius in performance. Cf. II.
ii. 518.

103. *Brutus killed me*] It is likely
enough that the roles of Caesar and
Brutus in *Caes.* (first performed 1599)
were taken by the same actors as
now played Polonius and Hamlet;
so that 'Hamlet' would already have
killed 'Polonius' in a previous play,
and, ironically, is to do the same
'brute part' in this.

104. *brute*] (1) brutish, no doubt;
but also (2) heroic, from Brut(us), the
legendary founder of Britain.

to kill . . . a calf] This alludes – by
way of a pun on *calf*, fool – to the
feat so called, which appears to have
been part of a traditional mumming
entertainment. It was probably
Shakespeare's skill in this histrionic
item ('he killed a calf' with 'a high
style' and 'a speech') that misled
Aubrey to suppose that he was the
son of a butcher. (See Chambers,
WS, i. 17, ii. 252–3; D. Hamer, *RES,*

n.s. XXII, 484.)

108. *attractive*] in the strict sense
(among others): having magnetic
power.

110–11. *lie in your lap*] Hamlet first
implies, then (l. 113) affects not to
have meant, an indecent meaning,
which he returns to at l. 115. See
OED, lap *sb.*[1] 2b; Hulme, pp. 119,
92–3.

113. *my head . . . lap*] Some light on
customs of gallantry may be given
by Fletcher, *Queen of Corinth,*
I. ii. 194–7, 'The fine courtier . . . tells
my lady stories, . . . lies at her feet
At solemn masques', and Gascoigne,
'The Green Knight's Farewell to
Fancy' (l. 16), which lists among
court pleasures 'To lie along in
ladies' laps'. But more significant is
the situation traditional in the Morality plays (as excellently shown by
M. Collins, *N&Q,* CCXXVI, 130–2),
where a youth, by lying in the lap of
a temptress, puts himself in her power
and is betrayed. The innuendo is thus
clear.

Ham. Do you think I meant country matters?   115
Oph. I think nothing, my lord.
Ham. That's a fair thought to lie between maids' legs.
Oph. What is, my lord?
Ham. Nothing.
Oph. You are merry, my lord.   120
Ham. Who, I?
Oph. Ay, my lord.
Ham. O God, your only jig-maker. What should a man
    do but be merry? For look you how cheerfully my
    mother looks and my father died within's two hours.   125
Oph. Nay, 'tis twice two months, my lord.
Ham. So long? Nay then, let the devil wear black, for I'll
    have a suit of sables. O heavens, die two months ago
    and not forgotten yet! Then there's hope a great
    man's memory may outlive his life half a year. But   130
    by'r lady a must build churches then, or else shall
    a suffer not thinking on, with the hobby-horse, whose

120. lord.] *Q2*; Lord? *F.*   127. devil] deule *Q2*, Diuel *F.*   for I'll] *Q2,F,Q1*;
'fore I'll *Warburton.*   128. have a] *Q2,F,Q1*; not have a *Keightley*; leave
a *conj. Lloyd, apud Cambridge*; have no *conj. Becket.*   131. by'r lady] *F*
(byrlady); ber Lady *Q2.*   a] *Q2*; he *F,Q1.*   132. a] *Q2*; he *F.*

115. *country matters*] physical love-
making (with a popular pun on the
first syllable). Cf. Donne, 'The Good-
morrow', l. 3, 'country pleasures';
Birth of Merlin, II.i.18, 'country
breeding'; Dekker, *Westward Ho*,
v.i.170, 'Though we lie all night out
of the city, they shall not find country
wenches of us'.
117. *fair*] (1) pleasing; (2) pure.
119. *Nothing.*] The absence of anything (in jocular allusion to virginity),
perhaps with specific reference to
the male 'thing'. Alternatively the
figure O, in allusion to the woman's
sexual organ (cf. II.ii.424–5 n.).
123. *only jig-maker*] one and only
composer of comical afterpieces (see
II.ii.496 n.); hence, champion maker
of merriment.
125. *within's*] within this.

126. *twice two months*] Without
taking it too strictly, this, along with
I.ii.147–56, 176–9, implies the passage of three months between Acts
I and II.
127. *the devil wear black*] As in
popular belief of course he did.
128. *sables*] the much-prized furs of
the animal so called, noted for their
luxuriant and dark colour and traditionally worn in mourning; hence
the 'most splendid and impressive
mourning wear' (Hotson). LN.
132–3. *the hobby-horse . . . is forgot*]
The hobby-horse was a traditional
character in the morris dance and
the May Games, which became, it is
not clear why, the type of what is
forgotten and the subject of a popular
catch-phrase. LN.

epitaph is 'For O, for O, the hobby-horse is forgot'.

The trumpets sound. A dumb-show follows.

Enter a KING *and a* QUEEN, *the Queen embracing him and he her.
She kneels, and makes show of protestation unto him. He takes her up,
and declines his head upon her neck. He lies him down upon a bank
of flowers. She, seeing him asleep, leaves him. Anon comes in another*
Man, *takes off his crown, kisses it, pours poison in the sleeper's ears,
and leaves him. The* QUEEN *returns, finds the King dead, makes
passionate action. The* Poisoner *with some* Three or Four *comes
in again. They seem to condole with her. The dead body is carried
away. The Poisoner woos the Queen with gifts. She seems harsh
awhile, but in the end accepts his love.*   *Exeunt.*

Oph. What means this, my lord?

Ham. Marry, this is miching malicho. It means mischief.   135

Oph. Belike this show imports the argument of the play.

Enter PROLOGUE.

Ham. We shall know by this fellow. The players cannot

---

133 S.D. (*substantial variants only*) 1. *The trumpets sound*] *Q2;* Hoboyes *play* F.
S.D.2. *Queen*] *Q2; Queene, very louingly* F.   *and he her*] *Q2;* not in F.
S.D.3. *She kneels . . . him*] F; not in *Q2.*   S.D.4. *lies*] *Q2;* Layes F.
S.D.4–5. *lies . . . flowers*] *Q2,* F (*subst.*); sits downe in an Arbor *Q1.*
S.D.5–6. *another Man*] *Q2;* a Fellow F.   S.D.8. *Three or Four*] *Q2;* two or three
Mutes F.   S.D.9. *condole*] *Q2;* lament F.   S.D.10. *harsh*] *Q2;* loath and
vnwilling F.   S.D.11. *Exeunt*] F; not in *Q2.*   135. *this is*] *F,Q1;* this *Q2;*
'tis *Q3.*   miching] *F,Q1;* munching *Q2.*   malicho] F; Mallico *Q2,Q1;*
mallecho *Malone.*   It] *Q2;* that *F,Q1.*   136 S.D.] *Theobald;* opp. fellow
137 *Q2; after 143* F; *after 134 Q1.*   137. this fellow] *Q2,Q1;* these
Fellowes F.

---

133 S.D. *A dumb-show*] LN.

S.D.2–11.] The many little textual
variants in F show the freedom
which the playhouse allowed itself
with stage-directions. Most are insignificant rephrasings, but the *two or
three Mutes* (instead of the Q2 *three
or foure*) illustrate F's usual economy
in casting. On the other hand the
sentence beginning *She kneels* must,
in view of *he takes her up*, represent an
omission in Q2.

S.D.4–5. *upon a bank of flowers*]
Quite a likely property: the Admiral's

Company had, in an inventory of
1598, 'ij mose banckes'. But Q1 *in
an Arbor* reflects a different staging.

S.D.10. *with gifts*] Cf. I.v.43.

135. *miching malicho*] sneaking mischief; stealthy iniquity. LN.

136. *this show . . . the play*] Not what
dumb-shows usually did, but a hint
from the dramatist that this one does.
Cf. l. 133 S.D. LN.

argument] subject, plot.

137. *know by this fellow*] Dumb-
shows, like the pageants from which
they derived, often had a 'presenter'

keep counsel: they'll tell all.

Oph. Will a tell us what this show meant?

Ham. Ay, or any show that you will show him. Be not you 140
ashamed to show, he'll not shame to tell you what it
means.

Oph. You are naught, you are naught. I'll mark the play.

Prol. 				*For us and for our tragedy,*
					Here stooping to your clemency,				145
					We beg your hearing patiently.				[*Exit.*]

Ham. Is this a prologue, or the posy of a ring?

Oph. 'Tis brief, my lord.

Ham. As woman's love.

Enter [the Player] KING *and* QUEEN.

P. King. *Full thirty times hath Phoebus' cart gone round*		150
		Neptune's salt wash and Tellus' orbed ground,

138. counsel] *F,Q1; not in Q2.*	139. a] *Q2;* they *F;* he *Q1.*
140. you will] *Q2;* you'l *F,Q1.*	146 S.D.] *Globe.*	147. posy] *Q2;*
Poesie *F,Q1.*	149 S.D.] *Alexander; Enter King and Queene. Q2,F (subst.);
Enter King and Queen, Players. Pope; Enter two Players, King and Queen. Globe;
Enter the Duke and Dutchesse. Q1; Enter Duke, and Dutchess, Players. Theobald.*
150, 168, 181, 220. *P. King]* Steevens²; *King Q2,F;* Duke *Q1, Theobald.*
151. orbed] *F;* orb'd the *Q2.*

to explain their meaning to the
spectators. Cf. the Act-Prologues in
Locrine; *Spanish Trag.* i.iv.138ff.;
MND v.i.126ff. But the 'fellow'
in this case does not do as expected,
so that the play begins with the stage-
audience unwarned. Cf. l. 133 S.D.
LN.

137–8. *The players . . . tell all.*] This
refers both to players in general, who,
by the nature of their art, make
things public; and also to the particular players and what their play
will disclose. Dover Wilson, however,
supposed that Hamlet feared that
the players, through the dumb-show
and its presenter, would divulge the
nature of their play too soon.

138. *keep counsel*] keep a secret. See
OED counsel sb. 5d. Cf. iv.ii.10.

140. *show . . . show*] The obvious in-
decency, acknowledged by Ophelia's
rebuke, may be heightened by a pun

on *shoe*, referring to the woman's
sexual part (*Trivium*, iv, 108–11).

Be not you] i.e. if you be not (subjunctive rather than imperative).

143. *naught*] lit. of no worth; hence
(morally) bad, improper, offensive.

147. *posy*] a short motto, usually in
verse (cf. *poesy*) such as was often
engraved inside a ring. Cf. *AYL*
iii.ii.255–7, 'pretty answers . . . out
of rings'. For instances see *Mer.V.*
v.i.147–50; Middleton, *Chaste Maid
in Cheapside*, i.i.188–91; and the
collections printed in Arber, *English
Garner*, i.611–19, Halliwell, *Literature
of the 16th and 17th Centuries*, pp. 223–
36. For an account see *Archaeological
Journal*, xvi, 307–17.

150–5.] LN.

150. *Phoebus' cart*] the chariot of the
sun.

151. *Tellus' orbed ground*] the earth.

> *And thirty dozen moons with borrow'd sheen*
> *About the world have times twelve thirties been*
> *Since love our hearts and Hymen did our hands*
> *Unite commutual in most sacred bands.*   155

P. Queen. *So many journeys may the sun and moon*
> *Make us again count o'er ere love be done.*
> *But woe is me, you are so sick of late,*
> *So far from cheer and from your former state,*
> *That I distrust you. Yet though I distrust,*   160
> *Discomfort you, my lord, it nothing must;*
> *For women's fear and love hold quantity,*
> *In neither aught, or in extremity.*
> *Now what my love is, proof hath made you know,*
> *And as my love is siz'd, my fear is so.*   165
> *Where love is great, the littlest doubts are fear;*
> *Where little fears grow great, great love grows there.*

P. King. *Faith, I must leave thee, love, and shortly too:*
> *My operant powers their functions leave to do;*
> *And thou shalt live in this fair world behind,*   170
> *Honour'd, belov'd; and haply one as kind*
> *For husband shalt thou—*

P. Queen.   *O confound the rest.*
> *Such love must needs be treason in my breast.*
> *In second husband let me be accurst;*

156, 172, 211, 222. *P. Queen*] Steevens²; *Quee.* Q2,F2; *Bap.* F (except 222 *Qu.*);
Dutchesse Q1, Theobald.   159. *your*] F; *our* Q2.   *former*] Q2; *forme* F.
162. *For*] F; *For women feare too much, euen as they loue, / And* Q2.
hold] Q2; *holds* F.   163. *In*] F; *Eyther none, in* Q2.   164. *love*] F,Q5;
Lord Q2.   166–7.] Q2; *not in* F.   169. *their*] Q2; *my* F.   171. *kind*] Q5;
kind, Q2; *kinde.* F.

---

152. *sheen*] brightness.

155. *bands*] i.e. bonds.

160. *distrust*] feel anxiety for.

162. *hold quantity*] are in proportion to one another. The line in Q2 which F discards expresses exactly the same thought. See Intro., p. 41.

163. *In neither . . . extremity*] nothing of either or both in excess.

169. *operant powers*] faculties. Cf. Heywood, *Royal King and Loyal Subject*, I.i.37–8, 'may my operant parts Each one forget their office'; Webster, *Appius and Virginia*, v.ii.108, 'all my operant powers'.

leave to do] cease to perform. Cf. III.iv.66.

> *None wed the second but who kill'd the first.*　　　175
> *Ham.* [*aside*] That's wormwood.
> *P. Queen.* *The instances that second marriage move*
> 　　　*Are base respects of thrift, but none of love.*
> 　　　*A second time I kill my husband dead,*
> 　　　*When second husband kisses me in bed.*　　　180
> *P. King.* *I do believe you think what now you speak;*
> 　　　*But what we do determine, oft we break.*
> 　　　*Purpose is but the slave to memory,*
> 　　　*Of violent birth but poor validity,*
> 　　　*Which now, the fruit unripe, sticks on the tree,*　　　185
> 　　　*But fall unshaken when they mellow be.*
> 　　　*Most necessary 'tis that we forget*
> 　　　*To pay ourselves what to ourselves is debt.*
> 　　　*What to ourselves in passion we propose,*
> 　　　*The passion ending, doth the purpose lose.*　　　190
> 　　　*The violence of either grief or joy*
> 　　　*Their own enactures with themselves destroy.*

176. *aside*] *Capell.*　　　　That's wormwood] (*in margin*) *Q2*; Wormwood,
Wormwood *F,Q1* (*subst.*).　　　177. *P. Queen*] *Steevens²*; *Bapt. F*; *Quee. F2*;
Dutch. Theobald; not in *Q2*.　　　181. *you think*] *Q2*; you. Think *F*; you sweete,
Q1.　　　185. *the fruit*] *Q2*; like Fruite *F*.　　　191. *either*] *Q2*; other *F*.
192. *enactures*] *Q2*; ennactors *F*.

175–80.] I do not think we should
infer that Hamlet actually suspects
his mother of murder. That is more
than the Ghost has charged her with
and than the Gonzago play represents. What *is* implied, I take it, is
that through her second marriage she
becomes an accomplice in her first
husband's death. Cf. III. iv. 29 and n.

175. *None wed*] plural indicative.
Kittredge construes 'Let no woman
wed', but for *none* as plural see *OED*
none *pron.* 2 b.

but who] except those who.

177. *instances*] motives, causes.

178. *respects of thrift*] considerations
of profit or worldly advantage.

179. *kill . . . dead*] The tautology is
idiomatic. Cf. *Tit.* III. i. 92 ('had he
kill'd me dead'), and see *OED* kill
v. 2 c. Hence it is unnecessary to
explain, with Dowden and Kittredge,

that the second killing is of a husband
already dead.

183–208.] LN.

184. *Of violent birth . . . validity*] For
a rewording of the thought, see
ll. 189–90.

185–6. *sticks . . . fall*] 'The subject,
which is singular, is here confused
with, and lost in, that to which it is
compared, which is plural.' (Abbott
415).

187–8. *Most necessary . . . debt.*] Our
resolves, being debts to ourselves only,
inevitably remain unpaid. *Necessary*
refers to what in the nature of things
cannot fail to happen, not to what is
morally requisite, as seems to be
supposed by those who find in this
couplet a sanction for Hamlet's
forgetfulness.

191–2. *The violence . . . destroy.*] The
very extremity of (either) passion

> *Where joy most revels grief doth most lament;*
> *Grief joys, joy grieves, on slender accident.*
> *This world is not for aye, nor 'tis not strange*   195
> *That even our loves should with our fortunes change,*
> *For 'tis a question left us yet to prove,*
> *Whether love lead fortune or else fortune love.*
> *The great man down, you mark his favourite flies;*
> *The poor advanc'd makes friends of enemies;*   200
> *And hitherto doth love on fortune tend:*
> *For who not needs shall never lack a friend,*
> *And who in want a hollow friend doth try*
> *Directly seasons him his enemy.*
> *But orderly to end where I begun,*   205
> *Our wills and fates do so contrary run*
> *That our devices still are overthrown:*
> *Our thoughts are ours, their ends none of our own.*
> *So think thou wilt no second husband wed,*
> *But die thy thoughts when thy first lord is dead.*   210
>
> P. Queen. *Nor earth to me give food, nor heaven light,*
> *Sport and repose lock from me day and night,*
> *To desperation turn my trust and hope,*
> *An anchor's cheer in prison be my scope,*

194. *joys . . . grieves*] *F*; ioy . . . griefes *Q2*.   199. *favourite*] *Q2*; fauourites *F*.
211. *me give*] *Q2*; giue me *F*.   213–14.] *Q2*; not in *F*.   214. *An anchor's*]
Theobald; And Anchors *Q2*; And anchors' *Jennens*.

inhibits its translation into action.
With the plural verb, cf. i.ii.38.
enactures (*OED*'s only instance), en-
actments, i.e. fulfilment in deeds.

195–204.] These sentiments on
friendship and fortune go back ultimately to Cicero's *De Amicitia*. With
l. 198 cf. Cicero's 'Non igitur utili-
tatem amicitia, sed utilitas amicitiam
secuta est'. For the tradition, see
MLR, LXV, 1–6.

196. *loves*] Cf. i.i.178 and n.

201. *hitherto*] up to this point (in
the argument on the 'question' posed
in ll. 197–8).

204. *seasons*] matures, as at i.iii.81.
A hollow friend is a potential enemy
and when put to the test ripens into
one unambiguously.

207. *devices*] designs.
still] always.

209–10. *think thou . . . dead*] This is
the case at the death of Amleth in
Saxo and Belleforest; but a connection (suggested in *SAB*, XXIV, 280–2)
seems improbable.

212. *Sport . . . night*] An inversion,
of course: may day withhold pastime
from me and night rest.

214. *An anchor's cheer*] the standard
of living of an anchorite. (*Cheer* is not
merely food but the whole manner
of a man's entertainment.) Steevens
cited from Hall's *Satires* (IV.ii.103),
'Sit seauen yeares pining in an
Anchores cheyre'; but neither this
supposed analogy nor the attempt to
restrict *scope* to its physical sense can

> Each opposite, that blanks the face of joy,   215
> Meet what I would have well and it destroy,
> Both here and hence pursue me lasting strife,
> If, once a widow, ever I be a wife.

Ham. If she should break it now.

P. King. 'Tis deeply sworn. Sweet, leave me here awhile.   220
> My spirits grow dull, and fain I would beguile
> The tedious day with sleep.

P. Queen.   Sleep rock thy brain,
> And never come mischance between us twain.

> > Exit. He sleeps.

Ham. Madam, how like you this play?

Queen. The lady doth protest too much, methinks.   225

Ham. O, but she'll keep her word.

King. Have you heard the argument? Is there no offence
in't?

Ham. No, no, they do but jest—poison in jest. No offence
i'th' world.   230

King. What do you call the play?

---

218. *once a widow . . . a wife*] *This edn;* once I be a widow . . . a wife *Q2;* once a Widdow . . . Wife *F,Q1.*   219.] *As F,Q1 (subst.); in margin opp.* 217–18 *Q2.*   223 S.D. *He sleeps*] *Capell subst.; after 222,* Sleepes *F; not in Q2.* 225. doth protest] *Q2;* protests *F,Q1.*

justify emending *cheer* or interpreting it as a form of *chair*.

215–16. *Each opposite . . . have well*] May everything I desire to prosper encounter the particular opponent which makes joy turn pale (or possibly, cancels the manifestation of joy). *blanks,* blanches (as in Sylvester's Du Bartas, I.vi.200, 'His brow Was never blankt with pallid fear'); less probably, makes blank, nullifies.

217. *here and hence*] 'in this world and the next' (Kittredge).

223. *mischance*] ill-fortune.

227–8. *Have you heard . . . offence in't?*] The first sign of uneasiness in the King. It has been used both as evidence that he did not see the dumb-

show, or he would have known there was 'offence' (e.g. *WHH,* p. 159), and as evidence that he did see it, or he would not have suspected 'offence' yet (e.g. Hart, *RES,* XVII, 17). (See III.ii.133 S.D. LN.) But the pointed remarks on second marriage are obviously provocation enough. The King appears to be alerted first on the Queen's behalf rather than his own, though Hamlet's reply can leave no doubt now of what is to come.

229. *jest*] make believe.

offence] Hamlet, as usual, shifts the meaning of the word: for *offence* (1) = cause for objection, he substitutes (2) = crime. We may also hear an echo of I.v.141–3.

Ham. *The Mousetrap*—marry, how tropically! This play
is the image of a murder done in Vienna—Gonzago
is the Duke's name, his wife Baptista—you shall see
anon. 'Tis a knavish piece of work, but what o' that? 235
Your Majesty, and we that have free souls, it touches
us not. Let the galled jade wince, our withers are
unwrung.

Enter LUCIANUS.

This is one Lucianus, nephew to the King.
Oph. You are as good as a chorus, my lord.   240
Ham. I could interpret between you and your love if I
could see the puppets dallying.

232. how tropically!] *This edn;* how tropically, *Q2;* how trapically: *Q1;*
how? Tropically: *F.*   234. Duke's] *Q2,F,Q1;* King's *Hudson.*   235. o'] *F;*
of *Q2;* A *Q1.*   237. wince] winch *Q2,F,* wince *Q1.*   238 S.D.] *F;* after
239 Q2.   240. as good as a] *Q2,Q1;* a good *F.*   241-2.] *Prose F; 2 lines
divided* Loue / If *Q2.*

232. *The Mousetrap*] 'The play's the
thing Wherein I'll catch . . . '
(II.ii.600–1). J. Doebler (*SQ,* XXIII,
161 ff.) discusses the theological symbolism of the mousetrap, as in
Augustine's allusion to the cross of
Christ as the mousetrap of the devil,
who is trapped by his own corruption.
The analogy with Claudius is pertinent; but we had better stop short of
seeing Hamlet therefore as a Christ-
figure.

marry, how tropically] *tropically,* by
a trope, metaphorically. The Q1
spelling suggests pronunciation and
brings out the pun (see Kökeritz,
pp. 223–4). Eds. always prefer F's
punctuation, but there is no point in
thus making *how* a question and
tropically the answer to it. Rather (as
Q1,Q2 suggest) *how tropically* (trapically) is Hamlet's delighted
exclamation at his own conceit.
Marry trap appears to have been an
exclamation of derision when a man
was successfully tricked or discom-
forted. Cf. *Wiv.* I.i.151, 'I will say
"marry trap" with you', i.e. I will
get my own back on you.

233–4. *the image of a murder . . .
Baptista*] LN.

236. *free*] guiltless, as at II.ii.558,
v.ii.337.

237. *Let the galled jade wince*] A
galled jade is a horse which is rubbed
sore, esp. on the withers through an
ill-fitting saddle. For a literal instance, see *1H4* II.i.5–7. The proverbial expression is very common:
Tilley H 700; *OED* winch *v.*[1] 2b;
Palsgrave, *Acolastus,* EETS, pp. 195–6.
E.g. Lyly, i.257, 'None will winch
excepte shee bee gawlded, neither
any bee offended vnlesse shee be
guiltie'; also ii.151, 'Rubbe there no
more, least I winch, for deny I wil
not that I am wroung on the withers'.
Wince and *winch* (Q2,F) are different
forms of the same word, which then
meant 'kick out restlessly' but has
weakened in meaning since.

239. *nephew to the King*] LN.

240. *chorus*] which explains or
'interprets' the action of a play.

241–2. *interpret . . . puppets dallying*]
In a puppet-show the man who
'interprets' is he who supplies the
verbal accompaniment of the puppet

Oph. You are keen, my lord, you are keen.

Ham. It would cost you a groaning to take off my edge.

Oph. Still better, and worse. 245

Ham. So you mis-take your husbands.—Begin, murderer. Leave thy damnable faces and begin. Come, the croaking raven doth bellow for revenge.

Luc. Thoughts black, hands apt, drugs fit, and time agreeing,
Confederate season, else no creature seeing, 250
Thou mixture rank, of midnight weeds collected,

---

244. my] *F; mine Q2.*　　　246. mis-take] *Capell;* mistake *Q2,F;* must take *Q1.*
your] *Q2,Q1; not in F.*　　　247. Leave] *Q2;* Pox, leaue *F,Q1 subst.*　　　248. the
croaking . . . revenge.] *As Q2,F,Q1; verse, divided* raven | Doth *Steevens⁴; as
quotation White.*　　　250. Confederate] *F,Q1;* Considerat *Q2.*

action and so makes clear to the
audience what is going on. Cf. *Pierce
Penniless,* 'like . . . one's voice that
interprets to [i.e. for] the puppets'
(Nashe, i. 173); *Gent.* II.i.85-6. So
Hamlet, if he saw the love-play of
Ophelia and a lover, would be able to
supply dialogue for it. Cf. ll. 140-2
above.

243. *keen*] sharp-tongued, bitter.
Cf. *LLL* v.ii.256, 'The tongues of
mocking wenches are as keen As is
the razor's edge'.

244. *a groaning . . . my edge*] The
(keen) edge is that of (1) a sharp
instrument, (2) sexual desire. The
groaning which would blunt it is that
of the woman losing her maidenhead.

245. *better, and worse*] more keen,
and more objectionable. The better
the worse is what Diogenes reputedly
said of dancers. Cf. *Tw.N.* I.v.68-72,
'the better fool'; Tilley B 333.

246. *mis-take your husbands*] 'For
better for worse' is how women 'take'
their husbands in the marriage-
service. In saying that they *mistake*
them Hamlet gibes at the lightness of
their vows. For *mistake,* cf. *R2*
III.iii.16-17, 'Take not . . . lest you
mistake'; *Bartholomew Fair,* II.ii.101-2,
'to . . . mistake away the bottles and

cans . . . before they be half drunk
off'; and other examples in Furness.

248. *the croaking raven . . . revenge*]
Recognized by Simpson (*Academy,*
19 Dec. 1874) as a telescoping of two
lines from the anonymous *True
Tragedy of Richard III,* 'The screeking
Raven sits croking for revenge./Whole
heads [herds] of beasts comes bellow-
ing for revenge' (MSR, 1892-3). It
is often remarked that the line is
inappropriate for the murderer. But
it is of course apt for the 'nephew to
the King' (see l. 239 LN) and sustains
the ambivalent character of Lucianus.
Claudius is simultaneously confronted
with the image of his crime and the
threat of its avenging.

249-54.] Many have maintained
that this is the speech inserted by
Hamlet, but others have denied that
his speech is to be found in the play
at all. Most critical opinion probably
agrees with Dowden, 'If we were
forced to identify Hamlet's lines, we
must needs point to the speech of
Lucianus'. A. Walker emphasizes the
sudden change of tempo, but not
everyone would accept her estimate
of the linguistic vitality of the lines
(*MLR,* XXXI, 513-17). Cf. II.ii.535-6
LN, III.ii.183-208 LN.

With Hecate's ban thrice blasted, thrice infected,
Thy natural magic and dire property
On wholesome life usurps immediately.
                    Pours the poison in the sleeper's ears.

Ham. A poisons him i'th' garden for his estate. His name's 255
    Gonzago. The story is extant, and written in very
    choice Italian. You shall see anon how the murderer
    gets the love of Gonzago's wife.

Oph. The King rises.

Ham. What, frighted with false fire?   260

Queen. How fares my lord?

Pol. Give o'er the play.

King. Give me some light. Away.

Pol. Lights, lights, lights. *Exeunt all but Hamlet and Horatio.*

Ham.   Why, let the strucken deer go weep,   265
            The hart ungalled play;
        For some must watch while some must sleep,
            Thus runs the world away.

---

252. *ban*] Q2,F; bane Q1,Q5,F4.   *infected*] F,Q1,Q3; inuected Q2.
254. *usurps*] Q2,Q1; vsurpe F.   254 S.D.] F subst.; not in Q2; exit. / Q1.
255. A] Q2; He F,Q1.   for his] Q2,Q1; for's F.   256. written] Q2; writ
F.   very] Q2; not in F.   260.] F,Q1 subst.; not in Q2.   264. Pol.] Q2;
All. F.   268. Thus] Q2,Q1; So F.

---

252. *Hecate*] the goddess who presided over magic arts; hence regarded
as the power of witchcraft and
'contriver of all harms' (*Mac.* III.v.7).
    ban] curse.
    thrice] Perhaps because Hecate was
often represented as *triformis*, with
three bodies.
    254. *usurps (on)*] takes possession
(of), steals.
    255. *for his estate*] Apparently
echoing a folklore motif. Cf. *The
Revesby Play*, 'for your estate we do
your body kill'.
    His name] i.e. the sleeper's name;
cf. ll. 233, 258. We need not suppose
(with Bullough) that victim and
murderer are both called Gonzago.
    256–7. *extant . . . Italian*] This was
probably true (cf. ll. 233–4 LN),
though Shakespeare's actual source

has not been traced.
    259. *The King rises.*] Cf. an actual
incident when, as a result of a
'scandalous representation' before
Elizabeth, 'the Queen was so angry
that she at once entered her chamber
using strong language, and the men
who held the torches . . . left [the
actors] in the dark' (Cal.S.P.,
Spanish, 1558–67, p. 375).
    260. *false fire*] a blank discharge of
weapons, fire without shot. Just so,
a play is only make-believe.
    264. *Pol.*] F obviously means to
increase the commotion.
    265–6.] This repeats the sentiment
of ll. 236–8. LN.
    265. *strucken*] A common, if irregu-
lar, form of the past pple. See Abbott
344.
    267. *watch*] stay awake.

Would not this, sir, and a forest of feathers, if the rest
of my fortunes turn Turk with me, with Provincial 270
roses on my razed shoes, get me a fellowship in a cry
of players?

Hor. Half a share.

Ham. A whole one, I.

For thou dost know, O Damon dear, 275
This realm dismantled was
Of Jove himself, and now reigns here
A very, very—pajock.

Hor. You might have rhymed.

Ham. O good Horatio, I'll take the ghost's word for a 280
thousand pound. Didst perceive?

270. with Provincial] *Q2;* with two Prouinciall *F.* 272. players] *Q2;*
Players sir *F.* 274. A whole one, I] *Q2,F;* Ay, a whole one *Hanmer;*
A whole one;—ay *Rann, conj. Malone.* 276–7.] *As Q2; divided* himselfe, /
And *F.* 278. pajock] paiock *Q2,* Paiocke *F,* Pajocke *F2;* Paicock *Q 1676;*
Pecock *Q 1695;* peacock *Pope.*

269. *this*] Surely not (as Kittredge)
Hamlet's declamation of the preceding stanza but his striking success
with the play. Cf. *WHH,* p. 197.

269–71. *feathers . . . roses*] The
flamboyance of feathers on the hat
and rosettes on the shoes characterizes the costumes of actors.

270. *turn Turk*] lit. become an
infidel; hence play false, be
treacherous.

270–1. *Provincial roses*] LN.

271. *razed*] slashed.

cry] pack (of hounds, etc.).

273. *Half a share*] A sharer in a
company of players, as distinct from
a hired man, was joint owner of its
property and participated in its
profits (see Chambers, *El. St.,* i.
352–5). The system also permitted of
half-shares, as when Henslowe (Diary,
1 June 1595) bought one for his
nephew Francis. Horatio perhaps
implies that the achievement Hamlet
boasts of is only half his (since he has
needed the collaboration of the
players).

274. *I*] There is not much point in
the interpretation 'Ay', whereas the
pronoun carries great emphasis as
insisting on Hamlet's own opinion
against Horatio's.

275–8.] 'The stanza seems . . . *too*
applicable to the political circumstances to be a quotation' (Verity).
Cf. ll. 265–6 above and, *mutatis mutan-
dis,* the Pyrrhus speech of II.ii.446 ff.
Line 279 is compatible with Hamlet's
having made this up.

275. *Damon*] A traditional shepherd
name from pastoral poetry, appropriately addressed to one who has
the ancient virtues of the golden age
before the realm was 'dismantled'.

277. *Jove himself*] A clear analogy
with Hamlet's father. Cf. III.iv.56.

278. *pajock*] Often supposed to be
for 'peacock', but more probably a
form of 'patchock', a base contemptible fellow, a savage; in which
case pronounce *padge-ock* rather than
pay-jock. LN.

279. *rhymed*] The expected rhyme-
word would be *ass.*

Hor. Very well, my lord.

Ham. Upon the talk of the poisoning?

Hor. I did very well note him.

Ham. Ah ha! Come, some music; come, the recorders.   285
    For if the King like not the comedy,
      Why then, belike he likes it not, perdie.
   Come, some music.

Enter ROSENCRANTZ *and* GUILDENSTERN.

Guild. Good my lord, vouchsafe me a word with you.

Ham. Sir, a whole history.   290

Guild. The King, sir—

Ham. Ay, sir, what of him?

Guild. Is in his retirement marvellous distempered.

Ham. With drink, sir?

Guild. No, my lord, with choler.   295

Ham. Your wisdom should show itself more richer to signify this to the doctor, for for me to put him to his purgation would perhaps plunge him into more choler.

---

285. Ah ha!] Ah ha, *Q2;* Oh, ha? *F.*   288 S.D.] *Q2; after 284 F; after 287 Johnson.*   295. with] *Q2;* rather with *F.*   297. the] *Q2;* his *F.*   for for] *Q2,F;* for *F2.*   298. more] *Q2;* farre more *F.*

283. *talk of the poisoning*] But cf. l. 255. The dialogue and not merely the S.D. at l. 254 (added in F) shows there to have been more than talk.

286. *For if . . . the comedy*] Apparently parodying *Spanish Trag.,* IV. i. 197, 'And if the world like not this tragedy . . . ' *Comedy* is both ironic and (for Hamlet) apt.

287. *perdie*] colloquial for *pardieu.*

288 S.D. *Enter . . . Guildenstern.*] It is unnecessary to see their entry as motivating Hamlet's 'Ah ha!' (Dover Wilson, following F) or, after a pause at 'belike', his impromptu conclusion of the couplet (Johnson). Their first words, however, suggest that Hamlet does not give them immediate or unsolicited attention.

293. *marvellous*] Cf. II. i. 3.

distempered] out of humour; but Hamlet, with his usual trick of deliberate misunderstanding, chooses to take it in its sense of 'drunk'. Cf. *H5* II. ii. 42, 54, 'excess of wine', 'distemper'; *Oth.* I. i. 100, 'distempering draughts'.

295. *choler*] Anger at Hamlet's behaviour seems to the court the natural explanation of the King's perturbation (*distemper*). But Hamlet takes *choler* in the sense of the physiological 'humour', i.e. bile.

298. *purgation*] the process of (1) cleansing the body by eliminating the excess humour; (2) purifying the soul from guilt by eliciting confession.

Guild. Good my lord, put your discourse into some frame, 300
    and start not so wildly from my affair.

Ham. I am tame, sir. Pronounce.

Guild. The Queen your mother, in most great affliction of
    spirit, hath sent me to you.

Ham. You are welcome.   305

Guild. Nay, good my lord, this courtesy is not of the right
    breed. If it shall please you to make me a wholesome
    answer, I will do your mother's commandment; if
    not, your pardon and my return shall be the end of
    my business.   310

Ham. Sir, I cannot.

Ros. What, my lord?

Ham. Make you a wholesome answer. My wit's diseased.
    But sir, such answer as I can make, you shall com-
    mand—or rather, as you say, my mother. Therefore 315
    no more, but to the matter. My mother, you say—

Ros. Then thus she says: your behaviour hath struck her
    into amazement and admiration.

Ham. O wonderful son, that can so stonish a mother! But
    is there no sequel at the heels of this mother's admir- 320
    ation? Impart.

Ros. She desires to speak with you in her closet ere you go
    to bed.

Ham. We shall obey, were she ten times our mother.
    Have you any further trade with us?   325

300–1.] *Prose F; 2 lines divided* frame, / And *Q2.*   301. start] *F;* stare *Q2.*
310. my] *F; not in Q2.*   312. Ros.] *Q2;* Guild. *F.*   314. answer] *Q2;*
answers *F.*   315. as you] *Q2;* you *F.*   319. stonish] *Q2;* astonish *F.*
321. Impart.] *Q2; not in F.*

---

300. *frame*] systematic form. Cf.
Meas. v.i.61, 'Her madness hath the
oddest frame of sense'.

307. *breed*] (1) species, kind; (2)
breeding, training in manners.

    wholesome] rational.

309. *pardon*] permission to depart.
Cf. i.ii.56; *Ado* ii.i.307.

318. *admiration*] astonishment. Cf.
i.ii.192.

322. *to speak with you*] Cf. iii.i.183–7.

Hamlet's 'behaviour' (l. 317) at the
play has merely provided the convenient occasion for what was already
planned.

325. *trade*] business. Although, as
Kittredge says, the word does not
accuse them of mercenariness, it puts
an end to any pretence of friendship;
and it coincides with Hamlet's use
of the royal plural for the only time
in the play.

Ros. My lord, you once did love me.

Ham. And do still, by these pickers and stealers.

Ros. Good my lord, what is your cause of distemper? You
    do surely bar the door upon your own liberty if you
    deny your griefs to your friend.   330

Ham. Sir, I lack advancement.

Ros. How can that be, when you have the voice of the
    King himself for your succession in Denmark?

Ham. Ay, sir, but while the grass grows—the proverb is
    something musty.   335

Enter the Players *with recorders.*

O, the recorders. Let me see one.—To withdraw
    with you, why do you go about to recover the wind
    of me, as if you would drive me into a toil?

Guild. O my lord, if my duty be too bold, my love is too
    unmannerly.   340

Ham. I do not well understand that. Will you play upon
    this pipe?

327. And] *Q2;* So I *F.*   329. surely] *Q2;* freely *F.*   upon]*Q2;* of *F.*
334. sir] *Q2; not in F.*   335 S.D.] *Q2 (after 333); Enter one with a
Recorder F.*   336. recorders] *Q2;* Recorder *F.*   one] *Q2; not in F.*

327. *pickers and stealers*] i.e. hands.
From the Church catechism, 'To keep
my hands from picking and stealing'.

329. *bar the door . . . liberty*] I do not
(with Dover Wilson and Kittredge)
see this as a threat that Hamlet will
be shut up as a madman. Rather it
recalls the idea of his being self-
imprisoned (see II.ii.250–3). It was
a recognized function of a friend that
you could unburden your heart to
him.

332–3. *you have the voice of the King*]
Cf. I.ii.108–9. By contrast Hamlet
seems sometimes to be regarded as
heir in his own right: see I.iii.20–4,
and perhaps III.i.154.

334. *the proverb*] 'While the grass
grows, the horse starves' (Tilley
G 423). Cf. ll. 93–4, 'I eat the air'.

335. *musty*] Hence too stale to
quote. Kittredge points to it in
Petrus de Vineis (*d.* 1249).

335 S.D. *the Players*] The actors of
course. The notion that this might
refer to special recorder-'players'
would not need refuting if it had not
been so strangely persistent.

336. *To withdraw*] to speak in
private.

337–8. *recover the wind . . . toil*]
Conflicting explanations have often
left the hunting metaphor obscure.
To *recover the wind* is to get to wind-
ward. The quarry is allowed to
scent the hunter, so that it will run
in the opposite direction and into the
net (*toil*).

339–40. *if my duty . . . unmannerly*] He
makes a merit of offence: if my efforts
are too obtrusive, it is my love that
makes me gauche.

341. *I do not . . . that.*] i.e. how love
can be unmannerly, implying that
if unmannerly it cannot be love.

Guild. My lord, I cannot.

Ham. I pray you.

Guild. Believe me, I cannot. 　　　　　　　　　　345

Ham. I do beseech you.

Guild. I know no touch of it, my lord.

Ham. It is as easy as lying. Govern these ventages with
　　your fingers and thumb, give it breath with your
　　mouth, and it will discourse most eloquent music. 350
　　Look you, these are the stops.

Guild. But these cannot I command to any utterance of
　　harmony. I have not the skill.

Ham. Why, look you now, how unworthy a thing you
　　make of me. You would play upon me, you would 355
　　seem to know my stops, you would pluck out the
　　heart of my mystery, you would sound me from my
　　lowest note to the top of my compass; and there is
　　much music, excellent voice, in this little organ, yet
　　cannot you make it speak. 'Sblood, do you think I 360
　　am easier to be played on than a pipe? Call me what
　　instrument you will, though you fret me, you cannot
　　play upon me.

Enter POLONIUS.

348. It is] *Q2;* 'Tis *F.*　　　349. fingers] *Q2;* finger *F.*　　　thumb] *F;* the
vmber *Q2;* the thumb *Q3.*　　　350. eloquent] *Q2;* excellent *F.*
358. the top of] *F;* not in *Q2.*　　360. speak] *Q2;* not in *F.*　　'Sblood] *Q2;*
Why *F;* Zownds *Q1.*　　think] *Q2,Q1;* thinke, that *F.*　　362. fret me,]
This edn; fret me not, *Q2;* can fret me, *F;* can frett mee, yet *Q1.*
363 S.D.] *As Capell; after 364 Q2,F.*

348. *as easy as lying*] I accept from
Kittredge, but cannot confirm, that
this was proverbial and hence that
lying is not to be emphasized. The
casual allusion may be more effective
than a direct accusation.

349. *fingers and thumb*] The correct
reading is indicated by the nature
of the recorder, which had seven holes
for the *fingers* and one at the back for
the *thumb.*

359. *organ*] Though the word could
signify, then as now, the instrument
of many pipes, it was commonly
used for a single-pipe instrument.

362-3. *fret . . . play upon me*] Via
'what instrument you will' Hamlet
switches from wind to stringed
instrument for the sake of the pun on
fret: (1) equip with frets (i.e. the
ridges on some stringed instruments
which mark the places for the fingers);
(2) irritate. Cf. 'There's no music
without frets' (Dekker, *Gull's Horn-
Book*, Grosart, ii.254). Eds. almost
invariably retain *can*, though this is
surely an intrusion in F (and Q1)
rather than an omission from Q2.
Hamlet not merely *can* be but *is*
being fretted, and the musical

God bless you, sir.

Pol. My lord, the Queen would speak with you, and 365
presently.

Ham. Do you see yonder cloud that's almost in shape of
a camel?

Pol. By th' mass and 'tis—like a camel indeed.

Ham. Methinks it is like a weasel.   370

Pol. It is backed like a weasel.

Ham. Or like a whale.

Pol. Very like a whale.

Ham. Then I will come to my mother by and by.—
[*Aside*] They fool me to the top of my bent.—I will 375
come by and by.

Pol. I will say so.   *Exit.*

Ham. 'By and by' is easily said.—Leave me, friends.
                                    [*Exeunt all but Hamlet.*]
'Tis now the very witching time of night,
When churchyards yawn and hell itself breathes out 380
Contagion to this world. Now could I drink hot blood,

---

367. yonder] *Q2,Q1; that F.   of*] *Q2,Q1; like F.   369.* mass] *Q2,F4;*
Misse *F.   'tis—] Jennens;* 'tis, *Q2;* it's *F;* T''is *Q1.   370, 371.* a weasel]
Q2,F,Q1; an ouzle *Pope.   371.* backed] *Q2,F,Q1;* black *Q3.   372.* whale.]
Q2,Q1; Whale? *F.   374. Ham.] F,Q1; not in Q2 (except c.w.).   I* will] *Q2;*
will I *F;* i'le *Q1.   374–8.] Prose Pope; lines ending* by, | by, | said, *Q2;*
ending by: | bent. | so. | Friends: *F.   375. Aside] Staunton; to Hor. | Capell.*
377, 378. *Pol., Ham.] F; not in Q2.   377* S.D.] *F; not in Q2.*
378. Leave me, friends.] *F; after 376 Q2.   378* S.D.] *Steevens[2] subst.;* Exe.
Rowe.   380. breathes] *F;* breakes *Q2.*

---

paradox is the greater if you actually
fret the instrument and still cannot
play it. Modern eds. who read *yet*
with Q1 assume that the non-
sensical *not* of Q2 is a misreading of it.
This is also to assume, however, that
the two good texts are each in error
independently.

364. *God bless you, sir.*] W. J.
Lawrence (*TLS*, 1930, p. 241) argues
that for this to have 'rationality' it
needs to be taken as accompanying
the return of the recorder rather than
as a greeting to Polonius. But would
Hamlet seriously address a player so,
and why should it be rational when

the following speeches are not?

366. *presently*] at once.

367–73.] LN.

374. *by and by*] This has its modern
sense, as Dover Wilson, against many
other commentators, recognizes. Cf.
v.ii.297.

375. *the top of my bent*] the height
of my capacity, the utmost limit I can
go to. Cf. II.ii.30.

379–83.] LN.

379. *witching*] associated with witchcraft. It may not be irrelevant to
recall that the rites of the witches'
sabbath included the drinking of
human blood (cf. l. 381).

And do such bitter business as the day
Would quake to look on. Soft, now to my mother.
O heart, lose not thy nature. Let not ever
The soul of Nero enter this firm bosom;   385
Let me be cruel, not unnatural.
I will speak daggers to her, but use none.
My tongue and soul in this be hypocrites:
How in my words somever she be shent,
To give them seals never my soul consent.   *Exit.*   390

[SCENE III]

Enter KING, ROSENCRANTZ, *and* GUILDENSTERN.

King. I like him not, nor stands it safe with us
    To let his madness range. Therefore prepare you.

382. bitter business as the] *F;* busines as the bitter *Q2.*   383. Soft, now] *Q2;*
Soft now, *F.*   387. daggers] *F,Q1;* dagger *Q2.*   389. somever] *Q2,F;*
soever *Q5.*   390. never my soul] *Q2,F;* never, my soul, *Capell.*   390 S.D.]
Q2,Q1; not in F.

                              Scene III

SCENE III] *Capell.*

382. *bitter . . . day*] In defence of Q2
Charney (*Style in 'Hamlet'*, p. 10)
suggests that 'the bitter day' is
Doomsday. But the antithesis is
between *day* and *night* (l. 379).
Revenge is 'bitter' in *Wint.* I.ii.457,
IV.iv.762.

384. *nature*] natural feeling, filial
affection. Cf. I.v.81. The same
'nature' as demands revenge requires
him to spare his mother (cf. I.v.85–6).

385. *Nero*] who put to death his
mother Agrippina, who had
poisoned her husband, the emperor
Claudius.

387. *speak daggers*] As he does. Cf.
III.iv.95. The image is anticipated in
Ado II.i.220 ('She speaks poniards,
and every word stabs') and *3H6*
II.i.96–9.

389. *shent*] reproved, censured.
This past pple. was still common

though the verb *shend* had otherwise
fallen into disuse.

390. *seals*] It is the seal that
authenticates a document and ratifies
its words. But Hamlet does not mean
to put his harsh words into action.

never my soul consent] subjunctive
(like l. 388) rather than imperative,
with *my soul* nominative rather than
(as often taken) vocative.

                    Scene III

1. *nor stands it safe*] The King,
having learnt from the play that his
crime is known, has every reason to
fear Hamlet's revenge; and though
the others cannot see what he sees,
there was still ample in the play and
in Hamlet's comments on it to
persuade them that the King is in
danger from his nephew.

I your commission will forthwith dispatch,
And he to England shall along with you.
The terms of our estate may not endure   5
Hazard so near us as doth hourly grow
Out of his brows.

Guild.   We will ourselves provide.
Most holy and religious fear it is
To keep those many many bodies safe
That live and feed upon your Majesty.   10

Ros. The single and peculiar life is bound
With all the strength and armour of the mind
To keep itself from noyance; but much more
That spirit upon whose weal depends and rests
The lives of many. The cess of majesty   15
Dies not alone, but like a gulf doth draw
What's near it with it. Or it is a massy wheel
Fix'd on the summit of the highest mount,
To whose huge spokes ten thousand lesser things

6. near us] *Q5;* neer's *Q2;* dangerous *F.*   7. brows] *Q2;* Lunacies *F;*
Lunes *Theobald;* brawls *(later edns* brows) *Wilson;* braues *Parrott-Craig, conj.*
Wilson.   14. weal] *Q2;* spirit *F.*   15. cess] *Q2;* cease *F.*   17. Or it is]
Q2; It is *F;* 'tis *Dyce* ²; O, 'tis *Wilson.*   18. summit] *Rowe;* somnet *Q2,F.*

3-4.] The King is proceeding with
the plan first formed at III.i.171. But
there is no indication, as Bradley
(p. 171) and others have supposed,
that the plan as yet includes the
arrangements for Hamlet's death
which we hear of at IV.iii.66-8,
v.ii.18-25. See A. L. French, *ES,*
XLVII, 28-30.

3. *dispatch*] speedily deal with.

5. *our estate*] The royal plural as in
l. 1: my position as king.

7. *brows*] What grows out of the
brows is generated in the head, i.e.
plots, contrivances. LN.

provide] equip, make ready. Cf.
AYL I.iii.83 ('provide yourself').

11. *peculiar*] of concern only to the
individual possessor of it.

13. *noyance*] harm.

14-15. *That spirit . . . lives of many.*]
Cf. Bacon on sovereign princes,
'Themselves are not only themselves,

but their good and evil is at the peril
of the public fortune' ('Of Wisdom
for a Man's Self').

14. *depends and rests*] The singular
verb is common when the plural
subject follows. Abbott 335.

15. *cess*] decease. *OED sb.*². Cf.
All's W. v.iii.72, 'in me, O nature,
cesse'.

16. *gulf*] whirlpool.

17. *Or it is*] Unless we are to achieve
metrical regularity, without textual
authority, by contracting to '*tis*, it
seems preferable to retain Q2's
alexandrine.

wheel] Pictorial representations
often show the king on the top of
Fortune's wheel with many 'lesser'
figures clinging to its periphery.

18. *summit*] Q2,F suggest that
Shakespeare spelt *sommet*. The word
was similarly misread at I.iv.70.

Are mortis'd and adjoin'd, which when it falls,   20
Each small annexment, petty consequence,
Attends the boist'rous ruin. Never alone
Did the King sigh, but with a general groan.
King. Arm you, I pray you, to this speedy voyage,
For we will fetters put about this fear   25
Which now goes too free-footed.
Ros.   We will haste us.
Exeunt Rosencrantz and Guildenstern.

Enter POLONIUS.

Pol. My lord, he's going to his mother's closet.
Behind the arras I'll convey myself
To hear the process. I'll warrant she'll tax him home,
And as you said—and wisely was it said—   30
'Tis meet that some more audience than a mother,
Since nature makes them partial, should o'erhear
The speech of vantage. Fare you well, my liege.
I'll call upon you ere you go to bed,
And tell you what I know.
King.   Thanks, dear my lord.   35
Exit Polonius.

---

22. ruin] *F;* raine *Q2.*   23. with] *F; not in Q2.*   25. about] *Q2;* vpon
F.   26. *Ros.*] *Q2; Both. F.*   35 S.D.] *Q2 (after* know); *not in F.*

20. *falls*] Kittredge sees here the
abandonment of the metaphor of the
wheel and takes this to reflect a
defect in the speaker, not the poet.
But cf. the break-up of Fortune's
wheel at II.ii.491.
22. *boist'rous*] Retaining the sense
of 'massy' (bulky, cumbrous, *OED* 3)
along with the suggestion of violent
tumult appropriate to large-scale
destruction.
24. *Arm*] = *provide,* l. 7; get ready,
as at *MND* I.i.117.
27. *he's going . . . closet*] Cf. III.i.184–
7, III.ii.322–3, 365–6, 383.
28. *convey*] This word often has the
suggestion of furtiveness or stealth.
Cf. *3H6* III.iii.160, 'thy sly conveyance'.
29. *process*] proceedings.

warrant] Q2 as well as F has the
uncontracted form in contrast to
I.ii.243, III.iv.5. But Shakespeare's
ms. need not have been consistent,
and whatever the spelling, the pronunciation *war'nt* would be almost
inevitable in familiar dialogue.
30. *as you said*] The idea in fact
originated with Polonius. See III.
i.186–7.
33. *of vantage*] in addition. Cf.
Oth. IV.iii.82 ('as many to th'
vantage', i.e. as many more), and see
OED vantage 2b, c. So Schmidt,
Onions. Alternatively, but less probably, from a position of advantage
(Dowden), 'from the vantage-ground
of concealment' (Abbott 165); cf.
Mac. I.vi.7, 'coign of vantage'.

O, my offence is rank, it smells to heaven;
It hath the primal eldest curse upon't—
A brother's murder. Pray can I not,
Though inclination be as sharp as will,
My stronger guilt defeats my strong intent,   40
And, like a man to double business bound,
I stand in pause where I shall first begin,
And both neglect. What if this cursed hand
Were thicker than itself with brother's blood,
Is there not rain enough in the sweet heavens   45
To wash it white as snow? Whereto serves mercy
But to confront the visage of offence?
And what's in prayer but this twofold force,
To be forestalled ere we come to fall
Or pardon'd being down? Then I'll look up.   50
My fault is past—but O, what form of prayer

39. will,] *Q2;* will: *F.*   50. pardon'd] *F;* pardon *Q2.*

37. *primal eldest curse*] Genesis iv. 11–12. This reference to Cain is ironically anticipated at 1.ii. 105 and echoed at v.i. 75–6.

39. *Though inclination . . . will*] The syntax allows this to be taken with what precedes or what follows. Objections to it as tautology are not valid. By determination or force of *will* a man may overcome a natural *inclination*. Here the two combine. Boswell pertinently cites Locke, *Human Understanding*, II.xxi.30 ('the will is perfectly distinguished from desire').

41–3. *double business . . . both neglect*] *Bound* is usually interpreted as the adj. from M.E. *boun* < O.N. *búinn* (*OED* bound *ppl. a.*[1]), as in 'bound' for a destination, rather than as the past pple. of *bind*. But the meanings of these etymologically different words cannot be kept distinct. There is a 'double' objective, but also a dual obligation. The analogy, however, seems less than perfect: the choice is not between *two* courses but between pursuing or refraining from *one*. What nevertheless the analogy, and indeed

the whole speech, brings out is that the King does not refrain through deliberate choice but through indecision. It is not, I think, generally remarked that Claudius himself presents an instance of Hamlet's generalization at III.i.84–8.

45. *rain*] with which mercy is compared by Portia (*Mer.V.* IV.i. 180) following Ecclesiasticus xxxv. 20. The scriptural echo combines with another of Psalm li. 7, 'wash me . . . whiter than snow'; Isaiah i. 18.

50–1. *I'll look up. My fault is past*] With the exception of Dover Wilson and the most recent Americans, eds. have traditionally followed F in linking these two sentences, as though Claudius's resolve to 'look up' were due to his fault's being past instead of to his confidence in the efficacy of prayer. The 'twofold force' of prayer once recognized – to prevent or forgive sin – his admission that his own case requires the second begins the new train of thought: the fact that his fault is already committed determines the 'form' that his prayer must take.

Can serve my turn? 'Forgive me my foul murder?'
That cannot be, since I am still possess'd
Of those effects for which I did the murder—
My crown, mine own ambition, and my queen.   55
May one be pardon'd and retain th'offence?
In the corrupted currents of this world
Offence's gilded hand may shove by justice,
And oft 'tis seen the wicked prize itself
Buys out the law. But 'tis not so above: 60
There is no shuffling, there the action lies
In his true nature, and we ourselves compell'd
Even to the teeth and forehead of our faults
To give in evidence. What then? What rests?
Try what repentance can. What can it not?   65
Yet what can it, when one cannot repent?
O wretched state! O bosom black as death!
O limed soul, that struggling to be free

58. shove] *F;* showe *Q2.*

56. *th'offence*] i.e. the benefits of the offence (by *retaining* which he perpetuates the *offence*).

57. *currents*] courses of events; perhaps playing on the sense of 'currencies'.

58. *gilded*] gold-bearing, both as acquiring ill-gotten gains and as bestowing them in bribes; with a play on *gilt, guilt* (for which cf. *Mac.* II.ii.56–7; *2H4* IV.v.129; etc.).

shove by] push aside. For a possible (but not clearly applicable) metaphor from the game of shove-groat (an ancestor of shove-halfpenny), beginning in *currents* (coinages) and continuing through *gilded, shove, prize, shuffling,* see T. W. Ross in *Anglia,* LXXXIV, 173–6.

61. *There*] (emphatic) above, in heaven.

shuffling] evasion by trickery, sleight-of-hand. Cf. IV.vii.136. A variant of *shovelling,* the word recalls *shove* (l. 58), in order to enforce the contrast

between 'this world' and 'above'.

the action lies] the deed is exposed to view, with a quibble on the legal sense of both words. By a further quibble, that paradoxically *lies* which shows its *true* nature.

62. *his*] its. Cf. I.i.40n.

and . . . compell'd] For this construction, see I.iii.62n.

63. *to the teeth and forehead*] in face-to-face confrontation.

64. *in*] adv. with *give* (not prep. with *evidence*).

rests] remains (as an alternative).

65. *can*] Absolute use. Cf. IV.vii.83; *Lr* IV.iv.8 ('What can man's wisdom . . . ?'); etc.

68–9. *limed soul . . . engag'd*] The practice of catching birds with birdlime, a sticky substance smeared on twigs, affords a frequent metaphor in Shakespeare. The idea here was proverbial. Cf. Thos. Wilson, *Discourse upon Usury,* 'Like as a bird, being taken with lime twigs, the more she

Art more engag'd! Help, angels! Make assay.
Bow, stubborn knees; and heart with strings of steel,   70
Be soft as sinews of the new-born babe.
All may be well.   *He kneels.*

                    Enter HAMLET.

Ham. Now might I do it pat, now a is a-praying.
    And now I'll do't.   [*Draws his sword.*]
                    And so a goes to heaven;
And so am I reveng'd. That would be scann'd: 75
A villain kills my father, and for that
I, his sole son, do this same villain send
To heaven.
Why, this is hire and salary, not revenge.

69. Help, angels!] *Theobald;* Helpe Angels, *F;* helpe Angels *Q2.*   70. Bow,]
Theobald; Bowe *Q2,F.*   72 S.D. *He kneels.] Q1;* not in *Q2,F.*   73. pat] *F;*
but *Q2.*   a] *Q2;* he *F.*   a-praying] *Q2;* praying *F.*   74 S.D.]
Capell (subst.).   74. a] *Q2;* he *F.*   75. reveng'd.] reueng'd: *F,Q1;*
reuendge, *Q2;* revenged, *Q4;* reveng'd? *Q5.*   77. sole] *Q2;* foule *F.*
78–9.] *As Q2; one line F.*   79. Why] *Q2;* Oh *F.*   hire and salary] *F;* base
and silly *Q2;* a benefit *Q1;* bait and salary *Wilson.*

struggleth to get out, the more she
is limed and entangled fast' (ed.
Tawney, p. 227); and other instances
in Tilley B 380. Battenhouse (*Shakespn.
Trag.*, pp. 377–8) shows its recurrence
in Augustine's *Confessions* to describe
the *death-like* state of the soul which
entanglement in worldly pleasures
keeps from God. *engag'd,* entangled.

69. *Make assay.*] Many eds. take
(and Kittredge asserts) this to be
addressed to the 'limed soul', presumably on the assumption that it
would be inappropriate for 'angels'.
But an *assay* is more than a trial or
attempt. It is a putting forth of all
one's powers (cf. *Mac.* IV.iii.143), a
concerted effort, sometimes a military
enterprise (cf. II.ii.71) or even an
actual onslaught (as in *H5* I.ii.151;
and characteristically in *FQ*, as at
v.iv.23). See *OED* Assay *sb.* 13–15.
Sisson justly explains that 'Claudius
calls upon the angels to help him . . .
in the struggle' (*NR*), yet appears to
regard *make assay* as an infinitive

complement of *Help* instead of, more
naturally, as a parallel imperative.

74 S.D. *Draws his sword.*] That the
sword, sheathed again at l. 88, was
drawn at this point, appears from
the wording of Q1: 'Ay so, come
forth and work thy last'.

75. *reveng'd.*] 'I am inclined to think
that the note of interrogation put
after "revenged" in a late quarto
is right' (Bradley, p. 134n.).

That would be scann'd] Either (1)
having stated his conclusion, Hamlet
recognizes that 'that requires to be
looked into' (Verity) and proceeds to
examine accordingly; or (2) it being
premised that he does as l. 74 proposes, 'that would be interpreted (as
follows)'. (1) is almost universally
accepted: on the sense of *would* see
Abbott 329, and for abundant demonstration in Bacon, *Studier i Modern
Språkvetenskap*, XVIII, 133–44. But (2)
has the support of *OED* (see scan *v.* 4).

79. *hire and salary*] On the variants,
LN.

A took my father grossly, full of bread,   80
With all his crimes broad blown, as flush as May;
And how his audit stands who knows save heaven?
But in our circumstance and course of thought
'Tis heavy with him. And am I then reveng'd,
To take him in the purging of his soul,   85
When he is fit and season'd for his passage?
No.
Up, sword, and know thou a more horrid hent:
When he is drunk asleep, or in his rage,
Or in th'incestuous pleasure of his bed,   90
At game a-swearing, or about some act
That has no relish of salvation in't,

---

80. A] *Q2;* He *F,Q1.*   81. flush] *Q2;* fresh *F.*   86–7.] *As Q2;*
one line F.   89. drunk asleep] *F;* drunk-asleep *Johnson;* drunke, a sleepe *Q2.*
91. game a-swearing] *Q2,Q1 subst.;* gaming, swearing *F.*

---

80. *grossly, full of bread*] in the full
indulgence of sensual appetites, not
purified (as by fasting), hence un-
prepared for death. Cf. Ezekiel
xvi.49, 'the iniquity of . . . Sodom,
pride, fulness of bread . . .'

81. *broad blown*] in full bloom.
Cf. i.v.76, 'the blossoms of my sin'.
Note the conception of sin as natural
to growing life.

flush] lusty, full of life. Cf. *Ant.*
i.iv.52, 'flush youth revolt'.

83. *in our circumstance*] as it appears
to our limited earthly vision.

86. *season'd*] matured (cf. i.iii.81),
hence thoroughly prepared.

88. *know*] meet with, have experience of.

hent] Best taken as a variant spelling
of *hint*, occasion, opportunity. But
since the noun apparently derives
from the verb *hent*, seize, lay hold of,
most commentators explain *hent* here
as an act of seizing, while differing
on whether it refers to Hamlet's
seizing of the sword (Kittredge) or
the sword's laying hold of the King
(Johnson). *OED's* alternative suggestion of 'intention, design' seems

insufficiently attested and also less
appropriate: what is to be 'more
horrid' is not the purpose but the
occasion of executing it.

89–95. *When he is drunk . . . whereto
it goes.*] On this desire to effect
the King's damnation, LN.

89–90. *drunk asleep . . . his bed*] Cf.
Beaumont and Fletcher, *Four Plays
in One* (*Death*, vi.120–1), 'Take him
dead drunk now without repentance,
His lechery enseam'd upon him'.
Though probably deriving from
Hamlet, this at least shows the
currency of the sentiment. In *Thierry
and Theodoret* (i.i.137) the worst fate
Brunhalt can propose for her hated
son is to 'kill him drunk or doubtful'
(i.e. unbelieving). For the King's
drinking see i.iv.8ff., i.ii.125n.

91. *At game a-swearing*] Cf. *White
Devil* (v.i.70–2), where among the
deaths Lodovico would have enjoyed
inflicting on Brachiano is to have
poisoned the handle of his racket,
'That while he had been bandying
at tennis, He might have sworn
himself to hell, and struck His soul
into the hazard'.

Then trip him, that his heels may kick at heaven
And that his soul may be as damn'd and black
As hell, whereto it goes. My mother stays.   95
This physic but prolongs thy sickly days.   *Exit.*
King. My words fly up, my thoughts remain below.
Words without thoughts never to heaven go.   *Exit.*

[SCENE IV]

Enter QUEEN *and* POLONIUS.

Pol. A will come straight. Look you lay home to him,
Tell him his pranks have been too broad to bear with
And that your Grace hath screen'd and stood between
Much heat and him. I'll silence me even here.
Pray you be round.
Queen.   I'll war'nt you, fear me not.   5

Scene IV

SCENE IV] *Capell.*   1. A] *Q2;* He *F.*   4. silence] *Q2,F;* 'sconce *Hanmer;*
shrowde *Q1.*   even] *Q2;* e'ene *F.*   5. Pray you be round.] *Q2;* Pray
you be round with him. / *Ham. within.* Mother, mother, mother. *F; Ham.*
Mother, mother. *Q1.*   war'nt] *Wilson;* warrant *F;* wait *Q2.*

93. *kick at heaven*] The metaphor
suggests both that Claudius will be
spurning heaven and that he will be
plunging head first (into hell).
  96. *This physic*] Prayer. Cf. 'purging' (l. 85).
  97. *My words . . . below.*] Cf. Angelo,
Meas. II. iv. 1–7.

Scene IV

S.D. *Enter Queen*] In her closet: see
III. ii. 322–3, III. iii. 27. It is hard to
know why producers nowadays put
this scene – so incongruously – in
the Queen's bedroom.
  1. *lay home to him*] = 'tax him
home', III. iii. 29.
  2. *pranks*] acts outraging order and
decency. Cf. *Tw.N.* IV. i. 54, where
Olivia refers to the 'pranks' of 'this

ruffian' Toby; *1H6* III. i. 15, 'thy
audacious wickedness, Thy lewd,
pestiferous, and dissentious pranks'.
This word sometimes translates L.
scelus or *facinus* (*OED*).
  broad] unrestrained, gross.
  4. *I'll silence me*] Ironically he does
not (l. 22) and so meets his death.
  5. *round*] forthright, plain-spoken.
F *with him* is idiomatic but has given
eds. much trouble with the metre
and is more like an addition in
recollection of III. i. 185 than an
omission from *Q2.* For *round* used
absolutely cf. *OED* round *a.* 13b.
The calling *within* in F is a fairly
obvious stage accretion: cf. IV. ii. 1
and see *SB*, XIII, 34–5.
  war'nt] *Q2 wait* appears to be the
misreading of an abbreviation in the
copy. Cf. I. ii. 243, II. i. 39 and n.

Withdraw, I hear him coming.

> [*Polonius hides behind the arras.*]

Enter HAMLET.

Ham. Now, mother, what's the matter?

Queen. Hamlet, thou hast thy father much offended.

Ham. Mother, you have my father much offended.

Queen. Come, come, you answer with an idle tongue.   10

Ham. Go, go, you question with a wicked tongue.

Queen. Why, how now, Hamlet?

Ham.   What's the matter now?

Queen. Have you forgot me?

Ham.   No, by the rood, not so.
You are the Queen, your husband's brother's wife,
And, would it were not so, you are my mother.   15

Queen. Nay, then I'll set those to you that can speak.

Ham. Come, come, and sit you down, you shall not budge.
You go not till I set you up a glass
Where you may see the inmost part of you.

Queen. What wilt thou do? Thou wilt not murder me?   20
Help, ho!

Pol. [*behind the arras*] What ho! Help!

Ham. How now? A rat! Dead for a ducat, dead.

> [*Thrusts his rapier through the arras.*]

---

6 S.D. *Polonius . . . arras.*] *Rowe* (subst.).   *Enter Hamlet.*] *F; after* round (*l.
5*) *Q2.*   11. a wicked] *Q2;* an idle *F.*   15. And, would it were not so,]
Capell; And (would it were not so) *Pope;* And would it were not so, *Q2;* But
would you were not so. *F.*   16. Nay, then] *Q2,F;* Nay then, *Dowden.*
19. inmost] *F;* most *Q2.*   21. Help] *Q2,Q1;* Helpe, helpe *F.*   22. S.D.]
Rowe.   22. Help] *Q2;* helpe, helpe, helpe *F;* Helpe for the Queene *Q1.*
23 S.D.] *This edn; making a Pass at the Arras | Capell; Killes Polonius. F.*

---

6 S.D. *hides behind the arras*] Cf.
III.iii.28, IV.i.9. Q1 has here 'I'le
shrowde my selfe behinde the Arras'.
In Belleforest the spy hid under a
quilt (*loudier*), on which Amleth
jumped.

14. *husband's brother's wife*] 'A
woman may not marry with her . . .
husband's brother' (*Book of Common
Prayer*). Cf. I.ii.8, 157 and nn.

16–20. *Nay . . . murder me?*] Evi-

dently the Queen makes as if to
depart and is forcibly prevented
by Hamlet. The accompanying action
is suggested by Q1 at IV.i.8, 'then
he throwes and tosses me about'.

23. *A rat!*] Not in Belleforest, yet
found in the 1608 translation, where
'he cried, A rat, a rat' is apparently a
recollection of the play. Cf. IV.i. 10. See
Intro., pp. 89–90. Rats proverbially
cause their own deaths by drawing

Pol. [*behind*] O, I am slain.

Queen. O me, what hast thou done?

Ham.   Nay, I know not.   25

    Is it the King?

          [*Lifts up the arras and discovers Polonius, dead.*]

Queen. O what a rash and bloody deed is this!

Ham. A bloody deed. Almost as bad, good mother,

    As kill a king and marry with his brother.

Queen. As kill a king?

Ham.   Ay, lady, it was my word.—   30

    Thou wretched, rash, intruding fool, farewell.

    I took thee for thy better. Take thy fortune:

    Thou find'st to be too busy is some danger.—

    Leave wringing of your hands. Peace, sit you down,

    And let me wring your heart; for so I shall   35

    If it be made of penetrable stuff,

    If damned custom have not braz'd it so,

    That it be proof and bulwark against sense.

Queen. What have I done, that thou dar'st wag thy tongue

    In noise so rude against me?

Ham.   Such an act   40

    That blurs the grace and blush of modesty,

24. *behind*] *Capell.*   25–6. Nay . . . King?] *As Capell; one line Q2,F.*
26 S.D.] *Wilson; lifts up the Arras, and draws forth Polonius | Capell; after 30, Lifts
up the arras, and sees Polonius. | Dyce.*   30. it was] *Q2;* 'twas *F.*   32. better]
Q2,Q1; Betters *F.*   37. braz'd] brasd *Q2,* braz'd *F;* brass'd *Globe.*
38. be] *Q2;* is *F.*

attention to themselves. Cf. Taverner, *Proverbs* (1552, fol. 54), 'Rats be wont to make . . . a noisome crying . . . to which noise many men hearkening forthwith though it be in the dark night throw at them and so kill them'.

  for a ducat] Not a bet that he *is* dead but the price for making him dead. Cf. for two pins.

  23 S.D.] See IV.i.9–12.

  29. *As kill a king?*] Nothing said by the Ghost has accused the Queen of complicity in the murder. Her reaction manifests her innocence, but the text hardly entitles us to infer that Hamlet is deliberately putting it to the test. Rather, he does not distinguish the elements of killing and marrying in what he apparently regards as one composite crime. Cf. III.ii.179–80.

  37. *damned custom*] Cf. ll. 163–72 below.

  braz'd] converted to, or covered with, brass.

  38. *proof*] impenetrable, like proof (i.e. tested and certified) armour. Cf. II.ii.486n.

  sense] feeling, 'perceptive sensibility' (Dover Wilson). Cf. ll. 71–4 below.

Calls virtue hypocrite, takes off the rose
From the fair forehead of an innocent love
And sets a blister there, makes marriage vows
As false as dicers' oaths—O, such a deed   45
As from the body of contraction plucks
The very soul, and sweet religion makes
A rhapsody of words. Heaven's face does glow
O'er this solidity and compound mass
With tristful visage, as against the doom,   50
Is thought-sick at the act.

Queen.   Ay me, what act
That roars so loud and thunders in the index?
Ham. Look here upon this picture, and on this,
The counterfeit presentment of two brothers.

---

44. sets] *Q2;* makes *F.*   48. does] *Q2;* doth *F.*   48–9. glow O'er] *Q2*
(Ore)*;* glow, Yea *F;* glow, And *Wilson.*   50. tristful] *F;* heated *Q2.*
51. Is] *Q2,F;* 'Tis *Pope.*   Ay] *Q2,F;* Ah *Malone.*   51–2. Ay me . . .
index?] *divided as Q2; as prose F.*   53. *Ham.*] *F; before 52 Q2.*

42–8. *takes off the rose . . . of words*]
This passage is impossible to reconcile
with the contention that the play
does not present the Queen as having
been unfaithful during King Hamlet's
life. Cf. l. 66 below, 'leave to feed'
and l. 75, *choice;* v.ii.64; i.v.42 ff.
and LN; *WHH*, pp. 293–4.

42. *rose*] emblem of ideal love.

44. *a blister*] Whores were tra-
ditionally branded on the forehead.
Cf. IV.v.118–19. In *Meas.* II.iii.12
Juliet has 'blister'd her report'.

46–7. *from the body . . . soul*] Reduces
to an empty form not merely the
marriage-contract but *contraction*, the
very principle of contracting solemn
agreements of which the marriage-
contract is the type.

48. *A rhapsody*] (of words) a confused and meaningless heap. So,
substantially, Cotgrave. Cf. Florio's
Montaigne, I.25 (Tudor Trans.,
i.151), 'those mingle-mangles of
many kindes of stuffe, or as the
Grecians call them *Rapsodies*'.

48–51. *Heaven's face . . . the act.*]
The Queen's act is here made to
epitomize the guilt of the world –
whether, with Q2, we take what 'is
thought-sick' at it to be heaven, or,
with F, the world itself (*this solidity
and compound mass*). LN. *as against the
doom*, as if in anticipation of the day
of judgment (which is prophetically
associated with signs in the heavens).
thought-sick, sick with sorrowful contemplation or mental distress. Cf.
III.i.85 ('sicklied o'er with . . .
thought') and n.

52. *index*] table of contents at the
beginning of a book, hence any
prefatory matter.

53. *this picture, . . . this*] The pictures
are presumably produced by Hamlet.
LN.

54. *counterfeit presentment*] representation in an image or portrait. The
noun *counterfeit* for a portrait (e.g.
Mer.V. III.ii.115, 'Fair Portia's
counterfeit') was in regular use.

See what a grace was seated on this brow,   55
Hyperion's curls, the front of Jove himself,
An eye like Mars to threaten and command,
A station like the herald Mercury
New-lighted on a heaven-kissing hill,
A combination and a form indeed   60
Where every god did seem to set his seal
To give the world assurance of a man.
This was your husband. Look you now what follows.
Here is your husband, like a mildew'd ear
Blasting his wholesome brother. Have you eyes?   65
Could you on this fair mountain leave to feed
And batten on this moor? Ha, have you eyes?
You cannot call it love; for at your age
The heyday in the blood is tame, it's humble,
And waits upon the judgment, and what judgment   70

---

55. this] *Q2;* his *F.*   57. and] *Q2;* or *F.*   59. heaven-kissing] *F,Q5;*
heaue, a kissing *Q2.*   65. brother] *Q2;* breath *F.*

55–62.] This portrait of Hamlet's father develops various hints of the first act. Cf. I. i. 65–6 (Mars), I. ii. 139–40 (Hyperion), 187–8 (the complete man).

56. *front*] forehead.

58. *station*] stance, manner of standing.

Mercury] the envoy of the gods, whose bearing typified grace and beauty.

59. *New-lighted . . . hill*] Mercury is often so represented in pictorial art. But cf. Virgil's description of him alighting on Mount Atlas, 'primum paribus nitens . . . alis Constitit' (*Aeneid*, IV. 252–3). Milton uses the same comparison for Raphael when, having alighted on 'the eastern cliff of Paradise', he 'stood' like Mercury (*Par. Lost*, v. 285).

60. *A combination and a form*] The idea is that of an image formed on wax by the combined impression of many seals. For *form* see I. v. 100 and n., III. ii. 24.

62. *give the world . . . a man*] By effecting a realization of the ideal man. Cf. Brutus with 'the elements So mix'd in him that . . . "This was a man!"' (*Caes.* v. v. 73–5).

64–5. *a mildew'd ear . . . brother*] Cf. the ears of Pharoah's dream, Genesis xli. 5–7, 22–4. *Blasting*, infecting with disease, and so causing to wither (cf. *blastments*, I. iii. 42); *wholesome*, healthy, as at I. v. 70, III. ii. 254.

66–7. *on this fair mountain . . . moor*] The animal metaphors here and at ll. 93–4 derive, directly or indirectly, from Belleforest and ultimately from Saxo. See Intro., pp. 88, 91–2. Cf. also I. ii. 150, I. v. 57.

66. *leave*] cease, as at III. ii. 169.

67. *moor*] The contrast with a *fair* mountain suggests a play on blackamoor. This may be what prompts Q1 'With a face like *Vulcan*'.

69. *the blood*] As the source of sexual desire. Cf. I. iii. 6 and n.

Would step from this to this? Sense sure you have,
Else could you not have motion; but sure that sense
Is apoplex'd, for madness would not err
Nor sense to ecstasy was ne'er so thrall'd
But it reserv'd some quantity of choice   75
To serve in such a difference. What devil was't
That thus hath cozen'd you at hoodman-blind?
Eyes without feeling, feeling without sight,
Ears without hands or eyes, smelling sans all,
Or but a sickly part of one true sense   80
Could not so mope. O shame, where is thy blush?
Rebellious hell,
If thou canst mutine in a matron's bones,
To flaming youth let virtue be as wax
And melt in her own fire; proclaim no shame   85

71. step] *Q2,F;* stoop *Collier².*   71–6. Sense . . . difference.] *Q2; not in F.*
77. hoodman-blind] *F;* hodman blind *Q2;* hob-man blinde *Q1.*   78–81. Eyes
. . . mope.] *Q2; not in F.*   81–2. O shame . . . hell,] *As Q2; one line F.*

71. step from this to this] Cf.
I.v.47–52.

Sense] the senses collectively (as
often), and the faculty of perceiving
through them. Cf. ll. 78–80 and n.

72. Else . . . motion] It was an
Aristotelian maxim that the external
senses are necessarily present in all
creatures which have the power of
locomotion (*De Sensu*, ch. 1, 436b).
See C. S. Lewis, *Studies in Words*,
p. 151. This shows the meaning of
both key words here and refutes
the usual interpretations of *motion*
as emotion, impulse, or desire.

73. err] i.e. *so* err. What is explicit
in the next line is here understood.

74. ecstasy] state of hallucination.
Cf. below, l. 140, II.i.102n.

75. some quantity of choice] a modi-
cum (*OED* quantity 8b) of the
power to choose.

76. To serve . . . difference] to make
use of in a case of such markedly
different alternatives.

76–7. What devil . . . cozen'd you]
The failure of Gertrude's perceptions,
seemingly inexplicable by natural

causes, is attributed to the devil, who
in the general belief not only deceived
men but also undermined their
judgment so that they deceived
themselves (cf. II.ii.597).

77. hoodman-blind] blind man's buff.

78–80. Eyes . . . one true sense] The
senses, referred to collectively in
ll. 71–5, are now individualized.
Cf. *Ven.* 433–46.

81. mope] be in a daze, unaware of
what one is doing. Cf. *Temp.* v.i.240,
'in a dream . . . brought moping
hither'.

82. Rebellious hell] For the identification of sexual desire with the
rebellion of man's lower nature, cf.
All's W. IV.iii.13–18 (and see above,
I.iii.44 and n.); for its attribution to
hell, cf. *Lr* IV.vi.117–28.

83. mutine] A common variant of
mutiny.

84–5. To flaming youth . . . fire]
This passage, with its suggestion of
what may be expected of youth,
does much to explain Hamlet's
attitude to Ophelia. Cf. III.i.103–15,
136–51. The comparison of virtue

> When the compulsive ardour gives the charge,
> Since frost itself as actively doth burn
> And reason panders will.
>
> *Queen.*   O Hamlet, speak no more.
> Thou turn'st my eyes into my very soul,
> And there I see such black and grained spots   90
> As will not leave their tint.
>
> *Ham.*   Nay, but to live
> In the rank sweat of an enseamed bed,
> Stew'd in corruption, honeying and making love
> Over the nasty sty!
>
> *Queen.*   O speak to me no more.
> These words like daggers enter in my ears.   95
> No more, sweet Hamlet.
>
> *Ham.*   A murderer and a villain,

88. And] *Q2; As F.*   panders] *F; pardons Q2.*   89. my] *Q2; mine F.*
eyes into my very] *F; very eyes into my Q2.*   90. grained] *F; greeued Q2.*
91. not leave] *F; leaue there Q2.*   92. enseamed] *F; inseemed Q2; incestuous Q3.*   95. my] *Q2; mine F.*

succumbing to the flames of youth
with wax consuming *itself* in its
own flame, though it no doubt adds
intensity, gives a less than perfect
analogy. But cf. IV. vii. 113–14.

86. *compulsive ardour*] 'the heyday
in the blood', l. 69.

gives the charge] makes the attack.

87. *frost*] the numbed passions of
the matron.

88. *reason panders will*] Cf. I. ii. 150.
The function of reason is subverted
when it is put at the service of 'will'
instead of subduing it. Cf. *Ant.*
III. xiii. 3–4. *Will*, instinct for self-
gratification; in general, passion as
opposed to reason (cf. *Troil.* I. iii. 120;
Meas. II. iv. 175); in particular, sexual
desire (cf. *Meas.* II. iv. 164; *Lucr.* 243,
247, etc.).

90. *grained*] ingrained, indelibly
dyed (originally in scarlet, *grain* being
the dye of the insect kermes, which
was mistaken for a seed).

91. *not leave*] The F reading is
generally preferred to Q2's dupli-

cation *there their*. The meaning is
basically the same, owing to the
ambiguity of *leave*, which means
either cease, give up (F) or cause to
remain behind (Q2); yet Q2 verges
on nonsense (for how could the
colour stay without the spots?)
and is certainly bathetic after *grained*,
which F by contrast reinforces by
insisting that the colour will never
disappear. Cf. *Mac.* v. i. 30–50.

92. *enseamed*] saturated with *seam*
(cf. *Troil.* II. iii. 180), i.e. animal fat,
grease. The word combines with
others in the context to suggest the
grossness of the sexual behaviour
through physical metaphors of dis-
gusting exudations. Explanations
making it out to be a technical term
from falconry (Schmidt, etc.) or the
woollen industry (Dover Wilson) are
quite beside the point.

93. *Stew'd*] bathed, steeped, with
a play on *stew*, brothel.

95. *like daggers*] As Hamlet purposed, III. ii. 387.

A slave that is not twentieth part the tithe
Of your precedent lord, a vice of kings,
A cutpurse of the empire and the rule,
That from a shelf the precious diadem stole   100
And put it in his pocket—
Queen. No more.
Ham. A king of shreds and patches—

Enter GHOST.

Save me and hover o'er me with your wings,
You heavenly guards! What would your gracious
        figure?   105
Queen. Alas, he's mad.
Ham. Do you not come your tardy son to chide,

---

97. tithe] *F;* kyth *Q2.*   103 S.D.] *As Singer; after 102 Q2,F; Enter the ghost*
in his night gowne. Q1.   105. your] *Q2;* you *F.*

---

98. *a vice*] (1) a model of iniquity,
with particular reference to (2) the
character so called in the Morality
plays. As the devil's henchman, he
was a mischievous buffoon. *A vice of
kings* thus stresses the paradox of a
king who is both villain and clown,
a grotesque figure against his majestic
predecessor.

99, 100. *cutpurse, stole*] Not incompatible with his having succeeded
by popular consent. It is not by
usurpation but by murder that he
has dispossessed the rightful owner.
Cf. 1.ii.1 LN. Yet the language here
implies an unscrupulous opportunism
in his assumption of the crown, which
did not appear in 1.ii but becomes
more explicit at v.ii.65. In Belleforest
Hamlet tells his mother that his
uncle, who 'has been false to his lord
and sovereign prince', is 'neither my
king nor my lord'.

103. *of shreds and patches*] In contrast to the complete man of ll. 60–2.
Some eds. suppose the phrase to have
been suggested by the parti-coloured

dress of the Vice (l. 98).

103 S.D. *Enter Ghost*] Appropriately enough in this context as a
visual reminder of the king that was.
There is no textual support for
assumptions that the Ghost intervenes because Hamlet is ignoring the
warning concerning his mother in
1.v.85–6 (Verity) or to prevent
Hamlet from revealing the facts
about the murder (*WHH*, pp. 251–2).
How the Ghost now appeared, in
contrast with the armoured figure of
1.i, is indicated by Q1 '*in his night
gowne*', i.e. robe of undress. It is not
perhaps what we should expect from
l. 137 below but not incompatible
with it.

104–5. *Save me . . . guards!*] Cf.
1.iv.39.

107–9.] 'If, after the first appearance, the persons employed neglect,
or are prevented from, performing
the message or business committed
to their management, the Ghost
appears continually to them' (Grose,
Provincial Glossary).

That, laps'd in time and passion, lets go by
Th'important acting of your dread command?
O say.

Ghost.   Do not forget. This visitation   110
Is but to whet thy almost blunted purpose.
But look, amazement on thy mother sits.
O step between her and her fighting soul.
Conceit in weakest bodies strongest works.
Speak to her, Hamlet.   115

Ham. How is it with you, lady?

Queen.   Alas, how is't with you,
That you do bend your eye on vacancy,
And with th'incorporal air do hold discourse?
Forth at your eyes your spirits wildly peep,
And, as the sleeping soldiers in th'alarm,   120

109–10. Th'important . . . say.] *As Theobald; one line Q2,F.*   117. you do]
Q2; you *F;* thus you *Q1,F2.*   118. th'incorporal] *Q2;* their corporall *F;*
the corporall *F2.*

---

108. *laps'd in time and passion*]
Commentators divide on whether
Hamlet has failed through too little
passion or too much. I take the
natural interpretation to be that he
has let both time and passion slip
away. This (significantly) accords
with a recurrent motif of the play –
the failure of human purposes through
a weakening of passion or resolve.
See III.i.84–8, IV.vii.117–20, and
esp. III.ii.189–90 (where the purpose
fails because the passion ends). Dover
Wilson (among others) argues for
the opposite: that Hamlet has fallen
into inactivity through a too great
indulgence in passion.

109. *important*] urgent, impatient
of delay.

110. *Do not forget*] The first words
now take up the last words of the
Ghost's former visitation (I.v.91),
though with significant variation.

112. *amazement*] Not merely
'astonishment' but 'bewilderment'.
Cf. I.ii.235, II.ii.559.

113. *step between . . . soul*] protect
her from her own inner struggle.

114. *Conceit in weakest bodies*]
Florio's Montaigne (I.20) says that
it is 'the *weakest* and seeliest, whose
conceit and belief is so seized upon,
that they imagine to see what they
see not'. *Conceit*, imagination.

119. *Forth at your eyes . . . peep*] A
metaphor based on the theory that
the physical signs of mental excitement were attributable to the agi-
tation of the *spirits*. These were
conceived of as fluids permeating
the blood which ascended to the
brain and determined its activity.

120–2. *as the sleeping soldiers . . . an
end*] 'The hairs are compared with
soldiers who leap from their beds . . .
and stand stiff and erect for action'
(Dover Wilson) – *alarm*, call to arms
(the literal sense). *Hair* is a collective
singular, but the comparison with
soldiers emphasizes a plural sense,
which is reinforced by *excrements*
and determines the form of the verbs.
Hence attempts to emend the
grammar, begun in Q3, are best
avoided.

　　Your bedded hair, like life in excrements,
　　Start up and stand an end. O gentle son,
　　Upon the heat and flame of thy distemper
　　Sprinkle cool patience. Whereon do you look?
Ham. On him, on him. Look you how pale he glares.　　125
　　His form and cause conjoin'd, preaching to stones,
　　Would make them capable.—Do not look upon me,
　　Lest with this piteous action you convert
　　My stern effects. Then what I have to do
　　Will want true colour—tears perchance for blood.　　130
Queen. To whom do you speak this?
Ham. Do you see nothing there?
Queen. Nothing at all; yet all that is I see.
Ham. Nor did you nothing hear?
Queen. No, nothing but ourselves.　　135
Ham. Why, look you there, look how it steals away.
　　My father, in his habit as he liv'd!
　　Look where he goes even now out at the portal.

　　　　　　　　　　　　　　　　　　　　　　Exit Ghost.

Queen. This is the very coinage of your brain.
　　This bodiless creation ecstasy　　140
　　Is very cunning in.
Ham. My pulse as yours doth temperately keep time,
　　And makes as healthful music. It is not madness

---

121. hair] *Q2,F;* hairs *Rowe.*　　122. Start . . . stand] *Q2,F;* Starts . . . stands
Q3.　　an] *Q2,F;* on *Pope², Theobald.*　　131. whom] *Q2;* who *F.*
140–1.] *As Pope;* one line *Q2,F.*　　142. My] *Q2;* Extasie? / My *F;* Idle, no
mother, my *Q1.*

121. *excrements*] outgrowths (L.
ex + *cresco*). Bacon describes 'hair
and nails' as 'excrements and no
parts' (*Sylva Sylvarum*, 1.58). That
they do not belong to the living
organism was held to be evidenced
by their lack of sensation. Hence the
preternatural effect of the 'life'
manifest here.

122. *an end*] See I.v.19n.

127. *capable*] responsive. Cf.
III.ii.11. On the stones, cf. Luke
xix.40; *Caes.* III.ii.230.

129. *effects*] purposed deeds.

130. *want true colour*] lack proper

character (*OED* colour *sb.* 16), with,
in the contrast between blood and
tears, a play on the literal sense.

133. *Nothing at all*] LN.

137. *habit*] characteristic dress, as
at I.iii.70. Cf. above, l. 103 S.D. n.

as he liv'd] as when he was alive,
rather than (as sometimes asserted)
as if he were. Cf. Jonson, *Fortunate
Isles*, l. 312, 'Enter Scogan, and
Skelton in like habits, as they lived'.

140. *ecstasy*] madness (its synonym
in l. 143). Cf. II.i.102, III.i.162, and
l. 74 above.

That I have utter'd. Bring me to the test,
And I the matter will re-word, which madness.   145
Would gambol from. Mother, for love of grace,
Lay not that flattering unction to your soul,
That not your trespass but my madness speaks.
It will but skin and film the ulcerous place,
Whiles rank corruption, mining all within,   150
Infects unseen. Confess yourself to heaven,
Repent what's past, avoid what is to come;
And do not spread the compost on the weeds
To make them ranker. Forgive me this my virtue;
For in the fatness of these pursy times   155
Virtue itself of vice must pardon beg,
Yea, curb and woo for leave to do him good.

Queen. O Hamlet, thou hast cleft my heart in twain.
Ham. O throw away the worser part of it
And live the purer with the other half.   160
Good night. But go not to my uncle's bed.

---

145. I] *F; not in Q2.*   147. that] *Q2;* a *F.*   150. Whiles] *Q2;* Whil'st *F.*
153. on] *Q2;* or *F;* o'er *Caldecott.*   154. ranker] *Q2;* ranke *F.*
155. these] *Q2;* this *F.*   160. live] *F;* leaue *Q2.*   161. my] *Q2;* mine *F.*

146. *gambol*] leap wildly, shy away.
A verb denoting the action of a
curvetting horse supplies Shakespeare
with a metaphor for the wild
irrational movements of the mind.
Cf.   *2H4*   II.iv.240–1,   'gambol
faculties . . . that show a weak mind';
Tw.N. I.v.189, where 'so *skipping* a
dialogue' is a sign of lunacy.

147. *Lay*] apply. *OED* lay *v.*[1] 15.
unction] ointment, as at IV.vii.140.

149. *skin*] grow skin over. Cf. *Meas.*
II.ii.136, 'medicine . . . That skins
the vice o'th' top'.

149–51. *skin and film . . . unseen*]
Kittredge cites Hughes, *Misfortunes
of Arthur,* III.i.111–14, 'where the
salve did soonest close the skin, The
sore was oftener covered up than
cured, Which festering deep . . . grew
greater than at first'.

153–4. *spread the compost . . . ranker*]

Developing the 'unweeded garden'
metaphor of I.ii.135–7.

155. *fatness . . . pursy*] Both words
suggest the physical (and metaphorically the moral) grossness that
comes   from   undisciplined   self-
indulgence: *pursy* (from *purse*), puffed
up, flabby. Cf. Chapman, *Byron's
Conspiracy,* I.i.131, 'pursy regiment' (of
peace). The explanation of it as a
variant of *pursive,* short-winded, is
not helpful here, though Shakespeare
exploits both meanings in the 'pursy
insolence' of *Tim.* V.iv.12. For the
idea cf. variously IV.iv.27, V.ii.186.

157. *curb*] (F *courb* < Fr. *courber*)
bow, bend. Cf. III.ii.61, *crook* the
knee.

158. *in twain*] between regret for
her conduct and loyalty to her
present husband.

Assume a virtue if you have it not.
That monster, custom, who all sense doth eat
Of habits evil, is angel yet in this,
That to the use of actions fair and good   165
He likewise gives a frock or livery
That aptly is put on. Refrain tonight,
And that shall lend a kind of easiness
To the next abstinence, the next more easy;
For use almost can change the stamp of nature,   170
And either [lodge] the devil or throw him out
With wondrous potency. Once more, good night,
And when you are desirous to be blest,
I'll blessing beg of you. For this same lord
I do repent; but heaven hath pleas'd it so,   175
To punish me with this and this with me,

163-7. That . . . on.] *Q2; not in F.*   163-4. eate Of habits evil,] *Theobald
(conj. Thirlby); eate Of habit's evil, White, conj. Theobald; eate Of habits deuill,
Q2; eat, Of habits divell, Q5; eat Of habit's devil, Rowe; eat Of habits, devil,
Johnson; eat, Oft habits' devil Staunton.*   167. on.] on: *Q5;* on *Q2.*
Refrain tonight] *F,Q5;* to refraine night *Q2.*   169-72. the next more . . .
potency.] *Q2; not in F.*   171. either lodge] *This edn, conj. Clarendon;* either
Q2; Maister *Q3;* master ev'n *Pope;* either master *Jennens;* either curb *Malone;*
either house *Chambers (RL), conj. Bailey.*

---

162. *Assume*] put on the garb of
(but not − as now usually quoted −
simulate, pretend to); adopt, i.e.
actually begin to practise.

163-7. *That monster . . . put on.*]
i.e. Custom, which erodes or eats
away all sense (perception) of evil
in what we habitually do, likewise
creates a habit whereby we readily
get into the way of doing what is
good. LN.

168. *shall*] (denoting necessary
consequence) cannot but. Cf. Abbott
315.

170. *use . . . nature*] Cf. 'Use is
another nature' (*Unfortunate Traveller*,
Nashe, ii.302). A very common
proverb going back to classical times.
See Nashe, ii.36; iv.216-17; Ascham,
Toxophilus (*English Works*, ed. Wright,
1904), p. 98; Tilley C 932.

stamp of] character bestowed or
imprinted by. Cf. I.iv.31, 'the

stamp . . . , Being Nature's livery'.

171. *lodge*] receive hospitably,
afford accommodation for. LN.

172. *With wondrous potency*] Stressing
the less expected effect (that *use* can
bring about good as well as evil).

174. *I'll blessing beg*] He acknowledges what, given more proper
behaviour on his mother's part,
would be proper for a son to do.

176. *To punish . . . with me*] 'Even
so doth God punish the wicked one
by another' (P. de Mornay, *The
Trewnesse of the Christian Religion*,
ch. 12). Hamlet is punished for his
savage passions (cf. III.ii.379-83 LN
and III.iii.89-95 LN) by their un-
toward consequence (the killing of
Polonius), which in turn will have
further consequences (cf. l. 181).
Kittredge and Dover Wilson find
Hamlet's punishment in his having
now put himself in the King's power.

That I must be their scourge and minister.
I will bestow him, and will answer well
The death I gave him. So, again, good night.
I must be cruel only to be kind.   180
This bad begins, and worse remains behind.
One word more, good lady.
Queen.   What shall I do?
Ham. Not this, by no means, that I bid you do:
Let the bloat King tempt you again to bed,
Pinch wanton on your cheek, call you his mouse,   185
And let him, for a pair of reechy kisses,
Or paddling in your neck with his damn'd fingers,
Make you to ravel all this matter out
That I essentially am not in madness,
But mad in craft. 'Twere good you let him know,   190

---

181. This] *Q2*; Thus *F*.   182. One . . . lady.] *Q2*; *not in F*.   184. bloat]
Warburton; blowt *Q2*; blunt *F*.   188. ravel] *F*; rouell *Q2*.   190. mad]
Q2; made *F*.

But we must surely suppose him to refer to the weight now on his conscience (cf. Bowers, *PMLA*, LXX, 740–2; and see l. 177 LN).

177. *their*] the heavenly powers'. The use of *heaven* in plural sense is common: see Walker, ii. 110–13.

scourge and minister] LN.

178. *bestow*] stow away, dispose of. Cf. IV.ii.1, IV.iii.12.

answer] atone for.

181. *This*] the killing of Polonius, as in l. 176. It is hard to see why most eds. continue to prefer F's vague and feeble *Thus*. (Cf. *MSH*, p. 275.)

remains behind] is still to come. Not, surely, a threat against the King and Queen (as Kittredge and others), but a prophetic glimpse of the whole tragic outcome.

182. *One word . . . lady*] F may be right to omit this. It seems intrusive after Hamlet's couplet, and the Queen's question in itself prompts him to resume.

184. *bloat*] (so spelt now through confusion with *bloat* describing a soft-cured herring, though *blowt* was formerly a different word) flabby, bloated. Abbott (342) does not seem justified in regarding it as a form of the past pple. (since the adj. antedates the verb).

185. *Pinch wanton*] i.e. leave marks of his fondling which proclaim you a wanton.

mouse] A term of endearment to a woman. Cf. Edw. Alleyn to his wife, 'My good sweet mouse', etc. (*Memoirs*, Shakespeare Soc., pp. 25–6); *Tw.N.* I.v.58; and Capulet's having 'been a mouse-hunt' in his time (*Rom.* IV.iv.11).

186. *a pair*] a few.

reechy] (= reeky) rank, filthy.

187. *paddling*] fingering amorously. Cf. *Wint.* I.ii.115, 'paddling palms and pinching fingers'.

188. *ravel . . . out*] disentangle, clear up. The Queen is not to solve the King's puzzle for him by disclosing what Hamlet has told her (in ll. 142–8).

For who that's but a queen, fair, sober, wise,
Would from a paddock, from a bat, a gib,
Such dear concernings hide? Who would do so?
No, in despite of sense and secrecy,
Unpeg the basket on the house's top,   195
Let the birds fly, and like the famous ape,
To try conclusions, in the basket creep,
And break your own neck down.
Queen. Be thou assur'd, if words be made of breath,
And breath of life, I have no life to breathe   200
What thou hast said to me.
Ham. I must to England, you know that?
Queen.   Alack,
I had forgot. 'Tis so concluded on.
Ham. There's letters seal'd, and my two schoolfellows,
Whom I will trust as I will adders fang'd—   205
They bear the mandate, they must sweep my way
And marshal me to knavery. Let it work;

197. conclusions, in the basket] *F2*; conclusions in the basket *Q2*; Conclusions
in the Basket, *F.*   202-3. Alack . . . on.] *As Capell; 2 lines divided* forgot. |
Tis *Q2; one line F.*   204-12.] *Q2; not in F.*

192. *paddock . . . gib*] frog or toad . . .
tom-cat. All these creatures had a
sinister obloquy as being the familiar
spirits of witches.

193. *Such dear concernings*] matters
which are so important to him (or
which concern him so closely). See
OED dear *a.1* 4b.

195-6. *Unpeg . . . fly*] Birds let out
of baskets, like cats out of bags, are
not easily recaptured.

196. *the famous ape*] Its fame has
not survived, but St Hildegard says
that when an ape sees birds fly, he is
enraged at being unable to do likewise (Janson, *Apes and Ape Lore*,
pp. 176-7). Evidently the fable was
of an ape which, having seen birds
fly when released from a basket,
attempted to copy them, with disastrous results. Hamlet warns his
mother that the disclosure of his
secret (opening the basket) will bring
disaster to her.

198. *down*] i.e. by falling from the
housetop.

202. *I must to England*] The King's
plan was already forming at III. i. 171,
but at III. iii. 3 the 'commission' (cf.
ll. 204-6 here) was still to be prepared. As to how Hamlet knew of it,
since the text, as eds. note, is silent,
speculation is invalid. The 'difficulty'
passes unnoticed in the theatre, and
such inventiveness as making Hamlet
search Polonius's pockets is misplaced.

204. *schoolfellows*] Cf. II. ii. 11.

206. *sweep my way*] i.e. in the course
of their escort duty, not (as supposed
in *WHH*, p. 258) by going in advance.

207. *marshal*] conduct.

knavery] to be suffered, of course,
not committed, by the speaker. Cf.
v. ii. 19.

207-11. *Let it work . . . at the moon.*]
Hamlet's confidence in the outcome
will prepare the audience for it, but
affords no justification for supposing

For 'tis the sport to have the enginer
Hoist with his own petard, and 't shall go hard
But I will delve one yard below their mines   210
And blow them at the moon. O, 'tis most sweet
When in one line two crafts directly meet.
This man shall set me packing.
I'll lug the guts into the neighbour room.
Mother, good night indeed. This counsellor   215
Is now most still, most secret, and most grave,
Who was in life a foolish prating knave.

209. and 't] *Q 1676;* an't *Q2.*   215. good night indeed.] *Q2 subst.;*
goodnight. Indeede *F.*   217. foolish] *F,Q1;* most foolish *Q2.*

that he has any precise plan for
bringing it about (which he ultimately does by sudden inspiration,
v. ii. 6–53), still less that he 'has
planned in advance for the intervention of the pirates' (*SQ*, XXVI, 279).
 208. *enginer*] maker of 'engines' of
war. This Q2 spelling indicates the
Elizabethan stress. Cf. *pioner,* I. v. 171.
 209. *Hoist with his own petard*]
'Blown into the air by his own
bomb' (*OED* hoise 2 b). *Hoist* is the
past pple. of *hoise,* from which *hoist*
as a present form apparently arose
through confusion. The 'engine'
called (from Fr.) a *petard* was an
explosive device, recently invented,
for breaking through gates, walls,
etc. Most eds. retain the Q2 form
petar, no doubt a pointer to pronunciation (and *OED* shows Drayton
rhyming it with *far*), but it seems
proper in a modernized text to
adopt the more regular spelling.
Jonson (*Epicoene,* IV. v. 222) has *petarde.*
The phrase sums up the ironic pattern
to be fulfilled in the catastrophe.
Cf. v. ii. 56–9; 312–13; 323–4; 332–3;
389–90.

 212. *in one line . . . directly*] on a
collision course (i.e. on a single path
in opposite directions).
 crafts] cunning plots, continuing
the metaphor of mine and counter-
mine. A pun on *crafts,* ships, is (at
this date) unlikely.
 213. *packing*] (1) off in a hurry;
but also continuing the idea of (2)
plotting (cf. *Shr.* v. i. 105, 'Here's
packing . . . to deceive us all').
Some suppose a further pun, (3)
loading up (with the body). But this
would surely not be *lugging* it.
 214. *lug the guts*] Hamlet's uncere-
monious treatment of the body has
its precedent in Saxo and Belleforest,
where he cut it in pieces, boiled it,
and threw it out for the hogs. Does
'by the heels' in the prose *Hamblet* of
1608 derive from what was seen on
the stage? See Intro., pp. 89–90.
 215. *indeed*] positively, in earnest.
He now really means what he has
already said three times – ll. 161,
172, 179. The F punctuation, with
the mass of eds. who follow it, misses
the point.

Come, sir, to draw toward an end with you.
Good night, mother.

> *Exit lugging in Polonius.* [*The Queen remains.*]

219 S.D.] *This edn; Exit Hamlet tugging in Polonius. F; Exit Hamlet with the
dead body. Q1; Exit. Q2; Exeunt severally; Hamlet tugging in Polonius. Capell,
(*with* dragging *for* tugging) Malone.*

218. *draw toward an end*] finish my
business.

219 S.D. *lugging in Polonius*] The
F direction, which Greg thought
'one could swear . . . was Shakespeare's' (*SFF*, p. 319), appears in
fact to be an editorial addition
deriving, via a misprint, from the
dialogue (*lug*, l. 214).

[ACT IV]

[SCENE I]

[*To the*] QUEEN, *enter* KING, *with* ROSENCRANTZ *and*
GUILDENSTERN.

King. There's matter in these sighs, these profound heaves,
 You must translate. 'Tis fit we understand them.
 Where is your son?
Queen. Bestow this place on us a little while.
        [*Exeunt Rosencrantz and Guildenstern.*]
 Ah, mine own lord, what have I seen tonight!   5
King. What, Gertrude, how does Hamlet?
Queen. Mad as the sea and wind when both contend

ACT IV

Scene 1

ACT IV SCENE 1] *Q 1676.*   S.D.] *This edn; Enter King, and Queene, with Rosencraus and Guyldensterne. Q2; Enter King. F; Enter the King and Lordes. Q1.*
1. matter] *Q2;* matters *F.*   sighs, these profound heaves,] *Q2;* sighes. These profound heaues *F;* sighs, these profound heaves; *Rowe.*   4.] *Q2; not in F.*   4 S.D.] *Q 1676.*   5. mine own] *Q2;* my good *F.*   7. sea] *Q2,Q1;* Seas *F.*

ACT IV SCENE 1] 'It is a disaster that editors have followed a late quarto in choosing this of all points at which to begin a new act' (Greg, *SFF*, p. 333). The action is continuous, the Queen remaining on stage. LN.

S.D. *Rosencrantz and Guildenstern*] Their appearance with the King here, though silent and but momentary (and accordingly dropped from F), is dramatically very pointed – after the stress just laid (III.iv.204–11) on their role as Hamlet's escort.

1–2. *There's matter . . . translate.*] The syntax is not without ambiguity, as the variant punctuation shows. But I take it that a relative is to be supplied before *You.* For (1) the sighs have not merely *matter*, or purport, but a purport which is not apparent, and (2) what needs translating is not the *sighs*, or *heaves*, but the *matter* they express. This is not inconsistent with 'understand *them*'. With *heaves*, cf. the 'penitential heaves' of *Revenger's Trag.*, II.iii.12.

1. *profound*] For the accentuation on the first syllable (in contrast with II.i.94), see I.iv.52n.

6. *What, Gertrude*] Not an interrogative, still less a feeble echo, but a (compassionate) exclamation.

Which is the mightier. In his lawless fit,
Behind the arras hearing something stir,
Whips out his rapier, cries 'A rat, a rat',   10
And in this brainish apprehension kills
The unseen good old man.
King.   O heavy deed!
It had been so with us had we been there.
His liberty is full of threats to all—
To you yourself, to us, to everyone.   15
Alas, how shall this bloody deed be answer'd?
It will be laid to us, whose providence
Should have kept short, restrain'd, and out of haunt
This mad young man. But so much was our love,
We would not understand what was most fit,   20
But like the owner of a foul disease,
To keep it from divulging, let it feed
Even on the pith of life. Where is he gone?
Queen. To draw apart the body he hath kill'd,
O'er whom—his very madness, like some ore   25
Among a mineral of metals base,

---

10. Whips out his rapier,] *Q2;* He whips his Rapier out, *and F;* whips me Out
his rapier, *and Q1.*   11. this] *Q2;* his *F,Q1.*   22. let] *Q2;* let's *F.*
25-7. whom—. . . pure—] *This edn;* whom, . . . pure, *Q2;* whom . . . pure. *F.*
25. some] *Q2,F;* fine *Furness, conj. Walker.*

---

11. *brainish*] deluded, frenzied.
Verity objects that there is no evidence for this sense; but the context
requires a word which will sustain the
ideas of *mad* and *lawless fit* as well as
describe *apprehension*, which the *OED*
glosses, 'headstrong, passionate', do
not do. The Queen attributes Hamlet's act to the false apprehension of
his own disordered brain. Cf. Drayton,
England's Heroical Epistles (Pref.), 'the
work . . . might be judged brainish, if
nothing but amorous humour were
handled therein'.
13. *us . . . we*] The royal plural is
used here and throughout the scene.
18. *short*] i.e. on a short tether.
out of haunt] away from any place of
resort.

22. *divulging*] becoming public.
23. *pith*] vital substance. Cf.
I.iv.22 and n.
25-7. *O'er whom . . . pure*] The Q2
commas after *whom* and *pure* suggest
that the words between should be
taken parenthetically; and this accords with sense, which the F pointing, though usually followed, can
hardly be said to do.
25. *ore*] Often used by the Elizabethans for precious metal, and specifically for gold, perhaps through confusion with Fr. and heraldic *or*.
Walker's conjecture (*Critical Exam.*,
II.299) *fine* for *some*, adopted by
Furness, is very plausible.
26. *mineral*] mine.

Shows itself pure—a weeps for what is done.
King. O Gertrude, come away.
  The sun no sooner shall the mountains touch
  But we will ship him hence; and this vile deed   30
  We must with all our majesty and skill
  Both countenance and excuse. — Ho, Guildenstern!

Enter ROSENCRANTZ *and* GUILDENSTERN.

  Friends both, go join you with some further aid.
  Hamlet in madness hath Polonius slain,
  And from his mother's closet hath he dragg'd him.   35
  Go seek him out—speak fair—and bring the body
  Into the chapel. I pray you haste in this.
                    Exeunt Rosencrantz and Guildenstern.
  Come, Gertrude, we'll call up our wisest friends,
  And let them know both what we mean to do
  And what's untimely done. [So envious slander],   40
  Whose whisper o'er the world's diameter,
  As level as the cannon to his blank,
  Transports his poison'd shot, may miss our name

---

27. a] *Q2;* He *F.*   32 S.D.] *Rowe; after 31 Q2; after* excuse *F.*
35. mother's closet] *Q2;* Mother Clossets *F.*   37 S.D.] *F subst.; not in Q2.*
39. And] *Q2;* To *F.*   40. So envious slander] *This edn; not in Q2,F;* For,
haply, Slander *Theobald;* So, haply, slander *Capell;* So viperous slander *Malone.*
41–4. Whose . . . air.] *Q2; not in F.*

27. *a weeps*] Not necessarily untrue
because we have not seen it. Those
who call it a lie forget both the dramatic conventions and III.iv.174ff.

35. *his mother's closet*] Perhaps implying that we are now somewhere
else, though there has been no break
in the action. Cf. headnote.

40. *So envious slander*] For the words
missing from the text most eds. have
accepted Theobald's suggestion, as
improved by Capell, *So, haply, slander.*
But *haply,* a too evident stopgap, adds
little to *may* (l. 43) unless some inappropriate doubt, and an adjective describing slander seems preferable.
LN.

41. *diameter*] whole extent from end
to end (*OED* 2g).

42. *As level . . . his blank*] as straight
as the cannon to its mark. The blank,
however, is not, as usually explained
(following *OED*), the white in the
centre of the target, but a target in the
line of direct, or *level,* aim (i.e. point-
blank, which is thus distinguished
from the angled sight-line requisite at
longer range). Properly *blank* refers to
the line or range of fire, as in *Wint.*
II.iii.5, *Oth.* III.iv.129 (see *SQ,* XIX,
33–40), but it is also used (as here)
for the object aimed at. Cf. *Lr* I.i.158.
For *his* here and in the next line, see
I.i.40n.

And hit the woundless air. O come away,
My soul is full of discord and dismay.   *Exeunt.*   45

[SCENE II]

Enter HAMLET.

Ham. Safely stowed.   [*Calling within.*]
But soft, what noise? Who calls on Hamlet? O, here
they come.

Enter ROSENCRANTZ, GUILDENSTERN, *and* Others.

Ros. What have you done, my lord, with the dead body?
Ham. Compounded it with dust, whereto 'tis kin.   5
Ros. Tell us where 'tis, that we may take it thence and
bear it to the chapel.
Ham. Do not believe it.
Ros. Believe what?
Ham. That I can keep your counsel and not mine own.   10

Scene II

SCENE II] *Pope.*   1 S.D. *Calling within.*] *This edn; Gentlemen within. Hamlet,*
Lord *Hamlet. F; not in Q2.*   2. But soft,] *Q2; not in F.*   3 S.D.] *Enter Ros.*
and Guildensterne. F; (at head of scene) Rosencraus and others. Q2.   5. Compounded]
F; Compound *Q2.*   6–7.] *Prose Dowden; 2 lines divided thence, /* And *Q2,F.*

---

44. *woundless*] invulnerable. Cf. I.
i. 150. With the metaphor cf. the
literal cannon of *John* II. i. 251–2,
whose 'malice vainly shall be spent
Against th'invulnerable clouds'.

Scene II

1 S.D. *Calling within.*] The words
supplied in F are evidently a playhouse addition suggested by l. 2, not
part of Shakespeare's text. Note that
they replace Hamlet's 'But soft',
which they make redundant. Cf. III.
iv. 5 n. and *SB*, XIII, 34–5.
3 S.D. *and Others*] These, though
dropped by F, no doubt to economize
in cast, are vouched for by IV. i. 33.

They will be required again for IV.
iii. 14–15.
5. *Compounded it with dust*] Cf. *2H4*
IV. v. 116.
whereto 'tis kin] 'Dust thou art, and
unto dust shalt thou return' (Genesis
iii. 19).
10. *keep your counsel . . . mine own*] An
adaptation of the proverb that a man
who cannot keep his own secrets is
unlikely to keep another's. Tilley C
682. Hamlet hints that they have purposes they do not divulge and claims
the same right for himself. Dover
Wilson finds a quibble in 'keep
counsel': (1) follow (your) advice;
(2) keep (my) secrets. But I know no
authority for (1).

Besides, to be demanded of a sponge—what replica-
tion should be made by the son of a king?

Ros. Take you me for a sponge, my lord?

Ham. Ay, sir, that soaks up the King's countenance, his
rewards, his authorities. But such officers do the   15
King best service in the end: he keeps them, like an
ape, in the corner of his jaw—first mouthed, to be
last swallowed. When he needs what you have
gleaned, it is but squeezing you and, sponge, you
shall be dry again.   20

Ros. I understand you not, my lord.

Ham. I am glad of it. A knavish speech sleeps in a foolish
ear.

Ros. My lord, you must tell us where the body is and go
with us to the King.   25

Ham. The body is with the King, but the King is not with

16–17. like an ape] *F;* like an apple *Q2;* as an Ape doth nuttes *Q1;* like an ape
an apple *Parrott-Craig, conj. Farmer (apud Steevens[2]).*

---

11. *of*] by. Cf. I.iv.18.

11–20.] This image of the sponge is
a very common one with Elizabethan
writers. LN.

14. *countenance*] favour, manifestation of goodwill.

15. *authorities*] influence, powers inherent in (his) position. The syco-
phant sponge profits from the king's
powers rather than, as Dover Wilson's
note suggests, appropriates them. Cf.
'Your authority and countenance
giveth me . . . great encouragement',
A. Fleming, *A Panoply of Epistles,*
1576, p. 27.

16–17. *like an ape*] Q2 *apple* is evidently a misreading and Dover
Wilson's defence of it special pleading
induced by his respect for Q2 in
general. It is *he*, the King, that the
comparison describes, not the thing
he swallows, as the Q2 printer
apparently supposed. This habit of
apes is well known, and Q1 shows
how well the actors understood. It
does not follow, as some eds. have
supposed, that there is an omission in

the better texts. The conjecture of
Farmer and others, *like an ape an
apple*, though accepted by Alexander,
Evans, and Spencer, is both unnecessary and improbable since it would
imply that the two good texts each
made a separate error. The same
mistake of *apple(s)* for *ape(s)* is found
in Peele's *Arraignment of Paris* (1584,
Dij; MSR, l. 873).

18–19. *When he needs . . . gleaned*]
Behind this lies a traditional gibe
about the monarch's treatment of
corrupt agents (see ll. 11–20 LN),
through which Hamlet threatens the
pair that they are playing a dangerous game.

26–7. *The body . . . the body.*] This
retort implies that the two commands
are one, the body being where the
King is. (1) The body (of Polonius) is
here in the palace 'with the King';
but the King, not being, as it is, dead,
is 'not with the body'. One may
catch a hint of what might have been
if Hamlet had not mistaken. Cf. III.
iv.26, 32, IV.i.13. (2) The body (of

the body. The King is a thing—
Guild. A thing, my lord?
Ham. Of nothing. Bring me to him.   *Exeunt.*

[SCENE III]

Enter KING *and two or three* [Lords].

King. I have sent to seek him and to find the body.
How dangerous is it that this man goes loose!
Yet must not we put the strong law on him:
He's lov'd of the distracted multitude,
Who like not in their judgment but their eyes,   5
And where 'tis so, th'offender's scourge is weigh'd,
But never the offence. To bear all smooth and even,
This sudden sending him away must seem
Deliberate pause. Diseases desperate grown

29. him.] *Q2;* him, hide Fox, and all after. *F.*

Scene III

SCENE III] *Pope.*   S.D. *and two or three*] *Q2; not in F; attended | Capell.*
7. never] *Q2;* neerer *F.*

the King) is necessarily where the
King is, but his kingship, that which
makes him king, is not contained in
the body. LN.

27–9. *The King is a thing . . . Of
nothing.*] (1) The essential king (see
previous note and LN) is no material
thing. But (2), in the sense of the
common phrase, this particular king
is a thing of no account. Thus a metaphysical profundity is turned into a
deliberate anticlimax. LN.

29. *him.*] Balance of probability
suggests that F's added words are a
stage accretion. LN.

Scene III

S.D. *and two or three*] Presumably
the 'wisest friends' of IV.i.38. F's
economical omission of these misre-
presents the speech which follows.

This, Kittredge notwithstanding, is
not a soliloquy: it publicly justifies
the King's proceedings while con-
cealing his real motives. Contrast
ll. 61–71 below.

4. *distracted*] irrational. Cf. III.i.5n.
6. *scourge*] punishment.
7. *To bear . . . even*] to conduct
affairs without provoking opposition.
9. *Deliberate pause*] A *pause*, a break
in activity, comes to be thought of as
(a period of) consideration. Hamlet's
removal, though sudden, must seem
the result of careful deliberation.

9–10. *Diseases . . . reliev'd*] A common proverb: cf. Cheke, *Hurt of
Sedition*, 1549, F4v, 'Desperate sick-
nesses . . . must have desperate reme-
dies'; *Euphues*, Lyly, i.213–14; Nashe,
ii.20; Chapman, *All Fools*, v.i.51;
Tilley D 357.

By desperate appliance are reliev'd,   10
Or not at all.

Enter ROSENCRANTZ, [GUILDENSTERN,] *and* Others.

How now, what hath befall'n?
Ros. Where the dead body is bestow'd, my lord,
We cannot get from him.
King.   But where is he?
Ros. Without, my lord, guarded, to know your pleasure.
King. Bring him before us.
Ros.   Ho! Bring in the lord.   15

Enter HAMLET *with* Guards.

King. Now, Hamlet, where's Polonius?
Ham. At supper.
King. At supper? Where?
Ham. Not where he eats, but where a is eaten. A certain convocation of politic worms are e'en at him.   20
Your worm is your only emperor for diet: we fat all
creatures else to fat us, and we fat ourselves for
maggots. Your fat king and your lean beggar is but
variable service—two dishes, but to one table.

---

11 S.D. *Guildenstern, and Others*] *Wilson; and all the rest* | *Q2; not in F.*
15. Ho!] *Q2 (subst.)*; Hoa, *Guildensterne? F.*   the] *Q2; my F.*   15 S.D.]
*This edn; They enter. Q2; Enter Hamlet and Guildensterne. F; Hamlet enters guarded
by soldiers* | *Wilson.*   19. a is] *Q2; he is F,Q1.*   20. politic] *Q2,Q1; not
in F.*   22. ourselves] *Q2; our selfe F.*   24. service . . . table.*] seruice, two
dishes but to one table, *Q2;* seruice to dishes, but to one Table *F;* seruices,
two dishes to one messe: *Q1.*

---

10. *appliance*] treatment, as in *Per.*
II.ii.91; *H8* I.i.124; etc.

11. S.D. *Enter . . . Guildenstern*] LN.

20. *politic*] (1) shrewd; but, *convocation* recalling the literal sense, also
(2) busy in statecraft.

e'en] i.e. even now, at this moment.

21–3. *Your. . . . your . . . Your . . .
your*] The fourfold *your* gives a classic
illustration of the indefinite use. Cf.
I.i.141 and n., I.v.175, III.ii.3, v.i.
56–7, 165–6.

21. *Your worm . . . for diet*] Wittily
improving on the usual aphorism, in

which an emperor is the food of
worms (e.g. Florio's Montaigne, II.12,
'The heart and life of a mighty and
triumphant emperor, is but the break-
fast of a seely little worm'). There is
play on *diet*, council, with reference to
the Diet at the German city of Worms,
presided over by the *emperor*. In 1521
it pronounced its ban on Luther after
his famous refusal to recant.

24. *service*] food served at table.
OED service[1] 27b. Cf. *Mac.* I.vii
S.D. ('*Enter . . . Servants with Dishes
and Service*').

That's the end.   25
King. Alas, alas.
Ham. A man may fish with the worm that hath eat of a
    king, and eat of the fish that hath fed of that worm.
King. What dost thou mean by this?
Ham. Nothing but to show you how a king may go a   30
    progress through the guts of a beggar.
King. Where is Polonius?
Ham. In heaven. Send thither to see. If your messenger
    find him not there, seek him i'th'other place your-
    self. But if indeed you find him not within this   35
    month, you shall nose him as you go up the stairs into
    the lobby.
King. [*To some Attendants*] Go seek him there.
Ham. A will stay till you come.   [*Exeunt Attendants.*]
King. Hamlet, this deed, for thine especial safety—   40
    Which we do tender, as we dearly grieve
    For that which thou hast done—must send thee hence
    With fiery quickness. Therefore prepare thyself.
    The bark is ready, and the wind at help,
    Th'associates tend, and everything is bent   45
    For England.
Ham. For England?

26–8.] *Q2,Q1 with variations; not in F.*   35. if indeed] *Q2;* indeed, if *F.*
within] *Q2; not in F.*   38. *To some Attendants*] *Capell.*   39. A will] *Q2;*
He will *F;* hee'le *Q1.*   you] *Q2,Q1;* ye *F.*   39 S.D.] *Capell.*   40. deed]
Q2; deed of thine *F.*   43. With fiery quickness] *F; not in Q2.*   45. is] *Q2;*
at *F.*

28. *and eat*] The Q1 *and a beggar eat*,
though it has been conjectured to be
right (Nosworthy, p. 161), gives an
inferior reading through anticipating
the point. Hamlet as yet speaks only
of 'a man'; his next speech will exploit the inference that what any *man*
may do may be done by a *beggar*. For
similar over-explicitness by the Q1
reporter, see IV.ii. 16–17.

31. *progress*] state journey, especially of a monarch (as made famous by
Elizabeth).

41. *tender*] are solicitous for, have
great regard for. Cf. I.iii. 107.

dearly] See I.ii. 182 n.

43. *With fiery quickness*] Mommsen
suspects F of interpolation perhaps
prompted by *R3* IV.iii. 54, 'fiery expedition' (*Neue Jahrbücher für Phil.
und Paed.*, LXXII, 116).

44. *at help*] i.e. 'in the quarter for
helping' (*OED*).

45. *tend*] attend, wait, as at I.iii. 83.

47. *For England?*] Though the
question-mark may be adopted,
Hamlet must not be taken to be surprised at what he has already accepted
at III.iv. 202–13.

King. Ay, Hamlet.

Ham. Good.

King. So is it, if thou knew'st our purposes.   50

Ham. I see a cherub that sees them. But come, for
    England. Farewell, dear mother.

King. Thy loving father, Hamlet.

Ham. My mother. Father and mother is man and wife,
    man and wife is one flesh; so my mother. Come, for   55
    England.   *Exit.*

King. Follow him at foot. Tempt him with speed aboard,
    Delay it not—I'll have him hence tonight.
    Away, for everything is seal'd and done
    That else leans on th'affair. Pray you make haste.   60
                  Exeunt all but the King.

    And England, if my love thou hold'st at aught—
    As my great power thereof may give thee sense,
    Since yet thy cicatrice looks raw and red
    After the Danish sword, and thy free awe
    Pays homage to us—thou mayst not coldly set   65
    Our sovereign process, which imports at full,
    By letters congruing to that effect,

---

51. them] *Q2;* him *F.*   51–6.] *Prose F; lines ending* England, | Hamlet. | wife, | mother: | *England. Q2.*   55. so] *Q2;* and so *F,Q1.*   57.] *one line Rowe; 2 lines divided* foote, | Tempt *Q2,F.*   60 S.D.] *Q1; not in Q2,F; Exeunt Ros. and Guild. Theobald.*   67. congruing] *Q2;* coniuring *F.*

---

51. *I see a cherub . . . them.*] A hint that Hamlet perceives more than the King supposes. Cherubim had the gift to 'see truly' (*Troil.* III. ii. 66–7). Cf. *Mac.* I. vii. 22–4.

52. *mother*] Hamlet, who had obeyed his mother by staying in Denmark (I. ii. 120), naturally thinks of her on leaving it. The King's mis-understanding provokes the sudden switch to chop-logic.

55. *man and wife is one flesh*] Cf. Genesis ii. 24; Matthew xix. 5–6; Mark x. 8.

57. *at foot*] close after. Abbott (143) compares 'at his heels'.

59–60. *everything . . . That else*] = everything else . . . that.

60. *leans on th'affair*] 'appertains to the business' (Kittredge).

61. *England*] the King of England. Cf. I. i. 51 (Denmark), etc.

65. *set*] set a value on, rate (cf. I. iv. 65); hence *coldly set*, regard with indifference (Schmidt). See *OED* set *v.* 89–90.

66. *process*] mandate. Though a *process* is often an actual document, I take the word to refer here to the order which the *letters* contain.

imports at full] conveys full direction for.

67. *congruing to*] in accordance with. The reading is supported by *H5* I. ii. 182 (F *Congreeing*, Q *Congrueth*). Those who prefer F *conjuring* point to

The present death of Hamlet. Do it, England;
For like the hectic in my blood he rages,
And thou must cure me. Till I know 'tis done,   70
Howe'er my haps, my joys were ne'er begun.   *Exit.*

[SCENE IV]

Enter FORTINBRAS *with his* Army [*marching*] *over the stage.*

Fort. Go, captain, from me greet the Danish king.
    Tell him that by his licence Fortinbras
    Craves the conveyance of a promis'd march
    Over his kingdom. You know the rendezvous.
    If that his Majesty would aught with us,   5
    We shall express our duty in his eye;
    And let him know so.
Cap.   I will do't, my lord.
Fort. Go softly on.   *Exeunt all* [*but the Captain*].

Enter HAMLET, ROSENCRANTZ, [GUILDENSTERN,]
                and Others.

71. were ne'er begun] *F;* will nere begin *Q2.*

Scene IV

SCENE IV] *Pope.*   S.D. *with . . . stage*] with his Army ouer the stage *Q2;* with an
Armie *F; Drumme and Souldiers Q1; and* Forces, marching / *Capell; a Captain, and
Soldiers, marching / Globe.*   3. Craves] *Q2,Q1;* Claimes *F.*   8. softly] *Q2;*
safely *F.*   8 S.D. Exeunt . . . Captain.] *Kittredge;* exeunt all. *Q1;* Exit. *F; not
in Q2.   Enter . . . Others.] Theobald subst.; Enter Hamlet, Rosencraus, &c. Q2;
not in F.*

conjuration at v.ii.38, which may,
however, have prompted it. See
MSH, p. 60.
    68. *present*] immediate.
    69. *hectic*] fever.
    71. *were ne'er begun*] The rhyme
seems to authenticate F's otherwise
inferior reading.

Scene IV

3–4. *the conveyance . . . kingdom*] Cf.
II. ii. 77–8, which explains *licence* (l. 2)

and *promis'd.* The *conveyance* is not
merely the carrying out of the promise but the 'conducting' of the
marchers (Q1, 'free passe and conduct'). LN.

    6. *express our duty*] pay our respects.
    in his eye] in his presence. Cf. I.
ii. 116 and n.
    7. *let*] imperative, parallel with
tell (l. 2).
    8. *softly*] gently. Cf. *Caes.* v.i.16.
OED, soft *a.* 5, softly *adv.* 3.

Ham. Good sir, whose powers are these?
Cap. They are of Norway, sir.   10
Ham. How purpos'd, sir, I pray you?
Cap. Against some part of Poland.
Ham. Who commands them, sir?
Cap. The nephew to old Norway, Fortinbras.
Ham. Goes it against the main of Poland, sir,   15
    Or for some frontier?
Cap. Truly to speak, and with no addition,
    We go to gain a little patch of ground
    That hath in it no profit but the name.
    To pay five ducats—five—I would not farm it;   20
    Nor will it yield to Norway or the Pole
    A ranker rate should it be sold in fee.
Ham. Why, then the Polack never will defend it.
Cap. Yes, it is already garrison'd.
Ham. Two thousand souls and twenty thousand ducats   25
    Will not debate the question of this straw!
    This is th'impostume of much wealth and peace,
    That inward breaks, and shows no cause without
    Why the man dies. I humbly thank you, sir.

9–66.] *Q2; not in F,Q1.*   20. ducats—five—] *Jennens;* duckets, fiue *Q2;*
ducats fine *conj. Theobald.*   24. Yes, it is] *Q2;* Nay 'tis *Q5;* Yes, 'tis *Pope;*
O, yes, it is *Capell.*   25. Ham.] *Q2; before 27 conj. Anon.*   26. straw!] *Wilson;*
straw, *Q2.*

18–26.] On the *little patch of ground,*
LN.

20. *ducats*] See II.ii.362 n.

five[2]] Usually taken as derisory repetition, but Theobald and others have
conjectured a misreading of *fine* (see
Nichols, *Illust. of Lit. Hist.,* ii.575;
Dyce[2]; *TLS,* 1947, pp. 591, 603). In
the sense of a contractual payment on
admission to a lease or tenancy, the
emendation would be almost irre-
sistible if it could be shown (as it has
not been) that *fine* without any preposition was as idiomatic then as it
would be now.

farm] take a lease of – often at an
annual rent, but alternatively, as
possibly here, on payment of a (non-
recurrent) fine.

22. *ranker*] more lavish.
in fee] outright, with absolute possession.

23. *the Polack*] = the Pole (l. 21),
the King of Poland. Cf. II.ii.63, 75
and I.i.66 LN.

25–6. *Two thousand . . . this straw!*]
Apparently an exclamation of astonishment. It has not been demonstrated that *debate* (= contest) can
signify *decide* or *settle* by combat
(Schmidt, Kittredge). This sense
seems in any case inappropriate for
Hamlet, but would fit with a proposal to transfer these lines to the
Captain (*Gentleman's Mag.,* LX, 403).

27. *impostume*] abscess; 'an inward
swelling full of corrupt matter' (Cotgrave, *v.* Apostume). LN.

Cap. God buy you, sir.   [*Exit.*]
Ros.   Will't please you go, my lord?   30
Ham. I'll be with you straight. Go a little before.

                                    [*Exeunt all but Hamlet.*]
            How all occasions do inform against me,
            And spur my dull revenge. What is a man
            If his chief good and market of his time
            Be but to sleep and feed? A beast, no more.   35
            Sure he that made us with such large discourse,
            Looking before and after, gave us not
            That capability and godlike reason
            To fust in us unus'd. Now whether it be
            Bestial oblivion, or some craven scruple   40
            Of thinking too precisely on th'event—
            A thought which, quarter'd, hath but one part wisdom
            And ever three parts coward—I do not know
            Why yet I live to say this thing's to do,
            Sith I have cause, and will, and strength, and means 45
            To do't. Examples gross as earth exhort me,
            Witness this army of such mass and charge,
            Led by a delicate and tender prince,
            Whose spirit, with divine ambition puff'd,
            Makes mouths at the invisible event,   50

---

30 S.D.] *Capell.*   31 S.D.] *Rowe subst.*   39. fust] *Q2;* rust *Rowe.*

30. *God buy you*] See II.i.69n.

33–5. *What is a man . . . no more.*] The essential distinction between man and beast lies in man's possession of *reason* (l. 38), lacking which the beast is actuated only by the senses (Cicero, *De Officiis*, I.iv.11). Cf. I.ii.140 LN, 150 LN.

34. *good and market of*] (hendiadys) advantage gained from the disposal of.

36. *discourse*] power of reasoning. 'The act of the understanding, by which it passes from premises to consequences' (Johnson, *Dict.*). Cf. I. ii.150 and LN.

37. *Looking before and after*] LN.

39. *fust*] become musty.

41. *Of*] from, in consequence of. Abbott 168.

41–2. *thinking too precisely . . . wisdom*] Cf. Florio's Montaigne (I.23): 'A *wisdom* so tenderly precise, and so *precisely* circumspect, is a mortal enemy to haughty executions'.

41. *event*] outcome, consequence, as also in l. 50.

47. *charge*] cost. Cf. l. 25.

48. *a delicate . . . prince*] In marked contrast with I.i.98–103: *delicate*, sensitive, of gentle nurture; *tender*, youthful and uncoarsened.

50. *Makes mouths at*] makes faces at, shows contempt for (as at II.ii.360).

invisible event] unforeseeable outcome. Cf. *unsure*, l. 51.

Exposing what is mortal and unsure
To all that fortune, death, and danger dare,
Even for an eggshell. Rightly to be great
Is not to stir without great argument,
But greatly to find quarrel in a straw   55
When honour's at the stake. How stand I then,
That have a father kill'd, a mother stain'd,
Excitements of my reason and my blood,
And let all sleep, while to my shame I see
The imminent death of twenty thousand men   60
That, for a fantasy and trick of fame,
Go to their gräves like beds, fight for a plot
Whereon the numbers cannot try the cause,
Which is not tomb enough and continent
To hide the slain? O, from this time forth   65
My thoughts be bloody or be nothing worth.   *Exit.*

53–4. Rightly . . . Is not] *Q2;* 'Tis not . . . Never *Pope;* Rightly . . . Is not,
not *Capell;* Rightly . . . Is, not *Malone.*

53–6. *Rightly to be . . . the stake.*] The
construction is that true greatness is
not this *but* that; and the single negative requires to be taken in a double
sense – i.e. *Is not to stir* = Is not not to
stir, as Capell read. LN.

54. *argument*] cause, subject of contention.

58. *blood*] As the seat of passion,
regularly opposed to *reason.* Cf. III.
ii.69 and I.iii.6n.

60. *twenty thousand*] Contrast l. 25.
I fear we must ascribe the confusion
to Shakespeare, often lax with numbers, rather than (with Verity) to
Hamlet.

61. *fantasy*] illusion. The 'honour'
(l. 56) is, after all, insubstantial. Cf.
II.ii.546, 'fiction . . . dream'.

trick] (1) toy, trifle (cf. *Shr.* IV.
iii.67, 'A knack, a toy, a trick, a
baby's cap'); but with something
also of (2) deceit, pretence.

63. *Whereon . . . the cause*] not big
enough to hold all those who fight
for it.

64. *continent*] container. Cf. V.ii.111.

[SCENE V]

Enter QUEEN, HORATIO, *and a* Gentleman.

Queen. I will not speak with her.
Gent.   She is importunate,
   Indeed distract. Her mood will needs be pitied.
Queen. What would she have?
Gent. She speaks much of her father, says she hears
   There's tricks i'th' world, and hems, and beats her heart,
   Spurns enviously at straws, speaks things in doubt   6
   That carry but half sense. Her speech is nothing,
   Yet the unshaped use of it doth move
   The hearers to collection. They aim at it,
   And botch the words up fit to their own thoughts,   10
   Which, as her winks and nods and gestures yield them,
   Indeed would make one think there might be thought,
   Though nothing sure, yet much unhappily.

Scene v

SCENE V] *Pope.*   S.D. *Horatio, and a Gentleman*] *Q2; and Horatio F; Horatio, and Attendants | Rowe; and a Gentleman | Hanmer.*   1, 4. *Gent.*] *Q2; Hor. F.* 1–2. She . . . pitied.] *As Q2; prose F; verse divided* distract; | *Her Capell.* 9. aim] *F;* yawne *Q2.*   12. might] *Q2;* would *F.*

S.D. *Horatio, and a Gentleman*] F's wish to save cast found an obvious opportunity here. Yet the dialogue requires a second speaker other than the Queen at ll. 14–15. The role of attendant on or adviser to the Queen is, however, a strange one for Horatio, and the dramatist appears to forget him after l. 16.

2. *distract*] out of her mind. Cf. III. i. 5, v. ii. 225.
   mood] state of mind.

6. *Spurns enviously at straws*] 'takes offence angrily at trifles' (Kittredge). *Spurns,* lit. kicks; *enviously,* spitefully.
   in doubt] with no clear meaning.

7. *nothing*] nonsense.

9. *collection*] putting together (of the 'unshaped' fragments), gathering by inference. Cf. *Cym.* v.v.431–2, 'so from sense . . . that I can Make no collection of it'.

aim] make conjecture. Those who read *yawn* with Q2 cite *Oth.* v. ii. 104, *Cor.* III. ii. 11, for the meaning 'gape in wonderment'. But the sense there is of stupefaction, here of movement in an effort to gather or grasp something. Hence *yawn* is more probably a misreading, perhaps influenced by the *y* of *they.*

11. *Which*] = the words.
   yield] declare, represent. Cf. *Ant.* II.v.28, 'well and free, If thou so yield him'. See 1.iii.23 n. Ophelia's gestures seem to give her words more meaning than in themselves they have.

12–13. *there might be thought . . . unhappily*] Though *thought* might at first be taken for a noun referring to the intended meaning of Ophelia's words, the complement (l. 13) shows it to be a past pple. A great deal could be

Hor. 'Twere good she were spoken with, for she may strew
    Dangerous conjectures in ill-breeding minds.   15
Queen. Let her come in.   *[Exit Gentleman.]*
    [Aside] To my sick soul, as sin's true nature is,
    Each toy seems prologue to some great amiss.
    So full of artless jealousy is guilt,
    It spills itself in fearing to be spilt.   20

Enter OPHELIA.

Oph. Where is the beauteous Majesty of Denmark?
Queen. How now, Ophelia?
Oph. (*sings*)   *How should I your true love know*
                From another one?

---

14. *Hor.*] Q2; *Qu.* F; *not in* Hanmer.   14–16.] *As* Q2; *lines ending* with, /
coniectures / come in. F.   16. *Queen.*] *Hanmer; before* 17 Q2; *before* 14 F.
16 S.D.] *Hanmer; Exit Hor.* / *Johnson.*   17. *Aside*] *As* Capell.   20 S.D.] Q2
(*after* 16); *Enter Ophelia distracted.* F; *Enter Ofelia playing on a Lute, and her
haire downe singing.* Q1; *Enter Horatio, with Ophelia, distracted.* Johnson; *Re-enter
Gentleman, with Ophelia.* Cambridge.   23. *sings*] Q2; *not in* F (*which prints all
the songs in italic*).   23–6, 29–32.] *As* Capell, Q1 (*subst.*); *4 lines as* 2, Q2,F.

---

mischievously (*unhappily*), though
nothing certainly, supposed.

    15. *ill-breeding*] prone to breed evil,
mischief-making.

    16. *Queen. Let her come in.*] Only the
Queen can give this order: I infer
that some misunderstanding of the
copy led Q2 to put the speech-
heading a line too late. Similar mislining of the speech-heading occurs at
l. 152 below, III.iv.52. See *MLR*,
LIV, 391–3.

    17. *my sick soul*] Hamlet's reproaches
of III.iv have a lasting effect.

    17–20.] In Q2 each of these lines
has prefixed to it the quotation-mark
which indicates a sententious saying.
Cf. I.iii. 36, 38–9.

    18. *toy*] trifle. Cf. I.iii.6 and LN.
amiss] misfortune.

    19. *jealousy*] apprehension of evil, as
at II.i. 113.

    20. *It spills . . . spilt.*] To *spill* is to
destroy (the original sense). The
wretchedness which the guilty inflict
on themselves in their apprehension
of disaster is no less than would be
that of disaster itself. The usual explanation that the guilty betray
themselves through the fear of being
betrayed goes beyond the text in the
assumption that betrayal is the only
route to ruin.

    20 S.D. *Enter Ophelia.*] Q1 no
doubt records some contemporary
staging. The hair down is conventional for madness, but the lute,
uncalled for in the text and incongruous with the ballad snatches Ophelia
spontaneously breaks into, looks like
an actors' embellishment.

    23. *sings*] For Ophelia's songs, LN.
23–40.] On this song, LN.

By his cockle hat and staff   25
And his sandal shoon.

Queen. Alas, sweet lady, what imports this song?
Oph. Say you? Nay, pray you mark.
   (*sings*)   *He is dead and gone, lady,*
                 He is dead and gone,   30
                 At his head a grass-green turf,
                 At his heels a stone.

      O ho!

Queen. Nay, but Ophelia—
Oph. Pray you mark.   35
   [*sings*]   *White his shroud as the mountain snow—*

                    Enter KING.

Queen. Alas, look here, my lord.
Oph. (*sings*)   *Larded with sweet flowers*
                 Which bewept to the grave did not go
                 With true-love showers.   40

29, 38, 48, 164, 187 *sings*] *Song (at right of text) Q2; not in F.*   33. O ho] *Q2;*
not in F; O, o *Capell.*   35–6.] *As F; one line Q2.*   36 S.D. *Enter King.]*
Q2; before 34 F.   38. *Larded*] *F,Q1;* Larded all *Q2.*   39. *grave*] *F,Q1;*
ground *Q2.*   *did not*] *Q2,F,Q1;* did *Pope.*

25–6. *his cockle hat . . . shoon*] The
insignia of a pilgrim. A favourite
convention pictured the lover as
going on pilgrimage to the shrine of
his saint (as in *Mer.V.* i.i. 120, II.
viii. 39–40. Cf. *Rom.* i.v.91–104). A
lyric in Greene's *Never Too Late*
(Greene, viii. 14) describes a pilgrim
lover as having 'A hat of straw . . .
With a scollop-shell before; Sandals
on his feet he wore'.
   25. *cockle hat*] A cockle-shell (or
more strictly, a scallop-shell) was
worn on the hat to denote, originally,
one who had been at the shrine of St
James at Compostela. The practice
appears to have derived from the use
of the scallop-shell in baptism and
hence as a symbol of repentance and
regeneration.
   26. *shoon*] The ballad retains the
archaic plural.
   31–2. *At his head . . . a stone.*] Tra-

ditional burial-customs referred to in
ballad and folklore. Cf. Child, *Eng.
and Scot. Pop. Ballads*, 1882–98, ii. 145,
'A green turf upon his breast To hold
that good lord down'; Keats, *Isabella*,
st. 38, 'a large flint-stone weighs upon
my feet'. An allusion to the custom
whereby obscurer graves had the
gravestone at the feet seems unlikely.
   33. *O ho!*] A deep sigh (Parrott-
Craig).
   38. *Larded*] strewn, bedecked. The
culinary verb for inserting strips of
fat extended its range till it came to
mean 'enrich' or 'garnish' in a general
sense and so 'intersperse or sprinkle
with ornaments'. Cf. v.ii. 20, and for
the practice of strewing flowers on the
dead v.i. 236–9.
   39. *not*] This of course violates both
the metre and the expected sense, and
has been thought an error. But (with
all three texts agreeing) we must

King. How do you, pretty lady?

Oph. Well, good dild you. They say the owl was a baker's
daughter. Lord, we know what we are, but know
not what we may be. God be at your table.

King. Conceit upon her father.   45

Oph. Pray let's have no words of this, but when they ask
you what it means, say you this.

(*sings*)   *Tomorrow is Saint Valentine's day,*
                         All in the morning betime,
                       And I a maid at your window,   50
                         To be your Valentine.
                       Then up he rose, and donn'd his clo'es,
                         And dupp'd the chamber door,
                       Let in the maid that out a maid
                         Never departed more.   55

King. Pretty Ophelia—

---

41. you] *Q2;* ye *F.*   42. good dild] *Q2;* God dil'd *F;* God yeeld *Q1.*
46. Pray] *Q2;* Pray you *F.*   48–51.] *As Q2,Q1; 2 lines F.*   52–5.] *As
Johnson, Q1 subst.; 2 lines Q2,F.*   52. clo'es] *Wilson;* close *Q2;* clothes *F,Q1.*

---

rather suppose it a deliberate interpolation by the singer, who recalls
and so emphasizes that the pattern
celebrated in the song is contradicted
by the instance in her mind. The song
thus reflects the actual shortcomings
of her father's burial (ll. 84, 210–12)
but still more, since it concerns a
'true love', her fantasies of Hamlet's
death. Cf. ll. 23–40 LN.

42. *good dild you*] A corruption of
God yield (i.e. requite) you, which
Q1 reads. (*OED* yield *v.* 7; God 8).
Q2, with the *good* of colloquial speech
(cf. 'good-bye'), probably gives the
authentic reading, which F and Q1
sophisticate.

42–3. *the owl was a baker's daughter*]
The relevance of this legend to the
context is obscure, but it possibly
alludes to the loss of virginity. LN.

43–4. *we know what . . . may be*] An
ironic echo of 1 John iii. 2, 'Now are
we the sons of God, and it doth not

yet appear what we shall be'.

44. *God be at your table.*] A sentiment
contrasting with that of the baker's
daughter (who grudged Christ
bread)?

45. *Conceit*] fancy.
upon her father] The King, not
alone, apparently takes her to allude
to the lack of burial rites and is blind
to Ophelia's frustrated love for Hamlet. Cf. l. 23 LN.

48–66.] LN.

51. *Valentine*] sweetheart according
to the ancient custom which recognizes as such the first person of the
opposite sex seen on St Valentine's
day.

53. *dupp'd*] opened. *Dup* = do up
(cf. don, doff).

56. *Pretty Ophelia* –] Comparison
with ll. 34, 41 suggests that this,
though almost always rendered as an
exclamation, is addressed to Ophelia,
in a vain attempt to divert the flow.

Oph. Indeed, without an oath, I'll make an end on't.

> *By Gis and by Saint Charity,*
> *Alack and fie for shame,*
> *Young men will do't if they come to't—*   60
> *By Cock, they are to blame.*
> *Quoth she, 'Before you tumbled me,*
> *You promis'd me to wed.'*

He answers,

> *'So would I a done, by yonder sun,*   65
> *And thou hadst not come to my bed.'*

King. How long hath she been thus?

Oph. I hope all will be well. We must be patient. But I
cannot choose but weep to think they would lay
him i'th' cold ground. My brother shall know of it.   70
And so I thank you for your good counsel. Come,
my coach. Good night, ladies, good night. Sweet
ladies, good night, good night.   *Exit.*

King. Follow her close; give her good watch, I pray you.

> [*Exit Horatio.*]

O, this is the poison of deep grief: it springs   75
All from her father's death. And now behold—

57. Indeed,] *Q2;* Indeed la? *F.*   62–3.] *As F,Q1; one line Q2.*   64. He
answers] *Q2 (in brackets); not in F,Q1.*   65. a] *Q2,Q1;* ha *F.*   67. thus]
Q2; this *F.*   69. would] *Q2;* should *F.*   72–3. (*4 times*) Good (*or* good)
night] *F (as one word);* God (*or* god) night *Q2.*   73 S.D.] *F; not in Q2.*
74 S.D.] *Theobald; Horatio and the gentleman follow her | Wilson.*   75–7.] *As
Steevens[4]; prose Q2; 2 lines divided* springs / All *F.*   76. And now behold] *Q2;
not in F.*

58. *Gis*] A corruption of *Jesus,* common in adjurations, pronounced and
sometimes spelt *jis.*

Saint Charity] Not a saint's name, of
course, but through such phrases as
by, for, or *of Charity,* often used in
oaths as if it were. 'The Catholiques
comen othe . . . to haue charitye alwayes in their mouth' (*Shepheardes
Calender,* May gloss).

60. *do't*] A euphemism. Cf. *Tim.*
IV.i.8.

61. *Cock*] Corruption of God; but
no doubt there is a thought of the
male organ too.

62. *tumbled*] tousled (with obvious
innuendo).

64. *He answers*] Dialogue in a lyric
is indicated in just the same way in
Troil. IV.iv.17.

72. *my coach*] Cf. 1 *Tamburlaine,* V.
i.315, where the mad Zabina calls
for her coach in order to join her dead
husband.

74 S.D. *Horatio*] See n. on S.D. at
head of scene. It is clear that the King
and Queen must now have the stage
to themselves.

75. *this is*] Often contracted to a
single syllable. Abbott 461.

76. *All . . . father's death.*] See above,
l. 45 n.

And now behold—] F's omission of
these words regularizes the metre.

O Gertrude, Gertrude,
When sorrows come, they come not single spies,
But in battalions. First, her father slain;
Next, your son gone, and he most violent author   80
Of his own just remove; the people muddied,
Thick and unwholesome in their thoughts and whispers
For good Polonius' death—and we have done but
          greenly
In hugger-mugger to inter him; poor Ophelia
Divided from herself and her fair judgment,   85
Without the which we are pictures, or mere beasts;
Last, and as much containing as all these,
Her brother is in secret come from France,
Feeds on this wonder, keeps himself in clouds,
And wants not buzzers to infect his ear   90

---

78. sorrows come] *Q2;* sorrowes comes *F.*   79. battalions] *Q2;* Battaliaes *F.*
82. their] *F; not in Q2.*   89. Feeds on this] *Q2;* Keepes on his *F.*

But they must have stood in the Q2
copy. Possibly *O Gertrude, Gertrude*
was meant to replace them.

78–9. *they come . . . in battalions*] An
elegant variation on a familiar proverb. Tilley M 1012, 1013, 1004. Cf.
IV. vii. 162–3. *spies*, soldiers sent ahead
to reconnoitre.

81–2. *muddied, Thick*] turbid, hence
clouded in mind, confused. Cf. *Shr.*
v. ii. 142–3, 'like a fountain troubled –
Muddy, ill-seeming, thick'.

82. *unwholesome*] tainted with suspicion.

83. *we*] The royal *we*.

greenly] foolishly. Cf. I. iii. 101, 'a
green girl'; *Ant.* I. v. 74, 'green in
judgment'.

84. *In hugger-mugger*] with undue
secrecy, clandestinely. Cf. l. 210. The
phrase was common but may here
echo North's *Plutarch* (Life of Brutus),
which Shakespeare had recently used
for *Caes*: 'Antonius thinking . . . that
his body should be honourably
buried, and not in hugger-mugger,
lest the people might thereby take
occasion to be worse offended'. Cf.
Revenger's Trag., v. i. 19, 'how quaintly

he died, like a politician in hugger-
mugger, made no man acquainted
with it'.

85. *Divided from . . . judgment*] Cf.
Hamlet's madness, v. ii. 230–2.

86. *pictures*] soulless outward forms.
Cf. *Mac.* II. ii. 53–4, 'The sleeping and
the dead Are but as pictures'; *Ven.*
211–14; *Mer. V.* I. ii. 65.

mere beasts] Cf. I. ii. 150, IV. iv. 35–9.

87. *as much containing as*] comprising
as much as, of a gravity equal to.

89. *this wonder*] The Q2 reading
must be taken to refer to this whole
sensational course of events. Cf. l. 94.
But perhaps we should accept F *his
wonder* (= his bewilderment) and regard *this* as an error, as at v. ii. 139,
Mer. V. IV. i. 30. Cf. Walker, ii. 219–28;
MSH, p. 112.

in clouds] mystified in uncertainties
(through indulging in 'wonder' instead of fact).

90. *wants not buzzers*] does not lack
rumour-mongers. Kittredge compares *Nobody and Somebody*, l. 1912,
'Strange rumours and false buzzing
tales' (Q n.d. sig. I^v).

With pestilent speeches of his father's death,
Wherein necessity, of matter beggar'd,
Will nothing stick our person to arraign
In ear and ear. O my dear Gertrude, this,
Like to a murd'ring-piece, in many places   95
Gives me superfluous death.   *A noise within.*
                    Attend!
Where is my Switzers? Let them guard the door.

                Enter a Messenger.

    What is the matter?
Mess.   Save yourself, my lord.
    The ocean, overpeering of his list,

---

92. Wherein] *Q2;* Where in *F.*   93. person] *Q2;* persons *F.*   95. murd'ring-
piece, . . . places] *Theobald (subst.);* murdring peece . . . places *Q2;* murdering
Peece . . . places, *F.*   96. Attend!] *Q2; Qu.* Alacke, what noyse is this? *F.*
96–8. Gives . . . lord.] *This edn; lines ending* death. / doore, / *Q2; ending* death. /
Switzers? / matter? *F.*   97. is] *Q2;* are *F.*   97 S.D.] *As Kittredge; after 96
S.D. Q2,F; Enter a Gentleman, hastily. Capell.*

---

92. *necessity*] The mother of invention (material facts being short).

93. *Will nothing stick . . . arraign*] will
by no means hesitate to accuse me
personally.

94. *In ear and ear*] in one ear after
another – of the many-headed multitude among whom the rumours
spread. But Kittredge takes the ears
to be those of Laertes, assailed now on
this side now on that.

this] Presumably the whole catalogue of 'sorrows' (l. 78) rather than
merely the last item. Hence l. 95.

95. *a murd'ring-piece*] a kind of cannon (also called a 'murderer') which
by the scatter of its case-shot could
hit many men at once. Cf. Fletcher,
Double Marriage, IV.ii.6, 'like a
murdering-piece, aims not at one,
But all that stand within the dangerous level'.

96. *superfluous*] Since one would
have been enough.

Attend!] i.e. Listen! F substitutes

an exclamation from the Queen.
Most modern eds. illogically include
both. (See *SB,* XIII, 36.)

97. *is*] For the singular, see III.
iii. 14 n.

Switzers] The Swiss were well
known as mercenaries, esp. for royal
guards. The bodyguard of the Danish
kings were in fact not Swiss though
sometimes thought to be so, probably
because their red and yellow uniform
resembled that of the Pope's Swiss
guard. See *SQ,* XVI, 157–8; Dollerup,
pp. 193–4.

99–102. *The ocean . . . officers.*] This
comparison of a rebellious people to
waters overflowing their banks is, significantly, a recurrent one with
Shakespeare. Cf. *Troil.* I.iii.111–13;
Cor. III.i.248–50; *Sir Thomas More,*
Addn II, 162–3.

99. *overpeering*] rising above. For the
pple. followed by *of,* see Abbott 178.

his] its. See I.i.40n.

list] boundary, barrier.

Eats not the flats with more impetuous haste   100
Than young Laertes, in a riotous head,
O'erbears your officers. The rabble call him lord,
And, as the world were now but to begin,
Antiquity forgot, custom not known—
The ratifiers and props of every word—   105
They cry, 'Choose we! Laertes shall be king.'
Caps, hands, and tongues applaud it to the clouds,
'Laertes shall be king, Laertes king.'
Queen. How cheerfully on the false trail they cry.   109
    O, this is counter, you false Danish dogs.   *A noise within.*
King. The doors are broke.

Enter LAERTES *with* Followers.

100. impetuous] *Q3F2;* impitious *Q2,F* (impittious); impiteous *Wilson.*
106. They] *F;* The *Q2.*   110 S.D.] *F* (*subst.*); *after 109 Q2.*   111 S.D.]
Spencer (*subst.*); *Enter Laertes with others.* (*after 110*) *Q2; Enter Laertes.* (*after 110*
S.D.) *F; Enter Laertes, arm'd; Danes following. | Capell.*

100. *impetuous*] violent, of great impetus. The Elizabethan spelling *impit(t)ious* adds something to the meaning; but the *impiteous* of some modern eds. emphasizes these secondary connotations at the expense of the primary meaning.

101. *Laertes*] For the suggestion that this rebellion of Laertes replaces the one originally envisaged for Fortinbras (I.i.98ff.), cf. Intro., pp. 100, 142, and see *Rice U. Studs.,* LX, 100–3.

   head] insurrectionary advance. (Not merely an armed force, as usually explained, but its forward movement.) Cf. *Cor.* II.ii.86, 'When Tarquin made a head for Rome'; *Oth.* I.iii.274.

105. *word*] motto, maxim. Proposed emendations all rest on a failure to grasp the sense of the passage. The *ratifiers and props* are not (as too often explained) the rabble, but *antiquity* (ancient tradition) and *custom*, by which a maxim, a guiding-phrase of conduct, needs to be upheld – as it conspicuously is not in the case of the *word* now being cried (see next line).

Cf. I.v.110 and n.

   106. *Choose . . . king.*] Denmark was an elective monarchy and in Belleforest Hamlet himself became king by public proclamation after he had killed his uncle. But this proclamation of Laertes against a reigning monarch is in defiance of all precedent (ll. 103–5).

109. *cry*] make the sound of hounds following a scent. Cf. *Wiv.* IV.ii.174, 'cry out thus upon no trail'.

110. *counter*] To hunt *counter*, to follow a scent in the direction contrary to that taken by the game, is not strictly the same as to follow a *false* scent, though the distinction is often not preserved in figurative use. Cf. *2H4* I.ii.85.

111 S.D. *with Followers*] Although these are kept off stage by F and Q1, perhaps for practical reasons of cast, the Q2 direction together with the dialogue suggests that they were meant to be seen erupting into the presence.

Laer. Where is this king?—Sirs, stand you all without.
Followers. No, let's come in.
Laer.   I pray you give me leave.
Followers. We will, we will.
Laer. I thank you. Keep the door.   [*Exeunt Followers.*]   115
                                O thou vile king,
      Give me my father.
Queen. [*holding him*]   Calmly, good Laertes.
Laer. That drop of blood that's calm proclaims me bastard,
      Cries cuckold to my father, brands the harlot
      Even here between the chaste unsmirched brow
      Of my true mother.
King.   What is the cause, Laertes,   120
      That thy rebellion looks so giant-like?—
      Let him go, Gertrude. Do not fear our person.
      There's such divinity doth hedge a king
      That treason can but peep to what it would,
      Acts little of his will.—Tell me, Laertes,   125

112. this] *Q2;* the *F.*   king?—Sirs,] *Q2 (subst.);* King, sirs? *F.*
113, 114. *Followers*] *Spencer (subst.); All | Q2,F; Dan[es] Capell.*   115–16.] *Divided*
as Q2; divided doore. | *Oh F.*   115 S.D.] *Kittredge (subst.); Exeunt. (after 114)*
Theobald; retiring without the Door (after 114) Capell.   116. *holding him*] *Johnson*
(subst.); the Queen throws herself in his path (at 120) Wilson.   117. that's calm]
Q2; that calmes *F.*   119. brow] *Q2,F;* brows *Q 1676.*

113. *give me leave*] A formula of dismissal, as at II.ii.170.
      118–20. *brands . . . mother*] This
solitary reference to the mother of
Laertes reinforces the contrast between him and Hamlet, for whom
such simple asseverations are not
possible. Cf. III.iv.42–4.
      119. *Even here*] i.e. in this of all
places.
      between the . . . brow] Comparison
with *Ado* III.v.12, 'between the
brows', suggests that a final *s* may
have been lost, and some eds. accordingly emend. But ambiguity as to
singular or plural is inherent in the
semantics of the word, 'between the
brows' and 'upon the brow' being
synonymous. Hence a grammatical
mix-up is neither unnatural nor
necessarily unShakespearean. Cf.

Roaring Girl, I.i.76–8, 'storms . . .
upon my . . . father's brow . . . fell
from *them*'.
      121. *giant-like*] For the story of
earth's giants who assailed the gods
in heaven, see Ovid, *Met.* i.152ff.,
Fasti, v.35ff. It was 'the great classical instance of *lèse-majesté*' (Thomson,
Sh. and the Classics, p. 118) and that
Shakespeare had it in mind is suggested by the references to Pelion
and Ossa in v.i.246, 278.
      122. *fear*] fear for, as at I.iii.51,
III.iv.5.
      123–5. *There's such divinity . . . will.*]
LN.
      124. *but peep to . . . would*] have no
more than a glimpse of what it would
like to do.
      125. *his*] its. See I.i.40n.

Why thou art thus incens'd.—Let him go, Gertrude.—
Speak, man.
Laer. Where is my father?
King.   Dead.
Queen.   But not by him.
King. Let him demand his fill.
Laer. How came he dead? I'll not be juggled with.   130
To hell, allegiance! Vows to the blackest devil!
Conscience and grace, to the profoundest pit!
I dare damnation. To this point I stand,
That both the worlds I give to negligence,
Let come what comes, only I'll be reveng'd   135
Most throughly for my father.
King.   Who shall stay you?
Laer. My will, not all the world's.
And for my means, I'll husband them so well,
They shall go far with little.
King.   Good Laertes,
If you desire to know the certainty   140
Of your dear father, is't writ in your revenge
That, swoopstake, you will draw both friend and foe,
Winner and loser?
Laer. None but his enemies.

---

128. Where is] *Q2;* Where's *F.*   137. world's] *Pope;* worlds *Q2;* world *F.*
139-40. Good . . . certainty] *As F; one line Q2.*   141. father] *Q2;* Fathers
death *F.*   is't] *Q2;* if *F.*   142. swoopstake] soopstake *Q2,F,* swoopstake
Dyce; Swoop-stake-like *Q1;* sweep-stake *Pope.*

132-5. *Conscience . . . what comes*]
The contrast with Hamlet is regularly
remarked. See esp. III.i.78-83.

132. *grace*] The grace of God
through which man attains salvation
and the rejection of which here leads
on to the next line.

profoundest pit] the 'bottomless pit'
of Revelation (ix.1, etc.).

134. *both the worlds*] i.e. this world
and the next.

136. *throughly*] thoroughly.

137. *the world's*] i.e. the world's will.

141. *father*] F's unmetrical *fathers
death,* though accepted by most eds.,
is perhaps an anticipation of l. 149

(*MSH,* p. 254).

142. *swoopstake*] alternative form of
sweepstake, the act of taking all the
stakes in a game, or the person who
does so. *OED* takes this to be a unique
adverbial use (= indiscriminately;
cf. Q1, *Swoop-stake-like*), but it might
be regarded as an interjection. Cf.
Heywood, *2 Ed. IV,* i.116, 'to cry
swoop-stake'. This is what the King
represents Laertes as doing when,
pursuing revenge against guilty and
innocent alike, he *draws* all the stakes
and not only the winnings he is entitled to.

King.   Will you know them then?

Laer. To his good friends thus wide I'll ope my arms,   145
    And, like the kind life-rend'ring pelican,
    Repast them with my blood.

King.   Why, now you speak
    Like a good child and a true gentleman.
    That I am guiltless of your father's death
    And am most sensibly in grief for it,   150
    It shall as level to your judgment 'pear
    As day does to your eye.

            A noise within. [Ophelia is heard singing.]
             Let her come in.

Laer. How now, what noise is that?

          Enter OPHELIA.

  O heat, dry up my brains. Tears seven times salt

---

146. pelican] *Q2;* Politician *F.*   150. sensibly] *Q2;* sensible *F.*
151. 'pear] *Johnson;* peare *Q2;* pierce *F.*   152 S.D. *within.*] *Q2; within.* Let
her come in. *F.*   Ophelia . . . singing.] *This edn.*   152. Let . . . in.] *This edn;*
Laer. Let . . . in. *Q2; as part of S.D. | F; Danes (within).* Let . . . in. *Capell;*
Voices (within). Let . . . in. *Munro; Shouting without.* Let . . . in. *Wilson.*
153. *Laer.* How] *F;* How *Q2.*   153 S.D. *Enter Ophelia.] Q2 (at 152, before*
Let . . . in), *F (before 153); Enter Ofelia as before. Q1; Enter Ophelia, fantastically*
drest with Straws and Flowers. *Rowe; Ophelia re-enters with flowers in her hand |*
Wilson.

146. *kind*] showing natural feeling
for its 'kind'.

    pelican] In traditional fable the
pelican feeds its young from its own
breast, in some versions reviving them
from seeming death (cf. *life-rend'ring*).
According as it is applied to parent or
child the same fable may illustrate
self-sacrifice or (*Lr* III.iv.74; *R2* II.
i.126) heartlessness. The extravagance
of the image here is no doubt meant
to characterize Laertes's 'emphasis'
and 'rant' (cf. v.i.248, 279).

    150. *sensibly*] feelingly.

    151. *level*] unimpeded. Cf. IV.i.42;
2H4 IV.iv.7, 'everything lies level to
our wish'.

    'pear] On the superiority of this (=
appear) to F *pierce*, see *MSH*, pp.
275–6. There is no clear distinction
between *'pear* and *peer*, to peep out, to

be (faintly) discernible (as in *Shr.* IV.
iii.170, 'Honour peereth in the mean-
est habit'; *Wint.* IV.iii.1, IV.iv.3; etc.)
and the meanings of the two words
interact. See *OED* peer *v.*[2]

    152 S.D. *Ophelia . . . singing.*] The
words which follow show that the
'noise' signals Ophelia's return.

    152. *Let her come in.*] This, which F
and all the eds. misconceive, must belong to the on-stage dialogue. Q2's
error is in placing the speech-prefix
Laer. a line too soon, so making these
words begin Laertes's speech instead
of continuing the King's. Cf. for a
similarly misplaced speech-prefix III.
iv.52–3, and see *MLR*, LIV, 391–3.

    154–5. *O heat . . . eye.*] To be spared
so painful a spectacle Laertes longs to
lose both sight and reason. The brain,
conceived of in the old physiology as

Burn out the sense and virtue of mine eye.   155
By heaven, thy madness shall be paid with weight
Till our scale turn the beam. O rose of May!
Dear maid—kind sister—sweet Ophelia—
O heavens, is't possible a young maid's wits
Should be as mortal as an old man's life?   160
Nature is fine in love, and where 'tis fine
It sends some precious instance of itself
After the thing it loves.

Oph. (*sings*)   *They bore him bare-fac'd on the bier,*
                   And in his grave rain'd many a tear—   165
Fare you well, my dove.

Laer. Hadst thou thy wits and didst persuade revenge,
     It could not move thus.

Oph. You must sing *A-down a-down*, and you *Call him*

156. with] *Q2;* by *F.*   157. Till] *F;* Tell *Q2.*   turn] *Q2;* turnes *F.*
160. an old] *F,Q1;* a poore *Q2.*   161–3.] *F; not in Q2.*   164. bier,] *Q2;*
Beer, | Hey non nony, nony, hey nony: F.   165. in] *Q2; on F.*   rain'd] *Q2;*
raines F.   166.] *Q2; italic (as part of song) F.*   167–8.] *As Q2; prose F.*
168. move] *Q2,F;* move me *conj. Walker.*   169–71.] *Prose F; 3 lines divided* a
downe, | And . . . it, | It *Q2.*   169–70. You . . . a-down-a] *This edn; as two
lines of song Staunton; all in italics Johnson; italics for all after* You must sing |
Steevens²; only 'Adown adown' *as quotation Wilson.*   169. A-down a-down] *Q2;*
downe a-downe *F.*   and] *Q2,F;* an *Capell.*

cold and moist, would perish if 'dried
up'.

   155. *virtue*] inherent power,
property.

   157. *turn the beam*] tilt the bar join-
ing the two scales of a balance.

   161–3.] These 'obscure and affected' lines (Johnson) have often given
trouble but may be paraphrased:
Human nature, when in love, is ex-
quisitely sensitive, and being so, it
sends a precious part of itself as a
token to follow the object of its love.
Thus, the fineness of Ophelia's love is
demonstrated when, after the loved
one has gone, her mind goes too. The
commentators, with Laertes, always
apply the general statement to
Ophelia's love for her father, but the
play leaves it open to us to apply it
also to her love for Hamlet.

   162. *instance*] example affording

demonstration, specimen.

   164–5.] LN.

   166. *Fare you well, my dove.*] Printed
by F as though part of the song, and
indistinguishable from it in Q2, but
more plausibly an endearment added
by Ophelia to it.

   169. *A-down a-down*] Cited by
Florio to illustrate 'the burden of a
country song' (*World of Words,* under
Filibustacchina), this common and all
but meaningless refrain is found in a
number of ballads in a variety of
forms. It is sung by Quickly in *Wiv.*
i.iv.38 and by the mad Lucibella in
Chettle's *Hoffman* (l. 1976). Here
Ophelia instructs her hearers to sing it
as a refrain to her song.

   169–70. *and you . . . a-down-a*] *You*
addresses others of those present. The
refrain is apparently to be sung by
alternating voices. LN.

a-down-a. O, how the wheel becomes it! It is the   170
false steward that stole his master's daughter.

Laer. This nothing's more than matter.

Oph. There's rosemary, that's for remembrance—pray
you, love, remember. And there is pansies, that's for
thoughts.   175

Laer. A document in madness: thoughts and remembrance fitted.

Oph. There's fennel for you, and columbines. There's
rue for you. And here's some for me. We may call it
herb of grace a Sundays. You must wear your rue   180
with a difference. There's a daisy. I would give you
some violets, but they withered all when my father
died. They say a made a good end.

[*sings*]   *For bonny sweet Robin is all my joy.*

---

170. wheel becomes it] *Q2,F;* wheeles become it *F2;* wheels become *F3.*
173-4. pray you] *Q2;* Pray *F;* I pray *Q1.*   174. pansies] *Q2;* Paconcies *F;*
pansey *Q1.*   180. herb of grace] *Q2;* Herbe-Grace *F;* hearb a grace *Q1.*
You] *Q2,Q1;* Oh you *F.*   must] *F,Q1;* may *Q2.*   183. a made] *Q2;*
he made *F.*

---

170. *wheel*] refrain. Strictly, a term
for a metrical or rhythmic (rather
than a verbal) element in a poem
which recurs at the end of each
stanza. LN.

170-1. *It is the false steward*]
Ophelia's mind is still running on
hapless maidens and deceits in love.
It is sometimes taken (I think unnecessarily) to refer to the ballad which
'the wheel becomes'. No appropriate
ballad, or tale, has been traced. The
false steward in the 'Second History'
of Wotton's *Cupid's Cautels* (1578),
which has been unconvincingly proposed as a source for the Ophelia
story (see *Emporia State Research
Studs.,* 1966, pp. 18-26), is not a candidate here: he ravishes his master's
daughter after making her drunk.

172. *This nothing . . . matter.*] This
nonsense conveys more than sense
would do. Cf. *Lr* IV.vi.175, 'matter
and impertinency mix'd'.

173-83.] The plants have their
meanings appropriate to their recipients. *Rosemary* and *pansies* are presented to Laertes; *fennel* and *columbines,* signifying marital infidelity, to
the Queen; *rue* or *herb o' grace,* for
repentance, to the King. The *daisy* is
the flower of (unhappy) love, *violets* of
faithfulness. LN.

176. *document*] piece of instruction
(the literal sense, from L. *docere*).

177. *fitted*] bestowed where they fit
or belong.

180. *a*] As at II.ii.383, the weakened
form of the O.E. prep. *on* (see *OED* A
prep. 8), common in Elizabethan
English and still surviving dialectally.
Cf. *nowadays.*

181. *a difference*] a variation in a
coat-of-arms (usually indicating a
junior member or branch of the
family).

184.] A line from a popular song.
LN.

Laer. Thought and affliction, passion, hell itself   185
     She turns to favour and to prettiness.

Oph. (*sings*)   *And will a not come again?*
                    And will a not come again?
                        No, no, he is dead,
                        Go to thy death-bed,   190
                    He never will come again.

                    His beard was as white as snow,
                    All flaxen was his poll.
                        He is gone, he is gone,
                        And we cast away moan.   195
                    God a mercy on his soul.

     And of all Christian souls. God buy you.   *Exit.*
Laer. Do you see this, O God?
King. Laertes, I must commune with your grief,
     Or you deny me right. Go but apart,   200
     Make choice of whom your wisest friends you will,
     And they shall hear and judge 'twixt you and me.
     If by direct or by collateral hand
     They find us touch'd, we will our kingdom give,
     Our crown, our life, and all that we call ours   205
     To you in satisfaction; but if not,
     Be you content to lend your patience to us,

---

185. Thought and affliction] *F;* Thought and afflictions *Q2;* Thoughts & afflictions *Q1,Q5.*   187, 188. *a*] *Q2;* he *F,Q1.*   189–90, 194–5.] *2 lines Johnson; one line Q2,F.*   192. *was*] *Q2;* not in *F,Q1.*   193. *All*] *F,Q1;* not in *Q2.*   196. *God a mercy*] *Q2,Q1;* Gramercy *F.*   197. Christian] *F;* Christians *Q2;* christen *Q1.*   souls.] *Q2;* Soules, I pray God. *F,Q1.* God buy you] *Q2;* God buye ye *F;* God be with you *Q1.*   197 S.D.] *F (subst.); not in Q2.*   198. see] *F;* not in *Q2.*   O God] *Q2;* you Gods *F.* 199. commune] *Q2,F2;* common *F.*

185. *Thought*] (often used for melancholy contemplation, hence) sadness, sorrow. Cf. III.iv.51 ('thought-sick'); *Ant.* IV.vi.35–6 (where Enobarbus expects 'thought' to break his heart); *Arrival of Edw. IV* (Camden Soc., 1838), p. 13, 'in great trouble, thought, and heaviness'.
     passion] suffering. Cf. *Mac.* III.iv.57.
186. *favour*] charm.
187–96.] LN.

195. *cast away*] i.e. to no purpose; scatter uselessly.
197. *of*] For the interchangeability of *on* and *of*, see Abbott 175, 181. Cf. I.i.92.
     God buy you.] See II.i.69 n.
199. *commune with*] participate in. (F *common* is but a variant form.)
203. *direct . . . collateral*] our own . . . our agent's.
204. *touch'd*] i.e. with guilt.

And we shall jointly labour with your soul
To give it due content.

Laer.   Let this be so.
His means of death, his obscure funeral—   210
No trophy, sword, nor hatchment o'er his bones,
No noble rite, nor formal ostentation—
Cry to be heard, as 'twere from heaven to earth,
That I must call't in question.

King.   So you shall.
And where th'offence is, let the great axe fall.   215
I pray you go with me.   *Exeunt.*

[SCENE VI]

Enter HORATIO *and a* Servant.

Hor. What are they that would speak with me?
Serv. Seafaring men, sir. They say they have letters for you.
Hor. Let them come in.   [*Exit Servant.*]

210. funeral] *Q2;* buriall *F.*   211. trophy, sword] *F;* trophe sword *Q2;*
trophy sword *Pope.*   212. rite] *F;* right *Q2.*   214. call't] *Q2;* call *F.*

Scene VI

SCENE VI] *Capell.*   S.D. *and a Servant*] *Capell; with an Attendant | F; and others |*
Q2.   2. *Serv.*] *F (Ser.); Gent. Q2.*   Seafaring men] *Q2; Saylors F.*
3 S.D.] *Hanmer.*

211.] It was an ancient custom, of
which relics may still be seen in
churches, that when a knight was
buried, his helmet, sword, and coat-
of-arms were hung over his tomb.

trophy] memorial. Originally one
erected in celebration of a victory and
consisting of arms and other objects
taken in war. Possibly we should read
trophy sword, i.e. take *trophy* as adjectival.

hatchment] a tablet or painting dis-
playing the coat-of-arms of the
deceased, normally placed outside
the house of mourning, and then,
after the burial, over the tomb.

212. *ostentation*] ceremony.

214. *That*] so that, as at IV. vii. 146
(Abbott 283).

Scene VI

IV. vi.] In Q1 this scene is replaced
by one in which Horatio tells the
Queen of the letter he has received
from Hamlet announcing his return,
and, further, reporting the exchange
of commissions (from v. ii. 13–53), so
that the Queen is now apprised of
the King's villainy.

2. *letters*] The plural (following L.
litterae) is common in a singular sense.
N.B. l. 8 below, 'a letter'. Cf. *Oth.* IV.
i. 232 ('the letter'), 272 ('the letters').

I do not know from what part of the world
I should be greeted, if not from Lord Hamlet.   5

Enter Sailors.

1st Sail. God bless you, sir.
Hor. Let him bless thee too.
1st Sail. A shall, sir, and please him. There's a letter for
you, sir. It came from th'ambassador that was bound
for England—if your name be Horatio, as I am let   10
to know it is.
Hor. (*reads the letter.*) *Horatio, when thou shalt have overlooked*
this, give these fellows some means to the King. They have
letters for him. Ere we were two days old at sea, a pirate of
very warlike appointment gave us chase. Finding ourselves   15
too slow of sail, we put on a compelled valour, and in the
grapple I boarded them. On the instant they got clear of our
ship, so I alone became their prisoner. They have dealt
with me like thieves of mercy. But they knew what they did:
I am to do a turn for them. Let the King have the letters I   20

5 S.D. *Sailors*] *Q2*; *Saylor F.*   8. A] *Q2*; *Hee F.*   and] *Q2*; *and't F.*
9. came] *Q2*; *comes F.*   ambassador] *Q2*; *Ambassadours F.*   12. *Hor.*]
Q2; *not in F.*   *reads the letter*] *F*; *not in Q2.*   16. *valour, and*] *Q2*; *Valour. F.*
20. *turn*] *Q2*; *good turne F.*

7. *Let him . . . too.*] 'And thee too'
would be normal courtesy. The extra
emphasis no doubt insinuates that the
sailor 'may well need God's blessing'
(Kittredge).

8. *and*] if (it). The suppression of
the pronoun is colloquially idiomatic.

9. *th'ambassador*] Evidently the
character assumed by Hamlet, who
has concealed his true identity. Misunderstood by F.

12. *overlooked*] looked over, perused.

14. *pirate*] The seas round Denmark
had plenty of pirate ships both in the
pages of Saxo and in Shakespeare's
time. For a possible analogy in
Plutarch's *Life of Caesar*, see Intro., p.
104.

19. *thieves of mercy*] The paradox of
thieves showing mercy is wittily expressed by applying to thieves a

phrase more commonly used of
angels.

they knew what they did] There is
no justification for inferring (as in
Miles, *A Review of Hamlet*, 1870, pp.
70–1 and recently in *SQ.* xxvi,
276–84) that they were therefore in
league with Hamlet and the whole
pirate encounter a plot to get him
back to Denmark. In that case Hamlet could hardly have spoken of their
'mercy'. The implication is that they
showed mercy in calculated exchange for services to be rendered.

20. *turn*] F's *good*, though accepted
by all eds., is not merely superfluous
but enfeebling. Hamlet not only does
a *good* 'turn', but thereby does *his*
'turn' ('an act duly . . . following a
similar act on the part of another',
OED turn *sb.* 28 b).

have sent, and repair thou to me with as much speed as thou
wouldest fly death. I have words to speak in thine ear will
make thee dumb; yet are they much too light for the bore of
the matter. These good fellows will bring thee where I am.
Rosencrantz and Guildenstern hold their course for England;   25
of them I have much to tell thee. Farewell.

He that thou knowest thine,
Hamlet.

Come, I will give you way for these your letters,
And do't the speedier that you may direct me   30
To him from whom you brought them.   *Exeunt.*

[SCENE VII]

Enter KING *and* LAERTES.

King. Now must your conscience my acquittance seal,
       And you must put me in your heart for friend,
       Sith you have heard, and with a knowing ear,
       That he which hath your noble father slain
       Pursu'd my life.
Laer.   It well appears. But tell me   5
       Why you proceeded not against these feats,
       So crimeful and so capital in nature,

21. *speed*] *Q2; hast F.*   22. *thine*] *Q2; your F.*   23. *bore*] *F;* bord *Q2.*
27. *He*] *F;* So *Q2.*   29. *give*] *F; not in Q2;* make *Q3.*

Scene VII

SCENE VII] *Capell.*   6. proceeded] *F;* proceede *Q2.*   7. crimeful] *F;*
criminall *Q2.*

23. *too light for the bore*] The bore of
this gun would take a heavier shot. So
although Hamlet's words are of a
weight to strike one dumb, they are
still far from matching the enormity
of the case.

29. *way*] The 'means' of access requested in l. 13. For *give . . . way* =
afford scope, see *Temp.* I.ii.186; *2H4*
v.ii.82 (*MSH*, p. 293).

Scene VII

3. *knowing*] knowledgeable.
5. *Pursu'd my life*] Cf. IV.i.13; III.
iv.26, 32.
6. *feats*] wicked deeds (as often at
this date).
7. *So crimeful . . . nature*] Cf. *Cor.* III.
iii.82, 'So criminal and in such capital kind'. Hence *criminal* (Q2) may be
right, though the unusual *crimeful* (F)

As by your safety, wisdom, all things else
You mainly were stirr'd up.

King.   O, for two special reasons,
Which may to you perhaps seem much unsinew'd,   10
But yet to me th'are strong. The Queen his mother
Lives almost by his looks, and for myself—
My virtue or my plague, be it either which—
She is so conjunctive to my life and soul
That, as the star moves not but in his sphere,   15
I could not but by her. The other motive
Why to a public count I might not go
Is the great love the general gender bear him,
Who, dipping all his faults in their affection,
Work like the spring that turneth wood to stone,   20
Convert his gyves to graces; so that my arrows,

8. safety,] *F;* safetie, greatnes *Q2.*   11. But] *Q2; And F.*   th'are] *Q2* (tha'r) *;*
they are *F.*   14. She is] *Q2;* She's *F.*   conjunctive] *F;* concliue *Q2.*
20. Work] *Q2;* Would *F.*

is then difficult to explain. See *MSH,*
pp. 163–4.
  capital] punishable by death.
  8. *safety, wisdom*] The Q2 *greatness,*
which makes the line a foot too long,
I take to be a rejected first thought
(cf. Intro., p. 41). Considerations of
the King's *greatness* enhance the importance of his *safety,* but the idea is
superseded by *wisdom* and included in
all things else.
  9. *mainly*] mightily.
  10. *unsinew'd*] feeble, without force.
  13. *be it either which*] whichever of
the two it may be.
  14. *conjunctive*] closely linked, like
planets 'in conjunction', i.e. in the
same or adjoining zodiacal signs. In
the imagery of the next line, however,
the idea of a conjunction between
planets gives way to that of a planet
held to a fixed orbit.
  15. *his*] its. See I.i.40 n.
  sphere] one of those which, in the
Ptolemaic astronomy, carried the
planets in their revolution round the
earth.
  17. *count*] account, reckoning.

  18. *the general gender*] the ordinary
sort (of people). Cf. II.ii.433. For
gender = kind, see *Oth.* I.iii.322, 'one
gender of herbs'.
  19–24.] 'A signal illustration of that
wealth and rapid change of metaphor which characterise Shakespeare's later style' (Verity).
  20. *spring . . . stone*] Several such are
reported, including one at King's
Newnham in Shakespeare's county of
Warwickshire. See Harrison, *Description of England* (prefixed to
Holinshed's *Chronicles*), 1587 edn, pp.
129–30, 215. There is thus no reason
to derive this·from Saxo.
  21. *gyves*] lit. shackles, hence disabilities, deformities. The metaphorical interpretation, which the context
suggests, presents no problem. No
precise parallel can be cited or
expected; but cf. Fletcher, *Wife for a
Month,* I.ii.89, 'a golden gyve, a
pleasing wrong'. Difficulties are created by the commentators, who
would have Hamlet literally in
fetters with the populace regarding
these as a mark of honour. Much in-

Too slightly timber'd for so loud a wind,
Would have reverted to my bow again,
But not where I had aim'd them.

Laer. And so have I a noble father lost, 25
A sister driven into desp'rate terms,
Whose worth, if praises may go back again,
Stood challenger on mount of all the age
For her perfections. But my revenge will come.

King. Break not your sleeps for that. You must not think 30
That we are made of stuff so flat and dull
That we can let our beard be shook with danger
And think it pastime. You shortly shall hear more.
I lov'd your father, and we love ourself,
And that, I hope, will teach you to imagine— 35

Enter a Messenger *with letters.*

Mess. These to your Majesty, this to the Queen.
King. From Hamlet! Who brought them?
Mess. Sailors, my lord, they say. I saw them not.
They were given me by Claudio. He receiv'd them

---

22. loud a wind] *F;* loued Arm'd *Q2.*   24. But] *Q2;* And *F.*   had] *F;*
haue *Q2.*   aim'd] *Q2;* arm'd *F.*   27. Whose worth] *Q2;* Who was *F.*
35 S.D. *with letters*] *Q2; not in F.*   36. *Mess.* These] *Q2;* How now?
What Newes? / *Mes.* Letters my Lord from *Hamlet.* This *F.*   this] *Q2,F;*
these *Wilson.*

genuity has also been wasted in efforts
at emendation. Elizabethan pronunciation alliterated *gyves* with *graces.*

22. *Too slightly timber'd*] with too
light a shaft.

so loud a wind] i.e. the powerful gust
of popular feeling.

26. *terms*] circumstances.

27. *go back again*] i.e. to what she
formerly was.

28. *challenger . . . the age*] *Of all the
age* relates to the challenger, not the
mount. There is no need to suspect an
allusion to the ceremony in which a
newly crowned King of Hungary on
a mountain near Pressburg would
brandish his sword at the four
quarters of the world challenging
any to dispute his right. But this

gives the idea.

33. *shall hear more*] Presumably a
reference to expected news from
England – which gives ironic impact
to what immediately comes instead.

36.] The extra dialogue in F must
be accounted a theatrical elaboration
(cf. IV.v.96). From IV.vi.9 it does not
appear that the bearer of the letters
knew the identity of their sender, and
it is arguably better if the King is not
thus forewarned. See *SB*, XIII, 36.

These] The plural can of course refer to a single epistle. Cf. l. 40 below
(*them*[2]); II.ii.112 and n.; IV.vi.2 and
n.

this] Consistency would require
these, and Dover Wilson infers a misprint. (Cf. *MSH*, p. 242.)

Of him that brought them.

King.   Laertes, you shall hear them.—   40
Leave us.   *Exit Messenger.*
[*Reads*] *High and mighty, you shall know I am set naked on
your kingdom. Tomorrow shall I beg leave to see your kingly
eyes, when I shall, first asking your pardon, thereunto recount
the occasion of my sudden and more strange return.*   45
                         Hamlet.
What should this mean? Are all the rest come back?
Or is it some abuse, and no such thing?

Laer. Know you the hand?

King.   'Tis Hamlet's character.
'Naked'—   50
And in a postscript here he says 'Alone'.
Can you devise me?

Laer. I am lost in it, my lord. But let him come.
It warms the very sickness in my heart
That I shall live and tell him to his teeth,   55

---

40. Of him that brought them] *Q2; not in F.*   40–1. Laertes . . . us.] *As
F; one line Q2.*   41 S.D.] *F; not in Q2.*   42. *Reads*] *Capell.*   44. *eyes, when
. . . first . . . pardon, thereunto*] *Q2; Eyes. When . . . (first . . . Pardon thereunto)
F.*   *your*] *F;* you *Q2.*   45. *the occasion*] *Q2;* th'*Occasions F.
and more strange] F; not in Q2.*   46. *Hamlet.*] *F; not in Q2.*   48. abuse, and]
Q2; abuse? Or *F.*   50–2.] *This edn;* . . . caracter. Naked / And . . .
alone, / . . . Q2;* . . . character; / Naked and (. . . says) / Alone . . . *Pope;
prose F.*   52. devise] *Q2;* aduise *F.*   53. I am] *Q2;* I'm *F.*   55. shall]
F,Q1; not in Q2.

---

42. *High and mighty*] The high-
flown style of royal address lends itself to sarcasm, which is less, however,
in the phraseology itself than in its
use by the prince.

naked] stripped of belongings.

43–4. *your kingly eyes*] your Majesty
in person. Cf. I.ii.116, IV.iv.6; and
see next note.

44. *thereunto*] This is to be taken, as
the Q2 pointing directs, with *recount*. F, by attaching it to *asking your
pardon*, robs it of meaning. The antecedent is *your kingly eyes* and eds. who
find an anomaly in recounting to
those ignore the conventional metonymy which uses 'eyes' for the royal
presence. Cf. *Troil.* I.iii.219, 'Do a
fair message to his kingly eyes'
(which F also unreasonably emends
by substituting *ears*). See ll. 43–4 n.

46. *Hamlet*] This incongruously bare
subscription, occurring in F only, may
be a players' addition.

48. *abuse*] deception. Cf. I.v.38, II.
ii.599.

49. *character*] handwriting.

52. *devise*] explain, resolve (with *me*
as ethic dative).

'Thus diest thou'.

King.   If it be so, Laertes—
As how should it be so, how otherwise?—
Will you be rul'd by me?

Laer.   Ay, my lord,
So you will not o'errule me to a peace.

King. To thine own peace. If he be now return'd,   60
As checking at his voyage, and that he means
No more to undertake it, I will work him
To an exploit, now ripe in my device,
Under the which he shall not choose but fall;
And for his death no wind of blame shall breathe,   65
But even his mother shall uncharge the practice
And call it accident.

Laer.   My lord, I will be rul'd,
The rather if you could devise it so
That I might be the organ.

King.   It falls right.
You have been talk'd of since your travel much,   70
And that in Hamlet's hearing, for a quality
Wherein they say you shine. Your sum of parts

56. Thus diest thou] *Wilson (reprint 1964), conj. Marshall;* Thus didst thou *Q2;*
Thus diddest thou *F;* thus he dies *Q1.*   56–8. If . . . me?] *As Q2; 2 lines
divided so:* | How *F.*   56–7. Laertes—. . . so, how otherwise?—] *Jennens
subst.;* Laertes, . . . so, how otherwise, *Q2;* Laertes, . . . so: How otherwise *F.*
58–9. Ay . . . peace.] *As Steevens; one line Q2.*   Ay, my lord, So you will]
Q2; If so you'l *F.*   61. checking] *F;* the King *Q2.*   67–80. My lord . . .
graveness.] *Q2; not in F.*

56. *diest*] This very simple emendation (which infers no more than a
misreading of *e* as *d* in Q2) restores
both sense and metre and is confirmed beyond question by Q1,
which merely substitutes indirect for
direct speech. Moreover, *diest thou*
supplies an essential link in the dialogue: it provides the antithesis
giving point to *I shall live* and calls
forth the fatal stratagem on which the
catastrophe depends. See *MLR*, LIV,
393–5.

56–7. *If it be so . . . otherwise?*] (1)
As usually taken, this shows the King
baffled between thinking that Hamlet

cannot have come back and that he
must have. Cf. l. 47. Alternatively,
(2) it may relate to the preceding
speech: between thinking that Laertes
cannot be and that he must be bent
on Hamlet's death, the King feels his
way to a new plot.

61. *checking*] shying, stopping suddenly in mid-course.

66. *uncharge*] (the opposite of
charge) exonerate.

practice] trick, underhand stratagem, as in v.ii.323.

70–104.] On this account of
Laertes's fencing, LN.

Did not together pluck such envy from him
As did that one, and that, in my regard,
Of the unworthiest siege.

Laer.   What part is that, my lord? 75

King. A very ribbon in the cap of youth—
Yet needful too, for youth no less becomes
The light and careless livery that it wears
Than settled age his sables and his weeds
Importing health and graveness. Two months since 80
Here was a gentleman of Normandy—
I have seen myself, and serv'd against, the French,
And they can well on horseback, but this gallant
Had witchcraft in't. He grew unto his seat,
And to such wondrous doing brought his horse 85
As had he been incorps'd and demi-natur'd
With the brave beast. So far he topp'd my thought
That I in forgery of shapes and tricks
Come short of what he did.

Laer.   A Norman was't?

80. Two] *Q2;* Some two *F.*   since] *Q2;* hence *F.*   82. I have] *Q2;*
I'ue *F.*   83. can] *Q2;* ran *F.*   84. unto] *Q2;* into *F.*   86. had he]
Q2,F; he had *Q5.*   87. topp'd] *Q2;* past *F.*   my] *F;* me *Q2.*

75. *siege*] rank, status.

76. *A very ribbon*] i.e. a mere decoration. There is no good reason for modern Shakespeare edns to perpetuate artificially the accidental difference between *riband* (Q2) and *ribbon;* the Elizabethan texts use these older and newer spellings indiscriminately. See Qq of *LLL* III.i.136 (*Ribbon*); *Wiv.* IV.vi.42 (*ribones,* F *Ribonds*); *MND* IV.ii.32 (*ribands,* mod. eds. *ribbons*); *Rom.* III.i.28 (*riband*).

78. *light and careless*] Fencing was an expected feature of a gay life. Cf. II.i.25 and LN.

79. *his sables . . . weeds*] its clothes of sober colouring. *Sables* were (1) robes trimmed with sable fur, as worn by men of dignity and standing; (2) more generally, black, and sometimes specifically mourning, attire. Cf. III.

ii.128 and LN. *Weeds,* a general word for clothes, was also, in appropriate contexts, used for mourning. *Sonn.* II. 1–4 contrasts 'youth's proud livery' with a 'weed' of 'forty winters'. For *his,* neut. possessive, see I.i.40n.

80. *health*] orderly well-being, stability. LN.

83. *can well*] have great skill. (O.E. *cunnan,* to know.) Cf. l. 154 below, *cunnings.*

86–7. *As had he been . . . beast*] Cf. Sidney, *Arcadia* (II.v.3), 'as if Centaur-like he had been one piece with the horse'; *incorps'd,* made into one body (with); *demi-natur'd,* possessed of half the nature (of).

88. *forgery*] fabrication. Cf. I.v.37, II.i.20.

shapes] forms, figures, postures.
tricks] feats of skill.

King. A Norman.   90
Laer. Upon my life, Lamord.
King.   The very same.
Laer. I know him well. He is the brooch indeed
    And gem of all the nation.
King. He made confession of you,
    And gave you such a masterly report   95
    For art and exercise in your defence,
    And for your rapier most especial,
    That he cried out 'twould be a sight indeed
    If one could match you. The scrimers of their nation
    He swore had neither motion, guard, nor eye,   100
    If you oppos'd them. Sir, this report of his
    Did Hamlet so envenom with his envy
    That he could nothing do but wish and beg
    Your sudden coming o'er to play with you.
    Now out of this—
Laer.   What out of this, my lord?   105
King. Laertes, was your father dear to you?
    Or are you like the painting of a sorrow,
    A face without a heart?
Laer.   Why ask you this?

91. Lamord] *Q2; Lamound F.*   93. the] *Q2;* our *F.*   97. especial] *Q2;*
especiallᵉ *F.*   99. you.] *Q2 (subst.);* you Sir. *F.*   99–101. The scrimers . . .
them.] *Q2;* not in *F.*   101. Sir, this] *Q2 (subst.);* This *F.*   104. you] *Q2;*
him *F.*   105. What] *Q2;* Why *F.*

91. *Lamord*] The apparent irrelevance of the horseman has led many
to suspect a personal allusion. The
favourite candidate is the cavalier
mentioned in Castiglione's *Courtier*
whose name, Pietro Monte, is rendered by Hoby (Tudor Trans., p. 58)
as Peter Mount (cf. F *Lamound*).
Dowden connects Q2 *Lamord* with
Fr. *mords*, a horse's bit. But if we
suppose some purposeful association
in the name (and why, otherwise,
should it be given?), will it not
suggest La Mort? Cf. ll. 70–104 LN.

94. *made confession of*] testified to.
The frequent assumption that *confession* implies reluctant testimony on

the Frenchman's part is unwarranted (and refuted by the context).

96. *defence*] fencing, swordsmanship.

97. *rapier*] The fashionable weapon,
which, among gentlemen, had ousted
the sword and buckler.

99. *If one could match you*] if there
were anyone capable of giving you a
match.

scrimers] Fr. *escrimeurs*, fencers.

100. *motion*] A term for the (manner
of) execution of the recognized movements in fencing. (Cf., in cricket, a
bowler's 'action'.) Cf. *Tw.N.* III.
iv. 263–4, 'he gives me the stuck in
with such a mortal motion'.

King. Not that I think you did not love your father,
　　　But that I know love is begun by time,　　　　　　110
　　　And that I see, in passages of proof,
　　　Time qualifies the spark and fire of it.
　　　There lives within the very flame of love
　　　A kind of wick or snuff that will abate it;
　　　And nothing is at a like goodness still,　　　　　115
　　　For goodness, growing to a pleurisy,
　　　Dies in his own too-much. That we would do,
　　　We should do when we would: for this 'would' changes
　　　And hath abatements and delays as many
　　　As there are tongues, are hands, are accidents,　　120

113–22.] *Q2; not in F.*

110–22. *But that I know . . . easing.*]
The similarity of these reflections to
those of the Player King (III. ii.
182–94) must be given a dramatic
rather than a psychological explanation. It is not so much that 'Claudius
cannot get "The Mousetrap" out of
his head' (Kittredge) as that the
dramatist reiterates a dominant
motif. Cf. III. i. 56–88 LN (penult.
para.); III. ii. 183–208 LN.
　110. *begun by time*] created by circumstance (Dover Wilson). Difficulty, and attempts at emendation
(e.g. *begone, begnawn*), have come from
the assumption that Shakespeare alludes to the fading of love with the
passage of time. But although this is
the burden of what follows, it is here
introduced by the complementary
truth that time, which causes love to
die, first brings it into being. Cf.
Euphues and his England, 'Love which
by time and fancy is bred in an idle
head, is by time and fancy banished
from the heart' (Lyly, ii. 74).
　111. *passages of proof*] well-attested
instances.
　112. *qualifies*] modifies, diminishes.
　113–17. *There lives . . . too-much.*]
These lines do not so much restate the

idea as combine it with another. Love
now grows dim not merely through
the ordinary process of time but
through being self-consuming: it *dies*
(l. 117) through the very intensity
with which it *lives* (l. 113). The *snuff*
is the charred portion of the wick
which dims the flame which has created it. There is a similar paradox in
the *sigh* of ll. 121–2.
　115. *still*] always. Cf. 1. i. 125, etc.
　116. *pleurisy*] This disease, properly
inflammation of the pleura, was,
owing to a mistaken derivation from
L. *plus, pluris,* thought to be caused by
some superfluity. Cf. Greene, *Mamillia,* 'the patient, which by over much
blood falleth into the Plurisie' (ii. 41).
The word was often used (as examples
in *OED* and Furness show) simply to
denote excess. Yet the retention by
many eds. of the Q2 spelling *pluris[y]*
in order to emphasize this sense entails loss as well as gain.
　117. *his*] its. See 1. i. 40n.
　118. *We should do . . . would*] While
the will still exists, we ought to act on
it.
　120. *tongues . . . hands*] Alluding to
the words and deeds of those who
would dissuade or prevent.

And then this 'should' is like a spendthrift sigh
That hurts by easing. But to the quick of th'ulcer:
Hamlet comes back; what would you undertake
To show yourself in deed your father's son
More than in words?

Laer.   To cut his throat i'th' church.   125
King. No place indeed should murder sanctuarize;
Revenge should have no bounds. But good Laertes,
Will you do this, keep close within your chamber;
Hamlet, return'd, shall know you are come home;
We'll put on those shall praise your excellence,   130
And set a double varnish on the fame
The Frenchman gave you, bring you, in fine, together,
And wager o'er your heads. He, being remiss,
Most generous, and free from all contriving,
Will not peruse the foils, so that with ease—   135
Or with a little shuffling—you may choose

---

121. spendthrift] *Q5;* spend thirfts *Q2;* spend-thrifts *Q3;* spendthrift's *Pope.*
124. in deed your father's son] *Malone;* indeede your fathers sonne *Q2;* your
Fathers sonne indeed *F;* your Father's Son in deed *F4.*   128. this, . . .
chamber;] *Steevens²* (*subst.*); this, . . . chamber, *Q2,F;* this, . . . Chamber? *F2;*
this? . . . chamber, *Q5.*   133. o'er] *Q2;* on *F.*

121–2. *this 'should' . . . easing*] Our
awareness of duty (what we *should*),
gratifying in itself, is, when unaccompanied by performance, harmful (because by *easing* the conscience it
weakens the moral perceptions). The
sigh which gives relief is at the same
time *spendthrift* of the life-blood (because sighs were thought to draw
blood from the heart). Cf. *2H6* III.
ii. 61, 63; *3H6* IV.iv.22 ('blood-
sucking sighs'); *MND* III.ii.97.
122. *the quick of th'ulcer*] i.e. the
heart of the trouble. The *quick,* the
most sensitive spot.
125. *To cut . . . church*] Contrast
Hamlet's scruple about killing *his* foe
at prayer (III.iii.75 ff.).
126. *sanctuarize*] give sanctuary to,
i.e. provide with immunity from
punishment.
128. *Will you do this,*] Not a question

but a condition. *This* has no direct
antecedent but refers to the taking of
revenge on Hamlet. Dependent upon
the wish for revenge is not merely the
injunction to stay hidden (as the
common editorial period after *chamber*
might suggest), but the whole chain
of events which culminates in its
achievement in l. 138.
130. *put on*] appoint.
132. *in fine*] finally (as at II.ii.69,
v.ii.15).
133. *o'er your heads*] This metonymic
use of 'head' was common in betting
parlance. Cf. v.ii.101–2; *2H4* III.
ii.44.
remiss] carelessly trusting.
134. *generous*] large-minded, magnanimous. Cf. v.ii.238, I.iii.74.
135. *peruse*] scrutinize. Cf. II.i.90.
136. *shuffling*] Contrast III.iii.61:
the King's own word condemns him.

A sword unbated, and in a pass of practice
Require him for your father.

Laer.   I will do't.
And for that purpose, I'll anoint my sword.
I bought an unction of a mountebank   140
So mortal that but dip a knife in it,
Where it draws blood, no cataplasm so rare,
Collected from all simples that have virtue
Under the moon, can save the thing from death
That is but scratch'd withal. I'll touch my point   145
With this contagion, that if I gall him slightly,
It may be death.

King.   Let's further think of this,
Weigh what convenience both of time and means
May fit us to our shape. If this should fail,
And that our drift look through our bad performance,

137. pass] *F;* pace *Q 2.*   139. that] *F; not in Q 2;* the *Q 3.*   141. that but dip]
Q 2; I but dipt *F.*   146–7. With . . . death.] *As F; one line Q 2.*
149. shape. If . . . fail,] *Rowe;* shape if . . . fayle, *Q 2;* shape, if . . . faile; *F.*

137. *A sword unbated*] As distinct
from a foil, which is blunted, or *bated*
(from *(a)bate,* to weaken), so as to
'hit, but hurt not' (*Ado* v.ii.13).
Though Shakespeare does not refer to
foil *buttons,* Dover Wilson is mistaken
in supposing these were not Elizabethan.

pass of practice] An arranged match
for a wager rules out the *practice* bout
which Johnson and others have supposed. The word must refer to the
trickery (cf. l. 66 above and v.ii.323).
Cf. *Lr* v.iii.151 ff., 'This is practice
. . . thou art not vanquish'd, But
cozen'd and beguil'd'. A *pass* may be
either a single sword-thrust or, by
extension, a bout (as apparently at
v.ii.162).

139. *I'll anoint my sword*] 'Some
barbarous nations there are who use
to poison their swords' (Plutarch,
Moralia, trans. Holland, Everyman,
p. 117). A precedent in the drama is a
Roman referred to in *Soliman and
Perseda* who fought with 'his weapon's
point empoisoned' (i.iii.32).

140–4. *an unction . . . death*] So
fabulous a thing is obviously not to be
identified with any known poison.
But cf. Gerard on a kind of aconite
(wolfsbane): 'If a man . . . be wounded with an arrow or other instrument
dipped in the juice hereof, doth die
within half an hour remediless'
(*Herbal,* 1597, p. 818). Cf. v.ii.321,
'not half an hour's life'. *unction,*
ointment.

140. *mountebank*] an itinerant quack
who, as the name implies, mounted a
bench or platform to prate his wares.
See *Volpone,* ii.ii.

142. *cataplasm*] plaster.

143. *simples*] medicinal herbs.

144. *the moon*] which was believed
to lend a more than ordinary power
or *virtue.*

146. *gall*] graze.

149. *our shape*] (a theatrical metaphor: see *OED* shape *sb.*8) the role
we are to act.

150. *drift*] scheme, underlying purpose. Cf. ii.i.38.

look] be visible.

'Twere better not essay'd. Therefore this project   151
Should have a back or second that might hold
If this did blast in proof. Soft, let me see.
We'll make a solemn wager on your cunnings—
I ha't!   155
When in your motion you are hot and dry—
As make your bouts more violent to that end—
And that he calls for drink, I'll have prepar'd him
A chalice for the nonce, whereon but sipping,
If he by chance escape your venom'd stuck,   160
Our purpose may hold there. But stay, what noise?

Enter QUEEN.

Queen. One woe doth tread upon another's heel,
     So fast they follow. Your sister's drown'd, Laertes.
Laer. Drown'd? O, where?
Queen. There is a willow grows askant the brook   165
     That shows his hoary leaves in the glassy stream.

---

153. did] *Q2;* should *F.*   154. cunnings] *Q2;* commings *F.*   155–6.] *As Johnson; one line Q2,F.*   157. that] *Q2;* the *F.*   158. prepar'd] *F;* prefard *Q2;* preferd *Q3.*   161. But stay, what noise?] *Q2;* how sweet Queene. *F;* how now, sweet Queene. *F2;* How now Gertred, *Q1.*   163. they] *Q2;* they'l *F.*   165. askant the] *Q2;* aslant a *F.*   166. hoary] *Q2* (horry); hore *F.*

---

152. *back*] backer-up.

153. *blast in proof*] come to grief when put to the test. Usually explained, after Steevens, as a phrase from the testing of cannon (which in the event of an explosion during proof, or trial, would harm the user), but contemporary evidence of the phrase is lacking.

154. *cunnings*] respective skill.

158. *prepar'd*] Q2 *prefard,* though rendered *preferr(e)d* by some recent eds., is presumably a misprint. The *ar* spelling is unmatched in Shakespeare's 46 instances of *prefer,* and F *prepar'd* suits better with the context (*for the nonce*) and the recollected sense of Q1 ('a potion that shall ready stand'). Cf. Sisson, *NR.*

160. *stuck*] a thrust with the sword-point in fencing, as at *Tw.N.* III.

iv.263. Apparently a variant of *stock* (cf. *Wiv.* II.iii.24), stoccado, from It. *stoccata* (cf. *Rom.* III.i.72; *Wiv.* II.i.201).

162–3. *One woe . . . follow.*] Cf. IV.v. 78–9 and n.; *Locrine,* v.iv.242 (the Queen when a damsel drowns herself), 'One mischief follows [on] another's neck'. (See *N&Q,* CCXXIV, 121–2.) But notwithstanding the parallel situations, the idea itself is too common for us to have to infer that *Locrine* echoes the *Ur-Hamlet.* Cf. Intro., p. 99 n. 2.

165–82. *There is a willow . . . death.*] LN.

165. *askant*] slanting over. A variant of *askance,* familiar as an adverb but not otherwise recorded as a preposition.

166. *his*] its. See I.i.40n.

Therewith fantastic garlands did she make
Of crow-flowers, nettles, daisies, and long purples,
That liberal shepherds give a grosser name,
But our cold maids do dead men's fingers call them.   170
There on the pendent boughs her crownet weeds
Clamb'ring to hang, an envious sliver broke,
When down her weedy trophies and herself
Fell in the weeping brook. Her clothes spread wide,
And mermaid-like awhile they bore her up,   175
Which time she chanted snatches of old lauds,
As one incapable of her own distress,
Or like a creature native and indued
Unto that element. But long it could not be
Till that her garments, heavy with their drink,   180
Pull'd the poor wretch from her melodious lay

167. Therewith . . . make] Q2; There with . . . come F.   170. cold] F; cull-cold Q2; culcold Q4.   171. crownet] Wilson; cronet Q2; Coronet F,Q3.   173. her] Q2; the F.   176. lauds] Q2; tunes F,Q1.   180. their] Q2,Q1; her F.   181. lay] Q2; buy F.

167. *Therewith . . . make*] F, though followed by many eds., misses the point: she did not bring garlands to the willow but made them with it (cf. Fuller in LN on ll. 165–82).

fantastic] ingeniously wrought.

168. *crow-flowers*] ragged robins. See ll. 165–82 LN.

long purples] Usually identified, more or less confidently, with a kind of wild orchis which suits the name by the purple spike of its inflorescence and is said to have been known as *dead men's fingers* (l. 170). See ll. 165–82 LN.

169. *liberal*] free-languaged.

a grosser name] We cannot know which Shakespeare had particularly in mind, but recorded names for the orchis, derived (like the term *orchis* itself) from the testicle-like tubers of most species, include dogstones (L. *testiculus canis*), dog's cods, cullions, fool's ballocks, and many variations on these.

170. *cold*] chaste, modest. Q2 *cull-cold*, though retained by Evans in

defiance of sense and metre, almost certainly represents a false start in the ms. (a deletion-stroke perhaps giving rise to the hyphen).

dead men's fingers] This alternative name for the orchis (see l. 168n.) is held to derive from the pale palmate roots characteristic of certain species but seems to have been extended to other species too. See ll. 165–82 LN.

171. *crownet*] made into a wreath or crown. A common variant of *coronet*, as *crowner* (v.i.4) of *coroner*.

172. *envious*] malicious.

176. *lauds*] songs of praise. A rare word, retrieved by Dover Wilson (see *MSH*, pp. 71–2) and since usually accepted. Objectors to it (e.g. Sisson, *NR*) face the difficulty of explaining how it could get into Q2 if not from Shakespeare's ms. See ll. 165–82 LN.

177. *incapable*] insensible. Cf. *capable*, III.ii.11–12, III.iv.127.

178–9. *indued Unto that element*] endowed appropriately for living in water.

To muddy death.

Laer.   Alas, then she is drown'd.

Queen. Drown'd, drown'd.

Laer. Too much of water hast thou, poor Ophelia,
  And therefore I forbid my tears. But yet   185
  It is our trick; nature her custom holds,
  Let shame say what it will. [*Weeps.*] When these are gone,
  The woman will be out. Adieu, my lord,
  I have a speech o' fire that fain would blaze
  But that this folly douts it.   *Exit.*

King.   Let's follow, Gertrude.   190
  How much I had to do to calm his rage.
  Now fear I this will give it start again.
  Therefore let's follow.   *Exeunt.*

---

182. she is] *Q2,Q1;* is she *F,Q3.*   drown'd.] *Q2;* drown'd? *F,Q5;*
drownde: *Q1;* drown'd! *Pope.*   187. *Weeps*] *This edn.*   189. o' fire]
Wilson; a fire *Q2;* of fire *F;* afire *Q5.*   190. douts] *F* (doubts); *drownes*
Q2,F2.

  184–5. *Too much . . . tears.*] Cf. for   186. *our trick*] the way of mankind.
the conceit, *Tw.N.* II.i.26–8, 'She is   187–8. *When these . . . out.*] i.e. These
drowned already, sir, with salt water,   tears will be the last sign of the
though I seem to drown her remem-   woman in me.
brance again with more'.

[ACT V]

[SCENE I]

Enter two Clowns [—the Grave-digger and Another].

Grave. Is she to be buried in Christian burial, when she
    wilfully seeks her own salvation?

Other. I tell thee she is, therefore make her grave straight.
    The crowner hath sat on her and finds it Christian
    burial.   5

Grave. How can that be, unless she drowned herself in her
    own defence?

ACT V

Scene I

ACT V, SCENE I] *Q 1676.*   S.D. *the Grave-digger and Another*] *This edn; with
Spades and Mattocks Q 1676; (a sexton and his mate) with spades and mattocks Wilson.*
1 *(and throughout scene).* Grave.] *This edn; Clowne. Q2,F; 1 Clown. Rowe.*
when she] *Q2; that F.*   3 *(and throughout scene).* Other.] *Q2,F; 2 Clown. Rowe.*
therefore] *Q2; and therefore F.*

S.D. *two Clowns*] The tradition
which makes the second as well as the
first a grave-digger, though it dates
from the 17th century, goes against
the implications of the dialogue. N.B.
ll. 3, 14 and n., and see *MLR*, LI,
562–5.

1. *Christian burial*] Christian funeral
rites were denied to suicides (see
below, l. 220n.), who were buried out
of consecrated ground (cf. l. 222),
usually at a cross-roads under a pile
of stones (l. 224) and with a stake
through the body, a practice which
continued into the 19th century.

2. *wilfully . . . salvation*] But see IV.
vii. 171–82, which makes clear that
her death was due to accident and the
mad mind's helplessness in it. If the
dramatist nevertheless allows scope
for different opinions in Elsinore, that

is a sign not of inconsistency (as maintained in *SQ*, XV, 345–8) but art. Cf.
IV. vii. 165–82 LN. The rustics believe
she committed suicide, but the
coroner finds otherwise (l. 4), while
still leaving room for doubt (l. 220).
In *BB* Ophelia does commit suicide –
by throwing herself from a cliff.

salvation] A mistake for 'damnation', as in *Ado*, III. iii. 3.

3. *straight*] straightway (as at II.
ii. 427, III. iv. 1), but with a play on
strait, confined.

4. *crowner*] A common variant of
coroner. Cf. *crownet*, IV. vii. 171.

4–5. *finds it Christian burial*] Implying
that his verdict was not suicide. The
coroner had to give warrant for the
burial. See nn. on ll. 1, 220.

6–7. *in her own defence*] A plea relevant to homicide, incongruous

Other. Why, 'tis found so.

Grave. It must be *se offendendo*, it cannot be else. For here
lies the point: if I drown myself wittingly, it argues   10
an act, and an act hath three branches—it is to act,
to do, to perform; argal, she drowned herself
wittingly.

Other. Nay, but hear you, Goodman Delver—

Grave. Give me leave. Here lies the water—good. Here   15
stands the man—good. If the man go to this water
and drown himself, it is, will he nill he, he goes,
mark you that. But if the water come to him and
drown him, he drowns not himself. Argal, he that is
not guilty of his own death shortens not his own life.   20

Other. But is this law?

Grave. Ay, marry is't, crowner's quest law.

Other. Will you ha' the truth an't? If this had not been a
gentlewoman, she should have been buried out o'
Christian burial.   25

Grave. Why, there thou say'st. And the more pity that
great folk should have countenance in this world to
drown or hang themselves more than their even-

9. *se offendendo*] *F*; so offended *Q2*.   11. to act] *Q2*; an Act *F*.   12. do,]
Q2; doe and *F*.   argal,] argall *F*; or all; *Q2*.   14. Goodman Delver] *F*;
good man deluer *Q2*.   18. that.] that, *Q2*; that? *F*.   23. an't] *Q2*; on't *F*.
24. o'] *Jennens*; a *Q2*; of *F*.   28–9. their even-Christen] *Q2*; their euen
Christian *F*; other people *Q1*.

(though not inadmissible) in suicide.
An instance, among many in this
scene, of Shakespeare's delight in 'the
uneducated mind, and its tendency
to express a sound meaning in an absurd form' (Bradley on *Cor.*).

9. *se offendendo*] for *se defendendo*;
another confusion of opposites.

10–20. *if I drown myself . . . life*] A
burlesque of the legal arguments in
the actual case of Sir Jas. Hales, who
drowned himself in 1554. LN.

12, 19, 48. *argal*] Cf. *argo* (*2H6* IV.
ii. 28; *Sir Thomas More*, Addn II, 127),
an uneducated pronunciation of L.
ergo, therefore. This further corruption allows a pun on the name of the
Elizabethan logician John Argall (for

whom see Kneale, *Development of
Logic*, p. 299).

14. *Goodman Delver*] A quasi-
proper name. The prefix *Goodman* was
especially used when designating a
man by his occupation. Clearly
Shakespeare does not think of the
second man as a grave-digger.

22. *quest*] inquest.

23. *an't*] The colloquial form has
the preposition with the weakened
vowel. Cf. I. v. 19n.

28–9. *even-Christen*] in a collective
sense (for which see *OED* Christen *a.*
3b), fellow-Christians. O.E. *efen* is
common in this usage. Cf. Chaucer,
Parson's Tale, ll. 395, 805, and other
examples gathered in Furness.

Christen. Come, my spade. There is no ancient
gentlemen but gardeners, ditchers, and grave-   30
makers—they hold up Adam's profession.   [*He digs.*]

Other. Was he a gentleman?

Grave. A was the first that ever bore arms.

Other. Why, he had none.

Grave. What, art a heathen? How dost thou understand   35
the Scripture? The Scripture says Adam digged.
Could he dig without arms? I'll put another
question to thee. If thou answerest me not to the
purpose, confess thyself—

Other. Go to.   40

Grave. What is he that builds stronger than either the
mason, the shipwright, or the carpenter?

Other. The gallows-maker, for that frame outlives a
thousand tenants.

Grave. I like thy wit well in good faith, the gallows does   45
well. But how does it well? It does well to those that
do ill. Now, thou dost ill to say the gallows is built

---

29. Come,] *F; Come Q2.*   31 S.D.] *This edn; strips, and falls to digging (after*
spade *29) Capell; he goes down into the open grave Wilson.*   33. A] *Q2; He F.*
34–7. *Other. Why . . . arms?*] *F; not in Q2.*   43. frame] *F; not in Q2.*

---

29. *my spade*] Presumably =
me my spade, rather than the vocative which the absence of the comma
in Q2 might suggest.

ancient] going back to the earliest
times. Douce (*Illustrations of Sh.*, ii.
263) observes that some books of
heraldry refer to Adam's *spade* as the
most ancient form of escutcheon. Cf.
l. 33.

31. *hold up*] sustain, keep going.

Adam's profession] 'Adam was a
gardener' (*2H6* IV.ii.129), and proverbially therefore not a gentleman.
'When Adam delved and Eve span,
Who was then the gentleman?'
Tilley A 30. This was the text on
which John Ball preached during the
Peasants' Revolt (Holinshed, 1587,
iii.437). But whereas the rhyme implies that in Adam's time there were
no gentlemen, the Clown's speech

wittily inverts this by implying that
there were *none but* gentlemen.

33. *bore arms*] See l. 29n.

34–7. *Why . . . without arms?*] The
omission in Q2, like that at ll. 104–5,
is evidently a compositor's error
occasioned by the repetition of a word
(here *arms*).

36. *The Scripture . . . digged.*] Adam
had to till (or in various versions dress,
work) the ground (Genesis iii.23).
Tradition, not the Bible, says he
'digged'.

39. *confess thyself—*] 'and be hanged'
completes the saying. Cf. *Oth.* IV.
i.38; *Jew of Malta*, IV.i.144–5.
Tilley C 587.

43. *frame*] A quibble on (1) a
gallows and (2) the timber structure
of a building.

45–6. *does well*] is a good answer.

stronger than the church; argal, the gallows may do
well to thee. To't again, come.

Other. Who builds stronger than a mason, a shipwright,   50
or a carpenter?

Grave. Ay, tell me that and unyoke.

Other. Marry, now I can tell.

Grave. To't.

Other. Mass, I cannot tell.   55

Grave. Cudgel thy brains no more about it, for your dull
ass will not mend his pace with beating. And when
you are asked this question next, say 'A grave-
maker'. The houses he makes lasts till doomsday.
Go, get thee to Yaughan; fetch me a stoup of liquor.   60

[*Exit the Other Clown. The Grave-digger continues digging.*]

(*Sings*)   *In youth when I did love, did love,*
          Methought it was very sweet:
     To contract—O—the time for—a—my behove,
     O methought there—a—was nothing—a—meet.

---

59. houses] $Q2,Q1$; Houses that F.   lasts] $Q2,F$; last $Q1,Q3,F4$.
60. to Yaughan] F; in, and $Q2$.   stoup] $F,Q1$ (stope); soope $Q2$; sup
Evans.   60 S.D.] *Rowe subst.*   63. *for*—a—] *Kittredge;* for a $Q2,F$; for, a,
Theobald; for, ah, *Capell;* for-a *Cambridge.*   64. *there*—a—*was nothing*—a—]
Kittredge; there a was nothing a $Q2$; *there was nothing* F; *there*, a, *was nothing*, a.
Jennens; there-a was nothing-a *Cambridge.*

---

52. *unyoke*] give over (like oxen
freed from the yoke at the end of the
day), have done with it.

56. *your*] See I. i. 141 n.

60. *to Yaughan*] Not satisfactorily
explained, but often conjectured to
give the name of a local alehouse-
keeper. LN.

61–95.] For the grave-digger's song,
LN.

63–4. *To contract . . . meet.*] The recurrent *a*, and perhaps also the *O* of
l. 63, is best explained as the grunting
of the grave-digger as he breaks his
song to take breath. Clark and Wright
(Clarendon) less plausibly supposed it
to indicate the singer's 'drawling',
like *stile-a*, *mile-a*, etc., in *Wint.* IV.
iii. 119–21, etc. But the *-a* sung by

Autolycus, like that of Lucibella in
Hoffman (MSR, ll. 1478, 2052), which
Dowden compares, occurs only at the
end of a line, to prolong the singing
when the words are done: what we
have here are interjections in the
middle. For *O* in l. 64, cf. l. 94.

63. *contract*] shorten. Kittredge
takes this to mean 'make (the time)
pass pleasantly'; but although pleasant times are known to seem short,
the converse does not follow. I suspect,
rather, that in garbling the verse (see
ll. 61–95 LN) the Clown gives another
instance of his penchant for replacing
the required sense with its opposite.
The point is not to *contract* the happy
time of youthful love but to prolong it.

behove] behoof, advantage.

[*While he is singing,*] *enter* HAMLET *and* HORATIO.

Ham. Has this fellow no feeling of his business a sings in   65
    grave-making?
Hor. Custom hath made it in him a property of easiness.
Ham. 'Tis e'en so, the hand of little employment hath the
    daintier sense.
Grave. (*sings*)   *But age with his stealing steps*   70
                Hath claw'd me in his clutch,
                And hath shipp'd me intil the land,
                As if I had never been such.

                                He throws up a skull.

Ham. That skull had a tongue in it, and could sing once.
    How the knave jowls it to th' ground, as if 'twere   75
    Cain's jawbone, that did the first murder. This
    might be the pate of a politician which this ass now

---

64 S.D. *While he is singing,*] *This edn.*   enter . . . *Horatio*] *Q2; Enter . . .*
Horatio a farre off (*before 56*) *F.*   65. a] *Q2;* that he *F.*   in] *Q2;* at *F.*
69. daintier] *F;* dintier *Q2.*   71. *claw'd*] *Q2;* caught *F.*   72. *intil*] *F;*
into *Q2.*   73 S.D.] *Capell; he throwes vp a shouel. Q1.*   75. to th'] *F;* to
the *Q2.*   'twere] *Q2;* it were *F.*   76. This] *Q2;* It *F.*   77. now] *Q2;*
not in F.

---

64 S.D. *Hamlet*] Dover Wilson,
following a suggestion of Wm. Poel,
has Hamlet 'clad in sailor's garb'. But
though this is plausible enough, it is
not necessary to account for a grave-
digger's failure to recognize the
Prince.

65. a] equivalent to *that he*, with
which F smooths out the colloquialism.

67. *property of easiness*] appurtenance, or characteristic, causing him
no disturbance. For the proverb that
custom makes all things easy, see
Tilley C 933, and cf. *Oth.* i.iii.229–31,
AYL ii.i.2.

68–9. *the daintier sense*] the more
delicate feeling.

70. *his stealing steps*] A proverbial
alliteration. Tilley A 70. See i.i.40n.
for *his*, neuter (as also in l. 71).

72. *shipp'd*] dispatched.

intil the land] Kittredge glosses
'ashore', but it is difficult to attach a

precise meaning to everything the
Clown sings. The original poem has
'into the lande, From whence I first
was brought'.   *intil*, to (dialectal,
rather than Danish).

73. *such*] Again imprecise, but may
be assumed = *in youth*.

74–110.] The skull affords a traditional motif of moral reflection. LN.

75. *jowls*] strikes, dashes, with a
play on *jowl*, jawbone.

76. *Cain's . . . murder*] Cain's crime,
not merely murder but fratricide, is
the prototype of Claudius's, as we
were reminded at iii.iii.37. Tradition
has it that he killed Abel with the
jawbone of an ass (*N&Q*, 6th ser. ii,
143; *Academy*, xlviii, 343), but it does
not follow that the jawbone here is the
ass's and not Cain's own. What does
is the justice of Cain's being in his
turn jowled by an *ass* (l. 77).

77. *politician*] crafty schemer, 'one
that would circumvent'.

o'er-offices, one that would circumvent God, might
　　it not?

Hor. It might, my lord.　　　　　　　　　　　　　　　　80

Ham. Or of a courtier, which could say, 'Good morrow,
　　sweet lord. How dost thou, sweet lord?' This might
　　be my Lord Such-a-one, that praised my Lord
　　Such-a-one's horse when a meant to beg it, might it
　　not?　　　　　　　　　　　　　　　　　　　　　　85

Hor. Ay, my lord.

Ham. Why, e'en so, and now my Lady Worm's, chopless,
　　and knocked about the mazard with a sexton's spade.
　　Here's fine revolution and we had the trick to see't.
　　Did these bones cost no more the breeding but to play　90
　　at loggets with 'em? Mine ache to think on't.

Grave. (*sings*)　　*A pickaxe and a spade, a spade,*
　　　　　　　　For and a shrouding-sheet,
　　　　　　　O a pit of clay for to be made
　　　　　　　For such a guest is meet.　　　　　95
　　　　　　　　　　　　[*Throws up another skull.*]

---

78. o'er-offices] *F; ore-reaches Q2.*　　　　would] *Q2; could F.*　　82. thou,
sweet] *Q2 (subst.); thou, good F.*　　84. a] *Q2; he F,Q1.*　　meant] *F,Q1,Q3;*
went *Q2.*　　87. chopless] *Q2;* Chaplesse *F.*　　88. mazard] *F;* massene *Q2;*
mazer *Q3.*　　89. and] *Q2; if F.*　　91. 'em] *F;* them *Q2.*　　95 S.D.] *Capell.*

---

78. *o'er-offices*] lords it over (by
virtue of his office). Cf. *Cor.* v.ii.60, 'a
Jack guardant cannot office me'.
Note the irony of over-officing an
intriguer for office. The preference of
editors and bibliographers for Q2's
o'er-reaches, an obvious substitution, is
astonishing. See Intro., pp. 59–60.

would circumvent God] As Cain
sought to do. Genesis iv.9.

83. *my Lord Such-a-one*] One might
not have expected the beggar of the
horse as well as the owner to be *my
Lord.* So Q1, 'why may not that be
such a ones Scull, that praised my
Lord such a ones horse'. But see *Tim.*
I.ii.208–10.

87. *chopless*] with the jaw gone. If
this form is more vulgar than *chapless*,
it suits well with *mazard.* Cf. l. 186
(Q2,F *chopfalne*).

88. *mazard*] head (jocular, from
mazer, cup, bowl).

89. *revolution*] as of the wheel of
Fortune or the whirligig of time.

trick] knack.

91. *loggets*] a game played by
throwing shaped pieces of wood (the
loggets) to lie as near as possible to
a fixed stake or other object. Cf.
Jonson, *Tale of a Tub*, IV.vi.69,
'tossing of his legs and arms, Like
loggets at a pear-tree'. I suspect that
the account in *Sh.'s Eng.* (ii.466) of
bones being used for loggets comes
from taking Hamlet's metaphor literally. 'Loggating' was one of the new
games made unlawful by statute 33
Hen. VIII c.9.

93. *For and*] and moreover. Not the
grave-digger's vulgarism, but a regular ballad idiom. (*OED* for *conj.* 5.)

Ham. There's another. Why, may not that be the skull of
a lawyer? Where be his quiddities now, his quillities,
his cases, his tenures, and his tricks? Why does he
suffer this mad knave now to knock him about the
sconce with a dirty shovel, and will not tell him of his   100
action of battery? Hum, this fellow might be in's
time a great buyer of land, with his statutes, his
recognizances, his fines, his double vouchers, his
recoveries. Is this the fine of his fines and the
recovery of his recoveries, to have his fine pate full of   105
fine dirt? Will his vouchers vouch him no more of
his purchases, and double ones too, than the length

96. Why,] *This edn;* why *Q2,F.*   may] *Q2;* might *F.*   97. quiddities] *Q2;*
Quiddits *F.*   quillities] *Q3;* quillites *Q2;* Quillets *F,Q1.*   99. mad] *Q2;*
rude *F.*   104–5. Is . . . recoveries] *F; not in Q2.*   106. his vouchers] *F;*
vouchers *Q2.*   107. double ones too] *F;* doubles *Q2.*

96. *Why*] Not, as usually supposed,
an interrogative but an interjection.
OED Why iv.7. Cf. iii.i.121, v.i.196.
97. *Where be*] The traditional *Ubi
sunt* motif, as at l. 183.
quiddities . . . quillities] quibbling
arguments. The second word appears
to be a mere variant of the first,
which referred originally to the
sophistical arguments of the schools
concerning the *quidditas* or essential
nature of a thing and afterwards to
fine legal distinctions. *LLL* iv.iii.
280–4 calls for 'some tricks, some
quillets' to 'prove Our loving lawful,
and our faith not torn'.
98. *tenures*] terms on which property
is held.
99. *mad*] wild, irrepressible (like the
'mad wag' Prince Hal, or Shallow in
his 'mad days', etc.). Cf. ll. 170, 173.
It is odd that editorial tradition has
preferred F's inferior *rude.*
100–1. *his action of battery*] i.e. his
liability to an action for assault. Cf.
Tw.N. iv.i.33.
102. *a great buyer of land*] Like
many who aspired to become landed
gentry. The practice had long been
notorious among lawyers, who were

accused of using their legal expertise
to their own advantage. Cf. Chaucer,
Prologue, ll. 318–20; Wyclif, *Three
Things*, Eng. Works (EETS), pp.
182–3.
102–3. *his statutes, his recognizances*]
Often coupled together, the *recogni-
zance* being a bond acknowledging a
debt or obligation, the *statute* (statute
merchant or statute staple, according
to the manner of record) securing the
debt upon the debtor's lands.
103–4. *fines . . . recoveries*] A *fine* (an
action leading to an agreement calling
itself *finalis concordia*) and a *recovery* (a
suit for obtaining possession) were
procedures for effecting the transfer
of estates when an entail or other
obstacle prevented simple sale. A
voucher in a recovery suit was the process of summoning a third party to
warrant the holder's title, and the
customary *double voucher* involved a
second warrantor.
104. *the fine*] the final result. This
begins a series of four different meanings for the same word (handsome
pate, powdered dirt).
104–5. *the recovery*] the whole gain.
106. *vouch*] assure, guarantee.

and breadth of a pair of indentures? The very con-
veyances of his lands will scarcely lie in this box, and
must th'inheritor himself have no more, ha?　　　110

Hor. Not a jot more, my lord.

Ham. Is not parchment made of sheepskins?

Hor. Ay, my lord, and of calveskins too.

Ham. They are sheep and calves which seek out assurance
in that. I will speak to this fellow.—Whose grave's 115
this, sirrah?

Grave. Mine, sir.

　　[*Sings*]　*O a pit of clay for to be made—*

Ham. I think it be thine indeed, for thou liest in't.

Grave. You lie out on't, sir, and therefore 'tis not yours. 120
For my part, I do not lie in't, yet it is mine.

Ham. Thou dost lie in't, to be in't and say 'tis thine. 'Tis
for the dead, not for the quick: therefore thou liest.

Grave. 'Tis a quick lie, sir, 'twill away again from me to
you.　　　　　　　　　　　　　　　　　　　　125

Ham. What man dost thou dig it for?

Grave. For no man, sir.

Ham. What woman then?

Grave. For none neither.

---

109. scarcely] *Q2;* hardly *F.*　　110. th'inheritor] *Q2;* the Inheritor *F.*
113. calveskins] Calue-skinnes *F,Q3;* Calues-skinnes *Q2.*　　114. which] *Q2;*
that *F.*　　116. sirrah] *Q2;* Sir *F.*　　117–18. *As F;* one line *Q2.*　　118. *Sings*]
Capell.　　O] *F;* or *Q2.*　　made—] made. *Q2;* made, | *for such a Guest is meete.*
F.　　120. 'tis] *Q2;* it is *F.*　　121. yet] *Q2;* and yet *F.*　　122. 'tis] *F;* it is
Q2.

---

108. *pair of indentures*] a deed dupli-
cated on a single sheet which was then
divided by a zigzag (indented) cut so
that the fitting together of the two
parts would prove their genuineness.
All the land the purchaser finally has
(his grave) is no bigger than the indentures which convey it. Editorial
ingenuities comparing the indentures
and the skull are beside the point.

109. *box*] (1) deed-box; (2) coffin
(not, as Dover Wilson, skull).

110. *inheritor*] acquirer.

114. *assurance*] (1) certainty of
possession; (2) legal deed securing

this. It is foolish to look for the first in
the second.

116. *sirrah*] A form of *sir* used to
inferiors.

118. *O a pit . . . made*] The extra
line in F (cf. IV.v.164, II.i.53) is
evidently an actors' addition. See
Intro., p. 62, and *SB*, XIII, 40–1.

119–20. *thine . . . You*] 'Note that
throughout this dialogue Ham. addresses the Clown in the second person singular, while the Clown replies
in the second person plural' (Furness).

120. *You lie*] The inevitable pun.

123. *quick*] living.

Ham. Who is to be buried in't?   130
Grave. One that was a woman, sir; but rest her soul, she's
   dead.
Ham. How absolute the knave is. We must speak by the
   card or equivocation will undo us. By the Lord,
   Horatio, this three years I have took note of it, the   135
   age is grown so picked that the toe of the peasant
   comes so near the heel of the courtier he galls his
   kibe.—How long hast thou been grave-maker?
Grave. Of all the days i'th' year I came to't that day that
   our last King Hamlet o'ercame Fortinbras.   140
Ham. How long is that since?
Grave. Cannot you tell that? Every fool can tell that. It
   was that very day that young Hamlet was born—he
   that is mad and sent into England.

---

135. this three] *Q2;* these three *F;* This seauen *Q1.*   took] *Q2;* taken *F.*
137. heel] *Q2,Q1,F2;* heeles *F.*   the courtier] *Q2,Q1;* our Courtier *F.*
138. been] *Q2;* been a *F.*   139. all] *F; not in Q2.*   140. o'ercame] *F;*
ouercame *Q2.*   143. was that] *Q2;* was the *F.*   144. is] *Q2;* was *F.*

---

133. *absolute*] strict, puristic (rather
than, as usually glossed, positive).

133–4. *by the card*] accurately, according to the rule, or chart, perhaps
alluding to the mariner's chart of the
seas, or, as usually though not necessarily taken, to the card on which the
32 points of the compass were marked
(the 'shipman's card' of *Mac.* I.
iii.17).

134. *equivocation*] ambiguous use of
words (1) in the plain sense, but (2)
also in the sinister sense, with intent
to deceive, which, though the practice had not yet acquired the notori-
ety that came with the trial of Garnet
in 1606 (see Arden *Mac.* xviiiff.), was
already familiar enough (cf. R. Scot,
Discovery of Witchcraft, 1584, xiii, ch.
15, 'How men have been abused with
words of equivocation'; Harrison,
Last Elizabethan Journal, pp. 111,
218–19). Hence *will undo us.*

135. *this three years*] The possibility
(rather than probability) of a topical
allusion naturally arises. Yet it is hard

to see why the Poor Law acts of 1597
and 1601 (proposed by Dowden and
Dover Wilson), even if they galled
the courtier with the poor rate,
should involve the diminution of
social differences, which appears to
be the point of the passage.

took] This use of the past tense for
the participle (Abbott 343) is common in Shakespeare. F modernizes
(as also at ll. 167, 179).

136. *picked*] refined, finical.

136–8. *the toe . . . kibe*] The peasant
is affecting the manners of the
courtier, until (to the latter's discom-
fiture) there is little distinction between them. A *kibe* was a sore on the
heel, typically a chilblain and, to
judge from frequent allusion, a prevalent affliction, perhaps due to poor
footwear. Cf. *Wiv.* I.iii.30.

139. *Of all the days i'th' year*] The
same idiom occurs in *Rom.* I.iii.17, 26.

139–57. *I came to't that day . . .
thirty years.*] On the implications of
this for Hamlet's age, LN.

Ham. Ay, marry. Why was he sent into England?   145

Grave. Why, because a was mad. A shall recover his wits
    there. Or if a do not, 'tis no great matter there.

Ham. Why?

Grave. 'Twill not be seen in him there. There the men are
    as mad as he.   150

Ham. How came he mad?

Grave. Very strangely, they say.

Ham. How 'strangely'?

Grave. Faith, e'en with losing his wits.

Ham. Upon what ground?   155

Grave. Why, here in Denmark. I have been sexton here,
    man and boy, thirty years.

Ham. How long will a man lie i'th' earth ere he rot?

Grave. Faith, if a be not rotten before a die—as we have
    many pocky corses nowadays that will scarce hold   160
    the laying in—a will last you some eight year or nine
    year. A tanner will last you nine year.

Ham. Why he more than another?

Grave. Why, sir, his hide is so tanned with his trade that
    a will keep out water a great while, and your water   165
    is a sore decayer of your whoreson dead body. Here's
    a skull now hath lien you i'th' earth three and twenty
    years.

146-7. a . . . A . . . a] *Q2;* he . . . hee . . . he *F.*   147. 'tis] *Q2,Q1;* it's *F.*
149. him there. There] him there, there *Q2;* him, there *F.*   156. sexton] *Q2,*
F2; sixteene *F.*   159. Faith] *Q2;* Ifaith *F,Q1.*   a . . . a] *Q2;* he . . . hee
F,Q1.   160. nowadays] *F; not in Q2,Q1.*   161. a] *Q2;* he *F,Q1.*
165. a will] *Q2;* he will *F.*   167. now] *Q2;* now: this Scul *F.*
hath lien you] *Q2;* has laine *F.*   i'th'] *Q2;* in the *F.*   three and twenty]
F; 23. *Q2;* twenty three *Q4.*

149-50. *There the men . . . as he.*] The
madness of the English presently became, if it was not already, a stock
joke (as in Marston, *Malcontent,* III.
i. 95; Massinger, *A Very Woman,* III.
i. 119-22).

158-66.] Note the physical variation on the theme of how long a man
is remembered after his death
(I.ii. 87-108, 145-57; III.ii. 124-33).

160. *hold*] endure, survive. Cf. *Cor.*
III.ii. 80, 'the ripest mulberry That
will not hold the handling'; *Tim.* I.

ii. 148.

161. *laying in*] i.e. in the ground.

162. *A tanner . . . nine year.*] It is
difficult (as desired by *N&Q,* ccxxi,
156) to see more than coincidence in
a nine-year-old play, *The Tanner of
Denmark,* recorded by Henslowe as
acted 23 May 1592.

165-6. *your . . . your*] Cf. I.i. 141,
IV.iii. 21-3 and nn.

166, 170. *whoreson*] expressive of
contemptuous familiarity.

Ham. Whose was it?

Grave. A whoreson mad fellow's it was. Whose do you 170
    think it was?

Ham. Nay, I know not.

Grave. A pestilence on him for a mad rogue! A poured a
    flagon of Rhenish on my head once. This same
    skull, sir, was Yorick's skull, the King's jester.   175

Ham. This?   [*Takes the skull.*]

Grave. E'en that.

Ham. Alas, poor Yorick. I knew him, Horatio, a fellow
    of infinite jest, of most excellent fancy. He hath bore
    me on his back a thousand times, and now—how 180
    abhorred in my imagination it is. My gorge rises at
    it. Here hung those lips that I have kissed I know not
    how oft. Where be your gibes now, your gambols,
    your songs, your flashes of merriment, that were
    wont to set the table on a roar? Not one now to mock 185
    your own grinning? Quite chop-fallen? Now get you
    to my lady's chamber and tell her, let her paint an
    inch thick, to this favour she must come. Make her
    laugh at that. —Prithee, Horatio, tell me one thing.

Hor. What's that, my lord?   190

170–1.] *Prose Q2; 2 lines divided* was; / Whose *F*.   173. A poured] *Q2,F;* he
pour'd *Q 1676*.   175. sir] *Q2*; Sir, this same Scull sir *F*.   was] *F*; was
sir *Q2*; was one *Q1*.   176 S.D.] *Capell; at 178 Singer*.   178. Alas] *Q2;*
Let me see. Alas *F,Q1* (*subst.*).   179. bore] *Q2*; borne *F*.   180. now—]
This edn; now *Q2,Q1; not in F*.   181. in] *Q2; not in F*.   it is] *Q2*; is *F*.
185. Not] *Q2*; No *F*.   186. grinning] *Q2*; Ieering *F*.   187. chamber]
F,Q1; table *Q2*.

174. *Rhenish*] Rhine wine. Cf. I.
iv. 10.

175. *Yorick's*] Amid the play's
mixed nomenclature, explanations of
this as a Danish name are not inherently improbable. But they fail to
agree as between a corruption of
Rorik (Saxo's Roricus, Belleforest's
Rorique, the Queen's father), or alternatively Eric, and an attempt to
render in English spelling the Danish
equivalent of George (*Jörg-*), *Y* of
course corresponding to Danish *J*.
Cf. 'Jerick' for a German peasant in
Alphonsus of Germany (Act II). And see

l. 178n.

176 S.D. *Takes the skull*.] The
demonstratives make clear that the
skull changes hands and at this point.
Hence at l. 178 F *Let me see* is an intrusion (*SB*, XIII, 36).

178. *Alas, poor Yorick*] Does an echo
linger in Shakespeare's mind of
'Alas, poor York', etc. (*3H6* I.iv.84)?

186. *chop-fallen*] literally and figuratively, down in the mouth. Cf. chopless, l. 87.

187–8. *paint an inch thick*] LN.

188. *favour*] appearance (esp. of the
face).

Ham. Dost thou think Alexander looked o' this fashion
    i'th' earth?

Hor. E'en so.

Ham. And smelt so? Pah!   *[Puts down the skull.]*

Hor. E'en so, my lord.   195

Ham. To what base uses we may return, Horatio! Why,
    may not imagination trace the noble dust of
    Alexander till a find it stopping a bung-hole?

Hor. 'Twere to consider too curiously to consider so.

Ham. No, faith, not a jot, but to follow him thither with 200
    modesty enough, and likelihood to lead it. Alexander
    died, Alexander was buried, Alexander returneth
    to dust, the dust is earth, of earth we make loam, and
    why of that loam whereto he was converted might
    they not stop a beer-barrel?   205
    Imperious Caesar, dead and turn'd to clay,
    Might stop a hole to keep the wind away.
    O that that earth which kept the world in awe
    Should patch a wall t'expel the winter's flaw.
    But soft, but soft awhile. Here comes the King,   210

---

191. o'] *F;* a *Q2.*   194. so? Pah] *Q5;* so pah *Q2;* so: pah *Q3;* so? Puh *F.*
194 S.D.] *Collier; Throws it down. Capell.*   196. Why,] *This edn;* Why
Q2,F,Q1.   198. a find] *Q2;* he find *F.*   199. consider too] *Q2;* consider:
to *F.*   201. it.] *Q2;* it; as thus. *F,Q1.*   203. to] *Q2;* into *F.*
206. Imperious] *Q2,Q1;* Imperiall *F.*   209. winter's] *F;* waters *Q2.*
210. awhile] *Q2,Q1;* aside *F.*

191. *Alexander*] From ancient times
Alexander was regularly cited in
meditations on Death the leveller.
See, e.g., Lucian's *Dialogues of the
Dead,* XII–XIV. Marcus Aurelius (VI.
24) comments on the sameness of the
dust of Alexander and his groom.

191–4. *looked . . . smelt*] Alexander
in life was noted for his 'very fair
white colour' and a body of 'so sweet
a smell' that his apparel 'took thereof
a passing delightful savour, as if it
had been perfumed' (North's Plutarch, Tudor Trans. iv. 301).

196. *Why,*] Not part of the question,
as eds. suppose, but an interjection –
as at III. i. 121, v. i. 96.

199. *curiously*] minutely, ingeniously.

201. *modesty*] moderation, as at II.
ii. 436 (see n.), III. ii. 19.

likelihood to lead it] The general
sense is clear if the antecedent of *it* is
not. The imagination is led to what it
envisages by considerations of what is
likely.

206–9.] The citation of *Caesar*
along with Alexander was traditional,
but the burst of rhyme must be taken
to be one of Hamlet's impromptus.
Cf. III. ii. 265 ff.

206. *Imperious*] imperial (as often).
Malone notes F's trick of substituting
the more familiar word.

209. *flaw*] squall.

The Queen, the courtiers.

Enter [Bearers *with*] *a Coffin, a* Priest, KING, QUEEN,
LAERTES, Lords *Attendant*.

       Who is this they follow?
And with such maimed rites? This doth betoken
The corse they follow did with desp'rate hand
Fordo it own life. 'Twas of some estate.
Couch we awhile and mark.   215
Laer. What ceremony else?
Ham. That is Laertes, a very noble youth. Mark.
Laer. What ceremony else?
Priest. Her obsequies have been as far enlarg'd
  As we have warranty. Her death was doubtful; 220
  And but that great command o'ersways the order,

---

211 S.D.] *This edn; Enter K. Q. Laertes and the corse. Q2; Enter King, Queene,
Laertes, and a Coffin, with Lords attendant. F; Enter King and Queene, Leartes, and
other lordes, with a Priest after the coffin. Q1.* 211. this] *Q2,Q1;* that *F.*
212. rites] *Q2, F corr.;* rights *F uncorr.* 214. it] *Q2,F;* its *Q5;* it's *F3.*
of] *Q2; not in F.* 219, 228. *Priest*] *F,Q1 (one speech);* Doct. *Q2.*
220. warranty] *Q2,F2;* warrantis *F;* warrantise *Dyce.*

---

211 S.D.] Q2's attenuated direction
is added in the right margin. It is left
for Q1 to supply the necessary *Priest.*
The *corse* of Q2, no doubt deriving
from the text (l. 213), became a
coffin in F and Q1 and hence evidently
on the stage. In view of l. 243 one
cann(t be certain this was Shakespeare's intention. But see note there.
Cf. Greg, *SFF*, p. 323.
 212–14. *This doth betoken . . . life.*]
Contrast above ll. 4–5 and n. This is
not so much an inconsistency as a
balancing of what is essential to
Christian burial against what is usual
but is here withheld. See ll. 222–31.
It is impossible to agree with Dover
Wilson that the *maimed rites*, so symbolic of Ophelia's tragedy, originated
in 'theatrical convenience' (*WHH*,
p. 295).
 214. *Fordo*] destroy.

it] its. See 1.ii.216n.
estate] rank, standing.
215. *Couch*] conceal ourselves.
219, 228. *Priest*] This F speech-head
corresponds to the dialogue (l. 233).
Shakespeare's known casualness about
speech-prefixes hardly permits us to
infer, with Dover Wilson (*WHH*,
pp. 69, 300), that Q2 *Doct.* must denote a Protestant divine.
220. *warranty*] This must refer to the
Church's sanction of its own offices, as
distinct from the coroner's warrant
for burial (ll. 4–5). The prohibition of
the burial service for suicides (on
which see Blunt, *Book of Church Law*,
1921 edn, pp. 182–3) became explicit
in the Prayerbook of 1662. Discretion
was allowed in *doubtful* cases (which
are provided for in the Roman *Codex
Iuris Canonici*, 1240 §2).
 221. *order*] prescribed practice.

She should in ground unsanctified been lodg'd
Till the last trumpet: for charitable prayers
Shards, flints, and pebbles should be thrown on her.
Yet here she is allow'd her virgin crants,   225
Her maiden strewments, and the bringing home
Of bell and burial.
Laer. Must there no more be done?
Priest.   No more be done.
We should profane the service of the dead
To sing sage requiem and such rest to her   230
As to peace-parted souls.
Laer.   Lay her i'th' earth,
And from her fair and unpolluted flesh
May violets spring. I tell thee, churlish priest,

---

222. been] *Q2;* haue *F.*   223. prayers] *Q2;* praier *F.*   224. Shards] *F;*
not in Q2.   225. crants] *Q2;* Rites *F.*   230. sage] *F;* a *Q2.*

---

222. *should . . . been*] The omission
of *have* between *should* or *would* and the
past pple. when other words intervene
is idiomatic. Cf. *Cor.* IV.vi.34–5, 'We
should . . . If he had gone forth con-
sul, found it so'; *H5,* III.ii.112–13, 'I
wad (= would) full fain heard some
question'; and see *MLR,* v, 346–7;
Neophilologus, xxx, 37–43. F's substitution of *have* for *been* and active for
passive, though followed by all eds.
but Evans, is a manifest attempt at
'improvement'.

224. *Shards*] pieces of broken
pottery.

225. *crants*] or *crance,* a garland or
chaplet worn as a sign of maiden-
hood, placed on the bier at burial and
afterwards hung up in church. LN.

226. *strewments*] flowers strewn on
the grave. Cf. ll. 236–9. For these as a
sign of chastity, cf. *H8* IV.ii.169–70.

bringing home] i.e. to her last resting-
place, the 'long home' of Ecclesiastes
xii.5. Cf. *Tit.* I.i.83, 'These that I
bring unto their latest home'. The
phrase was traditional, as in wills providing for the testator to be '(honest-
ly) brought home', given a proper

funeral (*OED* home *adv.* I c; *RES,*
n.s. x, 25).

227. *bell and burial*] the tolling of the
church bell and formal solemnities of
burial.

229–30. *profane . . . requiem*] Psalms
and masses for suicides were explicitly
forbidden in the canon law.

230. *sage*] grave, solemn. Cf. *Il
Penseroso,* l. 117, 'sage and solemn
tunes'. *OED* sage *a.* 3. Presumably
the word defeated the Q2 compositor.
Cf. *MSH,* p. 11.

233. *May violets spring*] Consciously
or not, an echo of Persius, *Sat.* 1.39–
40, 'nunc non e tumulo fortunataque
favilla / nascentur violae?' The violets
here contrast with the withered violets of Ophelia's lover (see IV.v.
173–83 LN). As the emblem of faithful
love they combine with the willow of
forsaken love (IV.vii.165 and LN) to
suggest the nature of Ophelia's
tragedy. They are also 'violettis of
parfit chastite' (Lydgate, *Troy Book,*
III, 4380). Cf. *unpolluted,* which rebuts
the fears of I.iii.31–2, II.ii.181–6,
while *fair and unpolluted* significantly
contradicts III.i.111–15. We cannot

A minist'ring angel shall my sister be
When thou liest howling.
Ham.   What, the fair Ophelia!   235
Queen. [*scattering flowers*] Sweets to the sweet. Farewell.
I hop'd thou shouldst have been my Hamlet's wife:
I thought thy bride-bed to have deck'd, sweet maid,
And not have strew'd thy grave.
Laer.   O, treble woe
Fall ten times treble on that cursed head   240
Whose wicked deed thy most ingenious sense
Depriv'd thee of.—Hold off the earth awhile,
Till I have caught her once more in mine arms.

                                   Leaps in the grave.

Now pile your dust upon the quick and dead,
Till of this flat a mountain you have made   245
T'o'ertop old Pelion or the skyish head
Of blue Olympus.
Ham.   What is he whose grief
Bears such an emphasis, whose phrase of sorrow

---

236. *scattering flowers*] *Johnson.*   Sweets . . . sweet.] *Q2* (*subst.*), *Q1*; Sweets,
to the sweet *F.*   239. have] *Q2*; t'haue *F.*   treble woe] *Q2*; terrible
woer *F.*   240. treble] *F*; double *Q2.*   243 S.D.] *F,Q1* (*subst.*); not in *Q2.*
246. T'o'ertop] *Q2* (To'retop); To o're top *F,Q1.*   247. grief] *Q2*; griefes *F.*

---

doubt that Laertes here voices the
sentiment of the play, though the
significance of this passage was
strangely overlooked by those who
used to imagine Ophelia seduced.

235. *howling*] among the damned in
hell (Matthew xiii.42). Cf. *Rom.*
iii.iii.48, *2H4* ii.iv.333.

238. *bride-bed . . . deck'd*] According
to the custom of strewing the
marriage-bed (and chamber) with
flowers. Cf. *Rom.* v.iii.12; *Epithala-
mion*, ll. 301–2.

241. *ingenious*] mentally alert (L.
ingenium). Cf. *R3* iii.i.155, 'quick,
ingenious, forward, capable'.

243. *Till I have caught . . . arms*] An
open coffin was, according to Dover
Wilson, 'the common if not the usual
practice of the time'. Juliet is borne

'uncovered on the bier' (*Rom.* iv.
i.110); and the stage affords many
instances of the supposed dead rising
from their coffins (*Knight of the
Burning Pestle*, iv.iv; *Chaste Maid in
Cheapside*, v.iv; etc.).

246. *Pelion*] A mountain famed
through the Greek myth in which the
giants in their war with the gods
piled Pelion on the neighbouring
Ossa (l. 278) in order to scale Olympus. Cf. Tilley O 81.

247. *Olympus*] A lofty mountain in
Greece, fabled home of the gods.

248. *emphasis*] the enforcement of
the sense 'by a word of more than
ordinary efficacy' (Puttenham, *Art of
Eng. Poesy*, iii.17), hence excessive or
violent language. Cf. *rant* (l. 279),
bravery (v.ii.79).

Conjures the wand'ring stars and makes them stand
Like wonder-wounded hearers? This is I,   250
  Hamlet the Dane.
Laer. [*grappling with him*] The devil take thy soul!
Ham.   Thou pray'st not well.
  I prithee take thy fingers from my throat,
  For though I am not splenative and rash,
  Yet have I in me something dangerous,   255
  Which let thy wiseness fear. Hold off thy hand.
King. Pluck them asunder.
Queen. Hamlet! Hamlet!
All. Gentlemen!
Hor. Good my lord, be quiet.   260
Ham. Why, I will fight with him upon this theme
  Until my eyelids will no longer wag.
Queen. O my son, what theme?
Ham. I lov'd Ophelia. Forty thousand brothers
  Could not with all their quantity of love   265

---

249. Conjures] *Q2;* Coniure *F.*   252. *grappling with him*] *Rowe.*
252-3. Thou . . . throat] *As F;* one line *Q2.*   254. For] *Q2,Q1;* Sir *F.*
and] *F; not in Q2.*   255. in me something] *Q2;* something in me *F,Q1.*
256. wiseness] *F;* wisedome *Q2,Q1.*   Hold off] *Q2,Q1;* Away *F.*
259. *All.* Gentlemen!] *Q2 (subst.); not in F.*   260. *Hor.*] *Q2;* Gen. *F.*

249. *Conjures*] casts a spell on.

the wand'ring stars] A regular term for the planets.

250. *This is I*] Cf. 'What is he', l. 247.

251. *the Dane*] the ruler of Denmark. Cf. I.i.16, I.ii.44. It is a sign of the change in Hamlet that he now assumes this title.

252. *grappling with him*] Q1 has the direction 'Hamlet leapes in after Leartes'. This and the *Elegy on Burbage* ('Oft have I seen him leap into the grave') are evidence of what was done in performance. But Granville-Barker (*Prefaces*, iii. 162–3 n.) argues that the action requires Laertes, the aggressor, to come out of the grave rather than Hamlet to leap in. Moreover, attendants must be able to part them. Neither the text nor the pattern of the action assists

those who would find here a symbolic burial and resurrection.

254. *splenative*] hot-tempered, characterized by spleen (source of ungovernable outbursts – of rage, etc.). Cf. *Rom.* III.i.154–5, 'the unruly spleen of Tybalt'; *Caes.* IV.iii.47.

256. *wiseness*] The Q2 reading, whether coincidental with or inherited from that of Q1, looks like a corruption of F's rarer word (*MSH*, pp. 163–4; *SFF*, p. 313). Possibly there is a distinction to be made between *wisdom*, sagacity in general, and *wiseness*, the exercise of it on a particular occasion.

262. *eyelids . . . wag*] The stirring of the eyelids is thought of as the smallest sign of life.

265. *quantity*] (contemptuous) a small or insignificant amount. Cf. III.iv.75, III.ii.41.

Make up my sum. What wilt thou do for her?
King. O, he is mad, Laertes.
Queen. For love of God forbear him.
Ham. 'Swounds, show me what thou't do.
       Woo't weep, woo't fight, woo't fast, woo't tear thyself,
       Woo't drink up eisel, eat a crocodile?   271
       I'll do't. Dost come here to whine,
       To outface me with leaping in her grave?
       Be buried quick with her, and so will I.
       And if thou prate of mountains, let them throw   275
       Millions of acres on us, till our ground,
       Singeing his pate against the burning zone,
       Make Ossa like a wart. Nay, and thou'lt mouth,
       I'll rant as well as thou.
Queen.   This is mere madness,
       And thus awhile the fit will work on him.   280
       Anon, as patient as the female dove

---

269. 'Swounds] *Q2;* Come *F.*   thou't] *Q2;* thou'lt *F;* thou wilt *Q1.*
270. woo't fast] *Q2; not in F;* wilt fast *Q1.*   271. eisel] *Theobald;* Esill
Q2,F (Esile); vessels *Q1.*   272. Dost come] *Q2;* Dost thou come *F;* Com'st
thou *Q1.*   279. Queen] *Q2; Kin(g) F,Q1.*   280. thus] *F;* this *Q2.*

268. *forbear him*] leave him alone.

269. *thou't*] This form of contraction follows Q2 (cf. *2H4* II.iv.266–8), though with *thou'lt* at l. 278 Q2 itself, and therefore perhaps Shakespeare, is inconsistent.

270–9.] The absurdity of the ranting match has troubled the critics. But we must not forget that the lady is dead. Cf. Intro., p. 158.

270. *Woo't*] colloquial for *Wilt* (which Q1 reads). *OED* will v.¹ A 3 δ.

271. *drink up*] drink avidly or unhesitatingly. Although this intensive *up* often implies 'to completion', the notion that it cannot be used otherwise is confuted by *Sonn.* CXIV, 'Drink up the monarch's plague, this flattery', etc.

eisel] vinegar; a drink of supreme bitterness. LN.

272. *Dost*] For this idiomatic omission of *thou*, cf. v. ii. 82 and see Abbott 241.

274. *quick*] alive.

276. *our ground*] the earth beneath which we are buried.

277. *his*] its. Cf. I. i. 40 n.

the burning zone] that part of the celestial sphere within which the sun supposedly moves, corresponding to the tropical zone on earth. See *Georgics*, I. 233 ff.

278. *Ossa*] Hamlet piles his Ossa on Laertes's Pelion (l. 246).

like a wart] Echoing Erasmus, *Colloquia,* Naufragium, which describes a tempest with huge waves in comparison with which the Alps are warts (*verrucae*).

281. *dove*] Proverbial for meekness. Cf. Tilley D 573.

When that her golden couplets are disclos'd,
His silence will sit drooping.

Ham.   Hear you, sir,
What is the reason that you use me thus?
I lov'd you ever. But it is no matter.   285
Let Hercules himself do what he may,
The cat will mew, and dog will have his day.   *Exit.*

King. I pray thee, good Horatio, wait upon him.

Exit Horatio.

[*To Laertes*] Strengthen your patience in our last night's
   speech:
We'll put the matter to the present push.—   290
Good Gertrude, set some watch over your son.
This grave shall have a living monument.
An hour of quiet shortly shall we see;
Till then in patience our proceeding be.   *Exeunt.*

---

282. couplets] *Q2;* Cuplet *F.*   287. The . . . and] *Q2,F;* A . . . a *Q1.*
287 S.D. *Exit*] *F; Exit Hamlet and Horatio Q2,Q1.*   288. thee] *Q2;* you *F.*
288 S.D.] *Q2, Q1 (see 287 S.D.); not in F.*   289. *To Laertes*] *Rowe.*
your] *Q2;* you *F.*   293. shortly] *F;* thirtie *Q2 uncorr;* thereby *Q2 corr.*

---

282. *couplets*] pair of young. The
dove lays two eggs and the new-
hatched birds have yellow (*golden*)
down.

disclos'd] hatched. Cf. iii.i.168.

286. *Hercules*] Celebrated for (1) his
performance of seemingly impossible
tasks; (2) rodomontade, as in Bottom's 'Ercles' vein', *MND,* i.ii.23–34.
See next note.

287. *The cat . . . his day.*] One cannot
agree with Kittredge that this cryptic
utterance, in which Hamlet returns
to the method of madness, is therefore
not to be related to the present situation. But it characteristically admits
of more than one interpretation (cf.
iv.ii.26–7 and LN.). (1) You cannot
stop a creature from acting according
to its nature: a cat will not be silenced
nor a dog kept down. Hence Hamlet
abandons the more than Herculean

task of trying to restrain Laertes. But
the saying about the dog, already a
familiar proverb (Tilley D 464),
usually implied that the dog would
have its turn of prosperity or success.
Hence (2), as Verity suggests and
Dover Wilson prefers, Hamlet dismisses the Herculean rant of Laertes
and boasts his own eventual triumph.

289. *in*] i.e. 'in the thought of'
(Abbott 162).

our . . . speech] iv.vii.127–61.

290. *the present push*] immediate
action. Dover Wilson detects a
quibble on 'push' = rapier-thrust.

292. *a living monument*] an enduring
monument (for 'succeeding ages' as
in *Atheist's Trag.* iii.i.2) rather than
a life-like statue. A second meaning,
for Laertes's ear, may hint at the
memorial the life of Hamlet will
provide.

[SCENE II]

Enter HAMLET *and* HORATIO.

Ham. So much for this, sir. Now shall you see the other.
　　　You do remember all the circumstance?
Hor. Remember it, my lord!
Ham. Sir, in my heart there was a kind of fighting
　　　That would not let me sleep. Methought I lay　　　　5
　　　Worse than the mutines in the bilboes. Rashly—
　　　And prais'd be rashness for it: let us know
　　　Our indiscretion sometime serves us well
　　　When our deep plots do pall; and that should learn us
　　　There's a divinity that shapes our ends,　　　　　10
　　　Rough-hew them how we will—
Hor. 　　　　　　　　　　　　That is most certain.
Ham. Up from my cabin,
　　　My sea-gown scarf'd about me, in the dark

Scene 11

SCENE 11] *Rowe.* 　　1. shall you] *Q2;* let me *F.* 　　5. Methought] *F;* my
thought *Q2.* 　　6. bilboes] *F;* bilbo *Q2.* 　　6–11. Rashly— . . . it: let . . .
will—] *Kittredge* (*subst.*)*;* rashly, . . . it: let . . . will. *Q2;* rashly, (. . . it) let . . .
will. *F;* Rashly, . . . it,—(Let . . . will.) *Jennens.* 　　7. prais'd] *Q2;* praise *F.*
8. sometime] *Q2;* sometimes *F.* 　　9. deep] *Q2;* deare *F.* 　　pall] *Q2 uncorr.*,
F (paule)*;* fall *Q2 corr.;* fail *Pope.* 　　learn] *Q2;* teach *F.* 　　13. me, in the
dark] *Q5;* me in the darke *Q2;* me in the darke, *F.*

1. *see the other*] As promised in IV.
vi. 22–3.

6. *mutines*] = mutiners, mutineers.
All three forms occur in Shakespeare's
texts.

bilboes] iron shackles attached to a
fixed horizontal bar used on board
ship to confine prisoners by the
ankles.

Rashly—] on impulse (in contrast to
deep plots). The word evokes a parenthetic reflection; the narrative resumes at l. 12 with the incidents
which *rashly* describes.

7. *let us know*] 'that is, take notice
and remember' (Johnson).

9. *pall*] lose force, falter. *OED v.*[1] 2.
The variant *fall* in some copies of Q2,
though followed (or emended to *fail*)

by some eds., is apparently a miscor-
rection.

learn] F's substitution of *teach* suggests that *learn* in this sense, common
in Shakespeare and still surviving in
dialect, may already have been losing
favour.

10–11. *There's a divinity . . . will*]
For the sentiment, LN. The concentrated expression of it uses a single
word (*ends*) to apply both to purposes
and their outcome, and a metaphor
from stone or timber work, in which
rough-hew was a familiar term.

13. *sea-gown*] 'a coarse, high-
collared, and short-sleeved gown,
reaching down to the mid-leg, and
used most by seamen and sailors'
(Cotgrave, v. *esclavine*). Dampier used

Grop'd I to find out them, had my desire,
Finger'd their packet, and in fine withdrew   15
To mine own room again, making so bold,
My fears forgetting manners, to unseal
Their grand commission; where I found, Horatio—
Ah, royal knavery!—an exact command,
Larded with many several sorts of reasons   20
Importing Denmark's health, and England's too,
With ho! such bugs and goblins in my life,
That on the supervise, no leisure bated,
No, not to stay the grinding of the axe,
My head should be struck off.

Hor.   Is't possible?   25
Ham. Here's the commission, read it at more leisure.
    But wilt thou hear now how I did proceed?
Hor. I beseech you.
Ham. Being thus benetted round with villainies—
    Or I could make a prologue to my brains,   30
    They had begun the play—I sat me down,
    Devis'd a new commission, wrote it fair—

---

17. unseal] *F;* vnfold *Q2.*   18–19. Horatio—Ah, royal knavery!—] *Wilson;* Horatio A royall knauery, *Q2; Horatio,* Oh royall knauery: *F.*   20. reasons] *Q2;* reason *F.*   22. ho!] hoe *Q2;* hoo, *F.*   27. now] *Q2;* me *F.* 28. I beseech] *Q2,F;* Ay, 'beseech *Capell.*   29. villainies] *Capell;* villaines *Q2,F.*   30. Or] *Q2;* Ere *F.*

---

his as a 'covering in the night' (*Voyages,* II. 1, p. 91; cited *OED* sea *sb.* 18 j.).

  scarf'd about] wrapped round (as distinct from properly put on).

  14. *them*] Rosencrantz and Guildenstern.

  15. *Finger'd*] purloined.

  in fine] finally (as at II. ii. 69, IV. vii. 132).

  20. *Larded*] garnished. Cf. IV. v. 38 and n.

  21. *Importing*] concerning. Cf. I. ii. 23.

  22. *bugs and goblins*] These words, along with the scornful astonishment of *ho!*, ridicule as imaginary the frightful dangers alleged to be inherent in Hamlet's continued existence. *Shr.* I. ii. 207 refers to *bugs* (i.e. bugbears, bogeys) as suitable for frightening 'boys', *Troil.* V. x. 29 to *goblins* as the creation of 'frenzy'.

  23. *supervise*] perusal. The sole recorded instance of the noun; see II. i. 4 n.

  no leisure bated] no time lost.

  24. *stay*] wait for.

  30. *Or*] alternative form of *ere* (< O.E. *ær*). Cf. I. ii. 147 n. F modernizes.

  30–1. *Or I could . . . play*] Before I had had time to work out what to do, my brains had started to do it. A *prologue* (like that to *Rom.*) outlines the action which the players then perform.

  32. *fair*] in a clerkly hand.

I once did hold it, as our statists do,
A baseness to write fair, and labour'd much
How to forget that learning, but, sir, now   35
It did me yeoman's service. Wilt thou know
Th'effect of what I wrote?

Hor.   Ay, good my lord.

Ham. An earnest conjuration from the King,
As England was his faithful tributary,
As love between them like the palm might flourish,   40
As peace should still her wheaten garland wear
And stand a comma 'tween their amities,
And many such-like 'as'es of great charge,
That on the view and knowing of these contents,
Without debatement further more or less,   45
He should those bearers put to sudden death,
Not shriving-time allow'd.

Hor.   How was this seal'd?

Ham. Why, even in that was heaven ordinant.
I had my father's signet in my purse,
Which was the model of that Danish seal,   50
Folded the writ up in the form of th'other,

37. Th'effect] *Q2;* The effects *F.*   40. like] *Q2;* as *F.*   might] *Q2;*
should *F.*   42. comma] *Q2,F;* commere *Theobald, conj. Warburton.*
43. 'as'es] *Rowe (As's);* Assis *F;* as sir *Q2.*   44. knowing] *Q2;* know *F.*
46. those] *Q2;* the *F.*   48. ordinant] *Q2;* ordinate *F.*   51. the form
of th'other] *Q2;* forme of the other *F.*

33. *statists*] politicians, men of affairs.

40. *like the palm . . . flourish*] Psalm xcii.12.

41. *still*] always.

wheaten garland] with which, as a symbol of plenty and prosperity, peace is traditionally represented.

42. *comma*] the least of the marks of punctuation, and therefore a type of something small and insignificant. LN.

43. *'as'es of great charge*] Punning on (1) the *as* clauses of great import, and (2) asses with great loads.

45. *more or less*] (without) the slightest deviation (from these instructions).

47. *Not shriving-time allow'd*] Perhaps too much has been made of the savagery of refusing them absolution, when the emphasis is on the denial not so much of the rite as of time for it (cf. 'short shrift'). Cf. ll. 23–5 above; yet also III.iii.89–95 and LN, while the lack of opportunity for confession is an aggravation of the killing of Hamlet's father (I.v.76–9, III.iii. 80–4).

48. *ordinant*] ordaining, directing the course of events. Cf. l. 10 above.

50. *model*] exact likeness.

that] indicating something assumed to be well known. *OED* That *dem.* II i b.

51. *writ*] writing.

Subscrib'd it, gave't th'impression, plac'd it safely,
The changeling never known. Now the next day
Was our sea-fight, and what to this was sequent
Thou knowest already.

Hor. So Guildenstern and Rosencrantz go to't.

Ham. Why, man, they did make love to this employment.
They are not near my conscience, their defeat
Does by their own insinuation grow.
'Tis dangerous when the baser nature comes   60
Between the pass and fell incensed points
Of mighty opposites.

Hor.   Why, what a king is this!

Ham. Does it not, think thee, stand me now upon—
He that hath kill'd my king and whor'd my mother,
Popp'd in between th'election and my hopes,   65

---

52. Subscrib'd] *F;* Subscribe *Q2.*   54. sequent] *Q2;* sement *F.*
55. knowest] *Q2;* know'st *F.*   56. Rosencrantz] *Q2; Rosincrance, F.*
57.] *F; not in Q2.*   58. defeat] *Q2;* debate *F.*   59. Does] *Q2;* Doth *F.*
63. think] *Q2;* thinkst *F;* thinks't *Dyce, conj. Walker.*   63–7. upon— . . .
coz'nage—] *Boswell;* vppon? . . . cusnage, *Q2;* vpon . . . coozenage; *F.*

---

53. *changeling*] a child substituted by fairies for one they steal.

56. *to't*] to their death. Cf. *Gent.* IV. iv. 3–4, 'one that I sav'd from drowning, when three or four of his blind brothers and sisters went to it'.

57. *make love . . . employment*] It does not appear from the text that they knew the nature of the commission they carried. But it is made abundantly clear that they were willing agents. Hamlet assumes them to be willing for the worst (III. iv. 204–9), and we are probably meant to assume it too and to accept the poetic justice of their end.

58. *defeat*] ruin. See II. ii. 566 n.

59. *insinuation*] worming their way in.

60. *baser*] lowlier.

61. *pass*] sword-thrust.

62. *opposites*] antagonists (a frequent 17th-century sense).

63. *think*] seem, with dative of the pronoun, as in *methinks*. Usually interpreted as an imperative, bethink.

But the sense is interrogative: Hamlet is asking an opinion. The grammar is less certain, wherefore many eds. follow F and accept Walker's interpretation *thinks't*, seems it? (*Sh.'s Versification*, pp. 281–2.) But I suspect that instead of trying to improve the grammar, we should accept a flexibility whereby *think thee* can borrow from the interrogative construction of the main clause: Does it not – (does it not) seem to thee? – stand me now upon . . .? (= Isn't it now incumbent on me, don't you think . . .?).

63. *stand me . . . upon*] put an obligation on me. To *stand upon*, to be incumbent on; cf. *R2* II. iii. 138, *R3* IV. ii. 60. See Abbott 204.

64. *whor'd*] See I. v. 42 ff., III. iv. 42–8 and nn.

65. *Popp'd in . . . hopes*] There was no suggestion in I. ii of any such 'hopes' or of any discreditable manœuvre on the part of Claudius. But it is now allowed to appear that he had anticipated the normal process

Thrown out his angle for my proper life
And with such coz'nage—is't not perfect conscience
To quit him with this arm? And is't not to be damn'd
To let this canker of our nature come
In further evil?   70

Hor. It must be shortly known to him from England
What is the issue of the business there.

Ham. It will be short. The interim is mine.
And a man's life's no more than to say 'one'.
But I am very sorry, good Horatio,   75
That to Laertes I forgot myself;
For by the image of my cause I see
The portraiture of his. I'll court his favours.
But sure the bravery of his grief did put me
Into a tow'ring passion.

Hor.   Peace, who comes here?   80

Enter OSRIC, *a Courtier.*

Osr. Your Lordship is right welcome back to Denmark.
Ham. I humbly thank you sir.—Dost know this water-
fly?

---

67. conscience] conscience, *F;* conscience? *Q2.*   68–80.] *F; not in Q2.*
73–5.] *As Hanmer; 3 lines ending* short, / more / *Horatio, F.*   73. interim is]
Hanmer; interim's F.   78. court] *Rowe;* count *F.*   80 S.D.] *Enter a Courtier.*
Q2; Enter young Osricke. F; Enter a Bragart Gentleman. Q1.   82. humbly]
F; humble *Q2.*

---

of 'election' and so come 'between'
Hamlet's hopes and their fulfilment.
See I.ii.1 LN, III.iv.99n.
  66. *angle*] fish-hook.
  proper] own.
  67. *coz'nage*] deception, with the
common word-play on *cousinage*, kinship. Cf. I.ii.65.
  perfect conscience] in complete accord
with one's sense of right. *OED* conscience 6.
  68–80.] The absence of these lines
from Q2 is difficult to explain except
as an accidental omission.
  69. *canker*] a spreading sore – and
thus a corruption inherent in our
'nature', rather than (as Schmidt) a
grub preying on it.

  74. *to say 'one'*] i.e. in counting. To
the hint that he has only a short time
in which to act Hamlet retorts that
man's whole life is short. Dover
Wilson, however, supposes this refers to a single rapier thrust (cf. l. 279
below), which is enough to 'finish
Claudius off' (*WHH*, p. 272).
  77–8. *the image . . . his*] The irony,
which Hamlet does not remark on
but which we can hardly miss, is that
the *image* which shows Laertes as a
revenger like Hamlet must also show
Hamlet as revenge's object.
  79. *bravery*] bravado, flamboyance.
See V.i.244–50, 278–9.
  82–3. *water-fly*] LN.

Hor. No, my good lord.

Ham. Thy state is the more gracious, for 'tis a vice to   85
know him. He hath much land and fertile. Let a
beast be lord of beasts and his crib shall stand at the
king's mess. 'Tis a chuff, but, as I say, spacious in the
possession of dirt.

Osr. Sweet lord, if your lordship were at leisure, I should   90
· impart a thing to you from his Majesty.

Ham. I will receive it, sir, with all diligence of spirit.
Your bonnet to his right use: 'tis for the head.

Osr. I thank your lordship, it is very hot.

Ham. No, believe me, 'tis very cold, the wind is northerly.   95

Osr. It is indifferent cold, my lord, indeed.

Ham. But yet methinks it is very sultry and hot for my
complexion.

Osr. Exceedingly, my lord, it is very sultry—as 'twere—
I cannot tell how. My lord, his Majesty bade me   100
signify to you that a has laid a great wager on your

88. chuff] *This edn;* chough *Q2,F* (Chowgh).   say] *Q2;* saw *F.*
90. lordship] *Q2;* friendship *F.*   92. sir] *Q2; not in F.*   93. Your] *Q2;*
put your *F.*   94. it is] *Q2;* 'tis *F.*   97. But yet] *Q2; not in F.*   sultry] *F;*
sully *Q2.*   hot for] *F;* hot, or *Q2.*   99. sultry—as 'twere—] *Steevens;*
soultery, as t'were *Q2,F.*   100. how.] how: *Q2;* how: but *F.*   101. a has]
Q2; he ha's *F.*

85. *gracious*] blessed. Cf. I.i. 169.

86–8. *Let a beast . . . king's mess.*] A
man of large possessions is received at
court though himself no better than
the cattle he owns. *Crib,* food-box,
continues the beast metaphor.

88. *chuff*] (of which Q2 *chough* is a
variant spelling) rustic, churl, esp.
one who is nevertheless well-to-do.
LN.

90. *Sweet*] Common in courtly
address. Cf. III.ii. 53.

92. *diligence*] attentiveness.

93. *bonnet*] An ordinary word for a
hat or cap. Cf. *Ven.* 339, 351. Hats
indoors were quite normal. Cf. II.i.
79n. Arguments that Osric must have
worn a Danish hat are without textual support.

his] its. See I.i.40n.

94. *it is very hot*] An adaptation of

an old joke. Cf. Guazzo, *Civil Conversation* (Tudor Trans., i. 165), 'seeing
him bare headed . . . made him put
on his hat – He should have put it
off again, to have shewed that he was
not bare in respect of them, but because of the heat'; Florio, *Second
Fruits,* 1591, p. 111, 'Why do you
stand bareheaded? . . . — . . . I do it
for my ease' (cf. l. 105 below). Bur-
lesqued in *The Malcontent,* Ind. 37–9.

94–5. *hot . . . cold*] For Hamlet's
mockery of the obsequious who will
agree to contrary propositions, cf.
III.ii.367–73. Theobald would derive
it from Juvenal, *Sat.* III. 102–3.

96. *indifferent*] moderately, fairly, as
at III.i. 122.

98. *complexion*] constitution. Cf. I.
iv. 27 n.

head. Sir, this is the matter—

Ham. [*signing to him to put on his hat*] I beseech you remember—

Osr. Nay, good my lord, for my ease, in good faith. 105 Sir, here is newly come to court Laertes—believe me, an absolute gentleman, full of most excellent differences, of very soft society and great showing. Indeed, to speak feelingly of him, he is the card or calendar of gentry; for you shall find in him the 110 continent of what part a gentleman would see.

Ham. Sir, his definement suffers no perdition in you,

---

103. *signing . . . hat*] *Johnson subst.*   105. good my lord] *Q2;* in good faith *F.* my ease] *Q2;* mine ease *F.*   106–34. here is . . . Well, sir?] *Q2;* not in *F.* 109. feelingly] *Q3;* fellingly *Q2 corr.;* sellingly *Q2 uncorr.*   111. part] *Q2;* parts *Wilson.*

---

104. *remember*] for 'remember your courtesy', a formula for 'cover your head'. The phrase has puzzled eds., who naturally suppose that courtesy would require one to remain uncovered; but its use not to demand but to waive this mark of respect is amply demonstrated, if not explained. Cf. *LLL* v.i.84–5, 'I do beseech thee, remember thy courtesy . . . apparel thy head'; *Lusty Juventus*, MSR, l. 616, 'I pray you be remembered, and cover your head'; *Every Man in his Humour*, i.ii.50–2, 'pray you remember your court'sy . . . nay, pray you be covered'. *OED* remember *v.* 1 d. The implication appears to be that the demands of courtesy are now satisfied (and that the hat should therefore be resumed).

105. *for my ease*] The polite rejoinder. See above, l. 94 n.

106–40. *here is newly . . . unfellowed*] This praise of Laertes fulfils iv.vii. 130–2. The reduction of it in F to a single sentence is 'an obvious playhouse cut' (Dover Wilson).

107. *absolute*] flawless.

108. *differences*] characteristics which are out of the ordinary, distinctions.

soft society] pleasing manners.

109. *feelingly*] with discrimination, justly, as at *Meas.* i.ii.34; *Tw.N.* ii. iii.149. Some eds. have preferred Q2's original *sellingly*, which is compared with *LLL* iv.iii.236 ('a seller's praise') and *Sonn.* xxi.14 and defended at length by Dover Wilson (*MSH*, pp. 293–4); but the word is neither authenticated nor (from Osric) apt.

109–10. *card or calendar*] model or paradigm. Two words for the same thing. A *card* is literally a chart or map, a *calendar* a register or directory.

110. *gentry*] behaviour proper to a gentleman. Cf. ii.ii.22.

111. *continent*] container, as at iv. iv.64. See next note.

what part] whatever part, any part which. This sense of *what* makes the emendation *parts* (see *MSH*, p. 301) unnecessary. A pun on *part* gives (1) ability, accomplishment (as in iv. vii.72), which a gentleman desires to see in another; (2) region (sustaining the metaphor of *card*, *continent*), which he desires to see on his travels.

112. *perdition*] in the literal sense, loss.

though I know to divide him inventorially would
dozy th'arithmetic of memory, and yet but yaw
neither, in respect of his quick sail. But, in the verity 115
of extolment, I take him to be a soul of great article
and his infusion of such dearth and rareness as, to
make true diction of him, his semblable is his mirror
and who else would trace him his umbrage, nothing
more.   120
Osr. Your lordship speaks most infallibly of him.
Ham. The concernancy, sir? Why do we wrap the gentleman in our more rawer breath?
Osr. Sir?
Hor. Is't not possible to understand in another tongue? 125

---

114. dozy] *Q2 uncorr.* (dosie)*; dazzie Q2 corr.; dizzie Q3.*   yaw] *Q2
uncorr.;* raw *Q2 corr.*   125. in another] *Q2;* in a mother *Tschischwitz, conj.
Johnson;* in's mother *conj. Staunton.*

---

113. *to divide him inventorially*] to list
his attributes separately.

114. *dozy*] bewilder, stupefy. Q2
gives a rare but acceptable form which
is difficult to explain except as the
ms. reading and which the corrector,
falling between *dizzy* and *dazzle*,
failed to improve.

114–15. *but yaw neither . . . sail*] do
no more than divagate in comparison
with his rapid motion. A ship is said
to *yaw* when it fails to keep a straight
course. The nautical metaphor (cf.
sail) establishes the reading, which the
Q2 corrector evidently did not understand. *Neither,* and nothing else, emphasizes the negative implied in *but.*
Cf. *Mer.V.* III.v.7 ('that is but a kind
of bastard hope neither'), *All's W.* II.
ii.33; and see Abbott 128, *OED*
neither A 3b. *In respect of* is regularly
used for 'in comparison with', but
may alternatively mean 'on account
of', which would imply that it was the
very attempt to keep up with the
swift sailing that threw the pursuer
off course. In either case, the excel-
lences of Laertes elude any attempt
to catalogue them.

116. *article*] theme; matter for an
inventory.

117. *infusion*] quality (as determined by what has been infused into
him).

dearth] = *rareness.*

118. *his semblable . . . mirror*] the
(only) person like him is his own
image in the glass.

119. *trace him*] follow his tracks.

umbrage] shadow (he himself being
the substance).

122. *The concernancy . . .?*] How does
this concern us?

122–3. *Why do we wrap . . . breath?*]
Why do we clothe him in words of
ours which can only fall short of his
refinement? An ornate way of asking
why we are speaking about the gentleman at all.

125–6. *Is't not possible . . . really.*]
Apparently a call for a different
(simpler) language, provoked by
Osric's failure to understand and
addressed, I assume, to Hamlet. *You
will to't,* you will apply yourself to it,
have a good go at it; *really,* assuredly.
LN.

You will to't, sir, really.

Ham. What imports the nomination of this gentleman?

Osr. Of Laertes?

Hor. His purse is empty already, all's golden words are
spent.   130

Ham. Of him, sir.

Osr. I know you are not ignorant—

Ham. I would you did, sir. Yet in faith if you did, it would
not much approve me. Well, sir?

Osr. You are not ignorant of what excellence Laertes is—   135

Ham. I dare not confess that, lest I should compare with
him in excellence; but to know a man well were to
know himself.

Osr. I mean, sir, for his weapon; but in the imputation
laid on him, by them in his meed, he's unfellowed.   140

Ham. What's his weapon?

Osr. Rapier and dagger.

Ham. That's two of his weapons. But well.

Osr. The King, sir, hath wagered with him six Barbary

---

126. to't] *Q2 uncorr.* (too't); doo't *Q2 corr.*   really] *Q2;* rarely *Theobald.*
135. is] *Q2;* is at his weapon. *F.*   136–40.] *Q2; not in F.*   139. his] *Q5;*
this *Q2.*   140. him, by them in his meed,] *Q2;* him by them: in this
meed *Capell;* him by them, in his meed *Steevens²*.   144. King, sir] *Q2;* sir
King *F.*   hath wagered] *Q2;* ha's wag'd *F;* hath layd a wager *Q1.*

---

127. *What imports the nomination of*]
What is the reason for mentioning.

134. *not much approve*] approve,
commend; *not much* because Osric's
judgment is of small account.

136–8. *I dare not . . . know himself.*]
Implying that only the excellent can
appreciate excellence and that only
through self-knowledge can a man
thoroughly know another. The first
proposition, however, does not entail
the second, which exceeds it. Hence
but.

139. *imputation*] estimation.

140. *in his meed*] in his service (*meed*,
reward, pay). So Dover Wilson in
accord with Q2 punctuation and the
plain sense. To take *in his meed* (=

merit) with *unfellowed*, as usually done,
is, after stress on *excellence*, tauto-
logical and leaves *them* unidentified.

142. *Rapier and dagger.*] The fashionable mode *c.* 1600, displacing
sword and buckler but itself presently
to be superseded (cf. l. 220 S.D. n.).
See Porter, *Two Angry Women of
Abington*, MSR, ll. 1339–42, 'sword
and buckler fight, begins to grow out,
. . . this poking fight of rapier and
dagger will come up'. With the
dagger (or *poniard*, as l. 146) in the
left hand, one warded off the opponent's rapier while thrusting with
one's own. Cf. *Rom.* III.i.158–60 and
see *WHH*, pp. 279–80.

144–5. *Barbary horses*] A much-
prized breed, noted for their swiftness.

horses, against the which he has impawned, as I 145
take it, six French rapiers and poniards, with their
assigns, as girdle, hanger, and so. Three of the
carriages, in faith, are very dear to fancy, very
responsive to the hilts, most delicate carriages, and of
very liberal conceit.   150

Ham. What call you the carriages?

Hor. I knew you must be edified by the margin ere you
had done.

Osr. The carriages, sir, are the hangers.

Ham. The phrase would be more german to the matter 155
if we could carry a cannon by our sides—I would it
might be hangers till then. But on. Six Barbary
horses against six French swords, their assigns, and
three liberal-conceited carriages—that's the French
bet against the Danish. Why is this—impawned, as 160
you call it?

---

145. has impawned] *Q2* (impaund); impon'd *F.*   147. hanger, and] *Q2;*
Hangers or *F.*   152-3.] *Q2; not in F.*   154. carriages] *F;* carriage *Q2.*
155-6. matter if] *Q2;* matter: If *F.*   156. a] *Q2; not in F;* the *Q1.*
157. might be] *F;* be *Q2 uncorr.;* be might *Q2 corr.*   157-8. on. Six . . .
swords,] *Pope subst.;* on, six . . . swords *Q2;* on sixe . . . Swords: *F.*
160. bet] *Q2;* but *F.*   impawned, as] *Malone;* impon'd as *F;* all *Q2;*
all 'impawned' as *Wilson;* all impon'd, as *Kittredge.*

---

145. *impawned*] staked. See l. 160
LN.

147. *assigns*] A fanciful term for
accessories.

hanger] 'Attached to a man's
girdle was the hanger, which con-
sisted of one or two straps and a plate
or pad to which was buckled the
scabbard of the sword' (Linthicum,
p. 265). The sense often prompts but
(contrary to *MSH*, pp. 238-9) does
not necessitate the plural form. Cf.
Inventory of goods of John Grant
(PRO, E 178/4006), 'Item, one
horseman's coat, boot-hose, mittens,
girdle and hanger'; *Every Man in his
Humour*, I.v.81; Marston, *What You
Will*, v.i.40.

148-50. *very dear . . . conceit*]
Hangers were often richly orna-
mented, wherefore: pleasing to the

fancy, matching the hilts in design,
finely wrought (*delicate*) with lavish
(*liberal*) ingenuity.

151. *What call you . . .?*] What do
you refer to as . . .?

152. *margin*] where, in books of the
time, one might find a gloss or explanatory note.

155-6. *The phrase . . . sides*] Since
carriage is the word for the frame on
which a cannon is mounted. Cf. *H5*
III. Prol. 26.

159-60. *the French bet . . . Danish*]
What the Frenchified Laertes has
brought back with him is set against
the home product. Danish horses
were esteemed and exported (Dollerup, pp. 118-19).

160. *impawned, as*] On the variant
readings, LN.

Osr. The King, sir, hath laid, sir, that in a dozen passes
　　between yourself and him he shall not exceed you
　　three hits; he hath laid on twelve for nine. And it
　　would come to immediate trial if your lordship　165
　　would vouchsafe the answer.

Ham. How if I answer no?

Osr. I mean, my lord, the opposition of your person in
　　trial.

Ham. Sir, I will walk here in the hall. If it please his　170
　　Majesty, it is the breathing time of day with me.
　　Let the foils be brought, the gentleman willing, and
　　the King hold his purpose, I will win for him and I
　　can; if not, I will gain nothing but my shame and
　　the odd hits.　　　　　　　　　　　　　　　　　　175

Osr. Shall I deliver you so?

Ham. To this effect, sir, after what flourish your nature
　　will.

Osr. I commend my duty to your lordship.

Ham. Yours.　　　　　　　　　　　　[*Exit Osric.*]　180
　　A does well to commend it himself, there are no

162. laid, sir] *Q2;* laid *F.*　　　163. yourself] *Q2;* you *F.*　　　164. laid on] *Q2;*
one *F.*　　　nine] *Q2;* mine *F.*　　　it] *Q2;* that *F.*　　　171. it is] *Q2;* 'tis *F.*
172–3. brought, the . . . purpose,] *Theobald;* brought, the . . . purpose; *Q2,*
F; brought. The . . . purpose, *conj. this edn.*　　　173. and] *Q2;* if *F.*
174. I will] *Q2;* Ile *F.*　　　176. deliver] *Q2,Q1;* redeliuer *F.*　　you] *Q2;*
you e'en *F.*　　　180. Yours] *Q2;* Yours, yours *F.*　　　180 S.D.] *F2 (Exit. after*
179), Capell.　　　181. A] *Evans, conj. Parrott-Craig;* hee *F; not in Q2.*

162–4. *The King, sir, hath laid . . .*
nine.] LN.

162. *passes*] bouts. Cf. l. 286 (*bout*)
and *Tw.N.* III.iv.262.

166. *answer*] acceptance of the
challenge (as Osric explains). Cf.
Troil. I.iii.332.

171. *breathing time*] time for exercise.
Cf. *All's W.* I.ii.17, 'sick For breathing and exploit'; *Per.* II.iii.101.

172–4. *Let the foils . . . and I can*] The
Q2 punctuation does not declare the
syntax, though the semicolon after
purpose (followed by F and some eds.)
seems to group the three preceding
clauses with *Let.* I take it this is subjunctive rather than imperative, introducing the conditions for 'I will

win . . .' This requires us to understand *be* before *willing.* An alternative
is to take only 'the gentleman willing,
and (= if) . . . purpose' as conditional
to what follows.

173. *and*] if.

174. *will*] consent to. This balances
the previous *will.* Future tense
would of course be *I shall.* See Abbott
319.

175. *the odd hits*] i.e. the extra three
he will have suffered (see ll. 163–4).

179. *commend*] (1) present to your
favourable regard. Cf. l. 192. But
Hamlet takes it as (2) praise. Plain
speech could have omitted it, as at
I.ii.253.

tongues else for's turn.

Hor. This lapwing runs away with the shell on his head.

Ham. A did comply with his dug before a sucked it. Thus
has he—and many more of the same bevy that I 185
know the drossy age dotes on—only got the tune of
the time and, out of an habit of encounter, a kind of
yeasty collection, which carries them through and
through the most fanned and winnowed opinions;
and do but blow them to their trial, the bubbles are 190
out.

Enter a Lord.

182. turn] *Q2;* tongue *F.*   184. A] *Q2;* He *F.*   comply] *F;* sir *Q2 uncorr.;*
so sir *Q2 corr.*   a] *Q2;* hee *F.*   185. has] *Q2;* had *F.*   many] *Q2;*
mine *F.*   bevy] *F;* breede *Q2.*   187. out of an] *Q2;* outward *F.*
188. yeasty] *F;* histy *Q2.*   189. fanned] *Hanmer, Warburton;* fond *F;*
prophane *Q2;* profound *Tschischwitz, conj. Bailey.*   winnowed] *F;* trennowed
Q2; trennowned *Q3;* renowned *Q 1676.*   190. trial] *Q2;* tryalls *F.*
191 S.D.–204.] *Q2; not in F.*

182. *for's turn*] to serve his purpose,
i.e. to do it for him. *OED* turn *sb.*
30 b(*g*).

183. *lapwing . . . head*] A favourite
proverb, possibly evoked (as Dover
Wilson suggests) by Osric's having
now put on his hat. But the essential
point about the shell is that the lapwing is ornithologically remarkable
for leaving the nest within a few hours
of birth and hence became the proverbial type of juvenile pretension.
Cf. Greene's *Never Too Late* (Greene,
viii. 35), 'Are you no sooner hatched,
with the lapwing, but you will run
away with the shell on your head?'
Tilley L 69.

184. *comply with*] pay courtesies to.
As at II. ii. 368. Cf. Fulwell, *Art of
Flattery*, Pref.: 'the very sucking babes
hath a kind of adulation towards
their nurses for the dug'. *Q2*, in
trouble with several words in this
speech, appears to have surrendered
on this one, for which I take *sir* to be
a substitution (and one which the
press-corrector did not much improve).

185. *bevy*] As a word used of birds,

perhaps suggested by *lapwing*.

186. *the drossy age*] With the sentiment cf. II. ii. 359–62, III. iv. 155–6, v.
i. 135–8.

186–7. *the tune of the time*] 'the cant
of the day' (Johnson).

187. *out of an habit of encounter*] from
habitual intercourse. (Cf. *OED* habit
sb. 10). *F outward*, though much
followed and superficially attractive
in reinforcing *habit* (= dress) and
providing a parallel metaphor for
tune, would imply a contrast with
some inner worth, which a *drossy age*
must lack. Cf. *MSH*, p. 329.

188. *yeasty collection*] accumulation
of froth, i.e. of 'fashionable prattle'
(Johnson).

188–9. *carries them through . . .
opinions*] enables them thoroughly to
hold their own among (and hence
perhaps, as Dover Wilson, impose
upon men of) the most tried and well-
sifted opinions. LN.

190–1. *do but blow . . . out*] This
continues the metaphor of *yeasty*:
when you put Osric and his like to
the test by as much as blowing on
them, the bubbles burst, i.e. when

Lord. My lord, his Majesty commended him to you by
young Osric, who brings back to him that you
attend him in the hall. He sends to know if your
pleasure hold to play with Laertes or that you will   195
take longer time.

Ham. I am constant to my purposes, they follow the
King's pleasure. If his fitness speaks, mine is ready.
Now or whensoever, provided I be so able as now.

Lord. The King and Queen and all are coming down.   200

Ham. In happy time.

Lord. The Queen desires you to use some gentle entertainment to Laertes before you fall to play.

Ham. She well instructs me.   [*Exit Lord.*]

Hor. You will lose, my lord.   205

Ham. I do not think so. Since he went into France, I have
been in continual practice. I shall win at the odds.
Thou wouldst not think how ill all's here about my
heart; but it is no matter.

Hor. Nay, good my lord.   210

Ham. It is but foolery, but it is such a kind of gaingiving
as would perhaps trouble a woman.

Hor. If your mind dislike anything, obey it. I will forestall
their repair hither and say you are not fit.

---

204 S.D.] *Theobald.*   205. lose] *Q 2;* lose this wager *F.*   208. Thou wouldst]
Q 2; but thou wouldest *F.*   ill all's] *Q 2;* all *F.*   211. gaingiving] *F;*
gamgiuing *Q 2;* game-giuing *Q 3.*   213. it] *Q 2; not in F.*

---

you try to converse with them their
fine phrases are shown to be empty of
substance or thought.

198. *If his fitness . . . ready.*] My convenience attends on his.

201. *In happy time.*] At an opportune
moment. A polite formula of welcome.
Cf. *All's W.* v.i.6, *Oth.* iii.i.29, etc.

202–3. *use some gentle entertainment*]
show some mark of courtesy. This
prepares for ll. 222 ff.

205. *lose*] F's addition of *this wager*
appears to have been necessitated by
the cut of ll. 192–204. (Cf. l. 135, F
at his weapon.) Strictly, it is the King

who will lose the wager and Hamlet
the match. But cf. l. 249.

206–7. *I have been in continual practice.*] This, though appropriate here,
contradicts ii.ii.296–7.

207. *the odds*] The 'three hits' of
l. 164.

208–9. *how ill . . . heart*] 'By a divine
instinct men's minds mistrust Ensuing danger' (*R3* ii.iii.42–3).

211. *gaingiving*] misgiving, with the
same prefix as in *gainsay.* The misreading of Q2 and the conjectural
emendation of Q3 suggest that the
word was unfamiliar.

Ham. Not a whit. We defy augury. There is special provi- 215
dence in the fall of a sparrow. If it be now, 'tis not to
come; if it be not to come, it will be now; if it be not
now, yet it will come. The readiness is all. Since no
man, of aught he leaves, knows aught, what is't to
leave betimes? Let be.   220

A table prepared. Trumpets, Drums, *and* Officers *with cushions.*
Enter KING, QUEEN, LAERTES, [OSRIC,] *and all the* State,
and Attendants *with foils and daggers.*

215. There is] *Q2;* there's a *F,Q1.*   216. now] *F,Q1; not in Q2.*
218. will] *F;* well *Q2.*   219. of aught he leaves, knows aught,] *This edn;*
of ought he leaues, knowes *Q2* (knows, *Warburton*); ha's ought of what he
leaues. *F* (leaves, *Rowe*); owes aught of what he leaves, *Hanmer;* knows aught
of what he leaves, *Johnson;* knows of aught he leaves *Spencer.*   220. Let be.]
Q2; not in F.   220 S.D.] *Q2 subst.; Enter King, Queene, Laertes and Lords,
with other Attendants with Foyles, and Gauntlets, a Table and flagons of Wine on it.
F.   Osric] Theobald.*

215. *We*] Note that Hamlet does
not speak for himself alone. Characteristically the personal predicament
expands to the general.

215–16. *There is special providence . . .
sparrow.*] Matthew x.29. The Elizabethans believed both in general
providence manifesting itself in the
whole system of creation and, within
this, in a singular or *special providence*
manifesting itself in the particular
event. The latter, along with its scriptural exemplification in the sparrow,
was especially insisted on by Calvin
(see *Institutes,* I, esp. xvi.1, xvii.6).
Cf. above, ll. 10–11, 48.

216. *it*] death.

218. *The readiness is all.*] Cf.
Matthew xxiv.44 ('Be ye also ready');
Luke xii.40.

218–20. *Since no man . . . betimes?*]
Since no man has any knowledge of
anything he is leaving, what signifies
an early death? LN.

220. *Let be.*] Enough, forbear. Cf.
Ant. IV.iv.6, *Wint.* v.iii.61, and v.ii.
343 below. Many eds. wrongly take
this to be part of Hamlet's reflections,
expressing his resignation to the
course of events. A misplaced ingenuity has even tried to make it
answer 'To be or not to be'. But it
merely recognizes an interruption
which requires their dialogue to
break off. Cf. variously II.ii.416 ('my
abridgment'), v.i.210 ('But soft'),
v.ii.80 ('Peace'), III.ii.90.

220 S.D. *the State*] the nobility, the
court.

foils and daggers] In accordance with
l. 142. Attempts to show that the
fencing must be with single rapier go
against the text. Though the exchange
of rapiers (ll. 306–10) on which the
catastrophe is to turn might be easier
with the single weapon, it evidently
did not presuppose it. F's substitution
of *Gauntlets* for daggers represents a
change in fencing style, but the significance of this in updating the action
has perhaps been overstressed (*WHH,*
p. 280). Rapier and dagger and single
rapier seem to have been current
simultaneously, and a change in stage-
performance may have taken place
already by 1603, the use of gauntlets
being suggested by the Q1 S.D., '*They
catch one anothers Rapiers*' (after l. 306).

King. Come, Hamlet, come, and take this hand from me.
                   [*Puts Laertes's hand into Hamlet's.*]
Ham. Give me your pardon, sir. I have done you wrong;
    But pardon't as you are a gentleman.
    This presence knows, and you must needs have heard,
    How I am punish'd with a sore distraction.   225
    What I have done
    That might your nature, honour, and exception
    Roughly awake, I here proclaim was madness.
    Was't Hamlet wrong'd Laertes? Never Hamlet.
    If Hamlet from himself be ta'en away,   230
    And when he's not himself does wrong Laertes,
    Then Hamlet does it not, Hamlet denies it.
    Who does it then? His madness. If't be so,
    Hamlet is of the faction that is wrong'd;
    His madness is poor Hamlet's enemy.   235
    Sir, in this audience,
    Let my disclaiming from a purpos'd evil
    Free me so far in your most generous thoughts
    That I have shot my arrow o'er the house
    And hurt my brother.
Laer.   I am satisfied in nature,   240

---

221 S.D.] *Johnson subst., after Hanmer.*   222. I have] *Q2;* I'ue *F.*
223–6.] *As Rowe; lines ending* knowes, / punnisht / done *Q2; ending* Gentleman. /
knowes, / punisht / done *F.*   225. a] *Q2; not in F.*   236.] *F; not in Q2.*
239. my] *Q2;* mine *F,Q1.*   240. brother] *Q2,Q1;* Mother *F.*

222–48.] LN.

224. *presence*] august and royal
assembly.

225. *distraction*] Cf. *distracted,* III. i. 5.

227. *nature*] natural feeling, filial
regard. Cf. I. v. 81, III. ii. 384 and nn.
Hamlet recognizes for Laertes promptings similar to his own.

exception] disapproval, sense of
grievance (cf. 'take exception to'). Cf.
All's W. I. ii. 38–40, 'his honour . . .
knew . . . when Exception bid him
speak'.

230. *If Hamlet . . . ta'en away*] Cf.
'Ophelia divided from herself and her
fair judgment' (IV. v. 84–5).

236. *Sir, in this audience,*] Cairncross

(*SQ*, IX, 587–8) supposes this part-
line misplaced and would transfer it
to l. 224, reading 'This presence
knows, sir, and this audience'.

239. *shot my arrow*] The figure of the
arrow that, once released, may go
farther than one meant is common.
Cf. Nashe (i. 355), 'As an arrow is
shot out of a bow . . . with such force,
that it flieth far beyond the mark
whereat it was aimed'.

240. *my brother*] Cf. l. 249, 'this
brothers' wager'. The ambivalence in
Hamlet's relation with Laertes, who
is both his foe and his second self, is
fundamental to our understanding of
the play.

Whose motive in this case should stir me most
To my revenge; but in my terms of honour
I stand aloof, and will no reconcilement
Till by some elder masters of known honour
I have a voice and precedent of peace   245
To keep my name ungor'd. But till that time
I do receive your offer'd love like love
And will not wrong it.

Ham.   I embrace it freely,
And will this brothers' wager frankly play.—
Give us the foils.   250

Laer. Come, one for me.

Ham. I'll be your foil, Laertes. In mine ignorance
Your skill shall like a star i'th' darkest night
Stick fiery off indeed.

Laer.   You mock me, sir.

Ham. No, by this hand.   255

King. Give them the foils, young Osric. Cousin Hamlet,
You know the wager?

Ham.   Very well, my lord.
Your Grace has laid the odds o'th' weaker side.

King. I do not fear it. I have seen you both,

---

245. *precedent*] president *Q2,F*, precedent *Johnson.*   246. *keep*] *F*; not in *Q2.*
ungor'd] *Q2*; vngorg'd *F.*   *till*] *F*; all *Q2.*   248-9. I . . . play.] *As F*;
one line Q2.   248. I] *Q2*; I do *F.*   250. foils.] *Q2*; Foyles: Come on. *F.*
256-7.] *As Q2; divided Osricke, | Cousen F.*   258. has] *Q2*; hath *F,Q1.*

---

245. *voice and precedent*] 'authoritative pronouncement, justified by precedent' (Dowden).

246. *ungor'd*] unwounded (rather than 'unstained'), from the verb to *gore*, pierce. Cf. Hamlet's fear of 'a wounded name' (l. 349); and *Troil.* III.iii.228, 'My fame is shrewdly gor'd'.

252. *foil*] background against which a jewel shows more brightly.

254. *Stick . . . off*] stand out conspicuously. Cf. *Cor.* v.iii.73, 'stick . . . Like a great sea-mark'.

256. *Osric*] Dover Wilson's assumption that Osric is an accomplice in the plot is unsupported by text or

plausibility; and it is not a play in which the guilty go unpunished. (Yet, transformed into Phantasmo, he has become an accomplice in *BB.*)

258. *laid the odds o*] backed. Commentators, assuming *odds* to imply inequality, have supposed it to refer either (as in l. 260) to the advantage of hits given to Hamlet (which makes nonsense of the King's reply) or to the unequal stakes. But that *lay odds* need mean no more than 'make a bet' appears from *2H4* v.v.106-8, 'I will lay odds that . . . We bear our civil swords . . . As far as France'. Cf. *Q1*, l. 164, 'on your side the King hath laide'.

But since he is better'd, we have therefore odds.   260
Laer. This is too heavy. Let me see another.
Ham. This likes me well. These foils have all a length?
Osr. Ay, my good lord.   *They prepare to play.*

[*Enter* Servants *with*] *flagons of wine.*

King. Set me the stoups of wine upon that table.
   If Hamlet give the first or second hit,   265
   Or quit in answer of the third exchange,
   Let all the battlements their ordnance fire:
   The King shall drink to Hamlet's better breath,
   And in the cup an union shall he throw
   Richer than that which four successive kings   270
   In Denmark's crown have worn—give me the cups—
   And let the kettle to the trumpet speak,
   The trumpet to the cannoneer without,

260. better'd] *F;* better *Q 2.*   263 S.D. *They prepare to play.*] *F subst. (after 262;
not in Q 2.*   *Enter . . . wine.*] Wilson subst. (*cf. 220 S.D. flagons of Wine F*).
269. union] *F;* Vnice *Q 2 uncorr.;* Onixe *Q 2 corr.*   271. worn—give . . . cups—]
This edn; worne: giue . . . cups, *Q2;* worne. / Giue . . . Cups, *F.*
272. trumpet] *Q2;* Trumpets *F.*

260. *better'd*] pronounced (by public
opinion) to be the better. The meaning, though it has escaped the dictionaries, is plain, and the inept
traditional explanation that Laertes
has improved (through his stay in
Paris) must be firmly contradicted.
The comparison is not between
Laertes as he is and was but between
Laertes and Hamlet.
   odds] Referring to Hamlet's advantage of three hits (l. 164). Cf. l. 207.
   266. *quit in answer . . . exchange*]
draw level in the third bout (presum-
ing Laertes to have scored in one of
the first two). Less satisfactorily
(though perhaps more strictly interpreting *in answer of*), equalize in a
later bout a score made by Laertes in
the third. A mere draw in the third
bout, which is what Dover Wilson
understands, would not be matter for
celebration. The idea that a third hit
by Hamlet would finish off the match

belongs to the critic's imagination
(see Sprinchorn in LN on ll. 162–4).
   268. *better breath*] enhanced vigour.
   269. *an union*] a pearl (cf. l. 284).
Apparently so called from the unique-
ness of each one. The term is normally reserved for pearls of finest
quality – such as might be in a royal
crown (l. 271). LN.
   271. *give me the cups*] An order in
parenthesis (as the usual punctuation
does not make clear) for the cups to
be placed by him in readiness. Cf.
next note.
   272–5. *let the kettle . . . to Hamlet*] Cf.
I. ii. 125–8, I. iv. 8–12. This resumes
and expands l. 267. Notwithstanding
'give me the cups', the King does not
drink yet but announces how he will
celebrate *if* (as in ll. 265–6), and as he
accordingly does at ll. 284–5. Q2's
S.D. opp. ll. 275–6 calling for trumpets now may be a book-keeper's
misunderstanding.

The cannons to the heavens, the heaven to earth,
'Now the King drinks to Hamlet.' Come, begin.   275
And you, the judges, bear a wary eye.

Ham. Come on, sir.
Laer. Come, my lord.   *They play.*
Ham. One.
Laer. No.   280
Ham. Judgment.
Osr. A hit, a very palpable hit.
Laer. Well, again.
King. Stay, give me drink. Hamlet this pearl is thine.
Here's to thy health.   *Drums; trumpets; and shot goes off.*
Give him the cup.   285
Ham. I'll play this bout first. Set it by awhile.
Come.   *They play again.*
Another hit. What say you?

---

274. heaven] *Q2,F;* heavens *Q3.*   275. begin.] *F;* beginne. *Trumpets | the while. Q2.*   278. Come, my lord] *Q2;* Come on sir *F.*   278 S.D.] *F,Q1 (after 280); not in Q2.*   285 S.D.] *Trumpets sound, and shot goes off. F (after* cup*); opp. 282–3 Drum, trumpets and shot. | Florish, a peece goes off. Q2.*   286. it] *Q2,Q1; not in F.*   287–8. Come. They play again.* Another] come againe. *They play againe.* Another. *Q1;* Come. [*play.*] Another *Capell;* Come, another *Q2;* Come: Another *F; They play.* Come—another *Pope.*

---

274. *heaven*] Possibly an error. Later Qq and some eds. regularize to *heavens,* but 17th-century usage permits either and the singular occurs in the corresponding I. ii. 127.

284. *give me drink*] to celebrate Hamlet's 'hit'. Cf. ll. 265–8.

this pearl] It is generally supposed (notwithstanding IV. vii. 158–61) that the 'pearl' is the poison, as seems indeed to follow from l. 331, and this may be its *raison d'être.* Cf. *Antonio's Rev.* I. i. 68–9. In *BB* the King's proposal is to put a powdered diamond into the wine. But the matter is not without difficulty. The reasonable inference from the dialogue both here and at ll. 268–9 is that the King drops the union into the cup from which he then drinks himself. A 19th-century tradition made Claudius 'pretend to drink' and then offer the same cup to Hamlet (Sprague, *Sh. and the Actors,* p. 179). W. J. Lawrence, however, maintained that as the King prepares to drink from one cup, he puts the poison in another (*Lond. Mercury,* XXXVII, 526–31). Spencer supposes that he drinks before the 'pearl' has time to dissolve. Dover Wilson concludes that how the poison got into the cup 'we are not told' (*WHH,* p. 283).

285 S.D. *Drums . . . goes off.*] In obedience to ll. 265–7, 272–5.

288. *Another hit*] There is no need for the second hit to be celebrated like the first, and the opportunity afforded by 'the first *or* second' (l. 265) has been taken already.

Laer. I do confess't.

King. Our son shall win.

Queen.   He's fat and scant of breath.   290
Here, Hamlet, take my napkin, rub thy brows.
The Queen carouses to thy fortune, Hamlet.

Ham. Good madam.

King. Gertrude, do not drink.

Queen. I will, my lord, I pray you pardon me.   295
                    She drinks [and offers the cup to Hamlet].

King. [*aside*] It is the poison'd cup. It is too late.

Ham. I dare not drink yet, madam—by and by.

Queen. Come, let me wipe thy face.

Laer. My lord, I'll hit him now.

King.   I do not think't.

Laer. [*aside*] And yet it is almost against my conscience.   300

Ham. Come for the third, Laertes. You do but dally.
I pray you pass with your best violence.
I am afeard you make a wanton of me.

Laer. Say you so? Come on.   *They play.*

Osr. Nothing neither way.   305

Laer. Have at you now.   [*Laertes wounds Hamlet; then,*] *in
scuffling, they change rapiers.*

King. Part them; they are incensed.

Ham. Nay, come again.   [*He wounds Laertes.*] *The Queen falls.*

289.] *Q2;* A touch, a touch, I do confesse. *F;* I, I grant, a tuch, a tuch. *Q1.*
291. Here, Hamlet, take my] *Q2 (subst.), Q1 (subst.);* Heere's a *F.*
295 S.D.] *Wilson, after Capell;* Shee drinkes. *Q1; not in Q2,F.*   296. *aside] Rowe.*
300. *aside] Rowe.*   it is] *Q2;* 'tis *F.*   against] *Q2;* 'gainst *F.*   301. third,
Laertes.] *Johnson;* third *Laertes, Q2;* third. *Laertes, F.*   do] *Q2; not in F.*
303. afeard] *F;* sure *Q2.*   304 S.D.] *Play F; not in Q2.*   306 S.D.] *Sisson;*
Laertes . . . rapiers, and Hamlet wounds Laertes. *Rowe;* In scuffling they change
Rapiers. *F;* They catch one anothers Rapiers, and both are wounded, Leartes falles downe,
the Queene falles downe and dies. *Q1; not in Q2.*   308. come again.] *Q2,F2;*
come, againe. *F;* come! again! *Kittredge.*   308 S.D.] *Sisson (cf. 306 S.D.
Rowe, Q1); Queen falls. Capell; not in Q2,F.*

289. *I do confess't.*] *A touch, a touch*
in F and Q1, though more felicitous
than most such additions, may be
actors' embroidery.

290. *fat*] sweaty; alternatively, out
of condition. LN.

291. *napkin*] handkerchief.

302. *pass*] thrust.

303. *make a wanton of*] toy with. A
wanton, a spoilt child.

305. *Nothing neither way.*] Commentators conjecture a lock of weapons or
a simultaneous hit; but, no reason
being given for this adjudication, the
producer has a free hand.

306 S.D. *they change rapiers*] LN.

Osr. Look to the Queen there, ho!

Hor. They bleed on both sides. How is it, my lord?　　　310

Osr. How is't, Laertes?

Laer. Why, as a woodcock to mine own springe, Osric.
　　　I am justly kill'd with mine own treachery.

Ham. How does the Queen?

King.　　　　　　　　　　She swoons to see them bleed.

Queen. No, no, the drink, the drink! O my dear Hamlet!　315
　　　The drink, the drink! I am poison'd.　　　　　　*Dies.*

Ham. O villainy! Ho! Let the door be lock'd.
　　　Treachery! Seek it out.　　　　　　　　　[*Exit Osric.*]

Laer. It is here, Hamlet. Hamlet, thou art slain.
　　　No medicine in the world can do thee good;　　　320
　　　In thee there is not half an hour's life.
　　　The treacherous instrument is in thy hand,
　　　Unbated and envenom'd. The foul practice
　　　Hath turn'd itself on me. Lo, here I lie,
　　　Never to rise again. Thy mother's poison'd.　　　325
　　　I can no more. The King—the King's to blame.

Ham. The point envenom'd too! Then, venom, to thy work.
　　　　　　　　　　　　　　　　Wounds the King.

All. Treason! treason!

---

310. is it] *Q2;* is't *F.*　　312. own] *Q2; not in F.*　　314. swoons] sounds
Q2,F, swounes *Q5,* swounds *F3,* swoons *Q 1676.*　　315–16.] *As Q2; 3 lines
divided* drinke. / Oh . . . drinke, / I *F.*　　316 S.D.] *Rowe (cf. 306 S.D. Q1).*
317. Ho!] how *Q2,* hoe *Q3;* How? *F.*　　318 S.D.] *This edn; at 354 Jennens.*
319. Hamlet, thou] *F;* thou *Q2.*　　321. hour's] *Q2;* houre of *F,Q1.*
322. thy] *F,Q1,Q5;* my *Q2.*　　327 S.D.] *Hurts the King / F; not in Q2.*

309. *ho!*] A call to stop the combat,
as in Chaucer, *Knight's T.,* ll. 1706,
2656.

312. *a woodcock . . . springe*] This
combines two proverbs (Tilley F 626,
S 788), so that the man who is caught
in his own snare becomes the foolish
bird who is easily caught.

318 S.D. *Exit Osric.*] Necessary for
the entry before l. 355, which most
eds. delete. But if an editor is to help
Shakespeare out, he should not remove a clearly purposed entry but
contrive an unobtrusive exit. Dover
Wilson has it in the middle of l. 354,

immediately following the '*shot within*', but it may occur more plausibly
in the general commotion here.

323. *Unbated and envenom'd*] See IV.
vii. 136–47.

practice] trickery, as at IV. vii. 66,
137.

324. *here I lie*] Emphasizing Nemesis. Cf. Edmund in *Lr* v. iii. 174,
'I am here'.

327. *venom, to thy work*] The hero
finally achieves revenge with the same
instrument, and the same venom,
though not the same treachery, as he
suffers it.

King. O yet defend me, friends. I am but hurt.

Ham. Here, thou incestuous, murd'rous, damned Dane,   330
  Drink off this potion. Is thy union here?
  Follow my mother.   *King dies.*

Laer.   He is justly serv'd.
  It is a poison temper'd by himself.
  Exchange forgiveness with me, noble Hamlet.
  Mine and my father's death come not upon thee,   335
  Nor thine on me.   *Dies.*

Ham. Heaven make thee free of it. I follow thee.
  I am dead, Horatio. Wretched Queen, adieu.
  You that look pale and tremble at this chance,
  That are but mutes or audience to this act,   340
  Had I but time—as this fell sergeant, Death,
  Is strict in his arrest—O, I could tell you—
  But let it be. Horatio, I am dead,
  Thou livest. Report me and my cause aright
  To the unsatisfied.

Hor.   Never believe it.   345

---

330. Here] *F; Heare Q2.* murd'rous] *F; not in Q2.* 331. off] *F; of Q2.* thy union] *F,Q1;* the Onixe *Q2.* 332 S.D.] *F,Q1; not in Q2.* 332-3. He . . . himself.] *As F;* one line *Q2.* 336 S.D.] *F,Q1; not in Q2.* 344. livest] *Q2;* liu'st *F.* cause aright] *Q2;* causes right *F.*

---

331. *Drink off this potion.*] Objection has been made to Hamlet's forcing the liquor on the King. But death from the cup as well as the sword is necessary so that (1) treachery falls on the inventor's head – cf. ll. 313, 333, 390; (2) the King is punished for the Queen he has destroyed by being joined with her in death.

thy union] (1) the pearl of ll. 269, 284; (2) the King's marriage, of which the poisoned cup thus becomes the symbol. Cf. Bradley, p. 151.

333. *temper'd*] mixed, concocted. Cf. *Cym.* v.v.250, 'to temper poisons'; *Rom.* III.v.97; *Ado* II.ii.19.

334-7. *Exchange forgiveness . . . follow thee.*] These important lines emphasize the distinction between Laertes and the King in their rela-

tion with Hamlet, too often overlooked by those who regard them as merely partners in crime. Note esp. *my father's death.* Cf. ll. 77–8, 222–49. *come,* subjunctive.

337. *free*] absolved.

338. *Wretched*] unhappy, pitiable. Cf. II.ii.168; IV.vii.181.

340. *mutes*] lit. actors without speaking parts, hence non-participants.

341. *sergeant*] an officer of the courts whose duties included the making of arrests. Death as a 'fell arrest' occurs also in *Sonn.* LXXIV. The metaphor was traditional. LN.

342. *strict*] both just and inescapable.

345. *unsatisfied*] inadequately informed. Cf. l. 384, 'yet unknowing'.

I am more an antique Roman than a Dane.
Here's yet some liquor left.

Ham.   As th'art a man
Give me the cup. Let go, by Heaven I'll ha't.
O God, Horatio, what a wounded name,
Things standing thus unknown, shall I leave behind me.
If thou didst ever hold me in thy heart,   351
Absent thee from felicity awhile,
And in this harsh world draw thy breath in pain
To tell my story.   *A march afar off and shot within.*
            What warlike noise is this?

                    Enter OSRIC.

Osr. Young Fortinbras, with conquest come from Poland,
To the ambassadors of England gives   356
This warlike volley.

Ham.   O, I die, Horatio.
The potent poison quite o'ercrows my spirit.
I cannot live to hear the news from England,
But I do prophesy th'election lights   360
On Fortinbras. He has my dying voice.

---

346. antique] anticke *Q2*, Antike *F,Q1*, antique *Q5*.   347–8. As . . . ha't.] *As Q2; divided* Cup. / Let *F*.   348. ha't] *Q2* (hate); haue't *F*.   349. God] *Q2;* good *F;* fie *Q1*   350. shall I leave] *Q2;* shall liue *F;* wouldst thou leaue *Q1;* shall't leave *conj. Nowottny;* shall leave *conj. Maxwell*.   354 S.D.] *Steevens;* A march a farre off. *Q2;* March afarre off, and shout within. *F.* Enter Osric.] *Q2,F;* not in Capell; Osric goes to the door and returns. *Evans*.   356–7. To . . . volley.] *As Pope;* one line *Q2,F*.   356. the ambassadors] *Pope;* th'embassadors *Q2,F*.

346. *antique Roman*] i.e. one who prefers suicide to unworthy life. Cf. *Caes.* v.iii.89; *Ant.* iv.xv.87; *Mac.* v. viii.1.

350. *shall I leave*] *Q2* is suspect because of the metre and the apparent error of *leaue* for *liue* at iii.iv.160. But metrical redundancy would encourage corruption in *F*, and *leave* here has the support of *Q1*. The conjectures *shall't* (= shall it) *leave* and, still more, *shall* (= shall I) *leave* (*MLR*, lii, 161–7; liv, 395–6) regularize metre at the expense of syntax.

352. *felicity*] Cf. the dying words of Juliet in Painter's *Palace of Pleasure*

(ii. novel 25), 'death the end of sorrow, and beginning of felicity'. Cf. below, l. 383 n.

354. S.D. *Enter Osric*] See l. 318 S.D. n.

358. *o'ercrows*] triumphs over (like a victorious cock).

360. *th'election*] for the new king of Denmark. Cf. i.ii.1 LN.

361. *He has my . . . voice.*] As Hamlet had had Claudius's voice, iii.ii.332–3. The importance naturally attaching to a monarch's own view of his successor is reflected here, as in the concern for Elizabeth's deathbed nomination of James.

So tell him, with th'occurrents more and less
Which have solicited—the rest is silence.   *Dies.*
Hor. Now cracks a noble heart. Good night, sweet prince,
And flights of angels sing thee to thy rest.   365
                                        [*March within.*]
Why does the drum come hither?

Enter FORTINBRAS, *and the English* Ambassadors, *and* Soldiers
with drum and colours.

Fort. Where is this sight?
Hor.   What is it you would see?
        If aught of woe or wonder, cease your search.
Fort. This quarry cries on havoc. O proud Death,

362. th'occurrents] *Q2;* the occurrents *F.*   363. solicited—]*Jennens;* solicited,
Q2; solicited. *F.*   silence.] *Q2;* silence. O, o, o, o. *F.*   363 S.D.] *F; not in Q2.*
364. cracks] *Q2;* cracke *F.*   365 S.D.] *Cambridge;* opp. 366 Capell.
366 S.D.] *This edn, after Sisson;* Enter Fortenbrasse, with the Embassadors. *Q2;*
Enter Fortinbras and English Ambassador, with Drumme, Colours, and Attendants. *F;*
Enter Voltemar and the Ambassadors from England. enter Fortenbrasse with his traine.
Q1.   367. you] *Q2;* ye *F.*   369. This] *Q2;* His *F.*

362. *occurrents*] = occurrences.
'Common in 16th and 17th c.'
(*OED*).

363. *solicited*—] urged (me to give it
him).

silence] Cf. Psalm cxv. 17 ('go down
into silence'), 2 Esdras vii. 32 ('dwell
in silence').

364. *sweet*] Frequent as an epithet
of affection. Cf. III.ii.53.

365. *flights of angels . . . rest*] No
specific source can be alleged or
should be sought for so traditional a
conception. But cf. e.g. the antiphon
of the old Latin burial service, 'In
paradisum deducant te angeli . . .
Chorus angelorum te suscipiat . . .
aeternam habeas requiem'; *Everyman,*
ll. 891–3, 'Methinketh that I hear
angels sing . . . where Everyman's soul
received shall be'. See R. M. Frye,
Sh. and Christian Doctrine, pp. 135–6.
Not all who quote this line recognize
that *sing* is optative.

368. *wonder*] calamity, extreme
wretchedness. The alliterative phrase

preserves this archaic sense. In the
ballad *Northumberland betrayed by
Douglas* (Child, iii.411), 'Woe and
wonder be them among' is the impre-
cation upon the betrayers. See *OED*
wonder *sb.* 5.

369. *quarry*] heap of dead (lit. of
deer killed in the hunt).

cries on havoc] loudly proclaims
wholesale slaughter. *Havoc* was a
battle-cry meaning 'No quarter' and
inciting to slaughter and pillage. Cf.
Caes. III.i.273 ('Cry "Havoc!" and let
slip the dogs of war'), *John* II.i.357
('Cry "havoc!" kings; back to the
stained field'), *Cor.* III.i.275. The
peculiarly Shakespearean use of a
hunting metaphor (cf. *quarry*), as also
in *Caes.* and *Cor.*, by imaging soldiers
as hounds, intensifies the savagery.
The word for the signal came to be
used for the consequent devastation,
so that, notwithstanding *Caes.* and
John but as the context shows, it is
not here a call for further slaughter or
vengeance but a description of the

What feast is toward in thine eternal cell,　　　　370
That thou so many princes at a shot
So bloodily hast struck?
1st Ambass.　　　　　　　　The sight is dismal;
And our affairs from England come too late.
The ears are senseless that should give us hearing
To tell him his commandment is fulfill'd,　　　　375
That Rosencrantz and Guildenstern are dead.
Where should we have our thanks?
Hor.　　　　　　　　　　Not from his mouth,
Had it th'ability of life to thank you.
He never gave commandment for their death.
But since, so jump upon this bloody question,　　　380
You from the Polack wars and you from England
Are here arriv'd, give order that these bodies
High on a stage be placed to the view,
And let me speak to th'yet unknowing world
How these things came about. So shall you hear　　　385
Of carnal, bloody, and unnatural acts,
Of accidental judgments, casual slaughters,

371. shot] *Q2;* shoote *F.*　　　382. arriv'd,] *Q2;* arriued. *F.*　　　384. th' yet] *F;*
yet *Q2.*

scene with which Fortinbras is confronted. To *cry on* is to cry out loud (sometimes in outrage), as in *Oth.* v. i.48 ('that cries on murder'), *R3* v. iii.231 ('cried on victory').

370. *What feast . . . cell*] The metaphor is not, as sometimes supposed, of Valhalla, where souls feast after death, but of Death feasting on the slain. Cf. *1H6* IV.v.7, *John* II.i.354. *toward,* in preparation.

372. *dismal*] (much stronger in meaning than now) dreadful. Cf. II. ii.452 and n.

380. *jump upon . . . question*] at the precise moment of this bloody affair. For *jump,* see I.i.68; *question,* topic for discussion, i.e. the 'sight' of ll. 367, 372.

383. *stage*] platform. Cf. accounts of Romeo and Juliet: 'The magistrates ordained that the two dead bodies should be erected upon a stage to the view and sight of the whole world' (Painter); 'the corses . . . Should be set forth upon a stage, high raised from the ground' (Brooke, ll. 2818–19).

386–8. *Of carnal . . . forc'd cause*] We need not suppose this a systematic classification. Examples of each kind will readily occur to everyone. *Carnal* applies to the incestuous marriage, *unnatural* (cf. I.v.25) to the fratricide. The consequential deaths of Polonius, Hamlet, Laertes, Claudius are all *bloody. Judgments* in *casual slaughters* are seen in the deaths of Polonius (cf. III.iv.175–6), Laertes and the Queen; *deaths put on by cunning* in those of Rosencrantz and Guildenstern and of Hamlet himself.

387. *accidental judgments*] divine judgments manifested in seeming accidents.

casual] (seemingly) due to chance.

Of deaths put on by cunning and forc'd cause,
And, in this upshot, purposes mistook
Fall'n on th'inventors' heads. All this can I   390
Truly deliver.

Fort.   Let us haste to hear it,
And call the noblest to the audience.
For me, with sorrow I embrace my fortune.
I have some rights of memory in this kingdom,
Which now to claim my vantage doth invite me.   395

Hor. Of that I shall have also cause to speak,
And from his mouth whose voice will draw on more.
But let this same be presently perform'd
Even while men's minds are wild, lest more mischance
On plots and errors happen.

Fort.   Let four captains   400
Bear Hamlet like a soldier to the stage,
For he was likely, had he been put on,
To have prov'd most royal; and for his passage,
The soldier's music and the rite of war
Speak loudly for him.   405

---

388. forc'd] *F;* for no *Q2.*   390. th'inventors'] *Q2;* the Inuentors *F.*
394. rights] *Q2,Q1;* Rites *F.*   395.] *one line Q2; divided* doth / Inuite *F.*
now] *Q2,Q1;* are *F.*   396. also] *Q2;* alwayes *F.*   397.] *one line Q2;*
divided mouth / Whose *F.*   on] *F;* no *Q2.*   399.] *one line Q2; divided*
wilde, / Lest *F.*   while] *Q2;* whiles *F.*   403.] *one line Q2; divided* royally: /
And *F.*   royal] *Q2,Q1;* royally *F.*   404. rite] *Wilson;* right *Q2;* rites *F.*

388. *put on*] instigated.

forc'd] contrived. Cf. *Oth.* I.iii. 111,
'indirect and forced courses'.

389–90. *purposes mistook . . . heads*]
Cf. above, ll. 312–13, 323–4, 332–3.
While here specifically applied (*in
this upshot*) to the final stratagems of
Claudius and Laertes, this is of course
a dominant motif of the play, particularly manifest elsewhere in the
fates of Rosencrantz and Guildenstern (cf. III.iv. 208–9) and generally
in the whole story of murder and revenge. Cf. III.ii. 206–7.

394. *of memory*] unforgotten.

395. *vantage*] favourable opportunity.

397. *whose voice*] See l. 361 above.

draw on more] induce further voices
(to be given for Fortinbras).

398. *same*] aforesaid. See ll. 382–5
above.

presently] at once.

399. *wild*] violently agitated.

400. *On*] on top of (Abbott 180, 'in
consequence of').

400–1. *Let four captains . . . like a
soldier*] Cf. *Cor.* v.vi. 148–9, 'Take him
up. Help, three o'th' chiefest soldiers;
I'll be one'.

401. *the stage*] See l. 383 above.

402. *put on*] set to it, put to the test.

403. *for his passage*] to mark his
passing. Cf. III.iii. 86.

405. *Speak*] subjunctive (Abbott
364).

Take up the bodies. Such a sight as this
Becomes the field, but here shows much amiss.
Go, bid the soldiers shoot.

Exeunt marching, [bearing off the bodies,] after
which a peal of ordnance is shot off.

406. bodies] *Q2;* body *F,Q1.*   408 S.D. *Exeunt marching*] *F; Exeunt Q2.*
bearing off the bodies] *Capell.*   after . . . off] *F (subst.); not in Q2.*

408 S.D.] Writing to Ellen Terry about Robertson's *Hamlet* on 8 Sept. 1897, Shaw said, 'I gave Forbes a description of what the end ought to be like. Fortinbras with a winged helmet and Hamlet carried off on the shields, with the "ordnance shot off within" just as the wily William planned it . . .'

LONGER NOTES

DRAMATIS PERSONAE

5. _Polonius_] Following Q1676 editors have usually described him as Lord Chamberlain, but the play, beyond naming him as of the Council (I.ii.S.D.), does not specify his office. Capell saw him as 'a great Officer', Dover Wilson supposes Shakespeare saw him as a Secretary of State, and that is apparently how Polonius sees himself (II.ii.166). In Q1 he is called Corambis (see Intro., pp. 34–5), a name said to be punningly derived from the well-known proverb _Crambe bis posita mors est_, Cabbage served up twice is death, and hence apt for one who regales us with stale and tedious wisdom (see _SQ_, XVIII, 23–4). It does not follow that Corambis was the original name; but it was natural to think so as long as Q1 was held to represent an earlier version of the play, and the belief has tended to persist when the reason for it has gone. Thus it is often assumed, though without evidence, that in substituting Corambis for Polonius Q1 was reverting to the usage of the _Ur-Hamlet_. On the showing of Q2 Polonius must be regarded as the original name in Shakespeare, and it presents us with the insoluble but perhaps connected problems of why so remarkable a name was chosen and why in Q1 (and presumably some performances) it was replaced. The associated change in Q1 from Reynaldo to Montano complicates any theory of personal satire; but Polonius of course connects its bearer with Polonia (Poland) and so may have pointed to a recognizable individual. This cannot have been Burghley, whom Polonius resembles in his office and his advice to a son, and the old theory that a caricature of Burghley as Corambis was subsequently redirected by a change of name is no longer tenable. Among the Poles who have been suggested the ambassador who received a famous Latin rebuke from Elizabeth in 1597 (_N&Q_, CXCVIII, 426; Dollerup, p. 165) seems barely eligible. The generally favoured candidate is the one first proposed by Gollancz (_Archiv_, CXXXI, 141–3; _A Book of Homage to Wm. Shakespeare_, pp. 173–7), the Polish bishop and statesman Wawrzyniec Goślicki (Goslicius), or, more strictly, the type-figure who is the subject of Goślicki's treatise _De Optimo_

Senatore, published at Venice in 1568 and in English as *The Counsellor* in 1598. This has been too readily proclaimed a 'source', but it may have been enough for 'Polonius' to suggest itself as a suitable name for a loquacious counsellor. The book claims to be 'replenished with the chief learning of the most excellent Philosophers and Lawgivers . . . very necessary for . . . the administration of a well-governed Common-weal . . . and consecrated to the honour of the Polonian Empire'; but it also contains the seeds of its own self-satire when the counsellor imagines himself being told that his 'art . . . is rather to be termed the science of prating' (p. 41; cf. *Ham.* III.iv.215–17) and fears lest his discourse may seem long and tedious (p. 69). A somewhat less likely candidate argued for by Keith Brown (*ES*, LV, 218–38) is Henrik Ramel (Ramelius), who had come from the service of the King of Poland to be a leading Danish diplomat and had headed an important embassy to England (cf. Dollerup, pp. 212–14). What none of these theories accounts for is the curious fact that the same play has a character called Polonius and a campaign against the Polack. The inspiration for the name might have come from within as well as without the matter of the play; but one can only speculate on a possible connection in the poet's mind between the part envisaged for Poland and for the man that Hamlet was to kill. (Cf. I.i.66 LN; *Rice U.Studs.*, LX, 104–5.)

9–10. *Rosencrantz, Guildenstern*] These splendidly resounding names, by contrast with the unlocalized classical ones, are evidently chosen as particularly Danish. Both were common among the most influential Danish families, and they are often found together (*Sh.Jahr.*, XLVI, 60 ff.; Dollerup, pp. 211–12). Frederick II (*d.* 1588) had nine Guildensterns and three Rosencrantzes at his court (*Contemporary Rev.*, LXIX, 32), and at the coronation of Christian IV in 1596, in a procession of 160 noblemen, one in ten bore one or other of these names (*SQ*, XVI, 157). Both occur in the records of Wittenberg students around 1590 (Dollerup, p. 128); and there is a family tradition, alas unverified, that in the last decade of the century two brothers-in-law called Rosencrantz and Guildenstern who had both been at Wittenberg accompanied one another on a London visit as part of a Danish mission (*TLS*, 1926, p. 62). An engraved portrait of Tycho Brahe dated in 1586 surrounds him with the coats-of-arms of sixteen families from which he is descended, including 'Guldesteren' and 'Rosenkrans'; but conjectures that Shakespeare knew this engraving – even that he saw a copy of it in the house of the astronomer Thomas Digges

(Hotson, *I, William Shakespeare*, pp. 123–4) – are not necessary to account for a conjunction as natural as it is felicitous in giving an authentic touch of Denmark. In Shakespeare's text as represented in Q2 it is notable that Rosencrantz and Guildenstern never appear singly (cf. IV.iii.11 S.D. LN). Q2 consistently spells Rosencraus, probably a misreading of Shakespeare's Rosencrans; F normally has Rosincrance. Q1 corrupts the names to Rossencraft and Gilderstone.

14–16. *Marcellus, Barnardo, Francisco*] Dover Wilson calls all three 'Gentlemen of the Guard', which Francisco, the 'honest soldier' of I.i.18, can scarcely be. He and Barnardo, as the 'two sentinels' who change guard in the opening, are presumably of the same rank, so that editors before Capell can describe them both as 'soldiers' in distinction from Marcellus, 'an officer'. Yet Barnardo shares watch with Marcellus, and both visit Hamlet with Horatio, who calls them 'gentlemen' (I.ii.194–6), so that Capell and subsequent editors can describe them both as 'officers' in distinction from Francisco, 'a soldier'. When Hamlet joins the watch, however, in I.iv, Barnardo is dropped while Marcellus and Horatio, the officer and the 'scholar' (I.i.45), are equated as both of them 'scholars and soldiers' who are Hamlet's 'good friends' (I.v.146–7). The truth of course is that Shakespeare, not untypically, leaves their exact status undefined (cf. Polonius), thereby creating a quandary for tidy-minded editors but for his play a convenient flexibility, of which Barnardo takes advantage. Faced also with an orthographic ambiguity, editors have traditionally preferred the form Bernardo against the more authoritative Barnardo, which is regular in F and with a single exception in Q2. Q1 uses both. The Latin name of Marcellus matches others in the play but sorts oddly with the Italianate ones of his companions. Shakespeare presumably picked these up from his miscellaneous reading; but one cannot make a great deal of the proximity of the names Francisco and Marcellus in the 1555 edition of Richard Eden's *Decades of the New World* (fols. 309^v–310), a work which Shakespeare at some time in some form looked into (Arden *Tp.*, pp. xxxii–xxxiii); nor of the conjunction of Francesco de Pazzi and Bernardo Bandini as assassins of Giuliano de Medici in the cathedral at Florence in 1478.

HAMLET, PRINCE OF DENMARK

I. i. 1–25.]   These first 25 lines are an excellent example of Shake-speare's technique in incorporating short colloquial exchanges in what is essentially a blank-verse scene. (Cf. I. ii. 224–43 and n.) While speeches of as much as five feet scan easily as blank verse (ll. 2, 6–8, etc.), shorter speeches often do not, and cannot be expected to, add up to regular metrical units. See McKerrow, *Prolegomena*, pp. 45–6. I have not here followed the usual editorial practice of wrenching into a typographical simulation of the blank-verse pattern what is clearly not meant to conform to it. Coleridge (i. 18, 38–9) notes in this opening the familiar language of common life, which leads gradually and naturally to that state in which the highest poetry will appear.

I. i. 26. *fantasy*]   This reflects a contemporary opinion concerning the nature of ghosts. While most authorities affirmed them to exist, it was generally acknowledged, even by those who believed in them most firmly, that they could in some cases be the product of the subjective mind. See e.g. Taillepied, chs. 3–5. Cf. *Caes.* IV. iii. 274–5, *Mac.* III. iv. 61 ff.   Le Loyer (*Des Spectres*, 1586), with a terminological nicety not usual, distinguishes between a phan-tom and a spectre. Hence Horatio's scepticism need not imply that he denies ghosts altogether. Yet that 'many good and godly men' held all apparitions to be hallucinations was conceded by Lavater (I. ii). Cf. Burton on spirits (*Anat. of Melancholy*, I. ii. 1 (2)), 'Many will not believe they can be seen.' This view, called 'damnable' by James I, had been maintained in Reginald Scot's *Discovery of Witchcraft* (with appendix on 'Devils and Spirits'), 1584. On the dramatic use Shakespeare makes of conflicting con-temporary attitudes to ghosts, see Dover Wilson, *WHH*, pp. 59 ff.

I. i. 32. *speak to it*]   They assume that the Ghost wishes to com-municate but is unable to. For, in popular belief, 'A ghost has not the power to speak till it has been first spoken to; so that, not-withstanding the urgency of the business on which it may come, everything must stand still till the person visited can find suffi-cient courage to speak to it' (Grose, *A Provincial Glossary*; Brand, *Popular Antiquities*, ed. Hazlitt). Cf. *Tom Jones*, XI, ch. 2, 'The other who, like a ghost only wanted to be spoke to, readily answered . . .'; Boswell's *Johnson*, 'Tom Tyers . . . said . . ., You are like a ghost: you never speak till you are spoken to'. Nor does the *Hamlet* ghost, either in I.iv–v or in III.iv. Yet for all the importance of addressing it (see below, l. 48, I.ii.214, 245), to do so in other than due form would be to risk offence and consequent danger to oneself. Hence the necessity for having present a man of superior learning (cf. l. 45).

I.i.42 S.D. *Enter Ghost.*] Possibly via a trap-door (cf. l. 33 n.), like the spirits in Greene's *Alphonsus*, Chapman's *Bussy d'Ambois*, Jonson's *Catiline*, and other plays, as is held by Lawrence (*Pre-Restoration Stage Studies*, pp. 104 ff.) and Sprague (*Shakespeare and the Actors*, p. 128). This, though not perhaps in conflict with, is not supported by, the dialogue, which suggests movement across the stage (ll. 43, 129–30). On departing the first time the Ghost 'stalks away' (l. 53). The second time it 'faded' (l. 162), but this word, like 'appears' and 'vanish'd' (I.ii.201, 220), is used not during but after the event. But cf. I.v.91 S.D. n. What the Ghost looks like is described at ll. 50, 63, 65 and I.ii.200–2, 226–33. Its being in armour is repeatedly stressed (cf. I.iv.52).

I.i.66. *sledded Polacks*] This much-disputed phrase is usually taken, and I think rightly, to refer to inhabitants of Poland riding in sleds. It is true that the spelling *sleaded pollax*, deriving from Q1, suggests that the early actors and printers did not so understand it. They must have thought the second word was *pole-axe*, or, as F4 prints it, *poleaxe*, of which *pollax* was a regular 16th-century spelling. But this spelling may have arisen in Q1 through an actor's misunderstanding of what he heard and said. (Cf. Intro., p. 23.) *Polack*, spelt in Q2 *Pollacke*, Q1 *Polacke*, F *Poleak*, is normal Elizabethan for 'Pole', as in II.ii.63, 75 and (in Q2) IV.iv.23. Despite some assertions to the contrary, the plural 'Polacks' (or 'Polakes') also occurs, as in R. Johnson, *Kingdoms and Commonweals* (*The World*, 1601), pp. 127, 128; Moryson, *Itinerary*, 1907–8 edn, iii.380. Scholars who accept *pole-axe* (for a recent defence of which see D. Haley, *SQ*, XXIX, 407–13) either assume a battle-axe with a sled, or sledge, i.e. hammer, to it (so Schmidt), despite the lack of authority for *sled* in this sense, or take *sleaded* as a corruption of 'leaded' or (by analogy with *FQ* v.xii.14) of 'studded' (*N&Q*, CCI, 509). In any event they see King Hamlet striking a weapon on the ice. This interpretation, since it avoids actual fighting, may be thought to be supported by *parle* (but see below). The objection to it, apart altogether from the difficulty of *sleaded*, is the pointlessness of the incident it leaves us with; if no Polanders and no sledges, why ice? A pole-axe connects with nothing else in the play, as is still true if you take it to refer to the man who bears the weapon (and have to invent a soldier on a sledge or hurdle of disgrace, *N&Q*, CCXIX, 128–30). An attempt to attach an incident with a pole-axe to the combat against Fortinbras seems refuted by the adverb *once*, which implies a separate occasion. Clearly allusion is being made to a second exploit which will parallel the combat against Fortinbras as an illustration of King Hamlet's martial prowess. And what, along with the natural sense of *sledded*, gives the preference overwhelmingly to Poles in sleds as the object of his smiting is their power to stir the imagination, which a pole-axe so signally lacks. It is true that the Polish exploit is not subsequently elaborated as the combat against Norway is and that no source for one has been found; but we cannot doubt its potentiality for elaboration and it may well have been in the dramatist's mind at this stage to make more of the Polish matter than he subsequently did. Was it this that led him to call the minister Hamlet kills by the remarkable name of Polonius? (Was there an idea for an avenging Polack son alongside the son of Norway? See *Rice U.Studs.*, LX, 104–5.) But the Poles are not dependent on such speculation for their relevance. They belong to the play's background wars in which Norway is balanced by Poland and which are already being prepared for, with the sleds giving a northern local colour. Shakespeare seems to have thought of these two countries as both bordering Denmark (see II.ii. 74–8, IV.iv. 3–4 and LN; also Keith Brown, 'Hamlet's Place on the Map', *Sh.Studs.*, IV, 160–82). For Poles in sleds he would hardly need particular authority. Ortelius's *Epitome of the Theatre of the World* tells how in the frozen fens of Lithuania, then 'under the crown of Polonia', men 'pass over the ice with sleds drawn by horses' (Eng. trans. 1603, f. 94^v); and Samuel Lewkenor's *Discourse of Foreign Cities* (1600) similarly describes how the Tartars around Vilna travel in sleds over snow 'not unlike the ocean'. Cf. Cawley, *The Voyagers and Elizn Drama*, p. 247 n., on the regular association of sleds with the people of this region. Still more to the present purpose the pictorial *Carta Marina* of the Swede Olaus Magnus (1539) shows armed men riding on the Baltic, which others cross in horse-drawn sledges. Even if he had no particular incident to draw on, Shakespeare would not be offending plausibility in imagining an encounter with sledded opponents on a frozen lake or sea.

The reading *Polack* (sing.), meaning the King of Poland, would correspond with II.ii.63, 75 and IV.iv.23 and provide an attractive parallel with *Norway* (l. 64); but it fails to explain *pollax* (i.e.

the hypothesis that *pollax* is an actor-reporter's homonym demands the plural *Pollacks*). There is obviously no substance in the
argument that only the Polack himself would be 'sledded', and to
object that one man could not 'smite' the Polish army shows a
neglect of common idiom (cf. Judges iii. 13, 'he . . . went and
smote Israel').

The difficulty of reconciling the *parle* of l. 65 with smiting foes
has I think been much exaggerated. Adams improbably suggests
that King Hamlet may have struck the Polish king 'with his glove
or hand'. Others remark that *frown'd*, implying the vizor up, is
more compatible with parley than with fighting, but the reverse
is surely true of *on the ice*. And the frown itself, traditional of Mars
(cf. 1.ii.230n.), is as much emblematic as realistic. It not merely
describes the warlike mien, but suggests the warlike action: as the
'armour' when he 'combated' (ll. 63–4), so the frown when he
'smote'. Kittredge explains, 'The parley broke up in a battle, in
which the King smote (routed) the Polanders'. But I suspect that
parle itself may imply a more than verbal encounter. For although
I can cite no parallel for such a use of *parle*, Shakespeare more
than once uses the verb *speak*, in similar understatement, to mean
'engage in combat'. In *Coriolanus* the reply to 'Has our general
met the enemy?' is 'They lie in view, but have not spoke as yet'
(1.iv.4); and Antony, in defiance of Pompey's navy, says 'We'll
speak with thee at sea' (*Ant.* 11.vi.25). Was it not this kind of
speaking that took place in the *parle* on the ice?

1.i.91. *Did forfeit . . . all*]   *All those his lands*, if strictly interpreted,
should include Fortinbras's Norwegian dominions; but it is not
likely to trouble us that by one of Shakespeare's little inconsistencies Norway continues as an apparently independent kingdom
(1.ii; 11.ii). *All* may derive from Belleforest, who, however, applies
it to the treasure (*toutes les richesses*) in the defeated warrior's ships.
(See Intro., p. 93.) The difficulty, if it is one, arises from transferring the forfeit to lands; it can hardly be resolved by supposing
(with Honigmann, *Stratford-upon-Avon Studies*, 5, p. 134) that
'lands which he stood seiz'd of' could mean merely 'lands . . .
seized . . . in war'; nor (with M. Coyle, *N&Q*, ccxxiv, 118–19)
that 'all' may refer only to lands 'against the which' Hamlet
gaged an equivalent portion of his. The text, conveniently or not,
is specific: all the lands he possessed.

1.i.96. *the same cov'nant*]   Some editors adopt the Q2 *comart*,
which Malone explained as a 'joint bargain'. Though it is hard to

see what bargain could be other than joint, and hence what the prefix adds, this seems more plausible than an alternative conjecture by Nares which, deriving *comart* from *mart* = battle, would interpret it as 'single combat'. F may have substituted a familiar for an unfamiliar word, but *comart* would be an easy misreading of *counant* in the manuscript copy, and Sisson notes (*NR*) that, on the evidence of *desseigne* in the next line, the Q2 printer was in difficulty at this point. The legal context also suggests that F may preserve the true reading.

1.i.97. *carriage of the article design'd*] The emendation *design'd*, which assumes the common misreading of final *d* as *e*, is preferable to the alternative emendation *articles*, a reading first found in Q3 and interpreted by those who adopt it as a possessive. If *design'd* could be taken with the whole preceding phrase, it might have its ordinary sense of 'purposed', but it is usual and syntactically better to regard it as a participial adjective qualifying 'article'. Johnson's gloss 'drawn up' is possible and generally accepted, but a more natural meaning is 'designated', implying that the article is the one already indicated in the account of the compact. So Schmidt, 'pointed out, mentioned before'. Cf. *R2* 1.i.203. The *covenant* is the agreement, the *article* the formal terms in which it is expressed, or if the *covenant* is itself taken to be a legal document, then the *article* is a particular clause in it. The *carriage* is what is conveyed in the *article*, its bearing (*OED* 21), or possibly the carrying out of its provisions (cf. *Wint.* III.i.17). Whatever construction is placed on the individual words, the legal terminology emphasizes the justice of King Hamlet's taking possession of Fortinbras's lands in contrast to young Fortinbras's lawless attempt to recover them.

1.i.117–23.] The description of *the prodigies preceding Caesar's death* is reminiscent of *Caes.* 1.iii and II.ii. There Shakespeare had added to portents recorded in Plutarch others deriving from such accounts as those in Ovid's *Metamorphoses* and Virgil's *Georgics* and still others from the description in Lucan's *Pharsalia* of portents preceding Caesar's attack on Rome. (See Muir, *The Sources of Shakespeare's Plays*, pp. 122–5.) The rehandling here admits some portents unmentioned in *Caes.* along with particular echoes of it. The 'strange eruptions' of *Caes.* 1.iii.78 have already found an echo at l. 72. With *The graves stood tenantless* cf. *Caes.* 1.iii.74, 'This dreadful night That . . . opens graves'; II.ii.18, 'graves have yawn'd and yielded up their dead'. With *the sheeted dead Did squeak and gibber in the Roman streets* cf. *Caes.* II.ii.24, 'ghosts did shriek and squeal about the streets'. The *stars with trains of fire* correspond to the 'comets' of *Caes.* II.ii.30; the *dews of blood* recall the war in the heavens which 'drizzled blood' at *Caes.* II.ii.21. The *disasters in the sun* and the moon's *eclipse* have no equivalent in *Caes.*; but Golding's translation of the *Metamorphoses* (xv.882) has 'Phoebus also looking dim did cast a drowsy light' and North's Plutarch tells how *after* Caesar's death 'the brightness of the sun was darkened, the which all that year rose very pale, and shined not out', while an eclipse of the moon is included among Lucan's portents (Marlowe's Lucan, ll. 567–9, 'Phoebe . . . Strook with th'earth's sudden shadow waxed pale'). The solar and lunar eclipses which in fact occurred during 1598–1601 may have intensified for the populace the terror of this passage; but it does not follow that Shakespeare was 'referring to contemporary events' (Dover Wilson).

1.i.120. *As*] *Omission* seems the likeliest explanation of the imperfect syntax. It is true that this might result from hasty or unfinished writing. (Note that F and Q1 drop the whole passage.) Cowden Clarke remarked on Shakespeare's frequent use of elliptical constructions with 'as', and Tucker Brooke, followed by Munro, accepts the construction as an ordinary Elizabethan anacoluthon. But it is usual to suppose that a line (or more) is lost after l. 119. As in *Caes.* (II.ii.18ff.), which goes straight from the graves which 'yielded up their dead' to the war in the heavens 'which drizzled blood', mention of portents on earth may have been followed by a reference to others in the heavens, of which 'as' introduces instances (cf. Abbott 113). Some scholars assume corruption instead of or as well as omission. Attempts to emend have usually focused on *disasters in*. Incorporating Capell's 'dimm'd' for 'in', Malone implausibly conjectured 'Astres with trains of fire – and dews of blood Disastrous dimm'd the sun'. There have been many other guesses at a finite verb (e.g. Staunton's 'distempered'), but none which fits both 'stars' and 'dews'; and the parallel with *Caes.* ('drizzled blood upon the Capitol') supports the natural assumption that dews would fall upon the earth rather than affect the sun. Dover Wilson, following Tschischwitz and influenced by Gerald Massey (*The Secret Drama of Shakespeare's Sonnets*, Supplement p. 46), 'restores the sense' by transposing ll. 124–8 before ll. 120–3, which are thus made to describe recent happenings in Denmark rather than in Caesar's Rome. But it is not easy to see why a disarrangement in Q2 is more plausible than an omission, and the revised order (1) ignores the tense of '*was* sick', (2) violates the connection between dews of blood and the other Roman portents, (3) leaves us with a false analogy between the ghosts of ll. 118–19 and the miscellaneous prodigies of ll. 120–3, and (4) removes the dramatic effect of the Ghost's entry upon talk of 'harbingers' and 'prologue'. For a detailed refutation, see Wilson Knight, *The Wheel of Fire* (rev. 1949), pp. 326 ff.

1.i.130 S.D. *spreads its arms*] Some editors, perhaps misinterpreting 'I'll cross it', make Horatio spread *his* arms in seeking to bar the Ghost's way. But one may question whether Shakespeare would insert a direction merely to specify the speaker's gesture. It *might* be a book-keeper's annotation (cf. 1.iv.57); but there is no good reason to suppose the Q2 *It* an error, and *his* is the normal Elizabethan neuter (cf. 1.i.40n.). If the Ghost's spreading its arms is taken as a prelude to departure, it may be this that provokes Horatio's 'Stay'. More probably it is the Ghost's reaction to being accosted. 'The gesture warns Horatio not to approach' (Sisson, *NR*), while perhaps suggesting that the Ghost is about to speak (cf. l. 152, 1.ii.216–17), though of course it will speak only to Hamlet (l. 176). The spreading of its arms, going beyond its behaviour on its first appearance, increases awe and still further quickens expectation in the audience.

1.i.133–42. *If . . . If . . . Or if . . . stay and speak.*] All three of Horatio's hypotheses were well recognized among the causes of apparitions. The first (ll. 133–4) anticipates the Ghost's own account of its unrest, 1.v.10–13. The second (ll. 136–7) recalls the explanation already offered in ll. 112 ff. Sir T. Browne believed 'that those many prodigies and ominous prognostics, which forerun the ruins of states, princes and private persons are the charitable premonitions of good angels' (*Religio Medici*). For the third (ll. 139–40), cf. *The Jew of Malta*, 11.i.26–7, 'ghosts that glide by night About the place where treasure hath been hid'; Dekker, *News from Hell*, 'If any of them had . . . bound the spirit of gold in caves, or . . . under the ground, they should for their own souls' quiet (which questionless else would whine up and down) . . . release it'. Paracelsus, however, explains such a ghost as not a soul but a sidereal spirit which survives the body for a time and which, retaining the thoughts and heart of the dead man, is constantly seen at the place of the treasure because his mind was concentrated on it during life (*Hermetic and Alchemical Writings*, trans. Waite, ii. 303). Note that Horatio here suggests only benign purposes for the Ghost, which he seems now to accept as the spirit of the dead King; but that he knows ghosts may have evil purposes and be devils in disguise he shows at I.iv.69 ff. It is through Shakespeare's art, no doubt, that the purpose the Ghost will ultimately reveal is, of all those associated with apparitions (see I.v.25 LN), the one that is as yet unmentioned.

I.i.155. *The cock*] '*How* to elevate a thing almost mean by its familiarity, young poets may learn in the cock-crow' (Coleridge, i.19). The account may be unexpected, but is the more effective, coming from the sceptical Horatio: having had the avouch of his own eyes (ll. 60–1; cf. l. 161, 'probation'), he now takes seriously the 'received tradition among the vulgar, that at the time of cock-crowing, the midnight spirits forsake these lower regions, and go to their proper places' (Bourne, *Antiquitates Vulgares*, 1725, p. 37). In *Lr* the foul fiend Flibbertigibbet 'walks till the first cock'. The tradition is of great antiquity, being already recorded in Prudentius' hymn *Ad Galli Cantum*, ll. 37–40 (ferunt vagantes daemonas / laetos tenebris noctium / gallo canente exterritos / sparsim timere at cedere). Le Loyer (1.3), accepting this belief from Psellus, calls the cock 'un oiseau céleste'. Its religious associations (with the light of God) may give point to the 'fearful summons' (l. 154), and are developed in the next speech (ll. 163–9).

For the legend of the cock's crowing all night for Christmas no other authority is known. But there are various stories in which the cock crows all night to signal a victory or a famous birth (see *PQ*, XLV, 442–7); and as the announcer of light the cock is emblematically the herald of Christ. A possible basis in fact is suggested by the observation of Richard Jefferies that 'towards the end of December the cocks . . . crow . . . hours before midnight . . . just when the nights are longest' (*Wild Life in a Southern County*, ch. 17). See W. S. Walsh, *Curiosities of Popular Customs*, 1897, p. 232: 'In England it is common to hear one say, when the cock crows in the stillness of the November and December nights, "The cock is crowing for Christmas". He is supposed to do this for the purpose of scaring off the evil spirits from the holy season.' But it is a moot point whether this explains Shakespeare or is explained by him.

I.i.171–2.   *the morn in russet mantle clad*
              Walks o'er the dew of yon high eastward hill]
The coming of dawn is not less dramatic for being conveyed

in conventional poetic images. Failure to recognize these has allowed too much licence to the eye of the beholder. Dover Wilson, recalling that the colour *russet* (reddish-brown) takes its name from a coarse homespun cloth, pictures Dawn as 'a labourer mounting the hill to his work of the day, his mantle thrown across his shoulder' (NCS, p. xxxvi). Many others have regarded the *eastward hill*, notwithstanding the lack of such a feature in the actual view from Elsinore, as a touch of local colour. English actors rehearsing on the spot in 1950 seemed to see there what Shakespeare had described (Hugh Hunt, *Old Vic Prefaces*, p. 51). M. Holmes (*The Guns of Elsinore*, p. 47) connects the hill with the (misleading) suggestions of Elizabethan maps, Dollerup (pp. 152–3) with the ridge behind the port of Helsingborg seen in contemporary painting. Yet the *russet mantle* was traditional, and in Gavin Douglas (*The Palice of Honour*, Prol. l. 2) had belonged to 'Aurora'; while Spenser had associated the cock's 'note shrill' (cf. l. 156) with Phoebus' car 'climbing up the eastern hill' (*FQ*, I.ii. 1). Shakespearean dawns include 'the grey-ey'd morn . . . Chequering the eastern clouds' in *Rom.* II.ii. 188–9 (Arden text), etc. The *F eastern* is perhaps a regularization, the Q2 *eastward* being unique in the Shakespearean texts.

I.ii.S.D.] *Claudius*, instead of the Feng(on) of Saxo and Belleforest, is an unexpected name for a Danish king, and Yngve Olsson has noted that in Krantz's *Chronica Regnorum Aquilonarium*, Strasburg, 1545, the same page (p. 619) includes references to the Danish 'Ambletus' and to the Roman Emperor Claudius (*Sh. Studs.*, IV, 208–9). But see *Dramatis Personae, Claudius*, n. To begin by providing a character with a name which is not subsequently used is not uncharacteristic of Shakespeare. Cf. 'Eskales' in the first entry-direction for the Prince in *Rom.*; 'Solinus' for the Duke in the first line of *Err.* In *LLL* the King of Navarre is called Ferdinand in the opening S.D. and in speech-headings in two scenes but not in the text. The editorial *Council, including* here corresponds to the Q2 *Counsaile: as*. This is taken by Dover Wilson and some subsequent editors for a misreading of 'Counsailors'; but *as*, in the sense of 'such as', 'for example', is acceptable as introducing the names of some of the persons present. The inclusion in the Council of Cornelius and Voltemand may be implied by their being given no separate entry in Q2 (cf. Greg, *SFF*, p. 330). The postponement of their entry to l. 25 in F is attributed by Dover Wilson (*MSH*, p. 35) to doubling of their parts with those of Barnardo and Marcellus. The naming of *Hamlet* last in

Q2 instead of in order of rank may indicate the order of entry; it has been taken to isolate Hamlet dramatically from the rest of the court (*MSH*, p. 34). It should be noted, however, that the Q2 stage-direction names the characters in the order in which the ensuing scene takes notice of them: it is possible that the author's S.D. ended with *Counsaile* and that *as Polonius, and his Sonne Laertes, Hamlet, Cum Alijs* represents an addition by the book-keeper. That the last two words at least are his is probable. For Hamlet *in black*, see ll. 68 ff.

I.ii. 1–39.] The elaborate *style of the King's speech* is variously regarded. L. C. Knights (*An Approach to 'Hamlet'*, p. 41) finds a masterly expression of Claudius's personality in its 'unctuous verse rhythms'. Coleridge (i. 20) noted a strain of undignified rhetoric betraying an uneasy conscience, while recognizing a certain appropriate majesty. Kittredge insisted that the whole speech is dignified and 'even eloquent', its artifice betokening not hypocrisy but ceremony. Yet no ceremony can gloss over the essential fact that the new king, with an admixture of 'mirth' and 'delight', has married his 'sometime sister' (cf. l. 8 and n.) while his brother's death is still fresh.

I.ii. 1. *Hamlet our dear brother*] *The succession* by a king's brother rather than his son was permitted by the system of an elective monarchy, which Denmark in fact had. See G. Sjögren, 'Hamlet and the Coronation of Christian IV', *SQ*, XVI, 155 ff.; Dollerup, pp. 131–4. Cf. 'th'election', v.ii.65, 360. The succession of a brother is paralleled within the play in Norway (l. 28). Dover Wilson's argument that Claudius is a usurper (*WHH*, pp. 30 ff.) is refuted by Honigmann (*Stratford-upon-Avon Studies*, 5, pp. 129 ff.) and by A. P. Stabler (*SP*, LXII, 654–61), who shows nevertheless that ambiguity on the point is inherited from Belleforest. I do not think, with Stabler, that uncertainty about Hamlet's rights can have been designed as part of his plight; nor, with Honigmann, that the present scene creates a 'mystery' about the succession which is to be clarified as the play proceeds. The play does, however, as it progresses, increase dramatically our sense of Claudius's unfitness. It is when he is established as a 'murderer and a villain' that Hamlet says he 'stole' the kingdom (III.iv. 96–100). It is when he has used his kingly power to plot Hamlet's death that the Prince asserts his own right (v.i. 251). Finally will come the hint that Claudius had anticipated the process of election (v.ii.65). But although this leaves the manner of Claudius's succession in some ambiguity, it is clear that he became king with public consent. The play does not question the legality of his title, even though it also regards the Prince of Denmark as the future king. See I.iii. 20–4, III.i. 154. At I.ii. 109 the King publicly nominates Hamlet as his successor; but this is not necessarily incompatible with the principle of election, in which the Prince's hereditary status and 'the voice of the King' (III.ii. 332–3) would be important. Jas. Howell in 1632 refers to the eldest son of the Danish king as 'King elect of Denmark', explaining that 'though that Crown be purely elective, yet for these three last Kings, they wrought so with the people, that they got their eldest sons chosen, and declared before their death' (*Familiar Letters*, ed. Jacobs, p. 294). From the reference to the Queen as *jointress* (l. 9) Dover Wilson infers that Gertrude had a life-interest in the crown, and it may be that Shakespeare had in mind how in earlier versions of the story Hamlet's father acquired the throne by marriage; but the rights he accords Gertrude as dowager he is content not to define. What is clear is that Claudius became king before taking her 'to wife' but consolidated his position by a prudent marriage.

I.ii. 11. *With an auspicious and a dropping eye*] It was proverbially said of the false man that he looks up with one eye and down with the other (e.g. Fergusson's *Scottish Proverbs*, ed. Beveridge, Scot. Text Soc., p. 56). This was a variant of the ancient proverb, To laugh with one eye and weep with the other (Tilley E 248), which was traditionally applied to Fortune (as in Chaucer, *Book of the Duchess*, ll. 633–4) in indication of her fickleness. See B. White, 'Claudius and Fortune', *Anglia*, LXXVII, 204–7. But though this may give the phrase, from Claudius's lips, an ironic undertone, it is a mistake to suppose that in itself it proclaims him hypocrite. In Elyot's *Governour* (II. ch. 12) a woman yields her maidenhead 'with an eye half laughing half mourning' while affirming constancy; and Paulina 'had one eye declined for the loss of her husband, another elevated that the oracle was fulfilled' (*Wint.* v. ii. 72–3). The idea of Fortune has suggested 'auspicious' for the happy eye and the 'scale' of l. 13; for the king as Fortune's surrogate, cf. esp. III.iii. 17–22. For *dropping*, downcast, cf. Fergusson and *Wint.* above.

I.ii. 65. *more than kin, and less than kind*] Most commentators, not unreasonably, take these words to apply, like *cousin* and *son*, to Hamlet himself. But some, justly stressing the unnaturalness as well as the hostility denoted by *less than kind*, apply them to

Claudius. The difference is perhaps not greatly material; for what Hamlet seizes on in the words *cousin* and *son* is the relationship they signify. His rejoinder is therefore best applied, I think, to *both* himself and Claudius, or rather to the relation in which they stand to one another. A 'cousin' is 'kin' but a 'son' is 'more'; and Hamlet's resentment at being made Claudius's son as well as nephew glances at the incestuous marriage which has created this 'more than' natural relationship. *Kind* is often used as a near-synonym for *kin*, as in *Gorboduc*, 1.i.18, 'In kind a father, not in kindliness'. But the distinction there between *kind* and *kindliness* approximates to the one Shakespeare makes between *kin* and *kind*. Both words refer to the members of one family, but whereas *kin* has regard only to the fact of relationship, *kind* has regard also to its manifestation in a community and mutuality of feeling. Cf. *kindless*, II.ii.577, void of natural feeling; Bastard, *Epigrams*, 1598, iii.29, 'Never so many cousins; so few kind'. The human paradox that kin are not always kind is often expressed in Elizabethan literature (cf. Tilley K 38), and the different meanings of *kind* are a favourite source of word-play. Instances are given by Kittredge and others. The adjective *kind*, in its Elizabethan use, included the modern sense ('benevolent'), but often retained the strong primary meaning of 'natural', and especially 'showing feelings natural among blood relations' (cf. Lear's 'unkind' daughters). Even so, the usual interpretation of the present passage, which takes *kind* as an adjective, instead of a noun in antithesis with *kin*, necessarily weakens its force.

1.ii.67. *in the sun*] (1) Although to Schmidt sunshine suggests 'careless idleness' ('I am more careless and idle than I ought to be'), the obvious meaning of the metaphor is that Hamlet, with the melancholic's characteristic preference for the shade, objects to the brightness into which he is brought, whether it be the glare of public notice (cf. Caldecott, 'I am torn prematurely from my sorrows, and thrown into the broad glare of the sun'), the gaiety of the Court, or, more pointedly, the sunshine of the King's favour. (2) Reinforcing this, is an unmistakable glancing at the sun as a royal emblem (cf. *1H4* 1.ii.190 ff.): Hamlet hints that he is too much in the King's presence. Cf. the similar word-play at II.ii.184: 'walk i'th' sun', come into the prince's presence. (3) There is an obvious pun on *son* (l. 64), supported, as Dover Wilson notes, by the Q2 spelling. Cf. *R3* 1.i.2, 'this sun of York' (Q1 sonne, F Son). Hamlet finds this relationship 'too much' for him and Claudius is making 'too much' of it (making him more his 'son' than he really is). 'Hamlet bitterly refuses the title which the King has emphasized' (Kittredge), and the King's further persuasions (ll. 107 ff.) are rejected in advance. An echo of the proverb 'Out of heaven's blessing into the warm sun' (cf. *Lr* II. ii. 156–7), first heard by Johnson, is surely somewhat faint. For the use and interpretation of the proverb see Tilley, *Elizn Proverb Lore* (no. 287); P. L. Carver, *MLR*, xxv, 478–81. From its implication of passing from good to worse a host of commentators have extorted a reference to Hamlet's present degradation, and in particular to his having been turned out from the place Heaven gave him and deprived of the throne. But Hamlet's wit is less recondite than theirs. The curious may consult the 43 meanings extracted from the phrase in E. Le Comte, *Poets' Riddles*, ch. 1.

I. ii. 113. *Wittenberg*] This German university, founded in 1502, had become famous through its association with Luther, Melanchthon, and the reformed religion. But to note with Dover Wilson that Hamlet's university was Protestant is less important than to learn from Brandes that it was the favourite university of Danes studying abroad. (Cf. I. ii. 126 n.) In the decade 1586–95 it had two students named Rosenkrantz and one Gyldenstjerne (Dollerup, p. 128). Its name was well known to the Elizabethans and had been familiarized in the theatre by *Dr Faustus*. Samuel Lewkenor (*A Discourse of Foreign Cities*) described it in 1600 as a 'learned seminary of the arts' in which 'many worthy writers have . . . received their education'.

I. ii. 129. *sullied*] The most debated reading in the play in recent years. Earlier editors, with their preference for F, naturally adopted *solid*, though Furnivall defended the Q *sallied* in the sense of 'assailed' and Furness recorded the conjecture *sullied*, which also occurred to Tennyson (*SQ*, XI, 490) and which Dowden thought might 'be right'. Dover Wilson's establishment of Q2 as the more authoritative text brought *sullied* into favour (see *MSH*, pp. 307–15; Greg, *Principles of Emendation*, p. 25; Bowers, *SS 9*, 44–8). Seven other Shakespearean instances of the word include two with the *a* spelling: *Ham.* II. i. 40, *sallies* (Q2); *LLL* v. ii. 352, 'pure as the *unsallied* lily' (Q,F 1). Cf. also Dekker, etc., *Patient Grissill*, I. i. 12, '*sally* not the morning with foul looks'. So whereas Dover Wilson took *sallied* as a misreading of 'sullied', it is reasonably regarded, Kökeritz notwithstanding (*Studia Neophilologica*, xxx, 3–10), as an alternative form (Crow, *Essays and Studies*, n.s. VIII, 8–9; Bowers, loc. cit.). *Solid* has obvious (too obvious?) aptness in the context and it too has the support of Shakespearean usage: *2H4* III.i.48, 'that one might . . . see . . . the continent, *Weary* of *solid* firmness, *melt* itself Into the sea'; *Troil.* I.iii.113. S. Weiss found it consistent with Shakespearean patterns of associated imagery (*SQ*, x, 219–27), and S. Warhaft related it to the essential characteristic of the melancholy humour (*ELH*, XXVIII, 21–30). Briefly, melancholy is the cold dry humour, and 'of this coldness and dryness riseth hardness whereof the flesh of melancholy persons is' (Bright, p. 128). In *Shr.* (Ind.ii.129) melancholy is associated with the congealing of the blood; and 'of the congealing of the blood' the flesh, according to Burton, is composed (I.i.2(3)). Melancholy among the humours thus corresponds to earth among the elements, and its remedy is for the excess of earth to *melt* into water, which in turn may *resolve* into vapour. But see ll. 129–30 n., *resolve*; and while all this may illuminate the passage, its support for *solid* would be stronger if the word actually occurred in Warhaft's illustrative quotations. The significance he attaches to *solid* is already implicit in *flesh*. And, just to show how one may argue either way, the alchemical transmutation of the baser element (*flesh*) into the purer (*dew*) has been held to support *sullied* (*ES*, LIX, 508–9). Though '*too* solid flesh' escapes tautology, *sullied* enlarges the meaning as *solid* does not. With the thought cf. (from the poem in Tottel's *Miscellany* beginning 'The life is long, that loathsomely doth last') 'Wherefore with Paul let all men wish, and pray To be *dissolv'd* of this *foul fleshy* mass' (ll. 37–8). The suggestion of contamination and self-disgust begins an important dramatic motif (cf. *MSH*, pp. 313–15). The textual evidence for *sullied*, moreover, cannot be dismissed. For *sullied* is less likely to be a corruption of *solid* than the other way about, and though Q2 may have derived it from Q1, this suggests that *solid* did not occur in Q2's manuscript authority, while Q1 is against its having been familiar in performance (though if Chapman, *Revenge of Bussy d'Ambois*, v.iv.7–9 is an echo, it must presently have become so). Further, the fact that Q2 *sallied* here and *sallies* at II.i.40 occur in the work of different compositors argues for a manuscript origin. It is sometimes contended that Shakespeare would not use *too too* with a participle; but *OED* shows it often used with verbs, and Q1, 'too much grieu'd and sallied', shows that a participle was in the reporter's recollection. The possibility of an intended play on both words cannot be ruled out; but what happens perhaps is that by a natural mental process the word (*sullied*) which gives at once the clue to the emotion which the soliloquy will express, brings to mind its near-homonym (*solid*), which helps to promote the imagery of *melt, thaw, resolve, dew*. Those who accept some F variants as authentic Shakespearean alternatives (cf. Honigmann, *The Stability of Shakespeare's Text*, pp. 70, 134–6) are likely to find an example here. (But see Intro., p. 43 n.)

I. ii. 140. *Hyperion to a satyr*] The contrast between the two brothers is repeatedly stressed by Belleforest along with the fact that the Queen has allied herself with the worse who has killed the better. See Intro., pp. 91–2. This becomes immensely more significant in Shakespeare: the antithesis here between the sun-god, with his majestic beauty, and a creature half man half beast epitomizes in the two brothers the complex nature of man – like a god and like a beast – which will be a theme of Hamlet's later reflections (cf. II. ii. 303–8; IV. iv. 33–9; and l. 150 LN below). The imagery enables the basic situation of the play to appear as one in which the beast in man has destroyed the god and now reigns in his kingdom. See Intro., pp. 129–32. Even in this first soliloquy the contrast between the two brother-kings (cf. l. 152) is not less important, though less often emphasized, than the revelation of Hamlet's state of mind and his attitude to his mother. Structurally the soliloquy effects a link between the presentation of one king in the preceding part of the scene and the description of the other in the dialogue which follows. The godlike attributes which Hamlet sees in his father are elaborated at III. iv. 55–62, when the contrast is resumed. The idea of man as partaking of both god and beast which thus underlies the play is very much the Renaissance concept. No single illustration can suffice, but cf. Pico della Mirandola, *De hominis dignitate*, and especially the opening pages: 'Neither heavenly nor earthly . . . thou canst grow downward into the lower natures which are brutes. Thou canst again grow upward from thy soul's reason into the higher natures which are divine.' 'If you see anyone . . . delivered over to the senses, it is a brute not a man that you see. If you come upon a philosopher winnowing out all things by right reason, he is a heavenly not an earthly animal.' 'We are made similar to brutes and mindless beasts of burden. But . . . as Asaph the prophet says, "Ye are all gods, and sons of the most high"' (trans. C. G. Wallis, 1940, pp. 5–7).

I. ii. 150. *wants discourse of reason*] The faculty of reason was traditionally recognized as the crucial difference between man and the beasts, for the classical statement of which see Cicero, *De*

Officiis, i.iv. 11. This lends further significance to the Hyperion–satyr comparison above (l. 140). It was through his reason that man could perceive the relation of cause and effect and thus connect past with future, whereas the beast, precisely because it lacks reason, must live largely in the present moment. Hence the axiom that its mourning would be brief. Cf. iv.iv. 33–9; and for Gertrude's failure to be guided by reason, iii.iv. 88.

Discourse of reason was a regular term, occurring also in *Troil.* ii.ii. 116, as well as in, e.g., Bright's *Treatise of Melancholy* (dedication), Holland's Plutarch (*Moral Virtue*), Florio's Montaigne, the translation of La Primaudaye's *The French Academy* (pp. 269, 278). For other instances, see Boswell, and *OED* discourse *sb.* 2 b. While sometimes apparently used as a cliché for 'reason', it properly denotes the faculty or process of reasoning from premises to conclusions. *Discourse* alone is also used in the same sense (see iv.iv. 36). The 'discursive reason' which was a property of man was distinguished from the higher 'intuitive reason' of angelic beings. In *Par. Lost* (v. 469 ff.) Raphael tells Adam that 'Reason is [the Soul's] being, Discursive or intuitive: discourse Is oftest yours, the latter most is ours'. But the difference, as Milton says, is of degree rather than kind.

i.ii. 187. *all in all*]   Often taken to mean, as in modern use, 'all things considered', 'on the whole'. But when Shakespeare uses *all in all* adverbially, it implies not qualification but intensification (= 'entirely'), as in *H5* i.i. 42; *Oth.* iv.i. 88, 262. The sense here is not that of weighing one thing against another but of accumulating them all. In iii.iv. 55–62 it is the accumulation of perfections that assures 'a man'. Hamlet's father, then, may be taken as a man complete in every particular, and so as the sum and pattern of excellence. Cf. Mabbe, *Celestina* (perhaps an echo), where a list of perfections is brought to a climax in 'Take him all together, and for all in all, you shall not find such another'. This sense of completeness or perfection is borne out by other Elizabethan instances: e.g. Stubbes, *Anatomy of Abuses* (New Shakspere Soc., i. 29) 'he is all in all; yea, so perfect . . .'; R. Carew, *The Excellency of the English Tongue* (Smith, *Elizn Critical Essays*, ii. 293), 'Will you have all in all for prose and verse? take the miracle of our age Sir Philip Sidney'. See, for an illuminating discussion, D. Barrett in *Neuphilologische Mitteilungen*, LXII, 164–8. Cf. Tilley A 133, 'All in all and all in every part', a proverb which T. W. Baldwin (*Literary Genetics of Shakspere's Poems*, pp. 157 ff.) shows to derive from the neo-Platonic doctrine of the soul.

1.iii.6. *a toy in blood*] '*A toy*, a thing of no regard' (*1H6* iv.i.145). This gives the fundamental sense (cf. iv.v.18) of a word with a wide range of meanings, abstract as well as concrete. It suggests the insubstantial or irrational – a whim, a fancy, or a short-lived passion (cf. i.iv.75). Or it denotes an idle diversion, often of an amorous kind (cf. *Oth.* i.iii.268, 'light-wing'd toys Of feather'd Cupid'). Here it continues the notion of frivolity in *trifling* and ephemerality in *fashion*, while its amorous connotations are strengthened by *blood*. The blood was popularly held to be the seat of the emotions, of passion as opposed to reason, which explains a very frequent use of this word in Shakespeare (cf. iii.ii. 69, iv.iii.69, iv.iv.58, iv.v.117). It is also associated with sensual appetite (cf. ii.i.34) and in particular with sexual desire, as at l. 116 below, iii.iv.69.

1.iii.21. *sanity*] This emendation of Theobald's is accepted by Dover Wilson and Alexander among others. It supposes that Q2 and F represent different misreadings. Q2 *safty* is good sense but not metre; for though the word is apparently trisyllabic in *FQ*, v.iv.46, Shakespeare affords no parallel and some 60 contrary instances. Other attempts to make Q2 scan are equally implausible, and the notion that the compositor may have omitted *the* before *health* is not supported by F. In defence of *safety* Sisson (*NR*) cites Prayerbook, 'the safety, honour, and welfare of our Sovereign and her dominions'. Cf. also Wither, *Emblems*, 1635, iv.xiv.6, 'where we In safety, health, and best content, may be'. But such collocations may be equally relevant to an author's association of ideas and to a compositor's error. Upholders of Q2 not only ignore the metrical deficiency but fail to explain *sanctity* in F. With this cf. Q2's misreading, *sanctity* for *sanity*, at ii.ii.210. *Sanity* was still used more commonly to refer to physical than to mental health and a conjunction of synonyms is not unique in Shakespeare.

1.iii.58–80.] *The 'few precepts' of Polonius to his son.*—Such parental advice, giving maxims of worldly prudence, was a tradition of the period. Surviving examples from life include a letter to Sir P. Sidney from his father (*Harl. Misc.* vii.603–4), Burleigh's *Precepts* for his son Robert Cecil and Raleigh's *Instructions to his Son* (both in *Advice to a Son*, ed. L. B. Wright, 1962), and the *Advice to his Son* of the 9th Earl of Northumberland (ed. G. B. Harrison, 1930). In Elizabethan literature similar sets of 'precepts' abound, most often delivered by a father to his son about to set off on his travels. For specimens see Lyly, *Euphues* (*Works*, ed. Bond, i. 189–90, 286) and *Euphues and his England* (ii. 30–1, 187–8); Greene, *The Card of Fancy* (*Works*, ed. Grosart, iv. 21–2) and *Greene's Mourning Garment* (ix. 137–8); Lodge, *Rosalynd*, (1590, B^v–B3) and *A Margarite of America* (1596, C3–4); Florio, *Second Fruits* (1591, ch. 6, pp. 93–105); and in Shakespeare himself, *All's W.* 1.i.54ff. The tradition goes back ultimately to Isocrates, *Ad Demonicum*, which the 16th century knew well (H. B. Lathrop, *Translations from the Classics*, pp. 45–6; *SQ*, IV, 3–9; VIII, 501–6, where G. K. Hunter sets out many parallels). It owed much also to Cato, *Disticha de Moribus ad Filium*, a favourite in the Middle Ages, to Erasmus (*Adagia, Disticha Catonis*), and to their 16th-century popularizers (see Doris V. Falk in *SQ*, XVIII, 23–30). The introductory *these few precepts* echoes Lyly, who has often been claimed as Shakespeare's source, but the correspondences (some set out by Bond, i.65) are nowhere verbally remarkable. Clearly no single or particular source need be looked for. Polonius's topics – speech, deportment, clothes, friends, quarrels, borrowing – are the regular ones, anticipated in more than one of the works cited, and most of the precepts themselves were recurrent. Several were proverbial maxims, though Shakespeare characteristically phrases them afresh. Only a few of the closer parallels can be given here.

With *Give thy thoughts no tongue* (l. 59), cf. *Euphues and his England*, 'Be not lavish of thy tongue' (elaborated in ll. 68–9).

With *Be thou familiar, but by no means vulgar* (61) cf. Isocrates, *Ad Demonicum*, 20 (trans. Bury, 1557), 'Be gentle and pleasant to all men: be familiar but only with the good'; Burleigh, *Precepts*, 'Towards thy superiors be humble yet generous; with thy equals familiar yet respective; towards inferiors show much humility and some familiarity'.

With the injunction on making and keeping *friends* (62–3), cf. *Ad Demonicum*, 24, 'Enter into friendship with no man, before you have perfectly searched out, how he hath used his former friends'; *A Margarite of America*, 'Learn of Augustus . . ., who was strange and scrupulous in accepting friends, but changeless and resolute in keeping them'; *Rosalynd*, 'Choose a friend as the Hyperborei do the metals, sever them from the ore with fire, and let them not bide the stamp before they be current'; *All's W.* 1.i.59–60, 'keep thy friend Under thy own life's key'; Tilley T 595.

With *do not dull thy palm*, etc. (64–5), cf. the proverb, 'Do not give thy hand to every man' (Tilley H 68).

With the injunction on conduct in *a quarrel* (65–7), cf. *Ad*

Demonicum, 43, 'Do your utter endeavour to live in safety. But if it fortune you to come in peril, so defend yourself . . . that it may redound to your renown'; Castiglione, *Courtier*, trans. Hoby (Tudor Trans., p. 53), 'Neither let him run rashly to these combats . . . he that goeth headlong to these things and without urgent cause, deserveth very great blame. . . . But when a man perceiveth that he is entered so far that he cannot draw back without burden, he must . . . be utterly resolved with himself, and always show a readiness and a stomach'; *Euphues and his England*, 'Be not quarrellous for every light occasion: they [the English] are . . . ready to revenge an injury, but never wont to proffer any: they never fight without provoking, and once provoked they never cease'.

With *Give every man thy ear . . . but reserve thy judgment* (68–9), cf. Sir H. Sidney, 'Be you rather a hearer and bearer away of other men's talk, than a beginner, or procurer of speech'; *Euphues and his England*, 'It shall be there better to hear what they say, than to speak what thou thinkest'; *Greene's Mourning Garment*, 'Little talk shows much wisdom, but hear what thou canst'; *All's W.* 1.i.60–1, 'be check'd for silence, But never tax'd for speech'; Tilley M 1277.

Polonius's advice on dress (70–2) has perhaps an individual note (*costly*, *rich*). Euphues was told 'Let thy attire be comely but not costly'. But the warning against excess and self-display is entirely traditional. Cf. *Ad Demonicum*, 27, 'Be neat and cleanly in your apparel; but not brave and sumptuous'; *A Margarite for America*, 'in thy apparel princely without excess'. And Polonius is not the first to cite a proverb about the apparel and the man: Peter Idley (15th century), in *Instructions to his Son*, requiring dress to be 'cleanly' but not 'too nice and gay', explains that 'clothing oft maketh man' (ll. 99–105). Cf. Tilley A 283; Moryson, *Itinerary* (1907 edn), ii.262, 'The wise man hath taught us, that the apparel in some sort shows the man'.

With advice against borrowing (75), cf. Burleigh's 'Neither borrow money of a neighbour or friend but rather from a mere stranger, where paying for it thou mayest hear no more of it'. That *loan oft loses both itself and friend* (76) is a piece of folk-wisdom, for which Kittredge quotes the jingle, 'I had my silver and my friend, / I lent my silver to my friend, / I asked my silver of my friend, / I lost my silver and my friend.' Cf. Tilley F 725.

The final precept, *to thine own self be true* (78), has proved ambiguous. Interpretation has ranged from a noble ideal of integrity to a cynical injunction to pursue self-interest. But the tradition of the maxim puts its meaning (Be constant) beyond doubt. Cf. Cato, *Disticha*, 1.4, as rendered, e.g., by Taverner (1540, etc.), 'He that striveth with himself shall full evil agree with other men . . . he that . . . is with every puff of wind carried now hither now thither, is not meet for the company of honest men'; and see D. V. Falk, *SQ*, XVIII, 29.

Such conventional precepts are entirely appropriate to Polonius as a man of experience. It is a mistake to suppose they are meant to make him seem ridiculous. Their purpose, far more important than any individual characterization, is to present him in his role of father. What is being dramatized in the advice as in the blessing is his son's departure from home and by impressing upon us here the relation between father and son the play is preparing for the emergence of Laertes later as the avenger who will claim Hamlet as his victim.

I.iii.65. *courage*] Editors, led by Dover Wilson and I think justifiably, have reverted to this Q2 (and Q1) reading. That *courage* could refer to a person is shown by *OED sb.* 1 c. One of its two examples retains the word from the French it is translating; the other shows Sir T. Hoby using it to render the Italian *animi* when, referring to the ancient Romans, he speaks of 'the prowess of those divine courages' (*The Courtier*, Tudor Trans., p. 327). It is hardly such that Polonius has in mind, but the manifestations of 'courage' may range from spiritual elevation through military valour to fashionable effrontery; Dover Wilson takes a *courage* here to be a spark, brave, or blood. Ingleby once asserted, but did not show, that *courage* 'in euphuistic talk, meant a gallant' (*N&Q*, 2nd ser. II, 206), and Dowden compares the use of *bravery* in that sense. Some support comes from *The Knight of the Burning Pestle* (Ind.), where 'a couraging part' is a noisy, swaggering role. It is true that Q2 might have taken *courage* from Q1, but equally they may concur because the word is right. It can scarcely be a memorial corruption of F *comrade*. Indeed *comrade* looks like a makeshift for a puzzle in the copy (cf. Greg, *Principles of Emendation*, p. 63), substituting a more for a less familiar word with some detriment to the sense.

The conjecture (*N&Q*, 10th ser. I, 425–6) that *courage* is a misprint for *comrague* (= comrade) was endorsed by Kittredge and favoured by Maxwell (*MSH*, 1963 repr., p. 428). This word, in spite of some scholarly demur, is well attested in contemporary literature. (Instances remarked include Dekker, *The Welsh Ambassador*, III.ii.110, IV.ii.76, V.ii.73; Webster, *Appius and*

Virginia, IV.ii.8; Heywood and Brome, *The Late Lancashire Witches*, Heywood's *Works*, 1874, iv.244; Sir Ed. Hoby, *A Curry-comb for a Coxcomb*, 1615, p. 69; H. Parrot, *Laquei ridiculosi*, 1613, epigram 27.) And it can be used without the jocular connotations inseparable from its variant *comrogue* (= comrade in roguery, fellow-rascal). Like *comrade*, it has the advantage that it could be accented on the second syllable; but also like it, when not vocative it usually has a possessive pronoun (all but one of the instances noted) and it is out of keeping with 'new-hatch'd'. It therefore asks us to suppose independent corruptions in different texts without satisfactorily fulfilling the requirements of the sense.

1.iii.74. *Are of a most select and generous chief in that.*] The proposed paraphrase regards Q2 *Or* as a misreading and interprets F as it stands. Q3, if it represents a deliberate emendation, already found *Or* unsatisfactory. Almost all scholars, with the notable exception of Sisson (*NR*), assume further corruption, notwithstanding the basic agreement of all three texts. This may be a case where the two later texts inherit error from Q1 (see Intro., p. 74). Q2 leaves us without a verb, and Sisson alone sees no difficulty in an absolute construction, 'They in France . . . [being] chief in that'. Bronson (*SQ*, VII, 280), among others, would find the verb in *chiefe* (Q2), which he holds 'a possible form' of the now obsolete *cheve*, to prosper, succeed (and hence excel). Most editors take *chief* as an adverb (principally, especially), which the preceding comma in Q2 supports. But if *chief* is not a noun, one has to be supplied from the context; and '*Or* of a most select and generous [rank and station]' hardly states a valid alternative to 'best rank and station', while 'They . . . of the best rank and station *Are* of a most select and generous [rank and station]' is tautologous. Some suppose tautology suitable for Polonius, but the rest of this speech is incisively expressed. The objection to taking *chief* as a noun is that the abstract use has no parallel in Shakespeare. Yet see *OED* chief *sb.* 10 and (following Malone) cf. Bacon, *Colours of Good and Evil*, 'the wits of chief', the most eminent minds. I should like to interpret it as 'model of excellence', but authority is lacking. Among proposed emendations, Ingleby and Staunton supported *sheaf* (see *N&Q*, 2nd ser. II, 206–7), while the old conjecture *choice* is adopted by Alexander and still advocated (as in *Studia Neophilologica*, L, 180–1). But Q1, by anticipating *chief* with *chiefe rancke* in the previous line, is almost conclusive for its authenticity. Very many editors have simplified the construction and regularized the metre by omitting *of a*, against all three texts and with little improvement of sense. The extra foot, though certainly not fatal, may be suspicious. But Dyce's notion that *of a* might have been accidentally interpolated through the influence of *of the* in the line before and Munro's that it might represent a false start are discountenanced by its presence in Q1. Dover Wilson thinks it a misprint, possibly for *often* (*MSH*, pp. 317–19). That *of a* also appears in the equally famous crux at I.iv.37 – even though the textual position is not the same, the latter occurring only in Q2 – may be more than coincidence. Other suggested emendations designed to restore the syntax include 'Or of a most select, *are* generous' (Dowden) and 'Are of *all* most select and generous' (*TLS*, 1938, p. 28; *N&Q*, CCII, 84). Much as we should like to recover the smallest word of Shakespeare's, it seems unlikely that any loss here is profound.

I.iii.109. *Running*]   For the metaphor cf. *3H6* I.iv.127, 'beggars mounted run their horse to death'; *Err.* IV.i.57, 'You run this humour out of breath'; Chapman, *An Humorous Day's Mirth*, sc. v.65 (after puns on a man's name), 'Here's a poor name run out of breath'. *Running* the phrase compares with *hunting* or *coursing* the letter (referring to alliteration, as in E.K.'s epistle before *The Shepherd's Calendar* and Sidney's *Apology*). With F *Roaming* cf. F *rome* (for *run*?) in *John* II.i.335. Both this and Q2 *Wrong* could well arise from manuscript *ron(n)ing* (Dover Wilson, *MSH*, pp. 315–16). Those who prefer the emendation *Wringing* or *Wronging* lose the force of the metaphor, which others would change altogether by emending *wind* to *ring*, on a supposed analogy with II.ii.424–5. See *SQ*, xxxi, 88–90. Q1 *tendring*, though occasionally followed, is obviously a memory confusion.

I.iii.130. *bawds*]   It is less easy to reconcile the QF *bonds* with the sense and demands of the passage than to see it as a misreading of *bawds* (especially if this were spelt *bauds*, as in *Tim.* II.ii.63 and elsewhere). 'Bonds of love' are common and Shakespearean (cf. *Sonn.* CXLII) and false vows could no doubt be said to simulate sacred love-pledges. But *bonds* are not easily thought of as *breathing*, as Theobald and others have remarked; and though *vows* may certainly 'breathe' (sound, be uttered), to say that they breathe 'like sanctified and pious bonds' verges on tautology. If, less plausibly but as Dover Wilson holds (*MSH*, pp. 290–1), it is the *suits* that 'breathe', this gives point to the contrast between *unholy* fact and *sanctified and pious* appearance, but, throwing the stress on the epithets, leaves *bonds* at the end of the line as an anticlimax. Moreover, it confuses the personification of vows as brokers and implorators which *bawds* would happily continue. This is the word which follows naturally on *brokers* (see l. 127n.) and which *implorators of unholy suits* defines, while the trickery associated with bawds leads on to *beguile*. I cannot agree with Dover Wilson that *bawds* gives an opposite sense to that intended. Indeed the whole passage, insisting that things are other than they seem, might be thought to call for a climactic paradox, which *bawds* who under an appearance of sanctity breathe their unholy persuasions will supply. Polonius is contending that the lover's vows are in reality seducers. The 'sanctified and holy traitors' of *AYL* II. iii. 13 are not quite analogous, since the virtues that betray are still virtues; but the similar oxymoron is worth noting, and the *bawds* and *traitors* thus associated through identical or synonymous epithets (*sanctified and pious*; *sanctified and holy*) are actually conjoined in *Troil.* v.x.37 ('O traitors and bawds').

1.iv.9. *the swagg'ring upspring reels*] *Reels*, with its suggestion of drunken motion, is variously taken as a plural noun, an intransitive verb, or (best) a transitive verb with *upspring* as its object. Johnson interpreteted *upspring* as 'upstart', referring to the King. But that an upspring was a German dance (or part of one) seems established by the play *Alphonsus Emperor of Germany*, printed 1654, formerly attributed to Chapman: 'We Germans have no changes in our dances, An Almain and an upspring, that is all' (Chapman's *Tragedies*, ed. Parrott, p. 435). Elze (edn of *Alphonsus*, p. 144) identified it with a wild dance traditional in German merrymaking called the *Hüpfauf* and was able to refute (edn of *Hamlet*, 1882, p. 133) Schmidt's assertion that the *Hüpfauf* was apocryphal. Presumably Shakespeare knew of the upspring as a feature of carousals and associated it with northern Europe. Kittredge, persuaded that the King would not himself 'go capering about the chamber', makes *upspring* the subject of reels. But this involves an awkward change of subject; the syntax points to *reels* as parallel with *keeps*. The transitive use, though rare, is hardly unidiomatic. (Cf., though with dissimilar object, *Ant.* 1.iv.20, 'To reel the streets'.) *OED* and Kökeritz (p. 189) prefer *reels* as a noun, as in *Ant.* II.vii.92, 'Drink thou; increase the reels'. This makes *upspring* an adjective, and as such (= 'upstart') *OED* records it in 1591 ('the new upspring nobility'), encouraging Dover Wilson to paraphrase *upspring reels* as 'newfangled revels'. But with the revelry insisted on as customary (ll. 13 ff.), the aptness of this is not obvious.

I.iv. 11. *kettle-drum and trumpet*]   The kettle-drum, though familiar in England from the mid-16th century, again gives local colour as a traditional accompaniment of Danish rejoicings (cf. Cleveland, *Fuscara*, 'As Danes carouse by kettle-drums'). 'Like a Denmark drummer' became a common phrase. On the entry of James I and Anne of Denmark into London in 1603, 'to delight the Queen with her own country music, nine trumpets and a kettle drum, did very sprightly and actively sound the Danish march' (Dekker, *Magnificent Entertainment*, *Dram. Works*, ed. Bowers, ii. 274). Cf. III.ii. 89 S.D. See Dollerup, pp. 195-7, and for an account of the kettle-drum and its history, P. R. Kirby in *Music and Letters*, IX, 34 ff.

I.iv. 12–13. *Is it a custom?—Ay*]   That it was so in fact appears from an account by Wm. Segar, Garter King at Arms, cited in Stow's *Annals* (1605), pp. 1433-7. Segar, who visited the Danish court in 1603 for the presentation of the Order of the Garter to Christian IV, says, 'It would make a man sick to hear of their drunken healths: use hath brought it into fashion, and fashion made it a habit'. He describes a banquet attended by King Christian on board the British ambassador's ship at which 'every health reported six, eight, or ten shot of great Ordnance, so that during the King's abode, the ship discharged 160 shot'. Jas. Howell (*Familiar Letters*, ed. Jacobs, p. 295) describes an occasion in 1632 when the King of Denmark 'from eleven of the clock till towards the evening . . . began thirty-five healths' and 'was taken away at last in his chair'. See also ll. 17–20 LN below. By making Claudius follow and Hamlet deplore this 'custom' Shakespeare uses his knowledge of Danish ways not merely for local colour but in the moral structure of his tragedy. There is of course nothing in the play to justify the inference that what was customary must have been made so by Hamlet's father. It is strange that Horatio, a Dane (I.i. 128, v.ii. 346), should not know of the custom. The play shows Shakespeare in two minds about him. In I.i Horatio seemed at home in Denmark and well informed on Danish affairs. But in I.ii. 164 ff. Hamlet is surprised to see him in Elsinore and now speaks as though Horatio were not a 'native'. Cf. notes on I.i. 82, I.ii. 186; and see Dover Wilson, NCS, p. xlviii; G. F. Bradby, *Short Studies in Shakespeare*, pp. 145 ff.

I. iv. 17–20. *This heavy-headed revel . . . Soil our addition*]   It is a fact
that the Danes had not merely the custom just described but, in
common with the Dutch and the Germans, the reputation of
drunkenness. Cf. *Oth.* II. iii. 72 ff. Fynes Moryson says, 'The Danes
pass (if it be possible) their neighbour Saxons in the excess of their
drinking' (*Itinerary*, 1907–8 edn, iv. 67). Many other allusions include *Greene's Mourning Garment*, 'Bring home pride from Spain,
. . . gluttony from England, and carousing from the Danes'
(Greene, ix. 136); Marston, *Jack Drum's Entertainment*, 'a Dane-
like barbarous sot' (Act IV); Rowlands, *Look to it, for I'll stab ye*,
'The Dane, that would carouse out of his boot' (Hunterian Club,
p. 21). But though the matter itself was common knowledge,
Shakespeare seems to have been particularly influenced here, as
later in this speech, by Nashe's *Pierce Penniless*, which, describing
the Danes as 'bursten-bellied sots', tells how 'the quick-witted
Italians . . . detest this surly *swinish* generation' (Nashe, i. 180).
Presently, inveighing against contemporary customs of excessive
drinking, Nashe says they would formerly have led a man to be
called 'foul drunken swine' (i. 205), and he goes on to the passage
cited in ll. 23–38 LN below. His types of drunkard include the
'swine drunk, heavy, lumpish, and sleepy' (i. 207), while 'the
heavy-headed gluttonous house-dove' (the reveller at home in contrast to the reveller abroad) is cited as a type of sloth (i. 210). See
Intro., pp. 104–5.

I. iv. 23–38. *So, oft it chances . . . scandal.*]   With this whole passage,
cf. the comment on the effect of drunkenness in Nashe's *Pierce
Penniless* (i. 205): 'A mighty deformer of men's manners and features, is this unnecessary vice of all other. Let him be indued with
never so many virtues, and have as much goodly proportion and
favour as nature can bestow upon a man: yet if he be thirsty
after his own destruction, and hath no joy nor comfort, but when
he is drowning his soul in a gallon pot, that one beastly imperfection will utterly obscure all that is commendable in him; and all
his good qualities sink like lead down to the bottom of his carousing cups, where they will lie, like lees and dregs, dead and unregarded of any man.' What Nashe says of drunkenness, Shakespeare
extends from drunkenness to any vice. On his indebtedness to
Nashe see also ll. 17–20 LN above and Intro., pp. 104–6. Cf. also
Greene's *Pandosto*, 'One mole staineth a whole face: and what is
once spotted with infamy can hardly be worn out with time'
(Greene, iv. 250). The present passage also recalls one in Belleforest's summing-up on Hamlet, who 'showed himself admirable

in everything, if one spot alone had not darkened a good part of his praises'.

i.iv.29–30. *o'erleavens The form of plausive manners*] The commentators give little clue to the meaning they attach to this – except for Dover Wilson, who says that 'to *o'erleaven* is to have too much of a good thing'. But leaven is not always good. Cf. Matthew xvi.6, 'the leaven of the Pharisees'; Latimer, *Last Sermon before Edward VI* (*Sermons*, Parker Soc., i.256), 'their sin doth leaven you all'; *Cym.* iii.iv.60, 'Thou, Posthumus, Wilt lay the leaven on all proper men'; Bacon, *Henry VII* (*Works*, ed. Spedding, vi.152), 'A little leaven of new distaste doth commonly sour the whole lump of former merits'. To *leaven* here, then, is 'to taint', 'to work corruption (in)'. And to *o'erleaven* is not, as *OED* would have it, 'to leaven too much', but 'to leaven over', to spread a corrupting influence over (or through). It is practically equivalent to 'lay the leaven on all' in the *Cymbeline* passage, where the evil in Posthumus brings others into disrepute and Sinon's hypocritical tears 'Did scandal' those of genuine grief (cf. *scandal*, l. 38). For *form*, see iii.i.155; and for *plausive* the 'plausive words' of *All's W.* i. ii.53, where the sense (though unknown outside Shakespeare) is usually and reasonably taken to be 'deserving of applause'. The passages cited describe Hamlet and Rousillon as models. But 'some habit' may spread an infection through accepted codes of conduct.

i.iv.32. *Fortune's star*] Kittredge takes this to refer to the 'defect' formed by 'habit', as distinct from those due to 'birth' and 'complexion', which are attributable to nature. But what precedes clearly regards all three as belonging to 'Nature's livery' (cf. ll. 25–30n.); a defect due to Fortune comes as an additional idea. It is true there seems to be a progression from unalterable nature (*birth*) to nature capable of modification (*habit*); for use, which creates habit, 'almost can change the stamp of nature' (see iii. iv.170 and n.). Yet 'use is another nature' and certainly not fortune.

i.iv.36–8.   *The dram of evil*
            Doth all the noble substance often dout
                    To his own scandal.]
This passage, in Q2 only, is probably the most famous crux in Shakespeare. Q2 *eale* is usually regarded as corrupt, even by those who have remarked that it 'may possibly be . . . some obsolete

word of unknown origin' (Verity) or that *eale* was a dialect verb meaning 'reproach' (Dyce; cf. *Dial. Dict.* ail v^3). The still more unsatisfactory *of a doubt* in the next line points to the compositor's having difficulty with his copy. It will be convenient to discuss these two presumed corruptions separately. Q3 evidently found *eale* unintelligible, but its *ease* is an obvious makeshift and, being without authority, can give no support to the conjecture *base*. Of the many suggested emendations *evil* is by far the most convincing. (1) It is the word which is the most likely to have given rise to *eale*. Q2 itself has a possible analogy in *deale* for 'devil' (twice) in II. ii. 595. Kittredge and Kökeritz (pp. 188–9) regard both *eale* and *deale* as mere contractions, but if this is all there is to *eale* it is strange that Q3 did not recognize it. Dover Wilson explains them as misreadings of manuscript *eule* (i.e. *evle*) and *deule* (*MSH*, pp. 320–1). The spelling *deule* for 'devil' actually occurs in Q2, III. ii. 127, as well as twice in the manuscript of *Sir Thomas More* in what we take to be Shakespeare's own hand (MSR, Addn II, 176, 179). As there written the word would not be easy to mistake, and there is in any case no such authority for the spelling *eule*. But one can conceive of various ways of writing *evil* (including the common spelling *euile*) which could have led to printer's error. (2) Moreover, *evil* fully satisfies the sense requirement for a word which will stand in opposition to *noble substance*. Cf. Sir Richd. Barckley, *The Felicity of Man*, 1598, p. 568, 'Evil is no substance . . ., but an accident that cometh to the substance, when it is void of those good qualities that ought naturally to be in them, and supplieth the other's absence with his presence'. For the use of *dram* with an abstract cf. *Mer.V.* IV. i. 6, 'any dram of mercy'; *Cym.* III. v. 89, 'A dram of worth'; *FQ*, I. iii. 30, 'A dram of sweet'.

Among the rare attempts to defend *eale*, a recent interpretation would explain it as a fermenting agent, seeking to connect the word with *gyle*, a brewing term for wort in process of fermenting. This would continue the train of ideas in *leaven* and *corruption* and fit the general sense of the passage; but there are difficulties about attributing to Shakespeare in this context a hypothetical variant (*eale*) of a dialectal form (*yele*) (Hulme, pp. 324–6). Word-play on *eale* in this sense and *ev'l* is accepted in a note in the Riverside edition, which nevertheless deserts the former for the latter in its text.

To the vast number of emendations proposed for *of a doubt* – itself an indication that no one of them has been found satisfactory – it is impossible to do justice, beyond the justice of ignoring most. The one thing we can be certain of is that the printer did not understand what he set up. Yet the general sense is clear: the small amount of evil in some way gets the better of 'the noble substance'. In what way depends upon the verb, which interpretation must locate; and it is natural to consider whether *doubt*, though taken by the printer for a noun, may not in fact be it. Boswell thought *doubt* might mean 'bring into doubt or suspicion', but I find no parallel for this. *Doubt* is, however, an acceptable spelling of *dout* (= put out, extinguish): as such it occurs in F in IV. vii. 190 and *H5* IV. ii. 11. Suggestions for a verb which would also incorporate *a* (*adoubt, adopt, abate, adoulter, adote, adaunt, endow, eat out*, etc.) or even *of a* (*overdout, overdaub*) have been singularly unpersuasive. Attempts to keep *doubt* as a noun by finding the verb in *substance* (Corson) or *scandal* (Dowden) strain the syntax beyond credibility. The idea that *Doth* may be the main verb rather than an auxiliary, recently revived by Sisson (*NR*), has more to be said for it if one notes *Meas.* I. iii. 43, 'To do in slander', but still leaves *of a doubt* a problem. The best interpretation of the line as it stands is probably Miss Hulme's 'Renders all the noble substance doubtful' (p. 326), but it leaves us, after *take corruption*, with a feeble anticlimax. It is not a tenable hypothesis that the difficulty is due to the interruption of the Ghost's appearance before the sentence is complete: this is to confuse the distinction between life and fiction. Shakespeare does not deliberately write two lines of nonsense. To take *doubt* as the verb entails emending *of a*, but I see no reason to resist this since these words give difficulty by any interpretation. That they also do so in I. iii. 74 suggests the possibility of a common error but may be a coincidence. The argument whether *of a* could arise from *ofn* as a contraction of *often*, as Greg thinks possible and Sisson not, seems to me to rest on a fallacy: a compositor seeking to force sense, or at least recognizable words, out of what he could not read, would not necessarily achieve letter-by-letter equivalence (cf. his *silly* for F *sallery* at III. iii. 79). This inevitably undermines confidence in attempts to recover the compositor's original. But I see no insuperable objection to the reading adopted here. To object to *often* on the grounds that Shakespeare is referring to something that *invariably* happens is to ignore *oft* in l. 23. Ridley and Sisson among others object to *dout* as implying the total destruction of the 'noble substance'; yet if it rather means, as I suppose, efface (Dowden), obliterate, i.e. render invisible (to public view), *dout* makes excellent sense. And the acceptance of Nashe as a source for this passage gives strong support. As in Nashe (see ll. 23–38 LN) the one imperfection will 'utterly obscure' the good qualities so that they are 'unregarded of any man', so here the little evil in a man causes the essential good to go unperceived. Or, as *take corruption* (l. 35) may suggest, the substance itself is so coloured by the small admixture of evil that it ceases to appear as the 'noble' thing it is. Cf. Ecclesiastes x.1, 'Dead flies cause the ointment of the apothecary to send forth a stinking savour: so doth a little folly him that is in reputation for wisdom and honour'.

This parallel, in which the flies bring the virtuous ointment into bad odour, supports the view that it is the *noble substance* which suffers *scandal* (disrepute) and to which *his own* thus refers.

I.iv.47–9. *thy canoniz'd bones . . . inurn'd*] A traditional motive of the classical ghost was to demand proper burial. The emphasis here upon the due formality, the finality (*hearsed in death, quietly inurn'd*) and the sanctity (*canoniz'd*) of the burial rites makes the appearance of *this* ghost the more unaccountable and gives it moreover the effect of a violation. It is unnecessary to speculate on the precise nature of the rites, but Winifred Nowottny suggests to me a possible reminiscence of those described by Samuel Lewkenor as practised at Würzburg at the funeral of a bishop-prince. The corpse, after a ritual progress through the town, reposed in the cathedral overnight, 'the clergy environing the hearse with many psalms and orisons', was then taken 'to the temple of the new monastery', and 'after many dirges and prayers' was brought back to the cathedral to be 'at length interred' (*Discourse of Foreign Cities*, 1600, pp. 7ᵛ–8).

I.iv.49. *inurn'd*] The supposedly incongruous associations of urns have led this F reading to be condemned (Sisson, *NR*; Bateson, *Sh.Jahr.*, XCVIII, 51 ff.). But an urn need not suggest cremation; the word was poetic for 'grave'. It is used for a resting-place for 'bones' in *H5* I.ii.228. See also *Cor.* v.vi.145 and *OED* urn *sb.* 1, *v.*² b. *Inurned*, not met with earlier, is a word formed in Shakespeare's manner and is much less easily explained as a corruption of *interr'd* (Q1,Q2) than the other way about. I take it that *interr'd* came into Q2 from Q1 (cf. *MSH*, pp. 154, 162), the corruption no doubt the more readily accepted in that *inurned*, an unfamiliar word with a congregation of minims, may have been difficult in the manuscript. The correspondence of the quartos goes against the view that the variants here may represent Shakespeare's own alternative wording (Honigmann, *The Stability of Shakespeare's Text*, p. 135), since a variant belonging to the foul papers should not have got into Q1.

i.iv. 73. *deprive your sovereignty of reason*]   In this use of *deprive* the
direct object is the thing taken away, not, as in the more familiar
construction (as at v.i. 242), the person dispossessed. Cf. *Luc.*
1186, 1752 ('That life . . . which thou hast here deprived'). With
your sovereignty of reason cf. iii.ii. 328, 'your cause of distemper' for
'the cause of your distemper' (Abbott 423). Yet it seems better to
regard *your* as qualifying the whole phrase *sovereignty of reason*,
which refers to the proper condition of man in which reason is
supreme. Cf. *Eikon Basilike*, 'to betray the sovereignty of reason in
my soul'. Bright (p. 61), insisting that the body and vital spirits
are subject to 'the mind's commandment', adds that nature
'commandeth only by one sovereignty: the rest being vassals at
the beck of the sovereign commander'. This 'sovereignty' belongs
to reason, to which the epithet 'sovereign' is therefore applied.
See iii.i. 159. Cf. *Par. Lost*, ix. 1127–30 (after the Fall): 'Understanding rul'd not, . . . in subjection now To sensual Appetite,
who . . . over sovran Reason claim'd Superior sway'.

i.v. 3. *sulph'rous and tormenting flames*]   'Sulphurish flame' is referred to in *Orpheus his Journey to Hell* (st. 45), by R.B., 1595, and,
as a torment of the classical underworld, it is familiar to the stage
ghost of the Senecan tradition (e.g. *Locrine*, iii.vi. 51, 'burning
sulphur of the Limbo-lake'). But Shakespeare sheds the classical
allusions customary with Kyd and others, while revivifying what
accords with contemporary belief. The flames, it would appear
from ll. 11–13, are those of purgatorial fire, of which Aquinas says
that 'the least pain surpasses the greatest pain of this life' (*Summa*,
iii. Appx 1, Q2, a 1), Dante that he would have flung himself
into molten glass to cool him, so immeasurable was the burning
(*Purgatorio*, xxvii. 49–51), and Sir Thomas More, in an intensely
vivid passage, that it 'as far passeth in heat all the fires that ever
burned upon earth, as the hottest of all those passeth a feigned fire
painted on a wall' (*Supplication of Souls, Works*, 1557, p. 337).

i.v. 10–13. *Doom'd . . . purg'd away.*]   The idea of a *purgatorial
expiation* of sins is ancient. Plato's *Phaedo* describes how impure
souls dwell in an infernal lake until purged of their evil deeds; and
in Virgil souls suffer for their former ill-doing until their guilt is
burnt away by fire (*exuritur igni, Aeneid* vi. 742). With so common
an idea we need not look for a particular source, but the phrasing
fast in fires and *burnt and purg'd away* closely parallels that of
More's *Supplication of Souls*, which says of souls that are un-
cleansed that 'in purgatory . . . the *fire* . . . shall . . . hold and keep

them *fast* and *burn* them with incessant pain: *till* the filthiness of their sin be clean *purged* and gone' (*Works*, 1557, p. 321). Ficino explained that at the death of the body, while pure souls ascended immediately to the eternal regions, impure souls, until they had undergone purgation, stayed close to earth and, assuming forms of air, were visible to men. The Catholic doctrine of purgatory gained support from accounts of ghosts which claimed to come from there. But Protestants, who held that the dead went straight to heaven or hell, whence they did not return, saw in these only evidence of the deceits of diabolic spirits. This passage is relied on along with l. 77 by those who contend that Shakespeare gives us a 'Catholic' ghost. Against them Battenhouse, emphasizing the Ghost's unChristian demand for revenge, argues that it is 'a spirit from pagan hell' (*SP*, XLVIII, 163). 'But perhaps even to raise this question . . . is to go . . . beyond what the play calls for. . . . We simply do not need to know the ghost's denomination, and to insist upon it is gratuitous' (R. H. West, *PMLA*, LXX, 1117). Cf. I.ii. 255n. There is of course no suggestion that action on Hamlet's part can ease the Ghost's torment, or that this is what causes it to communicate. Purgation, unlike revenge, is not concerned with this world. Cf. ll. 13–14. But contrast *The Spanish Tragedy* and its like.

I.v.25. *Revenge his . . . murder.*] The one thing certainly known about the pre-Shakespearean *Hamlet* is 'the ghost which cried so miserably . . . Hamlet revenge' (Lodge, *Wit's Misery*). To cry for revenge was the traditional function of the stage ghost which the Elizabethans took over from Seneca (as, e.g., in *The Spanish Tragedy*, *The Misfortunes of Arthur*, *Locrine*, *The Battle of Alcazar*) and which was ridiculed in *A Warning for Fair Women* (printed 1599). But Shakespeare's ghost is no mere theatrical stereotype. For the age-old notion that murderers are pursued by the souls of their victims, going right back to Plato (*Laws*, IX. 865 d), was one of the commonest of popular ghost-beliefs. According to the 1665 addition to the 'Discourse concerning Devils and Spirits' appended to Scot's *Discovery of Witchcraft* (3rd edn), 'such persons as . . . do most frequently appear again' are those who have been 'secretly murthered'; and though such apparitions are normally silent, when 'the murther . . . hath been more than ordinary, horrid, and execrable', 'then the remembrance of the same doth sometimes enable the apparition to frame a voice . . . and discover the fact' (II. 3, pp. 45–6). Cf. Aubrey, *Miscellanies* (1857 edn, p. 95), 'So certainly does the revenge of God pursue the abominated murderer, that, when witnesses are wanting of the fact, the very ghosts of the murdered parties cannot rest quiet in their graves, till they have made the detection themselves'.

I.v. 32–3.   *duller . . . than the fat weed*
                    That roots itself in ease on Lethe wharf]
The whole image is one of torpor. *Dull* in Shakespeare is often applied to sleep (cf. III.ii.221; *Cym.* II.ii.31, 'O sleep, thou ape of death, lie dull upon her'). There is an ironic anticipation of Hamlet's own use of 'dull' in his self-accusations of inactivity (II. ii. 562, IV.iv. 33). The sense of indolent unresponsiveness is reinforced by *fat* (*OED a*.11). This hardly supports the identification of the *weed* with the asphodel or poppy, which were said to grow beside Lethe, and the reminiscence detected by Baldwin (*W.S.'s Small Latine*, ii. 468–70) of Virgil's poppies in Lethean slumber (*Georgics*, I. 78) is surely imaginary. Shakespeare need have had no particular plant in mind. Drayton had written of 'black weeds on Lethe banks' (*Isabel to Mortimer*, l. 31). The (mistaken) defenders of F *rots* as against *roots* (who include Dover Wilson and Kittredge) compare *Ant.* I.iv. 45–7, 'Like to a vagabond flag upon the stream, Goes to and back, lackeying the varying tide, To rot itself with motion'. But the essential idea is quite different: the 'fat weed' – on the bank (*wharf*), not in the water – suggests (1) not motion, but immobility (contrast *stir*, l. 34), (2) not decay but rankness of growth. A more instructive comparison would be with *Ant.* II. i. 27, where 'a Lethe'd dullness' is seen as the result of 'sleep and feeding' (cf. *fat*, *ease*), which put a man's 'honour' in suspense. These are precisely the associations evoked by Hamlet's 'dull revenge' in IV.iv. 33 ff. (*dull*, *sleep and feed*, *oblivion*, neglect of *honour*). The pattern of ideas, emphasizing a mindless and self-indulgent existence, is therefore against *rots* but can well accommodate *roots*. Thriving weeds 'root' through neglect of cultivation in *H5* v.ii. 46. It is thus more reasonable to suppose that Q1 and Q2 unite in the correct reading than that Q2 is contaminated by corruption in Q1. There is no analogy such as Bowers supposes (*SQ*, IV. 51–6) between the *roots–rots* variants and the conjecture *god* for *good* at II.ii. 182.

I.v. 42. *adulterate*]   There has been unnecessary quibbling over an epithet which applies aptly enough to one who is a suborner to and partner in adultery. On the one hand it is objected that only the married partner can commit adultery; on the other it has been shown that unchastity in general and incest in particular were often referred to as adultery. It is true then that from this word *adulterate* alone one could not infer a guilty relationship between Claudius and Gertrude before her husband's death (cf. Joseph, *Conscience and the King*, pp. 16–18). But such a relationship is explicit in Belleforest, and I agree with Bradley (p. 166) and Dover Wilson (*WHH*, pp. 292–4) that it is clearly implied in the account given here. To suppose otherwise is to strain the meaning of 'seeming-virtuous' (l. 46), lose the force of the implied contrast with love that was faithful to marriage-vows (ll. 48–50), and leave ll. 55–7 without point. Moreover, l. 105 suggests that Hamlet, who already knew about the incestuous marriage, had received from the Ghost some new revelation of his mother's wickedness. Confirmation also comes from III.iv.42–7, 66–76; v.ii.64.

I.v.62. *hebenon*] The problems of this are the form of the word and the plant that it refers to. The word is the same as *ebony* (L. *ebenus* or *hebenus*, Gk. ἔβενος, which the Elizabethans often spelt (h)*eben(e)* as well as *ebon*. *The Jew of Malta* (III.iv.98) refers to 'the juice of hebon' as a poison, but even if Shakespeare took it from there and not from a common tradition, a play unprinted till 1633 can hardly have suggested his spelling. If, as seems likely, Q2 derived *Hebona* from Q1, F *Hebenon* may represent the Shakespearean form. Yet Shakespearean texts have *Ebony* (-*ie*) elsewhere (*LLL* IV.iii.243–4, *Tw.N.* IV.ii.38), with *ebon* for the adjective (*Ven.* 948, *2H4* v.v.37). In those instances, however, there is the traditional association of ebony with blackness: the unique form here suggests that Shakespeare may have thought of the poison-juice as belonging to a different plant. There is no evidence that ebony itself was ever regarded as poisonous. Henry Bradley (*MLR*, xv, 85–7) supposed that Marlowe's poisonous 'hebon' derived from a misunderstanding of Gower, who, from the ebony resting-place of the God of Sleep in Ovid (*Met.*, xi. 610), referred to hebenus as a 'sleepy tree' (*Confess.Am.*, IV.3017), and that Shakespeare associated 'hebon' with henbane. But all this, though it persuaded Dover Wilson, is no more than conjecture. It is true that Pliny speaks of pouring oil of henbane in the ears (*Nat.Hist.*, xxv.4), but he gives the result of this as mental derangement not death; and assertions to the contrary notwithstanding, the effects ascribed to henbane in Pliny and Elizabethan herbals show little correspondence with what Shakespeare here describes. Alternative identifications have fixed on guaiacum (*MLR*, xv, 304–6) and especially yew (New Shakspere Soc. *Transactions*, 1880–6, pp. 21 ff., 295 ff.), these being among a number of trees which early writers seem to have referred to as *hebenus*. Yew was known for a deadly poison; it is even called 'cursed' in Holland's translation of Pliny (1600, i. 463); and later accounts of yew-poisoning stress the rapidity of its action and eruptions of the skin. But it is probably a mistake to seek to equate *hebenon* with any familiar plant. No doubt Shakespeare drew on what he had heard or read of well-known poisons, but he surely relied (like Marlowe, to judge from his context) on a suggestion of the fabulous to intensify the horror.

I. v. 85. *Taint not thy mind*]   Most commentators, no doubt guided by the F punctuation, appear to take this as an injunction complete in itself. As such, in contrast with the Ghost's speech elsewhere, it is less than explicit. (Cf. *A Shrew*, xvi. 97, 'Taint not your princely mind *with grief*.') Dover Wilson understands it as a warning against loss of mental control (*WHH*, pp. 46, 209), others as enjoining Hamlet to avoid ignoble passion. I. J. Semper cites Aquinas to the effect that an act of justice may become sinful if hatred mingles in its execution (*Hamlet without Tears*, pp. 19–21. See *Summa*, II. ii. Q 108, a 1). Sister Miriam Joseph argues that Hamlet may avoid such 'taint' by undertaking vengeance as God's agent rather than in personal vindictiveness (*PMLA*, LXXVI, 501). But though Hamlet later refers to himself as heaven's 'minister' (III. iv. 177), it is difficult to read such an idea into the present context. What the Ghost has appealed to is Hamlet's natural feelings as a son (l. 81); and the same 'nature' as stirs Hamlet to avenge his father would bid him spare his mother (cf. III. ii. 384). Punctuation notwithstanding, it seems best to regard 'Taint not thy mind' as part of the injunction concerning Hamlet's attitude to his mother, parallel with 'nor let thy soul contrive'. He is neither to cherish animosity nor to take action against her (cf. P. N. Siegel, *PMLA*, LXXVIII, 149). The distinction between vengeance on the murderer and forbearance towards the guilty wife is also found in *Antonio's Revenge*.

I. v. 157. *Ghost . . . under the stage*]   This episode of the ghostly voice when the Ghost has gone has often been found puzzling. What is puzzling, I take it, after the appalling clarity of the Ghost's own narrative, is the impression now given of something happening beyond what is or can be explained (and the dramatic purpose of this). An eerie aftermath (cf. l. 172) prolongs the awful effect of the apparition even while Hamlet's jocularity, after the solemnity of the actual encounter, gives more than a touch of burlesque; and this 'comic relief' (for in the strictest sense it is that) has, in a manner characteristically Shakespearean, serious and even sinister overtones. The situation and dialogue are pertinently matter-of-fact, and yet have an aura of diabolism. We shall have accepted, along with Hamlet (l. 144), the Ghost's account of its purgatory, and its presence down below will seem to accord with this. But 'under the stage' is the traditional theatrical location of hell, with possibilities of a kind mockingly suggested in Dekker's *News from Hell*, 'Hell being under every one of their stages, the players . . . might with a false trap-door have slipped [the devil] down, and there kept him, as a laughing-stock to all their yawning spectators' (*Non-Dramatic Works*, ed. Grosart, ii. 92). The shifting locality of the voice adds to the impression of a subterranean demon. The familiarity with which Hamlet addresses it may recall the manner in which the stage Vice traditionally addressed the Devil. With the disarming *truepenny* (l. 158) cf. Miles in *Friar Bacon and Friar Bungay* calling his devil 'a plain, honest man'. The Latin tag *Hic et ubique* (l. 164), while literally apt, sounds like a conjuration formula, and, as Coghill has pointed out (pp. 10–11), it is only God and the devil that could be 'here and everywhere' at once. (Cf. *Tw.N.* v.i. 219–20.) It is perhaps not necessary to suppose that *old mole* (l. 170), so pertinent a nickname here, was actually a sobriquet of the devil, as has been contended but hardly demonstrated (see Coghill, loc.cit.; *N&Q*, ccxv, 128–9; ccxvi, 145–6; *ELN*, xii, 163–8), but to 'work i'th' earth' like a 'pioner' was the trick of underground spirits, who in popular belief often assumed the shape of miners. Lavater records how 'pioners or diggers for metal' affirm themselves often to be joined by spirits 'apparelled like unto other labourers in the pit', who 'wander up and down in caves and underminings, and seem to bestir themselves in all kinds of labour' (i.xvi). Reginald Scot (*Discovery of Witchcraft*, 'Discourse upon Devils', ch. 3) refers to alleged attacks by devils upon 'miners or pioners, which use to work in deep and dark holes under the earth'. (Cf. also Taillepied, ch. 13.) Cf. the saying, 'Like will to like, quoth the devil to the collier'; and *Tw.N.* iii.iv. 112, where Satan is called 'foul collier'. Yet a 'pioner' need be no more than a 'fellow in the cellarage'. Whether Hamlet believes, or affects to believe, that he is talking to a devil is perhaps too rational a question. We shall hardly accept Dover Wilson's theory that he is making a calculated attempt to deceive Marcellus into supposing that the Ghost is indeed a devil (*WHH*, p. 80). It is a principle too often neglected in criticism that the dramatist's purposes in his dialogue are not necessarily those of his characters. So the diabolic-seeming voice and Hamlet's 'half-hysterical jesting' (Dowden) may effectually leave still open the question of the Ghost's true nature, and even prepare for II.ii.594–5 ('The spirit that I have seen May be a devil'), but must not lead us to infer, with Dover Wilson (*WHH*, p. 83) and Coghill (pp. 13–14), that Hamlet himself at the present moment has doubts of the Ghost's story. Such a view would conflict with his assertion of the Ghost's honesty, his welcoming its collaboration in the swearing ritual, and with ll. 190, 196–7.

I.v.163 S.D. *They swear.*] When and how many times they swear must, in the absence of a stage-direction, be inferred from the text. Most editors (with Dover Wilson as the exception) defer the swearing till l. 189, presumably on the assumption that as they are about to swear they are interrupted by the Ghost and the consequent shifting of their ground. This would, I think, be the natural assumption from l. 164. Yet they have placed their hands on the cross of the sword (cf. l. 166) and though the text gives them no word (any more than it does at l. 189), it subsequently seems to regard them as actually having sworn. Cf. *again*, l. 166, and *as before*, l. 177. What I therefore think must happen is that the injunction to swear is echoed by the Ghost and obeyed by Hamlet's companions simultaneously. Moreover, Hamlet does not repeat exactly the same oath each time, but as Bradley noted, proposes a fresh variation of it. So they swear silence concerning first what they have seen (l. 161), secondly what they have heard (l. 168), and finally what they know about Hamlet himself (l. 187). Threefold oaths had a particularly binding force (sometimes explained by their invocation of the Trinity), and this one will have still further solemnity from seeming to be sworn at the behest not of Hamlet only but of a supernatural agent also.

II.i.7. *Danskers*] The context leaves no doubt that this, as in modern Danish, means Danes. But a Dansker in Shakespeare's time was strictly a citizen of Dansk or Danzig – as in Purchas (*Pilgrimes*, 1905–7, xii.53) and Fynes Moryson (*Itinerary*, 1907–8, iv.22, 'The English Merchants trading for Poland . . . first had their Staple at Dantzk in Prussen. . . . But when the Dantzkers . . .'). It was easy for the Elizabethans to confuse *dansk* (Danish), *Danske* (Danes) with Dansk (Danzig), Dansker (a Danziger). See G. Langenfelt ('Literary Contributions', *Stockholm Studies in*

Modern Philology, XVII, 1949, and 'Shakespeare's Danskers', *Zeitschrift für Anglistik und Amerikanistik*, XII, 1964), who further suggests that the emergence in the 17th century of the forms *Dansig* and *Dansicker* encouraged the association of *Dansk* and *Dansker* with Denmark. (See also Dollerup, pp. 161–4.) The confusion was not only linguistic. Drayton not merely gives Dansk as the place from which the Angles and Jutes came to England (*Polyolbion*, XI. 189), but, while correctly placing 'Dansig' at the mouth of the Vistula, refers to this as 'the greatest river of Danske', flowing 'into the Sound' (ibid., XIX. 191–2). G. Sjögren ('A Contribution to the Geography of *Hamlet*', *Sh.Jahr.*, C–CI, 1964–5) suggests that it may have been some such confusion that led Shakespeare to suppose that Denmark bordered on Poland (II. ii. 77–8, IV. iv).

II. i. 25. *fencing*]   It is not really strange to find this traditionally noble art listed among the 'slips' of the young. It completes a common pattern of wild living. Claudius will associate fencing with 'light and careless' habits (IV. vii. 75–8). In *The Debate between Folly and Love* appended to Greene's *Card of Fancy* it is joined with play-going, dancing, wrestling, 'and a thousand other foolish sports' (Greene, IV. 218); Nashe in *Pierce Penniless* links it with dancing and tennis among the exercises of 'the unthrift abroad' (i. 209); and Sir Andrew Aguecheek laments time bestowed on 'fencing, dancing, and bear-baiting' (*Tw.N.* I. iii. 88). Gosson had complained that fencers were addicted to quarrelling (*School of Abuse*, ed. Arber, p. 46), and Dekker warned likely victims against being set on 'by fencers and cony-catchers' (*Gull's Hornbook*, *Non-Dramatic Works*, ed. Grosart, II. 213).

II. i. 59. *tennis*]   Often referred to in Elizabethan literature, it was a favourite game of the aristocracy (*Sh.'s Eng.* II. 459–62), and notoriously popular in France. (Cf. *H8* I. iii. 30.) France became almost synonymous with tennis – cf. Dekker, *Gull's Hornbook* (*Non-Dramatic Works*, ed. Grosart, II. 240), 'the sweating together in France (I mean the society of tennis)' – and it was said that there were more tennis-courts in Paris than drunkards in England. That tennis, like fencing, was a typical pastime of youthful roisterers one could infer from the habits of Poins (*2H4* II. ii. 19); the occupations that go with it here are exactly repeated in Tomkis, *Lingua*, III. iv. 10–12, 'I . . . sought you in every ale-house, inn, tavern, dicing-house, tennis-court, stews, and such like places'. See also Nashe, i. 209.

II. i. 71. *Observe his inclination in yourself.*] Variously interpreted. I take it that the servant, sent to report on a superior's conduct, is not to attempt to oppose or influence it, but himself to fall in with it. This interpretation fits, as most do not, the natural parting injunction which Reynaldo accepts it as being. Most comments choose to stress *in yourself* and, ignoring the difficulty of *in*, assume that Reynaldo, besides seeking information from others, is now told to take note himself ('in your own person', Johnson). By contrast J. Torbarina insists that Reynaldo is to perceive the inclination of Laertes by examining his own (*Studia Romanica et Anglica Zagrabiensia*, VI, 3–13; *Eng. Studies Today*, 2, 1961, pp. 248–54). But this fits the words better than the situation (the instruction coming oddly as an afterthought and the two men being disparate in rank).

II. i. 77–100.] The incident of *Hamlet's appearance in Ophelia's closet* has given rise to much perplexity and some groundless inferences. It is often said, e.g., that Ophelia fails Hamlet when he comes to her for support, a view for which evidence is conspicuously absent. Some things, however, are clear. (1) This is the first account of Hamlet's 'transformation' (II. ii. 5), which we do not see until II. ii. 168. The audience are bound to connect it with his intention to 'put an antic disposition on' (I. v. 180), yet are likely to recognize in the 'look' (ll. 82–4) and the 'sigh' (ll. 94–6) an anguish which goes beyond anything put on. Hence the notorious problem of what is and is not feigned, which is by its nature insoluble. (2) The 'transformation' as described here (though not as later shown), while having a germ in Belleforest (see l. 79n.), takes the form of the 'careless desolation' conventionally associated with love-madness. Cf. *AYL* III. ii. 346ff. (esp. 'Your hose should be ungarter'd', etc.); *Gent.* II. i. 65–8; Marston, *What you Will*, I. i. 21, where the man in love is signalized by being 'unbraced and careless drest'. Such signs are necessary here for Polonius to jump to the conclusion not that Hamlet is mad, of which he is persuaded already (see II. ii. 48–9), but that his madness is caused by love. And it is of course the plot to test this conclusion (II. ii. 160–7; III. i. 29–37) that leads to Hamlet's encounter with Ophelia in the 'nunnery' scene (III. i. 88–151). But though many have joined themselves with Polonius in explaining Hamlet's behaviour to Ophelia by her rejection of his letters (l. 109), nothing in the text suggests that (see *HO*, pp. 140–1). (3) The clearest clues to the significance of the episode are the perusal of the face (l. 90) and the parting with eyes turned back upon the woman parted from (ll. 97–100). Deliberately or not, the eyes that 'bended their light' on her echo Ovid's description of Orpheus, *flexit amans oculos* (*Met.* x.57), at the moment of his losing Eurydice when coming back from hell (*MLN*, xciii, 982–9). This is Hamlet's despairing farewell to Ophelia, and emblematically to his hopes of love and marriage, a silent anticipation of what will be uttered in iii.i. Those who ascribe Hamlet's renunciation of love to its incompatibility with a dedication to revenge may point to i.v. 98–104. But there are obviously far deeper motives, among them his disgust with his mother, and with women (i.ii.146), which the Ghost's revelations have intensified (cf. i.v.105).

ii.ii.39 S.D. *Enter Polonius.*]   It was presumably the earlier references to Ophelia's accompanying her father that misled Q1 into bringing her in here with him. Many suppose that Q1, with Ophelia's entry here and with the plan for her to waylay Hamlet (ll. 162–4) followed immediately by its execution and the 'nunnery' scene (iii.i), preserves an earlier version. Comparison of the texts, however, points to Q1 as the derivative one (see Intro., p. 32 n. and Duthie, pp. 206–19). It seems clear that Ophelia's letter was introduced in place of Ophelia in person; and in Q1, no less than in the other texts, the discussion of the letter proceeds as though Ophelia were not present.

ii.ii.90. *brevity is the soul of wit*]   Shakespeare glances at the current stylistic controversy and the cult of brevity in reaction against Ciceronian eloquence (on which see M. W. Croll, 'Attic Prose in the 17th Century', *SP*, xviii, 79–128; G. Williamson, *The Senecan Amble*, 1951). Cf. Campion, *Observations*, 1602, p. 1, 'There is no writing too brief, that without obscurity comprehends the intent of the writer'; Jos. Hall, *Epistles*, 1611, vi.x, 'Brevity makes counsel more portable for memory, and readier for use'. Hence the demand of the anti-Ciceronians, like that of Gertrude (l. 95), is for 'more matter with less art'. Bacon notes it as the first distemper of learning 'when men study words and not matter' (*Advancement of Learning*, i.iv.3). Polonius's statement is itself an example of the sententious style he advocates (but seldom practises).

ii.ii.109–23.]   *Hamlet's letter to Ophelia* rather parodies than represents a typical Elizabethan love-address. From one who is 'the mould of form', its lack of eloquence may seem disappointing. But as a love-letter seen through Polonius's eyes it fits the occasion rather than the writer – or rather, it fits a writer whose mental state is baffling all around him. It is unquestionably an affirmation of Hamlet's love; but it has enough possible double meanings to be ultimately enigmatic. Cf. ll. 116–17nn., and see *SQ*, XXXI (1980), 90–3. It does not confirm, yet does not dispel, suspicions of love-madness. If the question arises – as for most commentators it does – of when Ophelia, who has repelled Hamlet's letters (II.i.109), could then have received this one, we are at liberty to infer that it preceded her father's prohibition. Indeed everything Polonius says is consistent with this. The letter is offered (and accepted, l. 128) as evidence not of Hamlet's present madness but of the love which, frustrated, led to it. The reasons for the production of a letter instead of a mere narrative of events are of course dramatic.

II.ii.110. *beautified*] Though Shakespeare several times uses the verb 'beautify', it is only here that he uses the participial adjective *beautified*. Some commentators, taking it to imply artificially rather than naturally beautiful, have shared Polonius's objection to it. Yet a not uncommon usage is illustrated by the Homily on Matrimony, which says that a virtuous wife shall be 'most excellently beautified before God'. The use of the word in religious contexts (cf. here *celestial, soul's idol*) seems to have been encouraged by confusion with 'beatified'. It may have been fashionable in complimentary addresses: dedications to 'the most beautified lady' and 'the most worthily honoured and most virtuous beautified lady' occur respectively in Nashe's *Christ's Tears* (1594) and the *Diella* of R.L. (1596). They forbid us to regard Hamlet's superscription as wildly extravagant; and though Shakespeare sees it to be vulnerable, by subjecting it to Polonius's criticism he to some degree protects it from our own. Cf. II. ii.494–6.

II.ii.112. *these;*] Many editors retain the Q2 *thus* while transposing the Q2 colon from before to after it, and this, it is true, suits with Polonius's way of demanding attention for what is coming. But the Q2 punctuation seems to regard this word as part of the letter, and *these* (F) is regular form in superscriptions. Malone objected that he had never seen *these* both at beginning and end of a superscription. But this is not the beginning: after Polonius's interruption the sense continues naturally '*To the celestial . . . Ophelia, these*'.

II.ii.137. *winking*]   Q2 *working* is strongly defended by Dover Wilson (*MSH*, pp. 74–5), who cites *LLL* IV.i.33, 'the working of the heart', and *Sonn.* XCIII, and shows that this was a common word with Shakespeare for any operation of heart, mind, or soul (cf. II.ii.548). Yet it is here more probably a misreading, assisted by *work* two lines below, of *winking* (F), which is equally Shakespearean and better fits the context of inaction. With the combination of winking and dumbness cf. *Rom.* III.ii.6–7, where winking of eyes will allow Romeo to be 'untalk'd of' as well as 'unseen'.

II.ii.167 S.D. *Enter Hamlet*]   Dover Wilson's transfer of the entry to l. 159 has no authority beyond his assumption that Hamlet must overhear Polonius's plot in order to provide an explanation for his subsequent behaviour to Ophelia (see esp. *WHH*, 101–14). But the belief that Hamlet's attitude to Ophelia is due to his knowledge of her role as decoy has itself no warrant in the text and in my view rests on a misconception (*HO*, pp. 145 ff. See also *Sh.Jahr.* (West), 1975, pp. 114–15). Whatever his attitude to her is, it has had its first demonstration already (II.i.77–100). Moreover, bringing the entry forward destroys its most essential effect: it is Hamlet's first appearance since his 'transformation' (l. 5), and 'the madness wherein now he raves' has now to be exhibited. The effect of this would be dissipated if, instead of watching Hamlet himself, we had to watch him watching others. One manifestation of the 'exterior' change has already been described by Ophelia, but since her account was of a single extraordinary occasion, it is not a guide as to how Hamlet should now appear on stage. On the contrary, the more sensational gestures and dishevelments of the speechless visit were designed to be described not witnessed and could only have been a distraction from the display of Hamlet's mind through dialogue. That they were, nevertheless, represented in contemporary performance is suggested by Anthony Scoloker's *Daiphantus* (1604, E4ᵛ), 'Puts off his clothes; his shirt he only wears, Much like mad Hamlet'.

II.ii.174. *a fishmonger*]   The shattering incongruity of calling Polonius *a fishmonger* wins an inevitable laugh, establishes Hamlet's 'madness', and might be point enough. But, Kittredge notwithstanding, it is natural to suspect some further implication. The view of Coleridge and others that Hamlet gibes at Polonius for fishing (for information) has provoked the just objection that fishing is not what a fishmonger does. Contemporary references make it easier to see that there was a joke attached to a fishmonger, and especially to having a fishmonger for your father, than to grasp what the joke was. Malone, citing Barnabe Rich, *The Irish Hubbub* ('him that they call *Senex Fornicator*, an old Fishmonger, that many years since engrossed the French pox . . .') is certainly right to say that a fishmonger could mean a wencher (see also *Trivium*, III, 94–100), which is a secondary meaning here (cf. l. 176 n.). But a fishmonger was not only given to venery; he was the cause of venery in others. It is generally supposed, though the evidence falls well short of proof (see Shaaber, *SQ*, XXII, 179–81, but in support M. C. Andrews in *Renaiss. Papers*, 1977, pp. 59–68), that a fishmonger, like a fleshmonger, was a trader in women's virtue, i.e. a bawd; and this sense too, as Dover Wilson insists, has its aptness here when Polonius is planning to 'loose' his daughter to the prince. But more to the present point is the belief that the trade of the fishmonger was a particular stimulus to breeding, as is suggested by a remarkable passage in Sir Hugh Platt's *The Jewel House* (1594): 'Salt doth greatly further procreation, for it doth not only stir up lust, but it doth also minister fruitfulness . . . And Plutarch doth witness that ships upon the seas are pestered and poisoned oftentimes with exceeding store of mice. And some hold opinion that the females, without any copulation with the males, do conceive only by licking of salt. And this maketh the fishmongers' wives so wanton and so beautiful.' This was tentatively cited by Dowden, seemingly without a full grasp of its relevance; but if we perceive that the connection of ideas is salt, sea, fertility of mice at sea, fishmongers' wives, we shall also see that fishmongers' wives, simultaneously beautiful and wanton (cf. III.i.107–14), are not only seductive but fertile. And (with daughter for wife and delivery for conception) this is obviously the point of Venus's remark, in Jonson's *Christmas Masque*, about the birth of her son Cupid, 'He came a month before his time . . . but I was a fishmonger's daughter'. Fishmongers' daughters, it appears, equally with fishmongers' wives, had advantages in the matter of procreation. Hence the deeper significance of *fishmonger* here is to introduce the sequence fishmonger>daughter>breeding (conception). Thoughts of mating and breeding, focusing on Ophelia, are seen to haunt Hamlet's mind. This 'method' of exploiting his madness does not of course imply that Hamlet must be aware of Polonius's plan for Ophelia; to suppose so would be to misunderstand the 'method'. What Hamlet *is* all the time (even obsessively) aware of is that Polonius is Ophelia's father. Cf. below ll. 399 ff., where, with the fishmonger and his daughter replaced by Jephthah and *his* daughter, the same question is raised, about the fate of Polonius's daughter, through the converse illustration. All this prepares for the putting of the question to Ophelia herself (III.i.121–2). For fuller discussion, see 'Hamlet and the Fishmonger', *Sh.Jahr.* (West), 1975, 109–20. Cf. Intro., pp. 150–1.

II.ii.181. *if the sun breed maggots in a dead dog*] For the ancient idea, see Hankins, *PMLA*, LXIV, 507 ff. (or *Backgrounds of Shakespeare's Thought*, pp. 161–71). The sun was regularly thought of as the source of life, as in *FQ*, III.vi.9, 'Great father he of generation Is rightly call'd, th'author of life and light'. The Elizabethans were clear, however, that if the sun's procreative power produced foul and corrupt forms of life, corruption was not in the sun but in that from which the sun bred. Cf. *Ant.* II.vii.26, 'Your serpent of Egypt is bred now of your mud by the operation of your sun'; *Tim.* IV.iii.1, 'O blessed breeding sun, draw from the earth Rotten humidity'. So Stubbes (*Anatomy of Abuses*, New Shakspere Soc., i.79) insists that the 'stench of a dead carcase' comes not from the sun but from its 'own corruption' and that the sun cannot make things 'fouler than they are of their own nature'. Hence Angelo (*Meas.* II.ii.165–8) refers to the carrion which corrupts 'with virtuous season' in contrast to the violet which, growing beside it in the sun, does not. It is a symptom of Hamlet's malaise that he thinks of life's fertility in images of maggot-breeding carrion while the complementary growth of fragrant flowers is ignored. Yet although the present passage links Ophelia with carrion, the play will associate her finally with violets. See v. i.232–3.

II.ii.181–2. *a good kissing carrion*] The sense, correctly understood by Raleigh (*Johnson on Shakespeare*, p. xxv) and well explained by Corson (quoted in Furness, i.149–50), may be brought out by analogy. A good eating apple is one which makes good eating; a good selling car is a model of car which sells well, the car being the thing sold as here the carrion is the thing kissed. Cf. *LLL* i.i.65, 'too hard a keeping oath'. It is because the dog's carcase makes good kissing that the sun can breed maggots in it, or, to put it another way, the production of maggots shows what good kissing it is. The failure to recognize this idiomatic usage and the consequent attempt to take *kissing* as an active present participle has obfuscated the plain sense with a wilderness of comment. Warburton's famous emendation *god*, though called by Johnson a 'noble emendation', still occasionally resuscitated by otherwise reputable editors, and misleadingly maintained by Bowers (*SQ*, IV, 51–6; *SB*, XXXI, 106; cf. I.v.32–3 LN), is as unnecessary as it is unjustified.

II.ii.196. *the satirical rogue*] If Shakespeare had meant a reference to Juvenal, as Warburton and others suggested, he would surely have made a better job of it. The vague resemblance between *Satire* x.188 ff. and what Hamlet purports to be reading is no more than is to be expected of two passages both ridiculing the disabilities of old age. This is equally the case with Guazzo's *Civil Conversation* and Erasmus's *The Praise of Folly*, which have also been identified with Hamlet's 'book'.

II.ii.206. *Will you walk out of the air*] The implication of being out of doors conflicts with earlier indications for this scene, or would conflict if it did not rather afford an interesting instance of the unlocalized stage. Cf. ll. 299–301; III.ii.367–8. A correspondence with *Every Man in his Humour* shows a verbal echo of a play Shakespeare is known to have acted in: Q 1601, I.iv.196–8, '*Biancha*: . . . Come in, out of the air. *Thorello*: How simple, and how subtle are her answers!' Did Shakespeare then play Thorello (Kitely), rather than Lorenzo (Knowell) Senior, as often conjectured?

II.ii.239–69. *Let me question . . . attended.*] The *omission of this passage in Q2* leaves as signs of a cut two consecutive sentences beginning with 'But', an anomalous capital after a semicolon, and a discontinuity of thought. Lines 269–70 ask a question in a way that suggests it has been put before – as indeed it has in ll. 239–41, which provide the necessary link between the discussion of Fortune's treatment of the new arrivals and the reason for their coming. This passage must therefore have been part of the original text and is usually thought to have been suppressed, on account of the derogatory references to Denmark, out of deference to Anne of Denmark, James I's queen. But see Intro., p. 45.

II.ii.249–50. *there is nothing either good or bad but thinking makes it so*] This common reflection was probably given currency by Montaigne's essay 'That the taste of goods or evils doth greatly depend on the opinion we have of them' (1.40). See it also in Spenser, *FQ*, VI.ix.30, 'It is the mind, that maketh good or ill, That maketh wretch or happy'; Donne, *The Progress of the Soul*, ll. 518–20; Robt. Johnson, *Essays* (1601, B1ᵛ), 'All worldly happiness hath his being only by opinion'; etc. See also Tilley M 254. It is clear from the contexts that 'good' and 'bad' here are not a matter of ethics: the inference that Hamlet maintains that there are no ethical absolutes (Levin, *The Question of Hamlet*, p. 75) is false.

II. ii. 298–303. *this goodly frame . . . a sterile promontory, this most excellent canopy . . . vapours.*] For the thought, devoid of its superb phrasing, cf. Bright, p. 106: 'The body thus possessed with the . . . darkness of melancholy obscureth the sun and moon, and all the comfortable planets of our natures, in such sort, that if they appear, they appear all dark, and more than half eclipsed of this mist of blackness, rising from that hideous lake.' It is sometimes suggested that the Shakespearean imagery derived from, and could apply to, the playhouse in which the words would be spoken: the actor of Hamlet on the platform stage actually appeared as on a *promontory*, while 'the heavens', the roof covering the rear part of the stage, with stars painted on its under-side, made visible the *o'erhanging firmamant* (Coghill, pp. 8–9). But in view of the frequent Elizabethan use of *frame, canopy, firmament* in descriptions of earth and heaven, it seems unlikely that Shakespeare needed such inspiration. Descriptions of the glory of the heavens in contrast with the insignificance of man are a classical and Renaissance commonplace, of which the oft-cited passage from Montaigne (III. 12) is merely one example (see esp. A. Harmon, *PMLA*, LVII, 994–6). As often Shakespeare achieves a magnificent result by combining elements, which, taken separately, are almost clichés.

II. ii. 304–6. *in form and moving how express and admirable, in action how like an angel, in apprehension how like a god*] The variant punctuation, once F ceased to be regarded as the superior text, has made this a major crux. The issue is not of course between F's question-marks (for exclamations) and Q2's commas but between different groupings of the words. Either (*a*) in accordance with F man is 'in form and moving . . . express and admirable', 'in action . . . like an angel', and 'in apprehension . . . like a god'; or (*b*) in accordance with Q2 as normally interpreted, man is 'infinite' not only 'in faculties' but also 'in form and moving', he is 'express and admirable in action', is 'like an angel in apprehension', and finally 'like a god' without any qualification. The higher authority is with Q2 as believed printed from Shakespeare's

autograph, and F's handling of the punctuation in general entitles it to little weight. Yet we cannot confidently assume that the
pointing of Q2 reproduces that of its copy, and the editor is
thrown back upon his judgment of the sense. Alexander, accepting the Q2 punctuation, nevertheless insists that Q2 means the
same as F: its commas after *moving*, *action*, and *apprehension* he
regards as 'commas with inversion' indicating a pause for emphasis within the phrase rather than marking off one phrase from
its neighbour ('Shakespeare's Punctuation', *Proceedings of Brit.
Acad.*, 1945, pp. 75–6; *TLS*, 1931, p. 754). Dover Wilson, however, is influenced by the Q2 pointing to maintain interpretation
(*b*). He argues forcibly against action and for apprehension as the
attribute of angels (on which see also C. Bourland in *Smith Coll.
Studs. in Mod. Langs.*, xxi, 6–9; T. Hawkes in *MLR*, LV, 238–41).
Yet this interpretation runs up against serious objections elsewhere, and the sense of the passage as a whole requires (*a*).
(1) Although one may readily accept the hyperbole of 'infinite in
faculties', it is difficult to think of a man as infinite in 'form'. On
the other hand *express* is appropriate for 'form' (as in 'the express
image' of Hebrews i.3) and shows indeed a turn of thought
characteristic of Shakespeare, who joins 'form' and 'pressure' at
I.v.100 and III.ii.24. From L. *exprimo, expressus*, to press out, the
word refers to the clear impression made by a die or seal and so to
the faithful reproduction of an original. Hence it describes a man
as not only well designed but well executed, and so sustains the
idea of a 'piece of work', which can inspire the wonder that leads
on to 'admirable'. (2) To attach 'in apprehension' to 'an angel'
leaves 'how like a god' in rhythmic imbalance. One may grant
Dover Wilson that the absolute 'like a god' would make a superb
climax, and it is true that Pico della Mirandola in the *Heptaplus*,
after ascribing to man the intellectual power of angels, ends by
calling him God's likeness (*Dei similitudo*). Yet the pattern of the
present speech – 'how like . . . in' – seems to require continuation
with 'how like a god' *in* some particular respect. And this would
also be more in line with Hamlet's way of thought. For it is only
when he contemplates the complete ideal in his father that he
sees a man as wholly godlike (III.iv.60–2). Characteristically
when he thinks of man as like a god in some way he laments how
unlike a god he is in others; and the present panegyric is no exception. After an unlimited comparison of man as 'like a god', to
celebrate him as 'the paragon of animals' would be bathos,
whereas to pass from '*in apprehension* . . . like a god' to man as 'the
paragon of animals' shows a natural progression of thought. For

man *is* an animal, as the play elsewhere will tell us (esp. IV. iv. 33–9), yet is raised above other animals by his 'godlike reason', through which he is 'the paragon' of them (cf. Pico, *On the Dignity of Man*, 'Man is rightly . . . thought to be . . . the animal really worthy of wonder' and I. ii. 140 LN). *Apprehension* I take to be the intuitive reason, which is higher than the discursive (cf. I. ii. 150 LN). With Wilson Knight (*Wheel of Fire*, rev. 1949, pp. 338–9) we may compare the faculty which can 'apprehend More than cool reason ever comprehends' (*MND* v. i. 5 ff.) and which links with the creative imagination. Shakespeare is of course drawing on a common stock of ideas and terms (cf. Bright, p. 70, 'the mind, in action wonderful, and next unto the supreme majesty of God, and by a peculiar manner proceeding from himself, as the things are, subject unto the apprehension, and action thereof'): but the combination of them is quite his own. An apparent imitation of the passage in a mock-eulogy of women in Marston's *Malcontent* (I. v), 'in body how delicate, in soul how witty . . .', etc., lends a little support to the F interpretation.

II. ii. 321. *in peace*]   Topical innuendoes have been sought in this reference to *the humorous man*, but although Jonson admits that the original ending of *Every Man Out of his Humour* was not 'relished', it is no more than a conjecture that the audience created a disturbance which prevented Macilente from ending his part 'in peace'. Dover Wilson's explanation that the humorous man was liable to interruption seems no more than a dubious inference from the passage.

II. ii. 322–3. *whose lungs are tickle a th' sear*]   See B. Nicholson, *N&Q*, 4th ser. VIII, 62; Ingleby, *Shakespeare Hermeneutics*, pp. 71 ff. Corrupted in both F and Q1, this phrase, as distinct from 'light of the sear', may not have been familiar. Possibly it was an echo from Howard's *Defensative against the Poison of Supposed Prophesies* (1583), where it occurs twice, while being otherwise unknown (see Harlow, *SEL*, v. 269 ff.).

II. ii. 330–1. *their inhibition comes by the means of the late innovation*]   The fundamental problem is to decide whether the *innovation* is or is not, as traditionally assumed, the emergence of the child actors referred to in l. 337. The chief ground for supposing that it is is that it was so understood by the reporter of Q1, which simply gives, as the reason for the players' travelling, 'Noveltie carries it away, For the principall publike audience that Came to them, are turned to private playes, And to the humour of children'. But against this are (1) the run of the dialogue in the full text, and (2) the meanings of the key words. (1) Although at a glance the account of the children may seem to enlarge upon the 'innovation' which prevents the players from continuing in town, closer consideration suggests that Hamlet asks and Rosencrantz answers two separate questions of which the second gives no sign of arising from the first: the innovation explains why the actors are on tour, the vogue of the children why they have declined in popularity. Mention of the children at once prompts further questions, but the dialogue seems to have accepted the 'innovation' as self-explanatory. Instead of seeking details about that, Hamlet turns to the other topic of the players' reputation (*estimation*, l. 332). (2) A closure due to the loss of audience is not at all the same as the formal ban implied in *inhibition*, so that the telescoped version of Q1 shows the reporter in some confusion, which may extend to *innovation*. In face of Q1 it is difficult to maintain that it could not mean merely 'novelty' (or that child actors, familiar at the Blackfriars twenty years before, could not be regarded as novel); but the word usually connoted a challenge to the established order and often had the specific sense of an uprising. In *1H4* v.i.78 'hurlyburly innovation' is synonymous with 'rebellion' and 'insurrection', and this is also the unmistakable sense in the only other Shakespearean instances, *Oth.* ii.iii.36 and *Sir Thomas More*, MSR, Addn ii, 216, while in *Cor.* iii.i.174 'a traitorous innovator' is 'a foe to the public weal'. It is in this sense that an 'innovation' could well lead to an 'inhibition', and 'the late innovation' implies a past and particular rather than a continuing event (cf. Boas, *Shakespeare and the Universities*, p. 23 n.).

The further problem is then to identify the event. Unless Fortinbras's 'enterprise' (1.i.102) should be thought to qualify, it is not easily traceable in the plot of the play, so that the allusion is generally assumed to be to some contemporary happening. Dover Wilson (NCS, p. 177) and Chambers (*Shakespearean Gleanings*, p. 69) confidently take this to be the Essex rebellion of February 1601. That the word would not be unique in such a context appears from a contemporary letter to Sir Robert Cecil which, referring to 'these late conspiracies' is scandalized by the idea of popular 'innovation' (Hist. MSS Commission, *Calendar of the MSS of the Marquis of Salisbury*, xi.538.) There is no evidence that the rebellion in fact led to a closure of the theatres, wherefore Honigmann (*SS 9*, 27–9), discounting a political interpretation altogether, accepts the oft-held view that the 'inhibition' is the order of 22 June 1600, which forbade more than two playhouses in London. But attempts to connect this with the 'innovation' of child actors are unconvincing. So, I think, is Harbage's supposition (*Shakespeare and the Rival Traditions*, pp. 114–15) that broils occasioned by the theatrical rivalries called forth a warning that an 'inhibition' might follow. But he at least perceives the fallacy of assuming that a topical allusion must show complete correspondence between fact and fiction. That an 'innovation' did not lead to a ban in actuality need not prevent its doing so in the play. It may seem odd that the 'innovation' should have been brought in if no more was to be made of it; but as I see it, Shakespeare, in need of an explanation for the players' travelling, referred it to a political disturbance, and if the passage is rightly dated after February 1601, must have done so in the knowledge, if not with the design, that the audience would instantly identify 'the late innovation' with the Essex rebellion. And this in itself may be why the matter received no further enlargement.

II. ii. 335–58.] These *lines on the child actors* are absent from Q2. Though the contrary view is sometimes taken (as by Honigmann, *SS 9*, 26–9), it is reasonable to suppose, by analogy with the cut at ll. 239–69, that this passage also was cut from the Q2 text rather than added in F. The connection of ideas, I think, puts the matter beyond doubt. Hamlet's question about the players' 'estimation' (ll. 332–3) seems designed to introduce the account of the child actors, and without this account his comment at l. 359 is abrupt. Moreover, although the Q2 text, comparing two changes in popular 'estimation', may read consecutively, as Honigmann maintains, the omission leaves us to compare the players' loss with Claudius's gain. The real comparison between the two cases is in the fickleness of a public favour which readily transfers itself from the old established to the upstart; and the full text is required to bring this out. (See Intro., pp. 2–3.) It is true that a motive for excision is less apparent than with ll. 239–69, and speculation is not profitable; but by 1604 the war of the theatres was no longer a burning topic, and the point has been made that a revival of animosities in print might not have been prudent just when, with the new reign, the boy troupe had been granted royal protection as the Children of the Queen's Revels. The quarto of *Poetaster* (1602) was 'restrained . . . by Authority' from including Jonson's 'Apologetical Dialogue'. See also Intro., pp. 44–5.

II. ii. 338. *on the top of question*]   *On the top of* is often taken (wrongly) in a merely comparative sense. It is not that the cry was above the matter, louder than the question called for (Verity), still less that, in the boys' shrill voices, it was in a higher than natural key (Kittredge); rather that it reached an incomparable height (cf. 'to the top of my bent', III.ii.375, and the idiom 'at the top of one's voice'). The suggestion is thus one of extreme noisiness (cf. *eyases*) and, if *question* may have its frequent sense of 'debate', 'dispute', this continues the notion of wrangling present in *cry out*. In Armin, *A Nest of Ninnies*, 1608, the phrase seems to have merely an intensive force ('making them expert till they cry it up in *the top of question*', Shakespeare Soc., 1842, p. 55); but this, like other phrases in the same work, is almost certainly an echo, and catches the words without the sense. Tucker Brooke (*Tudor Drama*, p. 381) conjectures 'matters of the most absolutely contemporary interest'.

II. ii. 358. *Hercules and his load*]   Hercules was represented bearing a globe because he relieved Atlas of his burden while Atlas fetched the apples of the Hesperides. It is generally believed, on authority which goes back to Steevens[2] (x. 256) and Malone (i(2).54; Boswell, iii.67) that 'Hercules carrying the Globe' was depicted on the sign of the Globe theatre. Although corroboration is lacking, I find it hard to believe that Steevens only conjectured this in an attempt to explain the present passage (see *RES*, n.s. XIX, 51–3). If we may accept it, Shakespeare's word-play not only represents the boys carrying the whole world with them but wittily allows them a complete triumph over his own fellow-actors at the Globe.

II. ii. 375. *I know a hawk from a handsaw.*]   As a proverbial phrase this is not recorded earlier, and so may be a derivative rather than a source of the present passage. But in any event it is a variation on a common type: Breton (*Pasquil's Foolscap*, 1600) refers to one who 'doth not know a buzzard from a hawk'. Among examples in Apperson's *English Proverbs* recorded from the early 15th century are 'to know not A from the gable-end' (alternatively, 'from a windmill'), 'to know not a B from a battledore' (or 'a bole foot', later 'bull's foot'). Cf. *SAB*, XVI, 29–32. Such phrases are commonly in the negative, implying a charge of stupidity, which Hamlet is therefore repudiating. Behind the *hawk* and *handsaw* are often seen (1) a metaphor from falconry, with *handsaw* plausibly regarded as a corruption of *hernshaw* or *heronshaw* (though

Kökeritz will have it to be a 'regular development' from Fr. *heronceau* with an excrescent *d*, *RES*, xxiii, 315–20) and/or (2) a collocation of workmen's implements, with *hawk* explained as a plasterer's tool (though the earliest instance in *OED* is 1700). Yet proverbs often delight to join incongruous items, and with hawk and handsaw, as with chalk and cheese, alliteration is quite as important as likeness or unlikeness. Later variations on Hamlet's pairing include an amusing one found in *A Burlesque Translation of Homer* (1762, etc.), where Agamemnon tells the seer Calchas:

> I don't believe, you mongrel dog,
> You ken a handsaw from a hog. (2nd edn, 1.254–5)

Hence it is not necessary to suppose that the phrase as used by Shakespeare, whatever the fact of its origin, envisages either two birds or two implements. From the double field of reference we may catch a hint that Hamlet sees in his schoolfellows both birds of prey and the King's tools.

Among other attempts to connect the two terms, the suggestion that Falstaff's sword 'hack'd like a handsaw' (*1H4* ii.iv.161) led Shakespeare to *hawk* via a pun on *hack* appears far-fetched. It may be no more than coincidence that in Bright (p. 61) the bird hawk and the saw are actually brought together into a contrast between two kinds of 'instruments' – one dead and destitute of motion 'as a *saw* before it be moved of the workman and a ship before it be stirred with wind', and the other lively and apt for motion 'as the hound to hunt with, and the *hawk* to fowl with'.

ii.ii.397. *For the law of writ, and the liberty*] The paraphrase proposed makes an antithesis between *law* and *liberty* in the matter of writing, or *writ*. But some, less strictly, oppose *liberty* to the whole phrase *law of writ* and so make a distinction between plays with a written text and acting extempore. The rules are usually taken to imply the three unities, in which Shakespeare, however, may have been less interested than his critics. Many, including Sisson (*NR*), suppose him to be contrasting classical and modern; Ifor Evans (*The Language of Shakespeare's Plays*, p. 96) even finds 'the whole contrast of classical and romantic drama' here defined. We must not take too solemnly (or too precisely) words occurring in a speech by Polonius which already mingles sense and nonsense. Its climax seeks to assert the pre-eminence of the actors in all kinds of drama whatsoever, for which *writ*, anything written, is an all-embracing term. But *writ* by a quibble suggests a legal instrument and *law* brings in its opposite, *liberty* (which Polonius perhaps adds as an afterthought), to acknowledge that some writing is without law, though these actors, it appears, can cope with this no less well. *Liberty* has also the sense, inescapable for the Elizabethans, of an area outside the jurisdiction of the city officers – and it was of course in the liberties that plays normally took place. So the actors' proficiency is quibblingly extended to their acting both under authority and without it.

Dover Wilson and Sisson are among those who seek to uphold the Q2 and F punctuation and hence attach 'for the law of writ, and the liberty' to what precedes instead of to what follows. (Wilson links Seneca with 'propriety' and Plautus with 'careless genius'.) But the natural interpretation which makes prowess with both law and liberty a sign of the players' versatility (the theme of the whole speech) is confirmed by Q1, which, while garbling the sense, witnesses to the rhythm and phrasing of the speech in contemporary performance ('For the law hath writ those are the onely men').

II.ii.399. *Jephthah, judge of Israel*] The story of Jephthah was one of the most famous of all Bible stories. As well as being several times balladized, Jephthah figured as a cautionary example in the Homily 'against Swearing and Perjury' (Book of Homilies, 1850 edn, p. 75), as also in *3H6* v.i.91. He had been a favourite subject for the academic drama; Buchanan's Latin tragedy was especially celebrated. (See W. O. Sypherd, *Jephthah and his Daughter*, 1948.) The popular stage would see a Jephthah play by Dekker and Munday (which Henslowe's Diary records) in 1602.

The ballad, apparently much reprinted, is extant in a 17th-century text among the Roxburghe collection (III.201; reprinted in *The Roxburghe Ballads*, vi.685–6) and with a few variants in the Shirburn MS (no. 41; ed. Clark, pp. 174–6). It may also be found in Evans's *Old Ballads*, 1810 edn, i.7–10 and Child's *English and Scottish Ballads*, 1859, viii.198–201. A corrupt version was included by Percy in his *Reliques*. I give the Roxburghe text with three emendations from Shirburn.

A proper new ballad, intituled, Jepha Judge of Israel.

> I read that many years agoe,
>   when *Jepha* Judge of *Israel*,
> Had one fair Daughter and no more,
>   whom he loved so passing well.

And as by lot God wot,   5
It came to passe most like it was,
Great warrs there should be,
     and who should be the chiefe, but he, but he.

When *Jepha* was appointed now,
     chiefe Captain of the company,   10
To God the Lord he made a vow,
     if he might have the victory,
At his return to burn
For his offering the first quick thing,
Should meet with him then,   15
     from his house when he came agen, agen.

It chanced so these warrs were done,
     and home he came with victory,
His Daughter out of doores did run,
     to meet her Father speedily,   20
And all the way did play
To Taber and Pipe, with many a stripe,
And notes full high
     for joy that he was so nigh so nigh.

When *Jepha* did perceive and see   25
     his Daughter first and formostly,
He rent his cloths and tore his haire,
     and shrieked out most piteously.
For thou art she (quoth he)
Hath brought me low, alas for woe,   30
And troubled me so,
     that I cannot tell what to do to doe.

For I have made a vow (quoth he)
     which must not be diminished,
A sacrifice to God on high,   35
     my promise must be finished,
As you have spoke, provoke,
No further care but to prepare,
Your will to fulfill,
     according to Gods will Gods will.   40

22. *with*] and *Rox.*   26. *first*] firm *Rox.*

For sithence God hath given you might,
    to overcome your Enemies,
Let me be offered up as right,
    for to perform all promises,
And this let be quoth she,   45
As thou hast said be not afraid,
Although it be I.
    keep promise with God on high on high.

But Father do so much for me,
    as let me goe to Wildernesse,   50
There to bewaile my virginity,
    three months to bemoan my heavinesse,
And let there go some moe,
Like Maids with me. Content quoth he,
And sent her away,   55
    to mourn till her latter day her day.

And when that time was come and gone,
    that she should sacrificed be,
This Virgin sacrificed was,
    for to fulfill all promises,   60
As some say for aye:
The Virgins there three times a year,
Like sorrow fulfill,
    for the Daughter of *Jepha* still, still, still.

41. *sithence*] silence *Rox.*

II. ii. 423. *chopine*]   The chopine originated in Spain and was very fashionable in Italy, esp. in Venice, where Coryate saw 'many of these chapineys of a great height, even half a yard high' (*Crudities*, 1905 edn, i. 400). Cotgrave defines *choppines* (Fr. *chappins*) as 'a kind of high slippers for low women'. For illustrations see Linthicum, p. 250.

II. ii. 431–2. *the play*]   There is no justification for identifying this with Marlowe and Nashe's *Tragedy of Dido*, which also gives 'Aeneas' tale to Dido' (see ll. 442–3), but from which Shakespeare's version is not taken (see ll. 448–514 LN). This is still true even though Shakespeare may have been influenced by the prominence *Dido* gives to the slaying of Priam and by one or two particular details (see ll. 469–70 LN, 476 LN, 515–16 LN).

II.ii.433. *caviare*] As to its lacking general appreciation, Bullokar (*English Expositor*, 1616) describes '*cavearee*' as 'a strange meat like black soap' and N. Breton (*The Court and Country*, 1618) has a tale of 'a little barrel of "*Cauiary*"' which a countryman sent back to the donor with this message, 'Commend me to my good Lady, and thank her honour, and tell her we have black soap enough already; but if it be any better thing, I beseech her Ladyship to bestow it upon a better friend, that can better tell how to use it'. Harbage (*Shakespeare and the Rival Traditions*, p. 292) comments that *caviare to the general* 'has passed into general currency in a sense quite contrary to the speaker's apparent intention . . . with purveyors of "caviar" receiving the cuff rather than "the general" who fail to relish it'.

II.ii.448–514.] *The Player's speech* has occasioned much controversy. Its primary function is of course to lead on to Hamlet's plot against the King and to give prominence to the players in preparation for their crucial role in it. At the same time it provides occasion for the contrast, elaborated in the soliloquy of ll. 543 ff., between the Player's reaction to a fictional calamity and Hamlet's reaction to a real one. Even more remarkably, though less remarked, Shakespeare takes the opportunity of the Player's speech to introduce in another key many of the motifs of his own play. The 'common theme' of 'death of fathers' (I.ii.104) is exemplified in the archetypal figure of Priam (who had fifty sons). The 'tale' of his 'slaughter' thus lights up the fall of a 'father' (l. 470) in the 'murder' (457) of a king. His deathsman Pyrrhus, 'trick'd' in 'total gules' (453), appears as the blazon of a killer. As a type he is, like Lucianus, ambivalent, embodiment at once of the murderer and (as the son of Achilles) of the avenging hero. In this second aspect his vehemence is the opposite of Hamlet's inactivity. Yet in that he 'stood', with drawn sword frozen, and for a whole line 'did nothing' (478), he temporarily images Hamlet, before his 'aroused vengeance' (484) re-establishes their antithesis. Then the outcry against the 'strumpet Fortune' (489) both echoes Hamlet's earlier reflections (225–36; 359–62) and states a theme for later variations (III.i.57–60; III.ii.67–71, 195–208; IV.iv.49–52). The destruction of Fortune's wheel anticipates another passage on the fall of a king (III.iii.17–22). And finally the description of the mourning queen (498–505), with its resounding climax (511), stresses by its contrast the short-lived grief of Queen Gertrude (I.ii.149–56; III.ii.124–9). The question whether such passages are quotation or original composition, which Kittredge thought 'insoluble', has surely an obvious answer. It is strange that distinguished critics have ever seriously maintained that Shakespeare lifted from some old tragedy, his own or another's, a speech so manifestly designed for the place it has in *Hamlet*. Its reproduction of the play's basic motifs in exaggerated form is also of course the clue to its much-debated style. Dryden, who declined to think it Shakespeare's, objected to its metaphorical excesses (*Essays*, ed. Ker, i. 224–6), and many, following Pope, have regarded it as pillorying bombast. By contrast, Coleridge thought its 'epic pomp' superb (i. 25, 37). Argument has centred on whether the speech is serious or satiric, whether it burlesques or emulates the style of earlier tragedy, and especially Marlowe and Nashe's *Dido*, which like it tells 'Aeneas' tale' (II. i. 126–288) and which it seems to echo at one or perhaps two points, though I think not more. (See l. 454n., 469–70 LN; 476 LN, 515–16 LN; Intro., p. 103.) But identity of subject does not conceal an essential difference of purpose: the speech in Shakespeare has to stand out from the drama which surrounds it and which is already removed from ordinary life; and this, as Schlegel so well saw (*Lectures on Dramatic Art and Literature*, 1815, ii. 197), demands a style which rises above normal theatrical elevation as the latter does above natural speech. This is the simple justification of the hyperbole and high-astounding terms. It is not necessarily incompatible with an element of parody, but the speech stands in too close a relationship to the tragedy which contains it for ridicule to be accepted as a dominant note. Its style, as well as being proper to its kind (as tragedy-within-tragedy), is inseparable from its content and from its purpose in the whole dramatic composition. Extravagance in the language reflects a fine excess in the subject. Priam, Pyrrhus, Hecuba are figures in an inset which exhibits in their most striking and extreme form the attitudes and gestures (of slaughter, vengeance, sorrow, hesitation, etc.) which belong to the larger work in which it is placed. See Intro., p. 145. There is an unfortunate tendency for criticism to seek to relate the speech to Hamlet's motivation; but it belongs less to the hero's design than to the dramatist's. For detailed examination of the speech see Bradley, *Shakespearean Tragedy*, pp. 413–19; Levin, *The Question of Hamlet*, pp. 138–64; A. Johnston, 'The Player's Speech in *Hamlet*', *SQ*, XIII, 21–30.

II. ii. 469–70.   *But with the whiff and wind of his fell sword*
                              Th'unnerved father falls.]
Seemingly a reminiscence (the likeliest one) of Marlowe and

Nashe's *Dido*, 'He . . . whisk'd his sword about, And with the wound thereof the King fell down' (II.i.253–4), where accordingly *wound* is often emended to *wind*. Yet cf. also *FQ*, I.vii.12, where the giant aimed such a blow at the Red Cross Knight 'That with the wind it did him overthrow', and Shakespeare's self-echo in *Troil.* v.iii.40–1, 'the captive Grecian falls, Even in the fan and wind of your fair sword'. *But in Ham.=Even in Troil.*

II.ii.476. *Pyrrhus stood*] Leech supposes this to derive from *Dido*, II.i.263, 'he stood stone still', Shakespeare having transformed the incident by placing 'Pyrrhus' pause' before instead of after the slaying of Priam. ('The Hesitation of Pyrrhus', in Jefferson (ed.), *The Morality of Art*, pp. 45–9.) But the parallel is dubious: in *Dido* Pyrrhus was 'leaning on his sword . . . Viewing the fire'.

II.ii.484. *Aroused vengeance*] The analogy between Pyrrhus and Hamlet is here made clear. But it is a mistaken criticism which says that Hamlet sees himself in Pyrrhus or which discovers in the renewal of vengeance after inaction a new resolution on Hamlet's part. The analogy here (by contrast with that in Hamlet's soliloquy which will follow) is not Hamlet's but Shakespeare's. Though the element of revenge is inherent in the story of Pyrrhus (his father Achilles had been slain by Priam's son Paris), it receives little stress in Virgil or the medieval writers. It becomes conspicuous, however, in some of Shakespeare's predecessors – momentarily in the Marlowe–Nashe *Dido* (II.i.259–60) when Pyrrhus dips 'his father's flag' in Priam's blood, more notably in Peele's *Tale of Troy*, where 'Achilles' son, the fierce unbridled Pyrrhus', 'his father's angry ghost enticing him', kills in 'murdering rage' (ll. 440–4).

II.ii.497. *Hecuba*] 'Hecuba, the woefullest wretch That ever lived, to make a mirror of' (*Gorboduc*, III.i.14–15). Shakespeare in some famous stanzas in *Lucrece* had shown her, 'staring on Priam's wounds', as the emblem of 'all distress and dolour' (1444ff.). One of the great heroines of Greek tragedy, she had always been recognized as the extreme type of sorrow (cf. ll. 515–16 LN); but her pre-eminence in classical literature owes much to her further afflictions after Priam's death. The woes of Hecuba do not form part of 'Aeneas' tale to Dido' in Virgil nor in the *Dido* of Marlowe and Nashe. In Caxton and Lydgate (*Troy Book*, IV.6422ff.) at the fall of Troy she flees with Polyxena not knowing where to go. Even in Peele, where the transition from

Priam's death to Hecuba's 'tears' seems to anticipate Shake-speare, she is thought of as 'thrice-wretched' because of what 'did after her betide' (*Tale of Troy*, ll. 458–63). In *Locrine* (III.i.43–53), which also passes from Priam to Hecuba, she weeps for Troy and for her children 'murdered by wicked Pyrrhus' bloody sword'. Shakespeare's unique emphasis upon her grief for Priam is significant of his purposes here.

II.ii.515–16. *has tears in's eyes*] There is no reason to ascribe (with Leech, loc. cit., p. 47) the Player's tears to an influence of the Marlowe-Nashe *Dido*, where Aeneas simply stops his tale from exhaustion due to 'sorrow' (II.i.293). In *Hamlet* there is weeping by the Player in his own person; and it is a mistake to seek any particular source for the tears, which were held from ancient times to be a sign of the good actor. Celebrated in the Greek Ion (Plato, *Ion*, 535), they are also reported of Roman actors by Cicero (*De Oratore*, II.xlv.189) and Quintilian (*Inst.Orat.*, VI.ii.35–6), the last of whom gains further currency through Montaigne (*Essays*, trans. Florio, III.4): 'Quintilian reporteth to have seen comedians so far engaged in a sorrowful part that they wept after being come to their lodgings; and of himself, that having undertaken to move a certain passion in another, he had found himself surprised not only with shedding of tears, but with a paleness of countenance [cf. *turned his colour*], and behaviour of a man truly dejected with grief.' Cf. ll. 548–51. Among those whose woes it affected Ion to recite were Hecuba and Priam; and, to pass from actor to spectator, it was 'the miseries of Hecuba', seen in a performance of the *Troades* of Euripides, that drew tears from the tyrant Alexander of Pherae, who had himself killed many people totally unmoved. Plutarch's account of this (in the Life of Pelopidas, *Lives*, Tudor Trans., ii.323) is remembered by Montaigne (II.27) and cited by Sidney as an instance of the power of tragedy. Marston's reference to 'a player's passion' weeping for 'old Priam When fell revenging Pyrrhus . . . mangles his breast' (*The Insatiate Countess*, I.i) is presumably, like the 'player-like' weeping of *Antonio's Revenge* (see Intro., p. 10), a recollection of *Hamlet*.

II.ii.535–6. *a speech . . . insert*] The voluminous attempts to locate the speech in the Gonzago play are only a degree less absurd than speculations about how the players came to have this play at all. Clearly we are to suppose that there is already in their repertory a play which 'comes near the circumstance' of

Hamlet's father's death (III. ii. 76–7) and which Hamlet adapts, by an inserted speech, to point its application. But it does not follow that the inserted speech must be identifiable in the Gonzago play as we have it in III. ii. It has been pertinently observed that in *MND* the play of Pyramus as presented before Theseus does not include the lines that occur in its rehearsal. But cf. III. ii. 183–208 LN, 249–54 n.

II. ii. 583. *scullion*] Q2 *stallyon* (=male whore) is accepted by Dover Wilson and (=whore) by Parrott-Craig, but the 'whore' and 'drab' of the context, which they take to authenticate this, would assist the misreading of *sc* as *st*, which is one of the easiest to make in the secretary hand. What looks like the same error, *stallion* for *scullion*, is found in *The Birth of Merlin*, II. i. 140. Some confirmation comes from Q1 *scalion*, which points to pronunciation. The Q2 copy may have spelt *scallyon*, as it presumably did *sallied* at I. ii. 129 and *sallies* at II. i. 40. The spelling *scallion-fac'd* occurs in the Beaumont–Fletcher Folio *Love's Cure* (II. i. 74).

II. ii. 585–8. *guilty creatures sitting at a play . . . have proclaim'd their malefactions*] North's Plutarch associates a 'guilty conscience' with the unsuppressable emotion which caused Alexander of Pherae to leave the theatre during a performance (cf. above, ll. 515–16 LN). But the closest analogies here are with the self-betrayal of those who witness an actual image of their own crimes (cf. ll. 590–3 and Claudius's exit at III. ii. 264). Various instances are reported, which playwrights liked to cite as evidence of the drama's power. *A Warning for Fair Women* (anon., pubd. 1599) recounts how at Lynn in Norfolk a woman was so moved by watching a guilty wife in a tragedy that she confessed to having murdered her own husband (sig. H2; Bullough, p. 181). This play had been 'lately' acted by Shakespeare s company and seems to have been echoed by him, though the story was apparently well known. (See Intro., p. 103.) The same incident is related in Heywood's *Apology for Actors*, 1612, G^v–G2^v, which names the players as Sussex's men and the play as *Friar Francis*, which Henslowe's Diary shows Sussex's to have been acting in London in 1593. Heywood adds another instance said to have happened at Amsterdam when some English players acted *The Four Sons of Aymon* (mentioned by Henslowe in 1602 but probably older). It was perhaps the influence of Shakespeare as well as such examples from the life that led Massinger to make the hero of *The Roman Actor* boast of a similar occurrence (II. i. 90–5). In *Der Bestrafte*

Brudermord Hamlet himself cites a particular case alleged to have happened in Germany at Strasburg.

II. ii. 595–6. *the devil hath power T'assume a pleasing shape*]   Le Loyer (III. 7) quotes Chrysostom to the effect that when an apparition claims to be the spirit of a particular person, one should suspect a deception of the devil. That the devil can appear in the likeness of a good man 'we need not doubt at all', says Lavater (II. ix), supporting his case with many references to the scriptures and the Fathers. While admitting that ghosts may be 'either good or evil angels', he supposed them normally to be diabolical; and James I insisted that they were invariably so. 'What means then these kind of spirits, when they appear in the shadow of a person newly dead. . . . Amongst the Gentiles the Devil used that much, to make them believe that it was some good spirit that appeared to them. . . . And this way he easily deceived the Gentiles. . . . And to that same effect is it, that he now appears in that manner to some ignorant Christians' (*Demonology*, III, ch. 1). Only the ignorant could imagine that a good angel might assume such a form or that the spirit of a dead man might return. Sir Thos. Browne (*Religio Medici*, I. 37) believed 'that those apparitions and ghosts of departed persons are not the wandering souls of men, but the unquiet walks of devils, prompting and suggesting us unto mischief, blood, and villainy.' Nashe (in *The Terrors of the Night*) specifies the shape of a father, mother, or kinsman as that in which the devil often appears in order that his victim shall the sooner hearken to him (i. 348). For other expressions of this belief, see Stoll, *Hamlet: an Historical and Comparative Study*, 1919, pp. 47–8. See also nn. on I. ii. 244, 245, I. iv. 40, 43, I. v. 54.

II. ii. 597. *Out of my . . . melancholy*]   'They say spirits appear To melancholy minds' (Fletcher, *The Night Walker*, III. ii. 5–6). Cf. Taillepied, ch. 3, 'Ceux qui sont mélancoliques . . . s'impriment en la fantaisie plusieurs choses merveilleuses et terribles'; *The Terrors of the Night* (Nashe, i. 354), 'From the fuming melancholy of our spleen mounteth that hot matter into the higher region of the brain, whereof many fearful visions are framed'. So the devil, in assuming a false shape, may be exploiting Hamlet's own 'weakness'. As Nashe says, 'The Devil when with any other sickness or malady the faculties of our reason are enfeebled and distempered, will be most busy to disturb and torment us' (i. 348). See Babb, *The Elizabethan Malady*, pp. 108–9, 49–53; Prosser,

p. 110. Accordingly it is not necessary to connect this passage with Belleforest; but see Intro., p. 95.

Melancholy of course was not merely a depression of spirits but a well-recognized disease supposedly arising from an abnormal preponderance of the one of the four bodily humours after which it is named. The word, however, like the complaint, was fashionable and had a wide range of meaning, from a transitory mood of dejection to a chronic condition indistinguishable from madness (see Burton, *Anat. of Melancholy*, I.i.1 (iv)). In the latter stricter sense Burton takes it commonly to denote 'a kind of dotage without a fever, having for his ordinary companions fear and sadness, without any apparent occasion' (I.i.3 (i)). Burton's book is only the most famous in the vast Renaissance literature on the subject. For Bright's *Treatise of Melancholy* (1586) see Intro., pp. 106–8. In modern criticism there has been much discussion of Hamlet as an example of the melancholic type. But although this is often illuminating (cf., e.g., nn. on II.ii.243, 256, 298–303; and see B. G. Lyons, *Voices of Melancholy*, 1971, ch. 4), the formulistic approach unduly restricts the characterization. It is perhaps as well to observe that though the word (in its full range of meanings) is a common one in Shakespeare, this is the only instance of its use by Hamlet to describe his own condition. It is used by the King at III.i.167.

III.i.56–88.] *To be, or not to be, that is the question*—This celebrated speech is, I suppose, the most discussed in Shakespeare, and the most misinterpreted. It is impossible to review the literature on it here. Earlier criticism is excerpted in Furness; a subsequent article useful for its abundant citation, though its own interpretation is quite unacceptable, is Irving T. Richards, 'The Meaning of Hamlet's Soliloquy', *PMLA*, XLVIII, 741–66; and some recent views are conveniently summarized by V. F. Petronella in *SP*, LXXI (1974), 72–88. There have been two fundamental disagreements. First, from Warburton, who thought of this as a speech about 'self-murder', a continuous tradition passes through Malone, Bradley, and Dover Wilson to the recent editor (Ribner) who pronounces quite simply that 'Hamlet is thinking of suicide' (cf. Petronella, p. 79; 'Suicide is Hamlet's concern in the great soliloquy of III.i'); and yet against this prevalent (but to my mind misguided) view are some who deny that the soliloquy is primarily concerned with suicide, or even that it refers to suicide at all. (For the view that the 'bare bodkin', l. 76, is meant not for the speaker but his opponent, see esp. I. T. Richards, loc. cit.). Secondly, opinion is divided on whether Hamlet is discussing his individual dilemma or whether, as Kittredge insists, 'the whole course of his argument is general, not personal'. Ranging from the general to the particular the main views may be categorized as follows: (1) The 'question' of 'To be or not to be' concerns the advantages and disadvantages of human existence, the discussion of which includes the recognition of man's ability to end his existence by suicide. (2) The 'question' concerns the choice between life and death and hence focuses on suicide throughout. (3) The 'question' is whether Hamlet shall end his own life. (4) It is whether Hamlet shall kill not himself but the King. (As between 'the proposed killing of Claudius' and 'the killing of himself', Wilson Knight ultimately decides in favour of both – *The Wheel of Fire*, rev. 1949, p. 304.) (5) Still more particularly, the 'question' is not simply whether Hamlet shall pursue revenge against the King but whether he shall proceed with the actual scheme (for the performance of a play) which he has already set in motion. (For this see esp. Alex Newell, 'The Dramatic Context and Meaning of Hamlet's "To be or not to be" Soliloquy', *PMLA*, LXXX, 38–50.) The argument (as in Newell) that dramatic effect demands the interpretation of the speech in relation to its immediate context is specious. The dramatic force of the speech comes rather from its enabling us to see Hamlet's situation in its most universal aspect. Any strict reading – one, that is, which adheres to the text without adding to it – must come close to (1).

Most difficulties have arisen through the temptation to supply what Hamlet himself does not. Johnson's famous observation that the speech 'is connected rather in the speaker's mind than on his tongue' has given too ready a licence to subjective ingenuity. The lack of coherence can easily be exaggerated, as in the desperate and wholly unjustifiable assumption that vaguely defined thoughts are carried on 'a current of feeling which is the main determinant of meaning' (Knights, *An Approach to 'Hamlet'*, pp. 74–80). Most commentators, Johnson among them, have found it perfectly possible to trace out a train of thought. That their results have diverged widely is due in large part to the different additions they have made to what Hamlet actually says. When Johnson begins his paraphrase, '*Before I can form any rational scheme of action under this pressure of distress*, it is necessary to decide whether, *after our present state, we are* to be, or not to be', it is easy to see that the words 'after our present state' are an addition which transforms 'the question' altogether. Yet Johnson's other addition – 'Before I can form any rational scheme of action' – has been less frequently remarked on. Indeed Malone, who castigated Johnson's 'wrong' beginning, appears to have accepted and even shared the error of applying the speech to the speaker's personal problems. Hamlet, he retorts, 'is not deliberating whether after our present state we are to exist or not, but whether he should continue to live, or put an end to his life'. Yet nothing anywhere in the speech relates it to Hamlet's individual case. He uses the pronouns 'we' and 'us', the indefinite 'who', the impersonal infinitive. He speaks explicitly of 'us all' (l. 83), of what 'flesh' is heir to (63), of what 'we' suffer at the hands of 'time' (70) or 'fortune' (58) – which serves incidentally to indicate what for Hamlet is meant by 'to be'. The numerous interpretations which depend on equating 'To be or not to be' with 'To act or not to act' take a wrong direction from the start. (Apart from Richards and Newell, loc. cit., see Prosser, pp. 160–71 (162–73) and for an extreme example Middleton Murry, *Things to Come*, p. 231, 'What is "to be or not to be" is not Hamlet, but Hamlet's attempt upon the King's life'.) Far from seeking to determine his own course, Hamlet is debating a 'question' and a question which in various aspects (e.g. that it is better to be unhappy than not to be at all) was traditionally debated in the schools (cf. Augustine, *De Libero Arbitrio*, III, chs. 6–8). The word 'question' itself is a customary one to denote the subject posed for argument in academic disputations or, it is interesting to note, at the moots of the Inns of Court (see D. Legge in *Studies in Honour of Margaret Schlauch*, pp. 213–17). And though 'the question' invites a verdict, this is not a matter for enactment but (as is clear when we go on 'Whether 'tis nobler . . .') of evaluation.

At the same time as we reject interpretations which give the speech a particularity it does not claim, we must equally resist those which distort the general proposition by irrelevant metaphysics. Thus, while one may accept a distinction between being and mere existence – Hamlet himself can recognize that human life is more than 'to sleep and feed' (IV.iv.35) – we need not include in *being* all Max Plowman would associate with 'consciousness' (*The Right to Live*, pp. 156 ff.); still less should we read into 'To be or not to be' the Boethian identification of being with goodness and evil with not-being (Knights, pp. 76–7) or the metaphysical problems of identity, self-fulfilment, or essence (Prosser, pp. 159–64 (161–6)). All such attempts to refine on Hamlet's question are doomed to founder as soon as the speech develops.

The 'question', then (crudely paraphrased as 'Is life worth living?') is essentially whether, in the light of what *being* comprises (in the condition of human life as the speaker sees it and represents it in what follows), it is preferable to have it or not. There is no reference here to suicide, nor even as yet to death. Nevertheless, since the question can only present itself to one who already has being, the implicit alternatives are those of continuing 'to be' and ceasing 'to be', so that the idea of death is already implied and as soon as 'the question' is amplified at once becomes explicit (*end*, l. 60). For of course we come to the end of life's 'troubles' not when we put an end to them but when they put an end to us (see below, ll. 57–60 LN). Hence the alternatives are to 'suffer' or to 'end', to endure or to die; and these are what the body of the speech discusses. From the cessation of troubles, it passes naturally enough to the attractiveness of dying (60–4), expressed in the familiar association of *end, consummation, sleep*. There is still no hint of suicide; but the idea of death's attractiveness leads no less naturally to the thought of how easily it may be come by and so to the 'bare bodkin' (76). Suicide is thus introduced – for the first time – in the question which begins at l. 70. But this is a rhetorical question, which already presupposes its answer, a hypothetical question brought in only to be dismissed – as, when the question is repeated (76 ff.), it quite explicitly is (*But that . . .*, 78). And its dismissal comes as naturally as its introduction; for the metaphor of death as sleep has been extended from *sleep* to *dreams* (65–6), which bring in the after-life and hence the 'rub' (65), the 'respect' (68), which determines the argument's course. The impulse to suicide is frustrated before it is even formed: before the consideration of it begins at l. 70 it is already preempted by the 'pause' of l. 68. It is impossible therefore to say that Hamlet ever contemplates suicide for himself or regards it as a likely choice for any man. The alternative meantime is made vivid by allusions throughout the speech to what life causes us to endure: the 'slings and arrows' of l. 58, the 'shocks that flesh is heir to' (62–3), the injustices listed in ll. 70–4, the 'fardels' we 'bear' (76) and the 'ills we have' (81). The soliloquy holds in skilful balance the opposites of life and death, the desire for death and the fear of death, the pains of death and the pains of life. But the conclusion to the debate is clear. Notwithstanding that the condition of human life prompts a longing for death, we 'rather bear' (81) the life we have. The 'question' is apparently decided: the alternative we choose is 'to be', 'to suffer', to 'bear'. And the whole is pithily summed up in the aphorism of l. 83: the conscience which makes us afraid of death because of the after-life causes us to go on living. This conclusion has of course this paradox: we do not so much choose one of the alternatives as passively accept it from fear of embracing the other; so that the question of which was 'nobler' (57) ends with the recognition, in the word 'cowards' (83), of what is the reverse of noble in our attitude to both.

I do not know why it should be made an objection to this speech that it lacks *logical* connection when the progress of its ideas is so supremely natural and lucid. The links, however, have sometimes been obscured by local misapprehensions. See esp. ll. 57–60 LN, 83 LN.

Some difficulty has also arisen at l. 84 from the transition to a new topic which the repeated 'thus' may disguise. The first *thus* (83) introduces, I take it, the conclusion which follows on all the preceding discussion: and with this the reflections prompted by the initial 'question' come to an end. But at the same time they lead, with the second *thus* (84), to a further reflection on a kindred matter in which the same trait of human nature may be seen. In fact the frustration of the impulse to seek death now offers itself as a particular example of a general tendency in men for any act of initiative to be frustrated by considerations which it raises in the mind. See below, l. 83 LN.

The failure of resolution to translate itself into action is an important motif which will recur at III. ii. 182–208 and IV. vii. 110–22. The lines which state it here (84–8) are of course among the most famous in the play because of the use to which they have been put in the description of Hamlet himself. It is important to remember that Hamlet himself does not so use them; he still makes no reference to his own case. Yet the drama which contains him permits, even invites us, as readers or spectators, to make the connection, very much as it has used the account of Pyrrhus (II. ii. 448–514), which likewise makes no mention of Hamlet's situation, to provide another perspective on it. On the present speech Coleridge comments that it is 'of such universal interest' and yet, among all Shakespeare's characters, could have been 'appropriately given' only to Hamlet (i. 26). Others, from Johnson to Kenneth Muir (*Hamlet*, pp. 34–5), have stressed that the ills it associates with human life do not correspond with Hamlet's experience in the play. Both views, I think, are right. Unlike all Hamlet's other soliloquies this one is not concerned with his personal predicament; yet the view of life it expresses is not an impartial or objective one such as we might ascribe to Shakespeare, but just such a view as one in Hamlet's dramatic predicament might hold. It is the view of one who began the play with a sense of 'all the uses of this world' as 'weary, stale, flat, and unprofitable' (I. ii. 133–4), of one who knows that his virtuous father is dead and his wicked uncle in possession of his father's queen and realm. It is a man in Hamlet's predicament who sees the world as 'an un-weeded garden' possessed by 'things rank and gross in nature' (I. ii. 135–6), who will regard the goodly earth as 'a sterile promontory' and the majestical firmament above it as a 'pestilent congregation of vapours' (II. ii. 298–303). The same vision will present the life of a man as a series of 'troubles', 'shocks,' 'fardels', 'ills' from which death – if it were only the end – would be a welcome release. This is what gives the speech, as it debates the pros and cons of human existence, its justification, and its power, in this place near the centre of the play. And although it looks beyond and never at the particular plans that Hamlet has afoot, it is not perhaps without relevance to the mood in which he now encounters Ophelia. See also Intro., pp. 141, 149.

For all their brilliant use, the ideas of the speech are for the most part traditional. Even the outline of its argument has its anticipation in Augustine (*De Libero Arbitrio*, III. vi. 19, 'It is not because I would rather be unhappy than not be at all, that I am unwilling to die, but for fear that after death I may be still more unhappy'). The likening of death to a sleep (ll. 60–6) (cf. *Meas.* III. i. 17; *Mac.* II. iii. 74; *2H4* IV. v. 35) was a Renaissance commonplace descending from such works as Cicero's *Tusculan Disputations* but often referred back to Socrates. It is found, among other places, in Cardan's *De Consolatione* (*Comfort*, trans. Bedingfield, 1573, D2), sometimes regarded as a direct source; in Holland's translation of Plutarch's *Moralia* (1603, p. 516); and in Montaigne's *Essays* (III. 12). For its classical origins, see Anders, *Shakespeare's Books*, p. 275. It was in the tradition of the ancients that Cardan thought of death as like a sleep in which 'we dream nothing', and Montaigne, here explicitly recalling Socrates, says, 'If it be a consummation of one's being, it is also an amendment and entrance into a long and quiet night. We find nothing so sweet in life, as a quiet rest and gentle sleep, and without dreams' (III. 12, Florio's trans.). By contrast Shakespeare, characteristically seeing both sides, thinks also of the possibility of dreams. But in adapting the metaphor accordingly he uses what is of course an equally traditional thought. The Homily against the Fear of Death sees 'the chief cause' of fear in 'the dread of the miserable state of eternal damnation' (Book of Homilies, 1850 edn, p. 90).

Cf. l. 78. For other traditional ideas, see notes on ll. 80, 83, and for a possible anticipation in Belleforest, Intro., p. 95.

III. i. 57–60.   *Whether 'tis nobler in the mind to suffer*
                  The slings and arrows of outrageous fortune,
                  Or to take arms against a sea of troubles
                  And by opposing end them.]

The bearing of these lines has been very frequently misunderstood, with a consequent failure to grasp an essential link in Hamlet's train of thought. Syntactically the lines are in apposition with l. 56, the *or* of l. 56 being paralleled by the *Or* of l. 59. An assumption (as in Knights, p. 78) that the 'whether' clause is adverbial ('That is the question', irrespective of whether . . .) is conclusively refuted in New Shakspere Soc. *Transactions* 1887–92, pp. 48*–52*. The alternatives put by 'the question', then, are now restated in metaphorical and amplified form. The difficulty arises because the alternatives do not appear at first sight to correspond: a choice of 'to suffer' or 'to take arms' does not seem the equivalent of 'to be or not to be'. Both are modes of being. Yet the second, 'to take arms', will inevitably lead to not-being, since paradoxically our troubles will then be ended not by our destroying them but by their destroying us. That Hamlet could possibly mean that by fighting against his troubles a man could overcome them would have seemed to me a very naïve view were it not for the number of distinguished critics who have apparently held it. (But in splendid contrast see Browning, *apud Transactions*, as cited above.) Hamlet believes that troubles and being are co-extensive, as this whole soliloquy shows; and the very concept of fortune (l. 58) supposes that a man is subject to it throughout life. If he could by fighting win, it could hardly be seriously questioned which were the 'nobler' course. The absurd futility of the contest is what Shakespeare's much-abused metaphor of taking arms against a sea very vividly suggests. (Cf. *Tp.* III. iii. 61–4, which mocks at the folly of trying to wound the winds or kill the waters with a sword.) The metaphor appears to be based upon well-known instances, notably that of the Celts, who, as described by various ancient authors, rather than show fear by flight, would draw their swords and throw themselves into the tides as though to terrify them. Shakespeare could have found this in Abraham Fleming's translation of Aelian (*A Registre of Hystories*, 1576, fol. 127^v); but other accounts make it clearer that the Celtic warriors perished in the waves (see New Shakspere Soc. *Transactions*, as above). Hence the true significance of 'end them' does not admit of doubt. It is precisely because the heroic gesture is necessarily disastrous that argument becomes possible about whether it is noble. This question had actually been raised, and pronounced upon, by Aristotle: 'A man . . . is not brave . . . if, knowing the magnitude of the danger, he faces it through passion – as the Celts take up their arms to go to meet the waves' (*Eudemian Ethics*, III. I. See also *Nichomachean Ethics*, III. 7). Shakespeare does not disagree with this; but it is not a case in which Aristotle has the last word.

III. i. 80. *No traveller returns*]   Some clever critics, remembering the Ghost, charge Shakespeare with inconsistency. Others, following Spalding (*Elizabethan Demonology*), exculpate him by observing that Hamlet has just expressed doubt of the Ghost's authenticity (II. ii. 594 ff.), even seeing here an affirmation of the Protestant view that ghosts are a deception of the devil. W. J. Lawrence, following Robertson, supposed the whole soliloquy misplaced, holding that Hamlet should properly speak this before he has seen the Ghost (*Speeding up Shakespeare*, pp. 57–9). Dover Wilson took it to show that Hamlet had now given up belief in the Ghost (*WHH*, p. 74; NCS, p. lii. So too Ribner). With the play-scene still to come, that *would* be inconsistent. If it were necessary we could retort to all this that a ghost under compulsion to vanish at cockcrow to be 'confin'd . . . in fires' (I. v. 2 ff.) can hardly be regarded as a 'traveller' who 'returns'. The truth surely is that we must not, and we do not (as Hamlet himself does not), connect the Ghost at all with this general reflection. Shakespeare allows Hamlet to utter it because it is what would occur to any well-read Renaissance man meditating upon death. (Cf. Prosser, p. 166 (168).) The metaphor of the journey with no return is in Catullus (III. 11–12), several times in Seneca (e.g. *Hippolytus*, 93, 625–6; *Hercules Furens*, 865–6), and in the Bible (e.g. Job x. 21; cf. Wisdom of Solomon ii. 1, 'neither was there any man known to have returned from the grave'). Cardan thinks of a dying man dreaming 'that he travelleth in countries unknown without hope of return' (*Comfort*, 1573, D3ᵛ). La Primaudaye, speaking of souls after death, says that we do not know 'into what country they go: because no body as yet ever brought any news from thence' (*The French Academy*, 1618, p. 596). Cf. also Marlowe's *Edward II*, where the condemned Mortimer 'as a traveller Goes to discover countries yet unknown' (v. vi. 65–6). Ingleby (*Shakespeare Hermeneutics*, pp. 91–2) would trace the image back to 'the allegorical country of the Meropes' described by Aelian, within the bounds of which was 'a place called Anostum', signifying a place from which there was no return.

III.i.83. *conscience*] Of the two senses the first is exhibited in *R3* I.iv.134, 'it makes a man a coward', v.iii.179, 'coward conscience', and v.iii.309; the second in *Tim.* II.ii.176–7, 'Canst thou the conscience lack To think I shall lack friends?' The choice between the two has been much debated. (1) is emphatically repudiated by Bradley (p. 98 n.) against *OED*. But it is upheld by reference to Elizabethan usage by, among others, Joseph (*Conscience and the King*, pp. 108–10), Prosser (pp. 167–70 (169–72)), and especially C. Belsey in 'The Case of Hamlet's Conscience' (*SP*, LXXVI, 127–48). This is also the sense in which the word is used by Belleforest in conjunction with the cowardice (*poltronnerie*) that hinders gallant enterprises (see Intro., p. 95) – in view of which it is less necessary, though still instructive, to note that Cardan's *Comfort* (1573, N6) attributes man's unhappiness to 'a cowardly and corrupt conscience'. The *Timon* passage relied on for sense (2) reveals itself as exceptional. The *R3* parallels, with their thrice-repeated association with cowardice, are strongly in favour of (1), and it is clearly implied in all seven other uses of the word in *Hamlet*. The antithesis between Hamlet, who here sees *conscience* as a deterrent, and Laertes, who consigns 'conscience . . . to the profoundest pit' (IV.v.132) is striking. Moreover, this sense follows naturally from the 'dread' of the after-life, which an uneasy conscience will increase. C. S. Lewis believes that *conscience* here means 'nothing more or less than "fear of hell"' (*Studies in Words*, p. 207). What alone is against this sense is that it does not so naturally lead on: the faltering of resolution as a result of 'thought' (l. 85) cannot easily be attributed to the recognition or fear of wrongdoing but rather to what Hamlet later calls 'thinking too precisely on th'event' (IV.iv.41). Excess of 'thought' comes from awareness of (and attention to) various considerations; but if that is what *conscience* now suggests, there is a shift of meaning. In fact there is no necessity to see ll. 84–8 as concerned with 'conscience' at all. Resolution weakens in the course of thinking just as courage to face death weakens through the operation of conscience. The commentators maintain (1) or (2) according as they associate *conscience* more with what precedes or with what follows. For the Bradleians, who tend to equate 'conscience' with 'thought', it is frequently 'reflection'. D. G. James (*The Dream of Learning*, p. 42) argues that the word here carries both meanings – 'both a command to do what is right and anxious reflections as to what is, in fact, the right thing to do'. I believe firmly in (1), which must be the meaning in l. 83, after which the inhibiting of action by the conscience which fears the after-life becomes but one instance exemplifying ('and thus') the general process described in ll. 83–7. See above, ll. 56–88 LN.

III. i. 107–8. *your honesty should admit no discourse to your beauty*]   The proverbial incompatibility of beauty and chastity (Tilley B 163) may owe something to Pettie's translation of Guazzo's *Civil Conversation*: 'Beauty breedeth temptation, temptation dishonour: for it is a matter almost impossible, and seldom seen, that those two great enemies, beauty and honesty agree together' (Tudor Trans., ii. 10). This proposition became familiar as a basis for Elizabethan wit. See, e.g., *AYL*, which states it at I. ii. 34, 'Those that [Fortune] makes fair she scarce makes honest' and applies it in Touchstone's dialogue with Audrey in III. iii. 24–34, 'Would you not have me honest? – No, truly, unless thou wert hard-favour'd', etc. See also Donne, *Paradoxes and Problems*, 'Why are the fairest, falsest?' (Problem 7) and *The Second Anniversary*, where it is a sign of ideal perfection when 'beauty and chastity together kiss' (l. 364).

III. i. 121. *a nunnery*]   The evidence that *a nunnery* might be a house of ill-fame had better be examined. It hardly establishes that this use of *nunnery* was 'common' (Dover Wilson) or 'well-known' (Adams). Passages relied on for such a meaning afford dubious authority for it here. When the Gray's Inn Revels of 1594 (cited *N&Q*, ccx, 332) refer to a brothel as a nunnery, this is part of an elaborate joke: '*Lucy Negro*, Abbess *de Clerkenwell*, holdeth the Nunnery of *Clerkenwell* . . . of the Prince of *Purpoole*, by Night-Service in *Cauda*, and to find a Choir of Nuns, with burning Lamps, to chaunt *Placebo* to the Gentlemen of the Prince's Privy-Chamber' (*Gesta Grayorum*, MSR, p. 12). The woman referred to as the abbess was well known for a brothel-keeper, and the wit depends on presenting her establishment in the guise of its contrary.

The same is basically the technique of the passage from Nashe's *Christ's Tears* cited in *OED* (as one of only two examples before 1700). For though Nashe is explicitly speaking of bawds who give gentlemen admission to 'their nunnery', he has already told us that it is 'a trick amongst all bawds, they will feign themselves to be zealous Catholics; and . . . if they be imprisoned or carried to Bridewell for their bawdry, they give out they suffer for the

Church' (Nashe, ii.151–2). Hence the use of the word 'nunnery'
simply sustains the pretence.

These two instances, the only ones recorded earlier than
Hamlet, do not entitle us to infer that a nunnery meant a brothel
outside carefully controlled contexts. But a passage from *The
Black Book* (pubd. 1604) (cited by R. Levin in *N&Q*, CCXIII, 249)
is rather different. There Pierce Penniless greets the idea that he
might become a usurer with a jest at what he might then do with
his unaccustomed wealth: 'I would build a nunnery in Pict-hatch
here' (Middleton, ed. Bullen, viii. 26). The area of Pict-hatch
was, as *The Black Book* tells us, 'the very skirts of all brothel-
houses'. A nunnery there would be an incongruity, which may
of course be the point. But it does not appear that Pierce proposes
to convert the local women; his other projects are rather concerned with increasing facilities for the town's disreputable sports:
he would 'turn the walk in Paul's into a bowling-alley' and 'have
the Thames leaded over, that they might play at cony-holes with
the arches under London Bridge'. Hence I incline to agree with
Levin that the full effect of this joke lies in its ambiguity; for
while a literal nunnery in Pict-hatch would have its comic point,
the context is likely to suggest to us a 'nunnery' of another kind.
Yet although the context can evoke this meaning, it cannot easily
create it, as in the previous instances, if it does not already exist.

The use of 'nunnery' for its opposite, aided by the witticism of
calling an unchaste woman a nun (e.g. *The Alchemist*, V.V.20),
might well develop into a stock joke; and we can see from
Fletcher that it did. *The Mad Lover* (*c.* 1616) supplies the second
of *OED*'s two instances and the one chosen by Dover Wilson for
his illustration: 'There's an old nunnery at hand. —What's that?
—A bawdy house' (IV.ii.43–4). In *Rule a Wife and Have a Wife*
(1624) Fletcher repeats the joke. A husband interjects sardonic
comment on a message delivered to his wife: 'Madam, the Lady
Julia—That's a bawd . . .—Has brought her coach . . . to be
inform'd if you will take the air this morning—The neat air of
her nunnery' (III.i.63–7). Fletcher, unlike Nashe and the *Gesta
Grayorum*, needs no religious context to justify his usage. He
expects us to accept quite simply that a 'nunnery' can be a
brothel, which helps to confirm our supposition that Middleton
had already done the same. But Fletcher does not trust the word
to be clear if it stands alone. We know his nunnery for what it is
when he explains the joke for us or when its owner has been
already (three times) called a bawd.

Can we assume that without such precise indications – and

twenty years or so before – the word *nunnery* would be so understood? The example of *The Black Book* makes conceivable that it
might. Yet even there, with less unmistakable direction, it is the
context that guides us to an ironic meaning: the nunnery is
placed in Pict-hatch, where the amenities are to be improved.
Hamlet gives no such guidance. On the contrary, its nunnery is
consistently presented as a refuge from marriage. Hence to depose
the literal meaning here in favour of the brothel is, in Kitto's
word, 'inept' (*Form and Meaning in Drama*, p. 280; cf. A. L. French
in *ES*, XLVI, 141–5). It is true that as Hamlet goes on to tax
Ophelia with the sins of womankind, he describes the arts of a
courtesan (ll. 144–8). But it does not follow that he is ironically
bidding Ophelia go where she may practise them. What the context most requires the nunnery to be is a place of renunciation. I
do not think we are meant to suppose (as in Adams, pp. 78,
259–60; Coghill, pp. 22–3) that with a sudden change of tone
after the question about her father (ll. 130–1) Hamlet goes on
repeating the word *nunnery* while switching its meaning to the
converse. I doubt if an actor could convey this, and the text
would not support him if he could. The dialogue would need to
give some warning of such a change of meaning, and conspicuously does not. How easily it could have done so we may see from
Wiv. II.ii.16, where Falstaff bids Pistol 'Go . . . to your manor of
Pickt-hatch; go'. Instead it moves to a climax in which the final
injunction to the nunnery follows immediately upon the most
emphatic proscription of marriage (ll. 149–51).

Yet additional evidence of the word's ironic usage has made
me less persuaded than I once was (*HO*, p. 144) that we can
altogether dismiss an inherent ambiguity. As the five-times-
repeated *nunnery* re-echoes through Hamlet's exhortations, if its
ironic use is familiar to us, it may bring to mind, along with the
nunnery where the wiles of women are renounced, another kind
of 'nunnery' where they flourish. It is possible that it was for this
that Shakespeare chose to reiterate the word. And a degree of
ambivalence would not be out of keeping with the baffling
behaviour of the 'antic' Hamlet as exhibited already – in the
ambiguous visit to Ophelia's chamber (II.i.77–100), the riddling
talk with her father (II.ii.171–217, 399–416), and the contradic-
tions of this very scene (ll. 95–6, 115–19). But contrary elements
of meaning need not be and are not equal. The fear that Ophelia
might be a fishmonger's daughter makes it more urgent that she
shall be Jephthah's (see nn. on II.ii.174, 399). The *nunnery* she is
to go to has its ordinary literal sense; and whatever ambiguity

we may hear in it, this meaning dominates from first to last. The *nunnery* Hamlet insists on for Ophelia is a sanctuary from marriage and from the world's contamination.

Some confirmation of this interpretation is perhaps afforded, as far as anything can be by so debased a version, by *Der Bestrafte Brudermord* (*BB*). There Hamlet tells Ophelia (in Furness's translation), 'Go to a nunnery, but not to a nunnery where two pairs of slippers lie at the bedside'. This at least confirms what a 17th-century 'nunnery' could be, though it also confirms our impression, derived from other examples, that if a 'nunnery' referred to a bawdy-house this was likely to be made explicit. More significantly it shows, despite Dover Wilson's contrary assertion (*WHH*, p. 134), that, as stage tradition understood him, a bawdy-house was not what Hamlet meant. The naughty meaning, even while it is dragged in for the sake of a cheap joke, is specifically rejected. Yet the very dragging of it in suggests that there was something in the episode in *Hamlet* which evoked it. *BB*, like Fletcher, rules out any ambiguity. Shakespeare perhaps did not.

III.i. 130–1. *Where's your father?*] The assumption that Hamlet knows that he is being spied on rests, I am confident, on a complete misinterpretation of the 'nunnery' scene (cf. III.i.96n.) based on a misunderstanding both of Hamlet's attitude to Ophelia (on which see *HO*, pp. 140–5; *Sh.Jahr.* (West), 1975, pp. 117–20) and of Elizabethan dramatic convention. Dover Wilson supposed that Hamlet knew from the beginning of Polonius's spying (see II.ii. 167 S.D. LN), others that he must have become aware of it at least by l. 103 (cf. Adams, p. 255), many more that he must detect it now. A stage tradition beginning early in the 19th century (see Sprague, *Shakespeare and the Actors*, pp. 152–4) made Polonius pop his head out at this point. Coghill, who found this crude, nevertheless thought the 'sudden irrelevance' of Hamlet's question made it 'certain' that this was his 'moment of enlightenment' (pp. 16–19). Among more fanciful theories is one (in the Penguin edition) that Hamlet thinks the Queen must be acting as chaperon and that his attack on the vices of women is intended for her ears. All such inferences are belied by the dramatic convention that a character's awareness of being overheard is normally made explicit in the dialogue (see H. Gardner, 'Lawful Espials', *MLR*, XXXIII, 345 ff.; *HO*, pp. 145–6). And the sudden disconcerting question may find less superficial explanation. It is very much in Hamlet's 'antic' vein. Cf. esp. 'Have you a daughter?' (II.ii.182) and l. 103 in this scene. It is true these other questions can be related, if obliquely, to what has just preceded them. Yet Hamlet's love for Ophelia has all along been entangled with her father. It is her father on whom he has projected his inarticulate feelings about her sexual nature – her 'honesty', her potentiality for mating and breeding (II.ii.174–89, 399–409); and now when these come to a climax in his encounter with Ophelia herself, he suddenly thinks of her father. (To Polonius, 'Have you a daughter?'; to Ophelia, 'Where's your father?') Perhaps the most surprising thing about the question is that it should so surprise us. But dramatic art combines the unexpected and the plausible. On a different dramatic level the question is important not to suggest that Hamlet has discovered Polonius's presence but to remind the audience of it. The eavesdropper must now hear something to his disadvantage; but the effect of this depends not on Hamlet's knowing that he is being overheard, but on *our* knowing it. For some perceptive comments on this scene see Kitto, *Form and Meaning in Drama*, pp. 274–81.

III.i.144. *paintings*] In attacks on the vanities of women cosmetics excited particular indignation as being in principle a blasphemy against God and in practice an accompaniment of easy virtue. Cf. Guazzo's *Civil Conversation*, 'A woman taking away and changing the colour and complexion which God hath given her, taketh unto her that which belongeth to a harlot' (Tudor Trans., ii.13). But in so common a matter it would be rash to assume any one specific source. Eight English authors outside the drama, as well as some Continental ones, are cited by Tilley (*RES*, v, 312–17). The case against face-painting was also familiar through the Homily 'Against Excess of Apparel' ('What do these women, but go about to reform that which God hath made?', Book of Homilies, 1850 edn, p. 315), and one of the most vehement attacks, that of Philip Stubbes, claimed the authority of the Christian Fathers, quoting Cyprian and Ambrose, the second to this effect: 'For what a dotage is it to change thy natural face which God hath made thee for a painted face, which thou hast made thyself?' (*Anatomy of Abuses*, New Shakspere Soc., i.66). Donne's argument 'That women ought to paint' (*Paradoxes*, no. 2) is correspondingly outrageous. The practice nevertheless was not unknown in the highest circles (see v.i.187–8 LN), and it has been suggested that F's textual variants here, eliminating the references to face-painting, represent deliberate alteration to avoid giving offence.

Traditionally associated with face-painting were other feminine vanities. Dover Wilson compares those specified here by Hamlet with Stubbes's reference to women's 'coyness in gestures, their mincedness in words and speeches, their gingerliness in tripping on toes like young goats, their demure nicety and babishness' (i. 78).

III.i.160. *out of tune*] Either *time* or *tune* must be a minim error, but as both make excellent sense we cannot be certain which. A Q2 misreading may be paralleled in *Mac.* IV.iii.235, F 'This time goes manly', where *time*, though occasionally defended, is usually emended to *tune*. Bright compares the mind which has lost control of faculties otherwise unimpaired to a musician with 'a false stringed lute' (p. 38), and in Shakespeare a musician who 'plays false' is 'out of tune' (*Gent.* IV.ii.57-8). In Bright, when reason is not in control, the parts of a 'most consonant and pleasant harmony' are put 'out of tune' (p. 250), and Shakespeare uses the same metaphor when Cordelia speaks of Lear's 'untun'd and jarring senses' (*Lr* IV.vii.16). Discordant sound rather than broken time may be suggested by *jangled*: Fynes Moryson describes bells at Polish funerals as being 'tolled and jangled, never rung out or answering one the other in musical tunes' (*Shakespeare's Europe*, ed. C. Hughes, 1903, p. 395). And Shakespeare elsewhere combines *out of tune* with *harsh*: see *Rom.* III.v.27-8, 'It is the lark that sings so out of tune, Straining harsh discords'; *Oth.* v.ii.118-19, 'murder's out of tune, And sweet revenge grows harsh'.

On the other hand, *out o' tune* in *Tw.N.* II.iii.108 is taken by some editors to be an error for *out o' time* (cf. l. 90); and in a musical age the dependence of music on correct time was often referred to (cf. III.iv.142-3). Shakespeare makes Richard II exclaim, 'How sour sweet music is When time is broke' (*R2* v.v.42-3), and Touchstone's objection that 'the note was very untuneable' is refuted by 'We kept time' (*AYL* v.iii.33-4). Cf. Middleton, *A Fair Quarrel*, I.i.100, 'I had thought soldiers Had been musical, would not strike out of time'; Massinger, *The Roman Actor*, II.i.227, 'The motion of the spheres are out of time'.

III.ii.1-35.] The *excursus on acting* no doubt betrays Shakespeare's own concern, but granted that Hamlet's views, as generally supposed, reflect those of his creator, they are also very much in character for a prince, whose standards can afford to be uncompromising. Cf. II.ii.431-7. The standards are in any case those sanctioned by the critical tradition. (See Joseph, *Elizabethan*

Acting, pp. 146–9.) The principle of ease and naturalness of gesture corresponds with what is advocated in Heywood's *Apology for Actors*, 1612 (c4): 'This is the action behooveful in any that profess this quality, not to use any impudent or forced motion in any part of the body, no rough, or other violent gesture, nor on the contrary, to stand like a stiff starched man, but to qualify everything according to the nature of the person personated: for in overacting tricks, and toiling too much in the antic habit of humours, men of the ripest desert, greatest opinions, and best reputations, may break into the most violent absurdities.' The 'amiable fiction' that Shakespeare is through Hamlet attacking the acting of Edward Alleyn is well refuted by Wm. Armstrong (*SS* 7, 82–9). Battenhouse's view that 'Shakespeare's play . . . implies a criticism of' Hamlet's principles and through them of the neoclassical dramatic style of Jonson (*Essays for Leicester Bradner*, pp. 3–26) is equally illusory.

III.ii.44–5. *the fool that uses it*.]   The *passage added in Q1* goes (in modernized form) as follows:

> And then you have some again that keeps one suit of jests, as a man is known by one suit of apparel, and gentlemen quotes his jests down in their tables before they come to the play, as thus: 'Cannot you stay till I eat my porridge?' and 'You owe me a quarter's wages', and 'My coat wants a cullison', and 'Your beer is sour', and blabbering with his lips, and thus keeping in his cinquepace of jests when, God knows, the warm clown cannot make a jest unless by chance, as the blind man catcheth a hare. Masters, tell him of it.
> *Players*. We will, my lord.

III.ii.128. *sables*]   Properly clothes faced or trimmed with sable (fur); and although the word came to be used generically for mourning blacks, it seems here to retain its strict signification too. For *I'll have* implies a change from present wear and so the replacement of Hamlet's customary 'inky cloak' (I.ii.77–8) by something more remarkable. The funeral procession in Day's *Parliament of Bees* (char. 8) includes 'the Graces . . . clad in rich sables'. See Hotson, 'Sables for Hamlet', *Time and Tide*, 1 Nov. 1952.

Hamlet's meaning has, however, been much disputed. The context has often been held to imply that after so long a period as 'twice two months' it is time to discard mourning, and various

attempts have been made to adjust the text or its interpretation
to what is thus presupposed. But we must remember the characteristic of Hamlet in his 'idle' moods to bewilder by defeating
expectation. Preferring the expected, Keightley supplied a
negative ('I'll *not* have') for a reversal of the sense, which Warburton had achieved more neatly by rendering *for* as *'fore* (before).
Others have sought to distinguish the *suit of sables* from the devil's
black and have decided that it signalizes the end of mourning by
its richness and display. Yet if Shakespeare had meant that, he
could have thought of something gayer; and it is rather absurd
for critics, from Johnson to Dover Wilson, to have insisted that
sables are not black but brown – a view which has the concurrence
of *OED* (sable, *sb.*² and *a.*) but which Hotson with abundance of
citation contradicts. It is clear that whatever the scientific fact,
sables were always *thought of* as black; literature betrays no incongruity in the use of the same word for the fur, the heraldic
colour, and the poetic epithet for night. No one has explained
why, being conventionally black and a badge of mourning, *sables*
should here denote the end of it. In fact, Hamlet's *suit of sables*
does not contrast with the devil's *black*, but outdoes it. Speedy
forgetting makes a man 'merry' (ll. 123–5), and sables, 'importing
. . . graveness' (IV. vii. 79–80), must presuppose the opposite. So,
as the text stands, it is not that a father so long dead had now
better be forgotten, but that since he is, remarkably, not forgotten, he shall be remarkably and splendidly mourned. And
since one has to be old to wear sables, they give a mocking emphasis to the long time his memory lasts.

III. ii. 132–3. *the hobby-horse . . . is forgot*] *The hobby-horse* is well
described by Nares as consisting of 'the figure of a horse fastened
round the waist of a man, his own legs going through the body
of the horse, and enabling him to walk, but concealed by a long
foot-cloth; while false legs appeared where those of the man
should be, at the sides of the horse'. The Puritan disapproval of
his lewd antics sometimes led the hobby-horse to be omitted from
the Games (see, for amusing illustration, Fletcher, *Women Pleased*,
IV. i); but neither such disappearance of the hobby-horse nor the
enactment by the hobby-horse of a ritual death and resurrection
(as described in *RES*, n.s. xxx, 6–9) seems sufficient to account
for the catch-phrase Hamlet quotes. 'For O, for O, the hobby-
horse is forgot' was the refrain of a popular song, as is evident
from *Old Meg of Herefordshire*, 1609, B4: 'John Hunt the hobby-
horse, wanting but three of an hundred, 'twere time for him to

forget himself, and sing but O, nothing but O, the hobby-horse is forgotten.' Cf. *LLL* III.i.25–6, where Armado's stammered 'But O – but O –' is completed by Moth with 'The hobby-horse is forgot'. From its frequent use we seem to have an instance of a catch-phrase continuing in popularity after the original point of it had been lost. What is certain is that the hobby-horse, while very much remembered, became a byword for being forgotten and as such the occasion for numerous jokes in Elizabethan plays.

III.ii.133 S.D. *A dumb-show*] Dumb-shows, gratifying the popular taste for spectacle (cf. ll. 11–12), were common enough; but commentary regularly stresses that this one is unique. The usual dumb-show either presented things that could not be conveniently given in dialogue, or alternatively, if it foreshadowed things which *would* be given in dialogue later, it did so emblematically. (See Creizenach, *The English Drama in the Age of Shakespeare*, pp. 388–90; *WHH*, pp. 146–7; B. R. Pearn, 'Dumb-Show in Elizabethan Drama', *RES*, XI, 385–405; D. Mehl, *The Elizabethan Dumb Show*, 1965.) What is peculiar in *Hamlet* is that the dumb-show exactly rehearses without dialogue what is then repeated with it. It is easy, however, to exaggerate the singularity of this; it could not have seemed strange to an Elizabethan audience already accustomed by the emblematic shows to see a theme given preliminary treatment in a different mode. It had been to some extent anticipated in *MND*, where the 'show' which precedes the Pyramus play introduces actors who presumably mime the action while the Prologue is describing it (v.i.126–50). The dumb-show in *Hamlet* likewise introduces an inset play, and what is exceptional in its character is evidently related to this exceptional use: its first function is to reveal the plot of the inset play in advance, so that the audience, freed from having to concentrate on what this play is about, may attend to the reactions of the stage-audience to it. Only a modern spectator for whom *Hamlet* has been staled by familiarity is likely to find the dumb-show otiose; and it becomes the more necessary in that the inset play itself is of course never completed (cf. *WHH*, pp. 145–9). But the dumb-show has also a second function, which extends beyond the present scene to the whole artistic design. While illuminating Hamlet's stratagem against the King, it also holds aloof from this sequential action to bring into focus at the centre of the drama a perfect image of the crime which is the foundation of its plot.

Yet the dumb-show has not fulfilled these functions without giving rise to a famous critical problem: how is it that the King, whose conscience is so well caught when he sees his crime re-enacted in the play, remains unmoved by the dumb-show? One answer has perhaps just been suggested. A few scholars have supposed a textual anomaly, whereby alternative versions are conflated (e.g. W. J. Lawrence in *Life and Letters*, v, 333–40; M. H. Dodds, *N&Q*, CLXIX, 334–5); but most attempt a rational account of the King's conduct which will square with the double representation. Their explanations belong to three kinds. (1) Since Claudius showed no reaction to the first representation of the murder, it follows that he could not have seen the dumb-show. (2) Since he was present he must be supposed to have seen it, and it follows that he did not recognize what he saw. (3) Since he must have both seen and recognized it, it follows that he was strong enough to stand the sight of his crime once but not twice. This last (3), the psychological explanation, often called the 'second tooth' theory, is both the simplest and the one tradition-ally most favoured. (Good exponents of it include W. W. Law-rence, 'The Play-Scene in *Hamlet*', *JEGP*, XVIII, 1–22 and 'Hamlet and the Mousetrap', *PMLA*, LIV, 709–35; A. Hart, 'Once More the Mouse-trap', *RES*, XVII, 11–20; Granville-Barker, *Prefaces*, III, 89–93). In a court of law, compelled to make deductions about fact from circumstantial evidence, it is difficult to see what other conclusion could be reached. Yet if this had been what the dramatist meant us to understand, he could easily have given the King an aside (like that at III. i. 50, for instance) to show the first tooth hurting and he did not. The trouble with all these theories is that they make additions to the text, or at least assumptions for which the text gives no warrant. They all apply to imaginary events the kind of rational inference appropriate only in the real world. In a work of fiction what we do not know because the fiction does not tell us cannot be presumed to exist. This is the basic objection to the suggestion that the King did not observe the dumb-show (1). Tieck's idea that he was too absorbed in talk was revived by Halliwell-Phillipps, who asked, 'Is it allow-able to direct that the King and Queen are whispering confi-dentially to each other during the dumb-show, and so escape a sight of it?' And this suggestion was taken up and insisted on by Dover Wilson (*WHH*, pp. 149–53, 158–60, 183–4), who wrote it into the stage-directions of his edition (pp. 68–9, 200–1), which has since been often followed on the stage, and with unfortunate results; for a King who whispers instead of watching can only divert the attention of the audience from the dumb-show which was put in for their benefit. It is true that the sophisticated modern theatre-goer, not needing the dumb-show to inform him, is likely in any case to watch the King, not merely in order to note how he is taking it but to see which critical theory the production has elected for. Yet this unholy legacy of criticism one would, if such a thing were possible, do better to renounce.

An alternative explanation of the King's alleged failure to see the dumb-show appeals to the nature of the Elizabethan stage: if the dumb-show were acted on the inner stage (Sisson, 'The Mouse-trap Again', *RES*, XVI, 129–36) or on the upper stage (Flatter, *Hamlet's Father*, pp. 40–59), it would be easy enough for the royal party to be placed where it was out of view. But apart from recent scepticism about the existence of these physical features of the Elizabethan playhouse, they cannot be used to account for happenings in the imaginary world of the play without adding a further dimension to the confusion of fact and fiction. Nor need we suppose, with a reviewer of Dover Wilson's book, that the afternoon light in Elsinore was dim (*N&Q*, CLXIX, 305).

The hypothesis that Claudius, though he must have seen the dumb-show, did not recognize in it the representation of his crime (2) was elaborated in a notorious article by Greg ('Hamlet's Hallucination', *MLR*, XII, 393–421), who maintained that what disturbed the King at the performance of the play was the menacing behaviour of Hamlet and not the sight of the poisoning, which by itself had left him unmoved; and that since it *had* left him unmoved, he could not have committed the murder in the manner represented, wherefore the account of it given by the Ghost was a figment of Hamlet's brain. Were it not for the controversy it provoked, one would hardly have thought this ingenious deduction in need of serious confutation. The play obviously expects us to accept that the King's conscience is caught 'upon the talk of the poisoning' (l. 283) and accordingly to join with Hamlet in taking 'the ghost's word' (l. 280). But perhaps the fundamental objection to Greg's case is its pointlessness. With the Ghost's main charge confirmed by the King's solemn confession that he 'did the murder' (III.iii. 54), the precise method of his doing it, for all its picturesque horror, does not affect the essential plot of fratricide and vengeance.

Nevertheless, the idea that what the King succumbs to is Hamlet's menacing behaviour has been incorporated in other explanations. Claudius, it is said, could endure the spectacle of his crime not only in the dumb-show but in the play itself, only to break at Hamlet's accusing fury (*SS 32*, 151–61). But this is no more than a variant of the 'second tooth' theory, with the additional objection that it distorts the whole dramatic pattern, in which the expectation created by ii.ii.584–94 that Claudius will be 'struck' by the 'cunning of the scene' is now (iii.ii.265–84) regarded as fulfilled, thanks to Hamlet's theatrical achievement.

There is somewhat more to be said for a theory that Claudius did not recognize the significance of the dumb-show because of the stylized way in which dumb-shows were performed (cf. Granville-Barker, p. 91). They were often enigmatic, not to say 'inexplicable' (l. 12) without the guidance of a presenter, such as Ophelia expects (l. 139) and does not get (see l. 137n.); wherefore Alice Walker supposes that 'the *Hamlet* dumb-show was probably presented in such a way as to leave no one much the wiser concerning its significance' (*MLR*, xxxi, 513–17. Cf. Mehl, pp. 117–18). This theory has at least the merit of recognizing dramatic convention; yet its appeal is still to literalism instead of to the nature of dramatic illusion. If *no one* is the wiser for the dumb-show, it will defeat its purpose: however it is performed, its purport must be made clear to us, the audience, though we may simultaneously accept that it is not clear to the play-audience on the stage. This is the principle of 'double consciousness', as well explained by Bethell (*Shakespeare and the Popular Dramatic Tradition*, pp. 156–60), and it is of course the same principle as operates in so familiar a dramatic convention as disguise. So, using Ophelia (who better?) as representative of the innocent play-audience, the dramatist simultaneously shows her puzzled by the dumb-show (ll. 134–9) and confirms us in our own surmise that it 'imports the argument of the play'. Yet there is still a further element which Bethell does not acknowledge and which the principle of double consciousness is inadequate to explain. There are limits to the willing suspension of disbelief: what we easily allow to Ophelia, who knows nothing of the murder, would be incredible in the King, aware not only of the crime but of its highly unusual method. It is surely not an oversight but Shakespeare's dramatic tact which leaves the King out of the dialogue at this stage: how *he* reacted to the dumb-show is a question the play not only does not answer but is careful not to ask. And though it reckons without the critic in the study, it counts on the spectator in the theatre not to ask the question either. He will see the King's suspicions rising first in the questions of ll. 227–8: the numerous critical accounts of a tense struggle going on before that between the King and Hamlet or within the King himself describe what is in the critics' minds and not in the play at all.

The problem which is thus, strictly speaking, no problem may nevertheless present itself, I suppose, to the producer and still more to him that plays the King. How should the actor behave during the dumb-show? If he wishes to be faithful to Shakespeare, as many do not, he will neither blench at seeing the dumb-show nor whisper so as not to see it. To the curious spectator's eye, giving no more clue than the text does, he must remain inscrutable.

(A recent review of various theories is in W. W. Robson, *Did the King see the Dumb-show?*, Edinburgh, 1975, which leaves, however, the specific issue unresolved.)

III. ii. 135. *miching malicho*]   Heavy weather has been made of this, aggravated by the practice of lumping the two words together as though they were one indivisible phrase. *Miching* at least (though *OED* for no discernible reason stops short of certainty) is perfectly straightforward – a present participle formation from the common verb to *mich*, lurk, be (furtively) up to mischief, still apparently current in some dialects alongside the related *mooch* (see *Eng. Dialect Dictionary*) and *meech* (see Webster). Cf. Anon., *Woodstock*, l. 2649 (one murderer to another), 'Come, ye miching rascal'; Heywood, *A Woman Killed with Kindness*, II. iii. 179, 'I never look'd for better of that rascal, Since he came miching first into our house'. Further confirmation, if such were necessary, comes from Florio (*A World of Words*, Acciapinare), 'to miche, to shrug, or sneake in some corner'; Cotgrave (under *recuict*), '. . . miching, . . . dodging'; and Minsheu, 'To Miche, or secretly to hide himselfe out of the way, as Truants doe from schoole'. It seems to be in the common sense of truant, mischievous skulker, that Shakespeare uses the noun *micher* in *1H4* II. iv. 396. In Massinger, *A Very Woman*, v. iii. 34, a slave notorious for villainous tricks is called 'you micher'.

The interpretation of *malicho* permits less certainty, though it need call for no serious doubt. It has long been taken to represent the Spanish *malhecho*, malefaction, mischief, which Kittredge therefore reads: the compromise spelling *mallecho* has been traditional since Malone. When *OED* remarks that 'there is no evidence that the Sp. word was familiar in English', it ignores (1) the possible significance of the *h* spelling in F's substitution of *Malicho* for the presumably phonetic *Mallico* of Q1, Q2, and (2) the parallel in Shirley's *Gentleman of Venice* (Q1655) where *Malligo* would appear to be a further variant of the same word: 'Be humble, Thou man of *Malligo*, or thou dyest' (III. iv. 125). This instance also helps to dispel the objection sometimes made that the Spanish *malhecho* means a particular deed of iniquity rather than iniquity in the abstract: an English vogue-word deriving from it need not of course do the same. There have been conjectures of textual corruption; but the hypothesis that a strange word might result from the misreading of a common one like *mallice* (J. Crawford, *RES*, n.s. xviii, 40–5) defies ordinary probability and the weight of all three texts. The italics of Q2 and F are easily accounted for as signalling a foreign word, but the printers may have taken it as a proper name. Attempts to explain it as one have ranged from Spenser's Malbecco (*FQ*, iii.ix–x) to Malichus, poisoner of Antipater (A. Walker, *MLR*, xxxi, 513–17). Yet while it is true that *miching* is an epithet for a person rather than an action, personification either in or out of Shakespeare is no unusual figure.

As for what it is that is characterized as *miching malicho*, no interpretation is acceptable which would have it to be the poisoner. Hamlet's answer, no less than Ophelia's question, clearly applies to the dumb-show as a whole. Primarily Hamlet refers to the action of murder and marriage which the dumb-show has exhibited. But, with a play on the word *means*, the dumb-show, by revealing what is to come, also 'means mischief' for the King. There is little to support Dover Wilson's fancy that Hamlet is surprised by the dumb-show and ascribes it to the 'mischief' of the Players, who thus give the game away too soon (*WHH*, pp. 156–8, 185–6).

iii. ii. 150–5.] *The play within the play* is at once marked off from the surrounding dialogue by the rhyming couplets and by an artificial elaboration of style characteristic of an older period. This is especially manifest in the opening periphrastic time-formulae, with which compare Green's *Alphonsus*, iv.i.9 ff.,

> Thrice ten times Phoebus with his golden beams
> Hath compassed the circle of the sky,
> Thrice ten times Ceres hath her workmen hir'd . . .
> Since first in priesthood I did lead my life;

and *Selimus*, ll. 37 ff.,

> Twice fifteen times hath fair Latona's son
> Walked about the world with his great light
> Since I began . . .
> To sway this sceptre.

Hence *thirty* is scarcely to be related to the duration of Hamlet's parents' marriage or to his own age (cf. v.i. 139–57 LN). There is no reason to suspect parody. Having set the tone, embellishment by periphrasis soon gives way, but the couplets, with an accumulation of *sententiae*, many inversions, and the occasional unfamiliar word, continue their distancing effect. See *MP*, LXVII, 150–9.

III.ii. 183–208.]   *The speech of the Player King.*—Speculation as to the speech inserted in the play by Hamlet (cf. II.ii. 535–6 and LN) has sometimes fastened on this passage on the grounds that nowhere else is there a continuous stretch of as much as a 'dozen or sixteen lines' which could be interpolation and that the general moral reflections here are much in Hamlet's vein. But cf. III.ii. 249–54n. One might have thought this argument sufficiently refuted on its own level by the failure of this passage to come 'near the circumstance' of Hamlet's father's death or to do anything at all to assist Hamlet's purpose of discovering the King's 'occulted guilt' (III.ii. 76–81). The echo here of sentiments expressed elsewhere by Hamlet reflects, as with the Pyrrhus speech (cf. II.ii. 448–514 LN, 484 LN), not Hamlet's mind but that of the creative dramatist fashioning his design. With the present speech cf. not only III.i. 84–8 but IV.vii. 110–22. With *purpose . . . memory . . . forget* (ll. 183, 187) cf. Hamlet's vow to *remember* (I.v. 92–112) and subsequent *blunted purpose* (III.iv. 107–111); with the interdependence of friendship and fortune (ll. 195–204) cf. II.ii. 359–62, III.ii. 60–71, and the whole career of Rosencrantz and Guildenstern; with the discrepancy between intention and achievement (ll. 206–8) cf. v.ii. 387–90.

III.ii. 233–4. *the image of a murder done in Vienna—Gonzago is the Duke's name, his wife Baptista*]   It appears to be true that the play *The Murder of Gonzago* (and accordingly the death of King Hamlet) is based on an actual murder, that of the Duke of Urbino in 1538. Gonzago, however, was not the name of the Duke, but of his alleged murderer, Luigi Gonzaga, a kinsman of the Duke's wife, Leonora Gonzaga. Cf. Intro., p. 102. *Vienna* might perhaps be a misreading of Urbino (U and V being interchangeable) or otherwise suggested by it. The reference to *the Duke's name* when the play is about a King is presumably a slip due to the source. It was obviously the intention to translate the Duke and Duchess of the original into a King and Queen the better to image events in Denmark. Q2, apart from this sole

instance, consistently refers to King and Queen, as also does F
except that the Queen is called Baptista in some speech-headings.
It may be through this error in the dialogue that the reported
text Q1, after having a King and Queen in the dumb-show,
transforms them into Duke and Duchess in the stage-direction
and speech-headings of the play which follows. All three texts
read 'King' at l. 239.

III.ii.239. *nephew to the King*]   Not, as we should expect, brother.
But the likeness of *The Murder of Gonzago* to the murder of King
Hamlet is already sufficiently established, and upon the image of
the murder can now be superimposed an image of its revenge,
with the single figure of Lucianus active in a dual role. The Court,
who are ignorant of the brother's murder, will see Lucianus as
the nephew only and hence can interpret the Gonzago play as a
threat by Hamlet against the King. For us of course it must depict
simultaneously crime and nemesis. When Lucianus becomes the
image of Hamlet he does not cease to be Claudius too – after all,
this is the very moment of the poisoning – as is sometimes implied by the few commentators who have remarked at all upon
his nephew's role. The identity of killer and avenger which the
tragic plot will exhibit in Hamlet himself and which has already
been symbolized in Pyrrhus (see II.ii.448–514 LN) is here sharply
focused in the person of Lucianus. This is of the most profound
significance, without a grasp of which the play cannot be understood. See Intro., pp. 145, 156.

III.ii.265–6.]   It is often conjectured that in the verse about *the
strucken deer* Hamlet is quoting a popular ballad (cf. II.ii.403–4);
but the ballad has not been traced and the pointed relevance of
these lines to the dramatic situation makes it perhaps more
probable that they were modelled on a ballad than cited from
one. Cf. 275–8n. Deer were proverbially 'stricken' (Tilley D189)
and it was a common belief that they wept when in distress (as
they do, e.g., in *Arcadia*, ed. Feuillerat, p. 61; *Polyolbion*, XIII.
160–1). Cf. *AYL* II.i.33 ff.; and on 'the sobbing deer' as a subject
of moral disquisition, C. Uhlig in *Renaiss. Drama*, 1970, pp.
79–109. In one of Peacham's emblems a wounded deer running
about with the arrow in its side represents a man of guilty conscience, whose characteristic is to 'seek his ease by shifting of his
ground' while neglecting the means which 'might heal the sin'
rankling within (*Minerva Britanna*, 1612, p. 4).

III. ii. 270–1. *Provincial roses*] Notwithstanding some ambiguity about the term *provincial*, Hamlet's general meaning is clear enough. Cf. the rhyme (in *Friar Bacon's Brazen-head's Prophecy* by Wm. 'Terilo', 1604), 'When roses in the gardens grew, And not in ribbons on a shoe'. The 'roses' which concealed· the shoe-fastenings were a development from the bows formed by the ribbons with which the shoes were tied on, or sometimes, in the case of slashed (*razed*) shoes, by strips of the leather itself. They seem to have become fashionable about the 1590s and to have rapidly grown in size and cost (see Linthicum, pp. 243–5). In the 1631 edition of Stow's *Annals* the continuator Howes notes that 'men of mean rank wear . . . shoe roses of more than five pound price' (p. 1039). The difficulty about the Provincial, or Province, rose has been aggravated by the commentators, who have contradicted one another as to whether it was the rose of Provence or of Provins, a town to the south-east of Paris famous for roses said to have been originally brought there by returning Crusaders; and this supposed origin may have encouraged the further confusion with the damask rose (*rosa damascena*). But the rose of Provins is *rosa gallica*, and horticulturalists (who do not include the editors of *OED*) regard the term *provincial* rose as applying to the rose of Provence, which is the cabbage rose, *rosa centifolia*. This seems to accord with the practice of the 16th-century herbalists and with the distinction made by Cotgrave between *Rose de Provence* 'The Province Rose, the double Damaske Rose' and *Rose de Provins*, 'The ordinarie double red Rose'. Yet *provincial rose* was a very versatile term. Some of the Herbals (Lyte, 1578, p. 655; Gerard, 1597, p. 1079) give it as an alternative name for the *damask rose*, others distinguish the province rose from the damask as being less scented but deeper in colour and 'more double'. It is sometimes equated with the Holland rose (Gerard, p. 1080; Parkinson, *Paradisus Terrestris*, p. 413), though this is more often distinguished from it by greater size and thickness. The normal colour is variously described as 'a mixt colour betwixt red and white' (Lyte), 'carnation' (i.e. flesh-pink) or 'blush'; yet a red and a white provincial rose are also recognized (in a list of 1634 by John Tradescant, printed in Gunther, *Early English Botanists*, p. 341; cf. Parkinson, pp. 413–14). What persists, through many shifts of identity, as the essential feature of a 'provincial rose', and one of particular relevance to Hamlet's shoe-roses, is the thick profusion of its layers of petals.

III. ii. 278. *pajock*] This creature, otherwise unknown, first appears

in this guise in F2 through what is presumably a modernized
spelling of *paiock(e)* (Q2,F). It is usually taken to be a peacock,
paiock being explained as either a variant form or a misreading.
This identification goes back to Q 1676 (*paicock*), and it is encouraged by the pronunciation *pay-jock*. Yet the mere existence
of a Scottish form *pea-jock* cited by Dyce does not make Shakespeare's use of it very likely. More plausibly Dover Wilson supposes a misreading of *pacock*, Sisson apparently of *paicock*, which
he has found as a spelling for the surname Peacock (*NR*); Alice
Walker assumes *c* omitted by a printer's slip (*RES*, n.s. II, 335).
Accordingly there is a growing tendency for editors to emend.
The peacock's gross and lecherous reputation is held to make it
an apt symbol for Claudius: it was said to break its mate's eggs
and to swallow its own dung. Yet one may question whether so
splendid a creature is altogether suitable for an antithesis to Jove
and for the degree of disgust implied here. It is not easy to see,
with Pope, an allusion to the birds' choice of the peacock instead
of the eagle as their king, while the relevance of its being the bird
of Juno, the wife of Jove, though asserted by Alice Walker, is even
less apparent. Moreover, we should note (with *OED*) that the
word *peacock(e)*, so spelt, gave no difficulty in the five indubitable
instances of its occurrence in the Shakespeare texts. Among many
other suggestions are *paddock*, toad, which is what Hamlet does
in fact call Claudius at III.iv. 192 (Theobald); *puttock*, kite, described by Nares as 'a base kind of hawk . . . used as a name of
reproach for a base and contemptible person' (a discarded
alternative of Theobald's revived by Tannenbaum, *SAB*, VII,
127–30); and *patchock*, a contemptuous diminutive of *patch*, clown
(*N&Q*, 4th ser. VIII, 255–6; Dowden). This last is the one that
best fits the requirements both in form and meaning. *Patchock* is
used by Spenser in *The Present State of Ireland* (ed. Renwick, 1970,
p. 64) for the barbarous and degenerate inhabitants; and it needs
only the voicing of its medial consonant to give *pajock* (pronounce
padge-ock), of which Kökeritz (p. 318) holds this to be 'un-
doubtedly' the derivation. See also Skeat's *Etymological Dictionary*,
under *patch*, and *JEGP*, XLIV, 292–5. Cf. III.iv.103, 'A king of
shreds and patches'.

III. ii. 367–73.]   This episode of *the cloud* comes as a little demonstration. Polonius, humouring the madman, would seem to know
his stops; but it is Hamlet who calls the tune, and it is only when
Polonius has piped to it that he consents to answer him. (Cf.
R. B. Bennett, 'The Dramatic Function of Hamlet's Cloud',

Archiv, CCXV, 89–92.) With the apparent change of location one could compare II.ii.206 (LN). But of course the cloud may be as imaginary as the shapes Polonius is persuaded to see in it. It would be hard to agree with Kittredge that there is 'nothing absurd' here about Polonius, who finds a cloud to have a back like a weasel's when he has just said it is 'like a camel'. The ease with which, like Osric later (V.ii.94–9), he is got to assent to contradictory propositions is perhaps point enough. Yet with the fishmonger and Jephthah in mind (see II.ii.174 and LN, 399 and n.) and Ophelia's flowers to come (IV.v.173–83 and LN), it is difficult to deny the possibility of some further significance attaching to the creatures mentioned. In the cryptic 'method' of his 'madness' the man who has warned Rosencrantz and Guildenstern that he knows a hawk from a handsaw (II.ii.375 and LN) would be capable of warning Polonius that a *camel* accustomed to bearing burdens may change into a *weasel* out for blood (cf. l. 381) or into a *whale* which destroys those who take it to be harmless (like the sailors who in legend mistake a whale for an island and when it submerges perish). There have been some attempts to find more esoteric meanings; but quite apart from a lack of convincing evidence for these or their intelligibility to an Elizabethan audience, there seems little point or plausibility in supposing the three animals all to represent lust or to represent in turn one who undertakes more than he can accomplish, who is unable to keep secrets, and who drags to destruction those who put trust in him (*SQ*, V, 211–13; X, 446–7). Such explanations seek to draw analogies between the various animals and Polonius; but the 'mystery' is not in him but in Hamlet, who has warned us to beware of over-interpretation (ll. 355–63).

The textual evidence suggests that in Q3 '*black* like a weasel' was an error for Q2 *backt* which subsequently led to the substitution by actors and editors of *ouzel* (=blackbird) for *weasel* (see *MLR*, XXXIV, 68–70) rather than (as there suggested) that *weasel* (*We(a)zell*) in the substantive texts was a mistake for an original *woosel(l)*. The emphasis moreover is on shape not colour.

III.ii.379–83.] '*Tis now the very witching time of night . . .* The absence of the heavy rhetoric of an earlier style does not disguise that we have here, in highly condensed form, the traditional night-piece apt to prelude a deed of blood. For a representative example, see *Locrine*, V.iv.1 ff., with earthquake and 'hellish night' presaging 'bloody massacres'; and in Shakespeare, *2H6* IV.i.1 ff., where, before the murder of Suffolk, the 'jades' of night 'breathe foul contagious darkness in the air'. Nor should the traditional nature of the selected details obscure their relevance. 'When churchyards yawn', Hamlet will be most susceptible to ghostly influences; when 'hell . . . breathes out Contagion to this world', the revenge to which he is 'prompted . . . by heaven and hell' (II.ii.580; cf. I.v.93) shows 'heaven' in eclipse. Hell is manifest in evil and destructive passions. The new resolution that comes to Hamlet when the Ghost's story is confirmed reveals not so much an acceptance of duty as an exultation in hate, vindictiveness, blood lust. In this mood the hero comes closest to the villain he would damn (III.iii.88–95), even resembles the evil figures of other plays: Iago, scheming against Othello, says 'Hell and night Must bring this monstrous birth to the world's light' (I.iii.397–8). With Hamlet hell's supremacy is a phase only; but it occupies the centre of the play and may be said to begin when the 'nephew to the King' wears the face of Lucianus (l. 239) and to last till he has with rash brutality slain Polonius. See also Intro., p. 156.

III.iii.7. *brows*] F *Lunacies*, along with *dangerous* in the line before, cannot derive from an autograph which produced Q2. Both words, adding nothing to what is already in the context, are apparently stopgaps supplied, consciously or not, by a recollection of *dangerous lunacy* in III.i.4. The correct reading, then, requires either the acceptance or the emendation of Q2. *Brows* has been thought meaningless, but I see no great difficulty about a metaphor which makes Claudius see danger springing out of Hamlet's head. What he fears are Hamlet's plots, schemes, contrivances. F. P. Wilson, remarking on the Elizabethan fondness for indicating states of mind by their physical signs, suggests that *brows* stands for what Claudius sees as the 'threatening aspect' of Hamlet (*Shakespeare and the New Bibliography*, ed. Gardner, 1970, p. 103). Cf. *John* v.i.49, 'Threaten the threat'ner, and outface the brow Of bragging horror', and the verb *browbeat*. Kermode (Riverside), perhaps influenced by F, suggests 'the madness visible in his face(?)'. Dowden, citing *OED* (brow, 5c and d), preferred a different metonymy whereby the brow, the 'fronting aspect', signified effrontery. But the *OED* instances are all singular as well as later and hardly justify those recent editions which gloss *brows* as 'effronteries'. It is as well to recognize that the context (*doth . . . grow out of*) equates the *hazard* not with the brows themselves but with their product.

Among emendations proposed, the likeliest is *braves*, acts or speeches of insolent defiance, strongly supported by Parrott-Craig and Sisson ('graphically most plausible, and apt in sense', *NR*). Cf. Anon., *Woodstock*, l. 567, 'Shall we brook these braves, disgraced and threatened thus', and l. 2828; Heywood, *1 Edw.IV*, (to a defiant rebel) 'Leave off these idle braves' (*Works*, 1874, i.54); and in Shakespeare *Troil.* iv.iv.136; *Shr.* iii.i.15; *1H6* iii.ii.123. Other conjectures include *lunes* (Theobald), fits of lunacy, as in *Wint.* ii.ii.30, and *brains*. Dover Wilson originally read *brawls* (cf. *MSH*, p. 324) but then retracted in favour of *braves* and finally decided it was 'safer to retain' *brows*.

iii.iii.79. *hire and salary*] The Q2 compositor evidently had trouble with his copy: *silly* is fairly obviously his misreading of *sallery*; but the same is not true for *base* and *hyre*. Hence Dover Wilson argues that the true reading must be one which could have been taken for *base* and plausibly proposes *bait*, perhaps spelt *bate* (*MSH*, pp. 325–6). Cf. Florio's Montaigne, ii.12, 'Have you paid him well, have you given him a good baite or fee?' (Tudor Trans., ii.286). *Bait* meant food, esp. food for travellers on a journey, and it has been suggested that it had a particular use in reference to man's last journey. This meaning has not been demonstrated and cannot reasonably be inferred from a passage in *The Unfortunate Traveller* (Nashe, ii.222), 'He could have found in his heart to have packed up his pipes and to have gone to heaven without a bait'; but the idea of giving Claudius the viaticum which Hamlet's father had been denied (cf. i.v.77) would accord with the irony of the passage.

iii.iii.89–95.] *Hamlet's desire to effect the King's damnation* was immensely shocking to Dr Johnson, who was not alone in the 18th century in thinking it 'too horrible to be read or to be uttered'. That it is less shocking to us now is no doubt due to the dimming of belief in hell. The first to explain it away as merely a pretext for delay may have been the actor Thos. Sheridan, as approvingly reported by Boswell (*London Journal*, 6 April 1763); but after Wm. Richardson had ventured 'to affirm' that Hamlet's words belied 'his real sentiments' (*Shakespeare's Dramatic Characters*, 1784, pp. 158–62), it became customary to maintain that the motive Hamlet avowed for deferring his revenge was 'only an excuse for his own want of resolution' (Hazlitt, *Characters of Shakespear's Plays*. Cf. Coleridge, i.29–30; Bradley, pp. 134–5). The dominance of this view in defiance of the text for well over a century is one of the most remarkable aberrations in the history of criticism. So strong was the tradition that long after the cogent attack on it by Stoll (*Hamlet: An Historical and Comparative Study*, 1919, pp. 51–6), distinguished scholars continued to interpret Hamlet's words as disguising, not expressing, his true feelings (e.g. Kittredge, p. xv; Alexander, *Hamlet Father and Son*, 1955, pp. 144–6; Sisson, *Shakespeare's Tragic Justice*, 1962, p. 68). Yet such an explanation could hardly have occurred to Elizabethans taught by their medieval ancestors to find satisfaction in the torments of heretics and sinners and well able to appreciate Hamlet's logical and theological rigour. Horrifying as it might be actually to promote an enemy's damnation, the attitude of Hamlet would not be unfamiliar. Gentillet's *Discours contre Machiavel* (1576; trans. Patrick, 1602) denounced the vengefulness of those who would force a victim 'to give himself to the devil' and thus 'seek in slaying the body to damn the soul, if they could' (III.6). The notorious episode in Nashe's *Unfortunate Traveller* of the man who induced his foe to abjure God's mercy by offering to spare his life and then killed him before he could repent (Nashe, ii.320–6) is in fact the elaboration of a well-known story – found, for example, from 1580 on in Jean Bodin's *République* (v.6; trans. Knolles, 1606, fol. 631ᵛ. See also Edw. Daunce, *A Brief Discourse of the Spanish State*, 1590, p. 24; and, though a later work, Heywood, *Gynaikeion*, 1624, p. 400; and cf. Sir T. Browne, *Religio Medici*, II.6; *Vulgar Errors*, VII.19).

Hamlet's sentiments, then, are no more than might be expected of a revenger, in literature if not in life. And they are consistent with others in the play. Hamlet himself as the object of revenge hears Laertes say to him, 'The devil take thy soul' (v.i.252), and his own account of the deaths he contrived for Rosencrantz and Guildenstern adds 'Not shriving-time allowed' (v.ii.47). (Cf. also I.ii.182–3, his horror of finding his foe in heaven; and IV.iii.33–5, his jocular confidence in his uncle's destination.) The contemporary drama, as scholars from Steevens to Stoll have shown, confirms this revenge code. *The Spanish Tragedy* ends with Revenge's promise, now that the villains are dead, to begin an 'endless tragedy' for them in the underworld. In Fletcher's *The Pilgrim*, as in *Hamlet*, a character asks if it is 'revenge' to kill an enemy when he would 'soar to Heaven' instead of waiting till he is 'fit . . ., his pious armour off' (II.ii.320–58); and one in Heywood's *The Captives* proclaims, 'Strangle him With all his sins about him. 'Twere not else A revenge worth my fury' (III.iii.71–3). See also notes on ll. 89–90, 91. Without recourse to Continental instances, Eleanor Prosser (Appx. B) has assembled from English literature 23 cases of a desire or plan to kill a foe in such a way as to damn his soul as well.

But although Hamlet's sentiments are those proper to a revenger and must be accepted at face value, that does not mean that the play or its author approves them. On the contrary, a sensational convention is brilliantly used by Shakespeare for his own dramatic ends. First, theatrically, the convention facilitates at the centre of the play a spectacularly ironic scene: the revenger, with his passion at its climax following proof of his enemy's guilt, is presented with his victim defenceless and alone; and yet it is revenge itself that provides an incontestable reason why this seemingly perfect opportunity is one impossible to take. But second, thematically, the convention enables revenge to be shown in its most repulsive aspect: for the appropriateness of Hamlet's utterance here is not to his lack of resolution, nor to the scruples of conscience, still less to the 'sensibility' of 'a gentle disposition' (Richardson), but to that savage mood which he has just exhibited to us, that mood in which he could 'drink hot blood' with the contagion of hell upon him (III. ii. 381–3). The revenger's horrifying sentiments contribute to the presentation of the hero in that significant phase of the play in which the evil of his double-sided nature – and his double-sided task — is temporarily uppermost. See III. ii. 379–83 LN; Intro., pp. 154–6. Cf. P. Gottschalk, 'Hamlet and the Scanning of Revenge', *SQ*, xxiv, 155–70.

III. iv. 48–51.   *Heaven's face does glow*
                         O'er this solidity and compound mass
                    With tristful visage, as against the doom,
                    Is thought-sick at the act.]

Ambiguities in phrasing and syntax, the variants, and the possibility of unresolved corruption have made this a stubborn crux. *This solidity and compound mass* is usually taken to refer to this earth, which is *compound* because composed of four elements. The periphrasis is not perhaps felicitous, but it has point in emphasizing the characteristics of the earth which contrast with its threatened disintegration at doomsday. The phrase would be much less apt as a description of the moon, and Dover Wilson's attempt so to interpret it (*MSH*, p. 327) – by drawing an analogy with I. i. 123, where the moon 'was sick almost to doomsday' (but also, be it noted, 'moist') – has nowhere found support. The chief problem is to decide whether it is earth or heaven which is made 'thought-sick' by the monstrous 'act'. As between the variants, the higher textual authority of Q2 is offset by the pleonasm of a

face that *does glow* with *heated visage* and the awkward lack of a
connective before *Is*; but these defects may be less serious than
F's discordant *Yea*, which switches the theme from heaven's face
to earth's while purporting to be reiterating the same idea. (With
the lack of copula between the co-ordinate clauses cf. IV.V.124–5.)
Dover Wilson (*MSH*, pp. 166–7, 327) and Greg (*MLR*, XXX, 85)
agree in regarding *Yea* as corrupt; yet they are apparently influenced by it to accept *solidity and compound mass* rather than
Heaven's face as the subject of *Is thought-sick*. I do not know why
Q2 *Ore* is said to be nonsense; like Sisson (*NR*) I see no difficulty
in heaven's glowing *over* a sinful world. Sisson and some others
take *glow* to indicate shame, as in *John* IV.i.114 ('blush And glow
with shame'), but Shakespeare associates a glowing countenance
with various emotions, including anger (cf. *Caes.* I.ii.183, 'The
angry spot doth glow on Caesar's brow'). There is no incompatibility in heaven's being simultaneously outraged at the
world's evil and grieved at the doom it must incur. On the contrary I think it more in keeping for Hamlet to envisage heaven
rather than earth as 'thought-sick'. He nowhere else suggests that
the world is distressed by the corruption in its midst; his characteristic complaint is that it is not (e.g. I.ii.135–7; II.ii.359–62;
III.iv.155–7). There is also the very striking parallel at the murder
of Duncan, when 'the heavens, as troubled with man's act,
Threatens his bloody stage' (*Mac.* II.iv.5–6). That which
threatens in *Macbeth* does *glow* (with menace?) in *Hamlet*, and the
heaven that in *Macbeth* is *troubled* by a human *act* has a *tristful
visage* when it contemplates one in *Hamlet*.

Neither F *tristfull* nor Q2 *heated* can very well be a misreading
of the other. In theory *tristful* may belong with *Yea* as part of an
attempt to improve a passage imperfectly understood. But so rare
and eloquent a word seems beyond an improver; a suggestion
that it is Shakespeare's own alternative is more plausible than
most conjectures of the kind (Honigmann, *The Stability of Shakespeare's Text*, pp. 135–6). But I agree with Greg that it is probably
the original word and Q2 *heated* a stopgap prompted by *glow*. See
Intro., p. 60. Such signs that the manuscript was difficult here
and that the compositor's efforts corrupted the text inevitably
undermine confidence in interpretations proposed. If emendation
were attempted, either *And* for *Ore* (Dover Wilson) or *'Tis* for *Is*
(Pope) would smooth the syntax; the first would go against, the
second with, my notion of the sense.

III.iv.53. *this picture, . . . this*]   In the debate on *the pictures* it is

important to distinguish, as has often not been done, the question
of how they might or should be represented from that of how they
were represented on Shakespeare's stage. On the second, which is
what concerns us, there has been much unnecessary controversy,
especially on whether the pictures were wall-portraits or 'miniatures', a term which has itself confused the issue. It is true that
Elizabethan plays afford instances of pictures hanging on the
wall of the stage, the most famous perhaps in *The White Devil*
(II.ii.dumb-show), where the portrait is revealed when '*they draw
a curtain*', while a scene in Heywood's *If You Know Not Me*, pt 2,
requires a whole gallery of portraits; but there is far too much of
taking portraits out of bosoms, passing them from hand to hand,
and holding them while apostrophizing or discussing them for
there to be any reasonable doubt of the kind of stage-business
called for in *Hamlet*. In *The Puritan* (1607) the Widow, '*drawing
out her husband's picture*', speaks to it and kisses it (I.i.135ff.). In
Gent. Silvia sends for the portrait which she hands to Julia, who
addresses it for 20 lines (IV.iv.113–14, 180–201). Bassanio takes
from the casket the portrait of Portia which he then rhapsodically
describes (*Mer.V.* III.ii.115–29). In *The Two Noble Kinsmen* and
Satiromastix, as in *Hamlet* and perhaps through its influence, there
are two companion portraits: Emilia addresses the portraits of
her two lovers as she turns from one to the other (IV.ii.1–54), and
Tucca forces the new Horace to look at the portrait of the true
Horace and contrast it with his own (V.ii.278–96). In both cases
dialogue and stage-directions together make the business clear:
'*Enter Emilia . . . with 2 pictures . . .* Lie there, Arcite . . . Stand
both together . . .'; '*Enter Tucca, his boy after him with two pictures
under his cloak . . .* Look here . . . here's the sweet visage of Horace
. . . here's the copy of thy countenance'. In these instances the
characters bring the pictures on and dispose them in the course
of their roles, and Hamlet by all the analogies must be supposed
to have done the same. It does not of course follow that all these
portable pictures were in any strict sense miniatures. The portraits
of Horace need a cloak to conceal them; the one that Silvia sends
by Julia is referred to as 'hanging in' her 'chamber' (IV.ii.117);
in *Blurt Master Constable* a 'wooden picture' delivered to a lady
by a servant is handed about, hung up, gloated over, and taken
down again all in full view (II.ii.85ff.; III.i.1. Cf. Webster, *The
Devil's Law-Case*, III.iii.379ff.). But true miniatures are also
familiar (e.g. *Tw.N.* III.iv.198; Marlowe, *Ed.II*, I.iv.127; Ford,
The Lover's Melancholy, II.i.224; IV.iii.132; V.i.251–78; Shirley,
The Lady of Pleasure, III.i.152–72), and when pictures are produced

without forewarning and, failing other indication, apparently from the person, the probabilities point to miniatures, which hence may have been used in *Hamlet*. A tradition 'for Hamlet . . . to produce from his pocket two pictures . . . not much bigger than two large coins or medallions' was said to be established from Restoration times and was taken by Thos. Davies to have been handed down from Shakespeare's day (*Dramatic Miscellanies*, London, 1784, iii. 106–7). Whatever the truth of that may be, it at least accords with the evidence that easily handled portraits were a favourite item in stage-business. The idea that Shakespeare had in mind the portraits of the Danish kings in a famous tapestry in the castle of Kronborg at Elsinore (Jan Stefansson, *Contemporary Review*, LXIX, 25–9, and others) is no more than a pleasant fancy. Theories of life-size portraits in the form of wall-paintings or tapestries hanging on the stage, though often confidently asserted, are without substance. *Der Bestrafte Brudermord*, in which Hamlet says 'Dort in jener Gallerie hängt das Conterfait Eures ersten Ehegemahls, und da hängt das Conterfait des itzigen', and the famous illustration in Rowe's Shakespeare (1709), with its portraits hanging over the Queen's head, afford some evidence, however we interpret it, of stage practice in a later period, but none at all for Shakespeare's. Against them may in any case be set an early 18th-century promptbook which requires Hamlet to bring on '2 pictures' with him (see McManaway, *PBSA*, XLIII, 318–19, reprinted in *Studies in Shakespeare, Bibliography and Theater*, pp. 118–20). The Rowe engraving, regularly relied on by the advocates of wall-paintings, has proved something of a red herring. Though it demonstrably owes something to stage tradition, it can hardly be a reliable witness of actual performance (cf. Sprague, *Shakespeare and the Actors*, pp. 162–8) and its portrait of Hamlet's father in half-length notoriously fails to show the 'station' described in ll. 58–9. It is often said that this reference to a standing posture is incompatible with and even disproves the use of miniatures; yet a full-length is not to be confused with a large-scale portrait, and full-length miniatures are in fact quite well known. (It will be enough to glance at the plates in C. Winter's Penguin *Elizabethan Miniatures*.) The literalists none the less object that with a miniature the audience could not see the detail Hamlet describes. It is a curious fallacy that what is visible to the characters in the play should be equally visible to the audience. On the contrary, the verbal description may work better if it is not. The language of poetic hyperbole seeks to evoke for the imagination what no stage-property could easily depict, and this is something that life-size paintings on the stage might more damage than assist. This does not mean that the pictures can be dispensed with altogether, as Irving and Salvini among others tried to do. To suppose them to exist in the mind's eye only is hardly in compliance with the text (ll. 53–4). Though we need not see in it what Hamlet sees, there must be some 'counterfeit' which we can see him exhibit.

The objection that Hamlet, who complained of those who bought his uncle's 'picture in little' (II. ii. 362), would be unlikely to have such a picture himself demands too much of psychological consistency. Verisimilitude could equally object to the Queen's having portraits of two husbands in her chamber. It may be more to the point dramatically – and a clue to the dramatist's mind – that the earlier reference to a 'picture in little', when Hamlet is contrasting the two kings, prepares for him now to produce such. It was probably to meet the supposed claims of verisimilitude quite as much as to achieve a striking stage-effect that there grew up in the 19th century the practice of having Hamlet wear one miniature and the Queen the other. This, no less than life-size wall-portraits, the text can accommodate if the producer so wishes, but the text does nothing to suggest it. A further variant in which Hamlet wears a miniature of his father while a portrait of his uncle hangs in the Queen's chamber goes against the obvious intention of juxtaposed companion portraits (ll. 53–4, 63–5).

The case for 'miniatures' is well put in Sprague, *Shakespeare and the Actors*, pp. 166–8, and *The Stage Business in Shakespeare's Plays: A Postscript*, pp. 19–20. On the other side see W. J. Lawrence, *Pre-Restoration Stage Studies*, pp. 112–16.

III. iv. 133. *Nothing at all*] The curious may make what they will of the fact that when Hamlet has shown his mother the 'picture' of his father, the spirit of its original appears to him and not to her. They must recognize, however, that it accords with classical and Elizabethan precedent (see Stoll, *Shakespeare Studies*, pp. 211–13) as well as with the popular belief that ghosts 'may be seen of some, and of some other in that presence not seen at all' (R. Scot, *Discovery of Witchcraft*, Appendix 'Of Devils and Spirits', ch. 28). Cf. James I, *Demonology*, III. 1, 'There are sundry that affirms to have haunted such places, where these spirits are alleged to be: and could never hear nor see anything'. The obvious Shakespearean comparison is with *Mac.* III. iv; but a closer dramatic parallel is in Heywood's *2 Iron Age*, Act v, where

Agamemnon's ghost appears to Orestes while Clytemnestra sees 'Nothing'. The present case, however, differs from both these in that the Ghost not only appears but speaks to Hamlet; and it has of course appeared previously to others. Explanations of a subjective apparition are thus ruled out. Speculations as to why then Gertrude did not see it have not perhaps sufficiently considered the consequence for the play's plot if she had. Hypotheses have ranged from the Ghost's 'tender regard for Gertrude's feelings' (Moorman, *MLR*, I, 201; cf. Bradley, p. 140) to the blindness imposed upon her by her guilt (Dover Wilson, *WHH*, pp. 253–5) – not to dwell on such extraordinary fantastications as the Ghost's own inadequacy as an 'alien' and 'unhealthy' spirit whose 'Olympian attitude' of 'scientific detachment' inhibits 'a shared faith and love' (Battenhouse, *SP*, XLVIII, 184–5). Dover Wilson's explanation has at least the support of early tradition; it is explicit in *Der Bestrafte Brudermord*: 'I can readily believe that you see nothing, for you are no longer worthy to look on his form.' Yet nothing in the *Hamlet* text suggests this and the very search for an explanation risks destroying plausibility as well as mystery and awe. In the contemporary view, as expressed by James I (loc. cit.) 'that is only reserved to the secret knowledge of God, whom he will permit to see such things, and whom not'. As the god of his own play, the dramatist permits a symbolic characterization of Gertrude as one who, believing she sees 'all', sees 'nothing'.

III. iv. 163–7.   *That monster, custom, who all sense doth eat*
                   Of habits evil, is angel yet in this,
                   That to the use of actions fair and good
                   He likewise gives a frock or livery
                   That aptly is put on.]

'How use doth breed a habit in a man' (*Gent.* v. iv. 1). The general sense is that though custom makes bad ways acceptable, it can equally lead to the adoption of good ways. This is a traditional idea, going back ultimately to Aristotle (*Nichomachean Ethics*, II. 1–4). And it requires us, as Theobald long ago perceived, to emend Q2 *devil* to *evil*. Most who do so accept *habits evil* as a plural (so that *habits* balances *actions* in the next line), but the possessive *habit's evil* was at one time advocated by Theobald in his correspondence with Warburton (Nichols, *Illustrations of Lit. Hist.*, ii. 574). With *d* and *e* often indistinguishable, the error of *devil* for *evil* is a simple one (cf. *MSH*, pp. 320–1; Sisson, *NR*); that the emendation has been long and frequently resisted is due to the attractiveness of an antithesis (insisted on by Johnson) between *devil* and *angel*. Yet this seeming justification for the Q2 reading may well have been, as Theobald supposed, the source of its error. Along with Dover Wilson, Kittredge, and Sisson, I take the true antithesis to be that of *angel* with *monster* and *evil* with *fair and good*. Custom is a monster because of what it habituates us to, and to add that it is a devil seems tautologous. Farnham, however, sees custom as a monster because of its 'double form, part devil and part angel'. All attempts – including his – to interpret Q2 as it stands involve some wrenching of the syntax. Johnson, with a comma after *habits*, makes *devil* parenthetic; more often a comma after *eat* instead leaves us with two unsatisfactory absolutes: custom eats away *all* sense or feeling (not only *all sense . . . of* a defined particular), and custom is the *devil* or 'evil genius' of habits in general. For Farnham it is 'a devil in, or in respect of, habits', for Kermode (Riverside) 'like a devil in establishing bad habits'; but although the words no doubt could hold such sense, one can hardly say that they transparently convey it. Moreover all these renderings (unless perhaps the last, where *bad* is then intrusive) have the drawback of presenting all habits as of the devil, whereas the point of the passage is that custom facilitates good deeds as well as bad. To make the reference to both aspects clear, the word *evil*, as Kittredge notes, seems essential. This reading is also more compatible, I believe, with the strict significance of *habit*. Its original meaning, dress, was still the usual one (as in III.iv.137, I.iii.70); and indeed the passage beautifully illustrates how a word which at first referred to clothing can come to denote customary behaviour. (Cf. I.iv.29 and n.) Here of course it carries on from *assume*, put on the garb of, in l. 162, and in turn leads on to the *frock or livery* of l. 166. Other proposed emendations, such as *Or* for *Of*, or Staunton's *Oft habits' devil*, hardly need discussing.

A suggested interpretation of *deuill* as mourning (Fr. *deuil*), in the dual sense of sorrow (*dole*) and the garments that betoken it, is at least ingenious; but the interpretation of *all sense doth eat* to mean that custom nourishes itself entirely on the senses (A. Upton in *Language Behavior*, ed. J. Akin, etc., 1970, pp. 301–2) is ruled out by the context, which insists that sense has failed to function (ll. 71–81).

The F cuts in this speech along with the obscurities of Q2 (cf. l. 171 and LN) suggest, as Sisson remarks, 'difficult copy' (*NR*, ii.224); but the obstacles may have been as much in the style as in the hand.

III.iv.171. *lodge*]   An editorial conjecture to supply a gap in Q2,
which is the only text at this point and deficient in both metre
and sense. It is obvious that *either* is balanced by *or* and hence that
a verb stating an alternative to *throw out* has been omitted.
Attempts to make *either* itself the verb, by emending it to *entertain*
(see *SQ*, IX, 586–7) or *exorcise* (suggested by Dover Wilson *faute
de mieux*), or by explaining it as a trisyllable meaning 'make
easier' (Hulme, pp. 224–5), can be confidently dismissed. Q3
maister, though often followed, lacks authority and, whether as a
substitute for *either* or an addition to it, is metrically unsatisfactory.
It is also, along with many suggested monosyllables – the much-
favoured *curb* (for a recent advocacy of which see *Studia Neophilologica*, L, 181–3), *lay*, *quell*, etc. – of inappropriate sense. For
although all these verbs provide a contrast with throwing the
devil out, they equally deprive him of his power; and the antithesis fundamental to this whole passage is between the good and
bad effects of custom, between the custom (=*use*, l. 170) which
induces surrender to the devil's power and that which establishes
power over him (cf. Bailey, ii.11–13; Sisson, *NR*). Hence the
alternative to throwing him out is to let him in, to give him
accommodation. This is recognized in such conjectures as *aid* and
throne; but of all the words which have been proposed those which
best fit the requirements are *house* and *lodge*. *House*, proposed –
apparently independently – by Bailey and Forsyth (*N&Q*, 3rd
ser. X, 427–8; *Shakspere: Some Notes*, pp. 101–4), and read by
Chambers (RL) and Sisson, is supported by the parallel usage in
Err. IV.iv.51, 'I charge thee, Satan, hous'd within this man'. Yet
lodge, as well as having the exact sense required, seems to have had
particular currency in contexts of devil-possession. Cf. Harsnet,
Declaration of Egregious Popish Impostors, chs. 12–13, e.g. 'Fie holy
Fathers . . . that you . . . make good the chase . . . even into hell
itself, and thence start the devil, and hunt him afresh, and lodge
him with Sara Williams'; etc. Because the priest in exorcism is
said to *lodge* the devil in some appointed place, it is sometimes
mistakenly supposed that the word in itself implies confinement
or restriction (e.g. Ingleby, *Shakespeare Hermeneutics*, pp. 123ff.).
Clark and Wright, who suggested it, thought of it as equivalent
to *lay*. More properly considered, to *lodge* the devil is of course to
grant him admission and opportunity (*OED* lodge *v.* 2, to 'show
hospitality to', 'to provide with a habitation'). This at least
supplies the necessary meaning in good metre, though in the
nature of things the attempt to supply a word that is lost can only
clutch at surmise.

Another possibility might be *clothe*, which, sustaining the previous metaphor, would suggest the provision of a *habit* for the devil which would disguise his presence.

III.iv. 177. *scourge and minister*] Critics have sometimes succumbed to the temptation to identify these respectively with Hamlet's two roles in the previous line. Yet both scourge and minister are *agents* of Heaven's will and hence primarily describe the second (i.e. the punisher) rather than the first. No doubt *scourge* stresses the sterner and *minister* the kindlier aspect of Heaven's righteousness; but the two cannot be regarded as necessarily distinct (as maintained by Bowers in an article which has been much too readily accepted: 'Hamlet as Minister and Scourge', *PMLA*, LXX, 740–9. Cf. Prosser, pp. 199–201 (201–3)). The words 'were often used interchangeably' (Jorgensen, *Clio*, III, 126): the heavens may employ a 'minister' for their anger (*2H6* v.ii.34) to give 'chastisement' (*R3* v.iii. 113), while their 'scourge' is not invariably the cruel tyrant that a term applied to Attila and Tamburlaine would suggest. Heaven may effect its purposes (as here) by unwitting agents and unexpected means. It may use sin to chastise sin by one who thus will merit chastisement himself (cf. Isaiah x. 5–12). Hence the paradox of being (as here) both punisher and punished. It is in this sense that 'scourge and minister' describes Hamlet in both roles. Yet because the scourge must often be scourged, it does not follow (as Bowers seeks to argue) that this role is given only to the guilty who are foredoomed to damnation. For some counter-argument see Sisson, *Shakespeare's Tragic Justice*, pp. 104–6; H. Skulsky, *PMLA*, LXXXV, 85; R. W. Dent, *SQ*, XXIX, 82–4. (Cf. H. Brooks in *Christopher Marlowe*, ed. B. Morris, p. 92.) It is also relevant, though not of course conclusive, that both phrase and idea are anticipated in Belleforest, who makes Amleth claim to be 'le ministre et executeur de si juste vengeance' (see Intro., p. 95).

ACT IV SCENE I] Johnson had already observed that an *act-division* here is 'not very happy'. Instead of inventing an exit for the Queen which all three texts lack, editors would have done better to follow F in omitting Q2's superfluous entry-direction for her. Cf. Irwin Smith, *SQ*, XVIII, 13. It is against all convention for a character to leave the stage at the end of one scene and immediately re-enter in another. It is not essential to suppose, as most editors do, a change of place (though cf. l. 35), and if it

were, there are many instances of such a change without a break
in the stage-action: e.g. *Rom.* i.iv–v ('*They march about the Stage,
and Servingmen come forth with Napkins*'); *1 Tamburlaine,* v.i.63 ff.
(where the Virgins go from Damascus to plead with Tamburlaine). Cf. also above, ii.ii.206 LN. Hence the Queen need not
leave the stage in order to interrupt the King in conference with
Rosencrantz and Guildenstern, and Dover Wilson's suggestion
that a scene may have been cut out is otiose, as is Greg's assumption that, rather than have the King 'enter the Queen's apart-
ment', Shakespeare must have intended a new scene to begin
here (*SFF*, p. 322).

iv.i.40. *So envious slander*] Munro uniquely, and oddly, supposes
no words lost. On the normal assumption, other suggestions for
the gap include references to *rumour* – Theobald's own alternative,
(*SR*, p. 108) – *calumny, malice,* or *suspicion.* Though we can never
know what Shakespeare wrote here, *envious slander* is at least
Shakespearean. He often personifies slander, and thinks of it as
having not simply a tongue but poison and weapons. See e.g.
Cym. iii.iv.31–3, 'Slander, Whose edge is sharper than the sword,
whose tongue Outvenoms all the worms of Nile'. In *Wint.*
(ii.iii.85–6) these two attributes coalesce in slander, 'Whose sting
is sharper than the sword's'. *R2* had already given us 'slander's
venom'd spear' (i.i.171), which parallels the *poison'd shot* of *Ham.*
As an epithet for slander in this context *viperous*, which Malone
imported from *Cym.* iii.iv.37, risks both redundancy and mixed
metaphor. *Envious* would link slander's actions with their cause
and it is a favourite with Shakespeare to describe malicious
tongues. See *1H6* iii.iv.33; iv.i.90; *2H6* iii.i.157 (not to mention,
as being of doubtful authorship, *H8* iii.ii.446). *1H6* also has
'envious malice' (iii.i.26), *R3* even 'envious slanders' (i.iii.26),
and *Troil.* 'envious and calumniating Time' (iii.iii.174).

iv.ii.11–20.] Apart from vaguer uses, *the image of the sponge,*
when used as here with precision, exploits the irony latent in the
thing: what the sponge soaks up can be just as easily squeezed
out of it. This goes back to Suetonius, who tells how it was said
of the emperor Vespasian that he used rapacious officials like
sponges, advancing them to high position so that they would be
richer when he came to condemn them (*Lives of the Caesars: Vesp.*
16). This story continued to be attached to Vespasian (as by
B. Riche, *Faults, Faults,* 1606, p. 44) but was also adapted by
Raleigh, again with the sponge metaphor, to an account of Henry

III (*Prerogative of Parliaments, Works,* Oxford, 1829, viii. 165); and the same image to describe extortioners and acquirers of wealth in general is found in emblem-book (see Whitney, *Choice of Emblems,* pt II, no. 43), satire (Estienne, *A World of Wonders,* trans. R.C., 1607, p. 81; Marston, *The Scourge of Villainy,* VII, 58–60) and sermon (Andrewes, *Sermons,* Oxford, 1841–3, v. 23–4) as well as in the drama (e.g. Massinger, *Duke of Milan,* III.i.25–7). Whitney's emblem, itself deriving from Alciati (see *Omnia Emblemata,* Antwerp, 1581, no. 147, p. 526), pictures a king squeezing a sponge and in the background the condemned hanging from a gallows. Shakespeare is thus in the tradition here, while adapting the image from extortioners to obsequious hangers-on. There are novel applications of it in Jonson – to the satirist castigating other men's vanities or the poet plagiarizing other men's wit (*Every Man Out of his Humour,* Ind. 143–6; *Poetaster,* IV.iii. 104–7). Cf. Mabbe, *The Rogue,* Tudor Trans., ii.34.

IV.ii. 26–7. *The body is with the King, but the King is not with the body.*] The cryptic utterance assists the impression of madness, but it is impossible to agree with Furness, Kittredge, and others that this or anything Hamlet says is meant to be mere nonsense. Cf. II.ii.205–6, 208–11. Many have supposed (though nothing in the context justifies this) a reference to King Hamlet, whom Polonius has joined in another world. But if, taking Hamlet's words in the most direct sense, we assume him to refer as Rosencranz does to (1) the body of Polonius, then that body is still here and the implication is that it is in the very neighbourhood of the King, who will not have far to search for it, while the paradox that the King is nevertheless not with it must be a thrust at Claudius, who has not shared its fate.

But it is entirely characteristic of Hamlet to confound his interlocutors by a shift of meaning, so that we may interpret 'the body' (2) as referring to the King. Political doctrine ascribed to a king two bodies, a body natural and a body politic, the first 'a Body mortal', the second 'a Body that cannot be seen or handled' but 'contains the Office, Government and Majesty' of the king (Plowden, *Reports,* 1816, pp. 212a–213). Hence when the king dies, the body politic does not die but is 'transferred and conveyed over' from one body natural to another (Plowden, p. 233a). See Maitland, *Selected Essays,* 1936, pp. 109–11; E. H. Kantorowicz, *The King's Two Bodies,* 1957. Thus, asked where 'the body' is in relation to 'the King', Hamlet indicates that the body (natural) is necessarily 'with the King' but that the essential of the king, his majesty and kingly office, does not inhere in or belong with that body. This does not imply (as suggested in *SQ*, xviii, 430–4) that Claudius as king is free from the imperfections and guilt of his mortal being, nor offer this as an explanation of Hamlet's difficulty about killing him. Nothing in the play attributes such a difficulty to Hamlet. Rather, Hamlet's words hold a barely concealed threat – since the King's body can be killed without impairing his kingship. Cf. Kantorowicz, p. 23, on the execution of Charles I.

IV.ii.27–9. *The King is a thing . . . Of nothing.*] Cf. III.iv.97–103. For the phrase *a thing of nothing* meaning a thing or person of no consequence see, e.g., Harvey, *Four Letters*, Bodley Head Q, p. 35; *Spanish Tragedy*, Addn II.8–10; Fletcher, *The Humorous Lieutenant*, IV.vi.28; etc. It goes back to the Psalms, 'Man is like a thing of nought: his time passeth away like a shadow' (cxliv.4, Prayerbook), and if the echo is still audible, Hamlet's gibe may also hint that the King's days are numbered (Dover Wilson).

IV.ii.29. *him.*] The words added in F, *Hide, fox, and all after*, are plausibly conjectured to be a cry in a children's game in which the player who is the fox hides and the others hunt him (cf. Sam. Pegge, *Alphabet of Kenticisms*, hide-and-fox). Then either Hamlet, as the fox, dashes off with the others in pursuit (Kittredge) or Polonius's body is the fox and Hamlet leads the hue and cry (Herford). This is theatrically effective and it cannot be said to be out of character (cf. I.v.118). Yet it may be 'an actor's interpolation to heighten the feigned madness' (Parrott-Craig). Not only are the words absent from Q2 but they have in the context a subtle incongruity (cf. II.ii.577n.). Madness may properly be incoherent but not therefore inconsistent. Hamlet's thrustful speeches here and in the next scene show a desire to confront and contend with his adversaries rather than elude them; so that *Bring me to him* makes an appropriate exit-line, from which the added words detract.

IV.iii.11 S.D. *Enter . . . Guildenstern*] In Q2 'and all the rest' must be taken along with '*They enter*' after l. 15, the second entry being really covered by the first. Since Rosencrantz is specified at l. 11 and Hamlet is brought in by others at l. 15, the only problem of '*the rest*' concerns Guildenstern. In leaving Rosencrantz unaccompanied and reducing Hamlet's escort to Guildenstern alone, F's economy is at its most ruthless; and its division of this pair –

though written into the dialogue, still followed by most editors (with Dover Wilson as a notable exception), and defended by Granville-Barker (*Prefaces*, iii. 126) and Munro – cannot be what Shakespeare envisaged. The pair are never otherwise separated on stage and although only one speaks here, his *we* in l. 13 shows that there are as usual two bodies with one voice. The pair enter together to report, while their assistants, in charge of Hamlet, wait without till called for.

IV.iv.3–4. *the conveyance . . . kingdom*] With *Fortinbras's march over Denmark* the play seems to place Denmark between Norway and Poland. Cf. LNN on I.i.66, II.i.7. The Elizabethan geography of those parts is often confused. Fynes Moryson thought that Elsburg (=Helsingborg), across the strait from Elsinore, was 'in the kingdom of Norway' (*Itinerary*, 1907, i. 124), and if Shakespeare thought the same, this heightened proximity of Norway might, as G. Sjögren remarks (*Sh.Jahr.*, C–CI, 272), 'explain the invasion scare' of I.i.98–110. On the other hand Belleforest locates the Hamlet story in Jutland, observing that this projects into the sea which has Norway on its northern shore; and if some recollection of the earlier venue stayed with Shakespeare even while he transferred the scene to Elsinore, it might help him to envisage a Norwegian army crossing Jutland as it moved south (cf. Dollerup, pp. 94–6). But it is not profitable to seek geographical precision for what Shakespeare is content to leave vague. The play is consistent with itself in making Fortinbras plan an invasion of Denmark (I.i.98ff., I.ii.17ff.), switch his troops against Poland (II.ii.64ff.), proceed there by way of Denmark, and return by the same route (v.ii.355). The shipbuilding of I.i.78 acknowledges that a Norwegian invasion would be by sea, and if we think of Fortinbras now as having just disembarked, a meeting between him and Hamlet, who is about to put to sea (IV.iii.55–8), is plausible enough.

IV.iv.18–26. *We go to gain a little patch of ground . . . this straw!*] Similar reflections occur more than once in Montaigne. He observes that we are 'daily accustomed to see in our wars many thousands of foreign nations, for a very small sum of money to engage both their blood and life in quarrels wherein they are nothing interested' (Florio, II.23). Again, 'What ruin did our last Duke of Burgundy run into, for the quarrel of a cartload of sheepskins?' (III.10). Hence, even if dates permitted, we could not, with Dover Wilson, suppose an allusion to the siege of Ostend

(1601), referred to in Camden's *Annales* as a contest 'for a barren plot of sand' (*de sterili arena*). In refutation see Chambers, *Shakespearean Gleanings*, pp. 70–5.

IV.iv.27. *impostume*]   More properly *apostume* (L. *apostema*), this was the regular word for any kind of swelling in any part of the body. Hence an attempt to interpret it as cancer (*SQ*, xx, 88–90) is not justified. Andrew Boorde (*The Breviary of Health*, 1552, ch. 29) describes 'a postume' as 'no other thing but a collection or a running together of evil humours' and proceeds to classify them according to the humour which is the supposed source of corruption. He also distinguishes 'interial' and 'exterial' and adds, 'These impostumes that be interial and cannot be seen be more periculous than they which a man may see and feel'. With the image in *Hamlet* cf. Cheke, *The Hurt of Sedition*, 1549 (H^v), reprinted in Holinshed (*Chronicles*, 1587, iii. 1054), 'So is sedition . . . the apostume of the realm, which when it breaketh inwardly, putteth the state in great danger of recovery'; Fulke Greville, *A Treatise of Monarchy*, st. 573, 'the impostum'd humours of a peace'; and with the idea, Bacon, 'Of Kingdoms and Estates' ('In a slothful peace . . . manners corrupt').

IV.iv.37. *Looking before and after*]   As Theobald notes, this is Homeric (*Iliad*, iii. 109, xviii. 250). But the *locus classicus* is Cicero's *De Officiis*, which specifically links man's power to regard both past and future with his possession of the gift of reason (cf. i.ii.150 LN). Among Shakespeare's contemporaries cf. Bright (pp. 70–1): 'If a man were double fronted (as the poets have feigned Janus) . . . the same faculty of sight would address itself to see both before and behind at one instant, which now it doth by turning . . . so the mind . . . varieth . . . as the same faculty applied to . . . things past, remembreth: to things future foreseeth: of present things determineth: and that which the eye doth by turning of the head, beholding before, behind, and on each side, that doth the mind freely at once.' It is the same passage that describes the mind as 'in action wonderful, and next unto the supreme majesty of God'. Cf. *godlike* (l. 38), II.ii.304–6 LN.

IV.iv.53–6.   *Rightly to be great*
                          Is not to stir without great argument,
                          But greatly to find quarrel in a straw
                          When honour's at the stake.]
This is perhaps an instance of what Bradley (p. 76) calls Shake-

speare's negligence in 'sometimes only half saying what he meant, and sometimes saying the opposite'. Pope with his usual licence rewrote the passage; but at least he led the early editors in grasping the double negation of the sense. The numerous attempts to interpret the words as they stand, with only a single negation, divide according as *not* is taken with *Is* or with *to stir*. The second half of the proposition creates no difficulty: there is greatness in fighting even over a trifling thing where honour is involved. It is what is being opposed to this that presents the problem. A long line of critics (from Johnson and Malone to Kittredge and his followers) finds that in a trifling matter it is great *not to stir* (1); a contrary line (running from Furness through Dowden, Verity, and Dover Wilson) finds that it *is not* great to stir (2). Interpretation (1), contrasting the greatness of not stirring with the greatness of stirring, misses the antithetical force of *not . . . but* and, by finding any praise for passivity, goes against the whole weight of the soliloquy. Interpretation (2), contrasting greatness and lack of greatness in stirring, offers a proposition of which the first half is so obvious as to be pointless; and by making the distinction turn solely on whether action is or is not associated with honour, enfeebles the antithesis.

It seems clear that what Hamlet and Shakespeare are first asserting, even though the words do not precisely say this, is that there is no greatness in refraining from acting because the grounds are insufficient. That there may be virtue in refraining is not denied: it corresponds indeed with Hamlet's sentiments in ll. 23–9. But any such virtue, *rightly* considered, is emphatically *not* greatness – which is, however, to be found in the perception, through a loftiness of spirit (*greatly*), even in a trivial circumstance, of some principle of honour which prompts to action. Thus the true antithesis is neither between two kinds of greatness (1), nor between two causes of action (2), but between greatness in taking action and lack of greatness in refraining from it; so that these lines fall in with and reinforce all the rest of the soliloquy by depreciating passive forbearance and emphasizing the nobility of action.

IV.v.23. *sings*] The commentators have always linked *Ophelia's songs* specifically with her grief for her father – guided no doubt by the Gentleman's preliminary comment, 'She speaks much of her father' (l. 4), by various further references in the dialogue (ll. 45, 68–70, 79, 182–3), and by the dominant death and burial motifs in the songs themselves. A typical comment says that

'Ophelia shows herself distressed by ideas of death and the grave in connection with her father's end' (Munro). But the songs of course are not factual and it is a fallacy to suppose that they necessarily allude to actual events. The simple equation of the buried man with Polonius belongs with that strange theory which once supposed that what happens to the maiden in the Valentine song must have happened to Ophelia herself. What the songs must connect with are the fancies which arise in Ophelia's mind released from rational control. Three of the five songs are about death (ll. 23 ff., 164 ff., 187 ff.), but the first is explicitly about the death and burial of a 'true love', which is hardly Polonius's role. Three in their different kinds are songs about a lover, and in each case (since the fifth song comes as a rejoinder to the fourth) a lover by whom the lady is forsaken. So while it is true that the songs most obviously connect with the recent death and burial of Polonius, they also express on a deeper level Ophelia's fantasies about Hamlet. (See next note.) Coleridge observed (i. 30) 'the conjunction here of these two thoughts that had never subsisted in disjunction, the love for Hamlet and her filial love'. The appropriateness of the person to whom the songs are sung may also be more than coincidence (cf. Long, *Shakespeare's Use of Music*, iii. 115): the first, about a dead but unmourned lover, is sung to Gertrude; the second, a song of seduction, to the seducer Claudius; the third, a funeral elegy, to the son of the man just buried.

The best and fullest account of the songs (though it does not give the music) is that of P. J. Seng, *The Vocal Songs of Shakespeare*, pp. 131–56. Though not extant elsewhere, they are clearly all fragments of popular ballads. The first two lines of the first occur with variations in analogous ballads (see next note) and *Bonny sweet Robin* (l. 184) is known from other allusions and the frequent citation of its tune.

The tunes to which the songs are usually sung, some at least of which descend from airs of Shakespeare's time, were written down early in the 19th century by Wm. Linley and Samuel Arnold from actresses who had sung them at Drury Lane. See Linley, *Shakespeare's Dramatic Songs*, ii. 23–4; Chappell, *Popular Music of the Olden Time*, i. 236. Except for the third song, '*They bore him bare-fac'd . . .*', which Linley tells us was usually omitted on the stage, the tunes were printed by Linley (ii. 50–2) and Chappell (i. 227–37, and *A Collection of National English Airs*, ii. 20–1, 110). They are accordingly given in, among other places, Chas. Knight's *Pictorial Edition of Shakespeare*, Tragedies i. 151–4 (except for *Bonny sweet Robin*); Furness; Caulfield, *A Collection of the Vocal Music in Shakespeare's Plays*, ii. 83–9; Naylor, *Shakespeare and Music*, rev. 1931, pp. 189–91; Sternfeld, *Music in Shakespearean Tragedy*, 1963, pp. 60–78 (with the most authoritative discussion); Sternfeld, *Songs from Shakespeare's Tragedies*, 1964 (arranged for modern performance); Long, *Shakespeare's Use of Music*, iii (1971), 124–7.

IV. V. 23–40.] *How should I your true love know.*—Among the multiple allusions of this song, in its context, are those to (1) the death of Polonius and his unsatisfactory burial 'in hugger-mugger' (see l. 39 n.); (2) Ophelia's forlorn love for Hamlet, which, since the song is explicitly that of a woman seeking her absent lover, is clearly the dominant motif. There is also, as well shown by Seng (pp. 133–4), an ironic application to (3) the Queen, to whom the song is pointedly directed (ll. 28, 35) and who herself has failed to distinguish her 'true love . . . from another one' and to lament him 'with true-love showers'.

The ballad belongs to a common duologue type, alternating question and answer. Ophelia launches into the middle of it, but the beginning can easily be inferred, especially with the help of analogues, the chief of which is the ballad of the Walsingham pilgrim who is met by a lover in search of his true love:

> As ye came from the holy land
> Of Walsingham
> Met you not with my true love
> By the way you came?

To judge from the numerous variations, it was a very popular ballad. This opening quatrain is one of the snatches sung by Merrythought in *The Knight of the Burning Pestle*, II. viii. In the second quatrain the pilgrim rejoins with his own question correspondent to Ophelia's beginning:

> How should I know your true love
> That have met many a one . . . ?

and exactly the same words occur in an analogous broadside ballad called *The Contented Cuckold* (see *The Pepys Ballads*, ed. Rollins, ii. 24–8). The inquirer replies with a description of the true love, 'She is neither white nor brown' (*Cont. Cuck.* 'black'), after which the pilgrim acknowledges having met 'such a one' and the ballad goes on to reveal a faithful love which is unreturned.

It will be apparent that Ophelia's song transposes the sexes as befits her plight; it is now the man who has gone away and the woman who seeks him. The song also diverges from the prototype in ascribing the lover's forsaking of the maiden to his death. We are hardly entitled to infer, in the absence of the direct source, that these are Shakespeare's innovations; but he may have been adapting a familiar ballad to his dramatic purposes or perhaps amalgamating several. Noble thought it 'evident' that Ophelia's three stanzas were fragments of 'three different songs' (*Shakespeare's Use of Song*, p. 119). However that may be, Shakespeare has provided her with the song of a woman who seeks her departed lover, despairs of his return, and, with the switch to a funeral elegy, gives to their separation the anguish of finality. It expresses a fantasy of the loved one's death and, the intrusive *not* of l. 39 becoming self-accusatory, of the failure in loving lamentation by the singer's therefore unfaithful self. Cf. the burial song of the unrequited lover in *Tw.N.* ii.iv.50 ff.

The words of the 'Walsingham' analogue are extant in three variant manuscripts in the British Museum, Bodleian, and Huntington libraries (the second attributing it to Raleigh), and in one printed version (Deloney's *Garland of Goodwill*, 1631, G5ᵛ–6ᵛ, Percy Soc. pp. 111–12). The manuscript versions are respectively printed in *Bishop Percy's Folio MS*, ed. Hales and Furnivall, iii.471–2; Raleigh's *Poems*, ed. A. M. C. Latham; *Hunt. Lib. Quarterly*, IV, 473–4. Among other places the ballad can also be found in Percy's *Reliques*, ed. Wheatley, ii.101–5; Deloney's *Works*, ed. F. O. Mann, pp. 365–6; *Music and Letters*, XLV, 111–13; and, perhaps most conveniently for the Shakespeare student, in Seng (pp. 137–8).

The traditional music of Ophelia's song (for which see previous LN) appears also to be a corruption of the popular Walsingham tune, which can be found in Chappell, i.121–3 (rev. Wooldridge, i.69); Naylor, *Shakespeare and Music*, rev. 1931, p. 190; Sternfeld, *Music in Shakespearean Tragedy*, pp. 61–2. For fuller bibliography, see Seng, p. 136.

IV.v.42–3. *the owl was a baker's daughter*]   A folk-tale of which there are several versions tells how, when Christ asked for bread, the baker's daughter took care that he should not be given too much and was thereupon turned into an owl. A variant in which Christ requested and she refused him water was current among the gypsies, and in their language an owl is called a baker's daughter (*Journal of the Gypsy Lore Soc.*, n.s. 1, 1907, 90). A story which identifies the two is not to be dismissed as irrelevant because it lacks obvious connection with Ophelia's case. The metamorphosis may acquire significance in the light of other emblematic usages (see R. Tracy, *SQ*, xvii, 83–6). Lines 8 ff. of this scene have invited us to make what sense we can of Ophelia's 'unshaped' speech – though we must also heed their warning against fitting it to the fanciful explanations in which commentators too readily indulge. What we may certainly perceive is that the associations of the mournful bird are appropriate for Ophelia. A widespread belief is that the owl sings only in winter (e.g. *Owl and Nightingale*, ll. 411–16); and hence, contrasting with the cuckoo (cf. *LLL* v.ii.878–9) and notoriously with the nightingale, birds of the mating season, it is readily regarded as mourning the death of love, as Ophelia's songs do now. Another belief is that the owl's cry, traditional signal of disaster, may betoken the loss of a maidenhead. This is said to be a common superstition in Wales (M. Trevelyan, *Folk-Lore and Folk-Stories of Wales*, pp. 83–4). Baker's daughters were traditionally women of ill repute: the Marian martyr John Bradford said of Philip of Spain that 'he must have three or four in one night . . . not of ladies and gentlewomen, but of bakers' daughters, and such poor whores' (Strype, *Eccles. Memorials*, 1822, iii (pt 2), 352). Hence the identification of the owl as having been a baker's daughter may connect the end of love with the loss of chastity, recalling what Hamlet has said about the transformation of honesty (iii.i.111–12) and leading on to Ophelia's next song.

iv.v.48–66.] Ophelia's *Valentine song* is not otherwise known, but the proverb-like l. 60 is cited by Burton as though it were a commonplace (*Anat. of Melancholy*, iii.ii.5(3)). If it is of Shakespeare's composition, it follows a familiar type, in which, however, it is more usual for the man to come to his mistress's window than the other way about. Like Ophelia's first song and her last, though in a very different mode, this is a song of disappointed love. Its indelicacy on Ophelia's lips has much exercised the critics, but how and when she could have learnt it is an irrelevant speculation. Its theme – that of the lover who takes a maiden's honour and then abandons her – we have seen impressed upon her mind by her brother and her father in i.iii.5–44, 91–131. The song presents a variation on what they warned her against. Yet the irony is not that the singer of the song has suffered what they feared and it narrates, but that she has not. Hamlet, far from despoiling, has rejected her (iii.i).

Sung apparently to Claudius, the song may also be seen as a variation, at a farther remove, upon his seduction of Gertrude (cf. I.v.45–6).

The tune to which it is traditionally sung (see IV.v.23 LN) was a common one. It is found in several 18th-century ballad operas and may well go back to Shakespeare's day. A version of it known as 'Who list to lead a soldier's life', or more simply 'Soldier's Life', was printed in Playford's *English Dancing Master*, 1651 (p. 65), and more than one tune under that name appears to have been familiar to Shakespeare's contemporaries. (See Chappell, i. 144, 227.)

IV.v.123–5. *There's such divinity doth hedge a king*
           That treason can but peep to what it would,
           Acts little of his will.]
Cf. *R2* III.ii.47–57, esp. 'His treasons will sit blushing in his face, Not able to endure the sight of day, But self-affrighted tremble at his sin'; Beaumont and Fletcher, *The Maid's Trag.* III.i.233–41, '*King*: Draw not thy sword; thou know'st I cannot fear A subject's hand. . . . *Amintor*: . . . There is Divinity about you that strikes dead My rising passions.' Chettle gives an account of Queen Elizabeth, who, after a shot had struck her barge and all were crying 'Treason', 'bade them never fear, for if the shot were made at her, they durst not shoot again: such majesty had her presence . . . that she . . . was as all princes are, or should be, so full of divine fullness, that guilty mortality durst not behold her but with dazzled eyes' (*England's Mourning Garment*, E2v–3). During the Essex rebellion she is reported to have said that 'He that had placed her in that seat would preserve her in it' (MS Sloane 718, fol. 26). For the political theory see J. N. Figgis, *The Divine Right of Kings* (1896).

IV.v.164–5. *They bore him bare-fac'd on the bier,*
           And in his grave rain'd many a tear—]
Usually taken by the critics, as by Laertes, to refer to the burial of Ophelia's father. But see LN on l. 23 above. Though no ballad is known in which these lines occur, they are unlikely to have been Shakespeare's invention. Cf. Chaucer, *Knight's T.* (ll. 2877–8), 'He leyde hym, bare the visage, on the beere; Therwith he weep that pitee was to heere'. The Drury Lane tradition supplying no old tune for this lyric snatch, it has usually been sung to a tune adapted from one or other of those for the songs at ll. 23 ff. (Walsingham) and ll. 187 ff. The *Hey non nony*, etc., which

F injects between the two lines of this song is presumably a stage-addition.

IV. V. 169–70. *and you Call him a-down-a*]   With both Q2 and F printing the whole speech in roman type, there has been much uncertainty as to which words exactly Ophelia is directing to be sung; and attempts to construe *and* as 'if', instead of the simple connective, have only added to perplexity. Some editors take *A-down a-down, and you call him a-down-a* all to belong to the required refrain. But the assumption that *and you* is an instruction to a further singer has some support from Q1 (even though the words are there misplaced), 'you shall sing a downe, And you a downe a'. Some suppose that the direction to the second singer is 'and you call him'. But the arrangement of the present text, which regards *call him* as part of the answering refrain, is attested by a ballad of King Edgar in Deloney's *Garden of Goodwill* (Song 3):

> Whenas King *Edgar* did govern this Land,
>   adown, adown, down, down, down;
> And in the strength of his years he did stand,
>   call him down a.

Attempts to identify *him* with Polonius, and Dover Wilson's consequent paraphrase of *and you call him a-down-a* as 'if you really think that he is fallen low a-down' (*MSH*, p. 228), mistake the dramatic function of the refrain when they seek to give its words a literal (and rational) application.

IV. V. 170. *wheel*]   Though Steevens could cite no authority for *wheel* meaning refrain, there is no reason to doubt the correctness of his explanation. The rival explanations of the sceptics – that wheel alludes to the spinning-wheel, the wheel of Fortune (or alternatively of Occasion), a dance movement, a musical instrument, and even Ophelia's farthingale – are mere guesses, despite the claim of the first to have support from the song in *Tw.N.* which is chanted by 'the spinsters and the knitters in the sun' (II. iv. 43) and from the ballads referred to in Hall's *Satires* as being 'Sung to the wheel, and sung unto the pail' (IV. vi. 54). As for Occasion (=Opportunity), it is true that she, like Fortune, is often pictured circling on a wheel (see *SQ*, XVIII, 35–6) and that this might have some relevance to 'revenge' (l. 167), but I do not think a mere mention of 'the wheel' could, without further particular, identify it as hers. The objection that F2 did not understand *wheel* in the sense of refrain applies equally to the other explanations offered. Among historians of prosody Guest defines a *wheel* as 'the return of some marked and peculiar rhythm' at the close of each stanza (*A History of English Rhythms,* ii. 290, 324); and Saintsbury as 'a short or short-lined stanza suffixed as coda to a longer one' (*A History of English Prosody,* i. 428). Guest distinguishes a *wheel,* which repeats the same rhythm, from a *burden,* which repeats the same words, but adds that the Elizabethans used the two terms indifferently.

IV.v. 173–83.] *Ophelia's distribution of flowers* still awaits satisfactory elucidation. The problems are of two kinds, mutually dependent: to determine the symbolic meanings of the plants and, in the absence of any guidance from stage-directions, to identify the various recipients. But first to dispel some critical misconceptions: (1) that the flowers exist only in Ophelia's fantasy and (2) that they have no serious significance. (1) The custom on which this episode is based is also used by Shakespeare in *Wint.* IV.iv. 73–9; and there is no apparent reason why Ophelia, who will presently gather many flowers for her fatal garlands (IV.vii. 167–8), should not be as well supplied with them as Perdita herself. In neither play are flowers mentioned in contemporary stage-directions. It was Rowe who made Ophelia enter 'fantastically drest with straws and flowers', presumably by analogy with the mad King Lear (as described in *Lr* IV.iv. 3–6); but her exclamation in Q1, 'Wel God a mercy, I a bin gathering of floures', is evidently occasioned by her appearance with them. With only imaginary flowers the dramatic effect would be hopelessly impoverished and the comments of Laertes would make little sense. Ophelia's madness shows itself not in gesturing with non-existent flowers but in unawareness of her surroundings and of the identity of those whom she gives her flowers to. Note that even the brother whom she bade affectionate farewell (I.iii. 4, 84–6) and who was but just now in her thoughts (l. 70) receives on his return no greeting nor any sign of recognition. (2) Accordingly the effect of her flower-giving is not to be measured by Ophelia's intent. Nor can it be summed up by the comment of Laertes on its 'prettiness' (l. 186), as maintained by J. W. Lever in an unexpectedly perverse and obfuscating article (*RES,* n.s. III, 123–9). He might instead have quoted her brother's previous comment: *A document in madness* (l. 176), a lesson conveyed through mad talk. We are reminded of Lear's 'reason in madness' (IV.vi. 176) and still more of those comments of Polonius on Hamlet's cryptic sayings (II.ii. 208–11) which alert us to the dramatist's purpose of using

madness to convey what rational discourse could not. With rosemary and pansies, the first two flowers, Ophelia indicates and
Laertes accepts an emblematic meaning, thereby inviting us to do
the same for those which follow. This could not have been beyond
the capacity of an intelligent audience which had the advantage
denied to us of seeing who the authentic recipients were and belonged to an age more accustomed than our own to emblematic
usages. There was a little vogue for floral verses. The youth in
Philaster could show in his garland 'What every flower, as country
people hold, Did signify' (I.ii.130–3). This is a lore, however,
which must be sought less (where Lever looks) in the standard
herbals than in popular beliefs. A difficulty for us is that much of
it has not survived and that the literary allusions from which we
may recover it, though for some plants abundant, are in other
cases sparse. Among many extant works which have supplied
quotations, regularly repeated since the time of Steevens and
Malone, the two most often cited, because of the number of relevant flowers they include, are the first few pages of Robert
Greene's *A Quip for an Upstart Courtier* (1592) and the poem in
Clement Robinson's *A Handful of Pleasant Delights* (1584) called 'A
Nosegay always sweet, for Lovers to send for Tokens . . .' In this
mystic language, not surprisingly perhaps, the same flowers do not
always signify the same thing; so that there is the further difficulty,
too often ignored by the Shakespearean annotators, of selecting
the meanings which are applicable to the play. Nevertheless,
while making due allowance for the inconsequentiality of madness, I think it wrong to assume that what we cannot explain is
designedly confused in order to symbolize 'the murky world of
intrigue and mental disorder' (*ELH*, XLIV, 63).

Rosemary was *for remembrance* because it was popularly supposed to
strengthen the memory. It is still associated with funerals and the
remembrance of the dead (cf. *Rom.* IV.v.79). Ironically, in giving it
to Laertes, Ophelia plays in his revenge (cf. ll. 167–8) the role of
the Ghost in Hamlet's (I.v.91). But rosemary is also given as a
token of remembrance between lovers. For the lover of 'A Nosegay'

> Rosemary is for remembrance
>   between us day and night:
> Wishing that I might always have
>   you present in my sight.

And a lover in Drayton's *Pastorals* (IX) is given it by

> his sweetheart, whose intent
> Is that he her should in remembrance have.

Very much as she has merged a lover's with a father's loss in her songs of lamentation, Ophelia confuses her brother with her lover. *Pansies*, given along with rosemary, continue the double application. *For thoughts* because of their name (Fr. *pensées*), they can strengthen in Laertes the thoughts prompted by his father's death; but they too are associated with the sentiments of love. Drayton implies that maidens call them heartsease for that reason, and among their other names is love-in-idleness. When the wife in Chapman's *All Fools* points to a pansy in her needlework, her jealous husband retorts 'O that's for lover's thoughts' (II. i. 234).

As Ophelia passes on, the formula *for you . . . for you* indicates a succession of recipients, and for dramatic effect these must include the key characters who are present and hence the King and Queen. It is always assumed that rue is for the Queen and fennel and columbines for the King; but I believe that a consideration of the emblematic implications will show this to be wrong. *Fennel* normally signifies flattery, as, in spite of an occasional dissentient, is abundantly attested. The Count in Jonson's *The Case is Altered*, when addressed as 'my good lord', exclaims 'Your good lord! O how this smells of fennel' (I. vii. 9). Jas. Yates, after praising its medicinal virtues, adds 'Yet some will say that fennel is to flatter' (*The Castle of Courtesy*, 1582, fol. 47); and in a poem 'Of Certain Flowers' by Turbervile we find

> Your Fennel did declare
> (as simple men can show)
> That flattery in my heart I bare
> where friendship ought to grow.
>> (*Epitaphs*, 1570, fol. 42ᵛ)

Flattery goes with insincerity and hence often with dissembling – Florio in *A World of Words* explains *dare finocchio* as 'to give fennel, to claw, to cog, to foist, to flatter, to dissemble' – and dissembling in love implies fickleness. Thus Turbervile (fol. 43) makes fennel the opposite of 'good faith', and in 'A Nosegay'

> Fennel is for flatterers,
> an evil thing it is sure:
> But I have always meant truly,
> with constant heart most pure.

Greene in *A Quip* is more specific: he thinks of fennel, 'for flatterers', as 'women's weeds . . . fit generally for that sex, sith while they are maidens, they wish wantonly, while they are wives they will wilfully, while they are widows they would willingly:

and yet all these proud desires are but close dissemblings'. It seems strange that this passage has escaped attention: if we may take it as a signpost for *Hamlet* it points plainly to the Queen. Her career as wife is told us by the Ghost (I.v.45–7), and for Hamlet she is the pattern of women's 'frailty' (I.ii.146), in whom 'reason panders will' (III.iv.88). Fennel thus leads on to *columbines*. This flower was noted for the horned shape of its nectaries: Steevens cited Thos. Cutwode's *Caltha Poetarum*, 1599 (st. 16), for its description of

> the blue cornuted columbine
> Like to the crooked horns of Acheloy

(i.e. Achelous, who changed himself into a bull). It is easy to see therefore how the columbine becomes a symbol of cuckoldry. Though the signification is sometimes disputed, it will explain the columbine joke in *LLL* (v.ii.647), which commentators curiously ignore; and the scene already cited from *All Fools* puts the matter beyond doubt. When Cornelio has ascribed the pansy his wife has worked to lover's thoughts, the dialogue continues:

> . . . What's that, a columbine?
> – No, that thankless flower fits not my garden.
> – Hem! yet it may mine. (II.i.234–6)

And the jealous husband goes on to explicit accusations. It is made clear that the columbine would fit either the man with horns or the wife or lover who, in Chapman's word, 'adhorns' him. The conflicting assumption that the columbine stands for ingratitude seems to rest solely on a misunderstanding of this passage. Those who assert that meaning have never succeeded in showing its relevance to either *All Fools* or *Hamlet*. I take it that the columbine is a 'thankless flower' because, like a 'thankless', or unrewarding, task, it affords no satisfaction. But this is said by a wife who is laying claims to virtue and thus disdains the flower that Queen Gertrude must accept.

This leaves the King as the recipient of *rue*. But who better? The significance of this plant is given it by its homonym, and the rue of regret includes not merely sorrow but repentance. And it is the King's need for repentance that is dramatized in the one scene where he holds alone the centre of the stage (III.iii). The alternative name for rue, *herb o' grace* (or *herb grace*) emphasizes this element of meaning; and though Malone may be right in one sense to insist that this is an everyday and not a special Sunday name, yet it has its special aptness on the day which is given to

God and the repentance of one's sins. For the aptness of rue for
the King it is also pertinent to remember that it traditionally had
the property of abating carnal lust (Cogan, *Haven of Health*, 1584,
p. 40, citing the authority of Galen); he no less than the Queen
may find his sexual transgressions rebuked. The rue that Ophelia
keeps herself is appropriate for her sorrow; but when the King is
bidden to wear his *with a difference*, the play uses this metaphor
from heraldry to point a distinction between recipients; and
although this remains, like much else, implicit, we shall surely
not be wrong to connect it, as has been usual since Malone, with
the difference between innocence and guilt.

The *daisy* has proved baffling. The much-repeated editorial
note that it is a symbol of dissembling is not by itself helpful. But
it appears to derive from Greene's allusion in *A Quip*, which
introduces 'the dissembling daisy, to warn such light of love
wenches not to trust every fair promise that such amorous
bachelors make them, but sweet smells breed bitter repentance'.
This gives an obvious clue: we recognize the plight imaged forth
in Ophelia's Valentine song (ll. 48–66) and in the warnings of
her father and brother (I.iii). Yet traditionally the daisy is the
flower not of deception but of love. As it appears in Greene, it
has become sadly tarnished since it was eulogized by Chaucer as
the flower of Alcestis, who by sacrificing herself for her husband
became the acknowledged queen of love. But one can see how
such a change could happen. Chaucer's *Legend of Good Women* is a
celebration of martyrs in love's cause, and these not surprisingly
include some who suffer through being forsaken by their lovers.
As an emblem of love's victims the daisy has a latent ambivalence;
the folly of being deceived, which is emphasized by Greene, may
go with a constant devotion (cf. III.i. 116–20). This is just what is
implied by Turbervile, whose lover suspected of change comments
on his mistress's flower,

> A daisy doth express
>   great folly to remain,

and gets from her an answer which both accepts the charge of
folly and vaunts undying love:

> Though daisy hit the nail aright,
>   my friendship aye shall last.

However we regard her and it, this is Ophelia's flower, wherefore
a number of editors (Dyce, Dowden, Dover Wilson) have
suggested that she keeps it for herself. But this does not inevitably

follow, and the language – *There's a daisy* (contrast *here's some for me*) – parallels it with the flowers given away. It should of course be given where its reproach fits, and in the absence of her lover it must go to whomever among those present her madness now substitutes for him. With nothing to mark a change of recipient (as *for you* has done before) the King as the person last addressed must be the likeliest candidate; and for Ophelia to offer him, like Laertes and the Queen, a second flower as an afterthought, though this may not be a strong argument, would give a kind of symmetry.

The desired recipient of *violets* is necessarily the same. It is certainly to her lover that Ophelia would give violets if she could. As 'A Nosegay' has it,

> Violet is for faithfulness,
>   which in me shall abide:
> Hoping likewise that from your heart,
>   you will not let it slide,
> And will continue in the same,
>   as you have now begun,
> And then for ever to abide:
>   then you my heart have won.

The significance of violets that have *withered* is plain enough. Ironically, it is what Ophelia's brother warned her to expect of Hamlet's love when he compared it to a violet 'sweet, not lasting, The perfume and suppliance of a minute' (1.iii.7–9); and it is how Ophelia found it when, 'their perfume lost', she returned the tokens of it (III.i.98–9). The only thing to surprise us is that the violets are said to have withered when her father died. It cannot be, as has been said, that Hamlet's killing of Polonius finally killed their love. For Hamlet's love was lost to her already and hers survived till death (cf. v.i.232–3). What happens, I think, is that amid the memories of forsaken love, symbolized in the rue, in the daisy, and in violets that have withered, her mind drifts back to her father's death to afford yet another instance of that confusion of grief in which the loss of father and lover merge. The violets have thus, like the flowers given to Laertes, a double implication: they recall along with a lost love Polonius's faithful service to the state (the first thing suggested to us about him, I.ii.47–9) while seeming to rebuke a court which knows faithfulness no more. Again it is to the King that this would most appropriately be said. Horatio, whom some editors have proposed as one to whom violets might be given, has been out of the dramatist's mind for at least a hundred lines (cf. l. 74 S.D. n.), and is surely the least eligible person to have it put to him that faithfulness is extinct.

The interpretation of the flowers here advanced has the result of giving them greater significance than they are usually accorded even by those who regard them as more than an incidental 'prettiness'. It is not a valid objection that some of them allude to things which Ophelia could not have known. The whole principle of dramatic irony depends on the use of dialogue to convey more than the speakers suspect. The distribution of the flowers, once these are correctly assigned, connects the characters involved (King, Queen, Laertes, Ophelia) beyond the present moment with their essential dramatic roles, and glances even at the absent hero (as well as the dead Polonius) in one aspect of his. Ophelia's lasting love for the lover who has forsaken her is an undercurrent throughout. As befits the warning given by the play (IV.v.6–10) of the risks of misconstruction, the meanings of the flowers are more suggested than defined – it is a virtue of the emblems to be, as is said nowadays, open-ended. But through the suggestions that they bring it is a function of this little episode, as of the Pyrrhus speech and *The Murder of Gonzago*, to represent in a different mode some basic motifs of the play.

IV.v.184. *For bonny sweet Robin is all my joy.*] That the song to which this line belonged and more especially its tune were very popular is attested by Sternfeld's catalogue of instances of instrumental music for it in no fewer than 6 books and 24 manuscripts (*Music in Shakespearean Tragedy*, pp. 68–78). The tune is also specified in connection with a number of other ballads from 1594 on. 'Bonny Robin' is one of the songs that the Jailer's daughter in *The Two Noble Kinsmen* (an imitation of Ophelia) says that she can sing (IV.i.134). The words of the song, however, have not survived. Chappell notes that the tune is variously called 'Bonny sweet Robin' and 'Now Robin is to the greenwood gone' and he supposes that the latter is the song's first line and that what Ophelia sings is the refrain (i.233–4; *Roxburghe Ballads*, i.181). It is pointed out that her words could fit either the first or the last strain of the melody. Robin is of course one of the commonest of all names, but Chappell's alternative title seems to identify the Robin of the song with Robin Hood, which gives ground for the supposition that the song is one for Maid Marian; and since Marian sometimes distributed flowers in the May Games, it is possible to see Ophelia as projecting herself into Marian's role.

Since Marian moreover had become associated with lewd jests and gestures, it is sometimes supposed that the song was an improper one and that Ophelia in singing it is continuing the vein of her Valentine song (Seng, p. 153). Yet the surrounding dialogue does nothing to compel this view, and the ready use of the tune in a variety of contexts is perhaps against it. We may accept that Robin was a familiar name not merely for a lover but for a man's penis (*PMLA*, LXXIII, 601–3). But because it sometimes had lewd connotations, it does not follow that it could not be used without them. On the contrary, Sidney, writing affectionately to his brother in 1580, calls him 'sweet Robin' (*Works*, ed. Feuillerat, iii. 130); and Raleigh wrote to Leicester in 1586, 'The Queen is on very good terms with you . . . and you are again her sweet Robin' (*Works*, Oxford 1829, viii. 655). No doubt Ophelia's singing of this line would remind the Elizabethan audience of the rest of so popular a song; but what this would suggest to them is, in the absence of the words, pure speculation. What we can say of the single line is that it appears to express exultant love. If the song is indeed the same as one beginning 'Now Robin is to the greenwood gone', we may add that the singer's confidence in her lover seems unimpaired by his departure. After the dirge and the pathos of the flower passage, this sudden burst of apparently joyous song is dramatically striking, and the abrupt return to despair in the next song the more poignant.

IV.v.187–96.] *And will a not come again?*—The change of tone comes so abruptly upon the love-song of l. 184 that, although this lyric reveals itself (192–3) as a dirge for an old man, it will almost inevitably strike us also as a lament for the lost lover. Cf. l. 23 LN. The usual tune derives from the Drury Lane tradition recorded by Linley and Chappell. Unlike those for the songs at ll. 23 ff., 48 ff., 184 it cannot be traced back to Shakespeare's time, but Chappell (i. 237) notes that 'it appears to be a portion of the tune entitled *The Merry Milkmaids*' in Playford's *English Dancing Master*, 1651 (in which see p. 31), and associated with 'several ballads'. There is a burlesque of this song in *Eastward Ho* (III.ii).

IV.vii.70–104.] The excessively elaborate *introduction of the fencing stratagem* suggests that, apart from its essential function in the plot, it had for the dramatist some ulterior significance. In particular, the centaur-like description of the Norman whose identity merges with that of his beast (ll. 84–7) seems to make of him an emblematic figure. One can hardly help being reminded of the comparison of Claudius to a satyr (I. ii. 140) and of kindred animal images, even while the horseman, in contrast with the satyr, is invested with a splendour of which no touch is ever given to Claudius or (till Laertes) his associates. Laertes's skill in fencing, which is to be the means of Hamlet's death, is presented ambivalently from the first. Simultaneously brilliant (71–2) and of dubious worth (75–8), it will befit the revenger in action, whom the play conceives of as both noble and base. As for the outcome, the name of the 'wondrous' messenger (91) is a presage of fatality, and the mere report of Laertes's prowess carries a venom (102) which anticipates the actual poisoned foil.

IV. vii. 80. *health*] It is unexpected to find *health* as well as *graveness* regarded as an attribute of age rather than youth, and many have accordingly supposed 'respectively' to be implied, so that youth's 'livery' imports health and age's costume graveness. The objection to this is not in syntax but in sense. For a speaker who depreciates even while excusing a 'light and careless livery' cannot see it as a sign of health. Rather it betokens youth's irresponsible wildness against which 'health' is opposed. Cf. I. iii. 21, where the 'health' of the state requires the circumscribing of youth's impulsive follies. The idea of a connection between health and the warm clothes worn in age had better be dismissed.

IV. vii. 165–82. *There is a willow . . . death.*] It is often conjectured that this *account of Ophelia's death* was inspired by that of the remarkably named Katherine Hamlett, at Tiddington, near Stratford, in December 1579. Going with a pail to fetch water from the Avon, she slipped, fell in, and was drowned. (*Minutes and Accounts . . . of Stratford-upon-Avon*, Dugdale Soc., iii. 50–1. See C. C. Stopes in Sh. Assoc. *Papers*, 1927, pp. 226–7; Fripp, *Shakespeare Studies*, pp. 128–36.) There may be more than coincidence here, and although Dover Wilson robustly observes that a December drowning could hardly have supplied Shakespeare with his setting, an imagination familiar with the Avon scene could well have transposed the incident, in recalling it years later, to a less austere season. Yet the imagination could not need such prompting: the primary source of the *willow* and hence of the mode of Ophelia's death is emblematic. By tradition the willow is 'a sad tree, whereof such who have lost their love make their mourning garlands' (Fuller, *Worthies*, 1662, p. 144), which they then wear or hang up like a trophy (ll. 171–2). And the tradition is one to which Shakespeare's mind readily responded: he had pictured Dido 'with a willow in her hand' (*Mer.V.* v.i. 10), he had shown Benedick mockingly inviting Claudio 'to a willow tree . . . to make him a garland, as being forsaken' (*Ado* II.i. 166–70, 193–4); and in the pathos of the willow Ophelia's end anticipates the death of Desdemona (*Oth.* IV.iii. 27–55).

Yet symbolism felicitously combines with realism. The common 'white' willow (*salix alba*), when precariously rooted in a river-bank, often leans across the stream (l. 165); and its leaves are *hoary* (silver-grey) on the underside, which it *shows* when reflected in the water. The flowers used for the garlands, though two of them have posed problems of identification, would seem to be natural to English water-meadows as well as emblematically apt.

Of these, *nettles* need little comment: all Shakespeare's other references to them (eleven) are notably if unsurprisingly un-favourable (see e.g. *Tp.* II.i. 138, and esp. *Lr.* IV.iv. 4–5). They are useless or noxious weeds, associated with pain, poison, or (*Tit.* II.iii. 272) betrayal. For *daisies* and forsaken love see IV.v. 181 and IV.v. 173–83 LN. As for the other two, with flower names from the time before Linnaeus, even when these are still familiar, it is often impossible to be certain what plant is being referred to. The mistaken assumption that *crow-flowers* are buttercups under an earlier name arises through confusion between the crow-flower and the crowfoot, which for Elizabethan botanists are entirely different plants. The crow-flower, which they classify as *lychnis* not *ranunculus*, which they often specifically identify with *lychnis flos-cuculi*, and which Lyte and Gerard alternatively call wild William, marsh gilloflower, or cuckoo gilloflower, is evidently therefore the flower we know as the ragged robin. (The doubts expressed by Gerard concern not the English flower referred to but its proper classification.) It is perhaps a symbol of dejection. *Long purples*, though the name does not occur in contemporary herbals, have been recognized from Shakespeare's account of them and their names (see ll. 168–70 and nn.) as a kind of wild orchis. Among the various species the favoured candidate is *orchis mascula*, though Beisly points to a confusion in the popular nomenclature when the name *dead men's fingers*, appropriate for a plant which has palmate roots, is extended to a species which has not (*Shakespeare's Garden*, p. 160). See also *N&Q*, x, 225–7; Grindon, *The Shakespeare Flora*, p. 129; Britten and Holland, *Dictionary of English Plant Names*. The modern conjectures – re-cently revived and refuted (*SQ*, xxix (1978), 413–17; xxx (1979), 397–402) – which would replace the orchis by the cuckoo pint (*arum maculatum*) depend largely on the curious assumption that only a phallic shape can inspire *a grosser name* (for which, however, see l. 169n.).

The allusion to alternative names is not the unsuitable elaboration it has been accused of being. On the contrary, in the suggestion of chaste maids untouched by country grossness, with an image of sexuality giving way to one of death (ll. 169–70), the whole of Ophelia's story is epitomized. It is a very limited notion of drama which regards as 'lyrical rather than dramatic' (Kittredge), and even awkwardly 'fulsome' (*N&Q*, ccxxvi, 134), a speech designed in all its details to provide the Ophelia we have seen with her most appropriate end. And though the Queen does not speak in character, it is an essentially dramatic conception which makes her, who has in large part caused Hamlet's revulsion from love and marriage, the messenger of Ophelia's lovelorn death (cf. *HO*, p. 148). Her account of it, reaching chorus-like beyond the dialogue, the play expects us to accept. So with the breaking of the branch (l. 172) the dramatist refutes in advance the suspicions of suicide which will nevertheless be allowed to determine the manner of Ophelia's funeral (v.i. 1–29, 211–31). In the circumstances of her death divergence of opinion among the folk of Elsinore is natural enough and must not be misconstrued as Shakespearean inconsistency (cf. v.i.2n.). Her failure to struggle against her fate may lend colour to the 'doubtful' verdict, but it is also given its exculpatory reason (l. 177). Her hymns of praise (and hence the Q2 reading *lauds*, l. 176) have often been objected to as incompatible with her earlier love-songs; but the critics have not perhaps sufficiently appreciated that what both have in common is their very incongruity. Ophelia's uninhibited songs in the royal presence, her lauds while sinking to a watery death show a complete unawareness of her physical surroundings in which the crazed mind is only too consistent. In each may be heard a voice from those deepest levels of the emotional being which sanity keeps secret. What can be incompatible between Ophelia's regard for Hamlet and for heaven? She appealed to heaven in her love's beginning (i.iii.114) and also in its crisis (iii.i.135, 143), and her mad songs are significantly interspersed with pious thoughts (iv.v.42–4, 68–71, 179–80, 197). It is in more than one way that her departure from the stage prepares for the account of her death. Shakespeare's conception of Ophelia is profounder than that of his critics; and the present speech, neither a digression nor an afterthought (as *SQ*, xv, 345–8), is its supremely imaginative culmination.

v.i. 10–20. *if I drown myself . . . life*] Shakespeare's knowledge of the *arguments about suicide* in the case of Hales v. Pettit, however come by, seems beyond question. The obvious analogies in the grave-digger's speech were first pointed out, though with some inaccuracy, by Sir John Hawkins, the friend of Dr Johnson. Sir James Hales had drowned himself in the river at Canterbury while of unsound mind, and the lawsuit, heard in 1560 and reported in Plowden (*Reports*, 1816, i. 253–64), contested the forfeiture of a lease as a penalty for his suicide on the grounds that the act of suicide could not be completed during his lifetime and that at the moment of his death his wife, as joint lessee, took possession by right of survivorship. The issue therefore was whether the forfeiture due to Hales's act was incurred before his death. The grave-digger's division of *an act* into *three branches* (which turn out to be identical) is a recognizable caricature of the argument of the defending counsel that the act of self-destruction 'consists of three parts. The first is the Imagination, which is a reflection or meditation of the mind, whether or no it is convenient for him to destroy himself, and what way it can be done. The second is the Resolution, which is a determination of the mind to destroy himself, and to do it in this or that particular way. The third is the Perfection, which is the execution of what the mind has resolved to do. And this Perfection consists of two parts, *viz*. the beginning and the end. The beginning is the doing of the act which causes the death, and the end is the death, which is only a sequel to the act' (Plowden, p. 259).

The grave-digger's distinction between whether *the man go to this water* or *the water come to him*, in spite of Hawkins and those others he has misled, was in fact not raised in the case of Hales, whose suicide was not in question. But the use of it here is brilliant; for it puts what is a crucial issue in Ophelia's death in a way that precisely mimics the typical legal argument. And in the grave-digger's resounding conclusion about one who *is not guilty of his own death* we may find a parody of a decision by one of the judges: 'Sir James Hales being alive caused Sir James Hales to die; and the act of the living man was the death of the dead man. And then for this offence it is reasonable to punish the living man who committed the offence, and not the dead man' (Plowden, p. 262).

v.i.60. *to Yaughan*] Difficulty concerns not only the meaning of this but, since it occurs in F only, its authenticity. It is usually taken to be a topical allusion; but if it is, as often assumed, a reference to a particular alehouse-keeper, it is less in Shakespeare's manner than in Jonson's and may be an actor's gag, which F happens to preserve. On the other hand, the Q2 *in, and* looks suspiciously like a compositor's stopgap for something he could not decipher or understand. Cf. *a* for *sage* by the same compositor at l. 230; and, though by another compositor, *all* for a conjectured *impaund* (F *impon'd*) *as* at v.ii. 160 and *sir* for *comply* at v.ii. 184. F's italics indicate a proper name and *Yaughan* is said to have occurred among immigrants from the Low Countries. That it was the name of an alehouse-keeper on the Bankside is possible; but attempts at further identification invite a little scepticism. It is not easy to see why 'a Jew, one Yohan' referred to in *Every Man Out of his Humour* (v.vi.48) as 'a slave about the town here' who is able to insert one dog into another's skin should be an alehouse-keeper; and if Yaughan was the alehouse-keeper whom *The Alchemist* (i.i.85) subsequently called 'deaf John', he had by then anglicized his name. This is what is supposed by Brinsley Nicholson, who identifies all three figures in a neatly connected but entirely conjectural account (*N&Q*, 4th ser. VIII, 81–2). Another fancy would see Shakespeare here translating into Danish a common English name (*Johan*, John. Cf. *Yorick*, l. 175n.). But those who find this plausible perhaps fail to reflect that the more it would evoke Hamlet's Denmark, the less it would suggest a notable of the Bankside. Emendations like *y'are gone* are unconvincing.

v.i.61–95.] The *verses sung by the grave-digger* continue motifs from Ophelia's songs in iv.v. Apt to the singer's occupation and, with their variation on the theme of the death of love, to the grave he is now digging, they have also a poignant irony in that sentiments appropriate to age are here offered to the grave of youth. They are a corrupt version of three stanzas (1, 3, and 8) from a 14-stanza poem by Thomas Lord Vaux, first printed in *Tottel's Miscellany* (1557) under the title 'The aged lover renounceth love'. The poem also survives in a number of manuscripts, including Brit. Mus. Harleian 1703 (fol. 100), where it is described as 'A dyttye or sonet made by the lorde Vaus in time of the noble queene Marye representinge the Image of deathe'.

The full poem may be found in reprints of *Tottel's Miscellany*, the edition of which by Rollins gives the most authoritative account (ii.283–6); in Percy's *Reliques*, in Furness, and in Seng (pp. 159–61); and, printed from the Harleian MS version, in Grosart's edition of Vaux's poems (*Miscellanies of the Fuller*

Worthies Library, iv. 42–5), and Noble, *Shakespeare's Use of Song* (pp. 119–20). The relevant stanzas, as printed in Tottel and with the significant variants of the Harleian MS (H) are:

1. I lothe that I did love,
   In youth that I thought swete:
   As time requires for my behove
   Me thinkes they are not mete.

3. For age with stelyng steppes,
   Hath clawed me with his crowche: [1st edn cowche;
        H cruch]
   And lusty life [H youth] away she [H hee] leapes,
   As there had bene none such.

8. A pikeax and a spade,
   And eke a shrowdyng [H wyndinge] shete,
   A house of claye for to be made,
   For such a gest most mete.

Some of the grave-digger's corruptions show a memory anticipating later passages of the poem. The opening words *In youth* are brought forward from the second line, where the resultant gap is supplied from the fourth. In the third line, *To contract the time* appears to be a garbling of a phrase from the third line of Vaux's second stanza, 'And tract of time begins to weave'. The *O* which follows *contract* (Q2 *ò*), if it is not a grunt of the grave-digger at work (see ll. 63–4n.), should perhaps, as Dover Wilson maintains (*MSH*, pp. 304–5), be *o'* for *of*. The third line of the grave-digger's second stanza, *And hath shipp'd me intil the land* (with the failure to rhyme remarked on by Dr Johnson), is imported from Vaux's thirteenth stanza, which reads:

13. For beauty with her bande
    These croked cares hath wrought:
    And shipped me into the lande,
    From whence I first was brought.

These and other perversions of the original may, but of course need not, have been designed by Shakespeare in fitting the song to the dramatic occasion and singer. A *pit* (l. 94) instead of a *house* of clay suggests the mind of the grave-digger, as Noble points out; but his idea that the repetition in the first line of the stanza is occasioned by faltering memory (rather than musical exigencies) obviously will not stand.

The seemingly casual shifts of phrase, for all the vagueness they leave us with, make for what it is possible to see as significant changes in meaning. The first stanza, instead of a philosophic acceptance of time's passing, has become expressive of regret. The transposition of *In youth* to the beginning puts the emphasis firmly on youthful love, while suppressing the idea of its being a thing for age to *loathe*. When the song in its new third line shows a wish to *contract* the time, whether or not this is an instance of the grave-digger's saying the opposite of what he means (l. 63n.), it goes against the original, which, seeking neither to contract nor pro-long, seems to recognize that what is appropriate to youth is now unmeet. The line which is incorporated into the second stanza, *And hath shipp'd me intil the land*, is feeble enough; but at least it fits in with the irony of applying the song to Ophelia's death, to which the original *lusty life* that *leaps* away is merely inappropriate.

Vaux's poem appears to have been well known in its own time. That a tune for it was also well known is evident from *A Gorgeous Gallery of Gallant Inventions* (1578), which includes a song to be sung 'to the Tune of I lothe that I did love' (ed. Rollins, p. 35). In fact two contemporary or near-contemporary settings are known. One is among the airs said to have been written in the margins of a 1557 copy of *Tottel's Miscellany* which has now disappeared and to have been transcribed by the composer Wm. Crotch for the edition of the *Miscellany* prepared c. 1814 by G. F. Nott. The only surviving copy of this ill-fated and apparently unpublished edition which is known to contain the music is one at Arundel Castle (described by Ruth Hughey in *The Library*, 4th series, xv, 394–7). The second tune is preserved in a manuscript in the British Museum (Addit. MSS 4900, fols. 62ᵛ–63; facsimile in Sternfeld, see below). Both were printed by Chappell (i. 216–17), from whom Furness (i. 382) gives the first only. Various musical historians since have printed one or other; both may be found together in Sternfeld, *Music in Shakespearean Tragedy*, 1963, pp. 152–5, in his *Songs from Shakespeare's Tragedies*, 1964, pp. 14–16, and in Simpson, *The British Broadside Ballad and its Music*, 1966, pp. 340–1. For fuller bibliography, see Seng, pp. 158–9. Whether either of these was actually sung by the grave-digger on Shake-speare's stage we cannot know. Chappell records that the tune which had become traditional in performance was that of the popular old ballad 'The Children in the Wood', which, following Chappell (i. 200–1), is accordingly printed by Furness (i. 385).

v. i. 74–110.]   This passage on *the skull* and the indignities suffered by the dead is especially reminiscent of one in a popular book of meditation by Luis de Granada, comparison with which shows Shakespeare characteristically elaborating and revitalizing a traditional reflection. See *Of Prayer and Meditation*, trans. Hopkins, 1582, fols. 202–4: 'Then do they make a hole in the earth of seven or eight foot long, (and no longer though it be for Alexander the great [cf. ll. 191–2], whom the whole world could not hold) and with that small room only must his body be content [cf. 108–10] . . . Then the grave maker taketh the spade, and pickaxe into his hand, and beginneth to tumble down bones upon bones [cf. 90–1], and to tread down the earth very hard upon him. Insomuch that . . . the rude grave maker . . . will not stick to lay him on the face, and rap him on the skull [cf. 88, 99–100] . . . And the fine dappered gentleman [cf. 81–2] who whiles he lived might in no wise abide the wind to blow upon him . . ., here they lay and hurl upon him a dunghill of filthiness and dirt [cf. 105–6]. And that sweet minion gentleman also that was wont forsooth to go perfumed with amber . . . must be contented here to lie covered all over with earth, and foul crawling worms, and maggots [cf. 87, 191–4.].'

v. i. 139–57. *I came to't that day . . . that young Hamlet was born . . . I have been sexton here, man and boy, thirty years.*] This apparent allusion to *Hamlet's age* has been the cause of much perplexity. No arithmetic is necessary to determine that Hamlet must be thirty, as seems to be near enough confirmed by the ensuing reference to Yorick, who, after delighting Hamlet's boyhood (ll. 179–83), has been dead three and twenty years (ll. 166–8). Whether the number of Hamlet's years was of concern to Shakespeare, or should be to us, is perhaps another matter. It is not incompatible that the King and Queen in *The Murder of Gonzago*, who image Hamlet's parents, have been married thirty years (iii. ii. 150–5), and some have thought it significant that it is not (but see LN). Yet a thirty-year-old Hamlet goes against the impression the play conveys of the hero's youth. We first meet him as a 'student' from the university, to which he is anxious to return. We first hear of him as 'young Hamlet' (i. i. 175), which the present passage is still content to call him (l. 143); and although the epithet has the function of distinguishing him from his father, it also matches him against those other sons, 'young Fortinbras' (i. i. 98) and 'young Laertes' (iv. v. 101), who are specifically characterized as youthfully hot-headed and impetuous. Hamlet's own youthfulness is crucial at i. iii. 5–12, 124, i. v. 16, still explicit at i. v. 38, iv. i. 19. The perfection

of manhood which Ophelia sees in him is that of youth's full bloom
(iii. i. 161).

Attempts to deny a certain discrepancy are futile. By the grave-
digger's account of the combat between their fathers, young
Fortinbras as well as Hamlet must be thirty, Horatio, who had
memory of the combat (i. i. 63–4), considerably more. Either
Shakespeare, as Blackstone supposed, here forgot what he wrote
in the first act, or else he chose to ignore it.

There are inevitably conjectures of revision, of which Q1, so
long as it could be taken for an earlier version, was naturally
thought to show evidence. It makes no reference to the sexton's
thirty years at his job (nor, for that matter, to Hamlet's birth);
it gives Yorick a mere 'dozen' years in the grave instead of
twenty-three; and it represents in the Gonzago play a marriage
of forty years not thirty. But the only conclusion to be drawn from
these divergences, now that Q1 is recognized as a reported text,
is that the reporter had a poor memory for numbers, as indeed
other instances in this same scene confirm (l. 135, three years,
Q1 seven years; l. 180, a thousand times, Q1 twenty times;
ll. 182–3, I know not how oft, Q1 a hundred times; l. 264, forty
thousand brothers, Q1 twenty brothers).

Nevertheless it is still widely accepted that the sexton's numbers
in Q2 have 'the appearance of being expressly inserted in order
to fix Hamlet's age' (Bradley, p. 407); and conjecture has been
busy to suggest why. We can dismiss at once the notion that
Hamlet had to be made thirty to fit Burbage. It is not to be
supposed that a highly accomplished actor still in his middle
thirties when Q2 was being printed would have difficulty in
sustaining a youthful role; and if he had, what would be obvious
from the start could not afterwards be helped by a belated last-act
statement. In fact an elegy on Burbage includes 'young Hamlet'
among his celebrated parts. It is more usual to account for a
thirty-year-old prince by the demands of the play itself rather
than the actor. Yet it is not a much more plausible theory, though
one commonly put forward, that Shakespeare proclaimed Hamlet
to be thirty in order to suit the character he found he had created.
No doubt Hamlet strikes us in the last act as more mature than
in the first. But how could it be otherwise when he has lived
through the experiences the play has visited on him? The reflections these have evoked from him throughout four acts have given
him a famed intellectual stature; but it is safe to say that it would
never have occurred to us that he must on that account be older
than we had hitherto supposed. To insist now that the seemingly

young hero is no less than thirty after all, far from removing an inconsistency, would be the surest way of drawing attention to one, as the fuss over Hamlet's age has only too well shown. Nothing about his age would be more difficult to credit than such dramatic naïveté on Shakespeare's part. It is clear, moreover, that Shakespeare still not only speaks but thinks of him as young – witness the fight soon to come at Ophelia's grave, the boarding of the pirate ship, the 'rashness' of rifling the packet with the King's commission (v. ii. 6–18). The whole catastrophe turns upon rivalry in fencing, which was, as the play takes unusual pains to emphasize, an accomplishment of youth (iv. vii. 72–80). The statements of the grave-digger must therefore have been introduced not because of but in spite of what they imply about Hamlet's age.

Schücking's rhetorical question, 'Why else are these precise pieces of information given, than in order to fix Hamlet's age unmistakably?' (*RES*, xi, 132) admits, to be sure, of an answer. But first one needs to observe that the numbers are not in fact precise and that they are not attached to Hamlet. 'Thirty years' is a round number, and a boast at that. And although '23' looks specific enough in the figures of Q2, if the copy, like F, had 'three and twenty', it would give a very different impression. The shepherd who says 'I would there were no age between ten and three and twenty' (*Wint.* iii. iii. 59–60) is not aiming at exactitude. (Cf. *Troil.* i. ii. 226; *1H6* i. i. 113.) In what is probably the most satisfactory treatment of the problem (*Prince Hamlet's Age, Kgl. Danske Videnskabernes Selskab. Hist.-fil. Meddelelser*, viii, no. 4) Østerberg has shown that thirty years was a traditional formula for a stretch of time covering most of a man's life. Instances include Marlowe's Faustus, 'I have been a student here these thirty years' (v. ii. 42); the Abbess in *The Jew of Malta*, '’Tis thirty winters long since some of us Did stray so far' (i. ii. 305); one of a group of fiddlers in Lyly's *Mother Bombie*, 'I have been a minstrel these thirty years' (v. iii. 16); one of a pair of watchmen in the old *King Leir*, 'I have bin a watchman about this Beacon this xxx. yere' (l. 2442). The last two are low comics who appear with like companions when their play moves towards its close, and they give hint of a dramatic tradition to which the Clown in *Hamlet* adheres. The sexton's thirty years belong to his role, not to Hamlet's. If Shakespeare had been concerned to impress his hero's age upon us, it would have been easy enough, when the dialogue harks back to his birth, to let Hamlet himself disclose it. The time the grave-digger has been at work and Yorick's skull in the earth relates to Hamlet only in so far as their roles impinge on his – as of course they significantly do, though in ways that a preoccupation with Hamlet's exact age is liable not to notice. The twenty-three years that Yorick has been dead are the years that separate Hamlet from his boyhood; and that this loss of boyhood is what Shakespeare associates with them is confirmed in *The Winter's Tale* when Leontes, also recalling his boyhood, casts his mind back 'twenty-three years' (I.ii.155). The grave-digger's numbers are less important for themselves than for the pattern of a life which they evoke. What matters is that when Hamlet came into the world a man began to dig graves and has now been at it for a lifetime. For let no one rise up and assure us that to have been a grave-digger 'man and boy, thirty years' one need not be much more than forty. As Hamlet's talk with the grave-digger thus links the grave-digger's occupation with the term of Hamlet's life, will it not seem to us that the hero has come face to face with his own destiny? The companion of his carefree childhood has already been a generation underground. Must not he himself, however 'young' or old, be ready for what will come? This scene leads on to the next (cf. v.ii.216–18) in ways apparently unsuspected by those who have been able to think of it as an interpolation or an afterthought (e.g. *RES*, XI, 129–38; *Yale Rev.*, LIV, 59).

That it is not primarily Hamlet's age that is in question is confirmed by the fact that the beginning of the grave-digger's occupation is said to have coincided not merely with Hamlet's birth but with King Hamlet's victory over Fortinbras, described in the opening scene. It is this which, if we consider it too curiously, makes Horatio, Hamlet's 'fellow-student', much older than Hamlet, which can hardly have been the dramatist's design. What was, I take it, was to link the end with the beginning, so that the activity of the grave-digger, despite the lateness of his entry, is found to span the whole play and with it the whole career of Hamlet since he was born into a world of strife. Exactly how old the prince is may seem of less moment than this.

v.i.187–8. *paint an inch thick*] A common motif in the tradition of the *danse macabre*, in which a skull appears beside a woman at her toilet, here makes use of a hyperbole which seems to have been current in the satire of women. Queen Elizabeth herself was reported by the Jesuit priest Anthony Rivers at Christmas 1600 to have been painted 'in some places near half an inch thick' (Foley, *Records of the Soc. of Jesus*, i.8); and Nashe in the 1594

Preface to *Christ's Tears*, ridiculing Gabriel Harvey's style, had compared his vainglory to a mistress 'new painted over an inch thick' (Nashe, ii. 180). The conjunction of this gibe with another figuring Harvey as a grave-digger making free with the carcases of dead authors has prompted, but does not compel, a hypothesis that Nashe was echoing an earlier version of *Hamlet* by Shakespeare in which this passage already appeared (*SQ*, xv, 446–7).

v.i.225. *crants*] The word, from German *kranz* (Danish *krans*) is singular, though in this spelling often mistaken for plural. The original floral wreath for the burial of a maiden came to be replaced by a less perishable artificial structure. For women of rank this might be a chaplet of pearl or gold and silver filigree, but surviving and recorded examples show characteristically a frame of wood shaped like a crown twelve or more inches high, covered with cloth or paper, adorned with artificial flowers (or occasionally black rosettes), and hanging from it ribbons, a pair of gloves, and sometimes a collar or kerchief. The practice of bearing such a symbol of virginity before the coffin and then hanging it in the church seems to have extended throughout northern Europe (see *Edin. Rev.*, cxxx, 96–7), in parts of which examples can still be seen. (I have myself seen some in Norway.) It is conceivable that Shakespeare sought to suggest a Danish custom; *crants*, like *lauds* (iv.vii.176) appears to have been unfamiliar to F. But the difficulty must surely have lain in the name rather than the thing. For the practice was certainly widespread in Elizabethan England and in various parts continued through the 18th century. Later survivals are also recorded, some of quite recent date. See esp. *The Reliquary*, i, 5–11; and also Chambers, *Book of Days*, 1888 edn, i. 271–4; *Journ. of Brit. Archaeol. Soc.*, xxxi, 190–5; New Shaks. Soc. *Transactions*, 1887–92, p. 180; C. S. Burne, *Shropshire Folk-Lore*, pp. 310–13; Hants. Field Club *Papers and Proceedings*, iv, 235–9; *English*, vii, 202–3; *Explicator*, xxviii (35).

v.i.271. *eisel*] Most of the extensive commentary on this need never have been penned if Theobald's recognition of Q2 Esill, F *Esile*, as an old word for vinegar had been accepted as it should have been. Some early commentators, looking for a fabulous drinking feat and puzzled by an obsolete word, were helped by the italic of F to suspect a proper name and so to conjecture that some river was intended. The Dutch Yssel was the one most favoured, though the *crocodile* even attracted some scholars to the Nile. But the increased knowledge now available of early English texts has confirmed Theobald's explanation beyond doubt. The word (from O.Fr. *aisil*, L. *acetillum*, dimin. of *acetum*, vinegar) was not uncommon in M.E. and survived into the early 17th century and in dictionaries much later. The many works in which it occurs include, beyond those cited in *OED*, the Chaucerian *Romaunt of the Rose* (l. 217) and Lydgate's *Troy Book* (II.62), which show it being used for a type and symbol of bitterness: Avarice lives on 'breed Kneden with eisel strong and egre'; Fortune deceitfully offers sweet things only to supplant them with a taste 'Of bitter eysel and of egre wyn, And corosyues þat fret and perce depe'. It was used in some early translations of the Bible, including that of Wyclif (Matthew xxvii.48, *aycel, or vynegre*) for the drink given to Christ upon the cross. In literary and popular allusions to the Crucifixion, from the *Cursor Mundi* (l. 24400), *The Castle of Perseverance* (ll. 3137, 3355) and all four Mystery cycles (see *MLN*, IX, 241–4) to Sir Thomas More (*Twelve Rules of John Picus*, l. 35) and Skelton (*Now Synge We*, ll. 39–40), the drink was regularly described as, in various spellings, 'eisel and gall'. At least fifteen instances have been noted. Equally regularly the drink was regarded as a torment. Hence *eisel* became the term for a bitter drink *par excellence*; it is in this sense that Shakespeare himself uses it in *Sonn.* CXI. It was sometimes equated with wormwood (*N&Q*, II, 241–2): in Wm. Thomas's Italian–English Dictionary (1550, etc.) *eysell* stands alone as the translation of *Assentio* (*assenzio*).

It is therefore a mistake to take *eisel* as no more than common vinegar, to be got down with a mere wry face. To *drink up eisel* is neither the impossible feat of swallowing a river, nor the mean and ludicrous task some commentators have supposed. It is something humanly possible which yet inspires extreme repugnance. And to *eat a crocodile* is evidently the same; whether this too was a recognized torment or newly suggests itself here as an apt companion-feat, it is likely to strike ordinary susceptibilities as peculiarly revolting. Yet those are things a lover will voluntarily undertake. With the crocodile, no doubt, the self-inflicted hardships (l. 270) are brought to the point of burlesque; but the note of contempt is less for the extravagances of the lover than for the man who cannot rise to them (cf. ll. 264–6). Attempts to explain the passage as taunting Laertes with vinegar as a source of melancholy and with a crocodile as a symbol of hypocrisy (Dowden; *TLS*, 1926, p. 512), though accepted by Dover Wilson and others, are quite beside the point. The proverbial insincerity of the crocodile's tears has nothing to do with eating it. Laertes is being mocked not by the things he is challenged to do but for his unreadiness to do them. At the same time what is absurd in the challenge itself cannot but reflect back upon the challenger. Protestations of love for one beyond receiving them may appropriately sound hollow.

v. ii. 10–11.   *There's a divinity that shapes our ends,*
                Rough-hew them how we will]

Cf. 'Our thoughts are ours, their ends none of our own', iii. ii. 208, where, however, belief in a beneficent power is absent. The present passage shows Hamlet recognizing a design in the universe he had previously failed to find (i. ii. 133–7; ii. ii. 298–303; etc.) Cf. Proverbs xvi. 9 (Bishops' Bible), 'A man deviseth a way in his heart: but it is the lord that ordereth his goings'; and, for the same metaphor as in Shakespeare, Florio's Montaigne, iii. 8, 'My consultation doth somewhat roughly hew the matter, and by its first show, lightly consider the same: the main and chief point of the work, I am wont to resign to heaven'.

v. ii. 42. *comma*]   A review of the diverse explanations finds none satisfactory and most tendentious. Some maintain that a comma, while marking off one clause from another, links them in sense. This goes back to Johnson, who says that the comma, in contrast to the period, signals '*connection* and continuity of sentences'. Alexander, in accordance with his theory of Shakespearean punctuation (cf. ii. ii. 304–6 LN), believes that Shakespeare's own practice with the comma shows 'how he came to use it as a metaphor for a bond instead of a break' (*TLS*, 1931, p. 754). Yet to gloss *comma* as a 'connecting link', as is becoming all too frequent, seems to me wholly unacceptable. Nor is it what the context requires: for what is not in itself a link is not made so by happening to *stand . . . 'tween*, and if the two kings are joined together, they are so by *their amities*, of which peace is not the agent but the consequence. Other senses of *comma* have been canvassed: Cowden Clarke appealed to musical usage, in which a comma is the least of the sensible intervals, to suggest that it is here a metaphor for a 'harmonious connection' (*The Shakespeare Key*, p. 443n.); Dowden reminds us that a comma in its original meaning was 'a phrase or group of words forming a short member of a sentence or period', and so sees peace like a dependent clause, deriving its significance from what it stands between. Perhaps it is not surprising that many emendations have been suggested. They include *commere, cement, co-mate, cov'nant, compact*. None is satisfactory; but one cannot quite quell a suspicion that *comma* may be one of Q2's stopgaps (see Intro., p. 60 and n.), which F in this case failed to correct.

If we are to interpret the word as it stands, I think it best to take it in its ordinary sense. A mere pen-stroke on the page, as a mark of punctuation it is the one of least significance. This accords with the only other use of the word in Shakespeare: when the Poet in *Timon* says 'no levell'd malice Infects one comma in the course I hold' (I.i.51), he refers to a comma as the smallest item of literary composition. That a comma may indicate a break or pause (*OED* 2c, quoting this passage) led Dover Wilson to interpret Hamlet's *comma 'tween their amities* as 'the briefest possible pause' in a conflict between 'inveterate foes'. This catches something of Hamlet's tone: but the irony that Dover Wilson detects in words like *faithful*, *love*, *amities* cannot be one of simple opposites. These are words which Claudius in his 'conjuration' might well use; the irony is in their use by Hamlet simulating Claudius to mock their fulsomeness, which *a comma* then deflates. In this context peace can hardly be represented as a temporary cessation of hostilities. What one might expect peace to be, standing (with a garland) between faithful friends, is something like a monument created by and celebrating *their amities*. When it appears as no more than *a comma*, the effect is one of bathos, which leads on to the open contempt of the next line.

v.ii.82–3. *water-fly*] 'A water-fly skips up and down upon the surface of the water, without any apparent purpose or reason, and is thence the proper emblem of a busy trifler' (Johnson). Shakespeare appears to have envisaged an insect (a dragon-fly?) with brightly flapping wings. Hamlet's image for Osric is also used by Thersites for Patroclus: 'thou idle immaterial skein of sleid [Q sleiue] silk, thou green sarcenet flap for a sore eye, thou tassel of a prodigal's purse . . . how the poor world is pest'red with such waterflies' (*Troil.* v.i.28–31). Cf. also the 'flies' ('fashionmongers') of *Rom.* II.iv.32. There may be an influence of Nashe's description of a Dane in *Pierce Penniless* (see Intro., pp. 104–6): 'he is the best fool braggart under heaven . . . his apparel is so puffed up with bladders of taffety, and his back like beef stuffed with parsley, so drawn out with ribands and devices, and blistered with light sarcenet bastings, that you would think him nothing but a swarm of butterflies, if you saw him afar off' (Nashe, i. 177–8). There are obvious hints for a costume-designer, and

Dover Wilson supposes that Osric may have worn the winged doublet then in fashion.

v.ii.88. *chuff*] The boorish connotations are often held inappropriate for the fantastical Osric, but a country fellow of more wealth than worth exactly fits the context. Cf. Cotgrave, '*Maschefouyn*, A chuffe, boore . . . one thats fitter to feed with cattell, then to converse with men'; but also '*Franc-gontier*, A good rich Yeoman, substantiall yonker, wealthie chuffe'. A *chuff* is thought of as 'rich' (*Woodstock*, MSR, l. 1527; Nashe, ii. 107; Marlowe, *Ovid's Elegies*, iii.vii.9) or 'fat' (Nashe, i. 163). Cf. *1H4* ii.ii.86, 'ye fat chuffs; I would your store were here'. But always implicit in the word is the paradox of riches possessed by one unfit to have them. See Marlowe's Ovid, iii.vi.50, 'Chuffe-like had I not gold and could not use it?'; Nashe, iii.211, 'countrey chuffes which make their bellies and their bagges theyr Gods'; *2 Return from Parnassus*, l. 226, 'thick-skin chuffes laugh at a schollers neede'; *Every Man Out of his Humour*, The Characters, 'SORDIDO. A Wretched hobnail'd Chuffe'; Massinger, *Duke of Milan*, iii.i.22, 'To see these chuffs, that every day may spend A soldier's entertainment for a year'. With the variant spelling attested in *OED*, this interpretation seems to me beyond question. Cf. the character Chough (Q *Chaugh*, *Chawgh*) in Middleton and Rowley, *A Fair Quarrel*, 'a Cornish gentleman', 'a rich simplicity of great estate' (ii.ii). Many editors, however, assume the different word *chough*, a bird of the crow family, esp. a jackdaw, and hence a chatterer. This, punned on in *A Fair Quarrel*, occurs some half-dozen times in Shakespeare and might be relevant to a description of Osric, though not to the present context. The linguistic excesses (preciosities rather than mere chatter) are not yet begun, or anticipated. It is no doubt because it seems at odds with the portrait of Osric that Furness finds this whole speech 'puzzling'. It may well be that Shakespeare's conception of the character changed as he proceeded.

v.ii.125–6. *Is't not possible to understand in another tongue? You will to't, sir, really.*] There has been much confusion about this speech, both as to what it means and to whom it is said. I agree with the minority who address it to Hamlet; for while it is true that Horatio always otherwise calls Hamlet *my lord*, not *sir*, it is at least as much to the point that he does not otherwise address Osric at all. This mocking comment is of a piece with his two other interjections in this dialogue, ll. 129–30, 152–3, both

directed to Hamlet. *In another tongue* can only mean in a language
different from the one you are using. The frequent interpretation
of this phrase as referring to Osric's inability to understand his
own language on someone else's tongue forces it to fit the context
but seems to me quite beyond what the words will bear. Horatio
is merely suggesting that they would all understand better if
things were said more simply. *You will to't*, to judge from the
'correction', proved as baffling to the printing-house reader as it
has been to editors since. Yet it is of course thoroughly idiomatic.
Cf. II.ii.425, v.i.54; *Rom.* III.i.169; *Gent.* II.vii.89; etc. Its
occasional obscurity arises through the indefiniteness of the pronoun, and to a lesser degree the preposition also. *To,* implying
motion towards, stands for *go to, come to, get to,* etc., and often
give oneself to (an activity), as in the instances cited; but *it,* unlimited by any specific antecedent, may refer to something,
precise or imprecise, which only the context or situation can make
clear. What the present context shows to be in mind is the practice
of an esoteric manner of speech. Hence *You will to't* is a compliment to Hamlet on his promise and assiduity in it: 'You will get
the trick of it', or perhaps, in the modern colloquialism, 'You
will be into it'. Alternatively, if *You will to't* is taken to refer not
to Osric's but to *another tongue,* it might carry a prophecy that that
is what Hamlet will come to in the end (and one could compare
ll. 152–3, implying 'I told you so'). But I think that less idiomatic.

All this is to interpret the passage as it first appeared in Q2.
But many, beginning with the Q2 press-corrector, have thought
emendation called for. The emendation *a mother tongue,* first
suggested by Johnson, is attractive. This would allow Horatio to
comment, when Osric fails to grasp Hamlet's meaning, 'Can the
man not understand in what after all is his own language?'; and
with the reference being thus to Osric's tongue, would neatly
lead on to the compliment on Hamlet's use of it.

v.ii.160. *impawned, as*]   If Q2 were our only text, its 'why is this
all you call it?' could be interpreted as it stands, with Hamlet
ridiculing Osric's verbosity by affecting to be unable to repeat it:
Why is this – all you said it was? But F, 'why is this impon'd as
you call it', together with the Q2 compositor's obvious difficulty
with his copy in this passage, suggests that there is an omission
in Q2 and that *all* (for *as?*) is a compositor's adjustment – not
so much to fill the gap as to preserve some sense across it (cf.
v.i.230, v.ii.184). What should fill the gap, as shown by F, is the
verb from l. 145, and it is odd perhaps that the compositor should

have been floored by a word he had set up once already. If I am right in regarding *all* as a makeshift reading, then obviously it cannot (as Dover Wilson and Kittredge would have it) belong with an emended text. As between *impawned* and *imponed* the first is the more authoritative as well as the more Shakespearean and exact. Its occurrence in Q2 ('impaund') would be difficult to account for except on the assumption that it stood in the foul papers as Shakespeare's own word, of which *imponed* in F ('impon'd') is probably a corruption. Yet it is a little surprising to find Osric mocked for the use of a word which Shakespeare had elsewhere used quite seriously himself (*1H4* IV.iii.108; *H5* I.ii.21). It is sometimes supposed that what is being mocked is not so much the word itself as Osric's pronunciation of it, represented by one or other of the variants. Yet everything else shows Osric's linguistic affectations to be a matter not of pronunciation but of highfalutin terms. I can only suggest that *impawned*, a word not yet in familiar use and elsewhere used of hostages and the stakes of war, is, in the context of a sporting wager, regarded as extravagant. The inflated diction, as with *carriages* for hangers, helps to give a comically fantastic air to ominous event.

v.ii.162–4. *The King, sir, hath laid, sir, that in a dozen passes between yourself and him he shall not exceed you three hits; he hath laid on twelve for nine.*] The terms of *the wager* pose an insoluble problem: these two statements of them appear to be incompatible. The first is, as Kittredge remarks, 'clear enough': the King bets that in a match consisting of twelve *passes*, or bouts, Laertes will not make three more hits than Hamlet. Johnson's objection to this, 'In a dozen passes one must exceed the other more or less than three hits', though much cited, is not valid; for 'more or less than three' will be decisive, and 'passes' are not the same as 'hits'. Though a pass would normally end with the scoring of a hit (and many discussions envisage nothing else), one with no score is possible and may occur at l. 305, though not all commentators agree that 'Nothing neither way' implies that the bout is at an end. The difficulty, however, comes when the second statement is added: *he hath laid on twelve for nine*. This is most naturally taken to refer to the excess of three hits – *twelve* by Laertes *for nine* by Hamlet, which is not of course compatible with 'a dozen passes' altogether.

Aside from this apparent contradiction, there is an ambiguity in the subject pronoun *he*. In the repetition of 'The King, sir, hath laid ... he hath laid' it is natural to presume that the subject is the same. But a moment's thought will show that if you bet on a man's not exceeding his opponent by three hits, you cannot lay *on* but are laying *against* his making twelve for nine. Hence there is something to be said for the view that *he* now refers to Laertes, so that the re-statement of the wager's terms gives them from the other side.

In either event it certainly looks as though the two statements were meant to correspond. The second sustains the idea of a contest of twelve while preserving a margin of three; but if it is the margin of hits that is now particularized as *twelve for nine*, there has been a shift from twelve as the number of passes to twelve as the winning score. Unless we are to suppose a textual error, I think we must conclude that, as between these two twelves, the author has not decided, or not said, what he meant.

Some attempts to evade the problem ascribe the confusion to Osric, here ridiculed by Shakespeare as 'unable to state intelligibly the very thing he was sent to tell' (Verity). Yet Osric temporarily drops his linguistic convolutions when at length he gets to the point; the sentence that causes all the trouble is the tersest thing he says. Shakespeare sometimes leaves plot details unstated, or even contradictory; but he can hardly have designed the wager to be obscure, and Hamlet, who mocks everything else Osric says, gives no sign of finding it so.

More commonly there have been attempts to find an interpretation of one or both of the statements which would permit them to be reconciled. The precise terms of the first leave little room for manœuvre. Not all the mathematical bravura of Sprinchorn in computing 'The Odds on Hamlet' can possibly persuade us in defiance of plain English that 'to exceed you three hits' means to score three hits in succession (Columbia U. *Forum*, VIII, 41–5, reprinted in Zitner, *The Practice of Modern Literary Scholarship*, pp. 335–41; refuted by J. A. Kilby, *N&Q*, CCXIII, 133–6). A Victorian writer in the *Quarterly Review* (LXXIX, 333) maintained that it meant to score not three hits more than Hamlet but three more than the par of six; and by also maintaining that *he hath laid on twelve for nine* meant that he had wagered for nine out of twelve, he managed to make the two statements equivalent. The second statement, one may grant, in the absence of a noun, admits more flexibility. From the time of Malone the notion has recurred that it may refer not to the number but to the ratio of hits, so that *twelve for nine* is tantamount to four to three. But no arithmetic can show how such a ratio can achieve a difference of three within a maximum of twelve. The use of the word 'odds' has bedevilled discussion through confusion among its various meanings. As used in ll. 207, 260 it refers to the advantage granted to Hamlet; in the sense of probabilities it appears to be irrelevant if not anachronistic; and it is hard to see how odds of 'twelve to nine in favour of Laertes' (Sprinchorn) can apply to a wager in which odds in one sense are set at 'six Barbary horses against six French swords' and in another at 'three hits'.

Two interpretations have been proposed which, instead of associating *twelve* with hits, simply refer it back to the 'dozen passes'. Dover Wilson supposed that Laertes, when he *laid on twelve for nine*, laid down the condition of twelve passes instead of the nine that were usual (*WHH*, pp. 278–9). But there is no evidence that nine was a normal expectation – the single instance cited (from Silver's *Paradoxes of Defence*, p. 3) only goes to show that three threes need not be the same as nine – and it is beyond all credibility that *laid*, as repeated in this context, does not retain its ordinary betting sense. The other interpretation, reviving the theory that in a wager *on twelve* passes Laertes wagers *for nine* hits, suggests that in his confidence he has thus stepped up the odds (handicap) (*N&Q*, ccxiv, 142–5). The objections to this again relate to both language and manners: it offends both the phrasal balance associating *twelve* with *nine* and the presumption that the parties to the wager would agree upon its terms before the messenger announced them. And it leaves us with what nothing else in the play suggests, two wagers instead of one (cf. ll. 172–5, 207, 257–60). This may be the best we can do with the puzzle of the text as it stands; but it is very hard to believe in as a rendering of Shakespeare's intent.

My own belief is that the discrepancy reflects a divided intent. A wager is laid on whether Laertes will score three more hits than Hamlet in a match of twelve; but is this to be over twelve passes or while scoring twelve himself? The second idea perhaps forms while the first is being penned, giving rise to an uncertainty which the text shows unresolved. So Laertes over twelve passes is to win by a margin of three, he is to score twelve against Hamlet's nine: it will not at once strike the audience in the theatre, and may not have struck Shakespeare, that the two things are not the same.

It is necessary, however, to add that the first alternative triumphs in the presentation of the contest itself. After two hits by Hamlet, the next 'exchange', irrespective of what will happen in it, is referred to as 'the third' (ll. 265–6, 301). Hence, while hits of course will decide victory, the duration of the match is being measured by the count of what the play variously calls 'passes', 'exchanges', or 'bouts'.

v. ii. 188–9. *carries them through and through the most fanned and winnowed opinions*] The problem caused by variants in both epithets is aggravated by the semantic flexibility of the other words in the context. Does the froth of fashionable clichés, in *carrying* the derided courtiers *through and through*, merely bear them along unimpeded, does it overcome opposition, does it even infect or permeate its environment? Are the *opinions* approved of, in contrast with the empty froth, or not? It is now generally accepted that Q2's meaningless *trennowed* (the *renowned* to which it was progressively emended having no textual status) must be a misreading of *winnowed* (F), and that *winnowed*, referring to the process of separating wheat from chaff, is essentially a term of approbation. This is supported by Shakespearean usage in such phrases as 'a winnowed purity' (*Troil.* iii. ii. 163) and 'Winnow the truth from falsehood' (*Cym.* v. v. 134) and most notably in 'Distinction, with a broad and powerful fan, Puffing at all, winnows the light [=worthless] away' (*Troil.* i. iii. 27–8). The favourable connotations of *winnowed* must override its association (in F) with *fond*, foolish, and exclude the suggestions of foppishness in such consequent interpretations as 'over-refined' (Chambers), 'fantastic' (Verity), 'exquisite' (Dowden); and an assumption that *fond and winnowed* may indicate opposites is discouraged by their being joined together by *most* and together set against *yeasty*. What I find persuasive, and indeed compelling, is Warburton's emendation of *fond* to *fanned*. That Shakespeare thought of winnowing as effected by a *fan* appears from the *Troilus* passage cited; and in *Cym.* i. vi. 176 he uses the verb *fan* in that sense (Iachimo, testing Imogen, is made to *fan* her and finds her 'chaffless'). Among Shakespeare's contemporaries the synonyms *fanned* and *winnowed* were not infrequently combined: Googe's translation of Heresbach's *Four Books of Husbandry* (1577) speaks of corn's being 'often fanned and winnowed' and of 'the often fannyng and wynnowing' as a remedy against weevils (p. 43); Markham's *Art of Husbandry* (1631) takes over the same phrasing (pp. 77–8) and adds two instances of 'fanned (or fan'd) and winnowed' of its own (pp. 18, 76); Markham's *English Husbandman* (1613) instructs that grain intended for seed 'must be winnowed, fand, and drest so cleane as is possible' (p. 31). Against such evidence of usage Dover Wilson's objection that *fanned and winnowed* is tautologous must, I think, give way; and his other objection that it errs against textual principle by emending F instead of seeking the guidance of the more authoritative Q2 (*MSH*, pp. 329–31) overlooks the relationship of *fanned* to the Q2 *prophane*. He preferred to revive an earlier conjecture and emend *prophane* to *profound* (cf. Bailey, ii. 17), which he envisages spelt *profond* or *profund*. But *fanned* and *profound* are of equal textual status in that either, postulated as the reading of Shakespeare's manuscript, requires us to suppose that Q2 and F give variant misreadings of it. Is it not the more likely thing, in view of the established association with *winnowed*, that the manuscript had *fanned*, spelt *fand*, as it is indeed in Markham (see above) and in Shakespeare's own *MND* (Q1 iii. ii. 142), and that the word went twice unrecognized, being in the one case corrupted to *fond* and in the other, with the familiar confusion of *d* and *e*, misread as *fane*? It is at least as likely that the prefix *pro-* was supplied by the Q2 compositor, of whose willingness to guess this passage gives other evidence, as that it was dropped in the F transmission.

v. ii. 218–20. *Since no man, of aught he leaves, knows aught, what is't to leave betimes?*] About this much-debated passage some things are clear: that Q2 (*since no man of ought he leaues, knowes*) and F (*since no man ha's ought of what he leaues.*) do not mean the same thing; that F is an attempt to tidy and make sense of what was found awkward and obscure; and that the sense it makes is not the sense required. The period in F conceals that the *since* clause provides the reason for the question which follows; but with the substitution of a comma many of the earlier editors (down to the Cambridge and Dowden) were content to accept F's wording. Yet in Q2 it is not a question of not *having* but of not *knowing*. This follows more naturally on the preceding acceptance of uncertainties; one cannot regret what one does not know. Hence Q2 may be held to have, along with higher authority, the better sense. Johnson's paraphrase is cogent: 'Since *no man knows aught of* the state of life which *he leaves*, since he cannot judge what other years may produce, why should he be afraid of *leaving* life betimes?' Yet to relate 'an early death' to an ignorance of whether life would bring 'happiness or . . . calamity' may restrict the sense of *know* unduly. A more metaphysical meaning also may be in character for a hero whose frustrated inquiry into the nature of man gives way to an acceptance of man's inability to know. What does it signify how soon we leave that which eludes our knowledge?

Textually, however, Johnson's conflation of the two texts by adopting the verbal order of F while replacing *has* by *knows*, although followed by Chambers and Kittredge among others, is a more than dubious procedure. Those who have believed in *knows* have more often followed Warburton in retaining while repunctuating the reading of Q2: 'Since no man(,) of aught he leaves(,) knows, what is't to leave betimes?' This gives the general sense (since no man has knowledge of aught he leaves) but, with or without the commas, in a way that is harsh and strained. For *knows* requires an object, and although I cannot quite share Dover Wilson's belief in Q2's propensity to omit words, I suspect that this may have happened in the present case. By repeating *aught*, which, if it was not Shakespeare's word, at least does not pervert what Q2 points to as his sense, I have supplied the missing object in the simplest and I hope most plausible way.

Dover Wilson attempted a different solution by retaining not only the wording but (substantially) the pointing of Q2, 'Since no man . . . knows what is't to leave betimes, let be'. This makes *what is't to leave betimes* the object of *knows* and extends the sentence to include *let be* as its main clause. It yields the interpretation, 'Since no one can tell . . . what is the right moment to die, why trouble about it?' But, although it has been followed by Evans and has influenced some criticism, I think we must pronounce it indubitably wrong. It proceeds from the false premise that Elizabethan commas have their modern value and, apart from suspending *of aught he leaves* in the air, equating *what is't* with *what it is*, and straining the meaning of *betimes*, it makes *let be* the climax of the moral reflection (cf. *MSH*, pp. 214–15) instead of a mere formula breaking off the conversation and effecting a transition to the fencing preparations and the entry of the court. Cf. l. 220n.

This exhortation against the fear of an early death belongs to the tradition of stoic consolation. Cf. Seneca, *Epistles*, 69, '*Nihil perdis ex tuo tempore, nam quod relinquis alienum est*'; Montaigne's *Essays* (Florio), 1.19, 'What matter is it when it cometh, since it is unavoidable? . . . No man dies before his hour. The time you leave behind was no more yours, than that which was before your birth, and concerneth you no more.'

v.ii.222–48.]   The uneasy comment which *Hamlet's apology and the reply to it* have attracted comes, I think, from a misunderstanding of their purpose. They have been remarked on as showing the characters of the speakers in an unfavourable light: they have rarely been considered for their part in the play's design, though their length and position suggest that this was something to which the dramatist attached importance. Hamlet's apology to

Laertes is not only done at length and in conspicuous form (see l. 221), but has already been prepared for in ll. 75–80 and 202–3; and the allusion to 'tow'ring passion' (l. 80), recalling to us what the Queen pronounced to be 'madness' (v.i.279), presages the form excuse might take. Yet, as pointed out by Bradley (pp. 420–1), what Hamlet sees as requiring pardon is not so much his behaviour to Laertes at Ophelia's grave as the injury he has done him by the killing of his father. The two avenging sons are here brought face to face.

Many will share Johnson's wish that 'Hamlet had made some other defence'. For it is much less 'odd' of Johnson, while accepting the pretended madness, to object to its use as an excuse than it is of Bradley and Kittredge to see no moral distinction between the two. The difficulty comes rather from the ambiguity of the word *madness*. When Johnson speaks of Hamlet as sheltering in 'falsehood', he is assuming that the madness is wholly feigned; yet we must surely recognize not only (1) an 'antic disposition' that is 'put on' but also (2) a genuine frenzy of ungovernable 'passion' which has led to the killing of Polonius as well as the fight with Laertes at the grave (cf. Dover Wilson, NCS, pp. lxii–lxiv). It is the second which gives substance to Hamlet's self-exculpation and though the distinction between them is sometimes blurred, the play by here ignoring it seems to rest Hamlet's defence upon a quibble. Yet once *madness* is accepted, the argument of ll. 230–3 has respected precedents: cf. Romans vii. 20, 'If I do that I would not, it is no more I that do it, but sin that dwelleth in me'. And however Hamlet's logic is judged by an age more suspicious of casuistry, we shall surely accept the underlying truth that he wrongs Laertes not by 'a purpos'd evil' but 'when he's not himself' and in so doing becomes his own 'enemy'. Criticism has made too little of the bond between the two revengers which Hamlet acknowledges in the word *brother*. Cf. above ll. 77–8 and n., 240n.

The element of casuistry in Hamlet's speech should prepare us for the same from Laertes. And the first thing to note about his .reply is that it answers Hamlet (see l. 227) point by point, dealing in order with *nature* (240), *honour* (242), and, although this time the actual word is not repeated, with 'exception' (247–8). Moreover, it distinguishes between what joins men together (*nature, love*) and what divides them.

In the appeal to authoritative opinion in matters of honour the conduct of Laertes is correct. Dover Wilson cites *Saviolo his Practise*, which exhorts those involved in quarrels 'to study and endeavour by all means possible to furnish themselves with men experienced and seen in chivalry and arms, that they may be counselled and advised by them' (sig. Aa 4); and Kittredge compares an account in Nashe (iii. 21) of 'the same manner that one of these Italianate conferences about a duel is wont solemnly to be handled, which is when a man, being specially touched in reputation, or challenged to the field upon equal terms, calls all his friends together, and asks their advice how he should carry himself in the action'.

This speech of Laertes appears to be designed to show that while his revenge is not to be forgone ('no reconcilement'), he acts from the compulsion of 'honour' and not malice; to confirm Hamlet's suggestion of men fated in spite of themselves to be opponents; and (most important) to anticipate their eventual reconciliation. The trouble of course is that the uttered sentiments are wholly at variance with the plot Laertes is even now engaged in, and the critics have accordingly been severe on his 'monstrous hypocrisy' (Kittredge). But the play's attitude to Laertes is less simple. Commentators point to l. 300 as preparing for his repentance, but without observing that it is already being prepared for here. Certainly this episode forces upon our notice the appalling irony of Claudius as peacemaker and of loving words which conceal a murderous intent. Yet in the gestures of the two young men who now hold the centre of the stage I think we should see, along with this ironic prelude to a treacherous revenge, a proleptic image of the revengers' exchange of forgiveness (see ll. 334-7). Shakespeare's problem is to show the two revengers as at the same time mutually destructive and at one.

v. ii. 269. *an union*] The most famous instance of the prodigality of *drinking a pearl* is that told of Cleopatra (Holland's Pliny, ix. 35). Another which Shakespeare presumably knew is that of Sir Thomas Gresham, who was fabled to have crushed a pearl in wine to drink the Queen's health when she visited the new Exchange in 1571. (Cf. Heywood, *2 If You Know Not Me*, sc. x.) For others see Horace, *Satires*, ii. iii. 239–41; Fuller, *Worthies*, 1811 edn, ii. 347.

v. ii. 290. *fat*] The precise meaning of this word is difficult to establish. But few now see in it an allusion to the actor's corpulence, any more than in the 'thirty years' since Hamlet's birth (see v. i. 139–57 and LN) a reflection of Burbage's age. Cf. *WHH*, p. 284n. In association with 'scant of breath' *fat* must refer to

Hamlet's state at the moment rather than to a permanent characteristic, and the offer of the 'napkin' to wipe his face indicates what his state is. With ll. 291, 298 cf. *2H4* II.iv.207, where Doll says to Falstaff when he has beaten Pistol downstairs, 'how thou sweat'st! Come, let me wipe thy face!' The equation of *fat* with 'sweating' is strongly supported by Tilley with evidence for the notion that sweat was produced by the melting of fat (*JEGP*, XXIV, 315–19), and Shakespearean instances include *Hamlet* III.iv.92. But no certain and authenticated parallel has been given for *fat* as an epithet for the condition, rather than the cause, of sweating. A passage cited from Richard Johnson's *Seven Champions of Christendom* describes a giant with sweat running into his eyes, who was 'so extreme fat, he grew blind' (1608, p. 52); but it is far from clear that *fat* here describes the giant's sweating without attributing it to his bulk. It seems likely, however, that an ancient usage was preserved by the farmer's wife in Wisconsin in 1923 who is reported to have greeted perspiring visitors with 'How fat you all are!' (*TLS*, 1927, p. 375).

The alternative interpretation, out of condition, would make *fat* denote not so much the accompaniment as the cause of being out of breath. Sisson (*NR*, ii.229) cites a Chancery case of 1578 in which a nag 'but new taken up from grass' and so not ready for hard work, was said to be 'fat and foggy'; and a 19th-century survival of this sense occurs in the *Autobiography* of Sir Harry Smith, who describes troops as 'fat and in bad wind' after a long time on board ship (i.199). It is not fatal to this interpretation that it does not square with the 'continual practice' of l. 207.

Less plausible than either of these is Hotson's assumption that *fat* means full (*Spectator*, 1952, p. 701): supposing that Hamlet has but just dined, he would draw a parallel with his father, killed in his resting-time when 'full of bread' (III.iii.80).

v.ii.306 S.D. *they change rapiers*] Among many discussions of the stage-business are the following: H. von Friesen, *Sh.Jahr.*, IV, 374–7 (quoted Furness, ii.338); W. H. Pollock, *The Theatre*, 1897, ii.162–3; G. Dubois, *L'Assaut du Vème Acte d'Hamlet*, 1932, pp. 27–9; Evan John, *TLS*, 1934, p. 60; J. L. Jackson, *MLN*, LVII, 50–5. An exchange of weapons as a result of disarming was not uncommon in Elizabethan fencing. With sword and gauntlet a recognized manœuvre was for the gloved hand to seize the opponent's rapier; and comparably though more rarely, in sword and dagger fight, the dagger in the left hand could be used to twist the opponent's rapier from his grasp. The proper counter to such a move was not resistance but immediate retaliation in kind, the left hand dispossessing the opponent's right. The result is a double disarming and a consequent exchange. That some such method was used in some performances of *Hamlet* appears from the S.D. in the reported text (*'They catch one anothers Rapiers'*). It is not quite what is suggested by F's *scuffling*, but scuffling might well result from the natural reluctance of Laertes to exchange the unbated sword.

The precise manner in which the exchange is effected is a matter for the producer. The important question for the critic is whether it is to be regarded as intentional on Hamlet's side or, as the wording of the S.D. (in F) would suggest, haphazard. The absence of any Q2 or indubitably Shakespearean direction lets us infer what we can from the dialogue. It is obvious that Hamlet must be wounded before the exchange takes place and hence immediately after Laertes's *Have at you now*. This cry, in contrast to the regular *Come (on)* (ll. 277–8, 287, 301, 304) suggests an attack without warning, which may well precipitate a scuffle. On the matter of whether Hamlet yet knows of the unbated sword commentators (and actors) divide. It is clear from l. 327 ('The point envenom'd too') that he discovers it before being told, but it must be supposed obvious to him at least by l. 310 ('They bleed'). The most natural supposition would have him grasp the truth the moment he is hit, and this gives added plausibility to the fury of the scuffle, which must justify the word *incensed* (l. 307). Yet it does not follow that there is a deliberate attempt by Hamlet to wrest his opponent's weapon from him. It is true that such a feat has often been made the basis of effective stage-action. Salvini as Hamlet, having carefully registered awareness of his wound, forced his antagonist to drop his rapier and then, placing his foot on it, with what is variously described as a graceful bow and a fierceness of command proffered his own in exchange (Marshall, p. 200; *Punch*, 1875, p. 255; Sprague, *Shakespeare and the Actors*, pp. 179–80). Any regular theatre-goer is likely to have seen some variation on this rendering; it lies behind the incident as envisaged by Dover Wilson· (*WHH*, p. 286) and performed in the Olivier film. Yet the imperious gesture is the reverse of what is called for by *scuffling* and *incensed*. Nor is there anything in the confession of Laertes (ll. 319–26) to imply that Hamlet has deliberately sought to punish his 'foul practice'. What kills Laertes is not Hamlet's will but his 'own treachery' (313) when it has 'turn'd itself' (324) against him, and fallen on the inventor's head (390). To see in the exchange of weapons a human rather than a providential design goes against both the text and the spirit of the play. A distinction between the hero's treatment of the man on whom he must exact revenge and the man from whom he must suffer it is consistently maintained.

v.ii.341. *sergeant*] For the metaphor of *Death as a sergeant* making an arrest, see e.g. the mediaeval treatise of *The Dying Creature* (MS Harl. 1706, fols. 96–105; printed W. de Worde, 1507, etc.; included in F. M. M. Comper, *Book of the Craft of the Dying*, 1917), 'Here hath been with me a sergeant of arms whose name is Cruelty [cf. *fell*], from the King of all Kings, Lord of all Lords, and Judge of all Judges; laying on me the mace of his office, saying unto me: I arrest thee and warn thee to make thee ready . . . The Judge that shall sit upon thee, He will not be partial [cf. *strict*] . . . but He will minister to thee justice and equity' (fol. 96; Comper, pp. 137–8); Stubbes, *A Crystal Glass for Christian Women* (1591), 'Send thy messenger death to fetch me, send thy sergeant to arrest me, send thy pursuivant to apprehend me . . .' (A4); Sylvester's Du Bartas, 'Death, dread Sergeant of th'eternal Judge' (I.iii.1087). See T. Spencer, *Death and Elizabethan Tragedy*, pp. 79–80; *SQ*, xx, 486–91; xxvi, 74–5; xxix, 84–5. In a Morality play called *The Cradle of Security*, witnessed by R. Willis as a small boy about 1570 and described by him in *Mount Tabor*, 1639 (pp. 110–13), the death of a prince was dramatically signalled by the arrival of a sergeant-at-arms: 'There came forth . . . two old men, the one in blue with a sergeant-at-arms his mace on his shoulder, the other in red with a drawn sword in his hand and . . . the foremost old man with his mace stroke a fearful blow upon the cradle' whereupon 'all vanished' but 'the desolate prince' who was 'thus sent for to judgment'. This spectacle so impressed the boy that the man remembered it in his old age 'as if I had seen it newly acted'. His account is quoted in full in F. P. Wilson, *The English Drama 1485–1585*, pp. 76–7.

APPENDIX

MANUSCRIPT NOTE IN GABRIEL HARVEY'S COPY OF CHAUCER'S *WORKES*, 1598
(See above, pp. 3–6)

The book is now in the British Museum (MS Add. 42518). The note is appended to 'A Catalogue of translatioris and Poeticall deuises, . . . by Iohn Lidgate . . .' and occurs on the verso of fol. 394 (which a library renumbering, by dint of including the preliminary leaves, calls fol. 422). Harvey's *Marginalia*, ed. G. C. Moore Smith, 1913, gives a facsimile (back pocket) and an accurate transcription (pp. 232–33).

Heywoods prouerbs, with His, & Sir Thomas Mores Epigrams, may serue for sufficient supplies of manie of theis deuises. And now translated Petrarch, Ariosto, Tasso, & Bartas himself deserue curious comparison with Chaucer, Lidgate, & owre best Inglish, auncient & moderne. Amongst which, the Countesse of Pembrokes Arcadia, & the Faerie Queene ar now freshest in request: & Astrophil, & Amyntas ar none of the idlest pastimes of sum fine humanists. The Earle of Essex much commendes Albions England: and not vnworthily for diuerse notable pageants, before, & in the Chronicle. Sum Inglish, & other Histories nowhere more sensibly described, or more inwardly discouered. The Lord Mountioy makes the like account of Daniels peece of the Chronicle, touching the Vsurpation of Henrie of Bullingbrooke. Which in deede is a fine, sententious, & politique peece of Poetrie: as proffitable, as pleasurable. The younger sort takes much delight in Shakespeares Venus, & Adonis: but his Lucrece, & his tragedie of Hamlet, Prince of Denmarke, haue it in them, to please the wiser sort. Or such poets: or better: or none.

Vilia miretur vulgus: mihi flavus Apollo
Pocula Castaliae plena ministret aquae: quoth Sir Edward Dier, betwene iest, & earnest. Whose written deuises farr excell most of the sonets, and cantos in print. His Amaryllis, & Sir Walter Raleighs Cynthia, how fine & sweet inuentions? Excellent matter of emulation for Spencer, Constable, France,

Watson, Daniel, Warner, Chapman, Siluester, Shakespeare, & the rest of owr florishing metricians. I looke for much, aswell in verse, as in prose, from mie two Oxford frends, Doctor Gager, & M. Hackluit: both rarely furnished for the purpose: & I haue a phansie to Owens new Epigrams, as pithie as elegant, as plesant as sharp, & sumtime as weightie as breife: & amongst so manie gentle, noble, & royall spirits meethinkes I see sum heroical thing in the clowdes: mie soueraine hope. Axiophilus shall forgett himself, or will remember to leaue sum memorials behinde him: & to make an vse of so manie rhapsodies, cantos, hymnes, odes, epigrams, sonets, & discourses, as at idle howers, or at flowing fitts he hath compiled. God knowes what is good for the world, & fitting for this age.